As we seem to slip more into a culture that pathogises every aspect of human experience, this book is not only welcome but essential. It takes an informed, critical, engaging and questioning position in relation to mental health and describes, with compelling detail, the relevance and importance of a person-centred approach in all working contexts with clients facing turmoil and distress. This is an incredibly invaluable handbook that helps us question what increasingly seems to be the unquestionable.

Dr Andrew Reeves, counsellor/psychotherapist, senior lecturer and writer

I cannot tell you how important I think this book is. The person-centered point of view has something important and unique to offer to both the understanding of psychopathology and the practice of therapy – something that is missing in other points of view. This book does a marvellous job of spelling this out and bringing person-centered theory up to date. The book cuts a wide swathe, looking at new theoretical contributions, different forms of psychological dysfunction, application of the person-centered approach to working with different populations, multicultural considerations, and political and professional ramifications. Highly recommended for anyone interested in the role of a 'positive' view of the human being in understanding psychopathology and psychotherapy.

Art Bohart, Professor Emeritus, California State University, Dominguez Hills

The first edition of this book vigorously challenged mainstream perceptions of the person-centred approach by presenting detailed accounts of the application of person-centred theory, ethics and practice when working with people experiencing severe psychological distress within a range of contexts. In this substantially revised, expanded and updated second edition, Stephen Joseph and his contributing authors have paid close attention to maintaining its relevance as an inspiring, accessible and research-aware resource. It is essential reading for practitioners and students in the counselling and psychotherapy arena, and those working in the wider mental health field.

Susan Stephen MSc, Diploma Courses Leader, University of Strathclyde

The new edition offers an invaluable counterpoint to the medicalisation of psychological health and wellbeing that continues to predominate in modern societies. Authors in this handbook deconstruct conventional approaches and help the practitioner to reframe the philosophy and practice of person-centred psychology while working alongside models of diagnosis and treatment that, in the main, consider personal distress as an illness to be treated. For the purist, the reformer, the pragmatist and all those working in psychiatric services, this book offers an illuminating path to the practice of a humane and truly person-centred approach to the problems so many people suffer from in the 21st century. This text is a must-have for the bookshelf of every therapist and mental health professional.

Stephen Paul, psychotherapist, past Director of the Centre for Psychological Therapies, Leeds Metropolitan (now Beckett) University. stephen-paul.co.uk

THE HANDBOOK OF PERSON-CENTRED THERAPY AND MENTAL HEALTH

THEORY, RESEARCH AND PRACTICE

An expanded and updated second edition of
Person-Centred Psychopathology

Edited by
Stephen Joseph

PCCS
BOOKS

First published 2017

PCCS Books Ltd
Wyastone Business Park
Wyastone Leys
Monmouth
NP25 3SR
contact@pccs-books.co.uk
www.pccs-books.co.uk

**The Handbook of Person-Centred Therapy and Mental Health:
theory, research and practice**

British Library Cataloguing in Publication data: a catalogue record for this book is
available from the British Library.

ISBN 978 1 910919 31 6

Front cover illustration © Polina Gazhur (Shutterstock)
Typeset in-house by PCCS Books using Minion Pro and Myriad Pro
Printed by Biddles Books Ltd, King's Lynn, Norfolk

Contents

RESEARCH

CONCLUSION

To my mother, Anne,
and in memory of my father, Clifford

Acknowledgements

My thanks to Richard Worsley, who co-edited the first edition with me, Pete Sanders for his guidance, and Heather Allan, Di English, Sandy Green and Maggie Taylor-Sanders at PCCS Books for all their help. My thanks also to past colleagues at the University of Warwick counselling service for their support. For this second edition, I am especially grateful to Catherine Jackson at PCCS Books for her commitment to this book. Thanks also to friends, colleagues and students in the counselling group in the School of Education at the University of Nottingham. Most of all, my thanks to all the authors for their important contributions and for being part of this volume.

Preface

Stephen Joseph

When the first edition of this book was published in 2005, the title was *Person-Centred Psychopathology*. Psychopathology is a term used in mainstream clinical psychology and psychiatry to refer to mental and behavioural disorders. A glance through textbooks of the time showed that the person-centred approach received little coverage in clinical psychology and psychiatry: it was seen as largely irrelevant. The aim therefore was to show it could be relevant. I wanted the book to show that the person-centred approach could face up to the challenge to offer theoretical explanations for the various disorders, while simultaneously questioning the concept of disorder and showing how person-centred therapy was an alternative helping system. I wanted the person-centred approach to push its way into mainstream mental health. The title was provocative.

Ten years on, and our criticisms of the mental health industry are now voiced by many others, but there remains much to be done to communicate how the person-centred approach can help occupy the space that is opening up as mental health professionals look for alternatives to the medical model. This second edition has a less provocative title and has widened its focus to debate and dialogue with other health professionals and explore aspects of theory, professionalism, the role of culture, and the politics of the person-centred approach in relation to mental health.

In this second edition, I also say goodbye to my friend and colleague Richard Worsley, who edited the first edition with me but whose life and career have taken him in new directions. I have missed working with him, and wish him well in his new life in the rectory.

In the first edition, we ended the preface by saying that the book stood for us as a learning about, and an assertion of, the human capacity to grow in the face of adversity. It still does for me. I hope that practitioners, trainers and those in training in the varied mental health professions will find this book of value to them.

Stephen Joseph
Nottingham, 1 July, 2016

INTRODUCTIONS

1 | Mental health and the person-centred approach

Stephen Joseph

Over recent decades, the person-centred approach has become a major force in the world of counselling and psychotherapy. Yet the person-centred approach to understanding distress and dysfunction has been overlooked within mainstream mental health services. In the first edition, Richard Worsley and I speculated that perhaps this was the result of the false belief held by many psychologists and psychiatrists that person-centred therapy is a good idea for the worried well, but that serious mental health problems require something more. There is, of course, a self-fulfilling prophecy to this. As the person-centred movement becomes marginalised within the National Health Service (NHS) because of these beliefs, training courses struggle to provide placements and supervision for trainees to work with clients with serious problems. It thus becomes the case that person-centred practitioners are often ill-equipped to work with anyone but the worried well, at least in the eyes of these other professionals.

It is this tendency towards a self-fulfilling prophecy that this book is intended to address. Reflection on the theory that underlies person-centred practice shows it has potential for helping people who would otherwise be considered to be suffering from serious mental health problems. However, the main issue is one of communication, as we are essentially dealing with a clash of paradigms: the potentiality model of the person-centred approach on the one hand and, on the other, the medical model.

The person-centred approach to helping is based on the assumption that human beings have an inherent tendency towards growth and development, such that movement towards becoming fully functioning will happen automatically when people encounter an empathic, genuine and unconditional relationship in which they feel valued and understood. However, it is recognised that such relationships are rare; the inherent tendency towards becoming fully functioning is more frequently thwarted and usurped, leading instead to psychological distress and dysfunction (Rogers, 1959). For the person-centred therapist, the power and direction for change comes from within the client; their task is solely to provide the new relationship that allows the person to flourish.

The medical model is based on the assumption that specific disorders exist, requiring specific treatments. So, when we consult a doctor with an ailment such as a stomach pain, we are likely to be uncertain what the cause of our pain is and anxious that they accurately identify the problem and quickly provide the correct treatment. To do this, the practitioner needs to be an expert diagnostician. They need to examine us in order to identify our specific symptoms and thence diagnose the most likely cause. To do this, they need to know the conditions we may be suffering from, and the symptoms of each. They will ask us questions about the nature of our pain, its location and duration, and they will examine us physically for bruises, swelling and so on. Having reached a diagnosis, they are in a position to prescribe the correct treatment. The treatment will depend on the condition from which they think we are suffering.

Mental health practitioners may be dealing with mental rather than physical health but, by and large, they still use the medical model. Traditionally, textbooks on psychiatry and abnormal and clinical psychology, for example, tend to be organised around each of the so-called disorders (for example, anxiety disorders, somatoform and dissociative disorders, mood disorders, schizophrenia, substance-related disorders, sexual disorders, personality disorders). The causes, correlates and effective treatments are discussed in turn for each disorder, the assumption being that psychological problems are like medical problems – they too require expert diagnosis, so the right treatment can be prescribed.

The mental health professional is therefore trained in the use of the American Psychiatric Association's *Diagnostic and Statistical Manual* (*DSM*) *of Mental Disorders*. First introduced in 1952 (*DSM-I*), followed by revised editions in 1968 (*DSM-II*), 1980 (*DSM-III*), 1987 (*DSM-III-R*), 1994 (*DSM-IV*), it is now in its fifth edition (American Psychiatric Association, 2013). *DSM-5* is a voluminous work, running to many hundreds of pages, that describes the range of psychiatric disorders and the detailed procedure for the diagnosis of each.

Whether or not they adhere strictly to the *DSM*, many mental health professionals take for granted that there is a need for specific treatments for specific conditions; alternative ways of thinking are rarely acknowledged. As already noted, the person-centred approach emphasises developmental processes and the actualising tendency of the individual; there is no need for diagnosis, because problems in living all have the same essential cause and the approach to therapy is always the same. Person-centred therapy is a relationship in which the client is able to grow and to self-right in such a way that they move away from façade, from pleasing others, and towards self-direction, openness to experience, acceptance of others, and trust of their self (Rogers, 1961). As a consequence, the person-centred approach uses different terminology to describe mental health.

Person-centred therapists do not use the language of psychiatry and do not make the assumption that specific conditions require specific treatments. This has meant that relatively little has been written from the client-centred school of thought about the various so-called disorders – a silence that has left client-centred therapy marginalised from mainstream mental health services. This does not mean that it is irrelevant, although it may seem so to those other professionals who do assume that specific conditions require specific treatments.

It is not the intention of this book to suggest that there is a need for a diagnostic approach; my aim is to show that the person-centred approach is applicable to understanding and working with people who are (or are likely to be) diagnosed as experiencing psychiatric conditions. Rogers wrote that, in his experience, whatever the client's problem was, whether it was to do with distressing feelings or troubling interpersonal relations, all were struggling with the same existential question: how to be themselves. But to what extent can person-centred personality theory account for the range of psychopathology that is described in the *DSM*? We can't simply assume that person-centred theory can explain everything, and we certainly can't expect other health professionals who hold the medical-model view to take us seriously when we don't provide theory and evidence.

Some person-centred practitioners have indeed revelled in living on the edges, taking great satisfaction in the radical nature of the paradigm. However, this stance has also hampered communication and respect between different disciplines. By not being able to articulate answers to those in the psychiatric and psychological professions who question how the person-centred approach can be used with people with severe and chronic psychological problems, the person-centred community has isolated itself and allowed itself to become marginalised. As I said, I am not advocating that anyone should adopt psychiatric or psychological techniques in their clinical practice. Still less am I condoning the medical model as a basis for understanding distress and dysfunction. What I am saying is that I think person-centred therapists have a duty to understand their psychological and psychiatric colleagues – what they do and why they do it – so that, in turn, they have the language to be able to articulate clearly what it is they do and why they do it.

I realise that many counsellors and psychotherapists, for ideological, social and political reasons, tend not to use psychiatric terms. For sure, I agree that how we label the phenomena that we are attempting to describe is not a trivial issue, but if you want to be understood, sometimes you have to meet the other person where they are, and talk to them there. For this reason, I have asked our contributors to write about the person-centred approach in relation to the professions of psychology and psychiatry, the medical model and the various so-called psychiatric disorders, and issues of assessment and diagnosis.

The point is simply to illustrate that most of these 'psychiatric disorders' are terms used by psychologists and psychiatrists to give themselves a common language with which to communicate to each other about best practice, as they see it. As counsellors and psychotherapists, we can use the language of psychiatry and psychology to help us communicate to a wider audience and to reach the new generation of psychologists and psychiatrists. This is particularly apposite at a time when the medical model is being questioned more widely (Bentall, 2003), particularly in areas of positive psychology (see, for example, Maddux & Lopez, 2015).

To me, it seems that we have much to gain from recognising that the person-centred approach, with its emphasis on helping people become fully functioning, is ultimately a positive psychology (Joseph, 2015). Positive psychologists are concerned with understanding what makes life worth living. The concept of positive psychology ought to sound familiar to the person-centred psychologist, counsellor or psychotherapist. After all, it was Rogers who introduced the idea of the fully functioning person. Historically, the person-centred approach has been viewed as a form of humanistic psychology, but today it is also a form of positive psychology. The person-centred approach is not a deficit approach to distress and dysfunction; it is a potentiality model. Therapy is not about correcting deficits, but about facilitating an inherent process towards growth and development. Each of the chapters in this book is in its different way ultimately concerned with understanding mental health problems as the expression of thwarted potential.

Content of the book

In this book, I have asked a range of authors to show to person-centred practitioners and trainees how the person-centred approach tackles some of the issues confronting psychologists and psychiatrists. We have to answer a number of questions:

- are all psychiatric diagnoses explicable by the person-centred model, or is there a limit to what the person-centred model can explain?
- is person-centred therapy useful, even if the theory is not able to explain the disorder?
- are some problems simply outside the scope of person-centred therapy?
- why does the person-centred community refuse to adopt the language of psychology and psychiatry?
- is person-centred theory an exclusive or an inclusive approach?
- what are the implications of the person-centred model for assessment and diagnosis?
- what is it like to be a person-centred therapist practising in the context of mainstream psychology and psychiatry?
- can person-centred psychology offer an alternative to the medical model?

These are the questions that this book sets out to answer. Each chapter addresses a particular set of theoretical issues or challenges posed by working in a specific professional context. Nearly all the contributors to the first edition of this book have kindly updated their chapters to include new ideas and research that have emerged over the past decade. I have also sought out contributions from new authors who have advanced our understanding in areas not covered in the first edition. As with any such book, the views expressed in each chapter are those of the authors. The range of views included here all come under the umbrella of person-centred practice.

In the second chapter of this introduction section, Pete Sanders raises some interesting issues about our relationship with mainstream psychology and psychiatry – whether we ought to find ways to work collaboratively with and alongside our psychology and psychiatry colleagues, despite the risk that we lose our values and identity, or whether we adopt a stance of principled opposition to the medicalisation of human distress, even if this has negative consequences for us. In this, Pete's chapter helps to set the scene for the rest of the book, as each author in their own way is at least implicitly expressing a view about the challenges of working in mental health contexts that often align with medical model thinking.

Moving into theory, in Chapter 3, Paul Wilkins addresses the main criticisms that have been made of the person-centred approach: that it is not suitable for people with serious problems, and that it lacks a theory of personality development. Paul shows us that these criticisms are unfounded, and that person-centred theory provides a substantial foundation for understanding psychopathology and its development. In Chapter 4, Mick Cooper presents his work on extending person-centred thinking to psychopathology, drawing on recent developments in self-theory and his work as an existential therapist. In Chapter 5, Peter Schmid follows a similar theme in his exploration of the roles of authenticity and alienation and how these concepts are at the core of the person-centred approach to psychopathology. In Chapter 6, Margaret Warner then argues that person-centred theory offers a model of human functioning that is relevant to all clinical psychology and the social sciences, in that it generates particular insights into human qualities that should be central to all humane mental health practice.

Putting theory into practice, in Chapter 7, Lisbeth Sommerbeck discusses the conflict between the values of psychiatry and the client-centred approach, and how she has been able to resolve the inevitable conflictual issues that arise for her, as a client-centred therapist working in a psychiatric setting, by drawing on complementarity theory. In Chapter 8, Paul Wilkins provides an overview of the role of diagnosis and assessment and, in light of criticisms about their use, discusses what person-centred theory offers us when thinking about assessment. In Chapter 9, Richard Worsley discusses evil and how this concept offers a way into talking about the impact of client material on practitioners. Finally, two new chapters conclude this section. In Chapter 10, Colin Lago discusses the conditions of worth, extending our understanding of Rogers' theory to take into account the social and cultural forces operating on a person. Finally, in Chapter 11, Emma Tickle and Stephen Joseph discuss attachment theory in relation to person-centred therapy.

The person-centred approach has applicability in many clinical contexts, and the next set of chapters explores this. In Chapter 12, Dion Van Werde describes his experience in a residential psychiatric setting, working with people who have problems that might be described as psychotic. In Chapter 13, Kirshen Rundle discusses psychosis from the person-centred perspective. In Chapter 14, Stephen Joseph discusses person-centred theory and how it is able to provide us with an understanding of post-traumatic stress, and how this resonates with other theories. In Chapter 15, Elaine Catterall discusses maternal depression through the lenses of the various theoretical perspectives and her personal experiences, before going on to show how person-centred therapy can fit into a multidisciplinary way of working with women. In Chapter 16, Jan Hawkins reviews the literature on child abuse and its wide-ranging and long-lasting effects, and the contribution of person-centred practitioners to work with survivors of abuse. In Chapter 17, Marlis Pörtner discusses person-centred therapy with people with special needs and how we can recognise and understand their impairments and limitations without pathologising them. Similarly, in Chapter 18, Jacky Knibbs and Anja Rutten draw on the first-hand accounts of children and young people diagnosed with Asperger syndrome and autism to underline the importance of understanding their world when working with them. In Chapter 19, Gillian Proctor discusses the historical roots of clinical psychology and its relationship with person-centred therapy, and how she manages the conflict between the two hats she wears as a clinical psychologist who specialises in client-centred therapy. Again, two new chapters conclude this section. In Chapter 20, psychiatrist Rachel Freeth describes her experiences of working in a person-centred way and the challenges and issues this raises. Finally, in Chapter 21, Andy Rogers and David Murphy discuss professionalism and statutory regulation in relation to person-centred therapy.

Turning to research, in Chapter 22 Jerold Bozarth and Noriko Motomasa summarise the psychotherapy research literature to make a strong case for the role of the relationship rather than technique, and specifically with regard to person-centred therapy. In Chapter 23, Barbara Brodley asks us to think carefully about how we use research findings to bolster our practice and reminds us that, although research is important, what we do is also a value-based activity. Barbara, sadly, died in 2007, and so her chapter is reprinted here as it was in the first edition. To me, her chapter is timeless in its message that research findings are not instructions for how to practise, and I am grateful to her estate for allowing me to reprint it. In Chapter 24, Lisbeth Sommerbeck presents an evaluation of client-centred therapy in psychiatric settings, with specific reference to Rogers and colleagues' famous Wisconsin project. Lisbeth shows us that, although its findings are often used to justify the claim that person-centred therapy is not appropriate with certain client groups, the research itself was flawed in many respects. So, although the project has much to teach us, it is going beyond the data to claim that they can be taken as evidence against client-centred therapy. In Chapter 25, Richard Worsley discusses his own venture into the world of qualitative research and encourages us to look at research in terms of what we can learn professionally and personally. Finally, concluding this section is a new chapter by Tom Patterson, who discusses the important issue of theoretically consistent measurement.

My aim has been to bring together writers who, while they all recognise the value of the person-centred approach, take a variety of perspectives. The book covers a wide range of issues and topics but, as with all such books, it provides only a snapshot of where we are right now. I hope that a new generation of scholars in the person-centred approach will emerge, who are able to take these ideas forward. I also recognise that, although the person-centred approach could be applied much more widely, it is unlikely that it offers solutions to all of the problems experienced by all those in mental distress, all of the time. Some problems may originate from neuropsychological or biochemical deficits and may require medical intervention. That said, even where person-centred personality theory may not be appropriate to explain the aetiology, person-centred therapy may still be an effective way of helping the person live more fully with their problems.

I intend this book to be useful to person-centred practitioners and trainees in informing their understanding of the application of the person-centred approach to the more severe and chronic problems of living. The psychiatric and psychological establishment tells us these are the sorts of issues and problems that are beyond the remit of person-centred therapy. Yet there has been little research into the person-centred approach to understanding mental health and its therapeutic effectiveness in relation to the specific so-called 'disorders'. Person-centred therapists have not always valued the ideas underlying evidence-based practice and what they see as the inappropriate medicalisation of therapy. Theirs is a phenomenological stance; they are interested in the experience of the client as defined by the client. Thus, research questions from the person-centred perspective are not shaped around psychiatric disorders. However, if person-centred psychotherapy is not to continue to be marginalised within mainstream mental health services, the onus must be on person-centred therapists to build stronger bridges with other approaches. It is hoped that this book will help to build those bridges, and that it will encourage phenomenologically based, person-centred practitioners to conduct research and theoretical work in this area.

I have learned a great deal from reading and editing the contributions to this book. My hope is that they will fuel debate and further research and writings on person-centred approaches to mental health. I also hope that practitioners and trainees of other disciplines will find the perspectives of our contributors thought provoking. The full significance of the client-centred approach is that it is always focused equally on the facilitation of growth and the development of human potential and the alleviation of distress and dysfunction. I hope this book further illuminates that understanding.

References

American Psychiatric Association (2013). *Diagnostic and Statistical Manual of Mental Disorders* (5th ed). Washington, DC: American Psychiatric Press.

Bentall R (2003). *Madness Explained: psychosis and human nature*. London: Allen Lane.

Joseph S (2015). *Positive Therapy: building bridges between positive psychology and person-centred psychotherapy*. London: Routledge.

Maddux JE, Lopez SJ (2015). Deconstructing the illness ideology and constructing an ideology of human strengths and potential in clinical psychology. In: Joseph S (ed). *Positive Psychology in Practice: promoting human flourishing in work, health, education, and everyday life* (2nd ed). Hoboken: Wiley (pp411–427).

Rogers CR (1959). A theory of therapy, personality and interpersonal relationships, as developed in the client-centered framework. In: Koch S (ed). *Psychology: a study of a science. Vol. 3: Formulations of the person and the social context*. New York: McGraw-Hill (pp184–256).

Rogers CR (1961). *On Becoming a Person*. Boston, MA: Houghton Mifflin.

2 | Principled and strategic opposition to the medicalisation of distress and all of its apparatus

Pete Sanders

These schools of thought will not be abolished by wishful thinking.
(Carl Rogers, 1951: 8)

The medicalisation of human distress is no less contentious now than it was in 2005, when the first edition of this book was published. Part of the problem is the lack of agreement on the position that the profession of counselling and psychotherapy should take towards the medicalisation of human distress and the related issues of psychopathology and psychodiagnosis. In this empty space rage arguments where the concern for vulnerable people is both a badge to be worn and a pawn to be played. This chapter asks why counsellors have abdicated the radical position occupied by client-centred therapy in the 1950s to become tacit supporters of the medical psychiatric system.

Here, I consider ways that person-centred therapists might position themselves and act in relation to human distress. Over the years I have promoted a particular approach, but I have become increasingly wary of critical positions that are as totalising and dismissive of other opinions as the medical model is itself. If our shared aim is to improve the treatment of people suffering from everyday distress and chronic distress, then we should debate the various options vigorously.

One option, frequently dismissed as impracticable, irresponsible and self-defeating, is that of rejection and principled opposition (but not disengagement). This position, however, must not become entangled with discussions about safety, risk or the dangerousness of distressed and distressing people. These important but separate issues are frequently conflated with an anti-medical stance by those wishing to defend the status quo. This chapter does not address these issues.

Another option is to establish alternative systems outside statutory medicalised services. There is little history for this option in terms of person-centred therapy, although it is ideally suited to a therapeutic community setting. Perhaps the closest approximation would be a Soteria House (Mosher and Hendrix, 2004) (see p19 this chapter). There are also similarities between person-centred therapy and the approach developed by the Hearing Voices Network (see p20 this chapter).

A further option is critical engagement with medicalised systems of mental health care by, for example, offering person-centred therapy within the NHS, making as few compromises as possible while retaining an honourable, professional critical analysis of medicalised diagnosis and treatment.

And a final option is to pragmatically embed a person-centred approach in the NHS. This involves making compromises; practitioners will have to make difficult decisions. The prize is that person-centered therapy is available from established statutory services and free at the point of delivery, rather than simply an option for those able to pay for private therapy. Counselling for Depression, which is offered through the Improving Access to Psychological Therapies (IAPT) programme in England, is an example of this option (see p30).

This chapter will briefly describe and consider each of these options. If the development of theory and practice is a matter of *evolution* rather than *progress*, then it is vital that diversity is at least preserved, and at best promoted. It is important to support those person-centred therapists who continue to explain the radical, ethical, humane principles of this approach against all the fashions that deny them, in all professional settings.

Metaphors for distress

Many writers (eg. Szasz, 1961; Boyle, 2014; Rapley, Moncrieff & Dillon, 2011) have challenged the assumption that human distress is an illness. Discussions about the role of psychiatry frequently take the illness metaphor as the starting point. The observation that illness might be a *metaphor* for distress, rather than a *fact* determined by 'scientific' analysis, is met in some circles with incomprehension. Although writers and practitioners have questioned the assumption, it still is taken as given by the general public and the vast majority of people working in the helping professions.[1] But, regardless of how many people use the metaphor, it is just a metaphor – a representation of reality, not reality itself. It is a way of thinking that is intended to be helpful. The key questions are: 1) is *illness* still a useful, helpful metaphor? 2) how can we evaluate the usefulness/helpfulness of the metaphor? 3) what metaphors might be more useful? and 4) how do we shift cultural thinking to a more useful metaphor?

I argue that illness is not a helpful metaphor, and that it is certainly discordant with the core values of person-centred therapy. Further, it was installed as the dominant cultural metaphor for professional and political reasons, and so will resist both evaluation by science and replacement by more culturally appropriate

---

1. It is essential continuously to remind ourselves that this 'medical model of mental illness' is a list of 'illnesses' based entirely on similarity of symptoms, not (as is the case with somatic illness) on aetiology.

metaphors – those that have a perceived better fit with contemporary professional experience.

Person-centred therapy suggests an *organismic growth* metaphor for human distress, and person-centred theorists and practitioners should declare this in juxtaposition to the dominant illness metaphor at every appropriate opportunity. There is, as Blackburn and Yates (2004) point out, a contemporary model for challenging the illness metaphor that has met with considerable success. They compare present-day traditional mental health services with learning disability services,[2] as shown in Table 2.1. A similar protocol can be adapted to compare traditional mental health services and client-centred therapy, as shown in Table 2.2.

Table 2.1 (Abridged from Blackburn & Yates, 2004: 32)

	Traditional mental health services	Learning disability services
Metaphor used	Illness	Communication
Professional discourses privileged	Psychiatrists	Speech and language therapists, social workers, psychologists, carers, parents
Method of defining	Diagnosis	Client's experience. Description as created in the conversation between client, carers, family, professionals etc
Beliefs about how change is brought about	Providing the right treatment to enable client change	By the system understanding and addressing the client's needs
Aims of intervention	To recover previous state of being	Development to new state of being
Professional relationship to client	Therapist	Advocate

---

2. Some 40 years ago in the UK, learning disability services were dominated by illness metaphors. This changed with the advent of a social model of disability. Further examples of 'metaphor reassignment' include women's reproductive biology and race/ethnicity.

Table 2.2

	Traditional mental health services	Client-centred therapy
Metaphor used	Illness	Organismic growth (adaptation) and/or client's own metaphor
Professional discourses privileged	Psychiatrists	No professional discourse privileged above client's experience
Method of defining client's experience	Diagnosis	Client experience/empathy
Beliefs about how change is brought about	Providing the right treatment to enable client change	Actualising tendency of client released by therapist-provided conditions
Aims of intervention	To recover previous state of being	Fulfilment of inherent potential
Professional relationship to client	Expert therapist	Therapist/companion

I am not suggesting metaphors are bad *per se*: metaphors and myths serve important functions in the understanding and management of our social world, but only in so far as they are useful and consensual, rather than harmful and unchallengeable. It is, however, increasingly difficult to keep the medical metaphor of distress within challengeable range – where challenges to it are not seen as fatally heretical or irresponsible.

Metaphors, practice and services to clients

A social model of learning disability has supplanted the medical model in professional circles, and this was achieved in a number of ways. Strategies have included:

- challenging at every possible opportunity the medical model, its hierarchical structure, potential for abuse and sheer lack of fitness for purpose
- supporting, working alongside and aligning with groups of users of disability services

- working within disability services, preparing them in small ways to meet the challenge of metaphor change when it arrived
- joining government and statutory bodies to present radical views
- carrying out research that challenged the dominant medical metaphor or tested alternative views
- exhorting professional bodies to present a coherent alternative framework of understanding and challenge government policy.

Whether such strategies would be suitable to challenge the illness metaphor in mental health remains to be debated in person-centred circles – in fact, the notion of *organised* opposition to the medical model has never been contemplated in the person-centred world. What cannot be in doubt, however, is that any alternative argument is weakened every time person-centred academics, writers and practitioners whose logical position is set against it make reference to, or accept without comment, the medical model and diagnosis. The progress of alternative practice is hindered and its character damaged every time practitioners silently accept the authority of psychiatrists over user groups and carers. Counsellors and therapists, both individually and, more importantly, as a group, have valuable contributions to make to this debate. Counsellors and psychotherapists should never be placed as acontextual, apolitical servants of individual clients. Rather, as Sanders and Tudor insist:

> Psychotherapists should be concerned with change, not adjustment; should be explicit about their values and should be intentional – socially and culturally… Psychotherapists and counsellors [must] base their practice on a thorough and critical understanding of psychiatry and psychotherapy *in context*… Psychotherapists' practice should reflect the awareness that the struggle for mental health involves changing society… Psychotherapists should organise and challenge oppressive institutions… in the organisation of mental health services, and professional monopoly in the control of service provision and direction, and the colonization of the voluntary sector in mental health. (2001: 157)

One key step is to organise collegial groups and professional associations to represent better the alternatives held at the centre of person-centred therapy.

A radical history

The history of client/person-centred therapy is a history of radical theory and practice. Carl Rogers and his colleagues in the client-centred therapy[3] movement were the

---

3. Rogers initially termed his therapy method 'non-directive therapy', changing it to 'client-centered therapy' around 1950. He introduced the term 'person-centered approach' in the late 1970s to signify applications of his approach beyond therapy, although in the UK the term 'person-centred therapy' (which Rogers never used) became popular. This chapter is founded in the radical roots of classical client-centred therapy, and so I shall use this term throughout.

first to give an account of what really happens in a psychotherapy session, by using wax-disc recordings of sessions and publishing and presenting for public scrutiny transcripts that revealed the arcane practices of psychotherapy (Kirschenbaum, 2007). Rogers trained lay people (non-medically qualified psychologists and social workers),[4] causing further controversy. As client-centred therapy developed, it made the client the centre of the healing process and effectively factored out the medical expert – the client was assisted by another, equal person. Psychiatrists forbade him to use the term 'psychotherapy' for this work, in order to protect their status, so he appropriated the word 'counseling'. On moving to Chicago in 1945, Rogers initiated research into psychotherapy, and in so doing turned the emerging client-centred therapy into the first evidence-based psychological (as opposed to medical) treatment programme – it became a *human science*.

Understandably, none of this went down well in the professional circles of the day. When news of the success of the Chicago Counseling Center spread, client-centred therapy was criticised for only being applicable to middle-class, articulate, worried-well clients. Rogers' research was criticised for being small-scale and only using clients whose symptoms were not severe. In response, he moved to the University of Wisconsin, where, as the first joint professor in psychology and psychiatry, he conducted research in a hostile environment – a state mental hospital where patients were kept in locked wards (Rogers et al, 1967) – with people who had the least hope of recovery (those with diagnoses of 'schizophrenia'). In its heyday, client-centred therapy was *the* radical, vibrant, anti-medical establishment, system-threatening, research-based psychological practice – and at its core it was non-invasive, non-medical, mindfully humane and just. It spoke out against the medicalisation of distress and professional expertism, while formulating a coherent theory and workable practice.

Meanwhile, the medicalisation of distress has continued to entrench its position. The anti-psychiatry movement in the 60s and 70s and the work of Szasz (1961) and Laing (eg. 1965) hardly caused the medical model to break its stride as it became not only the dominant ideology of distress, but the *only* ideology of distress. It has become a 'given' – that which we think *from*, rather than think *about*. The notion that human distress might not be an 'illness' is not merely radical, it is inconceivable. This status quo,[5] into which we were all socialised from birth, can be summarised thus:

---

4. In the US in the late 1930s only medically-qualified doctors, in particular psychiatrists, were permitted to offer psychotherapy. Rogers' clinical work and writing had already blurred the accepted boundaries between psychology, sociology and social work, so it was no surprise that the Rochester Council of Social Agencies insisted that the new community guidance centre (proposed by Rogers) be headed by a psychiatrist. After a year-long battle with the authorities, Rogers (not medically qualified) was made the director.

5. Referred to by some sociologists as 'doxa' (Bourdieu & Wacquant, 1992) and described by Charlesworth (2000) as 'constituted by those systems of classification which establish limits to what we contemplate in discursive consciousness, thus producing an inability to see the arbitrariness on which the classification and the structures have been established' (p31).

- the best way of thinking and talking about human mental distress is to medicalise it – to think and talk in terms of 'illness' and 'health', or, if we prefer, 'normality' and 'abnormality'
- severe and enduring mental illness has a biological base
- since mental distress is a medical condition, we need a psychopathology and system for classifying symptoms and, by association, treatments (diagnosis)
- psychosis is discontinuous with ordinary mental functioning, and so it requires special treatment by experts
- psychotherapy and counselling are ineffective treatments for severe and enduring mental illness. Worse than that, they are actually dangerous
- psychiatry is scientific, deals with the facts of the world, is based on evidence, is rational, and is therefore responsible
- criticisms of psychiatry are unevidenced, subjective, politically motivated, rhetorical, and therefore irresponsible. Further, they appeal to, and hold out false hope for, impressionable, vulnerable people.

How such ideas came to be installed as the status quo is another story of professional interests and political expediency. Readers are directed to accessible accounts by Pilgrim (1990), Newnes (1999), Bentall (2003), Boyle (2014) and Read and Dillon (2013).

Critical voices

In recent years, a growing number of psychology academics, authors and practitioners have taken up the reins of the anti-psychiatry movement of the 1960s and 1970s to present a critique of the medicalisation of distress. This group[6] advocates a thorough reform of the psychiatric system, based on a fundamental reframing of the nature of human distress and how it should be viewed. That some people suffer many manifestations of disabling distress every day of their lives is not in question. But what makes us think that these are the symptoms of an *illness*?

The following extracts capture many of the defining sentiments of these critics.

> The heightened sensitivity, unusual experiences, distress, despair, confusion and disorganisation that are currently labelled 'schizophrenic' are *not* symptoms of a mental illness. The notion that 'mental illness is an illness like any other', promulgated by biological psychiatry and the pharmaceutical industry, is not supported by research and is extremely damaging to those

6. Although I refer to these people as a 'group', this is just convenient shorthand. Worldwide, many work completely independently and only a few could be considered to be professional associates. What unites the group is their general critical position with regard to mainstream psychiatric practice and the medical model of mental illness, although the critique itself is not entirely unitary and cohesive.

with this most stigmatising of psychiatric labels. The 'medical model' of schizophrenia has dominated efforts to understand and assist distressed and distressing people for far too long. It is responsible for unwarranted and destructive pessimism about the chances of 'recovery' and has ignored – or even actively discouraged discussion of – what is actually going on in these people's lives, in their families and in the societies in which they live. Simplistic and reductionist genetic and biological theories have led, despite the high risks involved and the paucity of sound research proving effectiveness, to the lobotomizing, electroshocking or drugging of millions of people. (Read, Mosher & Bentall, 2004: 3)

Dorothy Rowe implicates the medical *profession* thus:

If such illnesses exist, then they can be treated by one profession only – psychiatry. But if such illnesses do not exist, if 'illness' is simply a metaphor for the various ways we can feel despair and alienation, then psychiatrists have nothing unique to offer. Anyone who has the necessary wisdom, sympathy and patience – a psychologist, a counsellor, a good friend – could give the help the sufferer needs. Psychiatry would vanish, just as the profession of hangman vanished from Britain once the death penalty was abolished. (Rowe, 1993: *xx*)

In 1993, Peter Breggin, an American psychiatrist, published *Toxic Psychiatry* – a comprehensive, passionate attack on the mental health system. He described the importance of seeking and finding meaning in the worlds of frightened, disturbed people. He realised that these people and their worlds have value; he treated patients with respect, rather than forcing dehumanising physical treatments on them; he understood that therapists must relate to clients as people, not as distant, powerful experts. Breggin is blunt:

Dozens of mass-marketed books misinform the public that a 'broken brain' or 'biochemical imbalance' is responsible for personal unhappiness. Yet the only biochemical imbalances that we can identify with certainty in the brains of psychiatric patients are the ones produced by psychiatric treatment itself. (Breggin, 1993: 14)

Richard Bentall, in *Madness Explained*, concluded:

If people can sometimes live healthy, productive lives while experiencing some degree of psychosis… if the boundaries between madness and normality are open to negotiation… and if… our psychiatric services are imperfect and sometimes damaging to patients, why not help some psychotic people just to *accept* that they are different from the rest of us? (Bentall, 2003: 511)

Bentall demonstrated that there is no dividing line between psychological health and disturbance; that diagnosis is largely an irrelevance and the medicalisation of human distress is at best a diversion. He then invited understanding *and* explanation of the experiences of people who receive diagnoses of psychosis. And he linked the experience of madness to events in people's everyday lives – the foundation of a psychosocial approach. Such an approach builds a psychology of the ordinary: a theory of you and me, of our lives and experiences – a theory of mental life in the round.

An enduring criticism of the earlier anti-psychiatry movement was that it gave the impression of being *anti* psychiatry, but not *pro* very much anything else; other than in the work of Laing and his associates (eg. Laing & Esterson, 1964), there seemed to be little systematic promoting of alternative treatments. It was also perceived as laying pretty much all of the blame at the doors of families and parenting. This left parents feeling alienated and blamed for the distress of their children and adult offspring, and unwilling, and often unable, to access the support they frequently needed as primary carers and advocates.

Alternatives: reinventing the wheel?

More recent critics continue to present a persuasive array of arguments pointing to the doxic (after 'doxa'[7]) nature of psychiatry, but offer a much more rounded perspective. Their critiques tend to be research based, and to propose tentative psychological explanations and non-medical treatment regimes. Some of these treatments originate in a broad cognitive approach and are evidence-based (see, for example, Birchwood, Fowler & Jackson, 2000; Bentall, 2003).[8] However, others are based on practitioners'/service-users'/survivors' experience (different types of 'evidence'), and provide interesting alternative stories for us to contemplate.

Soteria House

In 1983, the Soteria programme was closed after 12 years.[9] Well researched and reported in many journals (see Mosher 1999; Mosher & Burti, 1994),   the programme was based in a residential acute psychiatric unit in California

---

7. See footnote 5.

8. Many readers may lodge objections to this claim, but the purpose of this chapter is not to challenge the nature of the evidence base of different therapeutic approaches.

9. Funding was withdrawn. When asked why (if it was so successful), at a lecture in Birmingham, England, Mosher explained that, since the project had offended drug companies (by recommending an initial medication-free period on admission), psychiatrists (by using non-medically qualified staff), and hospital administrators (by locating it in a residential neighbourhood), the funding had to be withdrawn. The dominant medical ideology gets what it wants when the evidence might go against it, through alleged fraud (see, for example, Lock, cited in Lynch, 2004) and alleged corruption (see the account of the affair regarding the [non]appointment of psychopharmacologist David Healy at the University of Toronto at www.pharmapolitics.com).

that specialised in mainly drug-free treatment. It achieved good results with what psychiatrist Loren Mosher described as '... 24-hour-a-day application of interpersonal phenomenologic interventions by a non-professional staff' (Mosher 1999: 37). The project was initially part-funded by the US National Institute for Mental Health (NIMH), and the evidence showed that disturbed and disturbing persons were best helped by relationships with people, not by drugs. It showed that the best help for the majority of people was provided in a supportive, growth-oriented community, not in a hospital. It showed that helping improve mental life also meant improving the environment (micro and macro): interventions had better outcomes if they were psychosocial. Their experience also showed that diagnosis was anti-therapeutic, as were helping interventions that put a theory or ideology before the needs of the person being helped. Definitions of 'health' and disturbance were found to be better if they were functional (rather than normative); in other words, people were best served by being supported to live fulfilling lives, not by attempts to change them to fit society's ideas of normality. Although Mosher and others replicated the results in other facilities, the human contact-oriented, drug-free approach was never funded as a viable alternative. A few Soteria-style projects were set up, and some (for example, Soteria Berne) endured and continued to be researched (Ciompi & Hoffman, 2004). The method of working that Mosher described as '24-hour-a-day application of *interpersonal phenomenologic* interventions' is strikingly similar to person-centred therapy (Mosher & Hendrix, 2004).

Hearing Voices Network

In 1987, Dutch psychiatrist Marius Romme was inspired by his work with a patient, Patsy Hague, who heard voices. His conclusion was that, instead of instructing patients to ignore and suppress the voices or eliminate them with medication, the better treatment was to encourage them to talk about their voices and understand the meaning implicit in the experience (Romme & Escher, 1993; Romme et al, 2009). This led to the formation of the Hearing Voices Network[10] (HVN) in the UK – a thriving community of voice-hearers and supporters. An international organisation (Intervoice[11]) convened to coordinate the voice-hearer networks in different countries, and a self-help approach, in which voice-hearers listen to each other's experiences and swap ideas, is now well established. HVN and Intervoice have initiated research and developed an instrument (the Maastricht Interview[12]) that can be used in research or therapy/recovery by peers, carers and professionals.

---

10. http://www.hearing-voices.org/ (accessed 31 March, 2016).

11. http://www.intervoiceonline.org/ (accessed 31 March, 2016).

12. http://intervoiceonline.org/wp-content/uploads/2011/03/Maastricht_Interview_for_voice_hearers1.pdf (accessed 31 March, 2016).

Although HVN and Intervoice have made significant strides in helping voice hearers, educating professionals and changing attitudes and stigma, the learnings and general approach are not accepted by mainstream psychiatry, because explanations and recovery strategies do not conform to medical model protocols. Where voice-hearing is distressing (many voice-hearers are not distressed by their voices), HVN and Intervoice advance a broadly traumagenic model (Andrew, Gray & Snowden, 2008), and recovery involves acceptant listening and developing useful coping strategies.

Family Care Foundation[13]

Since 1987, the Family Care Foundation (FCF) in Gothenburg, Sweden, has been developing a model based on family life for (predominantly young) people suffering a range of distress and disturbance that might elsewhere be diagnosed as 'psychosis'. Another traumagenic model, it eschews diagnosis, medication and medicalised treatment as usual, and instead places individuals in 'normal', often rural, homes. The host families and distressed people are supported with family therapy, individual sessions and collaboration with the whole of the client's network via a systems approach, using the concept of the 'extended therapy room'. Continuously developed since its inception, the approach is characterised as 'ordinary life therapy' and is an established, if marginalised, approach to working with distressed people. The FCF work led them to understand that non-interpretative listening, not judging and being authentic are the keystones of how to be with distressed people.

Interested readers can find a comprehensive description in founder Carina Håkansson's *Ordinary Life Therapy: experiences from a collaborative systemic practice* (2009, The Taos Institute). A one-hour film exploring the approach through footage of some of the families, made by Daniel Mackler and called *Healing Homes*, is available on Youtube.[14] Recent developments in the approach led to Håkansson establishing the Extended Therapy Room Foundation[15] to further the work internationally.

Open Dialogue

This approach was developed in the 1980s, in Western Lapland, Finland, where psychiatric services were in a parlous state. As the homepage of the UK website says: 'Open Dialogue is not an *alternative* to standard psychiatric services, it *is* the psychiatric service in Western Lapland' (my emphasis). It is not a medication-free approach, but de-emphasises drugs and medicalisation. The treatment principles (Seikkula et al, 2003: 3–4) are:

---

13. http://www.familjevardsstiftelsen.se/english/ (accessed 31 March, 2016).

14. https://www.youtube.com/watch?v=JV4NTEp8S2Q (accessed 31 March, 2016).

15. http://extendedroom.org/en/home/ (accessed 31 March, 2016).

- early intervention – the provision of immediate help, no waiting lists
- working with the whole of the client's social network
- adapting the therapeutic response to the specific and changing needs of each case
- keyworker – whoever is the first responder becomes the keyworker
- psychological continuity – the same team is responsible for treatment, for however long it takes
- tolerance of uncertainty – an active attitude to work with the client's network in a collaborative process
- commitment to dialogue – creating a forum where clients and their families can increase their sense of agency through discussion
- flat, democratic structure within the team and client's network – no one can 'out-rank' anyone else.

Open dialogue is a complete philosophy and methodology. It is now the norm in Western Lapland, but is marginal elsewhere, although interest is clearly piqued in Western Europe. Full details and information about publications, research and training can be found on the UK website,[16] and a film, *Open Dialogue*, also by Daniel Mackler, is available free on Youtube.[17]

It is interesting that these alternative approaches do not use any of the 'branded' therapies prevalent in the US and Western Europe. They are clearly integrative, pragmatic and humanistic, and share the principle of non-directive, respectful listening, thereby helping clients discover their own narrative and useful coping strategies. Furthermore, away from these examples, we find that, wherever evidence is reviewed, similar stories emerge. Houghton (2005) commented on a Cochrane Review that concluded that cognitive behavioural therapy (CBT) had no better effect on improving mental states or reducing relapse and readmission rates for schizophrenia than 'supportive psychotherapy' (a term used to describe a variety of control conditions that include client-centred therapy/person-centred therapy). And in the same publication, commenting on similar evidence, Stickley explains:

> CBT expands on the unique meaning the person attaches to their experience… encourages dialogue about the person's experiences… stresses collaboration… [and] an understanding of their goals… expanding on the personal significance and meaning of their experiences. (Stickley, 2005: 25)

He goes on to say, 'I believe such factors are central to helping people with distressing psychotic experiences' (p25).

---

16. http://opendialogueapproach.co.uk/ (accessed 31 March, 2016).
17. https://www.youtube.com/watch?v=HDVhZHJagfQ (accessed 31 March, 2016).

So, a significant group of critical psychologists, academics and psychiatrists have discovered that the best way to help chronically distressed people is to offer them relationships:

- characterised by interpersonal, phenomenologic interventions
- offered by non-professional staff (not medically qualified)
  – who relate to the client as a person, not a distant and powerful expert
  – who help clients understand implicit meaning in their experiences, and
  – who value clients' experiences, and treat them with respect
- in growth-oriented, supportive communities, not hospital/medical settings.

They further discovered that diagnosis is anti-therapeutic; that help should include a focus on the *context* of the client's experiences – family, social context, class, race etc – (the central thrust of UK clinical psychologists' promotion of formulation (see Read & Dillon, 2013 on social contexts, and Johnstone & Dallos, 2013 or Johnstone, 2014 on formulation)), and that all of these treatments are often best done without the use of prescribed psychotropic drugs.

The list above describes person-centred therapy in all but name, particularly re-inventing it from their own clinical experience. This replicates Rogers' work of the 1940s and 50s, when he similarly distilled a series of principles for effective practice from his clinical experience. Many of the same commentators hold client-centred therapy/person-centred therapy in negative regard, use untrained practitioners in control groups and call the activity 'supportive counselling' or 'supportive psychotherapy'. The community of person-centred therapists accepted this state of affairs without individual or collective comment until, in recent meta-analyses, Robert Elliott and colleagues filtered studies to weed out those that did not use 'bona fide' person-centred therapy/client-centred therapy and experiential therapies that met their criteria (Elliott et al, 2015). The critical psychologists and psychiatrists have some things to learn from our 70 years of theory and practice development on 'such factors' that are 'central to helping people with distressing… experiences'. We will be wasting our time if we wait for them to come knocking on our door.

Classical client-centred therapy and psychopathology

Earlier in this chapter, I stated that client-centred therapy circa 1950 was the radical option in psychology. This radical nature has its foundation in the theory of client-centred therapy and in how the theory demands practice with integrity – that is, practice congruent with, in harmony with, the values and principles at the core of the approach. These core principles are all in opposition to the medicalisation of distress.

Actualising tendency

At the heart of any therapy theory is a view of human nature. One core debate on the constitution of human nature relates to our fundamental disposition. Does fulfilment come through release of potential or regulation of destructive impulses? Rogers' basic humanist declaration of the actualising tendency was, according to Merry (2003), a biological view that can be summarised as a directional tendency towards greater differentiation and fulfilment of the organism's constructive potential. Specifically, Rogers defined it as follows in 1959:

> This is the inherent tendency of the organism to develop all its capacities in ways which serve to maintain or enhance the organism. It involves not only the tendency to meet what Maslow terms 'deficiency needs' for air, food, water, and the like, but also more generalized activities. It involves development toward the differentiation of organs and of functions, expansion in terms of growth, expansion of effectiveness through the use of tools, expansion and enhancement through reproduction. It is development toward autonomy and away from heteronomy, or control by external forces. (Rogers, 1959: 196)

Rogers was wise to accusations of naïveté that the idea attracted:

> Some have thought of the client-centered therapist as an optimist. Others have felt that this line of thought follows Rousseau. Neither criticism seems to me to be true. The hypothesis in regard to the capacity of the individual is, rather, distilled out of an accumulated experience with many mildly and deeply disturbed individuals, who often display destructive or self-destructive tendencies. Contrary to those therapists who see depravity at men's [sic] core, who see men's deepest instincts as destructive, I have found that when man is truly free to become what he most deeply is, free to actualize his nature as an organism capable of awareness, then he clearly appears to move toward wholeness and integration. (Rogers, 1959, in Kirschenbaum & Henderson, 1990: 27)

To unilaterally contain or categorise such a general, positive tendency would, in practice, be illogical, unhealthy and anti-life. Practice in harmony with the actualising tendency construct would be cooperative and phenomenological, dedicated to removing obstacles to actualisation within the personality and the environment.

Non-directivity

Barry Grant (2004) wrote, 'Client-Centered Therapy is the practice of simply respecting the right to self-determination of others.' This is achieved by principled (rather than instrumental) non-directivity, a distinction made by Grant in 1990, when he outlined the difference between *using* non-directivity as an instrument or tool (as do integrationists, for example), rather than holding it as a fundamental quality or core value of human living. The principle of non-directivity or non-interference only makes sense as a way of living with the actualising tendency. If human nature has such a basic tendency to self- and other destruction, then such a principle would obviously be naïve. However, since a core element of client-centred therapy *is* the actualising tendency, the principle of non-directivity as a core value and attitude follows logically. Non-directivity has a historical line through 20th century anarchy back at least to 600 BC and the *Tao Te Ching*. This principle has many names – non-interference, non-action, or the principle of *wu-wei*, where *wu* means 'not' and *wei* means 'artificial, contrived activity that interferes with natural and spontaneous development' (Ames, cited in Marshall, 1992: 55). None of these terms are indicative of idleness or inertia or *laissez-faire*. They are the *mindful* application of actions that follow, rather than act contrary to, nature.

To have such a principle actively informing practice helps determine the whole attitudinal framework of the practitioner towards the client as a member of the human race. It points towards an organismic appreciation of humanness (the person as an organism in process), with *growth* (or adaptation) and *flourishing* as metaphors for change. It militates against an instrumental appreciation of humanness (the person as machine), with *manualised repair* and *adjustment* as metaphors for change. It points towards ethical human relational *healing* and militates against invasive, disrespectful, quasi-medical *treatment*. In short, such an irreducible principle determines our entire perception of what therapy is for and how to do it.

Holism

Classical person-centred therapy is intrinsically holistic. From Rogers' (1951) writings onward, the idea that the organism is an 'organised whole' (p486), and should be viewed and responded to as such, is paramount in theory and practice. In terms of the discussion here, any theory or treatment paradigm that is partial in its regard to the person would be antagonistic to person-centred therapy. In particular, the reductionist medical model of distress, with its almost exclusive focus on the physical dimension of the human being, is clearly out of step with person-centred therapy.[18] The physical, somatic, cognitive, affective and spiritual domains of human existence are given equal opportunity for expression in person-centred therapy, depending on the client's own biases and partialities with regard to their experience of themselves.

---

18. I concede that, with successive editions of diagnostic manuals such as the *Diagnostic and Statistical Manual of Mental Disorders* (*DSM*), there has been an increasing lean towards psychological symptoms/descriptors and diagnostic categories and away from physical disease analogues. However, the medical model is still a collection of reductionist medical protocols of diagnosis and treatment – namely, an illness metaphor methodology where symptom similarity is used to identify a 'disease category', which leads to a differentially applied 'treatment' as though it had been arrived at aetiologically.

An anti-diagnostic stance

A logical progression from the actualising tendency, non-directivity and holism is the classical client-centred position on diagnosis. There are two related senses of the term 'diagnosis' as used in the fields of counselling, psychotherapy and mental 'health'. First is the founding medicalised definition: diagnosis as the centrepiece of the medical model. Second is the evolving definition developed by the social/psychological sciences: the use of the faux-medical methodology of diagnosis, but with psychological descriptors and symptoms rather than out-and-out medical signs and symptoms. These two senses are hopelessly conflated, and have been since their inception: the history of social science is largely one of attempting to mimic the physical and/or medical sciences to gain credibility and professional status. It would be convenient if the term *psychodiagnosis* were used to describe diagnosis within *psychological* models of distress and the term *diagnosis* to describe *medical* models of distress, but both terms are used interchangeably, and I will not try to discriminate between usages in this chapter.

Classical client-centred therapy has strong complaints with both senses of the term, as I will outline below, but the main thrust of this chapter is to protest against the medicalisation of distress and the inappropriate diagnosis that inevitably comes in its wake.

Psychodiagnosis is clearly concerned with the political domain as well as the clinical, due to its association with the social control of people who are distressing (or inconvenient) to those around them, or society. Such issues have been comprehensively dealt with by such writers as Mary Boyle (1999) and Ian Parker and colleagues (Parker et al, 1995). However, few writers in the client-centred tradition critique the fundamental problem – the medicalisation of human distress.

Rogers himself rejected diagnosis from the start, for both clinical reasons and the ethical reasons detailed above. He addressed the issue in 'The Problem of Diagnosis' (1951: 219), in which he described the distinction between a model of pathology for organic disease and a model for psychopathology. He made his argument for a client-centred rationale for diagnosis when it was still possible to hope for a future where psychological therapies were not forced to practise under the shadow of the medical model. Even within this psychological domain, Rogers did not address the inherent redundancy of detailed diagnosis, given the phenomenological nature of client-centred theory.

Psychodiagnosis was left in a rather uneasy limbo until it was addressed in 1989 by Angelo Boy, who headed the most extensive client-centred therapy exploration of psychodiagnosis to date,[19] in the 'Symposium on Psychodiagnosis' published in *Person-Centered Review*. He located and then accepted the rationale

---

19. Notwithstanding that the Sixth World Conference of Person-Centered and Experiential Psychotherapy and Counseling, titled 'Process Differentiation and Person-Centeredness' and held in Egmond aan Zee, 6–11 July 2003, mostly deftly danced around the whole subject of psychodiagnosis and the medical model (without using those words).

for diagnosis in the medical model of mental illness, without much of a challenge. Again, the largely unquestioned starting point for the debate was acceptance of the logic of a medical model of mental distress. His conclusion was one that has become more familiar in recent years, in that he suggested that client-centred therapists should either help revise and improve the medical model, or provide an alternative diagnostic tool. Shlien is robust in his criticism:

> For the 'psychodynamic' therapist whose theory is based on pathology, or for the eclectic who thinks he has many different methods in his armory of equipment, diagnosis makes some sense.
>
> But client-centered therapy has only *one* treatment for *all* cases. That fact makes diagnosis entirely useless. If you have no specific treatment to relate to it, what purpose could there possibly be to specific diagnosis?
>
> Then, diagnosis is not good – not even neutral, but bad. Let's be straightforward about it. The facts may be friendly, but what are the facts? Diagnosis comes not just from a medical model, but from a theory of psychotherapy that is different from ours, antagonistic to ours. It is not only that its diagnostic predictions are flawed, faulty and detrimental to the relationship and the client's self-determination; they are simply a form of evil. That is, they label and subjugate people in ways that are difficult to contradict or escape. There is no value in being 'reasonable' about that, in wanting to participate in reformulation of the psychodiagnostic endeavor that will generate a universally agreed-upon answer. Why petition to be a partner to reformulation when it is wrong from the beginning? (Shlien, 1989: 160–161)

Therapists dedicated to emancipation, freedom, self-determination, growth, fulfilment and empowerment are in poor company with diagnosticians. Furthermore, an important dynamic of the healing process is highlighted here. The journey from emancipation, through empowerment, self-determination and growth, to fulfilment represents the very heart of the process of healing identified by Rogers (1951, 1959, 1978), and is increasingly implicated in psychological health by others (eg. Bentall, 2003). Diagnosis requires an already vulnerable person to submit to the arbitrary, damaging 'authority' of the expert diagnostician. Moreover, it is an unscientific, amoral authority, born out of historical precedent and political expediency, and maintained by professional interests. Client-centred therapy is the only approach that enshrines the client's right to access healing without sacrificing their personal power. They are the expert, and the client-centred therapist goes 'back to the client' for authority (Schmid, 2004). For a full discussion of the fundamental phenomenological and anti-expert positions of client-centred therapy, see Peter Schmid's chapter in this book (Chapter 5).

This right must be re-established by repeated re-presentation of these views in a hostile, medically dominated system. This situation is not new. Rogers (1957) wrote of his 'fear and trembling' because of a 'heavy weight of clinical opinion to the contrary' (in Kirschenbaum & Henderson, 1990: 230). There is still good reason for us to be afraid and tremble, but Shlien adds: 'There is no advantage in cooperating with the dominant clique. The lion and the lamb may lie down together, but if it is in the lion's den, the lion is probably quite relaxed, looking forward to breakfast in bed' (Shlien, 1989: 161).

Person-centred psychopathology?

The main theme of this chapter is the invalidity, the unevidenced and damaging nature of psychodiagnosis, and that this argument derives from the doxic idea that human distress is an 'illness'. Therefore, if there is no reasonable evidence that human distress constitutes an 'illness', then applying a medical model and its associated elements is at least inappropriate. Between the medicalisation of distress and diagnosis lies the apparatus of psychopathology – the very term 'pathology' indicates its medical origin. I could then argue that, if the cause (medicalisation of distress) and the effect (diagnosis and damaging inappropriate treatment) are invalid, we need not spend time dismantling the material in between.

Humanistic alternative diagnostic formulations mainly replace one set of labels with another, again failing to address the inherent redundancy of detailed diagnosis and the iatrogenic nature of categorisation. Person-centred therapy does have a system of understanding and, to some extent, categorising distress (Rogers, 1959), which could be considered to constitute a psychopathology, and Elke Lambers (2003) and Paul Wilkins (2003) both outline how person-centred therapy theory is, if treated as a static *system*, more than adequate as a system of explanation for medical model categories of 'illness'. However, person-centred therapy parts company with the usual symptom-driven diagnostic system when the theory makes it clear that, even though there may be a unitary source of tension, the ways in which this may be made manifest are unique to each individual. Understanding the individual characteristics of each person's experiences can only be achieved through empathy. A further departure from medically orientated psychopathologies arises when person-centred therapy theory proposes that the experience of resolution of the distress may not be due to the *instrumental* effects of the *techniques* of empathy, unconditional positive regard (UPR) and congruence, but, rather, result from the totality of the relationship – a unique, co-created healing moment, where complex human contact is the curative factor.

Among person-centred theorists, Margaret Warner presents an alternative psychopathology, not merely a diagnostic framework, based on client-centred and experiential theory. She accepts the primacy of diagnostic methodology, with its direct line of ancestry to the medical model; her position is founded on the pragmatism of compromise and revision. Her alternative psychopathology[20] is clearly outlined and

---

20. Alternative to the medical model, and also attempting to present a new and unifying 'person-centred psychopathology' as a development and extension of Rogers' work.

explained in Chapter 6 of this book. She aims to provide person-centred therapy with some of the apparatus that is valued, if not required, by insurance companies, government agencies and others holding the purse strings. Along the way, she manages to humanise the brutal medical model diagnostic terminology.[21]

A very particular approach to diagnosis can be found in emotion-focused therapy. First, some practitioners accept medicalised diagnoses such as depression and social anxiety disorder in order to engage with the mental health system. Second, every therapeutic encounter is perfused with micro-diagnoses, and strategies resulting from subsequent analysis can be found in process-experiential psychotherapy literature. Elliott and colleagues declare:

> Diagnosis based on [the *DSM-IV*] is an expert-based, non-empathic approach to working with clients. Thus it is inconsistent with the kind of therapeutic relationship desired in PE [process-experiential] therapy. Does this mean that client diagnosis should be ignored in PE therapy? Although this was our position 20 years ago… in the meantime we have found that knowing something about the patterns of difficulty their clients experience can help therapists to work with them more effectively. (2004: 275)

So it would appear that a principled position is set aside on the basis of pragmatism. However, on the same page, Elliott and colleagues state: 'At the same time, PE [process-experiential] therapists attempt as much as possible to bracket the client's diagnosis, setting it to one side. The client is not the diagnosis.' Although not made explicit, another factor may be at work here: namely, the requirement for research evidence. It is understandable – when therapeutic approaches vie for funding based on 'evidence', and when that evidence is only deemed trustworthy when presented in terms of diagnostic categories – that theorists and practitioners might be persuaded to be pragmatic, swallow their objections and play the game.

Elke Lambers gives a good account of the context of a person-centred perspective on psychodiagnosis (Lambers, 2003). She also offers a person-centred framework for psychodiagnosis built on theoretical constructs, and gives examples of working in a client-centred way with people who have received diagnoses of differing severity. She develops all of this in a scenario predicated on the pragmatic need to articulate (communicate) with the medical model in order to better serve our clients. This is helpful for those who are not familiar with medical-model methodology, and reassuring for the many practitioners who lack the confidence to work with disturbed and disturbing clients.

---

21. Changing language is an important project, since language is intimately connected with thinking. Change the way we talk about distress and a change in the way we think is brought one step closer. It could be argued that, for example, 'fragile process' is a less alienating label than 'borderline personality disorder' (see Margaret Warner's Chapter 6 in this volume). Lisbeth Sommerbeck points out (in a private communication) that the intention with which words are used is vitally important: for example, the term 'depression' can be prescriptive (as used by the medical model) or descriptive (as used by an individual client).

Finally (although this is not a comprehensive roll call), Lisbeth Sommerbeck's work is testimony to the success that is possible when compromise is relentlessly pursued while standing one's ground in terms of theory. In common with Lambers, she insists that client-centred therapists become familiar with the medical model and diagnostic categories in order to integrate better into the system. Sommerbeck introduces a novel way of approaching the discrepancies between client-centred therapy and the psychiatric medical model. She suggests that 'understanding (in the theory of client-centred therapy) and explaining (in the medical model theory of psychiatry) are complementary, not contradictory, activities' (Sommerbeck, 2003: 5). She argues for a very different strategy from the options presented in this chapter – one in which psychiatrists will be persuaded of the complementarity of the approaches by the experience of working with a dedicated, *congruent* client-centred therapist. (In her own practice she voices her critical view of psychiatry at every appropriate opportunity, at a general level, being careful not to compromise her relationship with individual clients.) Client-centred therapy will then sit comfortably in the range of possible treatment options. Sommerbeck outlines her position in Chapter 7 of this volume and in her book *The Client-Centred Therapist in Psychiatric Settings* (Sommerbeck, 2003).

By and large, however, all of the above arguments are, in Shlien's colourful analogy, already lying down with the lion (with no guarantee that they will not be on the breakfast menu) – their starting-point is an acceptance (however obviously compliant, reluctant and pragmatic) of the medical model of distress and its diagnostic methodology. Can Lambers' and Sommerbeck's calls for therapists to become familiar with the language and procedures of psychodiagnosticians be translated into a case of, 'If you want to defeat your enemy, sing his song'?

Counselling for Depression (CfD)

From the 1970s until the early 21st century, person-centred therapy dominated counselling in primary care in the UK. Around 2005, government initiatives required health and medical practice to be based on particular types of evidence, and cognitive behavioural therapies rapidly gained ground, to the exclusion of person-centred therapy. Since 2009, the Counselling for Depression project, supported by the British Association for Counselling and Psychotherapy (BACP), and headed by its (then) Head of Research Andy Hill, has attempted to restore person-centred and experiential therapies as a recommended choice in UK primary care provision (Sanders & Hill, 2014). The aim was to incorporate 'counselling for depression' (CfD) as a treatment within the framework of the government's Improving Access to Psychological Therapies (IAPT) programme. CfD is a new approach, integrating more classical person-centred therapy and some elements of emotion-focused therapy. Most importantly, it is approved by the National Institute for Health and Care Excellence (NICE) in its guideline for the treatment of mild-to-moderate depression (NICE, 2009). The success of the CfD initiative has been founded on the development of competencies, essentially 'manualising' a person-centred therapy set of skills and presenting the research evidence of the type reviewed by Hill and Elliott (2014).

Counselling for depression is not without its critics within the person-centred movement in the UK. The manualisation of person-centred therapy is seen by some as a philosophical and theoretical offence and impossible in practice. Yet it is celebrated by others, as it gets a foot in the door of the NHS in England, ensuring patients will have the choice of person-centred therapy for depression, free as a statutory service.[22]

The project is also funding ongoing research in the form of a large randomised controlled trial – the Pragmatic, Randomised Controlled Trial assessing the non-Inferiority of Counselling and its Effectiveness for Depression (PRaCTICED), led by Professor Michael Barkham at the University of Sheffield. CfD is research friendly in that it provides a regular, competence-based therapy, amenable to adherence and outcome measures. For many therapists, these qualities in themselves render it at terminal variance with true person-centred practice. However, if the trial results are favourable, it will continue to be a NICE-recommended frontline treatment for mild-to-moderate depression – a foot in the NHS door.

Positive psychology

Opinion is divided, if not polarised, when considering positive psychology (see Peterson (2006) for a comprehensive introduction). One of the founders of the approach, Martin Seligman, together with Mihali Csikszentmihalyi (2000), views positive psychology as including the biological, personal, relational, institutional, cultural and global dimensions of life. Positive psychology is becoming a ubiquitous commentary on 21st century life, sometimes unsympathetically associated with self-help guides to 'true' happiness, and a vehicle for neoliberal individualism (for a recent critique, see Friedli & Stearn, 2015). All this is because a group of psychologists wanted to focus on the positive aspects of human functioning and thriving, rather than pathological ones.

Throughout his career, Rogers demonstrated the unpopularity of stressing the notion that human beings are essentially positive, forward looking and forward moving. Several person-centred writers position the approach as a potentiality model. Chantler (2006: 47) explains that the actualising tendency, with an appropriate caveat, is the construct that moves person-centred therapy away from a 'deficit model' of human psychology:

> I suggest the actualizing tendency be read as a social construct, and to
> engage with where and what the process leads towards. This opens up the
> concept to further debate and contestation. The potentiality of subjects

---

22. For an authoritative and comprehensive account of CfD theory and practice, see Sanders & Hill, 2014.

(rather than a deficit model) that the self-actualizing tendency suggests
is important, but equally important to grapple with is the way in which
potentiality is influenced by, and thwarted by, the wider context.

Although simply put, this message, sympathetic to positive psychology, that human beings are best understood by looking at their potential, is *fundamentally at odds* with the medicalised deficit models of mainstream psychology, and offers normalisation of experience and hope. Is person-centred psychology a positive psychology? Perhaps, but regardless of the verdict, both offer substantial challenges to the medical model if properly contextualised in theory and practice.

Conclusion

Critical psychologists and psychiatrists have been developing their arguments in favour of dismantling the medical model, psychopathology and psychodiagnosis. The mainstream counselling and psychotherapy profession is still in thrall to medicalisation and diagnosis. Person-centred therapists have been treading water. Some simply reject the medical model and diagnosis, for the reasons outlined in this chapter. Others just as simply accept the primacy of the medical model, and either renounce or 'work around' their person-centred principles. And yet others mindfully enter the statutory system in order to change it from within and improve services. Mearns passionately and eloquently supports such engagement, or 'articulation' as he calls it (Mearns, 2003, 2004). Mearns' 2003 paper is the antidote to this chapter, and Lambers (2003), Warner (2005; Chapter 6 this volume) and Sommerbeck (2003, 2005, and Chapter 7, this volume) take similar, but crucially different, lines.

Nevertheless, this chapter seeks to keep the option of refusal and principled opposition on the table, not only for those in a position to use it in practice (although this would be reason enough), but also because the evolution of ideas requires diversity in the pool of ideas. Keeping the poles of the argument struck firmly into the ground provides the tension required for vibrant and creative exchange, to prevent the middle ground becoming a well-trodden, comfortable bog. My final reason is that the metaphor for distress that we as therapists carry with us into our work influences *every aspect* of our relationship with our clients. If we think sick, we will see sick, and nothing in that resonates with my understanding of person-centred therapy.

A criticism of this position is that it will needlessly antagonise the lion with which others are trying to make peace. However, I do not believe that the position of opposition and refusal is necessarily self-defeating, disenfranchising and irresponsible. It sits constructively alongside articulation, compromise and complementarity in the range of possibilities that comprise the person-centred therapy responses to the medicalisation of distress that offends our theory. Indeed, for better or worse, I decided to oppose and refuse in alignment with some service users, and to engage and articulate with others. In private correspondence, Margaret Warner correctly pointed out to me that something must be done *today* to help bring the person-centred therapy tribe back into the mix of funded treatment options wherever it has been excluded. Her work is, in part, an attempt to address such exclusion where it is based on the idea that person-centred therapy has no recognisable, unified psychopathology,[23] before a utopian medical-model-free order is installed. Client choice and emancipation is the shared aim – a humanising revision from Warner for the moment, while others plan and organise a future where to be frightened, confused and overwhelmed is not considered to be an illness.

At the start of this chapter, I quoted Carl Rogers (1951: 8): 'These ways of thinking will not be abolished by wishful thinking.' Again, history has proved him right – it is concerted action that has yielded results since the first edition of this book. The publication of *DSM-5* in 2014 was greeted with a chorus of criticism and frank horror, to the extent that the US National Institute of Mental Health announced that it would not use it. The British Psychological Society Division of Clinical Psychology published *Understanding Psychosis and Schizophrenia* (Cooke, 2014) as an antidote to the continuing medicalisation and diagnosis of distress in the UK. The 60-year-old International Society for the Psychological Treatments of the Schizophrenias and Other Psychoses recognised the changing tide by changing its name to the International Society for Psychological and Social Approaches to Psychosis. The users of psychiatric services continue to organise and reclaim the vocabulary and meanings of lives with unusual and/or distressing experiences. Their rising common chorus is empathy, authenticity and acceptance, while in the UK, person-centred voices are very few and far between.

Author's note for second edition

I thank Margaret Warner and Mick Cooper for their feedback on an early draft of this chapter in the first edition. I especially appreciate Lisbeth Sommerbeck for her continued friendship and enthusiastic engagement with the issues. I would also like to thank John Read for his friendship and continuing courageous assault on psychiatric hegemony.

---

23. This point will be contested by those who argue that there is a perfectly adequate client-centred therapy psychopathology, while others claim that it runs out of both steam and detail when human distress is severe and enduring, and is also light on developmental theory (see Paul Wilkins' Chapter 3 in this book for the alternative view).

References

Andrew E, Gray N, Snowden R (2008). The relationship between trauma and beliefs about hearing voices: a study of psychiatric and non-psychiatric voice hearers. *Psychological Medicine 38*(10): 1409–1417.

Bentall RP (2003). *Madness Explained: psychosis and human nature*. London: Allen Lane/Penguin.

Birchwood M, Fowler D, Jackson C (2000). *Early Intervention in Psychosis: a guide to concepts, evidence and interventions*. Chichester: John Wiley.

Blackburn P, Yates C (2004). Same story – different tale. *Mental Health Today* December: 31–33.

Bourdieu P, Wacquant L (1992). *Invitation to Reflexive Sociology*. Cambridge: Polity Press.

Boyle M (1990). The non-discovery of schizophrenia. In Bentall RP (ed). *Reconstructing Schizophrenia*. London: Routledge (pp3–22).

Boyle M (2014). *Schizophrenia: a scientific delusion?* (2nd ed). London: Routledge.

Boy A, Seeman J, Shlien J, Fischer C, Cain DJ (1989/2002). Symposium on psychodiagnosis. *Person-Centered Review 4*: 132–182. Reprinted in: Cain DJ (ed) (2002). *Classics in the Person-Centered Approach*. Ross-on-Wye: PCCS Books (pp385–414).

Breggin P (1993). *Toxic Psychiatry. Drugs and Electroconvulsive Therapy: the truth and the better alternatives*. London: HarperCollins.

Chantler K (2006). Rethinking person-centred therapy. In: Proctor G, Cooper M, Sanders P, Malcolm B (eds). *Politicizing the Person-Centred Approach: an agenda for social change*. Ross-on-Wye: PCCS Books (pp44–54).

Charlesworth SJ (2000). *A Phenomenology of Working Class Experience*. Cambridge: Cambridge University Press.

Ciompi L, Hoffmann H (2004). Soteria Berne: an innovative milieu therapeutic approach to acute schizophrenia based on the concept of affect-logic. *World Psychiatry 3*: 140-146. http://ciompi.com/pdf/WP-2004-10-Soteria.pdf

Cooke A (2014). *Understanding Psychosis and Schizophrenia*. Leicester: BPS Division of Counselling Psychology. Available free from www.bps.org.uk/system/files/Public%20files/rep03_understanding_psychosis.pdf (accessed 28 January, 2017).

Elliott R, Watson JC, Goldman RN, Greenberg LS (2004). *Learning Emotion-Focused Therapy: the process-experiential approach to change*. Washington, DC: APA.

Elliott R, Watson J, Greenberg LS, Timulak L, Freire E (2013). Research on humanistic-experiential psychotherapies. In: Lambert MJ (ed). *Bergin and Garfield's Handbook of Psychotherapy and Behavior Change* (6th ed). New York: Wiley (pp495–538).

Friedli L, Stearn R (2015). Positive affect as coercive strategy: conditionality, activation and the role of psychology in UK government workfare programmes. *Medical Humanities* 41: 40–47. doi:10.1136/medhum-2014-010622

Grant B (1990). Principled and instrumental non-directiveness in person-centered and client-centered therapy. *Person-Centred Review 5*: 77–88. Reprinted in Cain DJ (ed) (2002). *Classics in the Person-Centered Approach*. Ross-on-Wye: PCCS Books (pp371–377).

Grant B (2004). The imperative of ethical justification in psychotherapy: the special case of client-centered therapy. *Person-Centered and Experiential Psychotherapies 3*: 152–165.

Hill A, Elliott R (2014). Evidence-based practice and person-centred and experiential therapies. In: Sanders P, Hill A. *Counselling for Depression: a person-centred and experiential approach to practice*. London: Sage (pp5–20).

Houghton P (2005). Stop the juggernaught. *Mental Health Today* February: 22–23.

Johnstone L (2014). *A Straight-Talking Introduction to Psychiatric Diagnosis.* Monmouth: PCCS Books.

Johnstone L, Dallos R (eds)(2013). *Formulation in Psychology and Psychotherapy* (2nd ed). Basingstoke: Routledge.

Kirschenbaum H (2007). *The Life and Work of Carl Rogers.* Ross-on-Wye: PCCS Books.

Kirschenbaum H, Henderson VL (1990). *The Carl Rogers Dialogues.* London: Constable.

Laing RD (1965). *The Divided Self.* Harmondsworth: Penguin.

Laing RD, Esterson A (1964). *Sanity, Madness and the Family: families of schizophrenics.* London: Tavistock.

Lambers E (2003). The person-centred perspective on psychopathology. In: Mearns D (ed). *Developing Person-Centred Counselling.* London: Sage (pp103–119).

Lynch T (2004). *Beyond Prozac: healing mental suffering without drugs.* Ross-on-Wye: PCCS Books.

Marshall P (1992). *Demanding the Impossible: a history of anarchism.* London: HarperCollins.

Mearns D (2003). The humanistic agenda: articulation. *Journal of Humanistic Psychology* 43: 53–65.

Mearns D (2004). Problem-centered is not person-centered. *Person-Centered and Experiential Psychotherapies* 3: 88–101.

Merry T (2003). The actualisation conundrum. *Person-Centred Practice 11*: 83–91.

Mosher LR, Burti L (1994). *Community Mental Health: a practical guide.* New York: WW Norton & Co.

Mosher LR, Hendrix V (2004). *Soteria: through madness to deliverance.* Philadelphia, PA: Xlibris.

Mosher LR (1999). Soteria and other alternatives to acute psychiatric hospitalization: a personal and professional view. *Changes* 17: 35–51.

National Institute for Health and Care Excellence (NICE) (2009, updated 2016). Depression in adults: recognition and treatment. London: NICE.

Newnes C (1999). Histories of psychiatry. In: Newnes C, Holmes G, Dunn C (eds). *This is Madness.* Ross-on-Wye: PCCS Books (pp7–27).

Parker I, Georgaca E, Harper D, McLaughlin T, Stowell-Smith M (1995). *Deconstructing Psychopathology.* London: Sage.

Patterson CH (1948/2000). Is psychotherapy dependent upon diagnosis? In: Patterson CH (2000). *Understanding Psychotherapy: fifty years of client-centred theory and practice.* Ross- on-Wye: PCCS Books (pp3–9).

Peterson C (2006). *A Primer in Positive Psychology.* New York: Oxford University Press.

Pilgrim D (1990). Competing histories of madness. In: Bentall RP (ed). *Reconstructing Schizophrenia.* London: Routledge (pp211–233).

Rapley M, Moncrieff J, Dillon J (eds) (2011). *Demedicalising Misery: psychiatry, psychology and the human condition.* Basingstoke: Palgrave.

Read J, Dillon J (eds) (2013). *Models of Madness* (2nd ed). London: Routledge.

Read J, Mosher LR, Bentall RP (eds) (2004). *Models of Madness.* London: Brunner-Routledge.

Rogers CR (1951). *Client-Centered Therapy.* Boston: Houghton Mifflin.

Rogers CR (1957). The necessary and sufficient conditions of therapeutic personality change. *Journal of Consulting Psychology 21*: 95–103. In: Kirscenbaum H, Henderson V (eds) (1990). *The Carl Rogers Reader.* London: Constable (pp219–235).

Rogers CR (1959). A theory of therapy, personality and interpersonal relationships, as developed in the client-centred framework. In: Koch S (ed). *Psychology: a study of science. Vol 3: Formulation of the person and the social context.* New York: McGraw-Hill (pp184–256).

Rogers CR (1978). *Carl Rogers on Personal Power: inner strength and its revolutionary impact.* London: Constable.

Rogers CR, Gendlin ET, Kiesler DJ, Truax CB (1967). *The Therapeutic Relationship and its Impact: a study of psychotherapy with schizophrenics.* Madison: University of Wisconsin Press.

Romme M, Escher S (1993). *Accepting Voices.* London: Mind Publications.

Romme M, Escher S, Dillon J, Ciorstens D, Morris M (eds)(2009). *Living With Voices: 50 stories of recovery.* Ross-on-Wye: PCCS Books.

Rowe D (1993). Foreword. In: Breggin P. *Toxic Psychiatry. Drugs and electroconvulsive therapy: the truth and the better alternatives.* London: HarperCollins (ppxvii–xxix).

Sanders P, Tudor K (2001). This is therapy. In: Newnes C, Holmes G, Dunn C (eds). *This is Madness Too.* Ross on-Wye: PCCS Books (pp147–160).

Sanders P, Hill A (2014). *Counselling for Depression: a person-centred and experiential approach to practice.* London: Sage.

Schmid PF (2004). Back to the client: a phenomenological approach to the process of understanding and diagnosis. *Person-Centered and Experiential Psychotherapies* 3: 36–52.

Seligman MEP, Csikszentmihalyi, M (2000). Positive psychology: an introduction. *American Psychologist* 55(1): 5–14. doi:10.1037/0003-066x.55.1.5

Shlien JM (1989/2001). Response to Boy's symposium on psychodiagnosis. In: Cain DJ (ed). *Classics in the Person-Centered Approach.* Ross-on-Wye: PCCS Books (pp400–402).

Seikkula J, Alakare B, Aaltonen J, Holma J, Rasinkangas A, Lehtinen V (2003). Open Dialogue approach: treatment principles and preliminary results of a two-year follow-up on first episode schizophrenia. *Ethical and Human Sciences and Services* 5(3): 163–182. http://psychrights.org/Research/Digest/Effective/OpenDialogue2yfollowupehss0204.pdf

Sommerbeck L (2003). *The Client-Centred Therapist in Psychiatric Settings: a therapist's guide to the psychiatric landscape and its inhabitants.* Ross-on-Wye: PCCS Books.

Stickley T (2005). Learn to listen. *Mental Health Today* February: 24–25.

Szasz T (1961). *The Myth of Mental Illness.* New York: Harper & Row.

Wilkins P (2003). An absent psychopathology: a therapy for the worried well? In: Wilkins P. *Person-Centred Therapy in Focus.* London: Sage (pp99–107).

THEORY

3 | Person-centred theory and 'mental illness'

Paul Wilkins

Person-centred therapy has been criticised for its perceived lack of a theory of psychopathology that *is able to differentiate the needs* of clients experiencing mental ill health. In this chapter, the validity of this criticism is explored and rebutted with reference both to early theoretical statements and research and to the views of current practitioner/researchers. Differences within the person-centred family of therapies are indicated by briefly examining (for example) the situations in the UK and in continental Europe.

Four major contemporary positions to mental ill health within the person-centred tradition are explored. These are those based on:

1. (psychological) contact
2. incongruence
3. styles of processing
4. issues of power.

Cases for and against: a multiplicity of views

A therapy for the worried well?

One of the widespread beliefs therapists of other orientations have about person-centred therapy is that it is 'psychotherapy lite': that it may be perfect for those who are mildly and acutely disturbed but it lacks the teeth necessary to get to grips with people experiencing real, chronic distress. On the other hand, person-centred therapy is also seen as useful for people who are so deeply disturbed or dysfunctional as to be 'unsuitable' for psychotherapy (see Kovel, 1976: 116). In other words, person-centred therapy is not going to do anything for 'psychologically minded' people with real problems. Also, practitioners of person-centred therapy are seen as naïvely clinging to an optimistic (and outmoded) model of the person, a commitment to a non-directive approach that prevents effective intervention and an antipathy to assessment and diagnosis. Thus, person-centred therapy is criticised as lacking a theory of personality and, in particular, of child development. This leads to an inadequate view of how (for example) neuroses and psychoses may arise and thus how they may be addressed. These factors are seen to preclude any notion of 'psychopathology'. This is why Wheeler (in Wheeler & McLeod, 1995: 286) has two 'serious reservations' about person-centred therapy. First, she is concerned that there is an assumption of human goodness that does not hold water. Her second reservation is that there 'is a lack of theory of human growth and development to underpin the practice, and [a] subsequent disregard for assessment'.

The first of these doubts is easily dealt with. Person-centred theory makes no claim as to the inherent 'goodness' of people (see Wilkins, 2003: 60–63). The belief that it does seems to stem from a misunderstanding of the concepts of the actualising tendency and what it means to be 'fully functioning'. These terms imply direction, not an end point, and the actualising tendency is a biological force, common to all living things. In incorporating these concepts into theory, no moral judgment is made or implied.

Wheeler's second point presupposes that emotional distress and psychopathology can only be understood in the context of a theory of child development. This is a belief, not a proven fact. An alternative belief, perhaps more in keeping with a person-centred philosophy, is that mental distress is rooted in inequality and 'based on internalised oppression' (see Proctor, 2002: 84). This leads to a need to consider the power relationships and social position of the individual experiencing distress. However, Wheeler's assertion that there is no person-centred theory of child development is an error. Rogers (1959: 222) postulated that:

> … the individual, during the period of infancy, has at least these attributes:
>
> 1. He perceives *his experience* as reality. His experience is his reality.
>   a. As a consequence he has greater potential *awareness* of what reality is for him than does anyone else, since no one else can completely assume his *internal frame of reference*.
> 2. He has an inherent tendency toward *actualizing* his organism.
> 3. He interacts with his reality in terms of his basic *actualizing* tendency. Thus his behavior is the goal-directed attempt of the organism to satisfy the experienced needs for *actualization* in the reality as *perceived*.
> 4. In this interaction he behaves as an organized whole, as a gestalt.
> 5. He engages in an *organismic valuing process*, valuing *experience* with reference to the *actualizing tendency* as a criterion. *Experiences* which are *perceived* as maintaining or enhancing the organism are valued positively. Those which are *perceived* as negating such maintenance or enhancement are valued negatively.

6. He behaves with adience toward positively valued *experiences* and with avoidance toward those negatively valued.

In the same chapter, Rogers (pp224–226) explains the development of conditions of worth and (pp226–230) the development of incongruence and its consequences. Indeed, Rogers (1959) includes comprehensive theoretical statements about the human organism. He traces both 'healthy' development and 'dysfunctional' development and shows how there may be movement from ill health to health. In this way, Rogers' chapter can be seen as the bedrock on which person-centred theories of psychopathology may be built.

Other person-centred theorists have modelled child development. Biermann-Ratjen (1996: 13), drawing on Rogers' necessary and sufficient conditions, offers necessary conditions for self-development in early childhood. These are:

1. That the baby is in *contact* with a significant other.

2. That the baby is preoccupied with *evaluating experience* which might possibly arouse anxiety.

3. That the *significant other person* is *congruent in the relationship* to the baby, does not experience anything inconsistent with her self concept while in contact with the baby when it is preoccupied with evaluating [its] experience.

4. That the significant other is *experiencing unconditional positive regard* toward the baby's processes of evaluating his experience.

5. That the significant other is *experiencing an empathic understanding* of the baby's experiencing within his *internal frame of reference*.

6. That the baby gradually *perceives* both the unconditional positive regard of the significant other person for him and the empathic understanding so that in the baby's *awareness* there is gradually a *belief or prognosis* that the unconditionally positively regarding and empathically understanding object would when reacting to other experiences of the baby also exhibit positive regard and empathic understanding.

Biermann-Ratjen (p14) goes on to state that 'positive regard is the precondition for self development'. Rogers (1959: 223) wrote that the need for positive regard is 'universal in human beings, and in the individual, is pervasive and persistent'. In person-centred theory, it is the pursuit of positive regard at the expense of the organismic valuing process that underlies mental ill health. Put another way, if there is sufficient disharmony between the organism and the self(-concept), the resulting incongruence is likely to manifest as one or more of the complexes of thinking, behaviour and processing that in other models may be called neuroses and psychoses, mental illness or disease. Holdstock and Rogers (1977: 136) describe the acquisition of psychological disturbance thus:

the continuing estrangement between self-concept and experience leads to increasingly rigid perceptions and behavior. If experiences are extremely incongruent with the self-concept, the defence system will be inadequate to prevent the experiences from overwhelming the self-concept. When this happens the self-concept will break down, resulting in disorganization of behavior. This is conventionally classed as psychosis when the disorganization is considerable.

From the early days of person-centred therapy, there have been theoretical explanations of the acquisition and development of psychopathological ways of being, and these have continued to be refined and expanded (see, for example, Cooper, 2000: 87–94). As well as the theoretical structures mentioned above (and those below), in the simplest terms, 'disorder' can be understood with reference to the necessary and sufficient conditions. Thus, difficulties with 'communication' (including autism, and some other 'special needs') relate to 'contact' and 'perception' (conditions 1 and 6), while emotional distress and thought disorder are to do with incongruence (condition 2). Of course, there is often overlap between the two areas, but the theories and practices of person-centred therapy have evolved to take account of each. In fact, work with 'disturbed' populations has been a feature of person-centred practice from at least the 1950s. It may be that practitioners of other orientations disagree with these theories and practices, but that is a very different position from being critical of their supposed absence.

A historical perspective

Perhaps the best known and best documented early instance of person-centred practice with people considered to be 'mentally ill' is the so-called Wisconsin project. Barrett-Lennard (1998: 68–69, 267–270) writes of this 'massive study of psychotherapy with hospitalized schizophrenic patients', which lasted for much of the time Rogers worked at the University of Wisconsin (1957–1963) and led ultimately to the publication of a massive report (see Rogers et al, 1967). Besides Rogers, the project team comprised Eugene Gendlin, Donald Kiesler and Charles Truax, with contributions from many others. Although it was a difficult time for those concerned, riven with personal differences leading to partings of the ways of colleagues and erstwhile friends, and added little to knowledge of person-centred therapy, Barrett-Lennard (1998: 68) records that:

> The work is more of a milestone in respect to the conduct and reporting of research in its complex sphere, and in the development of strategies and instrumentation, than in terms of clear-cut findings from fully tested hypotheses.

Also, although Shlien (2003: 125) argues that the project as a whole 'became a failure' because the staff team was 'not prepared to provide Client-Centered Therapy that was adequate to test the hypotheses' and the research methods employed are now seen as flawed (see, for example, Prouty, 2002a: 583–584), it did offer evidence that high levels of congruence and empathy correlated with client improvement. Significant publications other than that of Rogers et al (1967) resulted from this study. Chief among these are Shlien's 1961 paper 'A client-centered approach to schizophrenia: first approximation', on his work with a deeply disturbed client (see Shlien, 2003: 30–59), and papers by Gendlin (1963) and Rogers (1961a), both of which 'include direct and sensitive portrayals of the human condition of the schizophrenic person' (Barrett-Lennard, 1998: 68). Also important in terms of the historical perspective on psychopathology in person-centred therapy is the symposium on psychodiagnosis published in *Person-Centered Review*, printed in 1989 and reprinted in Cain (2002). This is dealt with more thoroughly in the chapter on assessment (Chapter 9, this volume).

From the 1960s until the 1990s, as in so many other areas, research into person-centred therapy with people with schizophrenia and reports of case studies are largely absent from the (English language) literature. The published proceedings of a conference for client-centred and experiential psychotherapies in Leuven, Belgium contain two significant papers about working with people with schizophrenia: Prouty (1990) and Teusch (1990). This trend continued in the international conferences on client-centred and experiential counselling and psychotherapy that followed. For example, Berghofer (1996) reports on her work with long-term patients and (p492) concludes that '[t]he most important element in psychotherapy with schizophrenic patients is the active establishment and maintenance of a reliable interpersonal relationship'. Miksch (2000), too, stresses the importance of the relationship in working with this client group, while Warner (2002a) emphasises not only the quality of the relationship but also the importance of allowing this client group (and others experiencing 'thought disorders') to express themselves in their own voices. She (p471) writes:

> I suspect that the common psychiatric practice of ignoring or actively discouraging expressions that sound psychotic may actually stop clients from processing experiences in ways that could allow them to gain a more integrated sense of their own reactions and preferences.

Until the last decade of the 20th century, there does not seem to be much written about person-centred therapy with specific 'disorders' other than schizophrenia. The research effort in the 1960s and 1970s was largely directed towards establishing the efficacy of the therapist conditions of congruence, empathy and unconditional regard. This research yielded some interesting results, as a way of testing Rogers' hypothesis as to the necessity and sufficiency of the six conditions. However, because the therapist conditions were usually separated from the other three, and often attempts were made to consider them separately, it is flawed. Another main area for research throughout this time and henceforward was into the comparative effectiveness of person-centred therapy with respect to other approaches. This, too, is suspect because, as Elliott (2001: 67–68) confirms in his meta-analysis, 'researcher allegiance' (ie. the approach to therapy to which the researcher is predisposed) tends to influence findings. It is also true that, in terms of classic client-centred therapy, because there is only one 'treatment', regardless of the client's difficulty (see Wilkins & Gill, 2003: 177), there was little impetus to research the hows and whys of person-centred therapy with different issues and different client groups. However, Lambers (1994: 106–120) did make an important, accessible statement about 'person-centred psychopathology', setting out in straightforward terms how the major psychiatric categories of neurotic, psychotic, personality and borderline personality disorders may be understood in a person-centred way. She makes the 'key point' that, although person-centred theoreticians and practitioners are resistant to diagnostic labels, 'it is possible to understand, for example, neurosis in terms of person-centred theory. Such an analysis may help the counsellor to understand her own responses to the neurotic client'.

Lambers understands neuroses in terms of psychosomatic symptoms, anxiety and incongruent communication. She advances the idea that neurosis develops from strong conditions of worth, to which the punishment for not conforming 'took the form of *withdrawal of affection and acceptance*' [original italics]. What results is an externalisation of the locus of evaluation, a negative self-concept, and feelings may be denied or distorted. In every way, neurosis equates with incongruence. Lambers describes borderline personality disorder as characterised by a wide variety of symptoms, and states that the life of a person experiencing it 'may appear chaotic'. She sees borderline personality disorder as possibly developing from an inconsistency in conditions of worth and experiences, leading to an inability to develop a self-concept informed by experience. She writes that the self-concept of a person experiencing borderline personality disorder 'lacks boundaries, consistency, continuity and protection; it is constantly under threat as it has no effective means of evaluating and integrating new experiences'. Borderline personality disorder is further characterised by episodes of adequate functioning, interspersed with times of chaos and disturbance. Lambers takes the view that the defensive responses manifesting as disturbed behaviour 'only occur in situations where the self is threatened by new experiences'.

On psychosis, she reminds her readers that this is not a diagnostic category but a description of a mental state characterised by withdrawal from normal contact both with reality and with other people. She goes on to reiterate Rogers' view that psychosis is 'a state of disintegration, involving the breakdown of the neurotic defences of denial and distortion and the development of extreme forms of defence such as paranoid and catatonic behaviour'. Lambers understands the need for such an extreme in terms of an enormous threat to the self.

Personality disorder she describes in terms of 'subjective distress or significant impairment of the person's ability to function as a social being', and as characterised by a sense that the causes of misfortune and threat are located in others and outside the control of the sufferer. She writes that personality disorder arises from early significant relationships 'characterised by neglect or persistent abuse of power', in which 'conditions of worth have been linked with satisfying the needs of those with the power'. Because of the unpredictable nature of such relationships, people with personality disorders have learned to live only in the moment and have not been able to learn from experience. This results in a profound negation of self and a deep-seated sense of worthlessness. Lambers states that 'to bring this core sense of worthlessness into awareness would be very dangerous'.

Coming up to date

In the later years of the 20th century and into the 21st century, this situation changed radically. This change may be partly because of the need to demonstrate the effectiveness and applicability of the person-centred family of therapies to funders (healthcare providers, medical insurers and the like), but it also reflects a zeitgeist. Whatever the reason, the person-centred community has turned its attention once more to 'psychopathology'. This is evident, for example, from the review of research in the German language region produced by Eckert, Höger and Schwab (2003), where (p5) they indicate that the focus of research has become 'increasingly disorder-specific', listing studies addressing agoraphobia, panic disorder, borderline personality disorder, depression and psychosomatic disorders.

There has also been a debate around 'person-centred versus problem-centred' (see Takens & Lietaer, 2004: 79–80). At one extreme, Sachse (2004: 24) argues:

> [Client-centered therapy] urgently needs disorder-specific concepts...
> Therapists must act in a more disorder-specific fashion. To do this, they must
> first identify the disorder – they must make a diagnosis. To do this they must
> have disorder-specific knowledge.

Sachse sees diagnosis as leading to a conclusion as to which therapeutic approaches a client will respond to. Mearns (2004: 89–90) casts doubt on the validity of a 'problem-centred' approach to mental illness, pointing out that there has been little serious, mainstream questioning of the appropriateness of the medical model as a way of understanding mental health, and demonstrating that individuals respond differently to the same or similar stimuli. Because individuals who share a diagnosis (the example Mearns uses is alcoholism) almost certainly will not share 'the constellation of [their] symbolizing of their past, their present processing and their future vision for their self' (p90), so disorder-specific treatment is a nonsense. Schmid (2004: 46) takes a similar view, stating:

> Different ways of relating by the client in-form [sic] the therapist to relate and
> answer differently. This is crucial, because the relationship is unique. Each
> client deserves to get the answer and relationship they need and... not some
> preset 'type of intervention'.

For Mearns (2004: 94), the effective way of being with someone experiencing emotional distress or mental ill health is to work at relational depth: that is, to engage with the client in a fully empathic, accepting and congruent way (see also Mearns, 1996). In his final paragraph, Mearns (2004: 99) points out that clients' difficult processes (see below) are not problems in themselves but 'both barriers and gateways' to engaging at relational depth. In conclusion, Mearns writes: 'We do not need to be more than person-centered therapists; we just need to be good person-centred therapists.'

As the title of his 2004 paper suggests, Sachse probably sees himself (and certainly is seen by others) as having deviated from the basic tenets of client-centred therapy. Mearns, on the other hand, remains close to classic client-centred therapy, although he places more emphasis on the centrality of the relationship. Throughout their paper, Takens and Lietaer (2004) make it clear that others are positioned differently within this spectrum. They (p85) emphasise that, between the extremes, there are those who experience the two models as in tension rather than in conflict. This is their position, and it is a tension they believe to be fruitful.

By asking authors to examine psychiatric concepts and contexts of psychiatric practice from the person-centred perspective, the first edition of this book (published in 2005) developed the argument further. The language used by psychiatry professionals may be different, but person-centred theory does seem able to account for the experiences of distress and dysfunction described by the different psychiatric concepts.

Models of psychopathology in person-centred theory and practice

Treatment of people who are disturbed, suffering mental and/or emotional ill health or what you will, has, in the west, been dominated by practitioners who adhere to a medical model, whether they are medically trained or not. So an epistemology developed for the diagnosis and treatment of physical ailments has been applied wholesale to maladies of mind and spirit, without rigorous empirical testing. Barbara Douglas, counselling psychologist and historian of the treatment of people experiencing mental ill health, points out (personal communication, 2004) that early success in treating 'general paralysis of the insane' (late-stage syphilis) with a drug, and some subsequent success in the drug treatment of neurological disorders, reinforced the notion of the applicability of a '(symptoms)–diagnosis–treatment–cure-(lack of symptoms)' model to people whose disorder of thought and feeling is of other origins. This has not been established in the same way.

A second influence on psychotherapy has been psychoanalysis (which, to at least some extent, can in itself be considered an offshoot of medicine). It is from this source that some of the labelling language arises – 'borderline personality', 'narcissism' etc. Historically, both these ways of thinking about people have been opposed by person-centred practitioners (although latterly there has been some move towards a common language, especially by those who practise in medical settings). There are person-centred alternatives – person-centred theories and practices amounting to ways of working with the mentally and emotionally disturbed and distressed – some of them are described below.

Psychological contact and psychopathology

One of the most important contributions to person-centred understanding and practice in the last years of the 20th century resulted from Garry Prouty questioning what happens if the first of Rogers' necessary and sufficient conditions for constructive, therapeutic change (that there be contact between client and therapist) is not met. For me, the importance of this lies not only in the subsequent development of theory and action (pre-therapy – see Prouty 2002b, 2002c, 2002d), but in the very raising of the difficulty. As Sanders and Wyatt indicate (2002: viii), over the years, little attention has been paid to 'contact/psychological contact', and there is not really a definition of this concept – Rogers (1959: 207) is vague, suggesting that two people are in contact 'when each makes a perceived or subceived difference in the experiential field of the other', and this looseness leads to a lack of agreement that persists to this day. Wyatt and Sanders (2002) offer the first comprehensive exploration of contact (with perception, condition 6).

Prouty (2002b: 55) defines pre-therapy as 'a theory of psychological contact... rooted in Rogers' conception of psychological contact as the first condition of a therapeutic relationship'. This theory 'was developed in the context of treating mentally retarded or psychotic populations' (Krietemeyer & Prouty, 2003: 152) because, in Prouty's experience, such people are 'contact-impaired' and have difficulty forming interpersonal connections. Prouty (2002c: 56–60) describes contact in terms of three levels: contact reflections, contact functions and contact behaviours. These are summarised in Tudor and Merry (2002: 31–32). The theory led to a set of practices by which psychological contact could be established (see, for example, the case studies presented by Van Werde (1994: 125–128), and Krietemeyer and Prouty (2003: 154–160)). Prouty (2002a: 595–596) summarises the research evidence for this, noting that (p596) '[p]ilot studies with clients with severely limited mental abilities provide suggestive evidence for further empirical exploration'.

Warner (2002b: 89–91) also pays attention to the role of contact in 'difficult process' (see below for an explanation of Warner's models of processing). She points out (p89) that 'being blocked from psychological contact is almost always experienced as an affliction' and briefly describes the contact-impairment likely or possible in people experiencing fragile, dissociated and psychotic process.

Theories of incongruence

In person-centred theory, it is explicit that extreme incongruence is what leads to mental ill health, or, if you prefer, it is the conditions of worth leading to incongruence that are the roots of psychological disturbance. As stated in the 14th of Rogers' 19 propositions (Rogers, 1951: 483–522):

> Psychological maladjustment exists when the organism denies to awareness significant sensory and visceral experiences, which consequently are not symbolized and organized into the gestalt of the self-structure. When this situation exists, there is a basic or potential psychological tension.

This Merry (2002: 36) helpfully rephrases as: 'When we experience something that doesn't fit in with our picture of ourselves and we cannot fit it in with that picture, we feel tense, anxious, frightened or confused.' When a person has a poor self-concept that is out of touch with the organism, she or he is disturbed. In extreme cases, this manifests as 'madness'. Since incongruence is central to mental/emotional distress, it follows that person-centred practitioner/theoreticians base models of psychopathology around it. Thus, van Kalmthout (2002: 134–136) asserts that avoiding experiencing 'what there really is' and the resulting lack of contact between inner and outer reality 'can lead to problems and even psychopathology'. Speierer (1996: 300) goes so far as to state 'client-centered therapy is... the treatment of incongruence' and (1990, 1996) proposes a 'differential incongruence model' that offers 'a specific illness concept for client-centered psychotherapy' (1996: 299). Speierer's contention is that incongruence is the root of emotional distress and that it has three main causes (1996: 299):

- 'well-known client-centered social communicative factors', by which Speierer means the acquisition of conditions of worth and a 'form of incompatibility between societal and organismic values'
- 'a non-socially caused bio-neuropsychological inability to reach congruence'
- 'social and non-social life-changing events'.

Speierer's model goes far beyond the concepts of classic client-centred therapy, not least because he is suggesting that different 'disorders' are the result of differences in incongruence, and then he draws the conclusion that 'different therapy options can be offered according to the individual's needs and his disorder' (1996: 307).

Biermann-Ratjen (1998) also writes about incongruence and psychopathology. She devotes sections to 'post-traumatic stress disorder', 'psychogenic illnesses' and 'neurosis' as manifestations of incongruence. For example, she writes (pp126–127):

> Any symptom of psychogenic illness is the expression of experiencing incongruence:
> 1. The person may be unable to symbolize completely and communicate verbally certain experiences.

2. The person may be unable to understand and/or accept certain experiences as self-experiences.

3. The person may experience certain ways of defending against experience (stress reactions, acute incongruence) or different forms of stagnation in self-development (chronic incongruence).

4. In any case experiencing incongruence will include experiencing physical tension.

For Biermann-Ratjen, it is the stage at which self-development is interrupted that determines the nature of distress. Post-traumatic stress has been one of the psychiatric disorders most extensively explored from the perspective of person-centred theory. Joseph (2004) has shown how person-centred theory offers an almost identical model for how post-traumatic stress arises as contemporary social cognitive theories. Whereas social cognitive theories discuss how trauma shatters people's fundamental assumptions about themselves and the world, person-centred theory describes this same process as a breakdown and disorganisation of the self-structure. Person-centred theory has also been used to develop the new theoretical approach to trauma that emphasises the process of post-traumatic growth (Joseph & Linley, 2005; see also Chapter 14, this volume). The concept of depression has also received theoretical attention from Sanders and Hill (2014), who have discussed how the disorder of depression can be theorised from person-centred theory as an incongruence between self and experience. These developments are particularly important because their intention is to develop the understanding of person-centred theoretical approaches within mainstream psychology and NHS practice, thus bringing the person-centred approach to new audiences.

Other theoretical work within the person-centred community has continued to build theoretical approaches that advance person-centred theory, most notably on styles of processing.

Styles of processing

Rogers (1961b: 27) refers to life as 'a flowing, changing process in which nothing is fixed'. He also (pp126, 171) refers to an acceptance of the fluid nature of existence as an outcome of therapy and (p186) characterises the 'good life' as 'a process, not a state of being'. He also (pp132–155) describes the seven stages of process in therapy by which an individual changes from fixedness to a fluid way of being. From this, it is clear that people are defined as 'in process', rather than as of a particular 'personality type'. A person's process is their way of experiencing and encountering the world, a way of making sense of all the stimuli and information to which they are exposed. Process is cognitive, behavioural, emotional and (arguably, at least) spiritual. Worsley (2002: 21) points out that process is both in and out of awareness, and may be either reflexive or spontaneous. Also, a person's process may flow in the easy way Rogers described as desirable, or it may be 'difficult' (and, of course, all stages between). The notion of difficult process forms the basis of Warner's theory and practice (1998, 2000, 2002a, 2002b).

Warner describes three kinds of difficult process (summarised briefly in Warner, 2001: 182–183; see also Chapter 6, this volume). These are:

[Fragile process] Clients who have a fragile style of processing tend to experience core issues at very low or very high levels of intensity. They tend to have difficulty starting and stopping experiences that are personally significant or emotionally connected. In addition, they are likely to have difficulty taking the point of view of another person while remaining in contact with such experiences. (Warner, 2000: 150)

[Dissociated process] Clients who experience 'dissociated process' go through periods of time when they quite convincingly experience themselves as having selves that are not integrated with each other. Sometimes, they experience a disunity of self that feels 'crazy' to themselves and to others. At other times they may have periods of forgetfulness for the minutes or hours when alternate personality parts have been dominant. They may go for years without being aware of such parts by keeping very busy and leading quite restricted lives, only to have past experiences return in times of crisis. (Warner, 2001: 183)

[Psychotic process] When clients have a psychotic style of processing, they have difficulty forming narratives about their experience that make sense within the culture, or which offer a predictive value in relation to their environment. Clients experiencing psychotic process... (have) impaired contact with 'self', 'world' and 'other'. Such clients often experience voices, hallucinations or delusions that are neither culturally accepted nor are easy to process. (Warner, 2001: 183)

In her various papers, Warner describes the possible origins of these styles of processing and effective ways of working with each group of clients in a person-centred way.

Mearns (2004: 99) suggested a fourth style of processing, which he referred to as disconnected process. In this style of processing, the actualising tendency and an inferred balancing process of social mediation (see Mearns & Thorne, 2000: 178–186) 'are separating and creating disjunctions between the self and the phenomenological context'.

Although these styles of processing may be identified with traditional psychiatric/psychoanalytic categories, they are conceived of in a very different way, and the methods of working with people experiencing difficult process are firmly rooted in person-centred practice.

Power and mental and emotional distress

There is another view of the aetiology of mental and emotional distress that is compatible with person-centred theory and practice, but which moves away from the notion that such difficulties are intrinsic, intra-personal and a response to relationships with significant others. This is that their origin is social and/or environmental. Proctor (2002: 3) argues that 'there is much evidence to associate the likelihood of suffering from psychological distress with the individual's position in society with respect to structural power': women are more likely than men to be diagnosed with a range of disorders, and working-class people as a whole are over-represented in the mental illness statistics. Psychiatric systems are inherently systems of control and power (Proctor, 2002). It follows that, if distress flows from an experience of inequality, and an encounter with psychiatric services is disempowering, then psychiatry may be making people worse rather than better.

In a much more sophisticated way, this is the case made by the anti-psychiatry movement (proponents of which include Szasz and Laing) and by those involved in critical psychology (see, for example, Newnes & Holmes, 1999; Newnes, Holmes & Dunn, 2001). As articulated by Holmes and Dunn (1999: 2), critical psychology 'lays down a challenge to the idea that the psychiatric system is largely benign'. In the same book, Newnes and Holmes (1999: 281–282) offer a view as to the role of 'talking therapies' in the future of mental health services. Although they are wary of 'the dangers and limits of talking therapies' (p281), they see value in 'collaborative conversation' in which therapist and client meet with the intention 'to understand each other and work together on the [client's] goals'. They (p282) also emphasise the importance of 'empathy through personal disclosure' as a 'powerful way of relating to and helping people'. Proctor (2002: 90) refers to the demystification of therapy as a way of addressing the imbalance of power in the therapy relationship, and states: 'The demystification of my therapist as a person was a strong factor in my not feeling disempowered in the relationship.' In person-centred therapy, the relationship is understood to be what leads to constructive change. In this respect, person-centred therapy goes some way to meeting the needs, such as for the therapist and client to understand each other, discussed by Newnes and Holmes.

Certainly, Pete Sanders (speaking at the second conference of the British Association for the Person-Centred Approach) and Gillian Proctor (2002: 103) both emphasise the potential for person-centred therapy to offer a radical alternative to orthodox psychiatry (and medicalised psychotherapy), and 'to emphasise the autonomy and trustworthiness of the client' (Proctor, 2002: 103). However, Proctor warns that, although person-centred therapy 'addresses all aspects of power in the therapy relationship', there is a danger that 'the focus on the therapist as a person' may obscure 'the power inherent in the role of therapist' (2002: 137). She also sees that, within person-centred therapy, 'there is the potential for therapists to miss levels of oppression resulting from structural positions unless the socially positioned person is acknowledged' (2002: 137). This is something to be addressed if the criticisms of the critical psychology movement are to be rebutted. A person-centred model that addresses power issues would involve working at 'relational depth' but would also take account of inequalities of structural power both within and outside the therapy relationship.

The position of person-centred therapy with respect to the psychiatric system is explored and explicated by Sanders and Tudor (2001). They (p148) declare: 'We are proponents of the Person-Centred Approach precisely because it offers a radical view of psychology and psychotherapy and a critical contribution to contemporary concerns about mental health.' They are equally clear that they are not uncritical of person-centred therapy. For example, throughout their chapter they argue that to consider individuals without reference to the social and political milieus in which they live is a shortcoming of psychotherapy and one by which person-centred therapy is not untainted. Using Rogers' notion of process as an inspiration, Sanders and Tudor (pp156–157) characterise:

> … a [r]evolutionary effect on psychiatry and mental health services, based on movement towards:
>
> - A non-defensive openness in all interpersonal relationships – throughout the psychiatric system, regardless of status.
> - A holistic approach and attitude to the individual – for example, complementary health practitioners working in psychiatric services.
> - Human-sized, rather than institutional-sized, groupings – reflected in an emphasis on small units at all levels of the psychiatric system (i.e. primary, secondary and tertiary).
> - Attention to the quality of personal living – both in the community and in the asylum (crisis house, hospital, etc.).
> - A more genuine and inclusive caring concern for those who need help – which would require a radical shift of thinking and practice on community care... and an openness to creative, therapeutic alternatives to institutional care.

Behind all the views presented in this section is an assumption that 'madness' is socially defined, and that social and political circumstances at the very least contribute to mental ill health, and are possibly causal. There is also a belief that the imbalance and abuse of power relate to mental ill health, and therapy can only be successful if power in all its aspects is openly addressed. In this model of mental disturbance, while there is a challenge to person-centred theory and practice, it is one that it may meet more easily than many other approaches.

Conclusion

It is clear that, although the term may have been resisted, from its earliest days person-centred therapy has been concerned with the issue of 'psychopathology'. Rogers and his collaborators went to great pains to present theories of development and explanations for maladjustment, which they then attempted to test in a variety of therapeutic situations. More recently, early client-centred theoretical statements have been reinterpreted to offer (for example) theories of child development and support for different conceptions of working with people experiencing more extreme forms of emotional and mental distress. For the most part, these different conceptions of 'psychopathology' draw on the original six necessary and sufficient conditions for constructive personality change; the different emphases result from the originators' experience and allegiance (for example, whether closer to client-centred or experiential traditions).

Presumably, in the interests of dialogue and mutual understanding, these models also tend to draw to some extent on the language of psychiatry and psychoanalysis (although this is most usually to point out person-centred conceptions of phenomena recognised in these ways of thinking). An exception is the idea that the person-centred approach could (and should?) offer a radical alternative to existing philosophies and practices in the mental health system. Adherents of this view are inclined to believe that, by being true to its roots and by drawing on its strengths with respect to the exercise of power, and as a socio-political model as much as an intra- and interpersonal one, the person-centred approach can become a natural ally to the critical psychology movement in developing real and effective alternatives to current mental health practices.

References

Barrett-Lennard GT (1998). *Carl Rogers' Helping System: journey and substance.* London: Sage.

Berghofer G (1996). Dealing with schizophrenia – a person-centered approach providing care to long-term patients in a supported residential service in Vienna. In: Hutterer R, Pawlowsky G, Schmid PF, Stipsits R (eds). *Client-Centered and Experiential Psychotherapy: a paradigm in motion.* Frankfurt-am-Main: Peter Lang (pp481–496).

Biermann-Ratjen E-M (1996). On the way to a client-centred psychopathology. In: Hutterer R, Pawlowsky G, Schmid PF, Stipsits R (eds). *Client-Centered and Experiential Psychotherapy: a paradigm in motion.* Frankfurt-am-Main: Peter Lang (pp11–24).

Biermann-Ratjen E-M (1998). Incongruence and psychopathology. In: Thorne B, Lambers E (eds). *Person-Centred Therapy: a European perspective.* London: Sage (pp119–130).

Cain DJ (ed) (2002). *Classics in the Person-Centered Approach.* Ross-on-Wye: PCCS Books.

Cooper M (2000). Person-centred development theory: reflections and revisions. *Person-Centred Practice* 8: 87–94.

Eckert J, Höger D, Schwab R (2003). Development and current state of the research on client-centered therapy in the German language region. *Person-Centered and Experiential Psychotherapies 2*: 3–18.

Elliott R (2001). The effectiveness of humanistic therapies: a meta-analysis. In: Cain DJ (ed). *Humanistic Therapies: handbook of research and practice*. Washington, DC: American Psychological Association (pp57–82).

Gendlin ET (1963). Subverbal communication and therapist expressivity: trends in client-centered therapy with schizophrenics. *Journal of Existential Psychiatry 4*(14): 105–120.

Holdstock TL, Rogers CR (1977). Person-centered theory. In: Corsini RJ (ed). *Current Personality Theories*. Itasca, IL: Peacock (pp125–151).

Holmes G, Dunn C (1999). Introduction. In: Newnes C, Holmes G, Dunn C (eds). *This is Madness: a critical look at psychiatry and the future of mental health services*. Ross-on-Wye: PCCS Books (pp1–5).

Joseph S (2004). Client-centred therapy, posttraumatic stress disorder and posttraumatic growth. Theory and practice. *Psychology and Psychotherapy: Theory, Research, and Practice 77*: 101–120.

Joseph S, Linley PA (2005). Positive adjustment to threatening events: an organismic valuing theory of growth through adversity. *Review of General Psychology 9*: 262–280.

Kovel J (1976). *A Complete Guide to Therapy: from psychotherapy to behavior modification*. New York: Pantheon Books.

Krietemeyer B, Prouty G (2003). The art of psychological contact: the psychotherapy of a mentally retarded psychotic client. *Person-Centered and Experiential Psychotherapies 2*: 151–161.

Lambers E (1994). The person-centred perspective on psychopathology: the neurotic client. In: Mearns D (ed). *Developing Person-Centred Counselling*. London: Sage (pp105–109).

Mearns D (1996). Working at relational depth with clients in person-centred therapy. *Counselling 7*: 306–311.

Mearns D (2004). Problem-centered is not person-centered. *Person-Centered and Experiential Psychotherapies 3*: 88–101.

Mearns D, Thorne B (2000). *Person-Centred Therapy Today: new frontiers in theory and practice*. London: Sage.

Merry T (2002). *Learning and Being in Person-Centred Counselling* (2nd ed). Ross-on-Wye: PCCS Books.

Miksch G (2000). Client-centered psychotherapy with schizophrenic patients. Personal experiences and formulation of a helpful setting. In: Marques-Teixeira J, Antunes S (eds). *Client-Centered and Experiential Psychotherapy*. Linda a Velha: Vale and Vale (pp241–252).

Newnes C, Holmes G (1999). The future of mental health services. In: Newnes C, Holmes G, Dunn C (eds). *This is Madness: a critical look at psychiatry and the future of mental health services*. Ross-on-Wye: PCCS Books (pp273–284).

Newnes C, Holmes G, Dunn C (eds) (2001). *This is Madness Too: critical perspectives on mental health services*. Ross-on-Wye: PCCS Books.

Proctor G (2002). *The Dynamics of Power in Counselling and Psychotherapy: ethics, politics and practice*. Ross-on-Wye: PCCS Books.

Prouty G (1990). Pre-therapy: a theoretical evolution in the person-centered/experiential psychotherapy of schizophrenia and retardation. In: Lietaer G, Rombauts J, van Balen R (eds). *Client-Centered and Experiential Psychotherapy in the Nineties*. Leuven: Leuven University Press (pp645–658).

Prouty G (2002a). Humanistic therapy for people with schizophrenia. In: Cain DJ (ed). *Humanistic Therapies: handbook of research and practice*. Washington, DC: American Psychological Association (pp579–601).

Prouty G (2002b). Pre-therapy: an essay in philosophical psychology. In: Wyatt G, Sanders P (eds). *Rogers' Therapeutic Conditions: evolution, theory and practice. Vol 4: Contact and perception*. Ross-on-Wye: PCCS Books (pp51–53).

Prouty G (2002c). Pre-therapy as a theoretical system. In: Wyatt G, Sanders P (eds). *Rogers' Therapeutic Conditions: evolution, theory and practice. Vol 4: Contact and perception*. Ross-on-Wye: PCCS Books (pp54–62).

Prouty G (2002d). The practice of pre-therapy. In: Wyatt G, Sanders P (eds). *Rogers' Therapeutic Conditions: evolution, theory and practice. Vol 4: Contact and perception*. Ross-on-Wye: PCCS Books (pp63–75).

Rogers CR (1951). *Client-Centered Therapy: its current practice, implications and theory*. Boston: Houghton Mifflin.

Rogers CR (1959). A theory of therapy, personality and interpersonal relationships, as developed in the client-centered framework. In: Koch S (ed). *Psychology: a study of science. Vol 3: Formulation of the person and the social context*. New York: McGraw-Hill (pp184–256).

Rogers CR (1961a). A theory of psychotherapy with schizophrenics and a proposal for its empirical investigation. In: Dawson JG, Stone HK, Dellis NP (eds). *Psychotherapy with Schizophrenics*. Baton Rouge: Louisiana State University Press (pp3–19).

Rogers CR (1961b). *On Becoming a Person: a therapist's view of psychotherapy*. London: Constable.

Rogers CR, with Gendlin ET, Kiesler DJ, Truax CB (eds) (1967). *The Therapeutic Relationship and its Impact: a study of psychotherapy with schizophrenics*. Madison: University of Wisconsin Press.

Sachse R (2004). From client-centered to clarification-oriented psychotherapy. *Person-Centered and Experiential Psychotherapies 3*: 19–35.

Sanders P, Tudor K (2001). This is therapy: a person-centred critique of the contemporary psychiatric system. In: Newnes C, Holmes G, Dunn C (eds) (2001). *This is Madness Too: critical perspectives on mental health services*. Ross-on-Wye: PCCS Books (pp147–160).

Sanders P, Hill A (2014). *Counselling for depression*. London: Sage.

Sanders P, Wyatt G (2002). Introduction. In: Wyatt G, Sanders P (eds). *Rogers' Therapeutic Conditions: evolution, theory and practice. Vol 4: Contact and perception*. Ross-on-Wye: PCCS Books (ppvii–xiii).

Schmid PF (2004). Back to the client: a phenomenological approach to the process of understanding and diagnosis. *Person-Centered and Experiential Psychotherapies 3*: 36–51.

Shlien JM (2003). *To Lead an Honorable Life: invitations to think about client-centered therapy and the person-centered approach. A collection of the work of John M Shlien*. Edited by Pete Sanders. Ross-on-Wye: PCCS Books.

Speierer G-W (1990). Toward a specific illness concept of client-centered therapy. In: Lietaer G, Rombauts J, van Balen R (eds). *Client-Centered and Experiential Psychotherapy in the Nineties*. Leuven: Leuven University Press (pp337–360).

Speierer G-W (1996). Client-centered therapy according to the Differential Incongruence Model (DIM). In: Hutterer R, Pawlowsky G, Schmid PF, Stipsits R (eds). *Client-Centered and Experiential Psychotherapy: a paradigm in motion*. Frankfurt-am-Main: Peter Lang (pp299–311).

Takens RJ, Lietaer G (2004). Process differentiation and person-centeredness: a contradiction? *Person-Centered and Experiential Psychotherapies 3*: 77–87.

Teusch L (1990). Positive effects and limitations of client-centered therapy with schizophrenic patients. In: Lietaer G, Rombauts J, van Balen R (eds). *Client-Centered and Experiential Psychotherapy in the Nineties*. Leuven: Leuven University Press (pp637–644).

Tudor K, Merry T (2002). *Dictionary of Person-Centred Psychology*. London: Whurr.

van Kalmthout M (2002). The farthest reaches of person-centered psychotherapy. In: Watson JC, Goldman RN, Warner MS (eds). *Client-Centered and Experiential Psychotherapy in the 21st Century: advances in theory, research and practice*. Ross-on-Wye: PCCS Books (pp127–143).

Van Werde D (1994). Dealing with the possibility of psychotic content in a seemingly congruent communication. In: Mearns D. *Developing Person-Centred Counselling*. London: Sage (pp125–128).

Warner MS (1998). A client-centered approach to working with dissociated and fragile process. In: Greenberg L, Watson J, Lietaer G (eds). *Handbook of Experiential Psychotherapy*. New York: Guilford Press (pp368–387).

Warner MS (2000). Person-centred therapy at the difficult edge: a developmentally based model of fragile and dissociated process. In: Mearns D, Thorne B. *Person-Centred Therapy Today: new frontiers in theory and practice*. London: Sage (pp144–171).

Warner MS (2001). Empathy, relational depth and difficult client process. In: Haugh S, Merry T (eds). *Rogers' Therapeutic Conditions: evolution, theory and practice. Volume 2: Empathy*. Ross-on-Wye: PCCS Books (pp181–191).

Warner MS (2002a). Luke's dilemmas: a client-centered/experiential model of processing with a schizophrenic thought disorder. In: Watson JC, Goldman RN, Warner MS (eds). *Client-Centered and Experiential Psychotherapy in the 21st Century: advances in theory, research and practice*. Ross-on-Wye: PCCS Books (pp459–472).

Warner MS (2002b). Psychological contact, meaningful process and human nature. A reformulation of person-centred theory. In: Wyatt G, Sanders P (eds). *Rogers' Therapeutic Conditions: evolution, theory and practice. Vol 4: Contact and perception*. Ross-on-Wye: PCCS Books (pp76–95).

Wheeler S, McLeod J (1995). Person-centred and psychodynamic counselling: a dialogue. *Counselling 6*: 283–287.

Wilkins P (2003). *Person-Centred Therapy in Focus*. London: Sage.

Wilkins P, Gill M (2003). Assessment in Person-Centered Therapy. *Person-Centered and Experiential Psychotherapies 2*: 172–187.

Worsley R (2002). *Process Work in Person-Centred Therapy*. Basingstoke: Palgrave.

Wyatt G, Sanders P (2002). *Rogers' Therapeutic Conditions: evolution, theory and practice. Volume 4: Contact and perception*. Ross-on-Wye: PCCS Books.

4 | From self-objectification to self-affirmation: the *I-Me* and *I-I* self-relational stances[1]

Mick Cooper

At the heart of Rogers' (1959) model of psychological distress is the assertion that an individual may come to deny or distort self-experiences so that an incongruence develops between self-experiences and self-concept, with anxiety and breakdown possible outcomes (see Cooper, 2013). In contrast to other models of psychological defence, however, Rogers' understanding of these processes is relatively undeveloped. Moreover, in recent years, many theorists and practitioners in the person-centred field – as well as in the wider therapeutic and psychological community – have argued that human beings do not have just one self-concept, self or mode of experiencing (eg. Cooper, 1999; Cooper et al, 2004; Elliott & Greenberg, 1997; Mearns & Thorne, 2000; Stiles et al, 1990), but a plurality of different *I-positions* (Hermans & Kempen, 1993), and therefore a multitude of different ways in which they may defend – and construct – themselves. There is a need, therefore, to develop person-centred understandings of how people defend themselves against their own experiences, and the implications this might have for an understanding of psychological distress and health.

My own thoughts in this area arose following some work with a young woman who had experienced many years of sexual and physical abuse as a child.[2] She came to therapy deeply unhappy about her life. She spent most of her days pacing around her flat, frustrated, angry, but feeling incapable of venturing further outside or forging meaningful friendships. As she spoke about herself and how she was, I was struck by the parallels that her attitude towards herself seemed to have with Buber's (1958) notion of an 'I-It attitude'. For instance, she talked about her 'self-who-paced-

1. This chapter is an edited, revised and updated version of: Cooper M (2003). 'I-I' and 'I-Me': transposing Buber's interpersonal attitudes to the intrapersonal plane. *Journal of Constructivist Psychology* 16(2): 131–153 © 2003. Reproduced by permission of Taylor & Francis.

2. To ensure complete confidentiality, some details in the case examples used in this paper have been changed.

around-the-room' as if it was an object without volition and choice, and she seemed to have no empathy with this way of being – no ability to enter into 'its' frame of mind. She also accounted for her present experiences in entirely deterministic terms: as something that was *caused* by her past, and something over which she had no control. It occurred to me, then, that if I-It modes of interpersonal relating were a major source of interpersonal discord, perhaps I-It modes of *intra*personal relating were closely related to *intra*personal discord, and subsequent psychological distress. This led me to suggest that we can talk about an *I-Me* mode of self-relating, which is like an I-It attitude towards an other, except that it is towards ourselves or between different 'parts' of ourselves (Cooper, 2003, 2004). Concomitantly, I suggested that we could talk about an I-I form of self-relating, which is like the I-Thou form of self-relating, except, again, to ourselves or within ourselves rather than to others. Such an extrapolation from the interpersonal level to the intrapersonal level makes particular sense if we follow the argument of the Russian psychologist Vygotsky (1962) that our internal dialogue and thinking processes are essentially an internalisation of those modes of communication that have existed on the interpersonal plane.

This I-Me mode of self-relating is, in many respects, akin to Roger's (1959) notions of distortion and denial but, by drawing on Buber's (1958) distinction between the I-Thou and the I-It attitudes, it becomes possible to broaden and deepen an understanding of these processes. The aim of this chapter, then, is to develop a person-centred model of 'defensive' psychological processes, as well as to further our understanding of how such processes may lead to psychological difficulties. In doing so, however, this chapter also aims to advance a fundamentally humanistic model of psychological distress – that is, one in which psychological difficulties are seen as arising, not from a person's primary, pre-reflective responses to their world, but from their secondary, reflective experiences (see Cooper, 2015). Put differently, what is being proposed here is a model of psychological distress that starts from the assumption that human beings have an inherent tendency to experience, and act towards, their world in self-maintaining and self-enhancing ways – Rogers' (1959) *actualising tendency* – and that psychological distress emerges when people distrust, devalue and/or deny these experiences. Such a model may be of particular interest to psychologists, psychiatrists and other clinicians who are keen to retain some notion of human intelligibility and meaningfulness as part of their understanding of human psychological distress.

The chapter begins by outlining Buber's distinction between the I-Thou and I-It attitudes, and then goes on to show how this can be transposed to an intrapersonal level. It then explores ways in which the I-It mode of self-relating might lead to psychological distress, before discussing implications for therapeutic practice.

I-Thou and I-It

There are a number of elements to Buber's (1958) distinction between the I-Thou and the I-It attitude (these are developed in more detail in Cooper, 2015). It should be borne in mind, however, that Buber's philosophy was fundamentally holistic. Hence, these elements cannot be understood in isolation: each is fundamentally inter-related to, and implied by, the others. The differences outlined below, then, need to be understood as facets of a difference-as-a-whole, rather than as independent dimensions.

Experiencing versus relating

One of the first distinctions that Buber (1958) makes between the I-It attitude and the I-Thou attitude is that, in the former, an other person is *experienced*, while in the latter, the other is *related to*. That is, in the I-It attitude, I distance myself from the other and survey, study, measure and observe him or her – practices that tend to be quite common in the psychological and psychiatric fields. The other becomes something apart from me, something to which I direct my attention and from which I extract knowledge. By contrast, 'When *Thou* is spoken, the speaker has no *thing*; he has indeed nothing. But he takes his stand in relation' (p17). Here, I do not face the other, but stand alongside him or her. He or she is not the object of my experiencing, but an intrinsic part of my being-in-relation. 'I do not experience the man to whom I say *Thou*,' writes Buber. 'But I take my stand in relation to him, in the sanctity of the primary word. Only when I step out of it do I experience him once more' (p22).

This *I-Thou* attitude also differs from an *I-It* attitude in that I have an immediate and direct encounter with the other. There is nothing that mediates the meeting: I do not meet my *idea* of the other, but confront him or her directly (Levinas, 1967). Furthermore, for Buber (1958), there are no 'aims', 'anticipations' or 'lusts' that intervene between *I* and *Thou*. In this relationship, I am not encountering the other for some purpose or some need. I do not want anything from him or her – or, at least, those needs have been put to one side. 'Only when every means has collapsed,' writes Buber, 'does the meeting come about' (p25).

'It-ifying' versus humanising

In this objectifying I-It attitude, the other is also experienced as a 'thing': an object, an entity, an 'it' (Buber, 1958). 'He is then thought of as a being of size, surface area, weight, function, desire, consciousness, characteristics and capability of all sorts,' writes von Weizsäcker (1964: 407). Such a way of experiencing others, again, tends to be quite common in the psychological and psychiatric fields, where others may be construed in such object-ifying terms as 'a neurotic' or 'a borderline personality'. This 'it-ification' of the other has parallels with Sartre's (1958) notion of 'the look', in which the gaze of one human being constantly threatens to objectify – or, to use Laing's (1965) term, 'petrify' – the being of the other. While for Sartre this objectification is the primary mode of human relatedness, for Buber, 'If I face my human being as my *Thou*, and say the primary word *I-Thou* to him, he is not a thing among things' (p21). That is, I also have the possibility of encountering the other as a vibrant, dynamic humanity: a 'psychic stream' (1988: 70) that cannot be objectified or labelled, but which I can only relate to in its fluidity and spontaneity. In Bakhtinian (1973) terms, I have the capacity to affirm someone else's I, not as an object, but as another subject.

Fragmenting versus relating to wholeness

For Buber (1958), a further distinction between the I-It and the I-Thou attitude is that the former fragments what it experiences, while the latter relates to the other in its wholeness. In the I-It attitude, things are divided into sub-things: objects or people are analysed, reduced, broken down into essences, laws, psychometric scores, or such parts as 'id', 'ego' and 'superego' (Freud, 1923). By contrast, in the I-Thou attitude, the other is beheld and revered in its totality. Buber gives the example of relating to a tree, in which 'everything, picture and movement, species and type, law and number, [is] indivisibly united in the event. Everything belonging to the tree is in this: its form and structure, its colours a chemical composition, its intercourse with the elements and with the stars, are all present in a single whole' (p20).

Construing as determined versus acknowledging freedom

Buber (1958) also describes the I-It attitude as one in which the other is construed in determined, mechanistic terms, rather than as an other that is freely choosing and deciding its way of being. He, she or it is seen as something that is caused to be, that is driven by forces and mechanisms, rather than encountered in his, her or its freedom and spontaneity. Again, such a form of it-ification can be common in the psychiatric, psychological and psychotherapeutic fields. For instance, a therapist may construe their client's anger towards them as a consequence of his or her relationship with his or her father, rather than a choice that the client is making towards their immediate presence. 'Causality,' writes Buber, 'has an unlimited reign in the world of *It*' (p71).

Experiencing in the past or future versus encountering in the present

This leads on to a further distinction between the I-It and I-Thou attitudes. In the I-It attitude, the other is experienced in terms of pre-defined schemata: in terms of what has previously been experienced and known. In addition, as discussed above, in the I-It attitude, the other may be experienced in terms of future projects and needs: the other becomes an instrument for the actualisation of the I's possibilities. In the I-It attitude, then, the I is not really experiencing an other at all. Rather, it is experiencing a 'mirror' of its own schemata and interests (Woods, 1969) – the other only exists in as much as it is an object for the self. By contrast, in the I-Thou relationship, the other is met in the immediate present. Hence, there is a breaking-through of a true otherness into the I's world: a movement beyond a solipsistic engagement with the I's own past or future.

Generalising versus individuating

'Every real relationship in the world is exclusive,' writes Buber (1958); it 'rests on individuation, this is its joy – for only in this way is mutual knowledge of different beings won' (p128). By this, Buber means that the I-Thou attitude takes the other as unique, distinctive and inexchangeable. It is an encounter with *a* particular being at *a* particular 'now', which cannot be replicated or repeated. By contrast, the experiencing of an *It* – an entity that is stripped of its complexity and individuality and experienced as a we-remember-it or as a I'll-do-this-with-it – can be repeated over and over again.

Non-confirming versus confirming

For Buber (1958), an I-Thou attitude also involves a fundamental *confirmation* of the other. Friedman (1985) defined this as 'an act of love through which one acknowledges the other as one who exists in his own peculiar form and has the right to do so' (p134). There are clear parallels here with Rogers' (1957) notion of unconditional positive regard – particularly the emphasis on the acceptance of the other in his or her wholeness. However, Buber emphasises the way that confirmation involves an acceptance of the other in his or her 'own peculiar form'. In other words, it is an acceptance of the other in his or her otherness, and is clearly distinct from both absorbing the other into one's own schemata and being absorbed by the other such that one's own position and uniqueness is lost. Indeed, as Buber (1958) points out, to fuse or merge with another person is not to encounter him or her: one cannot encounter something that one is.

Relating in fragments versus relating as wholeness

As we have seen, Buber (1958) states that an *I-Thou* attitude is one in which an individual relates to the whole of the other. For Buber, however, such an *I-Thou* attitude also requires the I to bring his or her totality into the encounter. '[T]he primary word [I-Thou] can only be spoken with the whole being,' writes Buber; 'He who gives himself to it may withhold nothing of himself' (p23). The person who adopts an I-Thou attitude to the other, then, engages with the other in a transparent and open way, in which nothing is deliberately held back or obscured (although this does not necessarily entail a 'universal un-reserve' (Buber, 1947)). Furthermore, such a relationship requires the I to transcend a purely cognitive mode of relating, and to encounter the other as a cognitive-affective-embodied whole (Cooper, 2001). This contrasts with the I-It attitude, in which an individual engages with another in only a partial, non-transparent or superficial way.

Protectiveness versus willingness to take risks

As we have seen, for Buber (1958), an I-Thou attitude requires an I to engage with a Thou in an immediate and spontaneous way – in a way that is open to the other's freedom, uniqueness and otherness. For Buber, then, an I-Thou meeting is a 'perilous' and 'unreliable' encounter, in which 'the well-tried context' is 'loosened' and one's 'security shattered'. Furthermore, because the I is engaging with the other with the whole of his or her being, he or she has no firm foothold from which to control or determine the encounter – no external position of certainty or safety. Everything he or she is is thrown into the relationship, and this means that he or she may be changed by the encounter in ways that he or she cannot predict or control. As Buber writes: 'The human being who emerges from the act of pure relation that so involves his being has now in his being something more that has grown in him, of which he did not know before and whose origin he is not rightly able to indicate' (p140). This contrasts with the I-It relationship, in which the other is experienced in a predictable and controllable – ie. safe – way; in which a part of the self is always held back, such that there is never a full commitment to, or involvement with, the other.

Monologue versus dialogue

One of the most useful ways, perhaps, of drawing together the distinctions that Buber makes between the I-It and I-Thou attitudes is by relating them – as Buber does – to monologue and dialogue. In his 1929 essay *Dialogue* (published in 1947), Buber distinguishes between three realms of communication: *genuine dialogue, technical dialogue* and *monologue disguised as dialogue*. The first of these realms, genuine dialogue, corresponds most closely to Buber's (1958) notion of the I-Thou attitude. For Buber (1947, 1988), genuine dialogue involves a turning towards the other: an openness to being addressed by the other in his, her or its present and particular otherness, and a confirmation of the otherness of the other. This is similar to the model of dialogue outlined by Linell and Marková (1993), in which a person's position or formulation is modified in and through the dialogic exchange. For Buber, such genuine dialogue requires each respondent to bring what is really in his or her head to the dialogue, without artifice, seeming or pretence. However, as Buber emphasises, such dialogue does not require all of those involved to necessarily speak. For Buber, true dialogue and exchange can take place in silence.

In contrast to Linell and Marková (1993), however, Buber (1947) does not consider all forms of discursive interaction to be based on a dialogic form. Rather, he argues that the kind of dialogue in which interactants genuinely respond to each other's utterances are becomingly increasingly rare. Instead, he suggests, much modern communication takes the form of 'technical dialogue', 'which is prompted solely by the need of objective understanding' (p37). This is utilitarian, goal-focused communication, but communication in which real dialogue remains hidden away in 'odd corners', occasionally breaking through to the surface: 'as in the tone of a railway guard's voice, in the glance of an old newspaper vendor, in the smile of the chimney-sweeper' (p37).

It is the third form of communication, monologue disguised as dialogue, however, that Buber (1947) seems to consider most prevalent in the contemporary world. By this, Buber means a form of communication that has a semblance of interpersonal openness and receptivity, but is essentially a turning towards, and concern with, oneself: a 'reflexivity', rather than a reaching out to an other. Here, 'two or more men, meeting in space, speak each with himself in strangely torturous and circuitous ways and yet imagine they have escaped the torment of being thrown back on their own resources' (p37). In this form of communication, each individual's concerns are not with learning from the other, but with self-presentation and self-enhancement. Hence, spontaneity and transparency are replaced with artifice, phoniness and manipulation. Buber describes a number of forms of communication that make up this 'underworld of faceless spectres of dialogue' (p38). In *debate*, for instance, points are not made as they exist in the protagonist's mind, but are designed to strike home as sharply as possible – a 'word duel' that is far more about self-aggrandisement than any genuine learning. In *speechifying*, on the other hand, 'people do not really speak to one another, but each, although turned to the other, really speaks to a fictitious court of appeal whose life consists of nothing but listening to him' (Buber, 1988: 69).

Moments of I-Thou and dialogue

In concluding this section, two important points need to be noted. First, in drawing this distinction between I-Thou and I-It modes of relating, Buber (1958) is not suggesting that we can consistently relate to others in an I-Thou, dialogic way: 'It is not possible to live in the bare present,' (p 51) he writes. For Buber, then, it is inevitable that we will sometimes relate to others and the world in an I-It manner. In this respect, the I-Thou attitude is best understood as something that we can experience moments of, rather than as something we can experience on an ongoing basis (Anderson & Cissna, 1997). Furthermore, Buber does not see the I-It attitude as inherently negative. For him, it is through objectifying, and separating from, entities and people that human beings can progress from an undifferentiated state of connectivity towards a deeper and more profound encounter (Woods, 1969). The I-Thou and I-It attitudes, then, are seen as dialectically related. Hence, as with Heidegger (1966), Buber's concern is not that we should consistently maintain an attitude of *Gelassenheit* (openness) towards the world. Rather, it is that we should not become so seduced by a technical and manipulative way of experiencing the world that we forget a more contemplative and relational possibility. As Buber writes, 'without *It* man cannot live. But he who lives with *It* alone is not a man' (p52).

From external dialogue to internal dialogue

The basic premise of this chapter, then, is that we can usefully transpose this interpersonal distinction to the intrapersonal plane. That is, that we can meaningfully distinguish between two particular modes of relating to ourselves. In the first of these, we – or a particular 'part' of ourselves – relate to another part of ourselves in an it-ifying, fragmenting, generalised, non-confirming, fragmentary, protective and monologic way – construing the other part as determined, and on the basis of past experiences or future desires. In the second form of intrapersonal relating, by contrast, we relate to ourselves in a humanising, individualising, confirming, holistic, risk-taking, dialogic manner: in a way that takes us, or a part of ourselves, as a present, choice-making whole. The former mode of intrapersonal relating I have termed an I-Me self-relational stance, while the latter mode I have termed an I-I self-relational stance (Cooper, 2003, 2004). In other words, in the I-I self-relational stance, the I relates to itself as an *I*: as an active, phenomenologically experiencing, meaning-orientated being. By contrast, in the I-Me self-relational stance, the I relates to the I as a *me*: as an empirical, object-like entity (cf. Mead's (1934) distinction between the *I* as self-as-subject and the *Me* as self-as-object). As with the I-Thou attitude, the suggestion here is not that human beings can, or should, consistently relate to themselves in an I-I manner. Rather, the suggestion is that people may be able to experience moments of I-I relating to themselves, and that, as will be argued later, these moments of I-I encounter are of crucial importance in determining their psychological wellbeing.

An example may help to illustrate this distinction between I-I and I-Me forms of self-relating, and how the various differences between an I-Thou and I-It attitude, as outlined above, can be transposed to the intrapersonal plane. Martha was a 25-year-old female client who experienced intense and terrifying panic attacks, often in social situations where she felt an enormous pressure 'not to put a foot wrong'. Martha's relationship to this panicking, vulnerable I-position – from the adult, rational I-position that she tended to inhabit during the psychotherapy sessions – illustrates the I-Me mode of intrapersonal relating.

First, from her adult I-position, she tended to talk *about* her experiences of panic and terror, rather than relating to these experiences in an immediate and direct way. There was a sense of her surveying and studying this mode of experience from a distance – from the position of an 'objective', disconnected observer – rather than standing alongside her terrors and fears and allowing herself to fully connect with them. Second, from her adult I-position, there was a tendency to 'it-ify' her vulnerable I-position. She described it as something that took her over, something that came from outside, rather than a fluid, meaning-orientated phenomenological stream of experiencing. Third, then, her adult I-position did not relate to the totality of her vulnerable I-position, but focused primarily on its behavioural and physical manifestations, to the exclusion of its intentional, meaning-orientated facets. Fourth, from her adult I-position, Martha had a great tendency to look for explanations as to *why* she was experiencing such panic and terror, rather than considering the possibility that, in the midst of that vulnerable mode of being, she might be experiencing freedom and choice. Fifth, as touched on earlier, Martha, from her adult I-position, did not invoke a meeting with her vulnerable I-position in the present. Rather, it was something that she talked about in the past – how she *had* panicked, *had* felt afraid – and also something that she experienced in terms of her future – specifically, as a 'block' to becoming the person she wanted to be. Sixth, from her adult I-position, her experiences of panic were construed in generalised terms: her panic attacks were manifestations of a trans-personal disorder, rather than *a* particular mode by which she, as the individual she was, encountered her world. Seventh, from her adult I-position, Martha was entirely disconfirming of her vulnerable I-position. It was something she hated, detested and was desperate to get rid of – in no way did she confirm or validate her vulnerability and fear. Eighth, Martha's relationship to her vulnerable I-position, from her adult I-position, was an exclusively cognitive one. She analysed and deconstructed it, but did not allow herself to also engage with it in an emotional and embodied way. Ninth, from her adult I-position, Martha had no intention of allowing herself to open up to her fears and vulnerabilities and let herself be touched or affected by this way of being. In summary, then, we can say that Martha, from her adult I-position, was in no way willing to enter into a dialogue with her vulnerable I-position. She was willing to 'speechify' to it – to tell her fears that they were 'stupid' and 'unfounded' – but she was not willing to engage with them in a mutual and symmetrical way.

As the therapy progressed, however, Martha was increasingly able to experience moments of I-I encounter between her adult and vulnerable I-positions. Here, Martha, from her adult I-position, was able to temporarily stand in the shoes of her vulnerable self, and to remind herself of just how terrifying those moments of social anxiety were. She also became increasingly able to acknowledge that she was not 'stupid' or 'cowardly' for running away from social situations at these times, but that, from this I-position, this action seemed like the best way of dealing with her immediate situation. In this I-I mode of relating, then, Martha became increasingly able to confirm her vulnerable I-position, and to accept its legitimacy within her intrapersonal world, rather than seeing it as a foe to be eliminated at all costs.

In the case of Martha, it is interesting to note how her relationship to her feelings of panic and anxiety seemed to mirror those that others in her family had held towards them. Her parents, for instance, were generally warm and loving to her, but saw Martha as an outgoing and self-confident person (in contrast to her highly anxious brother), and virtually refused to acknowledge that she ever felt particularly vulnerable or afraid. Such a mirroring, however, is quite comprehensible if we follow the Vygotskian (1962) line of reasoning that psychological ways of being exist first on the interpersonal plane before becoming internalised on the intrapersonal plane. In other words, I-Me intrapersonal attitudes towards oneself may be the result of experiencing I-It attitudes from others. This raises the possibility, then, that clients who have experienced particularly severe forms of it-ification by others – for example, through sexual or physical abuse – may come to develop particularly objectifying self-relational stances, as in the example at the beginning of this chapter.

The I-Me self-relational stance and psychological distress

As a working hypothesis, it is suggested that an individual's levels of psychological distress are related to the extent to which they relate to themselves in an I-Me way. In other words, the more they it-ify themselves, the more they may tend to experience psychological difficulties. Put conversely, it suggests that psychological wellbeing can be defined as the ability to relate to oneself – as well as others – in a thou-ifying way. Such a proposition can be seen as an extension, and encompassment, of Rogers' (1959) assertion that psychological difficulties are related to high levels of negative self-regard. It also encompasses, extends and brings together many other models of psychological distress: for instance, the existential idea that psychological problems are related to perceiving oneself in an inauthentic way, or the feminist idea that psychological wellbeing requires an ability to develop a 'self-empathic' capacity (Jordan, 1991). As with the I-It relationship, however, this is not to suggest that all moments of I-Me relating are necessarily distress related; indeed, at times they may be of positive benefit. Richard Worsley (personal communication, 2004), for instance, gives the example of a young man who was bullied, and learned to reduce the pain of the verbal threats by 'standing off to one side of the character who was being attacked'. Nevertheless, as with the I-Thou and I-It relationship, it is proposed that, when a person experiences themselves predominantly or wholly in an I-It way, then he or she is likely to experience high levels of psychological distress. This is for a number of reasons.

First, if a person can communicate with other parts of their being and acknowledge that part's needs, then they are more likely to be able to work 'together' as a coherent, functioning whole. If, on the other hand, the person, in one I-position, refuses to confirm another way that they have of being, then the resulting conflict is likely to absorb much of the individual's attention, making them less able to fulfil their in-the-world projects. Cooper and Rowan (1999) sum this up:

> Where there is a lack of communication, where selves disown each other or where one self dominates to the exclusion of all others, then the result tends toward a cacophony of monologues – a discordant wail which will always be less than the sum of the individual parts. But where selves talk to selves, where there is an acceptance and understanding between the different voices and an appreciation of diversity and difference, then there is the potential for working together and co-operation – an interwoven harmony of voices which may transcend the sum of the parts alone (p8).

Second, an I-I self-relational stance is associated with the experiencing of positive feelings towards oneself, such as acceptance, confirmation, openness, harmony, and a belief in one's uniqueness, wholeness and humanity. By contrast, an I-Me self-relational stance is associated with derogatory, objectifying, rejecting, dis-confirming feelings towards oneself. An I-I self-relational stance, then, is more likely to be associated with a positive mood state than an I-Me self-relational stance.

Third, the existence of I-Me self-relational stances is likely to be closely associated with the creation and maintenance of *subjugated* (Hermans & Kempen, 1993) – or what have also been termed 'disowned' (Stone & Winkelman, 1989), 'shadow' (Cooper, 1999), 'neglected', 'subdued' and 'suppressed' (Hermans, 2001; Hermans & Kempen, 1993) – I-positions. These are the voices that are banished, ignored and rejected within the intrapersonal community (Satir, 1978): the I-positions that are consistently it-ified, dis-confirmed and talked at, rather than with. As in the case of Martha, Stone and Winkelman suggest that the 'vulnerable child' is one of the voices that is most consistently disowned, alongside other voices that an individual may have been taught were unacceptable, such as the 'daimons' (May, 1969) of rage and sexuality.

Such subjugation of internal voices is likely to lead to a number of psychological difficulties. First, from a humanistic perspective (eg. Rogers, 1959), each aspect of a person's being is seen as having a positive potentiality. This means that, in subjugating certain aspects of his or her being, an individual locks up part of his or her full potentiality, thereby losing touch with 'some very beautiful, useful qualities' (Vargiu, 1974: 54). For instance, a young woman who silences her angry voice surrenders her ability to stand up for her own needs and demands. Moreover, the positive potentiality of each voice consists not only in what it can contribute alone but also in what it can contribute in dialogue with other voices. Hence, where particular voices are subjugated, the person's ability to think creatively and innovatively through open intrapersonal communication is also likely to be attenuated.

Furthermore, because these I-positions are expressions of vital elements of our being, they will not simply go away if attempts are made to silence them. Rather, like a young child, the more they are told to shut up, the more they are likely to shout and demand repatriation. This will inevitably lead to an increase in anxiety in the person: a constant sense of being threatened by something alien and undesirable. Moreover, because the individual, from the position of the dominant voices, refuses to dialogue with the subjugated voices, he or she then has little ability to mediate or control their expression. Martha, for instance, does not look her fears and anxieties in the face; she hopes that they will go away. In a social situation, then, she does little more than cling to the desperate hope that, this time, she will somehow, magically, not start to feel anxious. When the voice of terror does begin to emerge, therefore, she feels completely helpless in the face of it. She has no way of engaging with it, of retaining some sense of being in control.

This leads on to a further reason why the existence of I-Me intrapersonal relationships – and the creation and maintenance of subjugated I-positions – may be closely associated with psychological distress. Because the subjugated I-positions are vital elements of an individual's being, it is inevitable that, at certain times, a process of 'dominance reversal' (Hermans, 1996) will take place. Here, 'a hidden or suppressed position can (without therapy) become, quite suddenly, more dominant than the position that corresponds with the trait the person considers as a prevalent and stable part of his or her personality' (Hermans, 1996: 46). The question, then, is what happens when an it-ified 'me' becomes a dominant 'I'? One answer may be that, because the usually dominant I-positions have not established a dialogical relationship with this I-position, then the subjugated I-position has no way of dialoguing back. In other words, no *bridge* has been created between the usually dominant I-positions and the usually subjugated I-position, so when the person comes to inhabit the latter, she or he has no way of connecting with the former. When Martha experiences extreme social anxiety, for instance, she is unable to connect with the adult, rational voice that 'knows' that not everyone is staring at her. And, because she is unable to connect with other voices, she is unable to stand back from her vulnerable I-position and regain some perspective on her situation.

Therapeutic implications

Based on this analysis, it can be proposed that one of the central aims of therapy should be to help clients develop the ability to relate to themselves in an I-I manner. Not only will such a development allow clients to experience more productive intrapersonal relationships, feel better about themselves and more fully actualise their potential, but it will help them to establish a dialogue with their subjugated selves such that, when they do become immersed in those ways of being, they have the capacity to take a step back and connect with other voices.

In the process-experiential therapeutic and gestalt therapy fields (eg. Greenberg & Elliott, 1997; Greenberg, Rice & Elliott, 1993), specific techniques have been developed – most notably, two-chair work – to facilitate more open and effective communication between the person and their different parts, or between the parts themselves. From the psychotherapeutic literature, it would seem that such techniques can be an effective means of facilitating the emergence of I-I relationships (Cooper & Cruthers, 1999; Elliott, 2002). There are a number of reasons, however, why such techniques may also be counter-therapeutic at times, reducing the prevalence of I-I relating rather than increasing it. First, these techniques, through encouraging clients to identify and define certain I-positions, may lead them to experience these I-positions in a more objectifying, fixed and detached way. The I-position becomes a definite *thing*, rather than a vague and ill-defined voice that is simply encountered, and while it may be important for clients to go through a dialectical process of objectifying different voices, separating from them and then re-encountering them at a deeper level, there is always the danger that the voices will remain isolated and objectified. Second, and closely related to this, as a client starts to identify and define certain voices, there is the danger that these voices are taken out of the context of the dialogic whole, so that the client develops an increasingly fragmented view of his or her own being. In other words, at the level of the person-as-a-whole, these techniques may lead to an increasing it-ification. Third, such strategies may require the therapist to relate to his or her client in a relatively technical, if not mechanistic, way. And if, following a Vygotskian (1962) line of reasoning, intrapersonal relationships emerge as the internalisation of interpersonal relationships, then the establishment of an I-It dialogue between therapist and client may ultimately increase the prevalence of I-Me relating. So too might many other commonplace psychological practices, such as conducting psychological tests on clients or providing clients with specific psychiatric diagnoses and formulations.

More significantly, then, the analysis presented in this chapter may point towards – and provide a rationale for – the importance of establishing an I-Thou, relationally deep encounter (Knox et al, 2013; Mearns & Cooper, 2005) with clients. Here, through a process of internalisation, clients may come to develop a confirming 'thou-ifying' voice towards themselves: a mode of self-relating that is willing to witness and confirm the otherness within. Certainly, I have witnessed this process in my own therapeutic work, where several clients have reported 'hearing' my voice in their day-to-day activities, telling them that it is OK to feel scared or angry.

However, as I have argued previously (Cooper, 1996), it may often be the case that clients tend to inhabit a relatively constant I-position within the therapeutic relationship, and generally the one of the rational, observing adult. Hence, while a client may experience confirmation of – and learn to confirm for themselves – their rational, adult I-position, there is the danger that their more subjugated I-positions – those that do not emerge within the therapeutic relationship – may fail to experience confirmation. If this is the case, it would seem important that, from a person-centred standpoint, we think about ways in which we can help clients to bring their more subjugated ways of being into the therapeutic environment. Creating safety, warmth and unconditional acceptance are no doubt key means of achieving this, but perhaps it also means that, at times, we need to take a somewhat more process-directive stance, inviting the subjugated voices into the room (see Mearns in Cooper et al, 2004), and helping clients to 'unpack' those experiences that are usually it-ified.

Conclusion

The argument presented in this chapter is an attempt to examine, expand and clarify a person-centred understanding of how people relate to – or within – themselves, and the particular forms that problematic self-relational stances might take. The I-Me mode of self-relating outlined here has many parallels with Rogers' (1959) notions of distortion and denial, but it also serves to develop our understanding of the form(s) that such defensive responses might take. Furthermore, by drawing on a model of interpersonal attitudes and relating, the notion of 'I-Me' and 'I-I' self-relational stances provides a means whereby we can understand both interpersonal discord and intrapersonal discord on one continuum – *as the tendency to 'it-ify'* oneself, others or the world.

The analysis presented in this chapter also provides a wide range of psychologists, psychiatrists and other clinicians with one means of understanding psychological distress that is rooted in a fundamental respect for human beings. Its starting point is that human beings experience their world in inherently intelligible and meaningful ways but come to grief when they start to distrust, deny or objectify these experiences. This is not to suggest that all forms of psychological distress are reducible to such I-Me modes of relating – problems like autism, for instance, would seem to have a significant biological component (Comer, 1998) – but even with such conditions, how a person relates to this 'given' way of being may have a significant impact on their overall levels of wellbeing. It has also been suggested in this chapter that problematic I-Me self-relational stances may be particularly prevalent in clients who have experienced severe objectification by others.

Finally, the discussion in this chapter lends strong support to a person-centred way of working, and highlights the dangers of adopting therapeutic techniques that, if internalised, can serve to further objectify and alienate the self. Through engaging with others in a relationally deep manner (Mearns & Cooper, 2005), therapists can help clients to develop the capacity to heal themselves at the deepest possible level. Through a humanising interpersonal relationship, they can come to witness, value and honour their own fundamental humanity.

References

Anderson R, Cissna KN (1997). *The Martin Buber – Carl Rogers Dialogue: a new transcript with commentary.* Albany, NY: State University of New York Press.

Bakhtin M (1973). *Problems of Dostoevsky's Poetics* (2nd ed). (Trans RW Rostel.) Ann Arbor, MI: Ardis.

Buber M (1947). *Between Man and Man.* (Trans RG Smith.) London: Fontana.

Buber M (1958). *I and Thou* (2nd ed). (Trans RG Smith.) Edinburgh: T&T Clark Ltd.

Buber M (1988). *The Knowledge of Man: selected essays.* (Trans M Friedman, RG Smith.) Atlantic Highlands, NJ: Humanities Press International Inc.

Comer RJ (1998). *Abnormal Psychology* (3rd ed). New York: WH Freeman.

Cooper M (1996). Modes of existence: towards a phenomenological polypsychism. *Journal of the Society for Existential Analysis* 7(2): 50–56.

Cooper M (1999). If you can't be Jekyll be Hyde: an existential-phenomenological exploration on lived-plurality. In: Rowan J, Cooper M (eds). *The Plural Self: multiplicity in everyday life*. London: Sage (pp51–70).

Cooper M (2001). Embodied empathy. In: Haugh S, Merry T (eds). *Rogers' Therapeutic Conditions: evolution, theory and practice. Vol 2: Empathy*. Ross-on-Wye: PCCS Books (pp218–229).

Cooper M (2003). 'I-I' And 'I-Me': transposing Buber's interpersonal attitudes to the intrapersonal plane. *Journal of Constructivist Psychology 16*(2): 131–153.

Cooper M (2004). Encountering self-otherness: 'I-I' And 'I-Me' modes of self-relating. In: Hermans HJM, Dimaggio G (eds). *Dialogical Self in Psychotherapy*. Hove: Brunner-Routledge (pp60–73).

Cooper M (2013). Developmental and personality theory. In: Cooper M, Schmid PF, O'Hara M, Wyatt G (eds). *The Handbook of Person-Centred Psychotherapy and Counselling* (2nd ed). Basingstoke: Palgrave (pp118–135).

Cooper M (2015). *Existential Psychotherapy and Counselling: contributions to a pluralistic practice*. London: Sage.

Cooper M, Cruthers H (1999). Facilitating the expression of subpersonalities: a review and analysis of techniques. In: Rowan J, Cooper M (eds). *The Plural Self: multiplicity in everyday life*. London: Sage (pp198–212).

Cooper M, Mearns D, Stiles WB, Warner MS, Elliott R (2004). Developing self-pluralistic perspectives within the person-centered and experiential approaches: a round table dialogue. *Person-Centered and Experiential Psychotherapies 3*(3): 176–191.

Cooper M, Rowan J (1999). Introduction: self-plurality – the one and the many. In: Rowan J, Cooper M (eds). *The Plural Self: multiplicity in everyday life*. London: Sage (pp1–9).

Elliott R (2002). The effectiveness of humanistic therapies: a meta-analysis. In: Cain DJ, Seeman J (eds). *Humanistic Psychotherapies: handbook of research and practice*. Washington, DC: American Psychological Association.

Elliott R, Greenberg LS (1997). Multiple voices in process-experiential therapy: dialogue between aspects of the self. *Journal of Psychotherapy Integration 7*(3): 225–239.

Freud S (1923). The ego and the id. (Trans J Strachey.) In: *The Standard Edition of the Complete Psychological Works of Sigmund Freud. Vol. 19*. London: Hogarth Press (pp12–59).

Friedman M (1985). *The Healing Dialogue in Psychotherapy*. New York: Jason Aronson Inc.

Greenberg LS, Elliott R (1997). Varieties of empathic responding. In: Bohart AC, Greenberg LS (eds). *Empathy Reconsidered: new directions in psychotherapy*. Washington, DC: American Psychological Association (pp167–186).

Greenberg LS, Rice LN, Elliott R (1993). *Facilitating Emotional Change: the moment-by-moment process*. New York: Guilford Press.

Heidegger M (1966). *Discourse on Thinking*. (Trans JM Anderson, EH Freund.) London: Harper Colophon Books.

Hermans HJM (1996). Voicing the self: from information processing to dialogical interchange. *Psychological Bulletin 119*(1): 31–50.

Hermans HJM (2001). The dialogical self: towards a theory of personal and cultural positioning. *Culture and Psychology 7*(3): 243–281.

Hermans HJM, Kempen HJG (1993). *The Dialogical Self: meaning as movement*. San Diego, CA: Academic Press.

Jordan JV (1991). Empathy and self-boundaries. In: Jordan JV, Kaplan AG, Miller JB, Stiver IP, Surrey JL (eds). *Women's Growth in Connection: writings from the Stone Centre*. New York: The Guilford Press (pp67–80).

Knox R, Murphy D, Wiggins S, Cooper M (eds) (2013). *Relational Depth: new perspectives and developments*. Basingstoke: Palgrave.

Laing RD (1965). *The Divided Self: an existential study in sanity and madness*. Harmondsworth: Penguin.

Levinas E (1967). Martin Buber and the theory of knowledge. In: Schlipp PA, Friedman M (eds). *The Philosophy of Martin Buber*. London: Cambridge University Press (pp133–150).

Linell P, Markova I (1993). Acts in Discourse – from monological speech acts to dialogical inter-acts. *Journal for the Theory of Social Behaviour 23*(2): 173–195.

May R (1969). *Love and Will*. New York: WW Norton and Co.

Mead GH (1934). *Mind, Self and Society*. Chicago: University of Chicago Press.

Mearns D, Cooper M (2005). *Working at Relational Depth: the heart of person-centred and existential therapies*. London: Sage.

Mearns D, Thorne B (2000). *Person-Centred Therapy Today: new frontiers in theory and practice*. London: Sage.

Rogers CR (1957). The necessary and sufficient conditions of therapeutic personality change. Journal of Consulting Psychology 21(2): 95–103.

Rogers CR (1959). A theory of therapy, personality and interpersonal relationships as developed in the client-centered framework. In: Koch S (ed). *Psychology: a study of science. Vol 3*. New York: McGraw-Hill (pp184–256).

Sartre J-P (1958). *Being and Nothingness: an essay on phenomenological ontology*. (Trans H Barnes.) London: Routledge.

Satir V (1978). *Your Many Faces*. Berkeley, CA: Celestial Arts.

Stiles WB, Elliott R, Firthcozens JA, Llewelyn SP, Margison FR, Shapiro DA, Hardy G (1990). Assimilation of problematic experiences by clients in psychotherapy. *Psychotherapy 27*(3): 411–420.

Stone H, Winkelman S (1989). *Embracing our Selves: the voice dialogue manual*. Mill Valley, CA: Nataraj Publishing.

Vargiu JG (1974). Psychosynthesis workbook: subpersonalities. *Synthesis 1*: 52–90.

von Weizsäcker V (1964). Selected readings. In: Friedman M (ed). The Worlds of Existentialism: a critical reader. Chicago: University of Chicago Press (pp405–407).

Vygotsky LS (1962). *Thought and Language*. Cambridge, MA: MIT Press.

Woods RE (1969). *Martin Buber's Ontology: an analysis of I and Thou*. Evanston, IL: Northwestern University Press.

5 | Authenticity and alienation: towards an understanding of the person beyond the categories of order and disorder[1]

Peter F Schmid

Don't ask the doctor, ask the patient. (Jewish proverb)

The individual, and not the problem, is the focus. The aim is not to solve one particular problem, but to assist the individual to grow, so that he can cope with the present problem and with later problems in a better-integrated fashion. If he can gain enough integration to handle one problem in a more independent, more responsible, less confused, better-organized way, then he will also handle new problems in that matter. (Rogers, 1942: 28–29)

If we take the person-centred approach seriously as a *client*-centred approach, we have to go back to our clients in order to engage them in an individualised, shared process of encounter and reflection. Following Rogers, it is argued that the essential conditions of psychotherapy exist in a single configuration, even though they occur uniquely with each client. From a dialogical point of view, therapists and clients are not only seen as being in relationships; as persons, they are relationships, which makes them different in each therapeutic contact. Furthermore, the traditional concepts of psychological health and disorder are rejected, seeing symptoms as a specific cry for help that has to be understood in a process of personal encounter between therapist and client. Following this concept, instead of the classical categorising and classifying of psychopathological models (such as the traditional medical paradigm deriving from psychiatry and a variety of clinical psychologies), it is appropriate to speak about clients as persons who are suffering from inauthentic or alienated forms of being in the world. The value of concepts and conceptions for helping us understand different types of clients are acknowledged and emphasised.

---

1. Revised version of a paper first printed in *Person-Centered and Experiential Psychotherapies* 2004; 3: 36–51, drawing on a paper given at the Person-Centered and Experiential World Conference 2003 in Egmond aan Zee (Schmid, 2003b).

However, the existing concepts for, and descriptions of, our clients still exist only at a primitive, unsystematic stage of development, and thus we need the development of a genuinely human science of person-centred therapy.

Personal anthropology: authenticity and alienation

Carl Rogers' approach to 'mental health' was humanistic, not medical. Taking the point of view of the social sciences, not the natural sciences, his holistic standpoint on human beings encompassed not only the biological and individual nature but also the relational and social nature of the person. From the very outset, Rogers' psychology was a social psychology (Schmid, 1994, 1996). In trying to understand the human being within his or her respective frame of reference, Rogers came to view every individual as a unique being. Therefore, as opposed to an observational and analytical approach, he stood in the tradition of phenomenology, existentialism, hermeneutics and constructivism (Zurhorst, 1993).

The substantial-relational notion of the person as a social criticism

But Rogers' personality theory is not only a social psychological theory; it is also implicitly social criticism, a critical theory of socialisation. Central to his understanding of the person is the process of authenticity, the perpetually striven-for congruence between the 'experiencing organism' and the self-concept. For a long time, this was misunderstood individualistically, as referring only to isolated individuals. On the contrary, Rogers (1965: 20) clearly stated that the nature of the human being itself is 'incurably social'. From a personal, dialogical viewpoint, we are not only *in* relationships; as persons, we *are* relationships. Therefore, the human person must be understood at one and the same time from both an individual or substantial view (which points to autonomy and sovereignty), *and* from a relational view (highlighting interconnectedness and solidarity) (Schmid, 2001, 2002a, 2003a, 2013). Self-determination *and* interrelatedness refer essentially to one and the same human nature; we only view and experience these as different dimensions. To regard the human as a substantial-relational being is what is meant by designating him/her a person. Therefore, any *person*-centred consideration on what 'healthy' or 'fully functioning' means must include a theory of social criticism and, consequently, a political and sociotherapeutic view (Schmid, 2012, 2015).

'Psychological health': a theory of authenticity instead of a 'health' concept

Authenticity as the process of balancing individuality and interrelatedness

To be a person means to be truly living the process of authenticity, developing one's potential in a constructive way. To live authentically means to be able to keep the balance or, better, to gain always anew the synthesis between the substantial and the relational task of living. A man or woman is authentic if they maintain this balance in the process of realising their own values and needs, their individuality and uniqueness, while *at the same time* living together with their others and the world, meeting the needs and challenges of these relationships in interdependence and solidarity. Who is fully him-/herself is fully social, and vice versa. Self-realisation and solidarity coincide. This is how Rogers viewed what he called the 'fully functioning person'. It was not by coincidence that Rogers referred to the biblical notion of *agape*, which embraces both dimensions: 'You shall love your neighbour as yourself' (Leviticus 19: 18; Matthew 22: 39).

From a superficial point of view, a person who lives this process of authenticity is called 'healthy' (etymologically connected with 'whole'), 'sane', or even 'normal' or 'in order' – whence the term 'dis-order' derives. This is in line with the meaning of 'in-firmity' or 'dis-ease'. But authenticity has nothing to do with being firm or at ease. These common terms are not only misleading, they are completely wrong (see Sanders, Chapter 2 this volume, 2006), because a severely ill person can live very authentically. This includes pain, fear, grief, struggle, sorrow, agony, transience, and stages of inauthenticity in which there is a new striving towards balance. It also means that each person is different in their way of being authentic.

Rogers always thought about the fully functioning person in terms of the *process* of becoming, never about a state or an end product. The significant meaning of authenticity is to live to become more and more authentic: that is, to become the author of one's own life (Schmid, 2001).

The outset of the person-centred point of view of a person's development is a salutogenetic one (Antonovsky, 1979), aiming at resources for and development of health, not a pathogenetic one, dealing with development of suffering and aiming at avoidance of illness.

In summary: the image of the human being in person-centred anthropology differs qualitatively from the respective image in the natural sciences. It is human science, not natural science. Thus, person-centred thinking sets out from a process theory of authenticity, not from a theory of failure or disorder. The person is understood as an existential process, a process of striving towards authenticity in every given moment of his/her existence, a joint process of self-development and relationship development. Therefore, person-centred in itself is process-centred (which is clearly different from process-directive). In the view of a genuinely personal anthropology, it makes no sense to separate the process from the person, and it is impossible to separate content and process: in a very significant sense, the process is the content is the meaning. (Therefore it also seems to be artificial to separate between relationship-, content- and process-experts.)

Alienation: the suffering person instead of a concept of 'dis-orders'

Trouble with the ongoing process of becoming authentic can be caused by the development of an inauthentic self-concept (due to introjected conditions of worth), or by the lack of the development of some parts of the organismic experiencing capabilities (due to missing opportunities) (Spielhofer, 2003). In both cases, the result is incongruence between experience and self. In both cases, inauthentic or missing relationships play a crucial role, because a person becomes, and is, the relationship they have, as stated above. A person becomes inauthentic if they are alienated from self and Others (ie. from the experiencing organism and the necessary genuine relationships). Psychological suffering is usually the result. Such a process must be understood as a fundamental self-contradictoriness (*Selbstwidersprochenheit*; Zurhorst, 1993) between the capabilities and the natural process of experiencing on the one hand, and the rigid and in itself torn structure of the self, and resulting rigid relationships, on the other hand.

Inauthenticity and maladjustment

Consequently, for a critical theory of socialisation, diagnosing and repairing a deviation from a norm is not an appropriate guideline. In trying to understand how far a person is alienated from self, the prevailing and ruling cultural norm cannot be a constant, although it must be taken into account. This notion of 'inauthenticity' differs qualitatively from the common meaning of (mental) illness or disorder (in the meaning of malfunction). What is experienced from an internal frame of reference as 'psychological suffering', from an external point of view is seen as alienation or maladjustment. If it is called 'disorder', one must *permanently* keep in mind that the 'order' always is also a cultural norm.

The 'deviation' can appear to be more on the substantial side, inasmuch as there are problems with a person's individuality and being all wrapped up in the social roles (for example, what is called melancholy), or it can look as if the difficulties are more relational when a person refuses to engage in their social tasks (for example, with schizophrenia) (see Zurhorst, 1993). No matter whether it is a deficit of substantial authenticity in the sense of 'not being who you are' or a deficit of relational authenticity in the sense of maladjustment, in either case the *person* is suffering. The 'maladjusted person' (see Rogers, 1959) – a term matching with the 'fully functioning person' – who has not succeeded in gaining the authentic balance always suffers from both sides: they lack self-confidence, due to an incongruence between self and experience (autonomy deficit), *and* they lack trust in the world and others, due to an incongruence between the others as perceived by the self and the others as really being Others (relationship deficit). So, suffering due to alienation is a signal of a deficiency or a loss of authenticity. A psychological symptom therefore is a cry for help (Schmid, 1992).

The symptom as a specific call for help to overcome inauthenticity

The Greek word 'symptom' originally meant 'coincidence, temporary peculiarity'; only later did it come to mean 'sign, warning, distinguishing mark', and finally took on the medical sense of a 'characteristic sign of a specific disease'. A symptom is a phenomenon, something that is shown by the person. As everyone familiar with the psychiatric field knows, symptoms often appear to be accidental; they can be subject to fashion (for example, think of co-morbidity and the intercorrelation of symptoms). One and the same client is quite often given a variety of diagnoses, frequently even contradictory ones.

In the light of a philosophy of the person, a symptom is always a specific cry, coming out of the attempt to be seen and receive help. It is an expression of being severely out of balance in the process of striving for authenticity, and the request for support is an attempt to deal with a situation by notifying oneself and others of the balance problem. In the specific cry lies the key to understanding the suffering person. It might often be a compromise between the problem and the request for help, but in any case it is, on psychological, mental, physical levels, a *unique* expression of this particular person in this particular situation – an expression of the wish to be understood and to understand oneself. It is a call to others to overcome the vicious circle and to get the process of authentic personalisation restarted. Thus, it always creates a unique situation of relationship. In this the key for therapy is to be found.

Symptoms are as manifold as persons, and situations are manifold. Many authors who regard differential treatment as necessary reproach the person-centred approach for adhering to a uniformity myth. What a gross misunderstanding! According to personal anthropology, each suffering person is not viewed uniformly but is seen as entirely different. And so the therapeutic answer is: not uniform but unique (Schmid, 1992).

More on the concepts of authenticity and alienation, health and illness, order and disorder and their connotations (with links to Marx, Angyal, Goldstein, Antonovsky, Whitehead, gestalt psychology, transactional analysis etc) can be found in a chapter by Tudor and Worrall (2006: 155–189), where they present enlarged and further differentiated thoughts on the issues at stake.

In summary: inauthentic persons are alienated from themselves and others. Suffering persons are communicating to themselves and others by symptoms that their process of striving towards authenticity in a given moment of their existence has severely failed or got stuck, that they need help in their processes of self and relationship development. Since the person is their existential process, the task is to understand the particular process, which is the same as understanding the particular person. The challenge is not so much what has gone wrong, but where the possibilities are to facilitate the process of life – ie. the self-healing capacities.

Therapy: personality development through encounter

If it is correct that the reason for alienation and suffering is inauthenticity, and therefore relationship, then it is also relationship that helps. Aptly, the kind of relationship that can reconcile the alienated person with self and the world was called 'encounter' by Rogers (1962).

Person-centred therapy is such a relationship: the facilitation of personalisation (ie. becoming a person) as a process of becoming independent and of co-creating relationships. Thus, therapy overcomes the stagnation (Pfeiffer, 1993). From a relational point of view, therapy is personal encounter; from a substantial point of view, it is personality development (which, by the way, sets the person-centred stance clearly apart from a merely systemic view, as well as from other ahistoric therapies). That is, personalisation occurs through encounter, and personality development by working at relational depth (Mearns, 1996).

Thus, although symptoms are manifold, the answer is always of the same kind: a certain relationship. Despite symptom specificity, the answer is a special kind of relationship. The same relational conditions that are crucial for the development of the infant and child are necessary and sufficient for psychotherapy. Psychotherapy is a special chapter of developmental psychology.

Therefore the relationship is always the same and always different: the same, because it is always the presence (unfolded as the core conditions; Schmid, 2002b, 2003a) of the therapist that is needed and constitutes the answer to the cry expressed by symptoms. It is unique, because it is the special relationship of the persons involved at any given moment of the process that is needed, co-created in the encounter process.

Does this mean 'intervention homogeneity' (Heinerth, 2002)? Yes and no. Yes, because therapy is independent of symptoms and circumstances, insofar as it is always the same 'type' of relationship that is needed: encounter. No, it is specific, because two or more unique persons are involved in unique moments of encounter. Differentiated answers are necessary, according to differential cries and different perspectives that the client expresses. They require differential empathy for the moment-by-moment process of the client's self-exploration and the forms of relationships that are offered.

In summary: person-specific is not symptom-specific, or problem-specific (Mearns, 2004), or disorder-specific, and not at all disorder-oriented, but instead is uniquely process-specific. Consequently, disorder-oriented or goal-oriented are not person-oriented or process-oriented. Since it is the relationship that facilitates the process of personalisation, differentiated relationships are needed: each person-to-person relationship is different, otherwise it would not be a personal relationship. But the kind of relationship is always the same: an encounter, although in very different ways. The client is seen as an active self-healer 'using' the therapist for support in this 'co-created interpersonal process' (Bohart & Tallman, 1997). As a part of the relationship, the therapist is different if the client is different.

Phenomenological epistemology: acknowledgement and knowledge

If we were fully functioning persons, we could always, with all persons and moment by moment, be the person the client needs in the given moment, and provide the communications the client needs, thus creating the optimal relationship at any given instant. But we are not fully functioning persons; we are all more or less maladjusted persons. This raises the question, what do we 'have' that can be of help and that can allow us to enter encounter processes in difficult relationships, in spite of our being restricted by our own fears and security needs?

The answer is: we have our ability to reflect. We have our intellect.

The relevance of knowledge and conceptions in person-centred therapy

Acknowledgment: the art of not-knowing

In immediately encountering another person, I do not think about what I could know about him/her; rather, I am ready to accept what they are going to disclose. This is a change of epistemological paradigms of tremendous importance for psychotherapy. It expresses acknowledgement as an active and proactive way of deliberately saying yes to the Other as a person. Specifically, this portrays psychotherapy as the art of not-knowing (Schmid, 2002a): the art of being curious, open to being surprised – a kind of sophisticated naïvety towards the client, where the challenging part is the unknown (see Takens, 2001) and not-yet-understood; the openness to wonderment, surprise and what the client has to disclose. 'Each experience, which deserves this name, thwarts an expectation' (Gadamer, 1999: 362). Thus, back to the client! For a new, truly human image of the human being, we need a new epistemology (Mearns, 2004).

Reflection: the human capability of dealing with experience

But life is not only surprise. We are able to think about our experiences and create expectations. We form specific concepts and theories. We inevitably do so, and should be aware of this, instead of ignoring it: we cheat ourselves if we think we do not think, expect and categorise. For a personal encounter relationship, both are necessary: acknowledgement *and* knowledge; experience *and* reflection.

Experiences lead to reflection. In order to be a personal encounter, therapy needs reflection both within and outside the therapeutic relationship. Reflection is necessary for a personal relationship not only *after* or *outside* therapy (eg. in supervision, theory building or scientific work); reflection is also needed *within* the relationship, together with the client. A therapeutic encounter relationship is not only co-experiencing; it also is 'co-thinking' (Bohart & Tallman, 1997, 1999). First, there is the immediate presence and experience of persons, and then there is the co-reflection by the involved persons about the meaning of their encounter experience. The experience needs a second view – a critical view from 'outside' of the immediate encounter but within the relationship. The experience needs to be looked at, thus objectifying it. Only after this does the 'initial encounter' become a 'personal encounter' relationship.

As encounter philosophy has discerned, all en-*counter* processes start by being affected by the essence of the Other – of the unexpected as something or somebody that I experience as *counter* to me. Encounter means to face the other person, thus appreciating them as somebody independent – as an autonomous individual, different from me, and worthy of being dealt with (Schmid, 1994, 1998, 2002a). What at first is always an 'initial encounter', a naïve encounter as experienced by an unaffected child, becomes a 'personal encounter' by the passage through reflection. It needs the potential to make oneself, Others and relationships into objects of reflected awareness, thus overcoming the mere naïvety and unity that lie before freedom and responsibility. Distance is necessary for reflection. In this way, analysing and evaluating become feasible, and with them so do the freedom and responsibility that characterise a mature encounter relationship. This free and responsible way of relating is the pre-condition for understanding what the call of the Other means, and for the ability to answer adequately.

Immediate encounter and reflection modes

In the *process of immediate encounter*, the epistemological road goes from client to therapist, so that the therapist asks, 'What does this person show, reveal, indicate?' (not, 'What do I see over there?'), or, 'What can we understand, comprehend, empathise?' The movement goes from the Thou to the I, constituting a Thou-I-relationship (Schmid, 2002a). In this way, we need to go 'back to the client' as our starting point, to a truly *client*-centred approach.

In the *process of reflecting*, however, the epistemological movement is the opposite, and so we ask, 'What do we perceive?' This requires that we look at the experiences and reflect on them (although sometimes or initially it might be only the therapist who starts reflecting).

Both epistemological movements are necessary: we need the subjective and the objective. In good moments of therapy they alternate, often quickly oscillating between both modes. The more reflecting follows experiencing and is connected with it, the more it feels like a holistic process, as 'one whole step'. (If the order is reversed or if encounter is missing at all, it is no longer *person*-centred therapy. If the critical reflection is missing, the therapist would no longer be the counter-part in the en-counter.) Therapeutic encounter always means to be *with* and – as a different person – *counter* the client (Schmid & Mearns, 2006).

In the '*immediate encounter mode*', it is impossible to do anything different from experiencing (otherwise one quits the encounter mode). Categorisation is impossible: clients do not show categories, they show themselves (or parts of them) – even if they use categories to describe themselves. Rogers (1962: 186–187) was very clear on this:

> ... the existential encounter is important... in the immediate moment of the therapeutic relationship, consciousness of theory has no helpful place... we become spectators, not players – and it is as players that we are effective... at some other time we may find it rewarding to develop theories. In the moment of relationship, such theory is irrelevant or detrimental... theory should be held tentatively, lightly, flexibly, in a way which is freely open to change, and should be laid aside in the moment of encounter itself.

While in the encounter mode, categorisation is impossible; in the 'reflection mode', the – whenever possible shared – enterprise is to understand the meaning of what was just experienced, and so we must use categories. We may feel reminded of an earlier situation with this person, or with somebody similar, or an experience we have had ourselves that we use as comparison. We recognise that a feeling was stirred up that we had in another situation; although it was somewhat different, it feels similar. And so we create and use categories, concepts and conceptions. We cannot not think. We cannot not categorise. We cannot (and should not) ignore that a certain behaviour reminds us, say, of puberty. If we use this concept after the respective encounter experience, it can help us to better understand what the client wants to have understood and how they stage and direct the relationship. Categories and concepts may not be systematically reflected upon, or hardly reflected on at all, but they always rule our acting.

Conceptions and categories

It is important, however, not to think that the self-created categories are given by nature. We need to be aware that the concepts and conceptions are our own constructs. We have to avoid reifying or ontologising the categories created by ourselves. In the immediate encounter mode, we experience; in the reflection mode, we perceive, which means 'to take'. But if we think that we just take what is there, we are wrong. We are construing what we think we see. We cannot perceive without pre-*inform*-ation. We do not look at the client with eyes that have never seen a client before. We are ourselves no *tabulae rasae*, but are biased by our experiences and the concepts derived from them.

Therefore, we must be aware that *we* are the ones who determine what we hear and see and how we arrange what clients tell and show. We decide about the frame of reference of our perceptions out of a pre-understanding and pre-interpretation (Spielhofer, 2003). Thus, we need to be aware that a person does not 'have' a disorder, she 'is' not 'out of order' (Fehringer, 2003). Fehringer (2016) emphasises that, since language constructs reality, the common language use supports a reification of pathologies existing independent of persons, but the persons are not only suffering victims of their symptoms but also creators of them in the given context and relationships. A phenomenological approach, rather, requires the question, 'In which situation does he/she *show* something?' On the basis of personal anthropology, it is not possible to say what a symptom or a cluster of symptoms means (ie. what the client wants to say) merely from an external frame of reference – without taking the relationship, and thus ourselves and the cultural context, into consideration.

Though it is impossible to think without concepts, we must keep in mind that they are likely to be more wrong than right (for example, they always oversimplify). Therefore, clients must have a chance to upset our concepts. To do this, we need first of all to disclose our concepts, and to keep them as transparent as possible. Implicit conceptions must become explicit in order to be falsifiable. Clients must have a chance (even more, must feel invited) to falsify the therapist's concepts and conceptions. These need not only to be open for correction, they must invite correction. They must be ready to be upset and exploded. The last word for the therapist always has to be the Socratic 'I know that I know nothing'.

Existential knowledge: context-, experience- and relationship-based

We have the choice either to use randomly what pops up in our mind, coincidental intuition or whatever, biased by ourselves, or we can reflect on the conceptions we have and investigate them in a scientific way, systematically: that is, methodically and in dialogue with others, which will reduce the probability of systematic errors or biases. Responsibility requires reflecting on our conceptions.

This means, in the reflection mode, we work with knowledge. From a personal point of view, this needs to be existential knowledge – knowledge that can provide a basis for our decisions to act. It must come out of experience and must remain bound to it and open to be changed by it. Reflected conceptions have to be process conceptions, which do not pin down but open up. Such knowledge means to be in-form-ed, to be brought 'in form' by experience and reflection on experience. Experience-based knowledge does not ask whether something is *absolutely* (ie. detached from the context) right or wrong; it can only *relatively* be 'right' or 'wrong' – within the *relation*-ship. Relevant knowledge is not only relationship-based, it is necessarily context-based and dependent on culture and social norms. (Many people were instantly 'cured' when homosexuality was removed from the list of diseases by the American Psychiatric Association (APA); now the 'Association of Gay and Lesbian Psychiatrists' is an affiliated organisation of the APA.)

So, for knowledge the same applies as for empathy: back to the client! Clients are the ones who in-form us about the next steps in therapy. They bring us 'in form'. Knowledge serves understanding, empathy and acknowledging (ie. unconditional positive regard; see Schmid, 2002a). Empathy is always knowledge-based. Existential knowledge 'in-forms' empathy, 'in-forms' understanding, and thus can be of help, just as theory 'in-forms' practice. Knowledge fosters therapeutic understanding. Ute Binder (1994: 17–18) is convinced that, at least in the clinical field, we stay far below the possible and necessary level of the realisation of the core conditions if we do not try to understand specific phenomena, the respective ways in which they are experienced and the conditions under which they develop. Binder and Binder (1991) emphasise that empathy needs knowledge about disorder-based specific peculiarities, or at least is furthered very much by it. This does not mean that the therapeutic conditions are not sufficient and need supplementation or addition by knowledge; rather, it means that knowledge is an intrinsic part of the realisation of the conditions. (Only barely enlightened, allegedly person-centred people play knowledge off against relationship and emotion.)

In summary: epistemologically, the person-centred process of understanding is a process of personal encounter. This includes the process of experiencing, acknowledging the Other, and empathy, and the process of reflecting on the co-experiences. Both modes require each other. The task is to personally and professionally handle the resulting dichotomy of not-knowing and knowing, acknowledgement and knowledge. To be truly a personal encounter, there needs to be reflection within and outside of therapy. Reflection is based on knowledge and leads to new knowledge. Although knowledge must not get in the way of the immediacy of encounter, it must be seen as an essential dimension of a personal encounter relationship. A personal use of concepts, conceptions and theories does not hinder experience, but fosters it.

Do we need disorder-specific conceptions and diagnostics?

Therefore, the crucial question or decision is, which theories we use. On which conceptions do we base our therapeutic endeavour? Which knowledge do we choose to determine what we do? On the basis of a personal understanding, presence and reflection belong to each other and require each other, as stated above. We need to offer the client the best conceptions available, the best to foster presence and personalisation. The phrase 'to the best of one's knowledge and belief' shows clearly that this is an ethical task, just as doing psychotherapy itself is an ethical enterprise (Schmid, 2002a, 2002c).

Disorder-specific?

Since we need reflection, concepts and knowledge to help us understand the processes in and with our clients and in ourselves as well as possible, it becomes clear that it is useful and necessary to have knowledge about specific processes in the person (which is different from the misleading term 'disorder'-specific knowledge). Rogers himself acted differently in different situations; he further developed his way of doing therapy and modified it (eg. after the Wisconsin project and encounter groups experiences), even though he did not systematise and classify this. He clearly stated, 'with some fear and trembling', because of a 'heavy weight of clinical opinion to the contrary', that 'the essential conditions of psychotherapy exist in a single configuration, *even though the client or patient may use them very differently*' (1957: 101; italics mine). The second clause of the sentence is often overlooked, although it is essential and marks the task: to understand how clients use the relationship differently. Again, back to the client! Different ways of relating by the client in-form the therapist to relate and respond differently. This is crucial, because the relationship is unique. Each client deserves to get the answer and the relationship they need, and – this seems self-evident from the relationship conditions – not some preset 'type of intervention'.

At the same time, we need concepts that help us to reflect on our therapeutic experiences, because it is better to act on the basis of critically reflected knowledge and scientifically investigated conceptions than on coincidental and randomly acquired knowledge. Thus, it is essential to develop carefully grounded and considered, genuinely developed systems of concepts. In this sense, process-differentiation makes sense, as do specific concepts when they help us to better understand different authentic and inauthentic processes.

On the other hand, *disorder*-centred conceptions are not *person*-centred: 'Person-centered is not problem-centered,' because clients are viewed through the prism of their distress rather than their potentialities (Mearns, 2004). To try to justify traditional diagnoses and 'intervention techniques' in person-centred therapy, arguing that modern applied sciences and mainstream health politics require us to do so, and thus to manualise person-centred therapy by describing categories of therapeutic techniques, is simply a contradiction. Finke and Teusch (2007), for example, favour a manualisation of the basic conditions for personality development as described by Rogers: which kind of intervention to use in which disorder-specific case – for example, 'repeating clients' statements', 'concretizing understanding', 'self-concept-oriented understanding', 'alter-ego relationship', 'self-disclosure', 'supportive' versus 'critically questioning resonance'. Such guidelines for intervention not only offer an isolated understanding of the conditions instead of seeing them as a comprehensive description of an encounter relationship ('presence') regarded from different perspectives (Schmid, 2002b); they once again reduce persons to categories of problems, and relationship therapy to disorder treatment – see also the psychiatrists Ludwig Teusch (Finke & Teusch, 1991, 2002) and Gert-Walter Speirerer (1994).

Quite a lot of person-centred 'disorder'-specific knowledge exists. There have been many attempts to describe and better understand characteristic processes. In recent years, many theoreticians and researchers have made much effort, and there is quite a body of literature. Out of different motivations – to be recognised by the authorities, to communicate with colleagues, to further develop understandings of person-centred therapy – numerous conceptions were developed and were more or less influential. The experiential movement deserves credit for strongly emphasising the necessity of conceptions. The work of Hans Swildens (1988), Ute and Johannes Binder (1994), Garry Prouty (Van Werde & Prouty, 2013), Dion Van Werde (Chapter 12, this volume), Elke Lambers (2003), Stephen Joseph and Richard Worsley (2005; Worsley & Joseph, 2007), Eva-Maria Biermann-Ratjen (1996), Paul Wilkins and Martin Gill (2003), for example, has contributed substantially to our understanding of person-centred processes and to the development of person-centred theory and practice.

Furthermore, much time has been spent on finding a way of dealing with the prevailing conceptions of medicine and psychiatry, the other therapeutic orientations, and the requirements of the public health system for effective treatments that are so fixed as a given and resistant to change (Fletcher, 2012). It seems clear that simply to adopt one of these other systems of thought will hardly or not at all correspond with person-centredness (Sanders, Chapter 2, this volume, 2006). As a result, quite a few attempts have been made to translate traditional models into person-centred categories. Although we cannot ignore these traditional conceptions, and therefore must understand them, and although we are often forced to use them in order to communicate with colleagues and institutions, or simply in order to get access to social security money, I am convinced that they are not at all consistent with the image of the human being as a person. (In the same way, in training, lack of self-assurance and competence should not be replaced by rules and techniques; instead, training should support personalisation and further trust in one's own capabilities, and a proper reflection on them, just as therapy does.) Sanders (Chapter 2, this volume, 2006) argues that a concept of mental illness is not only inappropriate but oppressive, and resistance to it 'can be justified in terms of philosophy, theory and effectiveness' (see also Gillon, 2013 and Wilkins, 2016, who discerns between (labelling) diagnosis and assessment as a mutual, non-expert based process).

I want to highlight two promising developments: first, the work of Margaret Warner (1998, 2001, 2013, Chapter 6, this volume) on difficult, fragile and dissociated process as an alternative way of thinking about clients who have traditionally been diagnosed with severe disorders; second, one of the most interesting and genuine attempts to develop a person-centred systematic description of inauthentic processes, done by Keith Tudor and Mike Worrall (2006), who took up the challenge I uttered in the first edition of this book (Schmid, 2005).

(The same caveat, by the way, is true for research, assessment, case formulation and testing (Gillon, 2013; Wilkins & Gill, 2003; Wilkins, Chapter 8, this volume). Research that is compatible with the person-centred image of the human being helps therapists *and* clients to comprehend what goes on in therapy.)

In the first versions of this chapter (Schmid, 2003b, 2005), I stated: 'It is now my turn to state "with some fear and trembling" (because of "a heavy weight of opinion to the contrary" and because the result may be disappointing) that, according to the preceding considerations, it is obvious that there is not yet a genuinely person-centred taxonomy (systematic classification), one that meets the criteria of person-centred anthropology and epistemology described earlier in this paper. Even more: I am convinced that all the knowledge we have gathered about processes in clients does not allow us to state that we already know enough about their experiences to elaborate systematic conceptualizations about specific processes.' Thirteen years later, I can add that intensive debates about these issues have been taking place, resulting in clarifications of the problems that we are dealing with in formulating such conceptualisations, but I cannot yet renounce my statement: we still face hard work – and this is not only true for person-centred pathology and therapy theory.

Diagnosis?

Intrinsically connected with concept specificity is the question of diagnostics. In the field of medicine, rational treatment cannot be planned and executed without an accurate diagnosis, which also means prognosis of likely progress and possible cures, and thus prescription of treatment. Such diagnoses are typically stated in terms of symptoms or aetiology. For psychotherapy, however, Rogers (1951: 223–225) was convinced that psychological diagnoses are not only unnecessary but also detrimental and unwise, because they place the locus of evaluation and responsibility in the therapist as the sole expert, which also has long-range social implications for the social control of the many by the self-selected few (again, an indication of the social criticism included in his theory and practice).

Rogers' alternative view sees the client as the expert on their life, because they are the one with the experience: 'Therapy *is* diagnosis, and this diagnosis is a process which goes on in the experience of the client, rather than in the intellect of the clinician' (Rogers, 1951: 223; see also his process description of therapy). This shows that the basic problem of diagnosis is the question of who is to be regarded as the experienced one. In a *person*-centred perspective, both are experts, yet in a different sense: the therapist is the expert on not being an expert on the life of another person (see also Bohart & Tallman, 1999).

The Greek word 'dia-gnosis' means 'distinguishing judgment'. Diagnosis is the hard work of the client, who works on the process of distinguishing: the client is constantly trying to find out – by experiencing and reflecting – which development is on the agenda next, what they need in the process of personalisation. Thus, there must be diagnosis, although in a person-centred sense this is differently understood from the common meaning. And, although it runs completely counter to the traditional and widespread understanding, from a *person*-centred point of view psychological diagnosis can only be a phenomenological process diagnosis, step by step unfolding through the joint process of experiencing and reflecting by both client and therapist. Just like therapy, diagnosis needs both modes, and requires both persons involved in the relationship, thus making it a *co-diagnostic process*.

In summary: although quite a lot of person-centred 'disorder'-specific knowledge exists, and there are phenomenological descriptions that provide a very valuable contribution to person-centred personality and therapy theory, a genuinely person-centred systematic description of inauthentic processes is only rudimentary, and a genuinely person-centred taxonomy of process-specificity does not exist at all.

Philosophy of science: towards a truly human science

So there still is a lot of work ahead. We are not yet able to set up a genuinely person-centred system. Thus, the only thing I can provide at this stage in the development of the paradigm is to name criteria such a systematic conceptualisation would require. Thus, I state some tentative theses as criteria for a genuinely person-centred conceptualisation of different processes of personality development.

1. Conceptions (that is, systems of concepts) must be created on the basis of *personal anthropology* – that is, on the basis of dialogical or encounter philosophy. Among other things, this means that conceptions must include thinking in relationship categories as well as in substantial categories. It necessarily includes thinking in processes. The matrix is a conception of personal authenticity, not a concept of dis-*order*, dis-*ease* or the like. Such a conception must be based on growth – a conception that rests on potential and actualisation. Since it will embrace the past and future of the person, as well as the present, thus thinking in life-long categories, it will also be of aetiological value.

2. Conceptions must be *phenomenological* – that is, they must go back to the client as a person. Such an approach keeps in mind that what the person shows is relevant, not just what can be analysed or explained. Person-centred conceptions must be as close to experience as possible, in keeping with the phenomenological radicalism of Rogers.

3. Hence, it must be possible to *falsify* the conceptions, or parts thereof. Conceptions are useful when they stimulate a process that leads to their being overcome by better ones. It must constantly be possible to revise specific concepts through experience. It is this sort of '*orthopractice*' that always challenges orthodoxy.

4. Conceptions must be *hermeneutic*. The original meaning of hermeneutics applies here: reconstruing the meaning the author of a damaged text had in mind. It also has to be clear that this understanding is ultimately for the client's sake, not for the therapist's; that understanding is impossible without knowledge of the cultural context, and that it is impossible to get rid of all prejudices. The task of existential hermeneutics, rather, is to become aware of the prejudices and pre-understandings of one's own existence and to make them transparent (see 3 above).

5. Person-centred conceptions need to be *existential* – that is, they must have a relation to the whole existence of a person, as well as to human existence in general.

6. Conceptions must include *social criticism and political and sociotherapeutical considerations*. They must have a critical eye on power and control, on interests and expertism (diagnoses are often motivated by economic and political interests (Fehringer, 2016)), and they have to be emancipatory in nature. Therefore, such conceptions must make transparent whose interests they serve and who will benefit from them. To adhere to emancipatory conceptions – facilitation of authentic persons versus assistance to social adaption – is a

political task of prime importance for an approach that is understood as a practice of social ethics.

7.   Conceptions must trigger *research that is genuinely humanistic* (Rogers, 1964). It goes without saying that person-centred conceptions must allow the influence of empirical research, even if the results are disconfirming. But more important is that person-centred researchers overcome empiricism and positivism and are able to initiate truly person-oriented approaches to research – for example, intensive case studies or creative types of research such as Elliott's (2002) Hermeneutic Single Case Efficacy Design (HSCED) (see Elliott, 2013).

Conclusion

'Back to the client' means back to the human being. We need to adhere to a human science to understand what goes on in human beings. If the movement goes from the client to the therapist, then in a client-centred approach, we need to go back to the client as the primary source of knowledge and understanding. Therapy is more than a matter of therapist variables; it is a matter of the client's self-healing capacities. This implies an epistemological paradigm change, resulting in a fundamental counter-position to traditional diagnosis and classification: it is the client who defines their life and the meaning of their experiencing, and thus 'in-forms' the therapist. The therapist is truly challenged to open up and to risk *the co-creation of becoming (part of) a unique relationship and also* – no less a risk – *to co-reflect on it.*

Why do we have all these discussions and debates about disorder-specific treatment? One main reason is that we want to reply to those who reproach us for not meeting their criteria for scientific work and research – criteria developed by people who start from a completely different view of the human being, if they have a view of the human being at all, and not only of some parts or aspects of behaviour. If we try to adapt ourselves to those criteria, we will lose our identity and abandon the radical paradigm change to the person in the centre. We might temporarily gain some applause, but we would lose the reason for being an independent approach, because we would lose our unique stance – the unique offer and ethical challenge of person-centredness. We would vanish into a general psychology.

The alternative, however, is not an easy task. We face the enterprise of encountering – in the sense of making steps counter to – the mainstream by responding in new categories, maybe more than ever. We face the job of working hard to develop a human, truly *person*-centred understanding of science, knowledge and research, including genuinely person-centred conceptions of what are called psychological disorders. *We face the challenge of creating an understanding of ourselves beyond the categories of order and disorder* – no less than an uncompromising continuation of the social criticism Carl Rogers pursued with his personality and therapy theory.

References

Antonovsky A (1979). *Health, Stress and Coping.* San Francisco: Jossey-Bass.

Biermann-Ratjen E-M (1996). On the way to a client–centred psychopathology. In: Hutterer R, Pawlowsky G, Schmid PF, Stipsits R (eds). *Client–Centered and Experiential Psychotherapy: a paradigm in motion.* Frankfurt/M: Peter Lang (pp11–24).

Binder U (1994). *Empathienentwicklung und Pathogenese in der Klientenzentrierten Psychotherapie.* Eschborn: Klotz.

Binder U, Binder J (1991). *Studien zu einer störungsspezifischen klientenzentrierten Psychotherapie: Schizophrene Ordnung – Psychosomatisches Erleben – Depressives Leiden.* Eschborn: Klotz.

Binder U, Binder H-J (1994) (eds). *Klientenzentrierte Psychotherapie bei schweren psychischen Störungen.* Frankfurt: Fachbuchhandlung für Psychologie.

Bohart AC, Tallman K (1997). Empathy and the active client: an integrative cognitive-experiential view. In: Bohart AC, Greenberg LS (eds). *Empathy Reconsidered: new directions in psychotherapy.* Washington, DC: APA.

Bohart AC, Tallman K (1999). *How Clients Make Therapy Work: the process of active self-healing.* Washington, DC: APA.

Elliott R (2002). Hermeneutic single case efficacy design. *Psychotherapy Research 12:* 1–20.

Elliott R (2013). Research. In: Cooper M, O'Hara M, Schmid PF, Bohart A (eds). *The Handbook of Person-Centred Psychotherapy and Counselling* (2nd ed). Houndmills: Palgrave Macmillan (pp468–482).

Fehringer C (2003). Brauchen wir Störungswissen, um personzentriert arbeiten zu können? Unpublished paper. Vienna: Person-Centred Association in Austria.

Fehringer C (2016). Überlegungen zum Umgang mit psychiatrischem (Vor)-Wissen in personzentrierten Therapien. Unpublished paper. Vienna: Sigmund Freud University.

Finke J, Teusch L (1991) (eds). *Krankheitskonzepte in der klientenzentrierten Psychotherapie.* Berlin: Springer.

Finke J, Teusch L (2002). Die störungsspezifische Perspektive in der Personzentrierten Psychotherapie. In: Keil W, Stumm G (eds). *Die vielen Gesichter der Personzentrierten Psychotherapie.* Vienna: Springer (pp147–162).

Finke J, Teusch L (2007). Using a person-centred approach within a medical framework. In: Cooper M, Schmid PF, O'Hara M, Wyatt G (eds). *The Handbook of Person-Centred Psychotherapy and Counselling.* Basingstoke: Palgrave (pp279–292).

Fletcher R (2012). Dealing with diagnosis. In: Milton M (ed). *Diagnosis and Beyond: counselling psychology contributions to understanding human distress.* Ross-on-Wye: PCCS Books (pp1–10).

Gadamer H-G (1999). *Wahrheit und Methode: Grundzüge einer philosophischen Hermeneutik. Vol. 1.* Tübingen: Mohr.

Gillon E (2013). Assessment and formulation. In: Cooper M, O'Hara M, Schmid PF, Bohart A (eds). *The Handbook of Person-Centred Psychotherapy and Counselling* (2nd ed). Houndmills: Palgrave Macmillan (pp410–421).

Heinerth K (2002). Symptomspezifität und Interventionshomogenität. *Gesprächspsychotherapie und Personzentrierte Beratung 1:* 23–26.

Joseph S, Worsley R (eds). *Person-centred Psychopathology: a positive psychology of mental health.* Ross-on-Wye: PCCS Books.

Lambers E (2003). The person–centered perspective on psychopathology: the neurotic client. In: Mearns D (ed). *Developing Person–Centred Counselling* (2nd ed). London: Sage (pp103–109).

Mearns D (1996). Working at relational depth with clients in person-centred therapy. *Counselling 7*: 306–311.

Mearns D (2004). Problem-centered is not person-centered. *Person-Centered and Experiential Psychotherapies 3(2)*: 88–101.

Pfeiffer WM (1993). Die Bedeutung der Beziehung bei der Entstehung und der Therapie psychischer Störungen. In: Teusch L, Finke J (eds). *Die Krankheitslehre der Gesprächspsychotherapie.* Heidelberg: Asanger (pp19–40).

Rogers CR (1951). *Client-Centered Therapy: its current practice, implications, and theory.* Boston: Houghton Mifflin.

Rogers CR (1957). The necessary and sufficient conditions of therapeutic personality change. *Journal of Consulting Psychology 21:* 95–103.

Rogers CR (1959). A theory of therapy, personality, and interpersonal relationships, as developed in the client-centered framework. In: Koch S (ed). *Psychology: a study of science. Vol III.* New York: McGraw-Hill (pp184–256).

Rogers CR (1962). The interpersonal relationship: the core of guidance. In: Rogers CR, Stevens B. *Person to Person: the problem of being human.* Moab: Real People (pp89–104).

Rogers CR (1964). Towards a science of the person. In: Wann TW (ed). *Behaviorism and Phenomenology.* Chicago: University of Chicago Press (pp109–140).

Rogers CR (1965). A humanistic conception of man. In: Farson R (ed). *Science and Human Affairs.* Palo Alto: Science and Behavior Books (pp18–31).

Sanders P (2006). Why person-centred therapists must reject the medicalisation of distress. Self & Society *34(3):* 32–39.

Schmid PF (1992). 'Herr Doktor, bin ich verrückt?': Eine Theorie der leidenden Person statt einer Krankheitslehre. In: Frenzel P, Schmid PF, Winkler M (eds). *Handbuch der Personzentrierten Psychotherapie.* Cologne: EHP (pp83–125).

Schmid PF (1994). *Personzentrierte Gruppenpsychotherapie: Ein Handbuch, vol I: Solidarität und Autonomie.* Cologne: EHP.

Schmid PF (1996). *Personzentrierte Gruppenpsychotherapie in der Praxis: Ein Handbuch, vol II: Die Kunst der Begegnung.* Paderborn: Junfermann.

Schmid PF (1998). 'Face to face': the art of encounter. In: Thorne B, Lambers E (eds). *Person-Centred Therapy.* London: Sage (pp74–90).

Schmid PF (2001). Authenticity: the person as his or her own author. Dialogical and ethical perspectives on therapy as an encounter relationship. And beyond. In: Wyatt G (ed). *Rogers' Therapeutic Conditions: evolution, theory and practice.* Vol 1. *Congruence.* Ross-on-Wye: PCCS Books (pp213–228).

Schmid PF (2002a). Knowledge or acknowledgement? Psychotherapy as 'the art of not-knowing' – prospects on further developments of a radical paradigm. *Person-Centered and Experiential Psychotherapies 1:* 56–70.

Schmid PF (2002b). Presence: im-media-te co-experiencing and co-responding. Phenomenological, dialogical and ethical perspectives on contact and perception in person-centred therapy and beyond. In: Wyatt G, Sanders P (eds). *Rogers' Therapeutic Conditions: evolution, theory and practice.* Vol 4. *Contact and Perception.* Ross-on-Wye: PCCS Books (pp182–203).

Schmid PF (2002c). 'The necessary and sufficient conditions of being person-centered': on identity, integrity, integration and differentiation of the paradigm. In: Watson J, Goldman RN, Warner MS (eds). *Client-Centered and Experiential Psychotherapy in the 21st Century.* Ross-on-Wye: PCCS Books (pp36–51).

Schmid PF (2003a). The characteristics of a person-centered approach to therapy and counseling: criteria for identity and coherence. *Person-Centered and Experiential Psychotherapies 2:* 104–120.

Schmid PF (2003b). Back to the clients: a phenomenological approach to process differentiation and diagnosis. Keynote lecture. 6th PCE Conference, Egmond-aan-Zee, 10 July.

Schmid PF (2005). Authenticity and alienation: towards an understanding of the person beyond the categories of order and disorder. In: Joseph S, Worsley R (eds). *Person-Centred Psychopathology: a positive psychology of mental health*. Ross-on-Wye: PCCS Books (pp75–90).

Schmid PF (2012). Psychotherapy is political or it is not psychotherapy: the Person-Centered Approach as an essentially political venture. *Person-Centered and Experiential Psychotherapies 11*: 95–108.

Schmid PF (2013). The anthropological, relational and ethical foundations of person-centred therapy. In: Cooper M, O'Hara M, Schmid PF, Bohart A (eds). *The Handbook of Person-Centred Psychotherapy and Counselling* (2nd ed). Houndmills: Palgrave Macmillan (pp66–83).

Schmid PF (2015). Person and society: towards a person-centered sociotherapy. *Person-Centered and Experiential Psychotherapies 14*: 217–235.

Schmid PF, Mearns D (2006). Being-with and being-counter: person-centered psychotherapy as an in-depth co-creative process of personalization. *Person-Centered and Experiential Psychotherapies 5*: 174–190.

Speirerer G-W (1994). *Das differentielle Inkongruenzmodell (DIM): Handbuch der Gesprächspsychotherapie als Inkongruenzbehandlung*. Heidelberg: Asanger.

Spielhofer H (2003). Störungsspezifische Konzepte in der Personzentrierten Psychotherapie. Unpublished paper. Vienna: Person-Centred Association of Austria.

Swildens H (1988). *Procesgerichte gesprekstherapie*. Leuven/Amersfoort: Acco/de Horstink.

Takens RJ (2001). *Een vreemde nabij: Enkele aspecten van de psychotherapeutische relatie onderzocht*. Lisse: Swets and Zeitlinger.

Tudor K, Worrall M (2006). *Person-Centred Therapy: a clinical philosophy*. London: Routledge.

Van Werde D, Prouty G (2013). Clients with contact-impaired functioning: pre-therapy. In: Cooper M, O'Hara M, Schmid PF, Bohart A (eds). *The Handbook of Person-Centred Psychotherapy and Counselling* (2nd ed). Houndmills: Palgrave Macmillan (pp327–342).

Warner MS (1998). A client-centered approach to therapeutic work with dissociated and fragile process. In: Greenberg LS, Watson JC, Lietaer G (eds). *Handbook of Experiential Psychotherapy*. New York: Guilford (pp368–387).

Warner MS (2001). Empathy, relational depth and difficult client process. In: Haugh S, Merry T (eds). *Rogers' Therapeutic Conditions: evolution, theory and practice*. Vol 2. *Empathy*. Ross-on-Wye: PCCS Books (pp181–191).

Warner MS (2013). Difficult client process. In: Cooper M, O'Hara M, Schmid PF, Bohart A (eds). *The Handbook of Person-Centred Psychotherapy and Counselling* (2nd ed). Houndmills: Palgrave Macmillan (pp 343–358).

Wilkins P (2016). *Person-Centred Therapy: 100 key points* (2nd ed). Abingdon: Routledge.

Wilkins P, Gill M (2003). Assessment in person-centered therapy. *Person-Centered and Experiential Psychotherapies 2*: 172–187.

Worsley R, Joseph S (2007). *Person-Centred Practice: case studies in positive psychology*. Ross-on-Wye: PCCS Books.

Zurhorst G (1993). Eine gesprächspsychotherapeutische Störungs-/Krankheitstheorie in biographischer Perspektive. In: Teusch L, Finke J (eds). *Die Krankheitslehre der Gesprächspsychotherapie*. Heidelberg: Asanger (pp71–87).

A person-centred view of human nature, wellness and psychopathology

6

Margaret S Warner

Most person-centred writings focus on health and actualisation, rather than on illness and psychopathology. This tendency results in large part because person-centred theorists are acutely aware of a number of problems that emerge when one tries to equate human psychological distress with physical illness, as it has been construed within the traditions of western medicine.

Several issues are central for person-centred theorists. Western medicine tends to relate specific diseases to specific cures, rather than focusing on the operation of the organism as a whole. As a result, it requires expert diagnosis of specific disease syndromes in order to specify and implement the right treatments. Given this overall approach, psychological practices based on traditional medical models tend to assume that the person's own judgment should not be trusted in making sense of his or her life, or in deciding what are the best ways personally for them to solve problems. And these tendencies are accentuated when clients have more severe emotional disturbance or life difficulties, since such clients are seen as even less able to make judgments on their own behalf.

This sort of medical-model framework is highly problematic to person-centred practitioners.[1] Person-centred theory is grounded in the hypothesis that human beings have a deeply rooted organismic tendency toward making a very personal sense of life and toward constructive problem-solving, particularly when supported by genuine, empathic, prizing relationships. Reliance on expert diagnosis and externally determined, symptom-specific interventions runs contrary to the practices supported by this theory.

Yet, despite its various conceptual problems, the illness metaphor is difficult to ignore entirely, since it has such a central role in organising the distribution of resources to people in need in modern industrial societies. And clients who

---

1. See, for example, Sanders (2010), Boy (1989), Shlein (1989).

suffer from extreme psychological distress have strong needs for emotional and physical support. Given this ideological tension, I think that it is worth trying to find a way to relate actualisation to psychopathology that is consistent with the person-centred view of human nature. And if, as person-centred theorists, we are able to clarify such an overall model of health and pathology, we may also be able to increase our effectiveness in critiquing and offering constructive alternatives to current systems of mental health services.

I believe that a version of psychopathology can be developed from within person-centred theory that avoids many of the pitfalls of the traditional medical model and is more true to the functioning of human beings as understood in the best of contemporary social sciences. This model of psychological functioning builds on Carl Rogers' (1957, 1959) theory of personality, without contradicting its key elements. It justifies working with descriptive categories of psychopathology for purposes of client funding and research. At the same time, this model makes a strong case for the validity of treating psychological distress and dysfunction at all levels of severity using person-centred psychotherapies that rely on self-directed process rather than disease-specific interventions.

Rogers' personality theory[2]

According to Rogers' (1957; 1959) personality theory, 'conditions of worth' inhibit individuals' natural tendency to process experience. These sorts of conditions of worth are internalised when they are conveyed by significant others, especially the primary caregivers of childhood. This tends to occur when significant others withdraw their positive regard in response to particular ways of being that the child may manifest. A 'condition of worth', then, is a particularly strong sort of attitude or value that has been internalised. Perhaps a person has internalised the idea that it is okay to be a 'good' person, but not an 'ambitious, self-serving' person. Or, he or she may feel that it is all right to feel 'sad', but not to feel 'angry'. On reflection, most people are able to notice such conditions of worth. They can see ways that they have shaped themselves to maintain the approval of others, often at the expense of developing their own values and understandings.

Rogers (1957, 1959) notes that the person-centred relationship, with its unconditional positive regard, empathy and genuineness, has healing value in and of itself. It also tends to reduce the negative effects of conditions of worth and allow processing of previously denied or distorted experience, with benefits for a broad array of psychological symptoms.

However, much severe psychological distress and dysfunction is not well explained by conditions of worth alone. For example, distress caused by childhood rape, traumatic brain injury, dementia or schizophrenia is not generated primarily

---

2. A number of sections in this chapter on Rogers' theory and on fragile self are adapted from an earlier chapter (Warner, 2013).

(if at all) by conditions of worth. This creates a theoretical dilemma. A 'condition of worth' can be clearly defined as an internalised *attitude* that relates to the withdrawal of positive regard when the values of significant others are threatened. As such, it can be seen as a rigorous and testable term. But it only seems central to the psychological issues of a limited set of clients. If, on the other hand, the term 'conditions of worth' applies to any sort of damaging life experience, it becomes so broad as to be virtually meaningless. This makes it difficult for Rogers' personality theory to explain why person-centred psychotherapy should work with many of the more severe forms of psychological dysfunction. I don't think that Rogers' earlier person-centred developmental theory needs to be abandoned. But I do think that it needs to be expanded, and that this can be accomplished without losing any of the strengths of his original theory. The changes to Rogers' theory of personality that I am proposing relate to the development of *capacities* relating to processing and self-cohesion, in addition to the conditions of worth proposed by Rogers (which are internalised *attitudes*). While I am placing particular emphasis on individual process in this initial formulation, I believe that the overall model that I am presenting is equally relevant to the understanding of human relationships and cultural phenomena.

The development of processing capacities

Initially, infants are almost totally dependent on their relationships with adults to manage their experiencing. They need the attentive presence of care-giving adults to avoid falling into either distracted boredom or states of physical and emotional trauma (Stern, 1985). This sort of child–adult attachment relationship provides the 'environment of evolutionary adaptedness' that is essential for normal human development (see, for example, Warner, 2000, 2013, 2015). This attachment relationship seems to require physical care, in combination with Rogers' core conditions – empathy, genuineness and prizing. Much in the way that the lungs of an unborn child anticipate but require oxygen after birth to come into full functioning, infants anticipate and require sustained, benign caregiving to develop into functioning adults. Both adults and infants are strongly oriented to forming this sort of attachment relationship, and, in the context of this sort of attachment relationship, the child's abilities to process experience follow a natural path of development.

I propose that several particular aspects of processing initially require a strong partnership with a caregiving adult in an attachment relationship in order to develop fully (Warner, 2000). Infants are initially almost totally dependent on adults to hold experience in any sort of sustained attention, to modulate the intensity of experience, and to name experience. With a benign attachment relationship, young children naturally acquire increasing abilities to perform these functions in a more or less autonomous fashion. With these abilities, and with increasing complexity of cognitive capacities, young children begin to be able to form an understanding of other people's experience without totally losing a sense of their own.

Common forms of difficult process

While the human organism is strongly oriented toward developing processing capacities, a good-enough early childhood attachment relationship – as well as the normative development of the biological structures that support processing – is required for this development to unfold optimally. Individuals (and those in relationships with them) are likely to experience their processing as difficult when such biologically and psychologically developed processing capacities are impaired. Likewise, physical or psychological damage that occurs later in life may disrupt the person's capacities to process experience in normative ways.

I have found that three kinds of difficult process emerge most often in my practice as a client-centred therapist – fragile process, dissociated process and psychotic process. These three styles are described at length elsewhere (Warner, 2000, 2013, 2014, 2015; Prouty, 1994). I will offer a brief description of difficult process here, and then consider some general aspects of difficult process that I have found important in therapeutic work.

Clients seem to develop a fragile style of processing experience when the sort of empathic caregiving needed to develop processing capacities in early childhood has been lacking. Clients who experience 'fragile process' (Warner, 2000, 2013, 2014, 2015) have difficulty holding experience in attention at moderate levels of intensity. As a result, they tend to feel core experiences at very high and very low intensity. They often have difficulty starting and stopping experiences that are personally significant or emotionally connected, and they often feel discomfort or shame in relation to their process.

Given this difficulty with holding onto their own experience, they often struggle to take in the point of view of another person without feeling that their own experience has been annihilated. As an example, a client might talk in a way that seems quite circumstantial for most of a session, and then suddenly feel a sense of connection to her experience where she feels intensely vulnerable. She may express this vulnerability quite indirectly and yet feel annihilated if the therapist doesn't sense the importance of the vulnerability and receive it in a welcoming way. Yet, if the therapist attempts to understand in a way that doesn't match the client's feelings with exactly the right words, or if the therapist offers advice or interpretations, the client may well lose her ability to stay with the experience, and may feel enraged or ashamed in the process. Alternatively, the client may feel flooded by emotion and fear that it could go on forever, doing damage to herself and the therapist. Afterwards she may feel exposed and ashamed at having lost control.

In personal relationships, clients with high intensity fragile process are likely to feel violated and misunderstood a lot of the time. Other people often experience them as being unreasonably angry, touchy and stubborn. This is not surprising, given that they often feel the need to defend their experience to avoid feeling that it has been annihilated. Others can become angry and rejecting in return, intensifying the client's sense that there is something fundamentally wrong with their experience. Many people alternate, holding in their reactions while feeling increasingly uncomfortable, and then exploding with rage at those around them. In contrast, people who experience low intensity fragile process can easily give up on connecting or expressing their personal reactions, and feel empty inside. A number of client-centred and experiential psychotherapists have described valuable ways of working with clients experiencing fragile or other closely related sorts of process (Bohart, 1990; Eckert & Biermann-Ratjen, 1998; Eckert & Wuchner, 1996; Lambers, 1994; Leijssen, 1993, 1996; Roelens, 1996; Santen, 1990; Swildens, 1990).

Clients who experience 'dissociated process' quite convincingly experience themselves as having selves that are not integrated with each other for periods of time (Warner, 1998, 2000; Roy, 1991; Coffeng, 1995). They may experience a disunity, alternating between different autonomous experiences of self that feel 'crazy' to them and to others. If alternate personality parts have been dominant, they experience periods of forgetfulness lasting for minutes or hours. Alternatively, they may get by for years, keeping very busy while leading quite restricted lives, only for the parts to emerge in times of crisis. Yet when they do emerge, the parts themselves express their experience of having been present all along, but having been separate from the awareness of the client in her everyday self.

In my experience, dissociated process of this sort virtually always results from extreme early childhood trauma or severely ruptured attachment in early relationships. Before they are seven or eight years old, children lack the cognitive and emotional capacities that would let them understand or moderate the intensity of emotionally or physically traumatic experiences. As a result, they rely almost totally on the comfort and protection of parenting figures to mitigate any experiences of emotional flooding. When traumatic experiences occur in the absence of such comfort and protection, young children are likely to stumble on an ability to move in response into trance-like states. These trance-like states have a particular tendency to separate into clusters of experience that have independent, person-like qualities. Such 'parts' tend to develop a variety of different strategies for responding to the emotional pain of traumatic experiences, revolving around a core belief that traumatic experiences could destroy the client if allowed to emerge. In adulthood, separate parts tend to emerge when, for one reason or another, trauma memories threaten to return.

Clients who have a psychotic style of processing have difficulty forming narratives about their experience that make sense within the culture, or that offer a predictive validity in relation to their environment. Prouty (1990, 1994) describes clients experiencing psychotic process as having impaired contact with 'self', 'world' and 'other'. Often such clients experience voices, hallucinations or delusions that are neither culturally accepted nor easy to process (Prouty, 1977, 1983, 1986). Still, various client-centred therapists who have worked with psychotic process have found that psychotic experiences tend to be meaningful and have the potential to process into more reality-oriented forms (Rogers, 1967; Prouty, Van Werde & Portner, 2002; Prouty, 1994; Raskin, 1996; Van Werde, 1998, 1990; Binder, 1998; Warner, 2002b).

Prouty (1994) suggests that therapists use 'contact reflections' that stay close to clients' concrete expressions as a way of restoring more reality-based connection.

Research suggests that a complex interaction between genetic propensities, disruptions of perinatal development and life stress are involved in the development of schizophrenic disorders. Other psychotic disorders can develop as a result of later physical trauma or organic degeneration (Green, 1998).

I suspect that numerous other forms of difficult process exist. Certainly, any significant impairment of physiological or biochemical processes in the brain is likely to make the ordinary processing of experience difficult. Yet the human organism is deeply oriented toward trying to make sense of experience and has numerous alternative ways of processing available to it. I believe that therapeutic relationships characterised by Rogers' core conditions will tend to foster processing that uses any of the biological capacities available to the person.

Virtually all clients and therapists have experiences of 'difficult' process at certain moments. Yet, for some clients, experiences of difficult process are so intense and vulnerable that they have problems working within standard psychotherapy formats. Often, these clients get labelled with serious and stigmatising diagnoses – such as borderline or narcissistic personality disorders, dissociative identity disorders or schizophrenia.

These categories can have some descriptive validity, but they often oversimplify and distort the actual situation of the client. Difficult styles of process can exist in varying combinations with each other, while clients tend to be diagnosed as having a single disorder. Difficult process can operate at differing levels of intensity or may apply to some aspects of a person's experience, but not others. Traditional schools of thought in psychology often suggest that non-normative forms of experience characteristic of severe disorders should be ignored or responded to with external interpretation and structuring.

The central life dilemmas of clients diagnosed with severe psychopathology are often experienced in the form of difficult process. Many person-centred practitioners propose that a lack of empathic responding – particularly when combined with structured, interpretive sorts of interventions – is likely to discourage clients from the sort of processing that is essential if they are to develop a personally authentic sense of self or understanding of their life situations (see, for example, Warner, 2000; Prouty, 1994; Eckert & Biermann-Ratjen, 1998; Coffeng, 1995).

Fragile self and the development of self in infancy

Rogers notes that 'conditions of worth' in childhood can lead to a self that is 'incongruent'. The experiences of a person whose organism is incongruent with the self are not well symbolised in awareness. According to Rogers, this leads to psychological dysfunction. So, for example, if I think of myself as a 'loyal' person, but find myself wanting to do something that betrays a friend, I may experience a great deal of anxiety. Such 'incongruence' can lead to intense anxiety and depression.

Heinz Kohut (1971, 1984) conceptualises another quality of self, that of 'cohesiveness'. I think that this concept can be added to the person-centred understanding of self without taking anything away from Rogers' initial conceptualisation. According to Kohut, infants are heavily reliant on caregivers to maintain a sense of emotional balance and wellbeing. He calls this particular sort of closeness (with a typically psychoanalytic denseness of language) a 'selfobject' relationship. A person is likely to experience extreme distress and volatility if something ruptures a selfobject relationship, leading to a state Kohut calls 'fragmentation'. He suggests that children develop cohesive selves through good-enough selfobject relationships in infancy. This enables them to keep a stable, coherent sense of self, and a relatively high level of autonomy in adulthood. A person is likely to experience a great deal of volatility in adulthood if he or she doesn't have this sort of cohesive self. In adulthood people will often seek out selfobject relationships that are highly supportive and dependent, which allows them to maintain emotional balance. According to Kohut, a stable, empathic, non-interpretive therapy can allow a client to use the therapist as a 'selfobject', re-initiating the developmental process that was missing or disrupted in childhood.

Integrating Kohut's thinking into person-centred theory, the self can be viewed as a human phenomenon that not only provides coherence (or 'congruence', in Rogers' terms) but also helps a person modulate emotional intensity and maintain a sense of personal existence and value. In addition to experiencing 'fragile process' at certain moments, some clients may also experience a 'fragile self'. In the terms of person-centred theory, then, 'cohesiveness' can be seen as a quality that allows a person to tolerate moderately high levels of experienced incongruence for a period of time. Without a certain level of cohesiveness, experiences of incongruence can be terrifying. It is not simply that I feel scared or distraught or angry; I feel that these experiences are forever, leaving me with no sense of self and no human value.

Person-centred therapists create stable, secure, empathic relationships that parallel those of healthy parent–infant attachment relationship (as does Kohut when he sees clients he diagnoses as 'narcissistic'). Following Kohut's thinking, the client-centred relationship itself is likely to help clients who lack self-cohesion maintain much higher levels of emotional balance and a stronger sense of personal worth than is possible without the relationship. The ongoing stability of these relationships also allows a more independent, viable, cohesive sense of self to develop over time.

But, Kohut notes, these relationships are easy to rupture. This sort of rupture creates a sudden, drastic change into volatility and panic, and clients are likely to engage in various behaviours that function as attempts to get away from the terror of this experience, such as cutting themselves or acting destructively toward others. Even mild comments and interventions by the therapist have the capacity to bring about this sort of fragmentation, according to Kohut. Given its empathy and nondirectivity, classical person-centred therapy seems particularly likely to be helpful to clients who struggle with living with a self that lacks cohesiveness.

Strategies for working with difficult process as experienced by individual clients

Person-centred therapists have found that the same relational conditions that facilitate process in high-functioning clients – empathy, congruence and unconditional positive regard – can be extremely helpful to clients engaging with such difficult process experiences (Warner, 1991; Prouty, 1994; Rogers, 1967). The human impulse to make sense of experience is so central to human survival that human beings continue to try to process, even when more ordinary ways of processing are compromised. To the extent that any organismic capacities exist, relationships that embody Rogers' core conditions will tend to provide support for the person's processing.

Clients often alternate between impulses to remain safe and impulses to engage with crucial though troubling aspects of experience and relationship. Person-centred therapists are committed to supporting the person's existential freedom in deciding whether, when and how to process their own experience. Yet, the human impulse to make sense of experience and to connect with others in relationship is so fundamental that clients are very likely to move in the direction of processing when in the presence of a genuine, empathic and prizing therapeutic relationship. As they process, clients are likely to develop more personally grounded, coherent, reality-based ways of experiencing themselves and their life situations.

Even if such processing has biological limits, any progress in the direction of having a sense of self and making sense of experience – particularly when it occurs in a context that allows the person to feel genuine, accepting contact with other human beings – has intense benefits for the individual. Indeed, such experiences often allow clients to move from feeling lost in states of alienation, confusion, emptiness and panic to having a sense of themselves as authentic human beings in relationship to other human beings.

A number of theorists have noted that work with difficult process makes particular demands on therapists' empathy, and on their ability to communicate that empathy to clients. Therapists may have intense personal reactions to client experiences that are foreign to them or, if familiar to them, similar to difficult experiences in their own lives that have not been fully resolved (Warner, 2014, 2016). As a result, they may find it difficult to stay empathic and prizing to the client's actual experience.

Therapists can easily distort their understanding of unfamiliar client experiences to fit more normalised experiences from their own lives. Given the vulnerability and shame that tend to accompany difficult process, clients may express their most important experiences indirectly or tentatively. As a result, clients may not find it easy to correct the therapist's understanding of difficult process. When experiences of difficult process aren't received, clients can easily give up on possibilities of genuine contact with the therapist. I believe that the therapy process is likely to feel safer to clients and they are more likely to take the risk of exploring more vulnerable aspects of their lives as therapists increase their empathic attunement to difficult process.

Clients in the midst of difficult process may also have difficulty receiving complexly formulated expressions of empathy from others without becoming confused or disconnected from their own experiences. Clients experiencing fragile process, or the very fragile experiences of dissociated parts, may only be able to receive silence or expressions of understanding that stay extremely close to their own words without feeling that their experience has been annihilated (Warner 2000, 2001). Prouty (1994) notes that personally meaningful, reality-based contact with self, world and others tends to be fostered by 'contact reflections' – empathic responses that are very concrete and close to the clients' actual words and facial and body gestures.

Work with the fragile self

In addition to experiencing 'fragile process' in a moment-to-moment way, clients may also experience a 'fragile self'. Like Kohut, person-centred therapists create stable, secure, empathic relationships that parallel those of the healthy parent–infant attachment relationship. The relationship itself helps clients maintain much higher levels of emotional balance and sense of personal worth than they are able to without it. The ongoing stability of these relationships also allows a cohesive sense of self to develop over time. But these relationships are easy to rupture, creating a sudden, drastic change into volatility and panic, and various behaviours that function as attempts to get away from the terror of this experience. Kohut notes that even mild therapist comments and interventions have the capacity to bring about this sort of fragmentation. The non-directivity of classical person-centred therapy, then, makes this therapy particularly likely to be helpful to clients who live with a sense of self that lacks cohesiveness.

A fragile sense of self can add greater intensity to a client's need to hold strongly to versions of their experience. As a result, clients can have a sort of 'tunnel vision'. With this, the person can experience his or her own (often intense and extreme) reactions to situations, but can't step out of these experiences to consider the experiences of others or take in other perspectives. If a client's formulation is seen to be wrong, it is not only that particular formulation that is at risk but the person's whole self and the relationships in which they are engaged. This can be a particular challenge to therapist congruence, as therapists often find that their impulse to 'help' a client view life situations in broader, more realistic, even-handed perspectives can be very strong. Yet such 'help' is particularly likely to leave the client feeling emotionally annihilated. Yet, when therapists stay within a client-centred framework, empathising with clients' experiences, clients' abilities to integrate their own experience with the experiences and perspectives of others tends to develop over time.

Actualization, processing and the nature of human nature

The person-centred approach not only provides a strong theoretical and practical basis for clinical work across all levels of psychological distress. It also creates a basis for understanding that certain aspects of the creation and function of meaning are humanly universal. At the same time, it clarifies the role of existential freedom in forming more particular, personal understandings of life situations. This way of understanding meaning can have relevance to the human sciences overall.

Rogers (1957, 1959) makes a strong claim about human nature when he declares that human contact that embodies broad human relational qualities – empathy, congruence and unconditional positive regard – is 'necessary and sufficient' to generate constructive personality change across diagnostic categories. While Rogers grounds his theory in the human 'actualising tendency', and makes many observations about process, he offers relatively little elaboration as to how human beings are organised so that they would have such a strong tendency to process in these ways. In the following sections, I will make an attempt to begin to develop a broader analysis of human nature, processing and self.

Recent work in ecological psychology, combined with the work of person-centred theorists, allows us to consider why human beings would respond to these core relational conditions in such a significant way, and what this says about psychopathology in general.

Tooby and Cosmides (1992) suggest that a series of adaptations in the Pleistocene era formed the basis of the relatively rapid human leap into culture. These combined adaptations offered an adaptive advantage that was strong enough to remain relatively stable throughout the millennia since. Human universality is not seen as contradicting the variability of human personalities and cultures. Rather, it is the basis of it:

> Culture and social behavior is complexly variable, but not because the human mind is a social product, a blank slate or an externally programmed general-purpose computer lacking richly defined, evolved structure. Instead, human culture and behavior is richly variable because it is generated by an incredibly intricate, contingent set of functional programmes that use and process information from the world. (p24)

Tooby and Cosmides (1992) suggest that the consistency of these evolved structures for processing information can be easily masked by the sheer variety of manifest behaviours and cultural forms. Yet these more subtle, deep structures are likely to remain constant – since they are essential to human adaptive success – while many more obvious and compelling aspects of human living will undergo constant change. Much of social science, they suggest, has looked for constancy in the wrong places:

> Mainstream sociocultural anthropology has arrived at a situation resembling some nightmarish short story Borges might have written, where their scientists are condemned by their unexamined assumptions to study the nature of mirrors only by cataloguing and investigating everything that mirrors can reflect. It is an endless process that never makes progress, that never reaches closure… whose enduring product is voluminous descriptions of particular phenomena. (p42)

On the one hand, Tooby and Cosmides (1992) suggest many specific adaptations form a taken-for-granted backdrop for human living:

> By adding together a face recognition module, a spacial relations module… a fear module… and emotion perception module… a friendship module, a grammar acquisition module, a theory of mind module, and so on, an architecture gains a breadth of competencies that allows it to solve a wider and wider range of problems. (p113)

Yet, they propose that such specific capacities of mind necessitate more function-general capacities:

> … the more alternative content-specialised mechanisms an architecture contains, the more easily domain-general mechanisms can be applied to the problem spaces they create without being paralyzed by combinatorial explosion. (p113)

I propose that 'processing' and self – a particular sort of self-directed, individual way of making sense and organising life experience in the context of human relationships – are central aspects of the way human beings have adapted to function as human beings. As such, these are core aspects of the universal human architecture outlined by Tooby and Cosmides (1992). They constitute the common mode of functioning that underpins the vast variety of more particular individual and group modes of living and experiencing life.[3] Because such processing and self are central to the adaptive advantage acquired in the human leap into culture, one can expect them to be universal and to be over-determined. One would expect people to keep trying to process and to integrate meaning into a sense of self, even under conditions of severe challenge. Any significant inability to do this would tend to be experienced as an affliction, and to cause severe dysfunction in a person's ability to live effectively among other human beings.

---

3. While the results of process research are consistent with this hypothesis, ecological psychologists would require a detailed analysis of ways that each alteration in capacities offered significant adaptive advantages in the Pleistocene era to provide definitive support for this sort of ecological hypothesis. Detailed ecological analysis of this kind would be a worthwhile project, but is beyond the scope of this paper.

All of the above qualities resonate deeply with the accumulated theory, experience and research in person-centred therapies. If this proposition is accurate, one would expect processing and self to emerge with a constancy that is less ephemeral and changeable than most social science phenomena. Extending the metaphor of Tooby and Cosmides (1992), one could say that, in analysing the processing of meaning and integration of such meaning into one's self, one is working with the mirror that is human nature itself, rather than the images reflected in the mirror, which make up much of the day-to-day content of life. With this in mind, I will next elaborate on the nature of these universal modes of processing, blending insights from Rogers, Gendlin and other person-centred process theorists, as well as various philosophers of meaning.

A person-centred model of processing and self

Human beings make sense of life using what I call 'soft meanings' (Warner, 1983). These are versions of life experience that don't have a hard existence that is likely to stay constant across observers, across time and space, or even within a particular person over time.

Soft phenomena include individual phenomena such as wanting, desiring, having emotions or thinking, as well as a variety of social qualities such as responsibility, justice or freedom. Whether a wedding occurred or not is a 'hard' phenomenon, since the various participants can agree that it happened and are likely to hold to that observation in the future. Whether the bride and groom were 'really in love' is a soft phenomenon. Various participants at a wedding are likely to disagree; even the bride and groom may offer quite different versions a few years later.

One major aspect of this human tendency to operate with soft meanings comes from what Dennett (1987) calls the 'intentional stance' – the idea that the behaviour of other people is guided by invisible internal entities such as beliefs or desires. In a similar vein, Baron-Cohen (1995) notes that human beings cannot construe the simplest daily situations without recourse to a sort of 'mindreading' that involves soft phenomena. For example, it is virtually impossible to understand a simple set of behaviours such as 'John walked into the bedroom, walked around and walked out' without recourse to intentions, wishes, beliefs, emotional states and the like. For example, one might propose that, 'Maybe John was *looking for* something he *wanted* to find and he *thought* it was in the bedroom', or, 'Maybe John *heard* something in the bedroom and *wanted to know* what had made the noise' (p1).

While the processing of such soft phenomena occurs within individuals, the phenomena themselves are about the totality of lived experience within human contexts. I suspect that the very softness of these phenomena – the fact that they have no hard existence and are subject to ongoing interpretation and re-interpretation – allows a bridge between individual consciousness and the culturally embedded life of human beings in relationships and communities. This particularly human capacity of individuals living within cultural groups to make sense of experience is what developed in the evolutionary leap into humanness. It seems likely that this flexible ability to make sense is responsible for much of the adaptive success and dominance of human beings over other species.

But a significant question arises as to how human beings form and reform such constructions of soft phenomena in relation to themselves, or in their understanding of the actions of others. This cannot be a simple matching of constructs with data, since the phenomena themselves don't have concrete existence and are subject to varying interpretations. Yet, despite their variability and openness to interpretation, soft phenomena have as much or more impact on a person's life as any more concrete and stable hard phenomena. For example, whether a person is sentenced to death may rest on the question of whether he 'intended' to pull the trigger of a gun.

Gendlin (1964, 1968, 1997) suggests that, rather than any machine-like computation, human organisms have 'implicit' within them a kind of seeking that is 'carried forward' as the organism finds something that at least partially completes that which is implicit and, in the process, changes the nature of the seeking. Meaning is a particular sort of carrying forward that is characteristic of human beings. One metaphor for carrying forward into meaning is the completion of a poem (Gendlin, 1995). If a poet has written eight lines and is looking for a final, ninth line, she may try any number of lines before finding one that 'works'. Once she has written the final line, it may well feel like the only line that could have been written. Yet, if she had waited until a week later, she might have come up with a different last line, one that also worked. Meaning, in Gendlin's philosophy, is like the last line of the poem in that it is neither totally constrained nor totally arbitrary.

Gendlin (1964, 1968) also emphasises that making sense (or carrying forward into meaning) is a whole-body process. There is no mind–body split. Following Gendlin's theory, I would place human experiencing on a continuum from that which is implicit to that which is articulated, as follows:

Physiological processes (eg. blood pressure)	*Physiological body sensing* (eg. pain in muscle)	*Vague sense of a situation* (eg. images, scenes, gestures, or body sensing giving a feel of a life situation)	*Partially articulated version of a situation* (eg. 'Something about x is getting to me'. Or, 'I have a vague feeling of y'.)	*Articulated version* (eg. 'I feel x about y for z reason'.)

At every point on this continuum, the body offers a lived way of responding to the person's whole situation. Under some circumstances, physiological processes are carried forward into subjective experience. Human beings can also take action in response to such subjective experience at any further point in this continuum, without further articulation of their experience. Yet, human beings have a tendency, especially when an organismic process is blocked, to attend to their experience and to try to carry it forward into meaning. So, for example, if a person is breathing effortlessly, he may pay very little attention to his breath. But if, suddenly, he is unable to breathe, he is likely to start looking for causes and explanations in the hope of finding a remedy. If a person is feeling content in an activity, she may continue without special attention to her experience. But if she is feeling bored or frustrated or lonely or frightened, she is likely to try to make sense of what is going on, and to try to change the situation in some way. Sometimes this sort of attending occurs spontaneously, sometimes with conscious intentionality.

However it occurs, attending to experience tends to create a shift in the quality of experiencing and to bring related experiencing into play in ways that can easily carry forward into increasing articulation of meaning. If a person attends to a tightness in the shoulders, he may come to sense a feeling of dread. If he attends to the feeling of dread, life scenes or thoughts relating to this sense may to come to mind. For example, he may picture the scene of a recent fight with his boss. If he pictures that scene, he may picture other times that he felt helpless and humiliated. From there he may articulate a version of what happened and why. For example, 'It wasn't fair to expect me to know what he wanted when he never told me. That's just the way my stepfather always was.' In each step of such carrying forward into meaning, the whole body changes – heart-rate, breathing, blood pressure, immune response and the like.

I propose that a number of the broad purposes of such carrying forward into meaning are universal. Human beings try to make *personal* sense of life situations so that they carry forward their whole body's lived experience in a way that feels authentic. They try to make *predictive* sense of life experience so that they will know why things happened and what is likely to happen next. They try to make *cultural* sense, so that their version of life experience isn't seen as crazy by those around them. They try to make *hopeful* sense, to find a version of their experience that lets them live into the future without total despair. They try to make *spiritual* sense by looking for some larger context within which to make sense of life, even in the face of tragic circumstances.

Of course, human beings have the existential freedom to act against any of these broad human purposes, but they tend to pay a price when they do. Metaphorically speaking, if people make sense in ways that contradict their organismic experience, their bodies are likely to speak back with discomfort, depression, illness or the like. If people make sense in ways that don't make predictive sense, reality is likely to speak back, as when a person who thinks she can fly jumps off a building and hits the ground. If people make sense in ways that don't make cultural sense, the culture is likely to speak back, calling them 'crazy', or shunning them. If people make sense in ways that don't offer hopeful or spiritual sense, their bodies are likely to speak back with alienation or despair.

Still, in particular circumstances, people may find that it is humanly worthwhile to pay any of those prices. They may be willing to go against some strong human purposes in order to actualise other purposes more fully. For example, an incest survivor in the 19th century might be willing to be called 'crazy' and hospitalised for the rest of her life rather than deny that her father raped her. A cancer patient who is given a two per cent chance of surviving the year, according to scientific research, may choose to hold the belief that he will be one of that two per cent who survives. Mystics may choose to live in isolation while fasting extensively, combatting hunger and other personal impulses in the hope of achieving greater spiritual enlightenment.

As part of making sense, human beings tend to look for narratives or stories, and to try to pull these together to form a coherent whole. In the process, they do something that I call 'selfing'. They tend to experience an 'I' at the center of clusters of feelings, motives, beliefs, personal qualities, experiences (and the like) within themselves, and they experience clusters of such 'I' experiences as being part of a somewhat coherent 'self'. Likewise, they are likely to postulate a 'self' or personality as organising the actions of others. Yet, if contrary experiences emerge, the person may well experience a dual self or selves that operate in various ways on other selves (Cooper et al, 2004). They can experience themselves as being a self at one moment, and at another they can experience themselves as standing outside and watching various self-experiences. For example, a person can sensibly say, 'I have to pull myself together because this lazy person that I have been for the last week is just not who I really am.'

These self-experiences operate like many other soft phenomena in the sense that human beings often experience them as if they had as much concrete reality as any hard phenomenon. A person may say, 'I am a Fitzgerald through and through. Everything about me is like my family.' Yet, such articulated self-experiences are a carrying forward to the totality of the person's lived experience in ways that are neither totally arbitrary nor totally pre-determined.

Experience could have been carried forward into an experience of self in more than one way, yet not just any self-experience will resonate with the person's lived experience. And, in a literal sense, there is no concrete existence to 'self', only an articulation of lived experience that carries forward more or less fully. And there certainly isn't a single 'real' self that already exists someplace 'under the surface'. Stable attachment relationships in infancy seem to create a sense of security in the person's sense of self that allows them to tolerate these sorts of ambiguity without feeling that their self has been annihilated (Kohut 1971, 1984).

This experience of self is so humanly universal that I suspect it is integrally related to human processing. Processing meaning allows a person to integrate clusters of experience in ways that carry forward the whole organism. This allows him or her to form a sense of 'I-ness' in relation to feelings, beliefs, life narratives and the like. Yet, however much organismic experience has been articulated, there is always more that could be articulated in addition, or in different ways.

Rogers (1959), in his 'theory of personality', notes a tension between 'self-actualization' and the actualisation of the whole organism. On the one hand, human beings have a wish for 'congruence' – a way of making sense of life that fits with the totality of organismic experiencing. On the other hand, human beings have a need to maintain some sense of coherence and stability in their sense of self. I would suggest that, while some level of processing is essential for human beings to function as human beings, processing, by its very nature, is morphogenic. As a person processes experience, experiential change occurs that can never be fully controlled or predicted. As such, processing is essential to human functioning, yet it exists in tension with a need to maintain the coherence and functional effectiveness of one's more personally and culturally established strategies and ways of viewing life.

Moreover, while a sense of self seems to be a human universal that is essential to processing, particular ways of experiencing or holding onto self are often seen as problematic in human living. For, example, many of the world's religions, in one way or another, suggest that letting go of a rigid or excessively individualist sense of self is essential to spiritual advancement.

Processing and relationship

Given the inherent role of processing in bridging between individuals and communities, it makes sense that relationships are so central in developing and fostering human abilities to make sense of their lived situations. The relational qualities posited by Rogers – empathy, congruence (or realness) and unconditional positive regard (or prizing) – seem likely to be human universals relating to this particularly human way of remaining individual while connecting deeply with the experience of others.

Empathy, in which people use various mental, emotional and intuitive capacities to create within themselves an experience of what it is like to be another person, seems essential to the human ability to take the intentional stance that Dennett (1987) and others see as central to the ways that human beings construe situations. Given this, it makes sense that empathy is a crucial aspect of the attachment relationships in which processing capacities are initially developed. It also makes sense that empathic, understanding relationships tend to facilitate processing in adults. Rogers (1959) notes that empathic understanding within a real and prizing relationship tends to lower the sense of fear that an individual feels in the face of incongruent experiences. I suspect that this lowering of fear tends to shift the balance towards the wish to make sense of that which is not yet clear in experiencing (Warner, 1997).

The sort of processing that I have been describing allows human beings to develop congruence – a coherent version of who they are that carries forward their whole-body sense of themselves. This sort of congruence allows human beings to operate within relationships in a reliable and comprehensible way. Notably, Mary

Main (1991) found that mothers who could present a coherent version of their life histories tended to have infants who were more securely attached. And children who had been securely attached tended to themselves be able to offer a coherent life history in their early teens.

The sort of prizing described by Rogers involves a human valuing of another in a way that is empathic and genuine at the same time. It is also a quality that is notably present in optimal infant attachment relationships. I suspect that a high-level combination of the three qualities, which Dave Mearns (1997) calls 'relational depth', is a universally valued aspect of intimate human relationships.

Processing and culture

While processing meaning is a human universal, societies vary considerably in the emphasis placed on elaborated individual understanding of life situations. A parallel can be drawn with language. While all known cultures use language, some emphasise talking a great deal and have elaborated literary languages, while others place much more emphasis on silence or action.

I suspect that individual processing has particular importance in modern societies, as individuals become less constrained by hierarchical power relationships and as a result have broader scope for personal choice. Moreover, as societies become more diverse, individuals have a greater need to differentiate their understandings of themselves in relation to others who approach life differently.

If it is correct that processing is fundamental to human nature, one would expect processing capacities to be central to human wellbeing and functioning in all cultures. But processing might be used quite differently within different cultural traditions.[4] For example, in many cultures, decisions made at the level of the family or group are given greater weight than individual personal inclinations. The best ways to support individuals and groups in their processing may be quite different and may need to be developed within particular contexts.

A person-centred view of psychopathology

This view of processing as central to human nature gives us the groundwork to formulate a person-centred view of psychological dysfunction. In day-to-day living, individuals often meet the press of life with actions grounded in familiar understandings, using well-established strategies for living that allow the person to proceed without processing the situation freshly. Ordinarily, the ability to process freshly is available, useful and personally satisfying to human beings. But it becomes crucial whenever pre-established understandings and strategies don't work to meet the implicit needs of the organism. Psychological distress, then, can be expected to result when pre-existing understandings and strategies don't work to meet the

---

4. See, for example, Mikuni (2015).

needs of the organism, and the person (or the group of people) is unable to use processing capacities to generate new, more workable alternatives. This version of person-centred theory suggests that Rogers' 'necessary and sufficient' relationship conditions of empathy, genuineness and prizing offer a support for the processing capacities and self-cohesion of individuals (and of dyads and groups) that is deeply grounded in human nature. Such processing and self-cohesion allow the development of a 'congruent' version of self that resonates with the person's whole-body experience and minimises psychological symptoms.

One can, then, form a three-sided model that will let us consider various sources of psychological distress.

Press of life
– unresolved by pre-existing understandings and strategies

Self-cohesion and processing capacities
– grounded in early childhood physical and psychological development of the organism

Facilitation of processing and self-cohesion
– via empathy, genuineness and unconditional positive regard

A continuum of psychological wellness and dysfunction, applying to families and groups as well as to individuals, can then be developed as follows.

1. Well-developed self and processing capacities used effectively (with or without the relational support of psychotherapy) to develop or enhance life possibilities in the absence of distress caused by an overwhelming press of life.

2. Well-developed self and processing capacities temporarily stressed or overwhelmed by the press of life, benefiting from the relational support for processing capacities offered in psychotherapy.

3. Difficult process and/or fragile self, resulting from any of numerous causes, such as:

    a) deficits in the early childhood caregiving (necessary for the development of capacities of processing and self)

    b) early deficits in the organic structures and processes that support processing meaning into a sense of self

    c) later deficits in organic structures that result from trauma, disease, substance abuse or the like, or

    d) later-life degeneration of capacities of the organism to process meaning into a sense of self.

Person-centred psychotherapy offers a form of relationship that facilitates currently functioning self and processing capacities, as well as fostering the development or reconstitution of impaired self and processing capacities within the biological limits of the organism.

A person-centred model as it relates to traditional categories of psychopathology

Traditional categories of psychopathology offer descriptions of characteristic states of distress to the person (such as anxiety or depression), or to others (as in conduct disorders), that may be useful to professionals communicating to each other about the superficial characteristics of client difficulties. But, a person-centred view of dysfunction suggests that such states can result from such infinitely varied, personally unique problems in living that the categories themselves don't offer much guidance to the therapy. Yet, person-centred theory suggests that, if a person is able to process the uniqueness of his or her life situation, this is likely to bring experiential changes that ameliorate anxiety and depression, to enable the person to alter beliefs that are not serving him or her well or to alter behaviours that are creating problems.

This person-centred view does not rule out the possibility of biological dysfunction or genetic predisposition to particular sorts of emotional distress. But it would suggest that the human organism is so deeply oriented to processing that human beings will continue attempts to make sense of and integrate understandings into a sense of self, even when some aspects of ordinary capacities are impaired. As with many capacities that are central to human functioning, multiple, alternative ways of accomplishing the same ends are available within the organism. When particular ways of processing are impaired, clients who have therapeutic support continue expressive efforts and, ultimately, are likely to develop alternative ways of processing their experience.

This person-centred view of psychopathology doesn't rule out medication, but its use does raise serious concerns. Given the side effects of medication and the possibilities of long-term organic damage, the risks and benefits of its use should be weighed carefully. And, it makes sense that more process-oriented approaches should be used whenever possible, whether as a substitute for medication or as an adjunctive treatment. Processing and integrating meaning into a sense of self are so central to human existence that medication should be carefully calibrated to protect and foster the client's abilities to be aware of moment-to-moment experiencing. The ability to form one's own opinions and choices is so central to human nature that support for the client's own ability to make choices about medication and therapy should be a central priority

Implications for mental health services

This view of processing and self as central to human nature offers a particular understanding of what it is to live fully as a human being. To be a human being is to experience oneself as a person able to make sense of one's own situation, to choose one's own next steps in living, and to live in relationships in which one can understand and be understood, value and be valued. This view has ethical, compassionate and pragmatic implications for mental health services.

Ethically, this would suggest a need to intervene in ways that support the qualities that are fundamental to human nature and to avoid interventions that impede the full functioning of core human qualities. In terms of human compassion, it emphasises the need to recognise the depth of human affliction that is experienced when one is unable to process and make sense of lived experience in these ways – a suffering that is often experienced as organismic panic, personal emptiness, fragmentation or existential despair.

Such a view of human nature opens a critique of common societal responses to psychological dysfunction. Medical systems often respond to physical illness while ignoring psychological dysfunction. When a person is unable to process experience, the sense of affliction is likely to be as damaging to core wellbeing and as threatening to prospects of physical survival as almost any physical illness.

Yet, when mental health services are offered, they often seem designed to shape clients' behaviours to be like those that are considered fully human, without considering the human qualities of the client's actual experience. Thus, clients are often taught to behave in culturally appropriate ways, whether or not this behaviour is congruent with their own feelings, wants or intentions. They may be required to participate in social activities, whether or not they feel or enjoy being sociable. They may be taught to speak in ways that don't sound 'crazy', whether or not this cuts them off from any sort of personally grounded experience. Medication is sometimes prescribed in ways that shut down negative emotions and expressions thought culturally 'crazy', without considering the need to foster the person's ability to make sense of her or his own life and to make choices in the light of those understandings.

Pragmatically, this view points to the effectiveness of Rogers' core conditions in fostering and re-constituting abilities to process experience and to develop a congruent, cohesive self. Therapy grounded in these conditions allows clients suffering from severe forms of disturbance to begin to form a sense of self that is personally authentic, and to make personally meaningful sense of their lived experience. A person-centred process stays attuned to the client's own rhythm, and open to the exactness and existential freedom of the person's own choices. Moreover, given the client-directed quality of such therapy, it is less likely to trigger or re-evoke experiences of abusive authority from the client's past than more confrontational or interpretive forms of therapy.

Person-centred theory, understood in this way, offers a model of human functioning that is relevant to all clinical psychology and the social sciences. It generates particular insights into the human qualities that should be central to all humane mental health practice. And it strengthens the rationale for person-centred therapy as an effective and compassionate approach to psychotherapy with clients at all levels of psychological dysfunction. It makes a particularly strong case for the humane value of the person-centred approach with clients experiencing the difficult process characteristic of the most severe psychological disorders.

References

Baron-Cohen S (1995). *Mindblindness: an essay on autism and theory of mind*. Cambridge, MA: The MIT Press.

Binder U (1998). Empathy and empathy development in psychotic clients. In: Thorne B, Lambers E (eds). *Person-Centred Therapy: a European perspective*. London: Sage Publications (pp216–230).

Bohart AC (1990). A cognitive client-centered perspective on borderline personality development. In: Lietaer G, Rombauts J, Van Balen R (eds). *Client-Centered and Experiential Psychotherapy in the Nineties*. Leuven: Leuven University Press (pp599–621).

Boy AV (1989). Psychodiagnosis: a person-centered perspective. *Person-Centered Review* 4(2): 132–151.

Cain D, Seeman J (eds) (2002). *Humanistic Psychotherapies: handbook of research and practice*. Washington, DC: APA Press.

Coffeng T (1995). Experiential and pre-experiential therapy for multiple trauma. In: Hutterer R, Pawlowsky G, Schmid PF, Stipsits R (eds). *Client-Centered and Experiential Psychotherapy: a paradigm in motion*. Frankfurt am Main: Peter Lang (pp499–511).

Cooper M, Mearns D, Stiles W, Warner MS, Elliott R (2004). Developing self-pluralistic perspectives within the person-centered and experiential approaches: a roundtable dialogue. *Person-Centered and Experiential Therapies* 3(3): 176–191.

Dennett D (1987). *The Intentional Stance*. Cambridge, MA: The MIT Press.

Eckert J, Biermann-Ratjen E (1998). The treatment of borderline personality disorder. In: Greenberg L, Watson J, Lietaer G (eds). *Handbook of Experiential Psychology*. New York: The Guilford Press (pp349–367).

Eckert J, Wuchner M (1996). Long-term development of borderline personality disorder. In: Hutterer R, Pawlowsky G, Schmid PF, Stipsits R (eds). *Client-Centered and Experiential Psychotherapy: a paradigm in motion*. Frankfurt am Main: Peter Lang (pp163–181).

Gendlin ET (1997). How philosophy cannot appeal to experience, and how it can. In Levin DM (ed). *Language Beyond Postmodernism: saying and thinking in Gendlin's philosophy*. Evanston, Illinois: Northwestern University Press (pp3–41).

Gendlin ET (1995). Crossing and dipping: some terms for approaching the interface between natural understanding and logical formulation. *Minds and Machines* 5(4): 547–560.

Gendlin ET (1968). The experiential response. In: Hammer E (ed). *The Use of Interpretation in Treatment*. New York: Grune & Stratton (pp208–227).

Gendlin ET (1964). A theory of personality change. In: Worchel P, Byrne D (eds). *Personality Change*. New York: John Wiley & Sons (pp100–148).

Green MF (1998). *Schizophrenia from a Neurocognitive Perspective*. Boston: Allyn & Bacon.

Kohut H (1971). *The Analysis of the Self*. New York: International Universities Press.

Kohut H (1984). *How Does Analysis Cure?* Chicago: University of Chicago Press.

Lambers E (1994). Borderline personality disorder. In: Mearns D (ed). *Developing Person-Centred Counselling*. London: Sage Publications (pp110–112).

Leijssen M (1993). Creating a workable distance to overwhelming images: comments on a session transcript. In: Brazier D (ed). *Beyond Carl Rogers*. London: Constable (pp129–147).

Leijssen M (1996). Characteristics of a healing inner relationship. In: Hutterer R, Pawlowsky G, Schmid PF, Stipsits R (eds). *Client-Centered and Experiential Psychotherapy: a paradigm in motion*. Frankfurt am Main: Peter Lang (pp427–438).

Main M (1991). Metacognitive knowledge, metacognitive monitoring, and singular (coherent) vs multiple models of attachment. In: Parkes CM, Hinde JS, Marris D (eds). *Attachment Across the Life Cycle*. London: Tavistock/Routledge (pp127–159).

Mearns D (1997). *Person-Centred Counselling Training*. London: Sage.

Mikuni M (2015). *The Person-Centered Approach in Japan: blending a Western approach with Japanese culture*. Monmouth: PCCS Books.

Prouty G (1994). *Theoretical Evolutions in Person-Centered/Experiential Therapy*. Westport, CT: Praeger.

Prouty G (1986). The pre-symbolic structure and therapeutic transformation of hallucinations. In: Wolpin M, Schorr J, Krueger L (eds). *Imagery: recent practice and theory. Vol: 4*. New York: Plenum Press (pp99–106).

Prouty G (1983). Hallucinatory contact: a phenomenological treatment of schizophrenics. *Journal of Communication Therapy 2*(1): 99–103.

Prouty G (1977). Protosymbolic method: a phenomenological treatment of schizophrenic hallucinations. *Journal of Mental Imagery 1*(2): 339–342.

Prouty G, Van Werde D, Portner M (2002). *Pre-Therapy: reaching contact-impaired clients*. Ross-on Wye: PCCS Books.

Raskin NJ (1996). Client-centered therapy with very disturbed clients. In: Hutterer R, Pawlowsky G, Schmid PF, Stipsits R (eds). *Client-Centered and Experiential Psychotherapy: a paradigm in motion*. Frankfurt am Main: Peter Lang (pp529–531).

Roelens L (1996). Accommodating psychotherapy to information-processing constraints: a person-centered psychiatric case description. In: Hutterer R, Pawlowsky G, Schmid PF, Stipsits R (eds). *Client-Centered and Experiential Psychotherapy: a paradigm in motion*. Frankfurt am Main: Peter Lang (pp533–543).

Rogers CR (ed) (1967). *The Therapeutic Relationship and its Impact: a study of psychotherapy with schizophrenics*. Madison: University of Wisconsin Press.

Rogers CR (1959). A theory of therapy, personality and interpersonal relationships, as developed in the client-centered framework. In: Koch S (ed). *Psychology: a study of science. Vol 3: Formulations of the person and the social context*. New York: McGraw-Hill (pp184–256).

Rogers CR (1957). The necessary and sufficient conditions of personality change. *Journal of Consulting Psychology 21*(2): 95–103.

Roy B (1991). A client-centered approach to multiple personality and dissociative process. In: Fusek L (ed). *New Directions in Client-Centered Therapy: practice with difficult client populations* (Monograph Series 1). Chicago: Chicago Counseling and Psychotherapy Center (pp18–40).

Sanders P (2010). *A Straight-Talking Introduction to the Causes of Mental Health Problems*. Ross-on-Wye: PCCS Books.

Santen B (1990). Beyond good and evil: focusing with early traumatised children and adolescents. In: Lietaer G, Rombauts J, Van Balen R (eds). *Client-Centered and Experiential Psychotherapy in the Nineties*. Leuven: Leuven University Press (pp779–796).

Shlein J (1989). Boy's person-centered perspective on diagnosis. *Person-Centered Review* 4(2): 157–162.

Stern DN (1985). *The Interpersonal World of the Infant*. New York: Basic Books.

Swildens JC (1990). Client-centered psychotherapy for patients with borderline symptoms. In: Lietaer G, Rombauts J, Van Balen R (eds). *Client-Centered and Experiential Psychotherapy in the Nineties*. Leuven: Leuven University Press (pp623–635).

Tooby J, Cosmides L (1992). The psychological foundations of culture. In: Barkow J, Cosmides L, Tooby J (eds). *The Adapted Mind: evolutionary psychology and the generation of culture*. New York: Oxford University Press (pp19–136).

Van Werde D (1990). Psychotherapy with a retarded schizo-affective woman: an application of Prouty's pre-therapy. In: Dosen A, Van Gennep A, Zwanikken G (eds). *Treatment of Mental Illness and Behavioral Disorder in the Mentally Retarded: proceedings of international congress, May 3rd and 4th, Amsterdam, The Netherlands*. Leiden: Logon Publications.

Van Werde D (1998). Anchorage as a core concept in working with psychotic people. In: Thorne B, Lambers E (eds). *Person-Centred Therapy: a European perspective*. London: Sage Publications (pp195–205).

Warner MS (2016). Difficult process: working with fragile and dissociated client experiences. In: Lago C, Charura D (eds). *The Person-Centred Counselling and Psychotherapy Handbook: origins, development and contemporary applications*. Maidenhead: Open University Press/McGraw-Hill (pp102–110).

Warner MS (2014). Client processes at the difficult edge. In: Pearce P, Sommerbeck L (eds). *Person-Centred Practice at the Difficult Edge*. Ross-on-Wye: PCCS Books (pp121–137).

Warner MS (2013). Difficult client process. In: Cooper M, O'Hara M, Schmid PF, Bohart A (eds). *The Handbook of Person-Centred Psychotherapy and Counselling* (2nd ed). Basingstoke: Palgrave MacMillan (pp343–358).

Warner MS (2002a) Psychological contact, meaningful process, and human nature: a reformulation of person-centered theory. In: Wyatt G, Sanders P (eds). *Rogers' Therapeutic Conditions: evolution, theory and practice. Vol 3: Contact and perception*. Ross-on-Wye: PCCS Books (pp76–95).

Warner MS (2002b). Luke's dilemmas: A client-centered/experiential model of processing with a schizophrenic thought disorder. In: Watson J, Goldman R, Warner MS (eds). *Client-Centered and Experiential Psychotherapy in the 21st Century: advances in theory, research and practice*. Ross-on-Wye: PCCS Books.

Warner MS (2001). Empathy, relational depth and difficult client process. In: Haugh S, Merry T (eds). *Rogers' Therapeutic Conditions: evolution, theory and practice. Vol 2: Empathy*. Ross-on-Wye: PCCS Books (pp181–191).

Warner MS (2000). Client-centered therapy at the difficult edge: work with fragile and dissociated process. In: Mearns D, Thorne B (eds). *Person-Centred Therapy Today: new frontiers in theory and practice*. Thousand Oaks: Sage (pp144–171).

Warner MS (1998). A client-centered approach to therapeutic work with dissociated and fragile process. In: Greenberg L, Watson J, Lietaer G (eds). *Handbook of Experiential Psychotherapy*. New York: The Guilford Press (pp368–387).

Warner MS (1997). Does empathy cure? A theoretical consideration of empathy, processing and personal narrative. In: Bohart AC, Greenberg LS (eds). *Empathy Reconsidered*. Washington, DC: American Psychological Association (pp125–140).

Warner MS (1991). Fragile process. In: Fusek L (ed). *New Directions in Client-Centered Therapy: practice with difficult client populations* (Monograph Series 1). Chicago: Chicago Counseling and Psychotherapy Center (pp41–58).

Warner MS (1983). Soft meaning and sincerity in the family system. *Family Process 22*(4): 523–535.

7 Complementarity between client-centred therapy and psychiatry: the theory and the practice

Lisbeth Sommerbeck

The crucial differences between client-centred therapy and psychiatry

The hermeneutic/phenomenological model of client-centred therapy stresses as the primary therapeutic variables the therapist's empathic understanding of the client's world, and the therapist's unconditional positive regard for the client. This means that the client is treated as a unique individual whom the therapist wishes to get to know and understand. Since it is the uniqueness of the client that is in the foreground in this model, it also means that the therapist can in no way be an expert on what is best for the client – that is, on what is the best conception of reality for the client, or what is wrong with the client, or what are the best options for the client, or what are the best courses of action for the client. (Throughout the chapter, this is what I mean by the phrase 'what is best for'.)

In the medical model of psychiatry, it is the other way round. In this model, the client is treated as representative of a group of people who have been allocated a certain psychiatric diagnosis. Their knowledge, drawn from the research and professional experience, of what is best for most people belonging to this diagnostic group, gives the psychiatrist the status of an expert on what is best for someone who is assumed to be representative of this group of people – that is, the psychiatrist is an expert on what is best for the client, because the client is seen as representative of a group of people with the same psychiatric diagnosis. In this model, the client is thus treated as more or less closely approximate to the average of a particular group of people.

Therefore, at a first glance, the hermeneutic/phenomenological model of client-centred therapy and the medical model of psychiatry seem mutually contradictory and in conflict with each other. This makes itself particularly strongly felt in the following two areas.

First, the client-centred therapist strives to understand from the client's frame of reference, whereas the psychiatrist strives to explain from his/her own (theoretical) frame of reference and treats the client from this point of view. Psychiatry has many explanations – more or less well documented by research – for the diverse conditions of patients: hereditary, bio-chemical, early environmental etc. These factors are seen as causal, aetiological factors that contribute, singly or in combination, to what are normally considered discrete, specific disease entities. The client-centred therapist, on the other hand, is in no way concerned with explaining the condition and symptoms of the client. He or she is solely concerned with trying to understand the client from the client's frame of reference and checking the accuracy of this understanding with the client, thereby communicating his or her unconditional positive regard for the client as a unique individual. This is, according to client-centred theory, helpful to clients, whether there exists a more or less well documented explanation for their ailment or not. Understanding people and explaining people are two very different things. It corresponds to the German philosopher Dilthey's (1894) distinction between the natural sciences as sciences that explain and the humanities as sciences that understand.

Second, the question of whether a client is psychotic or not (one of the most crucial differential diagnostic questions in psychiatry) is made from the point of view of 'consensual reality': ie. that which the majority in a given culture regards as reality. From the point of view of consensual reality, delusions and hallucinations (often prominent symptoms in psychosis) are not accurate perceptions of reality, but, from the point of view of the delusional or hallucinating client, they are real, and therefore they are real, too, for the client-centred therapist when he or she is trying to receive and accompany the client with acceptant empathic understanding. The client-centred therapist has to suspend his or her own sense of reality when in therapy sessions with these clients. Fundamentally, this is in no way different from work with clients who are not diagnosed as psychotic, because the therapist will always strive to understand the client from the client's frame of reference, no matter how unfamiliar the client's world may be to the therapist. However, the phenomenological field or psychological landscape of clients diagnosed with psychosis is often private and different from that of the therapist, and from that of 'consensual reality', to a more radical and extreme degree than is the case with most other clients. In the psychiatric setting, therefore, the client-centred therapist feels more acutely that he or she shuffles back and forth between the client's sense of reality when in session and the therapist's own sense of reality, which he or she probably shares to quite a large extent with most of his or her medical-model colleagues (consensual reality) when the session is finished. In session, for example, the client-centred therapist tries to empathically understand a client's experience of the threatening man in a black coat in the corner of the office in just the same way that the therapist tries to empathically understand a client's experience of, say, the client's mother. When the session is finished, however, the therapist probably regards the man in the black coat as a hallucination, as do his or her medical-model colleagues, and the therapist can likewise regard the client's perception of his or her mother as more or less real. However, the classical client-centred therapist's points of view and opinions, together with 'consensual reality', are utterly irrelevant in his or her therapeutic practice.

It is necessary for the client-centred therapist in the medical-model setting of a psychiatric hospital to find a way to encompass and reconcile within him/herself these seemingly conflicting viewpoints of (1) understanding as opposed to explaining, and (2) psychotic reality as opposed to consensual reality. When the therapist cannot do this, he or she will tend to see the theories of client-centred therapy and the medical model as being in conflict with each other, or, in the extreme, as two camps at war with each other. With such a point of view, the therapist will most likely find him/herself in the midst of a fruitless 'who is right?' discussion with his or her medical-model colleagues about the treatment of a given client – a discussion that will, more likely than not, end with the burnout of the client-centred therapist and his or her retreat from the field of psychiatry, where the medical model is, currently at least, the dominant model. Even worse, engaging in discussion with representatives of the medical model about what is best for one of the therapist's clients converts the therapist into just another expert on the client. Being an authority on what is best for one's clients in discussions with medical-model colleagues and a non-authority on one's clients in therapy sessions is, at best, self-contradictory and at worst hypocritical.

The theory of complementarity

To avoid this self-contradiction, I have found the concept of complementarity exceedingly helpful in my work as a client-centred therapist in a psychiatric hospital, and I will therefore explain it rather extensively here.

Complementarity in physics

In physics, the concept or principle of complementarity is the standard way of thinking about some strange phenomena in very small-scale elementary particle physics. I will illustrate this by using the electron as an example. An electron cannot be studied directly: physicists use different kinds of experimental set-ups to study it. When they do that, the following strange phenomenon occurs: in one kind of experimental set-up, the electron is seen to behave as a particle, and in another kind of experimental set-up, the electron is seen to behave as a wave. Logically, particle and wave are mutually exclusive categories; something cannot be both a particle and a wave, because the first is discrete (particles have a precise location and delineation), and the second is continuous (waves do not have a precise location and delineation). When physicists discovered this in the 1920s and 1930s, they were not happy about it. They therefore tried to find a 'hidden variable' (something in the electron yet to be discovered) that might sometimes appear as a particle and sometimes as a wave. As they were absolutely unsuccessful in this – the electron really *is* an elementary particle, it cannot be subdivided, no hidden variable exists – the Danish physicist Niels Bohr introduced the concept of complementarity to make some 'sense' of this particle/wave duality, as it is commonly called.

Bohr took the position that, in choosing his or her experimental set-up, the physicist chooses whether the electron will be a particle or a wave. Alternatively, depending on how he or she chooses to look at the electron, the physicist will decide on the nature of the electron – whether it is a wave or particle. However, he or she cannot, of course, see both at the same time. Bohr said that it is meaningless to ask what the electron 'really' is out there, when nobody is looking at it; you have to look at it to know, and then its nature depends on how you look at it: ie. on your own viewpoint or frame of reference. When not being observed, the electron is said to be in a state of superposition of particle and wave.

Complementarity in psychiatry

The earlier-mentioned dualities (understanding/explaining, private reality/consensual reality) can very helpfully be conceptualised as complementary viewpoints in an analogy with the wave/particle duality: what one sees from one point of view cannot be seen from the other, and vice versa, and what one chooses to see depends on one's purpose. In therapy sessions, the viewpoint of the client-centred therapist is, of course, that of understanding and private reality. In discussions with colleagues, it may be that of explanation and consensual reality. Person-centred personality theory, for example, explains psychological disturbance as the result of excessive exposure to conditional regard. The client-centred therapist, though, does not allow this explanation to get in the way of the client who explains his or her disturbance as genetically determined. Instead, the therapist empathises with the client's explanation of his or her disturbances. The client's personality theory is the therapist's personality theory for the duration of the session. Generally, however, and when thinking about psychological disturbances at large (ie. when taking the other perspective in the complementary duality), the person-centred therapist may very well disagree with the client.

In addition, the two viewpoints or dualities mentioned above could be said to be in a state of superposition when the therapist does not choose one or the other: that is, when he or she is neither trying to understand the private reality of a given client in therapy nor concerned with potential explanations of the client's condition in, say, talks with medical-model colleagues.

One could also say that the client-centred therapist sees the uniqueness of the client, whereas the psychiatrist sees their averageness in relation to a certain diagnostic group. From the client-centred therapist's point of view, it is the unique client that exists, not the average client. From the psychiatrist's point of view, it is the average client that exists, not the unique client. The psychiatrist, for example, sees a more or less close approximation to his or her idea of 'the average schizophrenic' or 'the average depressive' and treats his/her patient accordingly. The psychiatrist's glasses are coloured (and they are supposed to be coloured) by the psychiatrist's knowledge of what is assumed to be typical for people diagnosed with one of the many different diagnoses of psychiatry. The glasses of the client-centred therapist, in contrast, are not coloured (and they are supposed not to be coloured) by any previous knowledge of what may or may not be typical for this or that group of people. To the client-centred therapist, the client is unique: he or she is unlike any person seen before, a person to be known, not a person already more or less known, and they treat the client accordingly. Thus, the client-centred therapist's view is fundamentally, diametrically opposite to the view of the psychiatrist. This is the complementarity divide between two mutually exclusive approaches and points of views that cannot be integrated, but can, each in its own way, be useful in their respective contexts. (This is not synonymous with being uncritical of the dominance of the medical-model view in psychiatry.)

The detailed meaning of the term 'complementarity', in this case, is (continuing with the wave/particle duality from quantum physics) that 1) it is false to say that the client is both unique and average, because unique/average are logically self-contradictory terms; 2) it is false to say that the client is neither unique nor average, because one can choose a viewpoint where the client is unique, and one can choose a viewpoint where the client is average; 3) it is false to say only that the client is unique, because from another point of view the client is average, and 4) it is false to say only that the client is average, because from another point of view the client is unique. Thus, the logical possibilities for combinations with respect to the unique/average duality are exhausted, and this is what characterises what one sees from viewpoints that are in a complementary relationship to each other. Finally, as noted above and consistent with the concept of complementarity, it is meaningless to ask what the client 'really' is when he/she is not attended to, and it is the person who attends to the client who decides whether the client shall be unique or average.

Other dual terms, like 'private reality' and 'public (consensual) reality', or 'the inside perspective' and 'the outside perspective', can be used instead of 'unique' and 'average', and the application of the principle of complementarity outside the area of physics is, of course, not confined to the relationship between client-centred therapy and the medical model of psychiatry.

The practice of complementarity

Over the years, in the hospital where I work,[1] I have explained the principle of complementarity and its foundation in physics, and, in my experience, it has been very helpful in contributing to mutual respect between the practitioner of client-centred therapy and the practitioner of the medical/psychiatric model. Being

---

1. Since the publication of the first edition of this book, I have retired. I have, however, chosen not to change the present tense of the chapter to the past tense, in order to keep the writing as lively as possible for readers.

able to employ the principle of complementarity to understand their seemingly antithetical viewpoints with respect to individual clients is felt as a relief by the majority of professionals working in this setting, because the nagging question of who is right, whose viewpoint is the most truthful or real, is resolved in a meaningful way.

It must be remembered, however, that applying the principle of complementarity in the way I have described above is exclusively a result of seeing an analogy between some phenomena of the world of quantum mechanics and some phenomena of the world of psychiatry. I postulate no true identity between these two classes of phenomena. Future research may point to ways of thinking about the many puzzling and seemingly antithetical phenomena of the client-centred model and the medical model that are more fruitful than thinking about them in terms of complementarity.

Therapist duality

In accordance with the principle of complementarity, there is a duality to the client-centred therapist's practice in psychiatry: the therapist lives a sort of 'double life' when working in this medical-model context. From the moment a therapy client crosses the doorstep to his or her consultation room, the therapist sees the world from within the frame of reference of the client. When the therapy session is over, the therapist is back in a world where the dominating frame of reference is that of the medical model, and where the therapist may agree that the black-coated man that the client saw in the corner was an hallucination. Because of the seemingly antithetical elements of client-centred therapy and the medical model, these two worlds cannot be integrated into one. The therapist has no other option than to go back and forth between them, in the same way that the physicist shuffles back and forth, as he or she chooses, between seeing the electron as a particle and seeing it as a wave, since there is no possibility of seeing them as both at the same time. There are, however, several situations, also between sessions, where the therapist must protect the position that he or she cannot be an expert on what is best for the client, because it is the uniqueness, not the averageness, of the client that exists for the therapist. This is not always easy, and in the following paragraphs I'll describe some of the difficulties and some of the ways to overcome these difficulties that I have found fruitful in my 36 years' work in a psychiatric hospital. The main point is to simultaneously protect the client-centred therapy process and respect other professionals' treatment of the client from the medical-model perspective. To do this, it is first and foremost essential to avoid identifying with either the client or the medical model setting of psychiatry – that is, to avoid becoming an advocate, spokesperson, saviour or message-deliverer of the client in relation to the medical-model setting and to avoid becoming an advocate, spokesperson, saviour or message-deliverer of the medical-model setting in relation to the client. This has several practical consequences, as follows.

First, the therapist has to refuse to accommodate certain requests from the medical-model staff that seem perfectly natural to them. The therapist says 'no' when he or she, for example, is asked to evaluate the client's condition in their next session. Staff members may want this evaluation to help them make all sorts of decisions, and it is second nature for them, and part of their job, to make (diagnostic) evaluations when relating with clients. It is expected of them and they expect it of others. This is, of course, because they, from their medical-model perspective, attend to the averageness of the client. It can be difficult for non-informed staff members to understand and respect that the client-centred therapist, who attends to the uniqueness of the client, can have no plans or intentions of any kind when he meets the client.

The therapist can also be asked to talk certain things over with the client, or deliver a message, and, again, the client-centred therapist refuses to accommodate these requests in order not to have any agenda for the session with the client other than trying to empathically understand this unique client from this client's own frame of reference. Jerold Bozarth (1990: 63) puts it well when he writes:

> The therapist goes with the client – goes at the client's pace – goes with
> the client in his/her own ways of thinking, of experiencing, of processing.
> The therapist cannot be up to other things, have other intentions without
> violating the essence of client-centred therapy. To be up to other things
> – whatever they might be – is a 'yes but' reaction to the essence of the
> approach.

Second, the therapist refuses to participate in meetings or conferences about one of his or her therapy clients if the therapist thinks this participation could have negative consequences for the therapeutic process with the client. The full psychiatric treatment of the hospitalised patient involves all sorts of meetings: ward meetings for all staff and patients on the ward, meetings with relatives of the patient (with or without the participation of the patient), meetings with staff from other institutions to coordinate treatment plans (again, with or without the participation of the patient) etc. This is a delicate point, and sometimes difficult for the therapist to decide on: will participation place the therapist in the role of an expert on what is best for the client in the eyes of the client, or in the eyes of others, and perhaps even in the eyes of the therapist him/herself, to the detriment of the therapy process? The rule of thumb is to refuse to participate if it is likely that participation will result in the therapist being regarded as an expert on the client.

Normally I only meet with relatives and 'external' staff if they want my participation to facilitate their own process with the client. I refuse to meet with them if I am expected to tell them, as an expert, what is wrong with the client and the best way to 'put him/her right'. If this is their expectation, I refer them to my client's psychiatrist. This is no different from my practice of consultation/supervision/facilitation with 'internal' staff members with respect to their own processes with patients, whether they are my therapy clients or not. The significant point guiding the therapist's decisions on this issue is that he or she does not take on the role of expert on what is best for the client in any context whatsoever. At the same time, though, the therapist respects that medical-model representatives, from their perspective, naturally engage in processes with the therapist's clients where they behave as experts on what is best for the client.

Third, the therapist must be careful about sharing information and opinions about his or her therapy clients in the regular staff meetings and conferences in which the therapist normally participates as part of working in a psychiatric setting, particularly in a psychiatric hospital. The main point is not to say anything that others may inadvertently, and unbeknown to themselves, use – with the best of intentions – in their relationship with the client in ways that may harm the therapy process. It is useful to imagine what would happen if a staff member said to the client: 'I know from your therapist that...' I shudder at the thought that the psychiatrist of one of my clients might say to them: 'Lisbeth said, at the ward staff meeting, that it would be better for you if we reduce and eventually stop your medication. She doesn't think you suffer from an illness but from excessive exposure to conditional regard, so it will be an increasing understanding of this, in your psychotherapy, rather than medicine, that will help you' (or something to that effect). As a rule of thumb, when in doubt, it is better to say too little than too much. This is a delicate point, too; deciding what to relate and what to keep back is not always easy as it can depend on a multitude of factors specific to the given situation and the given moment. Most important among these, I think, is the relationship between the therapist and other staff: do they know and appreciate each other? Do they know, trust and respect the professional characteristics of each other's work? To the extent that this is the case, to the same extent can the therapist, according to my experience, accommodate other staff members' requests for information from the therapy.
 On the other hand, it is also the case that, in reality, very little information needs to be passed between the client-centred therapist and the representatives of the medical model for both parties to do their job. This is a consequence of the complementarity of their respective perspectives. The therapist has no use for knowledge from frames of references other than the client's own, and he cannot offer representatives of the medical model the kind of information they need to help them make medical-model treatment decisions for and with the client. Therefore, at root, only very minimal sharing of information is necessary for truly good reasons between the therapist and other staff members.

Fourth, the therapist does not try to control the way other staff members treat his or her therapy clients. The therapist offers the professionals in the medical model the same respect that he or she expects from them. The therapist is aware that the client is in hospital because psychotherapy alone – or, for that matter, psychopharmacological medication, or any other single treatment modality (physiotherapy, occupational rehabilitation etc) alone – has been deemed insufficient to help the client optimally. However, the therapist, being dedicated to the philosophy of client-centred theory, will probably often feel that medical-model professionals are treating a client with too little respect and understanding, and can feel tempted to try to protect the client by changing how other staff members are with them. This is a mistake: first, it amounts to identification with the client; the client must, after all, find his or her own way of dealing with his or her world and protect him/herself in it, including the world of the medical model. (Would the therapist contact the client's mother, for example, to try to influence her to treat the client with more respect and understanding?) Second, what seems disrespectful or insensitive to the therapist may not seem so to the client. Third, trying to change or control the ways of others is certainly not in line with the person-centred tradition. Fourth, acting on behalf of the client is, of course, synonymous with acting as an expert on what is best for the client, which is quite contrary to the essence of client-centred therapy. Protecting the client and protecting the therapy process are two very different, often even mutually exclusive, endeavours.

The following example is meant to illustrate some of the points made in the preceding paragraphs. In order to protect client confidentiality and anonymity, I have changed the factual content of the original case material. I believe the client, as represented here, is not recognisable. On the other hand, there is nothing unrealistic about the scenario.

> Marion is 30 years old, married, with a five-year-old son. She has been admitted to hospital on her own initiative because of frequent psychotic episodes where she hears voices ordering her to stab, variously, her husband, her son, and herself to death. She is treated with medication, which she feels helps her, and she has started psychotherapy. She has also started going home for weekends, but this occasions an upsurge of symptoms.
>
> In therapy, she hesitatingly begins to express very negative feelings towards her husband. This is a change from the first sessions, where she mostly talked about her voices and her fear of giving into them.
>
> On the ward, too, staff members have an impression that there are problems at home, partly because of the decline in her condition after weekends and because her husband never visits her, and also because she tries to shorten her weekend passes, telling her primary nurse that she is a burden on her husband when she is at home. He has to take care to keep knives locked away from her, he has to do all the cooking and other work in the kitchen, because it involves using knives, and he can't leave her on her own.
>
> Her condition and treatment are discussed in the regular weekly staff meeting, and the following dialogue takes place between the chief psychiatrist of the ward (CP) and the therapist (T):

CP: I really think we can't get further in the treatment of Marion without some sort of couples therapy. As it is now, I can't imagine her out of hospital in the foreseeable future, and we have many patients on the waiting list. (Turning to T): What about you having some couples sessions with Marion and her husband?

T: I'll gladly do that, if Marion wants me to.

CP: OK, then you talk with her about that and we can see how it progresses.

T: No, wait a minute. I won't introduce this idea, or any other, to her. You know I only work with issues that she brings up herself.

CP (smiling): Sorry, I forgot for a minute that you have this peculiarity. Then I'll propose it to her and suggest that she brings it up with you, if that is OK with you?

T: Sure, that's fine with me.

Two days later Marion (M) comes for her ordinary session and immediately brings up the subject of couples sessions.

M: CP said to me that it would be a good idea if I brought Douglas along to some talks with you.

T: Uhm, hmm… (a short silence).

M: But I don't know…

T: You are not sure it would be such a good idea?

M: No… I know I've told you that there are some things about Douglas that make me furious sometimes, but he also helps me a lot, and… I don't know… I don't feel like sitting here telling him about these things. I am sure it would make him feel bad, and I'd understand that; I'd feel bad if he gave me a scolding in front of a stranger, too.

T: You feel sort of disloyal at the thought of bringing him here for a scolding; he doesn't deserve that, because you also appreciate his helping you so much?

M: Yes, disloyal, and I'd also feel ashamed, a coward. I should talk all these things over with him when we are by ourselves. It's just so difficult, because he doesn't like to talk about that kind of thing.

Marion continues to discuss various aspects of her problems with her husband and decides that she will not bring her husband with her to a session. She prefers to try to find a way to have a talk with him at home about how she experiences their relationship. Then she turns to the therapist:

M: Will you tell CP that I won't bring Douglas in, explain it to him?

T: For some reason, you'd rather have me do it than do it yourself?

M: Yes, I'm afraid he'll be annoyed with me, because I won't bring Douglas in, but I'm sure he'd respect it if you told him.

T: Takes courage to say no to CP?

M: Yes, it really does – I'm afraid he'll discharge me from hospital soon if I don't accept his proposal, so will you tell him?

T: You think that if I tell him, he won't discharge you so soon?

M: Yes ... Oh, why should that make a difference...? It's just that sometimes it is a little difficult to talk with CP; he always seems to be in a hurry, a little impatient, and that makes me nervous. So, I'd appreciate it if you would talk with him.

T: You tend to feel nervous with CP, because you feel pressured when he seems to be in a hurry, and you'd prefer to avoid that by having me talk with him?

M: Yes, but... Well, I ought to do it myself. I'll talk with him myself.

T: You feel an obligation to do it yourself?

M (Laughing): Yes, and I'm also a little annoyed with you, because I think you won't do it, but then I also just thought that this is the kind of situation I always try to avoid – saying no to others, and particularly to authorities – and it doesn't do me any good in the long run.

Marion spends the rest of the session coming to terms with her annoyance with me and working out how best to tell CP about her decision not to have couples sessions. She is transferred to day-patient status two weeks later, and, after a month or so as a day patient, she is discharged from hospital altogether. She continues with the psychotherapy as an outpatient, and for a while she also continues to see CP about her medication, until this aspect of her treatment is transferred to her GP. Her psychotic symptoms have almost disappeared, she has managed to get her husband to talk about their relationship, and, generally, things are going much better at home. Currently the most frequent theme in her therapy sessions is her fear of being alone.

Comments on the example

The dialogue from the staff conference is typical of the therapist's efforts to avoid getting into situations where he or she will be placed in the position of expert on what is best for the client. The therapist avoids becoming an advocate, spokesperson, saviour or message-deliverer of the medical model to his/her client. Such situations occur in countless variations and disguises.

When the chief psychiatrist mentions the possibility of couples sessions during the staff conference, the therapist has a hunch, from their sessions with the client, that the client will not like this idea. The therapist, though, sees no point in speaking about this hunch, because they also want to avoid acting as an advocate, spokesperson, saviour or message-deliverer of the client in relation to the medical-model professionals. The therapist does not try to influence the psychiatrist, respecting that the psychiatrist will make the most constructive choice possible for him from his frame of reference, which, among other things, also includes balancing the needs of the patients in the hospital with those of patients on the waiting list.

Hopefully, the example illustrates the 'double life' of the therapist in a medical-model setting such as a psychiatric hospital, or the duality of the therapist's responsiveness in that setting, according to the principle of complementarity. Further, the client's process in the therapy hopefully illustrates how harmful it would have been to the therapy process if the therapist had either suggested couples sessions to the client (on behalf of the medical model) or suggested to the psychiatrist that couples sessions might not be beneficial (on behalf of the client).

The essence of the issues that have been discussed concerning the duality of the client-centred therapist's work in a medical-model setting, according to the principle of complementarity, can be summed up as follows:

- the therapy must progress in parallel, not integrated, with the medical-model treatments; the two worlds must be kept separate
- in his/her relations with the client, the therapist must take care not to identify with, or become the advocate, spokesperson, saviour or message-deliverer of the medical model
- in his/her relations with staff members, the therapist must take care not to identify with, or become the advocate, spokesperson, saviour or message-deliverer of the client
- the therapist listens to the client's experiences of the medical-model representatives of psychiatry as acceptingly and respectfully as he or she listens to any other of the client's experiences
- the therapist listens to the medical-model representative's experiences of his/her client as acceptingly and respectfully as he or she listens to any other of the staff members' experiences.

Dave Mearns (1994: 53–56) has stressed the importance of the therapist being 'beside' the client, not 'on the side of' the client. This is, to me, a very important point, and it is equally important to be 'beside', but not 'on the side of', the other professionals when working in a psychiatric context. The concept of complementarity is helpful in this respect.

All this is much easier said than done. The therapist can sometimes feel quite split when he or she passes back and forth between the world of therapy sessions and the world of the medical model: there is so little of his/her experiences in one world that he or she can use or share in the other. The therapist can sometimes feel disloyal to clients when he or she participates in 'medical-model talk' about a client with other staff members and does nothing to make them understand the client from the client's frame of reference. Likewise, the therapist can feel disloyal to his or her colleagues when listening with acceptant empathic understanding to a client's (negative) experiences of them in therapy sessions and does nothing to correct the client's impression in accordance with the therapist's own experiences of his or her colleagues. The concept of complementarity is useful to help the therapist to feel comfortable with this apparent 'split': both worlds can be considered true, but when in one you cannot see the other, and vice versa.

Person-centred contributions to medical-model psychiatric staff

As already stated, a consequence of conceptualising the hermeneutic/ phenomenological model of client-centred therapy and the medical model of psychiatry as standing in a complementary relationship to each other is that the psychotherapy must proceed in parallel, not integrated with the other medical-model treatments. This means that it can very legitimately be asked: what does the client-centred therapist actually have to say to medical-model representatives that might be important in order for both parties to do their job? In my experience the answer is: next to nothing (see also point 4 above). In spite of this, I'd like to extend this chapter with a description of two ways in which the person-centred practitioner can contribute fruitfully to the work of the medical-model representatives in a psychiatric hospital and, therefore, indirectly to the patients, without transgressing the frame of the concept of complementarity – that is, without running the risk of placing him/ herself in the role of an expert on what is best for the individual client/patient.

First, the client-centred therapist can contribute fruitfully to the regular ward staff conferences by relating to the other participants of these conferences in a predominantly person-centred way. All sorts of decisions about treatment plans for patients are made in these conferences, which makes them crucial for patients and staff alike.

As already mentioned, I have worked for 36 years in a psychiatric hospital, and for much of this time did not participate in ward staff meetings, with no consequences as far as my therapeutic work was concerned. It was not inconsequential, however, for my feeling of personal wellbeing in my work. I came to feel more and more isolated and estranged from most of my colleagues; I could have had my consultation room far away from the hospital, as an occasional telephone call was all that was needed to exchange any necessary information with staff on a client's ward. Therefore, for my own sake, I started to participate in the staff meetings of the two wards for which I did most of my work, to find out if I might have a contribution to make in this setting. It became apparent that this was the case, and in the following section I'll describe the contribution I, as a client-centred therapist (or, more correctly in this context, a person-centred practitioner) could make to the ward staff meeting.

I found that I could, with no agenda of my own, be helpful by facilitating the spontaneous tendencies towards a person-centred approach that already existed in the group, especially among the nurses. Although a holistic view of the patients as unique individuals is a commonly accepted value of nursing, and although most nurses have an intuitive feeling that listening to their patients is part of good nursing, many feel that they are 'doing nothing' when they are 'just listening'. In addition, nurses often do not fully realise how important their relationship with their patients is: that their ability to create a good relationship with their patients is of primary therapeutic importance and not secondary to, for example, psychopharmacological treatment and psychotherapy, or, even worse, irrelevant to the outcome of treatment. Nurses often welcome the great value that the client-centred therapist attaches to empathic listening and understanding and to the quality of the relationship with the patient, and can feel supported and strengthened by the therapist's interest in this aspect of their work. More specifically, I could be facilitative of the person-centred tendencies of the ward staff meeting by translating a categorising and diagnosing language into a language of characteristics of relationships. This could be the case, for example, if mention was made of a patient's narcissism. What does this mean in terms of nurses' daily relationships with the patient on the ward? Further, what does it mean that the client is 'unmotivated' or 'withdrawn' or 'psychotic' etc? Such questions underline the importance of the quality of staff members' relationships with patients and support staff members' tendency to deal with and talk about patients as unique human beings, alongside their obligation to deal with and talk about them as representatives of a diagnostic group.

I could also be facilitative of the person-centred tendencies of the ward staff meeting group by my interest in the patients' points of view – for example, by using appropriate occasions to ask: 'What does the patient him/herself want? Does anybody know what the patient will feel and think about this? These thoughts that you have about the patient's problems, are they yours, or are they the patient's?' Treatment plans with quite far-reaching consequences for patients are sometimes discussed in staff meetings, and most nurses welcome these kinds of question because they create a space for them to speak with the patient's voice, which they are most often very familiar with from their day-long contacts with patients on the ward. Nurses are most often the people who know best what treatment plans are acceptable to patients, whether these plans are about changes in the psychopharmacological treatment of patients, changes in their social network, changes in their daily activities, or whatever. In addition, it is most often nurses who will discuss the treatment plans extensively with patients, so it is important to most of them that the plans are in reasonable accordance with patients' wishes, and that they do not feel obliged to try, subtly or overtly, to enforce treatment plans on patients.

Further, I could enhance the importance attached to empathic understanding, by using nurses' accounts and descriptions of patients to guess at ways in which the patient might be understood empathically. This facilitates the nurses' spontaneous tendency to try to understand their patients empathically.

Finally, I could facilitate staff members' spontaneous feelings of compassion for their patients (an important aspect of unconditional positive regard), quite simply by listening with interest and acceptance to expressions of these feelings, and by openly expressing my own compassion for my clients. These attitudes are often regarded with a little suspicion in psychiatry because of its prizing of 'objectivity', although neither staff nor patients thrive well in a context of pure 'objectivity'. It is often a relief for staff members to allow themselves to feel compassion for their patients. All too often, staff members in psychiatry lean over backwards to distance themselves from being regarded as subjective or identifying with clients. Rogers (1961: 52) wrote:

> We are afraid that if we let ourselves freely experience these positive feelings toward another we may be trapped by them… So, as a reaction, we tend to build up distance between ourselves and others – aloofness, a 'professional' attitude, an impersonal relationship… It is a real achievement when we can learn, even in certain relationships or at certain times in those relationships, that it is safe to care, that it is safe to relate to the other as a person for whom we have positive feelings.

It is important that avoidance of identification with the patient is not confused with a distancing attitude that puts a taboo on feeling compassion for patients.

This role of mine, at ward staff meetings, has contributed to the wards becoming, in general, more 'person-centred' in the daily interactions between staff and patients. In addition, it has helped me out of my feelings of isolation and invisibility among all the other employees in the hospital. A precondition for this to happen is, of course, that the person in charge of the ward staff meeting, typically a psychiatrist – ie. a representative of the medical model – is sufficiently broad-minded to allow space and time for it. To the degree that this is the case, ward staff meetings can develop into a very exciting and enriching dialogue between the medical model and the person-centred approach.[2]

I think most client-centred therapists working in a medical-model setting will recognise this feeling of their psychotherapeutic work being (and having to be) separated, isolated and almost invisible from the activity of the rest of the setting. Some therapists may prefer to live with this 'invisibility' of their therapeutic work. For others, though, 'living with it' may entail a risk of burnout that has to be avoided by becoming visible, in some way or another, in spite of the 'invisibility' of their work with clients.

The second way in which the person-centred practitioner can contribute helpfully to the work of the medical-model representatives in a psychiatric hospital is as a 'helper for the helpers' and 'caretaker of the caretakers'.

---

2. Today I realise how lucky I have been to have this freedom granted to me by my managers all through my career. I mistakenly took that freedom for granted until it was withdrawn by a change of management, which resulted in my retirement and my deep feeling of gratitude to my previous managers (see Sommerbeck, 2012, 2015).

Nurses working in psychiatric wards, and particularly on locked psychiatric wards, are exposed to unusually high levels of emotional intensity and to unusually bewildering behaviours during almost the whole of their working day. Episodes with outbursts of violence, whether directed towards others, towards the person himself/herself, or towards material objects, are frequent, too. This is, of course, a constant strain and toll on nurses' own psychological resources, and the way they are exposed to, and must intervene with, various kinds and degrees of violence often has an impact on them that can best be described as traumatic.

It is important, therefore, that nurses themselves, as well as administrators, recognise that it is often not possible for them to process all these experiences on their own during a normally very busy working day. First, they simply haven't got the time to take care of themselves in the midst of taking care of the patients, and all that that entails. Second, they will normally all be so 'filled up' with their own experiences that they are unable to listen to each other very well. Planned 'time out' and an external facilitator are most often necessary to counter the risk of burnout among nurses, as well as the risk of high turnover of nursing staff, and the risk that nurses' behaviour will become rigidified into defensive routine strategies with the patients.

The approach of the client-centred therapist, non-directive, non-diagnostic and universally applicable as it is, is eminently suited to help psychiatric nurses 'survive' traumatic aspects of their work in a psychologically healthy way – namely, to learn from their experiences, rather than being harmed by them.

The client-centred therapist, therefore, can also contribute fruitfully to the representatives of the medical model by facilitating group debriefing sessions, and/or doing individual crisis therapy sessions with them. This work is not very different to ordinary client-centred therapy. The only difference, in my practice of it, is that I structure group sessions to make sure that everyone has time to talk and be listened to and understood, and I do not allow a short run of individual crisis sessions to turn into more long-term, personal therapy. This is partly because of my own time schedule, and partly because I do not wish to enter into a close, long-term therapy relationship with people whom I also meet every day as colleagues and, to a greater or lesser extent, as friends. Apart from a few crisis sessions, I would doubt my ability to consistently 'keep out of the client's way', if the client was a near colleague and/or friend of mine.

A third world

However helpful the principle of complementarity may be to dissolve many potential dilemmas of the client-centred therapist working in a medical-model setting, it is of paramount importance that the therapist has access to a 'third world': a world of his or her own. There must be at least one person with whom the therapist can talk freely about all of his or her experiences, from the therapist's own frame, with absolutely no risk to either the therapist's relationship with clients or to the therapist's relationship with medical-model colleagues. This person would ideally be another client-centred therapist who is knowledgeable about, or is working within, the medical-model setting. The therapist's need for somebody to pay attention to and try to understand his/her experiences from his/her own frame of reference has to be met frequently to counter feelings of isolation, with the concomitant risk of burnout. The ideal solution is a small peer consultation or supervision group that meets regularly. If this need is adequately met, all the difficulties listed above are more than compensated for by the richness, depth and diversity of the experience of working as a client-centred therapist in the medical-model setting, however much of a struggle this work also sometimes is.

The critique of psychiatry and the complementarity of client-centred therapy and the medical model

This chapter has dealt with one way for classical, non-directive client-centred therapists to work in psychiatric contexts with individual clients and individual representatives of the medical model without compromising the philosophy of client-centred therapy. In order to avoid any misunderstanding, it is important for me to stress that using the principle of complementarity between client-centred therapy and the medical model as a guideline for this work is *not* synonymous with an uncritical attitude towards, and acceptance of, the dominance of the medical-model perspective in psychiatry today. The chapter has been concerned with work with the unique client, and, at this individual level, the client-centred therapist is not an expert on what is best for his or her clients. This does not mean that the client-centred therapist cannot be an expert on what is best for 'the average client', or users of psychiatry in general. On this general level, I am extremely critical of the dominance of the medical model in the psychiatric establishment, and I voice this critique whenever the discussion is about 'the average user of psychiatry' and 'the average medical-model representative'. I do not, however, make the 'experts' mistake' (Sommerbeck, 2004) of confusing the perspective of the average and general with that of the unique and individual. If I confuse these two complementary perspectives by presenting myself to others (medical-model representatives, for example) as an expert on what is best for any individual client of mine, I would at best be self-contradictory and at worst hypocritical. In either case, I would betray the essence of client-centred therapy: the non-directive, non-expert, non-authoritarian empathic accompaniment of the client that maximally reduces the risk of conveying conditional regard to the client.

Conclusion

The chapter has been exclusively concerned with work with individual and unique clients and medical-model representatives. Other chapters in this book, and many other books and papers, are concerned with 'the average user of psychiatry' or users of psychiatry in general, and 'the average medical-model representative' or the psychiatric system. They express a critique of the dominance of the medical model in the psychiatric establishment with which I heartily agree. My own ambition in this chapter has been to point to a way in which the non-directive, classical client-centred therapist can work in 'the lion's den' (Sanders, Chapter 2, this volume) without compromising the therapist's non-authoritarian attitude towards the client or, to stay with this apt metaphor, towards 'the lion's prey'. Perhaps the better choice would be to engage more directly in saving the prey from the lion, but that question belongs to another, albeit very interesting, discussion. Indirectly, though, client-centred therapy does of course, by supporting their own organismic valuing process, enable clients to oppose more effectively any kind of authoritarianism, including, if they so wish, the authoritarianism of psychiatry. That is the whole point of client-centred therapy.

References

Bozarth J (1990). The essence of client-centered therapy. In: Lietaer G, Robarts J, Van Baleen R (eds). *Client-Centered and Experiential Psychotherapy in the Nineties*. Leuven: Leuven University Press (pp59–64).

Dilthey W (1894/1957). Ideen über eine beschreibende und zergliedernde Psychologie. In: Misch G (ed). *Gesammelte Schriften V*. Stuttgart: BG Teubner (pp138–240).

Mearns D (1994). *Developing Person-Centred Counselling*. London: Sage Publications.

Rogers CR (1961). *On Becoming a Person*. London: Constable.

Sommerbeck L (2004). Non-linear dynamic systems and the non-directive attitude in client-centred therapy. *Person-Centered and Experiential Psychotherapies* 3: 291–299.

Sommerbeck L (2015). *Therapist Limits in Person-Centred Therapy*. Monmouth: PCCS Books.

Sommerbeck L (2012). Being non-directive in directive settings. *Person-Centered and Experiential Psychotherapies* 11(3): 173–190.

Additional recommended reading

About not being an expert on the client and the philosophy of client-centred therapy

Rogers C (1951). *Client-Centered Therapy* (Chapter 2). Boston: Houghton Mifflin.

About client-centred therapy in psychiatry

Sommerbeck L (2003). *The Client-Centred Therapist in Psychiatric Contexts: a therapists' guide to the psychiatric landscape and its inhabitants*. Ross-on-Wye: PCCS Books.

About the complementarity principle

Lindley D (1996). *Where Does the Weirdness Go?* New York: Basic Books.

Polkinghorne JC (1984). *The Quantum World*. Penguin Books.

8 | Assessment and 'diagnosis' in person-centred therapy

Paul Wilkins

This chapter explores the meaning and relevance of assessment and psychodiagnosis across the family of person-centred approaches to therapy, and explains the differences between them. The continuing debate about 'assessment' is rehearsed (by, for example, reference to the symposium on psychodiagnosis first published in *Person-Centered Review* in 1989), and also presented in a contemporary framework by considering the work of (for example) continental European person-centred practitioners, often in close alliance with healthcare professionals, and the ideas relating to 'person-centred psychopathology' advanced by, among others, Elke Lambers, Garry Prouty and Margaret Warner. It concludes by advancing, as a potential resolution to the debates and disagreements about assessment in the person-centred tradition, a person-centred model for assessment, drawing on classic client-centred principles.

The problem of assessment as diagnosis

'Assessment' has long been contentious in the context of person-centred therapy. For some practitioners, it immediately conjures up the ogre of 'diagnosis', which they believe an inappropriate adoption from medicine and therefore incompatible with person-centred theory and practice. Mearns (1997: 91) articulates this view:

> The whole question of client 'assessment' runs entirely counter to person-centred theory and fits those approaches to counselling which more closely align to the diagnostic 'medical model'. Within the person-centred domain the question of assessment is ridiculous: the assessor would have to make a judgement not only about the client but on the relational dimensions between the client and the counsellor.

It is assessment as a process of reaching a diagnosis and formulating a treatment plan to which Mearns objects. Such notions are antipathetic to person-centred therapy because they arise from the frame of reference and 'expertise' of the therapist, and may not reflect the experience and needs of the client.

Bozarth (1998: 127) agrees that 'psychological assessment as generally conceived is incongruent with the basic assumptions of client-centered theory', but (pp128–131) he also examines circumstances in which assessment may legitimately be part of person-centred therapy. He lists three situations (p128) in which tests may be used in person-centred therapy. These are:

- the client may ask to take tests
- the policies of the setting may demand that tests be given to clients
- testing might take place as an 'objective' way for the client and counsellor to consider a decision about action that is affected by institutional or societal demands.

Whatever the reason, the 'critical factor' (p131) is that of honouring the client's self-authority.

Writing about humanistic therapies in general, Stiles (2001: 609–610) reaches a different view from that exemplified by Mearns and Bozarth. He states:

> Placing people in categories is potentially dehumanizing… Diagnoses may induce a false sense of security, a feeling that one knows more about another person than one actually does. (p609)

Broadly speaking, this accords with the classic client-centred position (Sanders, 2000). However, Stiles goes on to argue not only that 'diagnostic categories need not be dehumanizing' but that:

> People who appear as depressed or as borderline or as schizophrenic may experience the world in distinctive ways that differ from their therapists' experience. Knowledge of a client's diagnosis, and the distinctive experiences it may entail, may thus help a therapist understand what the client is trying to say more quickly or more deeply. (p610)

Stiles also points out that 'delivering treatments that lack diagnosis-specific efficacy may be viewed by some people as unethical' (p610). Stiles' arguments are reflected in the various person-centred approaches to psychopathology, all of which necessarily involve assessment, if not diagnosis.

The very fact that clients may have different needs raises problems. How and by whom are these needs to be recognised? Once recognised, how should they be met? Is it reasonable to suppose that all clients require sessions of the same length, at the same frequency, and would different clients benefit from therapists responding in different ways (see Wilkins, 2003: 122–125)? How and by whom is the nature of a 'contract' to be determined in person-centred therapy (see Worrall, 1997: 65–75)? A consideration of all these things (and others) is essential to good practice and, arguably at least, this process of consideration is assessment. Among the various branches of the person-centred family of approaches to therapy, attitudes and solutions to these problems differ. This chapter is an exploration of these differences and culminates in a person-centred theory of assessment.

The multiplicity of views

Experiential psychotherapy and continental Europe

Mearns and Bozarth draw on classic client-centred theory (Sanders, 2000) for their arguments. Other practitioners from the broader person-centred family take different views. For example, Rennie (1998: 35), who is influenced by the experiential tradition, writes of 'the need for person-centred assessment' (but is clear that it is problematic in as much as it shifts the locus of attention from the client to the counsellor), and Speierer (1990, 1996) has developed a 'differential incongruence' model of assessment. He proposes that this provides a 'theory of general psychopathology and specific psychic disorders' compatible with person-centred theory (1996: 304). This allows diagnosis (p306) and 'practically useful options' (p307), according to the nature of the client's incongruence. Also within the 'continental European' tradition, Eckert and colleagues (2003: 10–13) report client-centred therapy research in the German language region 'that has increasingly become more disorder specific'. Their references to this research (see also 2003: 5) make extensive use of diagnostic categories, including 'depression', 'borderline personality disorders' and 'agoraphobia'. However, Berghofer (1996: 483–485), writing about the significance of diagnosing schizophrenia, concludes that 'a diagnostic exploration of the schizophrenic patient hinders the establishment of an authentic relationship' (p484). All this indicates differences within the family of person-centred therapies, or at least that the position with respect to assessment within the approach is complex.

Within the UK

In the context of the UK, recent thought on assessment in person-centred therapy distinguishes between that and 'psychodiagnosis'. For example, from within the approach, Tolan (2003: 135–136) takes the view that, while diagnosing a client (or being informed of the diagnosis of the client by another) is not helpful, 'some judgements must be made' (p135). These centre on the likelihood of establishing a therapeutic relationship and are as much to do with the qualities of the therapist as those of the client. Milner and O'Byrne, writing about assessment in counselling as a whole, conceptualise it as 'a growth map' in the context of the person-centred approach (2004: 120–134). They state that '[t]his approach is sceptical of diagnostic thinking and says it could be harmful' (p129). Like Tolan, Milner and O'Byrne indicate that the usefulness of assessment in person-centred therapy is as a process by which therapists monitor their ability to sustain an effective therapeutic relationship (pp131–132). This too is the view of Wilkins and Gill (2003: 184–185), who offer a 'person-centred theory of assessment' based on Rogers' (1957: 96, 1959: 213) 'necessary and sufficient conditions' (see below).

Resistance to and acceptance of the medical model

Although this chapter is concerned with assessment in the person-centred tradition as a whole, in the UK context, 'person-centred' is indicative of a distinctive approach to therapy. This approach is heavily influenced by the thought and work of Dave Mearns and Brian Thorne (particularly through the agency of their book of 1988 and its successors), but also by the fact that few of its practitioners have previous either psychological or medical training and by 'how far therapy in Britain has had its intrinsic assumptions defined by the psychodynamic lobby' (Dave Mearns, personal communication, 2003). These factors bring a particular attitude to assessment and diagnosis that is indicated in the research of Wilkins and Gill (2003: 180–184). For many person-centred practitioners in continental Europe, 'assessment' is not at all problematic. Here, the language of psychiatry and medicine seems to sit a lot more easily with person-centred practice than it does in either the UK or the US. For example, in the Netherlands, Hans Swildens is both a psychiatrist and a client-centred psychotherapist who has promoted the adaptation of client-centred therapy to more seriously disturbed clients. In his keynote address to the 2003 conference of the World Association for Person-Centered and Experiential Psychotherapy and Counseling (WAPCEPC), he makes free use of the languages of psychiatry, psychoanalysis, person-centred psychotherapy and process differentiation, moving easily between them (Swildens, 2004: 4–18). Implicit in his use of terms such as 'borderline', 'psychopathology' and 'self-pathology' is not only a role for assessment but also one for diagnosis. In Germany, Sachse considers his approach to be a development of person-centred psychotherapy and unambiguously declares:

> Disorder specificity implies that *developing a diagnosis* is needed as part of CCT. Diagnosis ensures that therapists adopt the best possible client-centered approach! It makes it possible to identify at the earliest stage what different clients need and to what they will respond. Therapists can use this information to act in the best possible client-centered way. Rejecting diagnostics in CCT is highly unreasonable. (2004: 27)

In making his statement, Sachse is moving a long way from what may be described as the classic client-centred position that diagnosis is unnecessary because there is only *one* treatment, regardless of the nature of the client and the 'problem' –

namely, to respond in a manner consistent with the therapist conditions of empathy, unconditional positive regard and congruence.

While Sachse and Swildens may not be wholly representative of continental European thought on the matter of assessment and diagnosis in person-centred therapy, it seems likely that their views are indicative of a prevailing cultural difference with respect to the UK. Why else, when I spoke of the problem of assessment in person-centred therapy at the 2003 conference of the WAPCEPC, was I met with puzzled looks by (for example) the German and Dutch members of my audience? It was not until Elke Lambers made a useful intervention explaining that what I saw as a fundamental problem with respect to client-centred theory was no problem at all to many continental Europeans, for whom assessment was an everyday part of practice, that I recognised the difference in attitude and approach.

Diagnosis as a process

It would be mistaken to believe that all continental European person-centred practitioners are comfortable with schemes of assessment and diagnosis that in some way echo or mirror those of psychiatry. For example, the Austrian philosopher-scholar and person-centred therapist Peter Schmid (2004: 47) makes an argument for diagnosis as integral to person-centred therapy. He is clear that he is not writing of a system based on client symptoms and the aetiology of mental ill health but, rather, that 'diagnosis is the hard work of the client'. He states:

> [F]rom *a person-centered* point of view psychological diagnosis can only be a phenomenological process diagnosis, unfolded step by step through the joint process of experiencing and reflecting by both client and therapist. Just as therapy does, diagnosis needs both modes and requires both persons involved in the relationship, thus making it a *co-diagnosis process* (original italics).

Although I understand that there are other meanings and a multiplicity of views (see above), this chapter is principally concerned with assessment as a process via which the suitability and viability of person-centred therapy as a helpful intervention may be determined and which involves both therapist and client as assessors. In this sense, assessment is a process of negotiation and of addressing the questions arising from this negotiation. The emphasis is on the potential therapeutic relationship, rather than on diagnosis. The main area where a different approach to assessment may be applied is that of 'deeper disturbance'. This is touched upon here, and also in the chapter addressing person-centred theory and psychopathology. Also, my emphasis is, for the most part, on the situation in the UK – but I believe that the issues raised here are fundamental to client-centred theory.

Person-centred assessment in context

Perhaps there is an assumption on the part of person-centred therapists that therapists of other orientations, for whom assessment is a necessity dictated by theory, 'do' something to the client that is radically different from what happens in person-centred therapy of any stripe. But the experience and research of Wilkins and Gill (2003: 180–184) indicates that, for example, practitioners of psychodynamic therapies do not differ fundamentally from person-centred practitioners in their attitudes to and practice with their clients in the early stages of therapy.

Criticisms from other perspectives

Just as we (person-centred therapists) make assumptions about therapists who draw on traditions different from our own, so do they, sometimes, with respect to us. It is not uncommon to find that the reluctance of person-centred therapists to 'assess' their clients is looked on with misgiving. To some, it smacks of an irresponsible and slapdash attitude that does clients a great disservice. For example, Wheeler (in Wheeler & McLeod 1995: 286) expresses a 'serious reservation' that person-centred theory (or rather its lack of theory, in her view) leads to a 'subsequent disregard for assessment'. To us, the absence of a rationale for assessment is rooted in theory and practice, and our reasons are so obvious they do not need to be stated. To others, we demonstrate neglect and naïveté bordering on irresponsibility.

On the one hand, it may be sufficient to dismiss such criticisms as bogus, because the fundamental premise of client-centred therapy is different from that of other approaches; but, on the other, this does nothing for mutual understanding. It is not that we have a disregard for assessment, but that we have a different set of theories and procedures that take the place of the more conventional approaches (see Tudor & Merry, 2002: 115). However, person-centred therapy is subject to criticism because (in some eyes) it is seen to lack a theory of assessment and nor are its practitioners adequately prepared in their training to assess clients. For those who believe in the value of dialogue and understanding within the person-centred family and with practitioners of other approaches and disciplines, a clear statement of person-centred theory with respect to assessment is likely to be helpful.

Rebuttals

It is a mistake to believe that there is total opposition to assessment and diagnosis among person-centred theorists and practitioners. Its usefulness has been recognised from the earliest days – although this usefulness is not of the conventionally perceived kind. For example, Rogers (1957: 101–102), while 'forced to the conclusion that diagnostic knowledge is not essential to psychotherapy', goes on to point out that the one useful function diagnosis seems to have is to make some therapists feel secure in the relationship with the client, and thus (p102) 'the security they perceive in diagnostic information may be a basis for permitting them to be integrated in the relationship'. Berghofer (1996: 484) also draws attention to this factor, as do Binder and Binder (1991: 34). Schmid (1992: 112) states that 'differential classification of suffering' is justified when it leads to higher empathy and congruence by the therapist. The argument made by these authors is that knowledge of how clients are likely to behave and experience the world should not be understood as an explanation, still less as an instruction or prescription to the therapist, but rather as an aid to understanding and consequent action.

The challenge to a conventional view

Person-centred theory challenges the conventional view of assessment. As Tudor and Merry (2002: 5) indicate, there are person-centred theories 'which help to describe (rather than *prescribe* for) the client' and that are consistent with client autonomy and self-authority. It is incumbent upon person-centred therapists to clarify their theoretical and practical position with respect to assessment. We do have one, we can explain it – we do ourselves no favours by hiding our light under a bushel.

A historical perspective

The disregard for assessment

Literature on assessment is relatively rare in the classic client-centred canon, and is not much more prominent in the experiential and process-oriented literature. With the exception of Rogers (1951), a survey of major works of Rogers and his anthologisers indicates that assessment does not merit an entry in the indices. A consideration of assessment is similarly absent from Barrett-Lennard's (1998) comprehensive survey and from the widely read works of Mearns and Thorne (1988, 1999, 2000). This is indicative of the perceived irrelevance of assessment to person-centred theory and practice. Rogers (1946: 421) remarked that 'diagnostic skill is not necessary for good therapy', and this is probably a view held by a majority of person-centred practitioners to this day, and is understood by many to mean that assessment is unnecessary – even contraindicated.

Rogers' rationale for diagnosis

In his early definitive work, Rogers (1951: 221–3) does refer to 'the client-centered rationale for diagnosis'. This rationale clearly puts the client and the client's experience at the heart of the process – in fact, Rogers (p223) says it is really a rationale for psychotherapy without external diagnosis – that is, the psychotherapy does not result from some assessment of the 'problem' by the therapist. Rogers' scheme is based on the following propositions:

- behaviour is caused, and the psychological cause of behaviour is a certain perception or a way of perceiving. The client is the only one who has the potentiality of knowing fully the dynamics of his perceptions and his behaviours

- in order for behaviour to change, a change in perception must be experienced. Intellectual knowledge cannot substitute for this

- the constructive forces that bring about altered perception, reorganisation and relearning reside primarily in the client, and probably cannot come from outside

- therapy is basically the experiencing of inadequacies in old ways of perceiving, the experiencing of new and adequate perceptions, and the recognition of significant relationships between perceptions

- in a very meaningful and accurate sense, therapy is diagnosis, and this diagnosis is a process that goes on in the experience of the client, rather than in the intellect of the clinician.

Interestingly, Rogers immediately (pp223–225) follows his rationale with 'certain objections to psychological diagnosis'. Patterson (1948/2000: 3–9) had previously considered the question 'Is psychotherapy dependent upon diagnosis?' and reached the conclusion that it was not. Having outlined a theory of behaviour and examined the principles and practices of psychotherapy, he is led to the conclusion that, given the motivation to change or grow: 'For therapeutic purposes all that is necessary is that the patient come for help and be in sufficient contact to be able to verbalize his behavior and attitudes and feelings' (p8).

The 1989 symposium on psychodiagnosis

Although, until recently, assessment has been largely neglected by person-centred theoreticians, some attention had been paid to diagnosis – most notably in the form of a 'Symposium on Psychodiagnosis' published in *Person-Centered Review* in 1989. This symposium comprised a paper by Angelo Boy, to which Julius Seeman, John Shlien, Constance Fischer and David Cain responded (see Cain, 2002: 385–414 for reprints of these papers). Although I take the view that 'psychodiagnosis' and 'assessment' are different processes, with different ends, and it is the conflation of these terms that causes some of the heated opposition to assessment, it is worth briefly considering this debate.

Boy (in Cain, 2002: 385–396) offers a historical perspective on psychodiagnosis, examines its purpose and tools, and considers the relevance of the *Diagnostic and Statistical Manual* of the American Psychiatric Association (the third edition, *DSM-III*; the current version is *DSM-5*) to the practice of psychotherapy. Boy points out that the concept of psychodiagnosis emerges from the medical model and has at its heart the categorising of 'patient symptoms', which can then be summarised by a diagnostic label. He argues that it is pressure from those who are funding the provision of psychotherapy that influences the use of psychodiagnosis, and that psychiatry and psychoanalysis dictate its form.

Boy (in Cain, 2002: 387–388) is critical of the tools and methodology of psychodiagnosis, pointing out, for example, that it ignores the cultural and social influences on the client, and that its procedures fall short of the scientific standards of medicine *per se* and that, therefore, the objectivity claimed for it is spurious. Furthermore, traditional psychodiagnosis ignores the internal frame of reference of the client, in spite of the fact that, '[f]or nearly half a century Rogers… presented evidence that the only accurate and reliable viewpoint for understanding a client is from the client's internal frame of reference' (p388).

Boy goes on to explain his view that the case for psychodiagnosis is unproved and that the (then) existing schemes for the classification of 'disorders' are questionable. From a person-centred perspective, he does not see an objection in principle to 'the development of a broad classification system for categorizing human behavior' (p394), but argues that this system must be rooted in very different criteria from those used in, for example, *DSM-III*. Boy refers to Rogers' (1951: 221–223) client-centred rationale for diagnosis as one that could be of value.

Seeman (in Cain, 2002: 397–399) responds to Boy by outlining four aspects of psychodiagnosis:

- the value aspects of psychodiagnosis
- the technical validity of diagnostic tests
- the human judgments surrounding psychodiagnosis
- the positive function served by psychodiagnosis.

Seeman broadly agrees with Boy about the value of psychodiagnosis, suggesting that thinking *about* a person, rather than *with* a person, creates a split between client and therapist and establishes a 'one-up one-down hierarchy' (p397) inimical to person-centred therapy. Seeman regards Boy's arguments about the technical validity of psychodiagnosis as irrelevant, because psychodiagnosis has no role in person-centred therapy, but he does agree that psychological testing may sometimes offer other benefits. In considering the role of human judgment in diagnostic procedures, Seeman again agrees with Boy that there is a likelihood of error, and strengthens this argument by reference to the literature. Finally, Seeman expresses limited support for psychodiagnosis. He believes that people are comprised of complex, interlocking subsystems, 'biochemical, physiological, perceptual, cognitive, interpersonal' (p398), and that therapists have access to some subsystems but not others. It may be that the stresses on the system as a whole are located elsewhere in the hierarchy of subsystems, where therapists do not have access. Seeman sees that, for example, neuropsychological testing may indicate the advisability of interventions other than psychotherapy. He concludes with these words:

> [P]sychodiagnosis is irrelevant to the internal process of client-centered therapy [but] there are occasions when referral for psychodiagnosis is part of our ethical/professional responsibility. (p399)

Shlien (in Cain, 2002: 400–402) argues strongly against psychodiagnosis and, while he broadly agrees with Boy, clearly thinks Boy was too accommodating and conciliatory in his views. Shlien (pp401–402) states that Rogers 'did not really' develop a rationale for diagnosis, and that he was mistaken to use this description. Shlien concedes that psychodiagnosis makes some sense in some approaches to psychotherapy, but sees it as having no role in person-centred therapy. He writes (p402):

> [C]lient-centered therapy has only one treatment for *all* cases. That fact makes diagnosis entirely useless. If you have no specific treatment to relate to it, what possible purpose could there be to specific diagnosis? Nothing remains but the detrimental effects.
>   Then, diagnosis is not good, not even neutral, but bad.

Fischer (in Cain, 2002: 403–407) accepts the long-standing criticisms of psychodiagnosis but argues that 'nevertheless all therapy should be planned in accordance with assessment of the client's circumstances' (p403). She apparently has a different attitude to the first three contributors, *but* uses different language: she refers to assessment, not psychodiagnosis, and she writes of the client's circumstances, not the client *per se*, still less some assumed psychopathological category to which the client may be assigned.

Fischer (p404) argues that assessment is necessary to the practice of psychotherapy. She gives examples from clinical practice and (p405) states, 'in these cases, my familiarity with life patterns of disordered living allowed for planning that saved clients unnecessary anguish and effort'. Fischer is advocating 'life-oriented assessment'. She writes:

> Life-oriented assessment addresses the person going about his or her life. Test scores, diagnostic categories, theoretical constructs, and other nomothetic devices are derived notions to be used as tools to understand the person's circumstances. The tools should not be confused with the results. (p405)

And later:

> In short, life-centered diagnostics serves the client's interests. It empowers the client by recognizing personal agency and by exploiting positive possibility. It respects the ambiguity and intersubjectivity that are inherent to human understanding. Emphasis on life context alerts clients and others involved in the assessment to the larger contexts of comportment, and to our responsibilities for grappling with systems as well as with individuals. (p407)

Then, last, Cain (in Cain, 2002: 408–414) responds to Boy. His first assumption is that what clients learn about themselves is more important than what a diagnostician learns in an assessment process. If the purpose of diagnosis is to facilitate the process of 'knowing the self', then, argues Cain (p408), it is compatible with person-centred theory and practice. He establishes his argument with reference to the advantages and disadvantages of three approaches to diagnosis: mechanical, prescriptive and collaborative. The first two of these are 'expert-centred', and thus of limited use in the context of person-centred therapy; the latter is centred on the client and promotes self-knowledge. Cain (p413) outlines a collaborative approach to diagnosis, which can be summarised as follows.

Collaborative practitioners:

- view their clients holistically, realising that psychological, biological and sociocultural aspects of the person are interrelated. Focus is on the whole experience of the client – that is, as much on what is 'right' as what is 'wrong'
- take a phenomenological approach to their clients. Observation of immediate experience is of greater importance than explanation
- are more interested in enabling their clients to engage in an ongoing process of self-diagnosis, rather than limiting themselves to understanding a problem in isolation.

Cain also states:

> A major strength of the collaborative approach is that it helps create in clients a new consciousness about the significant and crucial role they can play in determining the nature and quality of care afforded them. It enables them to realize that they are the best judge of their needs... and that they can learn to take more charge of and influence the course of their lives... (p413)

In summary, the 1989 symposium represents three main views of psychodiagnosis. First, that psychodiagnosis is irrelevant to person-centred therapy and may actually be 'bad'. Second, there is a 'Yes, but...' position, in which the problems associated with psychodiagnosis are acknowledged, but there is also an acceptance that diagnosis and assessment are realities in the world of psychotherapy and perhaps person-centred practitioners should take this into account – and maybe, too, under some conditions, for some clients, some of the time, psychodiagnosis can be useful. This is also the view expressed by Bozarth (1998: 128–131, see above). Third, there is the notion that, if assessment focuses on the client and the client's self-knowledge, then not only is it compatible with person-centred theory, but it is also an advantage to the practice of person-centred therapy.

The contemporary view(s)

In terms of classic client-centred therapy, the situation was and remains very much as stated by Shlien (above). Assessment (for which read 'diagnosis') is pointless because, whatever and however the client presents, all that is required of therapists is that they adhere to the three therapist conditions of congruence, empathy and unconditional positive regard (conditions 3, 4, and 5 of Rogers' original six), and behave accordingly. Adherents of newer approaches in the person-centred family may take different views. For example, Lietaer (2001: 98–101), who is an experiential psychotherapist, refers to the role of 'confrontation' in his approach, and how this involves therapists in responding from their own frames of reference. He (p100) acknowledges 'the importance of timing' in making such interventions. This implies an assessment of the client's process and the client/therapist relationship.

Recently attempts have been made to frame person-centred theory and practice in terms of deeper disturbance or psychopathology (see Wilkins, Chapter 3, this volume). The very existence of 'person-centred psychopathology' suggests that, at least sometimes, it is helpful to know something about a person's way of being in the world, and that responsible therapist behaviour must take account of it. For some practitioners, this means behaving differently with clients manifesting different 'symptoms', by either adding to classic client-centred therapist behaviours or giving them a different emphasis. To decide on a particular approach for a particular client involves reaching some conclusions about the client from the therapist's frame of reference. This is diagnosis, or something very close to it.

Assessment and psychopathology

Although, at least from the perspective of classical client-centred therapy and the British school of person-centred therapy, there has been a general agreement that diagnosis and assessment have little, if any, relevance to person-centred therapy, there is an increasing acceptance among person-centred practitioners that the concept of psychopathology does have relevance (see Lambers, 1994: 105–120; Wilkins, 2003: 105–107). There is an apparent contradiction here, for how is it possible to conclude that a client is 'psychopathological' without making an assessment and/or diagnosis? The argument seems to be that, because different criteria from those of psychiatric/psychoanalytical models are used, and these are consistent with person-centred theory, the process and ends are also different. But what are these criteria?

Person-centred approaches to understanding mental ill health

Tudor and Merry (2002: 115) recognise three strands in the person-centred approach to understanding mental ill health. These are pre-therapy (Prouty, 1990), expansions and developments of the concept of incongruence (see Speierer, 1990; Biermann-Ratjen, 1998), and identifying styles of processing (Warner, 2000). These, and other person-centred theorists and practitioners who address 'psychopathology', base their ideas in person-centred theory.

Prouty defines pre-therapy as:

a theory and method that postulates psychological contact as the necessary
pre-condition of a psychotherapeutic relationship for contact-impaired clients,
such as clients with mental disability or chronic schizophrenia. (2001: 590–591)

He takes the view that, until the first of Rogers' necessary and sufficient conditions is met, there can be no effective person-centred therapy. Furthermore, there are groups of people who may, among other things, be distinguished as 'severely contact-impaired' (Van Werde, 1994: 121). For effective person-centred therapy to take place, absence of contact must be recognised and addressed. This clearly involves an assessment ('Are this client and I in psychological contact?') and a 'treatment' – pre-therapy. Prouty and other pre-therapists also use a language of diagnosis. For example, in his list of people for whom pre-therapy has been 'documented and applied', Van Werde (1994: 121) refers to 'dual-diagnosed mentally retarded populations', 'acute psychosis', 'chronic schizophrenics' and 'people with multiple personality'. Prouty's method of pre-therapy also involves ongoing assessment of a kind, because part of the method is to repeat what seems to work.

Speierer (1990, 1996) and Biermann-Ratjen (1998) both base their approaches to 'illness' on incongruence. Speierer (1996: 299) states, 'incongruence is the central construct of the client-centered illness concept'. Biermann-Ratjen (1998: 125) makes a similar statement:

Client-centred therapists regard different psychogenic illnesses as different
ways of experiencing different kinds of incongruence, or as different signs
of different efforts to defend oneself against self-experience which is
incompatible with the self-concept and therefore seems inimical.

In both cases, it would seem that the therapist may be called upon to make a judgment as to the client's incongruence. Partly, this may be a matter of definition: the second of Rogers' conditions requires that the client is incongruent and that this incongruence manifests as anxiety or vulnerability. However, Speierer (1996: 300) makes a claim that 'neurotic disorders, personality disorders and psychotic disorders differ from each other due to differences in the presence or absence of conscious incongruence', and Biermann-Ratjen (1998: 126) considers that 'any symptom of psychogenic illness is the expression of experiencing incongruence'. In both cases, some judgment as to the nature and/or manifestation of the client's incongruence is made by the therapist. This is assessment. Speierer (1990) goes further and offers a scheme for diagnosis and differential treatment, thus moving away from the classic client-centred position of 'one size fits all'.

Warner bases her ideas on the idea that, while processing experience is a fundamental aspect of human nature, 'many clients do not find that processing experience in the context of a therapeutic relationship proceeds smoothly or naturally' (Warner, 2001: 181). Such clients Warner views as having 'difficult processes', and she has described three types of such processes: fragile process, dissociated process and psychotic process. Brief accounts of these can be found in Warner (2001: 182–183; see also Warner, Chapter 6, this volume). In Warner's view, it is important that person-centred therapists recognise different difficult processes and respond accordingly. She writes (2001: 184):

> While client-centered therapy works well, engaging in difficult process requires courage and endurance on the part of the client. To sustain this effort, clients typically need relatively high levels of psychological contact from their therapists, a willingness to meet them at 'relational depth'... While each client is unique, I think that some general sorts of understanding about difficult process can be helpful to developing and maintaining process-sensitive empathy.

Implicit in this is a requirement for assessment rather than diagnosis, because people can and do shift in and out of difficult process and are not necessarily confined to one. The question to be asked is, 'At this time, does my client appear to be experiencing a difficult process?' If so, the required response is to tailor attention and therapist responses accordingly. What is important here is that the emphasis is on the current client experience, not on labelling the client once and for all as 'fragile', 'dissociated' or 'psychotic', and that the awareness of difficult process allows the therapist to respond in a way that can be received and understood by the client. Thus, Warner offers a response to the issue raised by Stiles (2001: 610 – see above): that knowledge of a client's distinctive experience leads to quicker, deeper understanding.

A person-centred theory of assessment

The legitimacy of assessment

Assessment, although probably not diagnosis in the clinical sense, does have a legitimate place in person-centred therapy. The evidence above demonstrates how practitioners take account of this when working with clients for whom establishing and maintaining a relationship that incorporates the necessary and sufficient conditions is problematic, and adapt accordingly. Also, it seems that 'assessment' may be part of the everyday experience of person-centred practitioners, even though they resist the term (see Wilkins & Gill, 2003: 180). As a result of our research, we (Wilkins & Gill, 2003: 184) found that:

> When meeting a new client... person-centred therapists engage in a process concerned with establishing whether the therapist and client can and will build an effective therapeutic relationship (as defined by Rogers, 1957, 1959).

This process can legitimately be called 'assessment', but it does not of itself constitute diagnosis. Diagnosis is a possible product of assessment, but it is not the only one, and nor is it a necessary one. Assessment may be thought of as a process by which therapists reach some conclusion as to the possibility or likelihood of effective working. In most models, diagnosis involves categorising the client according to a set of criteria arising from theory. Attempts to establish diagnostic categories in person-centred work centre on the client's experience and are framed in terms of contact, incongruence or experiencing. These are not universally accepted as 'client-centred'. However, at least from a person-centred perspective, assessment (as suggested by Fischer, in Cain, 2000; Worrall, 1997; and the research of Wilkins & Gill, 2003) appears to be of the relationship/potential relationship, not of the individual in the client role.

Since the first edition of this book, it is probably true to say that the use of assessment processes has become more commonplace in person-centred therapy, often because practitioners are required by employers to use psychometric tests to assess outcomes, or as part of research studies into the effectiveness of person-centred therapy. More often than not, such tests are ones that assess psychopathological conditions of depression, anxiety, or other psychiatrically defined states. Recognition of the pressures on therapists to introduce tests into their work has led to the proposal that, if tests are to be used, the person-centred community should play a more active role in choosing the types of tests. Person-centred theory hypothesises that clients are in the process of becoming more congruent and more fully functioning. As such, tests that assess concepts consistent with person-centred theory and that capture positive change in wellbeing, flourishing and authenticity are to be recommended, in preference to, or alongside, medical-model, symptom-based measures (Joseph, 2015; see also Patterson, Chapter 26, this volume).

The necessary and sufficient conditions as criteria for assessment

It does not take much thought to realise that person-centred theory has contained a statement of an assessment process since at least 1957. This 'theory of assessment' centres on features of the relationship between client and therapist, and not on the client alone. Rogers' (1957: 96, 1959: 213) necessary and sufficient conditions may be understood as a series of questions a responsible therapist must ask at the beginning of (and throughout) the therapeutic endeavour, as follows.

1. Are my potential client and I capable of establishing and maintaining contact? (For some, contact is assumed as an inevitable consequence of mutual presence; for others, some other qualities are necessary.)

2. Is my potential client in need of *and* able to make use of therapy? – ie. is the potential client in a state of incongruence and vulnerable or anxious? (Wilkins and Bozarth (2001: ix) speculate that it may be possible to be incongruent and yet not vulnerable and anxious. This may be so when, for example, a potential

client is referred by a third party without awareness of the nature of therapy. In this way condition 2 would not be met and therapy is contraindicated.)

3. Can I be congruent in the relationship with the potential client?

4. Can I experience unconditional positive regard for this potential client?

5. Can I experience an empathic understanding of the potential client's internal frame of reference?

6. Will the potential client perceive, at least to a minimal degree, my unconditional positive regard and my empathy?

If the answer to one or more of these questions is 'No', and the 'necessity' is not met by definition, therapeutic change will not occur. Making this judgment (which may very well be much more about the therapist's abilities and limitations than about the client) is an assessment. It is easy to see how pre-therapy fits into this scheme, because it is so evidently based on the need for contact. Warner's difficult process model, although based on classic client-centred ways of responding, seems to revolve around making a judgment about the likelihood that the client will perceive the therapist's empathy and unconditional positive regard, so it also fits. Perhaps the incongruence models are more problematic because the necessary and sufficient conditions do not include a consideration of a variety of manifestations of incongruence (apart from anxiety or vulnerability). However, in other ways person-centred theory does allow for different kinds of incongruence – the defence mechanisms of distortion and denial are an example.

The seven stages of process

The seven stages of process (Rogers, 1961: 132–155) may also be understood as relating to assessment, in as much as they indicate something about the client's likely way of being, and so what is appropriate from the therapist. These stages represent (p132) 'a continuum of personality change' and, although Merry (2002: 59) points out that there 'is a great deal of variation and individual differences in clients' processes', and Rogers (1961: 139) reminds us 'that a person is never wholly at one or another stage of the process' – or perhaps because of this – knowing something about a client's stage in the process continuum can inform the therapist and help in making appropriate ethical and professional decisions. Thus, people in the early stages of process (1 and 2) are unlikely to enter into counselling or, if they do, are unlikely to stay. Those at stage 3, the point at which Rogers (1961: 136) believed many people who seek therapy are, are likely to commit to a counselling contract and 'need to be fully accepted as they present themselves before moving deeper into stage 4' (Merry, 2002: 60). Rogers (1961: 139) expresses 'no doubt' that stages 4 and 5 'constitute much of psychotherapy as we know it', and (1961: 150) describes stage 6 as highly crucial. It is in this stage that irreversible constructive personality change is most likely to occur. Arguably, by stage 7 the need for the companionship of a therapist on the journey towards being fully functioning is over. Rogers (1961: 151) writes: 'This stage occurs as much outside the therapeutic relationship as in it, and is often reported, rather than experienced in the therapeutic hour.' So, in the seven stages of process, person-centred therapy has not only a guide to when and for whom therapy is appropriate, but an indication that different 'ways of being' by the therapist in the encounter suit different stages. Implicit in the scheme is that, for example, qualitative differences and differences of intent are required of the therapist dealing with a client in stage 3 than in stage 6. Reaching a judgment about all these things is assessment and requires appropriate action.

A person-centred rationale for assessment

Together, the necessary and sufficient conditions and the seven stages of process provide person-centred therapy with an assessment rationale for deciding the likelihood of establishing a successful therapeutic endeavour, for monitoring its progress, and, to a lesser extent, for determining the nature of therapist behaviour. This scheme is not only legitimate in terms of person-centred theory; it is also essential to good practice. In short, there is an answer to the criticism that person-centred therapists have a disregard for assessment: there is a theoretical model for assessment and an associated language to describe and communicate processes in person-centred terms, and the evidence from research and the literature reported here indicates that person-centred practitioners do conduct assessment.

Conclusion

Within the person-centred tradition, there are diverse views with respect to assessment. At the root of these lie differing attitudes to the legitimacy of diagnosis. The perceived problem of diagnosis is that it labels and fixes the client – the fear is that therapy becomes problem driven rather than client centred. On the other hand, diagnosis can be seen as helpful in that it allows the development of a mutual understanding between different healthcare professionals and disciplines, and because it enables the therapist's understanding of the client's process. Both of these concepts are essential to a person-centred psychopathology. For example, Warner's concept of client process allows for both correspondence to psychiatric ideas and the challenging of them, and knowledge of, for example, 'fragile process' may also be helpful to the therapist working with a client experiencing it.

No person-centred scheme of psychopathology is possible without a process of assessment. However, assessment is not inimical to person-centred theory. The radical challenge of a person-centred scheme of assessment is that it sets aside the notion of the therapist as an expert, able to reach a definitive conclusion as to the nature of the client's difficulties, and instead it concentrates on the likelihood of establishing a relationship in which the six necessary and sufficient conditions will be met. It also highlights the potential shortcomings of the therapist.

References

Barrett-Lennard GT (1998). *Carl Rogers' Helping System: journey and substance*. London: Sage.

Berghofer G (1996). Dealing with schizophrenia – a person-centered approach providing care to long-term patients in a supported residential service in Vienna. In: Hutterer R, Pawlowsky G, Schmid PF, Stipsits R (eds). *Client-Centered and Experiential Psychotherapy: a paradigm in motion*. Frankfurt-am-Main: Peter Lang (pp481–493).

Biermann-Ratjen EM (1998). Incongruence and psychopathology. In: Thorne B, Lambers E (eds). *Person-Centred Therapy: a European perspective*. London: Sage (pp119–130).

Binder U, Binder J (1991). *Studien zu einer Störungsspezifischen Klienzentrierten Psychotherapie*. Eschborn: Dietmar Klotz.

Bozarth JD (1998). *Person-Centered Therapy: a revolutionary paradigm*. Ross-on-Wye: PCCS Books.

Cain DJ (ed) (2002). *Classics in the Person-Centered Approach*. Ross-on-Wye: PCCS Books.

Eckert J, Höger D, Schwab R (2003). Developments and current state of the research in client-centered therapy in the German language region. *Person-Centered and Experiential Psychotherapies 2*: 3–18.

Hutterer R, Pawlowsky G, Schmid PF, Stipsits R (eds). *Client-Centered and Experiential Psychotherapy: a paradigm in motion*. Frankfurt-am-Main: Peter Lang.

Joseph S (2015). *Positive Therapy: building bridges between positive psychology and person-centred psychotherapy*. Hove: Routledge.

Lambers E (1994). The person-centred perspective on psychopathology: the neurotic client. In: Mearns D. *Developing Person-Centred Counselling*. London: Sage (pp103–108).

Lietaer G (2001). Unconditional acceptance and positive regard. In: Bozarth JD, Wilkins P (eds). *Rogers' Therapeutic Conditions: evolution, theory and practice. Vol. 3: Unconditional positive regard*. Ross-on-Wye: PCCS Books (pp88–108).

Mearns D (1997). *Person-Centred Counselling Training*. London: Sage.

Mearns D, Thorne B (1988). *Person-Centred Counselling in Action*. London: Sage.

Mearns D, Thorne B (1999). *Person-Centred Counselling in Action* (2nd ed). London: Sage.

Mearns D, Thorne B (2000). *Person-Centred Therapy Today: new frontiers in theory and practice*. London: Sage.

Merry T (2002). *Learning and Being in Person-Centred Counselling* (2nd ed). Ross-on-Wye: PCCS Books.

Milner J, O'Byrne P (2004). *Assessment in Counselling: theory, process and decision-making*. Basingstoke: Palgrave Macmillan.

Patterson CH (1948). Is psychotherapy dependent upon diagnosis? *American Psychologist 3*: 155–159. Reprinted in: Patterson CH (2000). *Understanding Psychotherapy: fifty years of client-centred theory and practice*. Ross-on-Wye: PCCS Books (pp3–9).

Prouty GF (1990). Pre-therapy: a theoretical evolution in person-centered/experiential psychotherapy of schizophrenia and retardation. In: Lietaer G, Rombauts J, Van Balen R (eds). *Client-Centered and Experiential Psychotherapy in the Nineties*. Leuven: Leuven University Press (pp645–658).

Prouty GF (2001). Humanistic therapy for people with schizophrenia. In: Cain DJ, Seeman J (eds). *Humanistic Psychotherapies: handbook of research and practice*. Washington, DC: American Psychological Association.

Rennie DL (1998). *Person-Centred Counselling: an experiential approach*. London: Sage.

Rogers CR (1946). Significant aspects of client-centered therapy. *American Psychologist 1*: 415–422.

Rogers CR (1951). *Client-Centered Therapy*. Boston: Houghton Mifflin.

Rogers CR (1957). The necessary and sufficient conditions of therapeutic personality change. *Journal of Consulting Psychology 21*: 95–103.

Rogers CR (1959). A theory of therapy, personality, and interpersonal relationships, as developed in the client-centered framework. In: Koch S (ed). *Psychology: a study of a science. Vol 3: Formulations of the person and the social context*. New York: McGraw-Hill (pp184–246).

Rogers CR (1961). *On Becoming a Person: a therapist's view of psychotherapy*. London: Constable.

Sachse R (2004). From client-centered to clarification-oriented psychotherapy. *Person-Centered and Experiential Psychotherapies 3*: 19–35.

Sanders P (2000). Mapping person-centred approaches to counselling and psychotherapy. *Person-Centred Practice 8*: 62–74.

Schmid PF (1992). Das Leiden. Herr Doktor, bin ich verrückt? Eine Theorie der leidenden Person statt einer 'Krankheitslehre'. In: Frenzel P, Schmid PF, Winkler M (eds). *Handbuch der Personzentrierten Psychotherapie*. Köln: Edition Humanistiche Psychologie (pp83–125).

Schmid PF (2004). Back to the client: a phenomenological approach to the process of understanding and diagnosis. *Person-Centered and Experiential Psychotherapies 3*: 36–51.

Speierer G-W (1990). Toward a specific illness concept of client-centered therapy. In: Lietaer G, Rombauts J, Van Balen R (eds). *Client-Centered and Experiential Psychotherapy in the Nineties*. Leuven: Leuven University Press (pp337–360).

Speierer G-W (1996). Client-centered therapy according to the Differential Incongruence Model (DIM). In: Hutterer R, Pawlowsky G, Schmid PF, Stipsits R (eds). *Client-Centered and Experiential Psychotherapy: a paradigm in motion*. Frankfurt-am-Main: Peter Lang (pp299–311).

Stiles WB (2001). Future directions in research on humanistic psychotherapy. In: Cain DJ, Seeman J (eds). *Humanistic Psychotherapies: handbook of research and practice*. Washington, DC: American Psychological Association (pp605–616).

Swildens H (2004). Self-pathology and postmodern humanity: challenges for person-centered psychotherapy. *Person-Centred and Experiential Psychotherapies 3*: 4–18.

Tolan J (2003). *Skills in Person-Centred Counselling and Psychotherapy*. London: Sage.

Tudor K, Merry T (2002). *A Dictionary of Person-Centred Psychology*. London: Whurr.

Van Werde D (1994). An introduction to client-centred pre-therapy. In: Mearns D. *Developing Person-Centred Counselling*. London: Sage (pp120–124).

Warner MS (2000). Person-centred therapy at the difficult edge: a developmentally based model of fragile and dissociated process. In: Mearns D, Thorne B. *Person-Centred Therapy Today: new frontiers in theory and practice*. London: Sage.

Warner MS (2001). Empathy, relational depth and difficult client process. In: Haugh S, Merry T (eds). *Rogers' Therapeutic Conditions: evolution, theory and practice. Vol. 2: Empathy*. Ross-on-Wye: PCCS Books (pp181–191).

Wheeler S, McLeod J (1995). Person-centred and psychodynamic counselling: a dialogue. *Counselling 6*: 283–287.

Wilkins P (2003). *Person-Centred Therapy in Focus*. London: Sage.

Wilkins P, Bozarth JD (2001). Introduction to volume 3: unconditional regard in context. In: Bozarth

JD, Wilkins P (eds). *Rogers' Therapeutic Conditions: evolution, theory and practice. Vol. 3: Unconditional positive regard*. Ross-on-Wye: PCCS Books (ppvii–xiv).

Wilkins P, Gill M (2003). Assessment in person-centered therapy. *Person-Centered and Experiential Psychotherapies 2*: 172–187.

Worrall M (1997). Contracting within the person-centred approach. In: Sills C (ed). *Contracts in Counselling*. London: Sage (pp65–75).

9 | The concept of evil as a key to the therapist's use of the self

Richard Worsley

Psychology from Sigmund Freud onwards has struggled to specify itself as a science, and hence 'respectable'. As such, it has striven for an objectivity that at times has bracketed out the subject and the subjective. Counselling and psychotherapy have shown greater ambivalence: science or art? The person-centred approach has a strong investment in seeing counselling as encounter, as personal. To the psychologist, psychiatrist and some therapists brought up within the medical model, or other models that strongly emphasise the objective and quantifiable, then to explore psychopathology from the category of personal reaction, and in particular the seemingly irrational, may feel like alien territory. I intend in this chapter to work from a debate about the nature of evil towards a position that the therapist is bound to respond with her whole self to the client, and thus be open to the client's pathology in all of its range of meanings. Indeed, it is about openness to the client's self in all of its facets; the word psychopathology itself can be objectifying of people.

In this chapter, I will examine the use of the concept of evil in person-centred debate since 1980; I will use the concept as a sign of the impact of client psychopathology upon the therapist, making particular reference to David Parkin's anthropological view of the concept. From there, I will describe the underlying category error that characterises some uses of the term evil, and will describe some of the underlying interpersonal mechanisms. A brief case study of Ruth then leads to the notion of renormalising the client's process; this I link to the work of Garry Prouty, Margaret Warner and Lisbeth Sommerbeck. The last of these in particular offers an eloquent plea to take seriously the impact of the client upon the therapist's internal world.

The theme and challenge of evil

Concern for the theme of evil has hovered at the edge of the person-centred approach over the years. Talk of evil is felt by many person-centred practitioners to be riddled with difficulties. What or who is evil? Is the word evil useable of a person at all? How does this sit with unconditional positive regard? The person-centred approach and the medical model seem at first sight to be in the same boat in abstaining from talk of evil. However, the existential therapist Rollo May challenged Carl Rogers, near the end of the latter's life, to reconsider evil and to acknowledge the tendency of person-centred therapists to miss a complete dimension of being human (May, 1982). The heart of the conflict between Rogers and May is Rogers' view that people are fundamentally constructive, however damaged they might be by their experience. By contrast, May puts forward the concept of the daimonic. This, he stresses, is not at all the same as the demonic, having nothing to do with dualism or non-human entities. Rather, May hypothesises that the constructive is very close to a destructive tendency in humans:

> The daimonic is the urge in every being to affirm itself, assert itself, perpetuate and increase itself… [the reverse side] of the same affirmation is what empowers our creativity. (May, 1969: 123)

For May, the constructive tendency in people is an assertion of self that, differently expressed, can be destructive. As a corollary of this argument, May challenges Rogers to see that in the latter's extensive work with hospitalised people with schizophrenia – the Wisconsin project (Barrett-Lennard, 1998: 68–69, 82–85, 267–273) – he and other person-centred therapists tended to miss this same destructive element in their clients.

Some 18 years later, the theme returned in person-centred literature in the form of a debate between Dave Mearns and Brian Thorne (2000, chapter 3). They agree that therapy requires a category of thought that can be termed 'spiritual' or 'existential'. (It is far from clear to me that these two concepts necessarily serve the same function.) However, behind them is a concern with the nature of evil. Dave Mearns rejects the use of the word evil, certainly of any human being, for to do so would be to declare all possibility of hope exhausted. By contrast, Brian Thorne takes a Christian mystical approach to the issue:

> It is the experience that such a transformation is possible and that person-centred therapists can embody such attitudes and behaviour towards their clients which underpins and authenticates what is, in effect, an evolutionary view of humankind. What is more, such an evolution takes place not by avoiding evil but by engaging with it and by disarming it through the power of relationship where spirit meets spirit, thus rendering evil both unnecessary and irrelevant. (Mearns & Thorne, 2000: 63)

Here, Brian Thorne accords a reality to evil that some would question. It is clear that he has taken up some aspects of May's challenge to Rogers. The question of evil is still important.

The impact of evil

The word evil is used with increasing frequency in a secular society, not least by the tabloid press. I was struck by the need of the press to mark out as evil the two boys who murdered the toddler Jamie Bulger, in 1993. The unimaginable had happened. It was two children who had murdered a third child. The impact of this as horror was patent. The underlying logic was frightening. Children must not murder children. (That is the role of adults?) When the unimaginable happens, then the offenders are simply removed from the realm of normal humanity. They become 'evil'. This manoeuvre itself leaves a nasty taste in the mouth. Society, it seemed, needed victims who were offenders, onto whom we could project our shame at our failure to maintain the innocence and inviolability of any of these three boys. The rhetoric of evil discomforts.

I have a personal and theological interest in the question of evil (Worsley, 1996). As such, I have been asked from time to time to present a session on the theme with counselling diploma students. The driving force of the question that led to this session tended to be the impact of considering client psychopathology. In the same way that the Jamie Bulger case labelled the offenders as 'evil' in the popular imagination, these students' encounter with psychopathology threw up the same strange concept. Indeed, I could resonate with their need to process something further. In 1987, I had a six-week encounter with a person labelled as a psychopath. I am still aware of the impact of him on me. I experienced a disturbance of my personal poise, and of my relationship with others – the latter stoked by an anxiety leading to aggression. I had met in this Other a version of humanity that I could scarce stomach.

Of course, I can own in retrospect a certain naïvety in my response to him, yet perhaps this response is more real, more open to experience, than is the self-protecting denial of that shudder under the shelter of objectivisation and 'science'. How then is this shudder to be processed? How is evil to be seen?

An anthropological view of evil

It is not my intention to reduce the notion of evil to the status of a psychological misunderstanding. I am happy to leave other sorts of debate about evil to philosophy, ethics and theology. However, I contend that, in using the word evil of some psychopathological phenomena, a category error is being made. Yet, it is not an error to be erased. It requires our full attention. It speaks.

In 1985, David Parkin edited a volume entitled *The Anthropology of Evil*. He pointed out that the term evil was a difficult one for anthropologists. They preferred terms that were incontestable. He gave as an example the term 'witchcraft'. Once this is defined as a behaviour, it becomes a mere social artefact to be explored. By contrast, 'evil' is a contestable concept. Its meaning is far from clear. It is used in different cultures in radically different ways. Yet, it serves a key function that ought not to be ignored. In his introduction to the book, Parkin describes his conceptualisation of evil thus:

> The main suggestions… are that evil refers to various ideas of imperfection and excess seen as destructive; but that these are contestable concepts which, when personified, allow mankind [sic] to engage them in dialogue and reflect on the boundaries of humanity. (Parkin, 1985: 23)

He points to the word 'evil' as representing a field of meanings that is particularly sensitive to cultural construction. This word is used – often through a process of personification – in order to assist us to navigate our acts of living through crises of value and human identity.

The process of personification seems a powerful one. I am struck by the prevalence of the notion of Satan in religious thinking, in spite of severe theological problems with it. Yet Satan is but one personification. Any difficult being can come to personify evil. Those offenders who become the subjects of tabloid vilification are but one example. I suggest that there are times that this process focuses upon bearers of particular psychopathologies. It is no coincidence that mental illness used to fall under the category of possession and, for a small number even in western culture, still does. The schizophrenic, seen as evil because violent, even murderous, serves the same psychological function for society as does the possessed in earlier times.

How does the use of the marker 'evil' function? Parkin points to imperfection and excess. This is rather restrained language. Much in life we can experience as deeply troubling. Often this centres on difference. The person with schizophrenia is different from me, to such a degree that I cannot understand who she is for me. Of course, in coming to know myself at depth, I come also to recognise those aspects of my own 'normal' experiencing that are tinged with the psychotic. This recognition then generates an existential anxiety, under the threat of meaninglessness or loss of self (Tillich, 1952: 41). This results in a splitting process in which the Other, the object, takes on the quality 'evil' in order that the perceived self may remain safe. This process has been thoroughly described by Menzies' (1970) landmark study of the behaviour of nurses in the face of their anxiety over illness, helplessness, meaninglessness and death. The patient – and already the word patient is a distancing and subduing word to use of another person – ceases to be human or dynamic, but becomes instead 'the liver in bed 10' or 'the pneumonia in bed 15' (Menzies, 1970: 12–13). No longer a person, but an organ or disease, the sick individual is less of a threat to the anxious carer. Where lies the sickness?

It would be remarkable if the psychologist, the psychiatrist, the psychotherapist or the counsellor were immune to this process. We are not. To be safe from the impact of anxiety, it must be faced, and not reduced to a pseudo-scientific commitment to objectivity. May and Thorne share at least this conviction. The ubiquitous concept of evil is a beginning point from which to take the subjective seriously.

Parkin argues that those things are labelled evil that embody a threat to our sense of our own being. It is in dealing with the experience of evil that the therapist can negotiate the truth about psychopathology. Before the question of hope can be dealt with, there must be a facing of the shudder, the sensation of encountering patterns that assail our own humanity.

Before moving on from the anthropological notion of evil, I want to acknowledge that some pathological structures evoke a question of evil in an ethical sense, and not just as a projection prompted by anxiety. I remember work with a woman, a deputy head teacher, whose mother carried a marked personality disorder. The mother was not the person she had been; nor, in the face of the agony of fear that dominated her life – a fear of being found out by a brutal father – was she able to find respite in madness. For mother and daughter, the suffering dragged over many years. The daughter strove to care, in the face of much adversity. Her heaviest burden turned out to be that she could not tell what the boundary was between her mother as ill and her mother as malign, manipulative, radically dishonest and wilfully treacherous. What sort of evil – projected or ethical? Even years of living with her mother could not disentangle the two.

Category error

The concept of evil has two significantly different denotations. The first is ontological. By this I mean that whatever is described as ontologically evil is, in and of itself, incapable of goodness – of being saved, to use Martin Buber's (1961: 200–205) category. Some strands of religious thought – but not my own – attribute ontological evil to non-human agency. Yet, it is deeply embedded within the person-centred approach that human beings ought not to be described as evil. For many practitioners, this is a matter of absolute, principled faith in human nature, and is described by some as a spiritual commitment (Purton, 1998). In this, the person-centred approach falls firmly within the more optimistic strand of Judaeo-Christian tradition that sees all creation as good. This chapter is not the place for further comment on the ontological meaning of evil.

The second, that expressed by Parkin (1985), is functional, and is crucial to our thinking about the impact of psychopathology. When something or someone is called evil, this is a naming. The focus is upon the need of the name-caller to separate herself off from the evil. (Such actions or propositions can also have an ontologically orientated truth-function, but that is simply a different matter.) Thus, when the killers of Jamie Bulger are called evil, something has to be exiled from human society, in order that society can maintain its humanity. But the question is, 'What?' If the killers are all that is to be disowned, then they are ontologically evil, and thus beyond hope. This is not a convincing version. Those who kill while they are children can be rehabilitated. Hope is not lost. Therefore, what is to be driven out of society like a scapegoat is the force and horror of our inability as a society to protect our own. It is part of us that is projected into the two offenders. The name-calling of evil serves a function.

However, this function can be healthy or sick. (I suspect that these two terms form a continuum, rather than a polarity.) If I describe the use of children for adult sexual pleasure as evil, I claim that this is a healthy use of the term. I note that it is absolutely and in principle unacceptable to have sex with children. In Parkin's terms, I deal with the murky issue of the paedophile's claim that sex with children is normal by exiling it from society. I exile the claim and the act, but not the person. I also note that I drive out into the desert like the scapegoat that part of me that could become addicted to the wholly unacceptable, and I struggle to recognise and accept that part of me is like that – open to corruption. However, to call Jamie Bulger's killers evil, even if humanly understandable, is unhealthy, because its sole function as name-calling is to disown and fail to take responsibility for that aspect of the murder that sits at all of our doors. A name-calling of evil can be used healthily or unhealthily. The unhealthy use is a category error. Child sexual abuse is evil because it is a behaviour and a belief-set that is to be excluded. The named is actually that which is to be exiled. With the boy-killers, it is not the named – the killers themselves – who are to be exiled as not-of-us. Rather, they become the screen upon which we project unfaceable elements of ourselves. It is this radical misattribution that constitutes the category error. Yet, the emotions of revulsion and anger are similar: what we feel does not mark out the healthy from the unhealthy.

It is my contention that the experiencing of some psychopathology as evil is a similar category error. The error manifests itself in many ways. The tabloid name-calling of the violent psychotic is a valid enough plea for public safety and increased mental health resources, but is wholly inappropriate in that it is projected onto the person with schizophrenia. This same sort of misattribution happens in the demonisation of Islam in the face of terrorism. When the medical model objectifies the psychotic and reduces her to her symptoms and behaviours, ignoring her inward experiencing, this is also a category error. The same happens when counselling students feel 'freaked' by their contemplation of the possibility of working with certain psychopathologies, for they fail to see the people behind the symptoms and behaviour.

Mental health practitioners must therefore know themselves well enough to spot the category error within themselves. The more exotic feelings around the person-as-evil are clear enough signals of personal work to be done. The depersonalisation of the client in the name of professionalism, the use of *DSM-5* (American Psychiatric Association, 2013) in place of human encounter, is less easy to spot.

Within the literature of psychotherapy, a number of ways of conceptualising this category error exist. I will outline some of these very briefly, before moving on to explore the insights of the person-centred approach into the re-personalisation of those who bear the traits often designated psychopathological.

Conceptualising the category error

The counselling students who wanted to think about evil, having experienced the 'shudder' in the face of human psychopathological patterns, are following up a category error. Some forms of distortion within the human personality or functionality feel just like evil, as it might be conceived ethically, existentially or theologically. At least they are aware of the disturbance within; the category error is useful. By contrast, those who exile the disturbed person by objectifying him or her in the name of the medical model seem often blissfully unaware of their own disturbed experiencing (Menzies, 1970).

I delight in the telling of a story that I found in Ronnie Laing's *Self and Others* (Laing, 1961: 106). I delight in the confusion it creates. A nurse offers a cup of tea to a chronically ill, catatonic person. On taking the cup, the person says: 'This is the first time in my life anyone has ever given me a cup of tea.' Most hearers struggle to escape the 'madness' of this. Surely nobody has gone through life without being given a cup of tea? Of course, the shift of frame of reference, of verbal emphasis, is crucial. The following concepts offer to me, however provisionally and speculatively, ways of engaging with the category error.

1. I and Thou

Martin Buber (1958) proposes that we engage with the world through the uttering of two primary words: I-Thou and I-It. Each precedes both ontologically and psychologically any notion of the separate self. We are created in relationship, but engage sometimes by seeing the other as radically like ourselves and at other times in an object-like way. I-Thou relating is marked by intimacy and mutuality, and offers to the other a confirmation of their being by affirming not only that which is actual within them but also their very potentialities. However, I-Thou relating is always prone to fall back into I-It relating. Buber notes that the 'bad' person is 'lightly touched by the holy, primary word' (Buber, 1958: 30). His way of thinking gives us the construct that, if the evil person declines to say 'Thou', the disturbed person can no longer find Thou. We are invited to a phenomenological description of the experience of, and an act of empathy towards, those who might be called mad.

2. Existential angst

Paul Tillich (1952) argues that, in order to have the courage to exist, we necessarily have to affirm ourselves in the face of that which limits our very being. For Tillich, threat comes as either relative or absolute, in three pairs corresponding to the categories – being, the spiritual, and the moral. His three pairs are fate and death; emptiness and meaninglessness; guilt and condemnation. The category error here is in mistaking the threat for the reality. Let us for a moment suppose that killing is evil in a moral or theological or ethical sense. In order for evil to be perpetrated, then the killing – or at least its serious contemplation – must take place. Yet, Tillich's point is that anxiety arises from the ongoing awareness of our own finitude:

> The anxiety of death is the permanent horizon within which the anxiety of fate is at work. (Tillich, 1952: 43)

In other words, the anxiety over our own finitude echoes whenever we meet versions of that finitude in others. Guilt, meaninglessness and fate all lead us back to our mortality. The anxiety of the client leads us to our own existential angst, and thus it is only too natural to feel and experience others' disturbance as, in some incoherent but powerful way, evil. We find the shudder and know it.

3. Projective identification

Throughout her life, Melanie Klein above any other developed the concept of projective identification as a description of one of the classic defences in which we all indulge (Klein, 1946, for example). Projection is simply the attributing of feelings or other experiencing to another, when it belongs to one's self. For instance, if I feel tired but cannot acknowledge that in the face of much work, I will tend to see tiredness in others, and react powerfully to it. Projective identification goes a step beyond this. The other experiences subliminal signalling that induces in them a required behaviour. In the face of some pathological patterns, this is a marked and difficult experience. In meeting in a pastoral context, the person whom I have most sincerely wanted to label as a psychopath, I felt an overwhelming sense of fear within seconds of our first exchange, as if being backed into a corner. The defensive structure of the other will evoke experiences in me. From time to time, these can be felt as invasive, threatening, malign. They are, however, mere defences! The category error is engaged. The psychopath is seen as evil.

4. The system is more than the sum of its contents

The life work of RD Laing was in challenging the medical model version of schizophrenia. In his 1964 book with Aaron Esterson, he explores through a number of interviews with families the possibility that schizophrenia is a manifestation in one member of a family of the dysfunction of the whole family unit. In other words, one individual has to become ill, like a scapegoat, to carry the dysfunction of the whole group. In some situations, the scapegoat is driven out into the desert of loneliness, meaninglessness and blame. They become 'evil'. It is easy for the therapist to collude with the system against the individual; once the phenomenon is uncovered, it is just as easy to reverse this splitting off by blaming the family instead. Complex systemic interactions multiply the category error.

5. Parallel process

The everyday supervision of counsellors provides a more banal example of the category error. In the classic supervision text, Hawkins and Shohet observe:

> In the mode of paralleling, the processes at work currently in the relationship between client and therapist are uncovered through how they are reflected in the relationship between therapist and supervisor. (Hawkins & Shohet, 1989: 68)

The parallel process is a major way of exploring those elements of the counselling relationship that seem not to be available to the direct awareness of either the supervisor or the therapist in the first instance. Typically, I may note that the supervisee is behaving in an unusual manner: is this how it is with the client? Yet, from time to time the parallel process will manifest itself in my awareness of my own feelings: I really do not like this client of yours! Of course, these feelings can be just about bad supervision: I want to rescue my supervisee from a tight corner by demonising the client. However, on other occasions, the important and revealing question is: How does my feeling real distaste for your client echo with how they are with you? My internal process temporarily consigns the client to the category 'evil' – or a weaker form of that, such as difficult-to-accept, or aggressive, or manipulative, or whatever. This is another version of the category error, but if I can be aware of it, it can put into the supervisory matrix useful information in the form of how the supervisee reacts to – owns or denies – my category error.

In short, there is a large number of theoretical concepts from different schools of therapy that can elucidate the category error by which certain structures or processes in the client are experienced – temporarily or otherwise – as evil. The whole point is that the therapist, in meeting the client at depth, needs to be aware of the impact of this category error. This is about personal development within the therapist: the developing of the need to contain and 'exorcise' the anxiety that is felt in the face of the client. The objectification of client symptoms has exactly the opposite effect to the desired one. The aim is to renormalise the client within the therapist's awareness, and thus within her own awareness.

Ruth

Ruth was a primary school deputy head from a local village. We worked together for nearly two years. She was 37 and single. Although very intelligent and an able and respected teacher, she experienced long-term depression and occasional self-harm and suicidal ideation. Her issues were from childhood – a deeply depressed and non-communicative mother, combined with some very painful bullying in secondary school. Yet, what seemed to haunt the early days of therapy for me was her self-presentation. On entering my workroom, she moved from being a crisply smart professional woman to being a six-year-old child. Her whole body language was that of late infancy. She twirled her hair, shuffled, yawned, squirmed in her seat, stretched out her hands, fiddled with her fingers and in every way undermined who she appeared to be.

More striking even than her behaviour was my embarrassed incongruence before it. It was the most powerful statement in the room, and yet I did not know how to get it back to her in a consumable form. One of us, perhaps both of us, had got me stuck. I was stuck with her stuckness at an early age. It was the very bizarreness of it that got in my way. It made me feel as if anything I might say to her that was honest would also be devastatingly hurtful.

In the end, the clue, the prod, the constructive moment came from her. She told me about doing an evening class in drama (which would be very helpful for her curriculum development work). She liked the drama teacher. She said that he teased her. There was a pregnant pause. Well, if he could, perhaps I could. If the therapist cannot be creative, then it must be up to the client. Ruth and I developed a whole dialogue about her experience of herself as 'odd'. Yes, in spite of the assumed behaviour of a competent professional, odd was how she felt – different, vulnerable, just not like anyone else. At last she had provided me with the elbowroom in which to empathise with this aspect of her – the little girl frozen before her mother's need and isolation. Her reaction, her self-concept was no longer 'odd', but rather just what she would have felt in the past, the distant past.

Ruth had managed to surround herself with a wall of others' incongruence. Her bizarre self-presentation expressed her self-experience. Others, like me, moved politely by on the other side and did not face up to what she screamed out. As the oddness-dialogue opened up, Ruth's whole way of being was normalised, not by her coming to conform straight away to more socially acceptable patterns, but by her seeing her current behaviour and emotional experience as normal. That is to say, she was not just different – as if ill – but, rather, she could work her way agonisingly towards acknowledging that, in some aspects, she had had an impossible life to live as a child. Emotional pressure at school could find no relief at home, where her prime carer was dominated by her own sense of neediness. There are many ways in which we might speak of the client becoming renormalised. It is a distortion to see this as a readjusting of the client. Rather, it is a change of relationship between the client and her environment.

Renormalisation

Renormalisation occurs in three matrices: the internal world of the client; the flow of communication between the client and others; the radical encounter within the therapist of the phenomena that the client presents. However, these three matrices are not functionally distinct. Change happens in complex ways.

Pre-therapy (Prouty, Van Werde & Pörtner, 2002) appears to address the communication process between the therapist and client in enabling psychological contact to happen. However, in so doing, this renormalises the internal world of the client. The client experiences through the concrete reflections of the therapist her location, her rootedness in her surroundings. Her internal world changes. Instead of imprisonment in the self, the possibility opens up of exploring the leading of an impossible life (Shlien,1961; Laing & Esterson,1964).

Yet, these changes have a massive impact upon the therapist, who becomes increasingly able to enter the client's frame of reference, not least in coming to experience the client's way of processing with deeper empathy (Worsley, 2002). Margaret Warner (2002) describes her work with Luke, a young man with a diagnosis of schizophrenia, as the learning of a new language before it became possible to understand Luke as if from within. She noted that he tended to be both over-exact and quite imprecise in his use of language. For example, when someone observed that Catholicism was 'going to the dogs', Luke, a Catholic, spent quite a while in self-observation so as to note how and when he would begin to metamorphose into a dog. From this, Warner develops her two key concepts of meta-facts and meta-causes.

> While meta-facts and meta-causes usually seem implausible as accounts of
> literal truth, they often work quite well as metaphors that serve as handles for
> his felt sense of the whole of his situation. (Warner, 2002: 463)

Why does Warner develop the notion of meta-facts and meta-causes? One feasible enough answer is that this contributes to her understanding of Luke's process. Yet, another version of this is to note that it gives Margaret Warner a handle on the therapeutic task of listening. In understanding Luke's process, she minimises the negative impact of that process upon her.

Lisbeth Sommerbeck (2003: 85) describes eloquently the effect of the psychotic client upon her. Because the client's talk is often fragmented and dissociated, then Sommerbeck notes that her literal empathic responses take on this quality too. She begins to experience the client's level of disturbance within her interventions. In working with manic clients, she reports that she will often cry out: 'Wait a minute! Let me see if I understand you...' It is as if the client's chaotic process has to be seized in order to be rendered bearable, and only then comprehensible, to the therapist. (Sommerbeck points out that this sense of immersion in chaotic process can occur at times with non-psychotic clients too.)

The point of this brief summary of the complex process of renormalisation is that it is a false defence to see the process as only happening either within the client or within the communication process. The therapist too must face the impact of the client upon her, and seek to ameliorate its effects through ongoing personal development.

It is no wonder that the category error sometimes occurs that causes us to experience some pathological patterns as evil – the shudder. It is at least better to use this series of defences than to drive the client out into the wilderness of the categories of the medical model misused. At the heart of work with challenging clients is the therapist's openness to facing who they are.

Conclusion

The rhetoric of evil is an important part of the internal discourse for the therapist concerning the impact on her of the whole of the client, including those aspects often referred to as psychopathological. The medical model reduces the role of the helper in contact with the client to that of the expert who keeps herself safe by distancing and objectifying the client's extreme and disturbing distress. Yet, it is a most valuable insight of the person-centred approach that what we term psychopathological in human beings is also the unique and undiagnosable response of a human being to her environment. When the therapist can remain open to the impact of the client upon her, she will be available to share in the journey towards renormalisation, and then integration and wholeness. To avoid the evil, however understandable, is to demonise the distressed person. The Other is forced to carry that which I cannot face. So much of the medicalisation of human distress is designed unconsciously to keep the medic safe, at the cost of the client's humanity.

References

American Psychiatric Association (2013). *Diagnostic and Statistical Manual of Mental Disorders* (5th ed) (*DSM-5*). Arlington, VA: American Psychiatric Association.

Barrett-Lennard GT (1998). *Carl Rogers' Helping System: journey and substance*. London: Sage.

Buber M (1958). *I and Thou*. Edinburgh: C & C Clark.

Buber M (1961). *Between Man and Man*. London: Collins.

Hawkins P, Shohet R (1989). *Supervision in the Helping Professions*. Milton Keynes: Open University Press.

Klein M (1946). Notes on some schizoid mechanisms. In: Klein M (ed) (1988). *Envy and Gratitude and Other Works 1946–1963*. London: Virago.

Laing RD (1961). *Self and Others*. Harmondsworth: Penguin.

Laing RD, Esterson, A (1964). *Sanity, Madness and the Family*. Harmondsworth: Penguin.

May R (1969). *Love and Will*. New York: WW Norton.

May R (1982). The problem of evil: an open letter to Carl Rogers. *Journal of Humanistic Psychology 22*: 10–21.

Mearns D, Thorne B (2000). *Person-Centred Therapy Today: new frontiers in theory and practice*. London: Sage.

Menzies IEP (1970). *The Functioning of Social Systems as a Defence against Anxiety*. London: The Tavistock Institute.

Parkin D (ed) (1985). *The Anthropology of Evil*. Oxford: Basil Blackwell.

Prouty G, Van Werde D, Pörtner M (2002). *Pre-Therapy: reaching contact-impaired clients*. Ross-on-Wye: PCCS Books.

Purton C (1998). Unconditional positive regard and its spiritual implications. In: Thorne B, Lambers E (eds). *Person-Centred Therapy: a European perspective*. London: Sage (pp23–37).

Shlien JM (1961). A client-centered approach to schizophrenia: first approximation. In: Burton A (ed). *Psychotherapy of the Psychoses*. New York: Basic Books (pp285–317). Reproduced in: Sanders P (ed) (2003). *To Lead an Honorable Life: invitations to think about client-centered therapy and the person-centered approach*. Ross-on-Wye: PCCS Books.

Sommerbeck L (2003). *The Client-Centred Therapist in Psychiatric Contexts: a therapist's guide to the psychiatric landscape and its inhabitants*. Ross-on-Wye: PCCS Books.

Tillich P (1952). *The Courage to Be*. New Haven: Yale University Press.

Warner MS (2002). Luke's dilemma: a client-centered/experiential model of processing with a schizophrenic thought disorder. In: Watson JC, Goldman RN, Warner MS (eds). *Client-Centered and Experiential Psychotherapy in the 21st Century: advances in theory, research and practice*. Ross-on-Wye: PCCS Books (pp459–472).

Worsley R (1996). *Human Freedom and the Logic of Evil: prolegomenon to a Christian theology of evil*. Basingstoke: Macmillan.

Worsley R (2002). *Process Work in Person-Centred Therapy: phenomenological and existential perspectives*. Basingstoke: Palgrave.

10 | A person-centred perspective on diagnosis and psychopathology in relation to minority identity, culture and ethnicity

Colin Lago

As we grew up, I would notice his face smeared with an unspoken trail of dirty tears when he got home. He never spoke of his terror; of the cruelty he endured every day, as a child and as an adult. Each day he wondered 'will I be safe today?' – a plea that persists today. He said there was little escape from the relentless battle that became his life at school in the 1970s. He took the name-calling, hits, the humiliation; it was relentless and he stopped feeling the pain, remembering once just standing there with the blows raining down on him, feeling only paralysis. He faced similar racist hate outside school… (Bains, 2007).

This chapter sets out to explore the various hypotheses generated by Carl Rogers and later writers within the person-centred approach concerning the development of pathology and disturbance, with specific reference to people of 'minority group' status in society. The Mental Health Foundation reports that, 'in general, people from black and minority ethnic groups living in the UK are more likely to be diagnosed with mental health problems, admitted to hospital, experience poor outcome from treatment, [and] disengage from mainstream mental health services, leading to social exclusion and a deterioration in their mental health'.[1] This is such a sobering, sad and alarming statement. This chapter, in seeking to explore the enormous complexities related to diagnosis and psychopathology development within minority groups, is underpinned by the following key ideas, which are developed in the text.

'Conditions of worth', the predominant conceptual framework espoused by Carl Rogers as the background from which psychological distress and disturbance is developed, is extended in this chapter to incorporate a wider conceptualisation

---

1. See www.mentalhealth.org.uk/help-information/mental-health-a-z/B/BME-communities (accessed 18 October, 2015).

involving society itself as a 'conditioning' agent. Ideas about society itself as conditional, therefore as toxic to some of its populace, are introduced. From this perspective, we might term these as 'culture-specific conditions of worth'.

Later writers, after Rogers, have also acknowledged other factors as contributing to mental health conditions: for example, trauma caused by life events, violence or accidents. As these can be an inevitable event in living, they can be easily incorporated into this wider societal overview relating to psychopathology causality. However, I make the distinction here that these traumatic events, while they might fit within the spectrum of 'culture-specific conditions of worth', might also exist independently of this conceptualisation, being the consequences of accidents, incidents and negative experiences associated with living life.

A general theme throughout this chapter is that the microdynamics of an individual's experiencing can be somewhat replicated, mirrored and paralleled by the dynamic processes of society. In other words, what is inside is outside. Although one might not experience any direct interpersonal discriminatory incident in life, it is still possible to be affected psychologically and emotionally by a perceived climate of unease, discrimination or hostility.

While the general human focus of this chapter is on the experiences leading to mental distress in groups and people defined as 'diverse' (BACP, 2004; Moodley & Rubin, 2008), the rather more specific categories of 'race', ethnicity, culture and identity (as a subset of diversity categories) are considered here in further depth.

Structural and material inequalities in society create and perpetuate psychological, social and relational dis-ease and ill health. The notion, then, of society as toxic, particularly to some of its members, is explored. Power and powerlessness are key recurring themes in this conceptualisation.

Contrary to a more traditional medical psychiatric view, where diagnosis predates and predicts the therapeutic treatment, early person-centred theory embraces the concept that diagnosis is the therapy (see, for example, the story by Wolter-Gustafson in Lago, Natiello & Wolter-Gustafson, 2014), and Brites and colleagues (2016) posit a more developed processual model of this activity.

Each of the above paragraphs introduces us to the many complexities inherent in exploring ideas about the development of psychopathology in particular groups within society. Inevitably, the following ideas and conceptualisations themselves are attempts to comprehend a vast field of individual human suffering, and will certainly not cover all manifestations of mental distress in people from ethnic and other minority groups.

Person-centred conceptualisations of the development of distress and disturbance

This subject is already extensively covered in the first edition of this book, so I will summarise very briefly here. Joseph & Worsley (2005) note that 'person-centred personality theory holds that psychological problems develop as a result of an internalization of conditions of worth' (p4). Both Brites and colleagues (2016) and Purton (2004: 39–41, 2014: chapter 4, 2015) concur with this historical summation, but also append their own critique, with the former noting that, 'whilst the theory is consistent with PCA theory, it is too generalist in nature' (p95), and the latter commenting:

> … in Rogers' own writings, and in standard PC theory when I was 'young' (!), it was held that all psychopathology arises from the introjection of conditions of worth, resulting in incongruence, and that the difficulties are then relieved through exposure of the client to the six conditions, thus enabling them to become congruent. That was a simple, neat, theory, but it can't explain the effectiveness of PC therapy in cases where pathology does not arise from introjection of conditions of worth. (Purton, personal communication, 2015)

(I will return later in the chapter to the later views of Purton and others in a wider purview of causality of psychopathology.)

'Conditions of worth', then, constitute the original perspective developed by Rogers in his seminal 1959 paper. As an aside, it is interesting to note that he (Rogers) had also noted that he considered diagnosis as being in direct conflict with the basic philosophy of the person-centred approach (Rogers, 1951).

Following feedback on my first draft of this chapter, I was stimulated to consider and explore further the source of 'conditions of worth'. This source is popularly perceived in the person-centred field to be the 'mother', or another primary caregiver. However, a careful re-reading of Rogers' 1959 paper led me to discover that he used other terminology, such as 'significant other' and 'social other'. He writes:

> … the expression of positive regard by a significant social other can become more compelling than the organismic valuing process [of the person themselves] and the individual becomes more adient to the positive regard of such others than towards experiences [their own] which are of positive value in actualizing the organism. (p224) (*My own words are included in brackets to enhance the reader's understanding here.*)

While this statement apparently casts a positivist value on another's positive regard, later reading reveals how a complex separation may grow between a person's need for positive regard and their accurate attunement with their own experiential frame of reference.

Rogers hypothesises that the need for 'positive regard' is universal in human beings, and is pervasive and persistent (p223). But we have to ask ourselves what happens when people receive 'negative regard' in their daily lives? We have to appreciate the extent to which negative conditioning from 'social others' severely affects people's sense of themselves as human beings of worth and value. Such dynamics constitute negative societal conditioning.

While there might be an interesting debate as to the validity of separating family-specific conditions of worth and culture-specific conditions of worth, Rogers' use of the wider terminology of 'social other' allows us, at least for the purposes of this chapter, to appreciate the potential negative impact of others in society behaving conditionally towards specific others, at worst leading to serious mental ill health (as evidenced in the opening quote to this chapter).

Although apparently 'switching gear' rather dramatically from the preceding paragraph, I wish to draw to attention the following extract by Cornelius-White and Ciesielski (2016) on the practice of client-centred therapy. They assert that the radical practice of acceptance and learning about a person through empathy pushed the psychological field to a *social justice empowerment* position that has been increasingly more accepted over time. They cite Eugene Gendlin, who argued that client-centered therapy:

> … put Rogers ahead of the country… In 1945, black people, women, gay
> people and others found help at the [Chicago] Counseling Center because
> these therapists knew that every client had to teach them a new world…
> These therapists never forced a policy on a client. (Rogers & Russel, 2002: xiii-
> xiv, cited by Kirschenbaum, 2007: 164)

Likewise, they add, one of the oldest studies on non-directive, person-centered education examined the reduction of fascist beliefs during World War II (Cornelius-White & Harbaugh, 2010).

These historic references to the early practice of client-centred therapy, particularly with reference to the work at the Chicago Counseling Centre, demonstrate that, while the practice of therapy in Chicago was delivered to people of all origins and diverse identities, such practice did not, apparently, cause Rogers to incorporate 'societal conditions of worth' into his seminal 1959 paper. For the purposes of this chapter on diversity and psychopathology development, however, I do believe this societal distinction of conditions of worth facilitates our understanding of the complex dynamics beyond the immediate and original family setting.

While much later work has been based on these early conceptualisations of Rogers, it is important that we also note his own concerns that his statements were not to be refined and reified into a definite objective truth. Interestingly, in his introduction to the 1959 paper, in response to the editor's request to 'cast his thinking in terms of the independent-intervening-dependency variable', he wrote that he found himself acknowledging that he found this terminology quite unacceptable, as it 'seems to deny the restless, dynamic, searching, changing aspects of scientific movement'. He also noted that 'at the time of its formulation every theory contains an unknown'.

In these statements Rogers was acknowledging the complexity of life as a dynamic process and that any propositions of theory should not become dogma.

These wise statements easily lead the way to later, person-centred conceptualisations of the development of psychopathology that cannot only have been seen as a response to conditions of worth. This is an aspect I return to later.

Sensitive to the fact that person-centred theory could be seen to have paid insufficient attention to the wide range of psychopathological conditions, as described, for example, in the various editions of the *Diagnostic and Statistical Manual of Mental Disorders* (DSM) (APA, 1952, 2013), Elke Lambers (1994: 105–120) wrote a series of short chapters from a person-centred theoretical perspective that sought to elucidate the general phenomenological characteristics that would contribute to further understanding of four key arenas of psychopathology: ie. neurosis, borderline personality disorder, psychosis and personality disorder. In a slightly different vein, Margaret Warner (2001) has also developed descriptions of styles of internal psychological processing, naming them as 'fragile', 'dissociated' and 'psychotic' processes.

To briefly recap this section, we have noted that Rogers' early ideas about the development of psychopathology have been revised and developed. These 'individualized' hypotheses, however, completely ignore the societal context of a person's life. It is to this additional source of distress and disturbance that much of the rest of this chapter is devoted.

Psychiatric diagnosis from then to now: an increasingly contested paradigm

In their opening chapter to the first edition of this book, the co-editors noted the inherent and potential value for client-centred therapists to become 'au fait' with and knowledgeable about the diagnostic categories used in psychiatry and clinical psychology. Their argument was that such knowledge might prove useful as a tool for communication with those other professions (Joseph & Worsley, 2005: 3).

This perspective chimes with my own early experiences as a counsellor of students in higher education in the late 1970s. Within the first few weeks of my counselling career, I was consulted by a young man who left me feeling that something was 'not quite right' in his presentation. His statements had seemed bizarre, surreal, slightly disconnected and, indeed, troubled. Fresh out of training and keen to do the best I could by this client, I encouraged him to consult one of the student health service doctors, who I knew had experience in psychiatry. Later that day, the doctor phoned me and congratulated me on picking up the signs of early onset of psychosis. He asked what it was that had alerted me to this young man's condition. My training had hardly touched on the whole field of mental ill health (as psychiatrically described and categorised), and I had never before been exposed to such presentations in my practice, so I felt somewhat embarrassed to find myself murmuring something like: 'I just felt that something was not quite right.' I felt both relieved that I had apparently acted appropriately (at least in the doctor's eyes), and somewhat embarrassed that I had lacked the tools and a language to describe my experience with this young man. In this episode, I was exposed to my own ignorance of mental health categories and behaviours as described by psychiatry, and thus lacked a common language to speak to other professionals about these phenomena. Yet, if I had continued to see this young man, I am not sure I would have done anything different to what I had attempted to do during our counselling work.

The power and the politics of the professional: a cautionary note

While briefly addressing the practice of psychiatric diagnosis, and specifically in relation to the subject of this chapter, it is necessary that we acknowledge the enormous personal, professional and role power wielded by those in the professions charged with this task. Back in the early 70s, Thomas and Sillen (1972) critically challenged the psychiatric and medical system in the US for neither recognising nor addressing the inherent discriminatory impacts of their work with patients from ethnic minority groups. In their own defence, psychiatric practitioners argued that they had spent many years in training in order to help others. How, then, could their work be discriminatory when it came from such a sincere and honourable place? This somewhat dated collective unawareness of racism (and, I imagine, sexism, gender-based prejudice, ageism, disablism and homophobia) and how it manifested itself in societal attitudes, procedures and dynamics (politics, education, medicine, the media, social services, employment practices and so on) seems now, looking back over several decades, unbelievably naive, yet undoubtedly at the time was a sincere (but uninformed and ideological) response.

Littlewood and Lipsedge first published their study of the impact of racism on mental health in the UK in 1982. Reflecting their different professional disciplines of psychiatry and anthropology, they noted that alienists (interestingly, a term once used to describe psychiatrists) are active agents who create aliens, and alienation is thus a social and political process. They applied this analysis to the situation of immigrants to the UK who had been alienated by a dominant white culture that more readily diagnosed psychosis in black people than in white people. (Such findings are also evidenced in Bhugra & Bhui, 2007; Sashidharan, 2001 and Sproston & Nazroo, 2002.)

D'Ardenne (2013: 5) notes (citing Fernando, 2010) that:

> … multiple studies… have shown that distressed black patients are more likely to end up in forensic environments, be offered less psychotherapy and be more heavily medicated… Even in the 21st century, there is evidence that black people of African and Caribbean heritage are six times more likely to be sectioned than white people and Asian people are four times more likely to commit suicide than white people.

She also cites Fernando's finding (2002) that, when identical case histories of people with either English or 'foreign' names were given to psychiatrists, they diagnosed psychosis more frequently in the latter group than they would have done by chance (D'Ardenne, 2013: 4).

The next section explores in more detail the impact of societal processes on individual functioning, but the question here remains: if someone is diagnosing, then where are they looking from? How socially aware are they, and what is their position of power in relation to the person being diagnosed?

The relationship between society and the individual

> Counselling and psychotherapy have often been criticised for focusing on the psychology of the individual and on the internal life of the client while ignoring the impact of the social, economic and cultural environment in which people live. (Feltham & Horton, 2000: 24)

There is a complex but, nevertheless, robust link between a person's experiences of a range of health conditions (including mental ill health) and their social position in society (Clark, 2016). This link has long been recognised; indeed, it was enshrined in the policy documents underpinning the creation of the welfare state and the National Health Service in 1948. More recently, Lago and Thompson (1996), Lago (2006) and Lago and Smith (2010) noted how the experienced toxicity of an oppressive society can affect and induce extreme distress in many people from minority groups, and Proctor (2002: 84) substantiates this view in her assertion that mental distress is rooted in inequality because inequality leads to internalised oppression. (See also the brief references later in this chapter to work by Aileen Alleyne on 'the internal oppressor' and 'internalized oppression'.)

Strong evidence for these ideas has, more recently, been provided by the publication of an extensively researched text by Wilkinson and Pickett (2009). They provide reams of evidence that the more unequal a society, the greater will be its levels of social malaise. Countries with the greatest income inequality (which include the UK, Portugal and the US), where the top 20 per cent of households have over seven times the income of the bottom 20 per cent, also have higher rates of addiction, homicide, obesity, teenage pregnancy and mental illness, proportionately more people in their prisons and lower levels of trust (p19).

Willie et al (1995) argue that the increased incidence of mental ill health in people from ethnic minorities is due, indirectly, to issues related to social class and poverty, and more directly (citing Moritsugu & Sue, 1983) to the stressors inherent in belonging to a minority group (see also Read, Johnstone & Taitimu, 2013).

In the field of psychotherapy research, both Dhillon-Stevens (2004) and Watson (2005) have noted the particular sensitivity and awareness of therapists and trainees from minority groups to their own situation in society, in direct contrast with their peers from the indigenous white community, who demonstrate much lower levels of awareness. (See also Ellis & Cooper, 2013, who write about the black student experience on counselling training courses.) These findings point to the complex, dynamic, dual influences of internal and external loci of evaluation potentially operating in people from minority groups. From an external perspective, their everyday, existential concerns could be:

- Will I survive today?
- Will I be safe today?
- Will I be accepted/loved today?
- And if I am, can I trust it?

Within this discussion, we cannot easily avoid the consideration that 'racism itself is a mental illness striking at the nation's health' (Castellano & Kramer, 1995: 4; Lago & Thompson, 1996; Lago, 2006; McKenzie-Mavinga, 2005). This perspective of society as toxic to particular groups is evidenced in phrases such as 'collective clinical depression', a term used by Cornel West (2000) to describe the collective experience of African Americans. In the UK, Lennox Thomas (2008) has used the term 'collective combat fatigue' in relation to the effects of racism described by a group of African Caribbean men. Similarly, the gay rights movement has coined the term 'oppression sickness' to describe the collective experience of prejudice and discrimination against the gay community and its individual members.

I am reminded, while considering this perspective, of the educational film published a long time ago by the Canadian Film Board, entitled *Blue Eyes, Brown Eyes*. In this film, a teacher, Jane Elliot, conducted an experiment with children, artificially and arbitrarily separating them into these two categories and then proceeding to favour one group over the other.[2] She maintained this stance for a day, and then, the following day, reversed this process so the other group was favoured. The impact of this on the emotions and behaviour of the children in both groups was frighteningly strong. When in the favoured group, they interacted more confidently and more positively, while those in the oppressed group visibly wilted. If this short experiment was so devastatingly effective in changing children's behaviour and confidence levels, just consider the likely effects of long-term exposure to negative conditioned responses from others in society, based on appearance, identity, behaviour etc. One such example is given by Suzy Henry, who has cited in her writings (2011) the devastating psychological and emotional effects of her earlier disfigurement.

These 'socio-situational' considerations (see Clark, 2016) relating to members of minority groups in society raises the spectrum of a wider conceptualisation of Rogers' original hypotheses concerning the development of psychological disturbance.

In considering the rather more 'macro' circumstance of society itself, we can now seriously consider the personal impact of conditions of worth when imposed and implied by wider society and experienced negatively by minority

---

2. See www.janeelliott.com/ (accessed 30 September, 2016) for further details of this original work with school children and her later anti-racist work with adults.

group members. Thus, just extracting the examples taken from the two preceding paragraphs, we can see that social class, poverty, minority group identity, oppression, discrimination and racism (as manifestations of societally experienced 'conditions of worth') are sufficient to contribute to psychological distress and disturbance.

Further, recognising the political complexities, negative social attitudes and occasional violence in the experience of many who are seen as different from the mainstream majority, we can also appreciate that the incidence of later traumatic events (beyond the early years of childhood) will also impact negatively on their mental health. This further dimension enhances and expands the early person-centred conceptualisations of the causes of psychopathology and accords with writers (cited earlier in the chapter) such as Purton, (2014), Brites and colleagues (2016) and Warner (2005).

Extending the essence of the above argument that society's systemic (behavioural, attitudinal) processes can be likened, to some extent, to Rogers' original ideas on conditions of worth, and also then including the recognition of the trauma caused by such experiences (as described by the later writers on the person-centred approach and psychopathology), the following sections provide illustrations of experiences that can be significantly distressing for people from ethnic minority communities.

Culture shock and transitional effects

The general movement and migration of people worldwide is, of course, not a new phenomenon. Lago (2006: 1–6) briefly charts the complex yet, historically speaking, natural flow of peoples to and from the UK over many centuries. Citing the Commission for Racial Equality (1999), he notes:

> Britain has always had ethnic minorities. People with diverse histories, cultures, beliefs and languages have settled here since the beginnings of recorded time.

At the time of writing, the world is currently witnessing migration on an enormous scale as, driven out by war, political conflict, famine and poverty, millions of people flee their homes and countries across the Middle East and Africa. The individual human consequences of these macro population movements will be very considerable, and, inevitably, will have enormous consequences for the mental health of a generation to come.

There is an extensive, though slightly dated, literature on the subject of 'culture shock' (see below). The term itself has entered the lexicon of everyday language and, in the process, no longer fully expresses the psychological, emotional and physiological effects of transition, and particularly the movement from one geographical and cultural setting to another. More recently, the consequences of cultural movement have been studied by Cooper (2003), Madison (2005), Babak (2015) and Conn (2016).

There are various stage models of the culture shock process (see, for example, Gullahorn & Gullahorn, 1963; Furnham & Bochner, 1986; Adler, 1975), and these can be constellated into a series of developmental positions that occur following such transitions. Briefly described, these stages include:

- a brief possible honeymoon phase (for some), where the new host country is seen through slightly rose-tinted spectacles

- a second stage when acknowledgement dawns that some things are slightly more complex than had, at first, appeared, and that this transition might involve some personal discomfort and necessary new learning

- a third stage where the trend towards perceiving some inherent challenges in this new life continues to a point of considerable strain, where the person begins to experience serious challenges to their previous ways of being in the world, to their patterns of being, relating, thinking and so on. This can lead some even to psychological stress and breakdown

- a fourth stage that offers relief to this strain, in that it is recognised over time that, throughout the crisis of the third stage, something has been learned about this new social milieu and the person in transition is able to understand the different cultural expectations of them, and is able to begin to accommodate this new knowledge into their behaviour

- a final, hypothetical stage of transition that we could describe as 'bi-cultural' competence – that is, the person feels completely at home, is psychologically safe, and is able to function equally well in both cultural settings.

This model, like most psychological models involving change and stress (eg. bereavement, change of employment, loss of limbs due to accident or surgery, leaving home, loss of a loved one, and so on), seeks to describe a general pattern of experiences over time that people experiencing such transitions may go through. While such models can be of immense value in attempting to explain what is happening to someone in transition, they cannot describe the nature of the experience itself, which can be extremely distressing, unpredictable, lonely and long lasting.

The effects of migration within one's home country can also have such effects. Although somewhat sparse (at least, when I last studied it, in the late 1990s), the literature on homesickness drew similar conclusions in describing the emotional and cognitive impacts of transition from, say, parental home to residential school or university. Students in one large-scale study (Fisher, 1989) reported higher emotional instability than they had experienced before going to university, and felt they were unable to function as well cognitively. These effects were quite long lasting for the majority of respondents, continuing on average for up to a year after the student first left home. I have worked with students seriously devastated by homesickness, and am only too aware of the distress it can cause.

Both bodies of literature, in reflecting on the consequences of cultural/ familial and geographic relocation, also emphasise the variety of unique and idiosyncratic reactions experienced by people, and how, for some, these changes can take an extraordinarily long time. I knew someone who, having been introduced to these models of culture shock, informed me that, even now, having been in the UK for 18 years, she still felt herself to only be in the fourth stage of this five-stage process.

More seriously, she added that, during this period of time living in the UK, she had suffered a serious mental breakdown and had been medicated and hospitalised. This presented a considerable shock to her self-image, as she had never suffered psychologically before, in her country of origin.

Zwingmann and Gunn, two medical practitioners at the University of Reading in the 1970s, even proposed (although not successfully), a new psychiatric diagnostic category of 'uprooting disorder', in an attempt to recognise how psychologically destabilising transitional processes can be for some people (1983).

Asylum-seeking: process and anxiety

So many asylum seekers, refugees and immigrants, particularly those whose immigration status is ambiguous or undocumented, suffer a chronic state of hyper-vigilance, alertness to danger and possible catastrophe that can be powerfully debilitating. (Imberti, 2008: 8)

Mudadi-Billings and Eschoe (2011: 196) report that 'the experiences of asylum seekers prior to, on arrival, or during their stay in the host country are often overlooked, trivialised, are of diminutive interest, or receive little consideration by the host populace'.

It is important to note that people going through the asylum-seeking process are exposed to additional stresses and strains beyond the general effects of the transition process described above. Many may already have experienced exhausting, demoralising, frightening journeys to reach the new host country, having previously faced gross disruption, displacement and torture in their home countries. They are then exposed to poverty and poor housing in their new home, and they can also suffer discrimination and violence. Their own transitional process is weighted further with uncertainty and complexity, precisely because of their insecure status in their new surroundings.

Can we dare to imagine ourselves in such a plight? Would our capacities of emotional resilience withstand these pressures? Their journey, at the very least, could be described as doubly traumatising, and, if they are able to access medical and psychological support, further efforts will be required if they are to comprehend and benefit from it.

Inter-generational differences in attitude and development of life-styles post immigration

From his long-term studies of migration in the US, American historian Marcus Lee Hansen, winner of the 1941 Pulitzer Prize for his book *The Atlantic Migration, 1607–1860* (Hansen, 1940), began to recognise the (perhaps inevitable) changes in outlook, attitude and experience of successive generations following immigration to the US from many other parts of the world.

He found an increased (renewed) interest among the third and fourth generations of immigrant families in the cultural origins of the family and its consequences for a revised sense of personal identity. He wrote: 'What the son wishes to forget, the grandson wishes to remember' (Hansen, 1938). This indicates a movement among many of original immigrant status towards the search for a congruent sense of identity: 'Who am I really?' acquires a deeper profundity in this context.

Other data emerging from the US on intergenerational life circumstances have been reported by David North (2009). In his article 'The Immigrant Paradox: the stalled progress of recent immigrant children', North notes that:

- success in the educational system declines from the first to the third generation
- violence and drug abuse rise among the later generations
- risky sexual behaviour increases from the first to the third generation, and
- when socioeconomic standing is taken out of the equation, the health of children in most immigrant groups gets worse from the first to the third generations.

It is important to note that these studies are from the US, and we cannot assume that these specific patterns occur in other countries that have experienced demographic change through immigration.

Migration has been a feature of human existence since the beginnings of time, but we also know that the experience of migration, whether through choice or force, has considerable psychological consequences that can feature (as evidenced in the above research) over several generations and impact on mental health.

The impact of an oppressed ancestry

Charura and Lago (2015) note that the transgenerational transmission of trauma is still considered a relatively new and controversial issue, although Braga and colleagues (2012) claim that it has been explored in more than 500 articles and these have reported mixed findings. This field of study has its origins in epigenetic studies that found a continuation of alarm responses in mice over several generations, despite there having been a complete absence of the threat that caused the original anxiety in the first generation.

Humans can also inherit epigenetic alterations/modifications that influence their behaviour, and this is possibly a route for a susceptibility to psychological distress relating to trauma (González-Pardo & Pérez Alvarez, 2013). Such studies enhance our thinking on the implications of epigenetics and the possibilities of transgenerational trauma.

Duran (2006) refers to intergenerational trauma as a 'soul wound' – an experience that impacts on the lives of many people in a particular cultural group that has been subjected to violence, injustice and oppression. Examples of such brutalities include slavery, genocide, violence, terrorism, civil war, and illegal and uninvited acts of systemic oppression. Delroy Hall (2011), for example, has used the term 'existential crucifixion' to describe the long-term impact of slavery and colonialism on people of African descent from the West Indies. Ellie Rose (2010), in her autobiographical article about the Katyn massacre in World War 2, describes the effects of intergenerational trauma on her father, who grew up hearing his Polish mother's stories of surviving Russian persecution and of the death of his grandfather in the massacre. Anne Karpf's autobiography, *The War After: living with the Holocaust*, deals with the same phenomenon, as Rose notes, and points out that it is an experience of inherited trauma that features in many studies of Holocaust survivors' children.

In a review of a recent book by Yaron Matras, titled *I Met Lucky People*, Sukhdev Sandhu (2014) charts key incidents in the centuries-old, societally orchestrated, systemic oppression of the Roma people, ever since they migrated from India in the Middle Ages. They were decreed 'enemy agents' by the Holy Roman Empire in 1496; in 1545, an assembly of members of the Holy Roman Empire, the Diet of Augsburg, declared that 'whosoever kills a gypsy, will be guilty of no murder', and in 1568 Pope Pius V banished them completely from the Holy Roman Empire. In England, the 'Egyptians Act' of 1530 required them to leave voluntarily or face deportation.

As a group, they have suffered in every country where they have sought to settle. Sandhu writes: 'Like the Jews, another group repeatedly castigated and cast out through history, the Roma were targeted by the Nazis. They were sterilized and, during a period that is referred to as the "Great Devouring", at least 100,000 (some estimates claim 1.5 million) were exterminated.'

Some years ago, a colleague told me the story of an eight-year-old boy of Jewish origin who had been referred to a play therapist by his parents. Their concern was that 'he just takes nothing seriously and continually wants to make mischief and have fun', and that he did not apply himself to schoolwork or any serious activity at all. This child had already been referred to other counsellors and social workers, a further indicator of the parents' own level of anxiety.

My colleague observed that, while this response would be perfectly understandable in most parents (ie. parents want their child to do well at school), what could be missed here was the potential impact of the child's Jewish ancestry. Both sets of grandparents escaped the ravages of concentration camps and the

Holocaust by emigrating to the UK in the late 1930s. Tragically, however, they had lost many friends and family members. Eventually, both sets of grandparents were able to achieve some success in business life. However, none of them would ever speak about their earlier (traumatic) life experiences. Rather, they exuded and extolled earnestness and a belief in hard work as a leitmotif for living. The notion of fun, then, was the furthest thing from their minds. The child's parents had been raised in this ethos of industriousness by their respective parents (the child's grandparents), and were thus horrified by their son's apparent frivolity. While this story has perhaps many other possible psycho-theoretical elements and perspectives, it could be seen to suggest the possibility of longer-term, transgenerational influence.

Clemmont Vontress and Lawrence Epp (1997) propose that an injury committed towards one's own forebears might manifest itself in 'historical hostility' and 'transgenerational hatred' in succeeding generations. This chimes with the general findings of the epigenetic studies reported, which suggest that, in addition to the intergenerationally received stories from previous generations and the naturally occurring feelings of later generations when they learn of their forebear's experiences, the hatred of specific 'others' or specific groups can be imprinted and inherited genetically over long periods of time and across generations. Vontress also argues that such a phenomenon might explain the higher incidence of heart conditions in African American males in comparison with European American males, reflecting a long-term history of slavery and colonisation (Vontress & Epp, 1997).

Ethnic identity, social circumstances and psychopathology

Human beings need to feel loved and socially connected, and usually seek to avoid undue psychic pain in their lives. These generalised existential needs can drive a person's avoidance or denial of distress and disturbance for a long time, sometimes until the levels of stress and exhaustion associated with their avoidance can no longer be sustained. Then, hopefully, they experience 'break-through' into other ways of being or, sadly, they may descend into serious mental disturbance.

I have noted how, in the mainstream transcultural counselling literature, different authors use a range of terms to try to capture the essence of (psychological and emotional) damage inflicted by societal conditioning effects. For example, these include:

- the development of a 'proxy self' – a persona that serves to keep dangerous issues and people at bay (Lago & Thompson, 1997: 122)
- 'racism as trauma' (Bains, 2007)
- 'recognition trauma' (also described as identity traumatisation) – '[a] process where the emotions of individuals relating to black issues either come to the fore or create a block' (Mckenzie-Mavinga, 2009: 36)

- 'continuous trauma' – the continuous presence of trauma in the oppressed person's life (Straker, Watson & Robinson, 2002)

- identity wounding – the impact of being regarded negatively and being discriminated against simply because you are who you are (Alleyne, 2011)

- 'internal oppressor' – referring to the 'oppressor' within the selves of minority group persons: 'prejudices, projections, inter-generational wounds and the vicissitudes from our historical past are all aspects of this inner tyrant – the internal oppressor' (Alleyne, 2011)

- 'internalised oppression' – 'the process of absorbing the values and beliefs of the oppressor and coming to believe that the stereotypes and misinformation about one's group is true (or partly true.) Such a process can lead to low self-esteem, self-hate, the disowning of one's group, and other complex defensive behaviours in relation to one's group' (Alleyne, 2011).

Conclusion

This chapter has expanded the early 'individualised' understandings of the development of psychopathology within the client-centred therapy perspective to take a wider view of the potentially negative effects of societal circumstances on (some) people. I have tried to incorporate the plethora of circumstances and causal factors that impact on people from minority groups, particularly with reference to race, ethnicity and culture. They include power, powerlessness, poverty, discrimination, racism, immigration, intergenerational consequences and minority identity, singly and in complex combinations.

Taking this wider perspective, both persons in the client–therapist dyad are directly implicated. Training and continuing professional development, then, for therapists and other professionals engaged in diagnosis and 'treatment', is of absolute importance to ensure the delivery of therapy that is truly anti-oppressive and anti-discriminatory (Lago, 2016).

This is no easy matter, as Jessica Buckley (2004) writes: 'Cross cultural psychological work is painful, problematic and stressful.'

References

Adler P (1975). The transitional experience: an alternative view of culture shock. *Journal of Humanistic Psychology 15*(4): 13–23.

Alleyne A (2011). Overcoming racism, discrimination and oppression in psychotherapy. In: Lago C (ed). *The Handbook of Transcultural Counselling and Psychotherapy.* Maidenhead: Open University/ McGraw Hill (pp117–129).

American Psychiatric Association (1952/2013) *Diagnostic and Statistical Manual of Mental Disorders* (1st/5th eds). Washington, DC: APA.

Babak M (2015). Developing an intervention programme for the needs of Iranian immigrants in the UK. Unpublished doctoral thesis. London: University of Middlesex/Metanoia Institute.

Bains S (2007). An autoethnographic exploration into transforming the wounds of racism: implications for psychotherapy. Unpublished doctoral thesis. London: University of Middlesex/Metanoia Institute.

BACP (2004). A working definition of diversity. Equality and Diversity Forum. Rugby: BACP.

Bhugra D, Bhui K (2007). *Textbook of Cultural Psychiatry.* Cambridge: Cambridge University Press.

Braga L, Mello M, Fiks J (2012). Transgenerational transmission of trauma and resilience: a qualitative study with Brazilian offspring of Holocaust survivors. *BMC Psychiatry 12*(1): 134–144.

Brites R, Nunes O, Hipólito J (2016). Psychopathology and the person-centred perspective. In: Lago C, Charura D (eds). *Person Centred Counselling and Psychotherapy Handbook: origins, developments and current applications.* Maidenhead. Open University/McGraw-Hill (pp117–129).

Carter R (1991). *The Influence of Race and Racial Identity in Psychotherapy: towards a racially inclusive model.* New York: John Wiley.

Castellano B, Kramer BM (1995). Connections between racism and mental health. In: Willie CV, Rieker PP, Kramer BM, Brown BS (eds). *Mental Health, Racism and Sexism.* Pittsburgh, PA: University of Pittsburgh Press (pp3–26).

Charura D, Lago C (2015). Working with transgenerational trauma: the implication of epigenetic considerations and transcultural perspectives in psychotherapy. *The Psychotherapist 59*(Spring): 23–25.

Clark D (2016). Thinking about the other: conversations and context. In: Lago C, Charura D (eds). *Person Centred Counselling and Psychotherapy Handbook: origins, developments and current applications.* Maidenhead. Open University/McGraw-Hill (pp277–287).

CRE (Commission for Racial Equality) (1999). *Ethnic Minorities in Britain.* Factsheet (revised edition). London: CRE.

Conn S (2016). A phenomenological study of help-seeking behaviours and coping strategies of international students of non- European backgrounds. Unpublished doctoral thesis. University of Middlesex/Metanoia Institute.

Cornelius-White JHD, Harbaugh AP (2010). *Learner-Centered Instruction: building relationships for student success.* Thousand Oaks, California: Sage Publications.

Cornelius-White JHD, Ciesielski M (2016). Rogers, rigor, research and recordings. In: Lago C, Charura D (eds). *Person Centred Counselling and Psychotherapy Handbook: origins, developments and current applications.* Maidenhead: Open University/McGraw-Hill (pp14–23).

Cooper R, Cooper N (2003). *Culture Shock Thailand and How to Survive It.* London: Kuperard.

D'Ardenne P (2013). *Counselling in Transcultural Settings.* London: Sage.

Dhillon-Stevens H (2004). Personal and professional integration of anti-oppressive practice and the multiple oppression model in psychotherapeutic education. *British Journal of Psychotherapy Integration* 1(2): 47–62.

Duran E (2006). *Healing the Soul Wound: counselling with American Indians and other native peoples.* New York: Teachers College Press.

Ellis E, Cooper N (2013). Silenced: the black student experience. *Therapy Today* 24(10): 14–19.

Feltham C, Horton I (2000). *Handbook of Counselling and Psychotherapy.* London: Sage.

Fernando S (2010). *Mental Health, Race and Culture* (2nd ed). Basingstoke/New York: Palgrave.

Fernando S (2003). *Cultural Diversity, Mental Health and Psychiatry: the struggle against racism.* Hove/New York: Brunner-Routledge.

Fisher S (1989). *Homesickness, Cognition and Health.* London: Lawrence Earlbaum Associates.

Furnham A, Bochner S (1986). *Culture Shock: psychological reactions to unfamiliar environments.* London: Methuen.

González-Pardo H, Pérez Alvarez M (2013). Epigenetics and its implications for psychology. *Psicothema* 25(1): 3–12.

Gullahorn JT, Gullahorn JE (1963). An extension of the U-curve hypothesis. *Journal of Social Issues 19*: 33–47.

Hall D (2011). The effects of an African Caribbean heritage: living as a problem. In: Lago C (ed). *The Handbook of Transcultural Counselling and Psychotherapy.* Maidenhead. Open University/McGraw-Hill (pp 231–254).

Hansen ML (1938). *The Study of Man: the third generation in America.* Lecture to the Augustana Historical Society. Republished in *Commentary Magazine* 1952; 1 November. www.commentarymagazine.com/articles/the-study-of-man-the-third-generation-in-america/ (accessed 12 October, 2016).

Hansen ML (1940). *The Atlantic Migration, 1607–1860: a history of the continuing settlement of the United States.* Cambridge, MA: Harvard University Press.

Henry S (2011). Disfigurement and visible difference: the impact upon personal and personality development and the implications for therapy. *Person-Centered & Experiential Psychotherapies* 10(4): 274–285.

Imberti P (2008). The immigrant's odyssey. *Therapy Today* 19(6): 2–9.

Joseph S, Worsley R (eds) (2005). *Person Centred Psychopathology: a positive psychology of mental health.* Ross-On-Wye: PCCS Books.

Karpf A. *The War After: living with the Holocaust.* London: Mandarin; 1997.

Kirschenbaum H (2007). *The Life and Work of Carl Rogers.* Ross-on-Wye: PCCS Books.

Lago C (2006). *Race, Culture and Counselling: the ongoing challenge* (2nd ed). Maidenhead: Open University/McGraw-Hill.

Lago C (2016). On becoming a person-centred therapist for these contemporary times: suggestions for professional development in the context of diversity. In: Lago C, Charura D. (eds). *Person Centred Counselling and Psychotherapy Handbook: origins, developments and current applications.* Maidenhead: Open University/McGraw-Hill (pp288–299).

Lago C, Smith B (2010). *Anti-Discriminatory Counselling Practice.* London: Sage.

Lago C, Thompson J (1996). *Race, Culture and Counselling.* Maidenhead: Open University/ McGraw-Hill.

Lago C, Thompson J (1997). The triangle with curved sides: sensitivity to issues of race and culture in supervision. In: Shipton G (ed). *Supervision of Counselling and Psychotherapy: making a place to think.* Buckingham: Open University Press (pp119–130).

Lago C, Natiello P, Wolter-Gustafson C (2014). The person-centred approach: courage, presence and complexity – a template for relationship in a postmodern/post-structuralist world. In: Charura D, Paul S (eds). *The Therapeutic Relationship Handbook: theory and practice.* Maidenhead: Open University/McGraw-Hill (pp51–62).

Lambers E (1994). The person-centred perspective on psychopathology. In: Mearns D (ed). *Developing Person Centred Counselling.* London: Sage (pp105–120).

Littlewood R, Lipsedge M (1982). *Aliens and Alienists: ethnic minorities and psychiatry.* Harmondsworth: Penguin Books.

Madison G (2005). *Existential migration.* Unpublished doctoral thesis. London: Regent's College.

McKenzie-Mavinga I (2005). Understanding black issues in postgraduate counsellor training. *Counselling and Psychotherapy Research* 5(4): 295–300.

McKenzie-Mavinga I (2009). *Black Issues in the Therapeutic Process.* London: Palgrave MacMillan.

Moodley R, Lubin D (2008). Developing your career to working with multicultural and diversity clients. In: Palmer S, Bor R (eds). *The Practitioner's Handbook.* London: Sage (pp156–175).

Moritsugu JN, Sue S (1983). Minority status as a stressor. In: Felner RD, Jason LA, Muritsugu JN, Farber SS (eds). *Preventive Psychology: theory, research and practice.* New York: Pergamon (pp162–174).

Mudadi-Billings S, Eschoe P (2011). On being an asylum-seeker. In: Lago C (ed). *The Handbook of Transcultural Counselling and Psychotherapy.* Maidenhead: Open University Press/McGraw-Hill (pp196–208).

North D (2009). The immigrant paradox: the stalled program of recent immigrants' children. [Blog.] Center for Immigration Studies; September. http://cis.org/ImmigrantParadox (accessed 1 February, 2016).

Proctor G (2002). *The Dynamics of Power in Counselling and Psychotherapy: ethics, politics and practice.* Ross-on-Wye: PCCS Books.

Purton C (2004). *Person-Centred Therapy: the focusing-oriented approach.* London: Palgrave Macmillan.

Purton C (2014). *The Trouble with Psychotherapy: counselling and common sense.* London: Palgrave.

Purton C (2015). Personal email communication with the author; 27 October, 2015.

Read J, Johnstone L, Taitimu M (2013). Psychosis, poverty and ethnicity. In: Read J, Dillon J (eds). *Models of Madness: psychological, social and biological approaches to psychosis* (2nd ed). London/New York: Routledge (pp191–209).

Rogers CR (1951). *Client-Centered Therapy.* London: Constable.

Rogers CR (1959). A theory of therapy, personality and interpersonal relationships, as developed in the client-centered framework. In: Koch S (ed). *Psychology: a study of a science. Vol. 3: Formulations of the person and the social context.* New York: McGraw-Hill. (pp184–256).

Rose E (2010). Katyn: The tragedy never ends. [Online.] *The Guardian*, 22 April. www.theguardian.com/lifeandstyle/2010/apr/24/katyn-massacre-poland-president (accessed 21 November 2016).

Sandhu S (2014). I Met Lucky People by Yaron Matras – review. [Online.] *The Guardian*; 29 January. www.theguardian.com/books/2014/jan/29/i-met-lucky-people-review (accessed 29 November, 2016).

Sashidharan S (2001). Institutional racism in British psychiatry. *Psychiatric Bulletin* 25: 244–247.

Sproston K, Nazroo J (2002). Ethnic minority psychiatric illness rates in the community. (EMPIRIC) Quantitative report. London: Department of Health.

Straker G, Watson D, Robinson T (2002). Trauma and disconnection: a trans-theoretical approach. *International Journal of Psychotherapy* 7(2): 143–156.

Thomas A, Sillen S (1972). *Racism and Psychiatry.* New York: Bruner-Mazel.

Thomas L (2008). *Cultural Narratives and Psychological Therapies.* Lecture at Confer conference. London. April.

Warner MS (2001). Empathy, relational depth and difficult client process. In: Haugh S, Merry T (eds). *Rogers' Therapeutic Conditions: evolution, theory and practice. Volume 2: Empathy.* Ross-on-Wye: PCCS Books (pp181–191).

Warner MS (2005). A person-centred view of human nature, wellness and psychopathology. In: Joseph S, Worsley R (eds). *Person Centred Psychopathology: a positive psychology of mental health.* Ross-on-Wye: PCCS Books (pp91–109).

Watson V (2005). Key issues for black counselling practitioners in the UK with particular reference to their experiences in training. In: Lago C (ed) (2nd ed). *Race, Culture and Counselling.* Maidenhead; Open University/McGraw-Hill Education (pp187–197).

Wilkinson R, Pickett K (2009). *The Spirit Level: why more equal societies almost always do better.* London: Allen Lane/Penguin.

Willie CV, Rieker PP, Kramer BM, Brown BS (eds) (1995). *Mental Health, Racism and Sexism.* Pittsburgh, Pa: University of Pittsburgh Press.

Vontress C, Epp LR (1997). Historical hostility in the African American client: implications for counselling. *Journal of Multicultural Counseling and Development* 25(3): 170–184.

West C (2000). *Race Matters.* New York: Beacon Press.

Zwingmann CAA, Gunn ADG (1983). *Uprooting and Health: psycho-social problems of students from abroad.* Geneva: WHO.

11 | Using attachment theory in person-centred therapy

Emma Tickle and Stephen Joseph

The idea for this chapter arose from a recent teaching session with some of our students on a person-centred training course. They had recently started a new placement, working with children and young people, and their supervisor had advised them to familiarise themselves with the work of John Bowlby and attachment theory. We agreed that this was a good idea. Knowing more about attachment theory would give our students a wider perspective that would help them engage in dialogue with other health professionals about the similarities and differences of the person-centred approach. However, as the conversation progressed, it became clear to us that the students were interested in attachment theory because they thought that the person-centred approach was not able to provide a sufficient understanding of developmental processes and how early experiences with a caregiver related to mental health.

The aim of this chapter is to show that Rogers' personality theory is a developmental theory that is sufficient in its own right, and that attempts to integrate attachment theory are unnecessary and may actually detract from person-centred practice. First, we will describe attachment theory and three types of attachment. Second, we will discuss how these three types of attachment describe experiences that can otherwise be viewed through the lens of person-centred theory and conditions of worth. Third, we will argue that, although the two approaches might describe the same phenomenon, the implications of categorisation are both limiting and inconsistent with the ethics of the person-centred approach. We will show how conditions of worth and attachment styles are essentially theories about the same process, but the terminology is different, and, most importantly, there is a difference in how the theory is put into practice.

Attachment theory

There is general consensus in the counselling and psychotherapy literature that our early childhood experiences of being in relationship with a significant other have an impact on how we relate to self, others and the world around us. Much of the credit for this is due to John Bowlby, who began writing about maternal care and mental health in the 1950s. One of his earliest studies was of the mental health of homeless children in post-Second World War Europe, the results of which came to wider attention in his 1953 book on child care (Bowlby, Fry & Ainsworth, 1953).

Bowlby went on to write what is known as the Loss Trilogy. This was a set of three books, published in 1969, 1973 and 1980 respectively, which formed the building blocks for attachment theory, the full synthesis of which was published in 1988 in Bowlby's book *A Secure Base: parent-child attachment and healthy human development*. Bowlby's work highlighted the damage of maternal deprivation. Bowlby argued that attachment to a significant other was both an evolutionary necessity for survival and necessary for psychological wellbeing. Bowlby believed that infants possessed a motivational system programmed to establish secure attachments with a small number of significant others, and that achieving this promoted healthy development.

Bowlby was unequivocal in his view that parental love was vital for healthy psychological development; it was, he said, as important as vitamins and proteins for physical health. He argued that the absence of parental love was invariably present in, if not the basis of, psychiatric disorders. He described attachment as an evolutionary behavioural system comprising three elements: the behavioural response to threat (eg. protest, crying); the significant other's response to these behaviours (eg. soothing), and the 'psychophysiological state that is the end result of those behaviours' (eg. a return to calm, feelings of safety) (Holmes, 2001).

One of the most influential contributions to attachment theory was made by Mary Ainsworth and colleagues (1978), who created the Strange Situation test to trigger and then observe this behavioural system in action. It consisted of a standardised laboratory procedure involving the observation of a child in the presence of its parent, followed by separation of the child from the parent, the introduction into the room of a stranger, and finally the reunion of the parent and the child. Children in the experiment were aged between 12 and 18 months old. Observations of the child's reactions to these stages led Ainsworth and colleagues to identify the three infant attachment categories of secure, avoidant, and resistant/ambivalent.

Secure attachment

In the Strange Situation test, before separation, a securely attached child will freely explore their environment with evident curiosity. When separated, they will show signs of missing the parent. They will also show a clear preference for the parent over the stranger. When the parent is brought back into the room, they will initiate contact and return to play as before. Attachment security is a result of sensitive and responsive caregiving. Securely attached children do better in terms of their social competence.

Avoidant

The avoidant child appears barely affected by the Strange Situation test. The child displays little distress when the parent leaves the room. Their play is unaffected by the presence or absence of the parent. The child's approach to the parent is tentative and they are equally well comforted by the stranger.

Resistant or ambivalent

The resistant or ambivalent child clings to the parent, and does not explore the toys. They are preoccupied with the parent and have difficulty finding comfort when reunited, seeking and resisting contact through a show of anger.

How childhood attachment affects adult relationships

It is thought that attachment patterns in childhood have consequences for how we develop relationship skills as adults. According to attachment theory, a person's attachment style as an adult is shaped by his or her early attachment patterns. Although recent researchers have begun to question this causal link and call for better research on the predictive power of early attachment (Meins, 2017), the idea remains influential among practitioners.

As with infants, it is thought that, as adults, we can be grouped into different attachment styles. Those with a secure attachment style are comfortable being close to others and don't worry about being abandoned. They have the capacity to be both intimate and autonomous.

In contrast, those who are anxious-avoidant are uncomfortable being close to others; for them, the trade-off is autonomy at the expense of intimacy (Holmes, 2001). They find it difficult to trust others completely and to allow themselves to become dependent. They are nervous when anyone gets too close and may feel uncomfortable when people seek intimacy.

Those who are anxious-preoccupied feel that others are reluctant to let them get as close as they would like; for them, autonomy is relinquished for intimacy (Holmes, 2001). They worry that their partner doesn't really love them or won't want to stay with them. Their desire for intimacy may frighten people away (Hazan & Shaver, 1987).

Attachment styles are an internal working model for all relationships that provides the lens through which people perceive the world and think about others and themselves. It is thought that a person's attachment style is evident in how they talk about their lives and what they focus on. It is thought that at least 39 per cent of people are insecurely attached (Meins, 2017). Ultimately, for those using attachment theory in their therapeutic practice, a person's attachment style is a guide for whether they are 'inoculated' against mental health problems (that is, they are resilient to the assaults and adversities that lead to mental health problems) or vulnerable to developing them.

There has been much further development in using attachment theory in therapy than we have described above, but it is beyond the scope of this chapter to go into the detail. Interested readers are referred to Holmes (2001). What is important for the purpose of this chapter is to note the central idea in attachment theory: that the classification of secure, avoidant or ambivalent attachment patterns or styles provides the basis for psychotherapeutic formulation, whether working with children or with adults.

Attachment style is thought to be an important predictor of how therapy progresses (Gonzalez, 2015). Working with children and young people, the practitioner will take into account their attachment pattern in terms of how best to respond to them. With adults, practitioners will interview their patients in order to discover their attachment style, and will relate to them in specific ways and offer interventions depending on their style. Holmes (2001) uses the metaphor of the boxing ring. The ring itself represents the secure base, but the therapist must be able to move freely around the ring so as not to get cornered. For example, an insecure patient will want to cling on and control the therapist, so the therapist must help the patient trust him/herself. In short, by knowing a person's attachment style, we know how they are likely to relate to us as therapists, what they need, and what we should do. Attachment theory offers a typological understanding of how experiences in childhood are important in the development of people's internal working models, and how these relate to mental health problems.

Attachment types and conditions of worth

Person-centred theory has been criticised by some authors for not offering an adequate theory of child development (see Wilkins, Chapter 3 in this book). This is, however, a misunderstanding of person-centred theory. Rogers (1951, 1959) provided a conceptual framework that reflected his understanding of how personality was shaped developmentally through a process of socialisation.

In brief, the meta-theoretical foundation of the person-centered approach is the view that the human being (the 'organism') has a basic propensity and potential towards self-organisation, self-regulation and growth towards the realisation of their full potential. This process is understood to occur naturally when they are supported by the right social environmental factors, but easily derailed when their context is controlling and coercive.

In Rogers' theory, 'conditions of worth' describe the ways in which early relationships may thwart the normal developmental process, leading to expressions of incongruence. Conditions of worth are the rules for living, values and beliefs about how to be in the world in order to be loved. Infants are born with a need for positive regard. We are social creatures who enter the world with a need to connect with others and be valued. This is understood to be a biological drive that is rooted in our evolutionary history, as it ensures the survival of the infant. Even in the early months and years, as the parent soothes, or scolds, and feeds the infant, the developing child is learning how he or she must behave to receive positive regard. As the child develops language, he or she receives verbal as well as non-verbal communication about what he or she must say and do to receive positive regard. Children who are loved unconditionally learn to be the autonomous agents of their own lives. They are not told that they must be other to how they are. As such, they grow in ways that express their own potentialities. They are said to be congruent because their self-concept is a realistic working model of the of the world they are experiencing.

In contrast, children who are loved conditionally learn to be other than how they are. They introject conditions of worth. These children learn that they must work hard, please others, be subservient, hate a group of people, hate themselves, or whatever combination of the myriad ways in which a child is socialised to meet the expectations of others. Each person's unique combination of conditions of worth together form the self-concept that becomes their internal working model. The child will not have awareness of these introjections as conditions of worth: for them, this is who they are and how the world is.

In person-centred theory, conditions of worth are understood to be unique to each person and their own experience. It is through the unconditionally accepting relationship offered by therapy that these conditions can dissolve, allowing the person to move toward new and more congruent expressions of him/herself. As such, there is no need to describe general patterns of conditions of worth, as the approach to therapy is always the same, no matter what the person's conditions of worth are. Unlike therapy based on attachment theory, in which the practitioner offers a different way of responding based on the client's attachment styles, the person-centred therapist strives to offer an unconditionally accepting, genuine and empathic relationship, no matter what the attachment style of their client is. Rogers does not specify ages, stages or sensitive periods. In contrast to attachment theory, person-centred therapy might appear to be rather loose. It sees the development process as unique to each individual – a weaving together of maturation and innate curiosity, driven by the actualising tendency of the organism. The therapist strives to understand the unique individual's conditions of worth through empathic listening, not through a pre-defined typology.

It would be entirely possible to understand attachment styles as expressions of congruence, if that were needed. Table 11.1 shows each category of attachment that children aged 12–18 months experience in the Strange Situation procedure and, underneath, the same behaviours described through the lens of conditions of worth.

Table 11.1: Attachment types and corresponding conditions of worth in the Strange Situation

Anxious-avoidant insecure	Secure attachment	Anxious-resistant insecure
Displays little distress when the significant other leaves. Play is unaffected by their presence or absence. Reunion is tentative and casual. Equally comforted by the stranger.	Maintains contact with significant other and explores the space. Shows distress on separation. Calmed and soothed when reunited. Curious of strangers in the presence of significant other but distressed in their absence.	Shows more anger and/ or passivity. Clings to the significant other rather than explores the toys. Difficulty finding comfort when reunited. Seeks and resists contact through a show of anger. Resists the stranger's efforts to make contact.
Conditions of worth – to be independent and not need others	**Few or no conditions of worth**	**Conditions of worth – to please others and seek intimacy**
The child experiences being dismissed and rejected when they seek intimacy. As such, they learn that to be valued they need to be independent. They learn to hide their experiences of anxiety, anger and joy, as these emotions are perceived as unacceptably needy. The child stays close enough to feel a sense of safety and far enough away to avoid rejection. Authentic spontaneity is suspended.	Significant other is responsive and congruent. The child learns that they are valued and has no need to distort their experiences to fit the needs of the other. The relationship facilitates the child's internal locus of evaluation such that they congruently evaluate their feelings of anxiety, anger and joy. The child is able to seek intimacy and independence in the relationship.	The parent's behaviours are inconsistent. The child is confused as to what behaviours are regarded positively, except for staying close. They learn that intimacy is to be valued. The child maintains close proximity as attempts at self-regulation and curiosity are unsupported.

Secure attachment and congruence

As already noted, in the strange situation a securely attached child will be spontaneous, curious and autonomous in their explorations of their environment. In essence, this is the behaviour of a child who would be described in person-centred theory as having few or any conditions of worth. Instead, they feel valued for who they are, rather than what they do, and so are learning to be congruent in their self-expression.

Seen this way, both attachment and person-centred theories are describing the same fulfilment, through a facilitative relationship, of the child's developmental capacities. For Rogers (1951: 503), it is the caregiver's capacity to value the child as a separate, autonomous individual that leads to 'a secure self which can serve to guide his behavior freely admitting in to awareness in accurately symbolized form, all the relevant evidence of his experience in terms of its organismic satisfactions, both immediate and longer range'.

Insecure attachment and incongruence

Whereas the securely-attached child might be said to have developed no or few conditions of worth, insecure attachment types reflect expressions of incongruence arising from particular conditions of worth. The link between the conditional nature of parent–child interactions and insecure attachment was noted by Mary Main (1979), who argued that attachment types are conditional behavioural strategies for regulating the caregiver's response to the child's anxiety, anger and joy. Thus, the child manipulates their emotions and their expression in response to the conditions of the relationship. It is important to note that, for the child, the perception that this is what they are doing will not be in their awareness.

For the anxious-avoidant child, the conditions of worth are likely to be that it isn't acceptable to expect others to meet their needs – that to be valued one must be strong, independent, and not dependent on others. With such conditions of worth, feelings of anxiety at separation are unacceptable, and the child learns that these feelings must not even exist. For the anxious-ambivalent child, it isn't acceptable to exist as a truly separate being. Their needs for intimacy and autonomy are unreliably met by the other. As a result, they experience inconsistent conditions of worth, which inhibits them in their capacity to create a consistent self-structure within which to process self-experience.

Attachment types, or, to use person-centred terminology, particular patterns of conditions of worth, shape the developing child's interactions with the world. Attachment theorists understand how these three attachment types, once established, influence how we process emotional information throughout our lives. Similarly, our configurations of conditions of worth influence how we process emotional information, in exactly the same way.

Turning to adults, Table 11.2 shows how the three adult attachment types, as described by Hazan and Shaver (1987), can be understood using the terminology of incongruence. These are presented as statements that a person might make if they have self-awareness of their conditions of worth. Many people will, however, lack such self-awareness and not experience their way of relating to the world as an expression of their conditional positive self-regard.

Table 11.2: Adult attachment types and corresponding conditions of worth

Anxious-avoidant insecure adult attachment	Secure adult attachment	Anxious-resistant insecure adult attachment
I am somewhat uncomfortable being close to others. I find it difficult to trust them completely and to allow myself to depend on them. I am nervous when anyone gets too close, and others often want me to be more intimate than I feel comfortable with.	I find it relatively easy to get close to others and am comfortable depending on them and having them depend on me. I don't worry about being abandoned or about someone getting too close to me.	I find that others are reluctant to get as close as I would like. I often worry that my partner doesn't really love me or won't want to stay with me. I want to get very close to my partner, and this sometimes scares people away.
Condition of worth – to be autonomous	**Congruent adult**	**Condition of worth – to seek Intimacy**
I must be independent and able to look after myself. I will do things to show others how independent I am. I experience positive self-regard when I am self-reliant. But when I feel vulnerable and in need of intimacy with others, I experience anxiety about being rejected.	I am loveable and love others. This is true even if my behaviour is not liked at that moment. I am important because I am unique. Other people are important and unique too. I can feel regard for myself, even when others are critical	I must be loveable to others. I will do and say things to gain their positive regard. I experience positive self-regard when people love me. But when people are not thinking of me and I am not their priority, I feel anxious and begin to feel bad about myself.

Implications

Returning to the students we introduced earlier, they had come to the understanding that person-centred theory was lacking because it did not have an understanding of attachment processes. We hope it is clear that person-centred personality theory offers an understanding of developmental processes that is, in essence, identical to attachment theory but, whereas attachment theory is used to describe specific discrete attachment types, person-centred theory does not.

For professionals who associate highly differentiated diagnostic categories with sophistication, this leaves person-centered theory looking simplistic and naïve. Seen from a diagnostic point of view, Rogers' theory would indeed be incomplete and lacking in detail as, unlike attachment theory, it does not offer an understanding of the different patterns or styles of attachment and the preferred way of relating to each of those categories. As such, therapists seeking a way of working based on diagnosis may be interested in incorporating attachment theory in their practice. We argue, however, that to do so is antithetical to person-centred practice. The fact that it does not describe specific types is not a failing in the person-centred approach but its unique strength, representing as it does the underpinning philosophy that it is the client who is their own best expert. Seen this way, the theories may be similar, but it is in the implications for practice that they differ.

As we have seen, attachment theory and the person-centred approach are similar in their understandings of how early experiences matter, the ways in which people develop an internal working model or self-structure, and how that in turn influences mental health and their needs in therapy. What is different are the philosophical underpinnings. Attachment theory is an expert-driven approach and, as such, has a categorical system that allows the therapist to plan in advance what they will do and how to be in relationship. The implication of attachment theory is that the therapist adapts their relational stance towards the client on the basis of the client's attachment style.

In contrast, the person-centred therapist follows the client and uses empathic understanding to know what the client needs and their own congruence to determine how to relate to the client moment by moment. For the person-centred therapist, categorical thinking forecloses empathy, as we are no longer able to enter our client's frame of reference through an 'as if' attitude. Categories mean that we would know before the client what direction they need to take. There may be generalities of behaviour that can be described as categories, but the person-centred therapist must be able to bracket this way of thinking when with a client if they are to be able to enter the client's world and understand their experiences from their point of view. To strive to categorise someone in order to understand them is the opposite of an empathic process. Seen this way, clues to understanding the world of an individual client cannot be found in theories, frameworks, categories, taxonomies or systems. Empathy is the keystone for understanding the narrative of the client and for the foundation of relationship. Using a knowledge of attachment styles to categorise a client may detract from our ability to empathise with and get to know him or her as a unique human being.

The task of the person-centred therapist is to understand their clients' unique configurations of conditions of worth and in what ways their particular patterns of incongruence are expressed. As such, the person-centred therapist has no need for pre-defined categories, as these will restrict their empathic understanding and ability to relate to their client authentically in whatever way that they come to know them. The person-centred therapist will strive to relate to their client in a way that is most meaningful, given the client's expressions of incongruence, but how they do this will unfold within the therapeutic relationship, rather than be determined by diagnosis. To do otherwise would be to be ahead of the client, and not alongside them. From a person-centred perspective, this is at best a meaningless interaction, and damaging at worst.

Conclusion

In this chapter, we hope to have shown that it is of value for person-centred therapists to be knowledgeable about attachment theory and able to understand the similarities and differences of the two theories. However, integration is, in our view, misguided, as the two theories have contrasting philosophical views on how to work with other people. Understanding developmental processes is already at the heart of person-centred theory and therapy. As such, there is no need for therapists to look to other theories of child development. It is not a failing in person-centred theory that it does not offer a categorical system of understanding styles of attachment; rather, it is a demonstration that the uniqueness of every therapeutic relationship is central to its philosophy.

References

Ainsworth MD, Blehar M, Waters E, Wall S (1978). *Patterns of Attachment: a psychological study of the strange situation*. Hillsdale NJ: Lawrence Erlbaum Associates.

Bowlby J, Fry M, Ainsworth MDS (1953). *Child Care and the Growth of Love*. Baltimore, MD: Penguin.

Bowlby J (1969). *Attachment and Loss. Vol I: attachment*. London: Hogarth Press.

Bowlby J (1973). *Attachment and Loss. Vol II: separation, anxiety and anger*. London: Hogarth Press.

Bowlby J (1980). *Attachment and Loss. Vol III: loss, sadness and depression*. London: Hogarth Press.

Bowlby J (1988). *A Secure Base: parent–child attachment and healthy human development*. London: Routledge.

Gonzalez DM (2016). Client variables and psychotherapy outcomes. In: Cain DJ, Keenan K, Rubin S (eds). *Humanistic Psychotherapies: handbook of research and practice* (2nd ed). Washington, DC: American Psychological Association (pp455–482).

Hazan C, Shaver P (1987). Romantic love conceptualized as an attachment process. *Journal of Personality and Social Psychology 52*(3): 511.

Holmes J (2001). *The Search for the Secure Base: attachment theory and psychotherapy* Hove: Routledge.

Main M (1979). The ultimate causation of some infant attachment phenomena. *Behavioral and Brain Sciences 2*: 640–643.

Meins E (2017). The predictive power of attachment. *The Psychologist* January: 20–24.

Rogers CR (1951). *Client-Centered Therapy*. Cambridge Massachusetts: The Riverside Press.

Rogers CR (1959). A theory of therapy, personality and interpersonal relationships, as developed in the client-centered framework. In: Koch S (ed). *Psychology: a study of science. Vol 3: Formulations of the person and the social context*. New York: McGraw-Hill (pp184–256).

CONTEXTS

12 Facing psychotic functioning: person-centred contact work in residential psychiatric care

Dion Van Werde

In the early 1990s, Professor Germain Lietaer (1990) already pointed out a new trend in person-centred/experiential psychotherapy: there is now a greater differentiation between varied client populations and settings. Along these lines, and after several years of practice and refinement, I will give you some examples of our way of working with people suffering psychotic functioning.

I will start with introducing Prouty's pre-therapy (Van Werde & Prouty, 2013; Van Werde, 2014, 2016; Prouty, 2008; Sanders, 2007), our major source of inspiration. Basically, Prouty defines contact as the antidote to psychotic alienation and formulates a way of restoring impaired contact functioning. I will describe how, on our ward, this approach has been translated into a multidisciplinary contact milieu to serve clients who are recovering from a psychotic breakdown, and in the process of strengthening their contact functioning.

Pre-therapy was originally formulated in relation to severe contact-loss and applied to different kinds of populations and in different settings (see, for example, Van Werde, Sommerbeck & Sanders, 2015; Prouty, 1976, 1994; Prouty, Van Werde & Pörtner, 2002; Krietemeyer & Prouty, 2003; Coffeng, 2001; Peters, 1999; Pörtner, 2000; Sommerbeck, 2003; Van Werde, 2002a, 2002b, 2004; Van Werde & Morton, 1999). In this chapter, I want to highlight that a person-centred conceptualisation and practice proves to be possible in a residential setting and with clients who have a milder form of contact loss, for instance those recovering from or fighting against the threat of psychotic breakdown. Mutatis mutandis, the ideas behind this practice, can be transposed to work with other kinds of endangered contact functioning.

Prouty's pre-therapy

Dr Garry Prouty's work can be considered as a theoretical evolution in person-centred/experiential psychotherapy (Prouty, 1994). Rogers (1957) had considered 'contact' as the first of the six necessary and sufficient conditions for constructive personality change. When starting his clinical work, Prouty, however, discovered that the clients he worked with in those days – people tragically suffering psychosis, with an average admission duration in huge hospitals of about 30 years and no proper care offered – were not able to engage in a therapeutic relationship, since contact in itself was problematic. Hence, a kind of pre-relationship activity was necessary before entering regular Rogerian psychotherapy. Clients Prouty worked with seemed unable to touch their experiences, if not being completely affectively frozen. This echoes with Eugene Gendlin's consideration of the concrete and bodily felt process of experiencing as the key issue in psychotherapy. Prouty consequently stated that pre-experiencing activity was needed to unfreeze frozen affective functioning, so that people could access their inner life again. Pre-therapy thus can be defined as pre-relationship and pre-experiencing activity.

In this respect, the notion of pre-expressive functioning (Prouty, 1998) is highly important. It is an intuitive and heuristic concept derived from Prouty's personal experience, as well as from clinical and quantitative case studies of pre-therapy. It points to disorganised and incoherent experiencing as capable of being transformed into a meaningful pattern. In that respect, Prouty considers all symptomatic behaviour as a manifestation of relationship and feeling efforts, even though not yet on an expressive level. If the caregiver is able to work with these forms of functioning, the person might be able to develop into expressiveness, and thus access relationship formation and experiential functioning. The use of the notion 'pre' indicates a highly therapeutic vision, since it underlines the teleological capacity of symptomatology: symptoms carry in themselves the key to understanding and meaning. If, for example, a man is standing in the corridor, face anxious, looking to the ceiling, and addresses you when passing by with the words, 'Do you hear them?', this can be seen as somebody trying to relate by asking a question and trying to pre-experientially 'express' his fear by his facial expression, the tone of his voice and his physical closeness to you. Even when he is not conscious of how he looks and how he gives away his inner world by his appearance and behaviour, it is obvious that this man is trying to deal with the strange experiences he has and the consequent feelings he is suffering from. His contacting you is a significant moment in a possible process of disclosure of everything that is locked up in the alienating symptomatology of experiencing auditory hallucinations.

In pre-therapy, the therapist uses five kinds of reflections through which the client is invited to (re)contact reality, affect and other people. Contact reflections are extraordinarily literal and concrete reflections that aim to reach the severely withdrawn or regressed client. Through the technique of reflecting, the realities of world, self and others are offered in a non-directive, yet very concrete, non-judgmental, non-evaluative and non-interpretative mode. The pre-therapy reflections are attuned to the low level of contact functioning of the client. The caregiver and reality are hereby allowed by the client to bridge into his or her idiosyncratic world. If the client permits himself to contact the reality that is mentioned in a reflection ('You are standing in the corridor', 'You look scared', 'You look into my eyes and ask whether I hear them'), this means that he has already come out of his idiosyncratic, sheltered position a little bit, and has let the world and the one who verbalises it come in. He has recognised that he is on the ward corridor, that he is addressing the nurse, and that, in doing so, he has been showing and sharing some of his psychotic functioning for maybe the first time. This is individual pre-therapy. Basically, the client now can freely choose to stay in his reality or engage in a shared reality. This latter reality can be about outer and 'objective' realities, such as people, places, events and things, or it can be about communication with others, but it can also be about contacting his own inner feelings. The five kinds of contact reflections as defined by Prouty (1976) are:

1. *Situational Reflection (SR)* reflects the client's situation, environment or milieu. People, places, events and things are reflected to facilitate reality contact: for example, 'A wooden chair', 'The sun is shining in', 'Bea is entering the room'

2. *Facial Reflection (FR)* reflects pre-expressive feeling embodied in the face to facilitate affective contact: for example, 'Your eyes are wet', 'Céline smiles'

3. *Body Reflection (BR)* reflects with words or, through mimicking with his own body, the movements or positioning of the client. It helps clients to integrate body expression within the sense of self: for example, 'You are making a fist', or making and upholding a fist, just as the client does, or combining the two ways

4. *Word for Word Reflection (WWR)* reflects single words, sentence fragments and other verbal disorganisation, to develop communicative contact: for example, '(Mumble), wood, (mumble), three, (mumble)' – the therapist reflects 'Wood, three', even if the meaning is not clear

5. *Reiterative Reflection (RR)* repeats previous reflections that proved to make contact. It helps to re-contact the client.

Contact reflections (what the therapist does) facilitate the contact functions (client process), which result in the emergence of contact behaviours (which can be measured – for a review of the research, see Dekeyser, Prouty & Elliot, 2008).

Once overall contact is (re)established, people can shift to more classical psychotherapy, or enjoy the restored contact as it is and profit from the possibilities this holds. Prouty (personal communication) mentions a young woman with special needs who was granted permission to go to her mother at weekends again, after she – with the help of a pre-therapy treatment – became able to contact her feelings of anger, and even express them, so preventing herself from unexpected explosions of feeling, causing repeated unreliable behaviour and management problems within this one-parent family.

Pre-therapy applied in a residential ward setting

Since we are working on a treatment ward in residential care for people with psychotic presentation, the question arose of how to translate Prouty's individual method into our setting and our specific client group (Van Werde 2002c, 2007). Within a rather traditional medical environment, we created the necessary space to formulate an explicit person-centred approach and apply pre-therapy whenever indicated. Of course, on our ward, the larger percentage of what happens and has to be done is quite similar to comparable wards anywhere else. Medication has to be distributed, people have to be motivated, beds have to be made, therapies offered, educational sessions given, visitors welcomed and so on. The person-centred approach and the skill of working along the lines of Prouty's pre-therapy, however, bring about a different quality in the care given: the interactions, the overall atmosphere and the design of the therapy. We compare the impact of this with the impact of the leaven in the bread. A small adjunctive element can cause a big qualitative difference in the outcome. Seventy or more per cent of the work basically remains the same, whatever approach you follow, whatever therapeutic song you sing. The specifically person-centred element represents only 30 per cent or less of the whole work. It is that 30 per cent that makes the difference. In our situation, this means that staff need to be trained in pre-therapy and schooled in contact facilitation. This is to say that a new vision can be integrated, which does not alter the everyday activities very much, and yet can have an enormous, determining impact on the essence and outlook of the care that is given.

The level of functioning of the clients on our ward can be situated at a grey-zone level. We use that term to describe a level in between 'up in the air' psychotic functioning versus well-rooted, so-called anchored functioning. Typical of this level is that characteristics of pre-expressive as well as of expressive behaviour alternate rapidly, or are even present simultaneously. A client described to me his weekend visit home in terms of '... so and so Mr Devil, and then I went to the shop to buy some stuff for dinner, Mr Devil, and my wife said...' He clearly every now and then mixed everyday reality with his idiosyncratic psychotic reality. Another client asked a nurse, 'Are they coming to get me?' in a very slow monotone voice, and on the one hand talked about the reality of the schedule for leaving to go home, but at the same time was psychotically anxious about being taken away by God-knows-who to be killed. Each reality clouded the other, and they were present together. It was thought that there was incest in that family, so the uncertainty about the hour of being picked up by her parents (father?) probably triggered the remembrance of the other reality of being suddenly visited or taken away, and, as a result, this pushed her into a 'grey-zone' blend of asking a realistic question, but mixed with paranoid psychotic experiencing.

In general, both sides of this transition zone need to be dealt with, need a contact offer. The people we work with are recovering from the most acute phase of contact loss of their psychotic breakdown and are struggling to have their contact functioning restored. So, they not only need our continuous support to overcome the still intimidating psychosis on the one hand, but can also profit from a contact-strengthening offer to fortify their newly regained but still fragile anchorage in shared reality, so that they can build up their healthy functioning further.

First, contact needs to be established, and then more functional functioning becomes possible – participating in group activities, making arrangements for the coming weekend, getting together for coffee, dressing or clearing the table, emptying the dishwasher and so on.

I will highlight some applications of pre-therapy in facing psychosis as we do it on our ward. I also hope to spell out what it means to create a contact milieu (see also Van Werde, in Prouty, Van Werde & Pörtner, 2002: 61–120).

In our contact offer, we make a difference between spontaneous and informal use of pre-therapy reflections as described in this contribution versus more structured contact work on the ward (ibid). Needless to say, looking at people through the spectacles of 'contact' has had an important influence on how we design and deliver our services.

It is not so easy to put across this kind of work to others. In general, when speaking about the praxis of pre-therapy, and especially when reflections are written down, they tend to look mechanical and a mere repetition of the client. Beautiful moments of delicate interaction, receptiveness of the existential situation, the required discipline and concentration, and the relatively distant playfulness, combined with a sincere and close compassion, are hard to transfer onto paper. The poetry and the art tend to get lost. Therefore, we recommend combining the reading of texts such as this one with exposure to pre-therapy carried out by dedicated and experienced therapists, who have had feedback about their work by Prouty himself, who regularly present their work for peer supervision to the members of the Pre-Therapy International Network and annually attend the network's meeting in order to stay up to date with what is happening with pre-therapy around the globe.[1]

This chapter is attempting to illustrate the benefits to be had from understanding and knowing how to use pre-therapy and pre-therapy reflections, especially in dealing with people recovering from psychosis or people trying to avoid drifting away towards a full-blown psychosis again. I will call this 'contact work', rather than psychotherapy or pre-therapy. I will give some very practical examples about how this contact work can be an overarching concept in an individual session, and how reflecting can be integrated in daily nurse–patient interactions.

Understanding contact work in an individual consultation

Tina is an ex-patient of our ward. She comes unexpectedly to my office for advice. She asks me a direct question: 'What can I do, so I don't become psychotic again?' Previous psychotic functioning seems to be re-surfacing and is making her anxious.

---

1. See www.pre-therapy.com (accessed 21 November, 2016).

The same topics tend to flood her daily functioning: she is delusional about the media and suffers from feelings of guilt about things that have happened in the past. At the same time, she seems relatively anchored: she can ask a question; she understands that she had to wait half an hour before I could talk with her, since I was busy with another appointment; she has contact with the growing threat of losing contact, and so on. This functioning on these two levels simultaneously is typical of the population we serve.

She starts by telling me the story of her first psychosis again. She has been educated in media, is gifted at drawing, and has been very keen to work in audio-visual media. Once she was in love with a man who looked like a TV newsreader (the anchorman). She starts sending him CDs, writing him letters and phoning him frequently. This behaviour increases. Finally, the man sues her for stalking. The lawsuit says that she must stop. Frightened by this verdict, she backs off. Later, she finds herself falling in love with a newsreader from a national network when she sees him reading an item about a matter of jurisdiction. She starts sending packages to the network, with all kinds of graphics, CDs and messages. At work – she designs websites – she continuously feels spied upon by TV people, and fears for her life. Her functioning becomes problematic. At her brother's one night, she says the newsreader on television asked a newspaper about what was on her mind. This is too much for her. She cannot bear it any longer, and wants to find out what is going on. She decides to be admitted.

We continue to look at what is going on now. She tells how her past is coming back and about how this destabilises her. She feels, for example, confused about what the people who she sent the packages to a year ago have done with them. 'I don't know what they did with my mail. I have put everything of myself in it,' she says. 'It was full of very personal thoughts and hopes.' She also sees things on television that others can't see. 'Sometimes they look away from the camera. I frightened them.' She also feels guilty about the mail and is 'inclined to examine everything carefully'. Obviously, she is suffering from a mixture of realities which she lives in: the psychotic past, and the actual.

To complete the picture of how her life looks, we decide to make an inventory of the things that are not burdening her and that even give her joy and support. She sums them up: sleeping, to wake up in the morning, eating, going to the solarium, writing Christmas cards, decorating the Christmas tree, buying presents. She also likes housework, such as doing the dishes and cleaning her room. Her job still gives her satisfaction as well. Sports such as swimming with others is still fine. When she doesn't quarrel with her friend, this contact is welcome too. She even makes plans for the future – looking for an internship, developing her CV, engaging in voluntary work – and this perspective helps her. Bringing all this together, we can recognise the so-called pre-expressive, grey-zone intermediate and anchored functioning. Respectively, they appeared as answers to the questions: 'Where do you come from and how has it been before?'; 'What is threatening you?'; 'What are your present doubts and fears?'; 'What are your resources?' The conclusion that she formulates after having looked at her past and present contact-functioning is that, when talking about it, she clearly felt the difference between healthy and constructive versus difficult contents and actions. She states: 'I'd better stop letting myself be sucked into areas that can make me psychotic (again)'; 'I'd better focus and direct myself to anchoring'. The conversation helped to strengthen her contact-functioning and indirectly proved to be beneficial in reducing psychotic symptomatology. She got an overview and could decide herself which direction to go from there. She chose to invest in building up strength and to stay away from the quicksand of psychotic ideation. In contact terminology, we would say that the client herself realised that anchoring and contact-loss are directly and inversely related. Investing in building up strength prevented her from getting psychotic again.

Nurses bridging individual process and ward structure

The following vignettes are taken from a video presentation the nursing staff made to illustrate how they are influenced by pre-therapy in their daily work, especially when working with clients functioning in the 'grey zone' between an anchored and an idiosyncratic/psychotic level. The art of making contact here requires the capacity to estimate and work on the same contact-level as the client, and then still empathically follow the client's level when slowly shifting upwards towards congruent communication, once the contact is established and becoming more solid. Unlike the previous example, nurses live and deal with 'objective' or 'shared' reality all the time. In concrete terms, this means that, besides reaching the client, they also have to take care of ward organisation, and especially help the client consent to and participate in it, even when afraid or not understanding, withdrawn, bizarre or unmotivated. This requires a continuous building of bridges, particularly when the people are only just re-anchoring to the world that they were losing grip of, or that they were pulling themselves back from. So, the idea is to first make contact and then address surrounding reality together.

1. Making arrangements for the coming weekend

The nurse enters the room of An – a patient – to call her for the coffee break, where she is expected. A bridge has to be built between ward life and the patient, who sits alone in her room. On the one hand, An looks frozen, doesn't show feelings or comment on the things on her mind, doesn't react to a directly asked question, and sits in her room like this for hours. On the other hand, being admitted on the ward presupposes things like drinking coffee together, participating in the therapies on offer, and responding to questions the nurses ask concerning, for instance, the arrangements made for the coming weekend. The nurse tries to bridge both sides of the given situation by making contact with An first, and then going over the nurses' agenda about finding out when exactly An wants to leave the hospital for the weekend and when she will be back.

To do this, the nurse stays with the concrete. In the beginning, it is in the format of mere pre-therapy reflecting. Later on, the level of functioning permits carefully asked questions. The nurse continuously estimates the level of contact-functioning of the client and shifts her level up when this seems appropriate. This then takes the form of concrete questions or congruent remarks, but always centres on the here and now, so as not to lose the client.

The reflections or first tentative questions can be about something that they see through the window (for example, SR:[2] 'Outside the room people are walking'; 'It's started raining again'); about something that happened just before this encounter (RR: 'At noon, I came to get you and you were sitting in exactly the same position as you are sitting now'), or happened yesterday ('Did your son give you his little teddy bear that you are holding in your hand now, to bring with you to the hospital?'). Sometimes the client herself is addressed, be it her body position (BR: 'Your elbow is on the table'; 'You're sitting like you were at noon'), the expression on her face (FR: 'You sigh… like you're thinking…'), or the words she starts to speak (WWR: 'Letting go hurts …'; 'I can't let it go, mustn't ever let it go'). The Facial Reflection 'You sigh' opens the door to her contacting and expressing feeling. She thaws a little bit and makes eye contact. Her contact level improves and makes a question–answer interaction possible. They finally can talk about the arrangements made for the weekend. The client now is ready to leave her corner by the bed, and they can go for coffee in the living room together.

2. Bizarre laughing in the television room

Tine and Freya are watching television. Christophe (the nurse) comes over to sit with them for five minutes, and asks if they would be willing to help him set the table for dinner later. Freya occasionally gives a sudden laugh without objective reason, and mumbles words, spoken to herself. The nurse talks to Tine about the television programme she is watching, and reflects to Freya when she is laughing and mumbling. By doing so, the situation seems contained. There is care for the structure on the one hand: Tine is talked to, and the laughing is seen and dealt with by reflections. The empathic, accepting and non-judgmental non-interpretative contact offered to Freya, on the other hand, can help her to get in touch with mounting affect, to realise where she is, how she is behaving and how it looks to her fellow patient and the nursing staff. Once she is in contact with all this, she can perhaps start mastering the situation and herself more.

When the nurse in the end asks for cooperation, Tine is willing to help and even Freya seems to understand that Tine is willing to help, thus coming out of her private world a little.

---

2. See page 201 for key to abbreviations.

3. Overcoming clouded delusional functioning

A middle-aged woman is recovering from a depression with psychotic features. She has a delusion of poverty: everything is gone, empty, broken, or has ended. For a while she is convinced her husband has died, although this is not the case.

On another occasion, she sees the dishwasher full and stands motionless and frozen in front of it, with three cups in her hand, not knowing what to do.

In this fragment, Jo, the nurse, contacts her by reflecting what she is doing (SR: 'You are laying the table'; BR and SR: 'You are standing here, with a little box and spoons in your hand'; WWR: 'You say, there aren't enough spoons in the box!') and how she looks (FR: 'You look puzzled'; 'It is like you are asking a question'). This enables the woman to contact herself more, and consequently become more grounded, albeit still fragile contact. Once this first contact is established, the nurse then turns to the reality of what has to be done. By asking, cup by cup, if a spoon is already there, the patient realises that every cup already has a spoon. So, the delusional thought of not having enough spoons for every cup diminishes by contacting and anchoring in reality step by step and cup by cup. Only in this way could the woman grasp the whole situation and could see and conclude that everything was OK. The nurse continues the contact-strengthening work, and invites the woman to go to the kitchen with her to fetch sugar and milk to put on the table.

Discussion

By constantly paying attention to the contact level of the client, we discovered how complex therapeutic progress can be. We now hypothesise that distinction can be made between the level of contact with reality, contact with affect and contact with others (communicative contact). It is probable that, in a psychotherapeutic process, these three contact functions do not necessarily have an identical evolution. What is important for us at this point is the idea that maybe reality, affective and communicative contact can be separately influenced. This is significant, in particular if we think of ward settings where there are a lot of opportunities to have nurses focus on and work with reality and communication on a daily basis. Contact can be worked with. Theoretically, this also bridges the supposed gap, often complained of in person-centred care, between following individual process ('being with') or working with the given reality ('doing with'). Within the borders of our specific setting, without losing the person-centred attitude, and by always taking the very concrete as the starting point for any action, the two inversely related realities are synthetically worked with. You reflect to restore, or you practise to strengthen the poor contact functioning.

We continuously try to steer the patients (and ourselves) away from a therapist–patient interaction that is characterised by interpreting, taking over, controlling, structuring, product-focusing, judging and authoritarian; from an activity that is characterised by being repetitive, superficial, empty, dull, obligatory; from a level of functioning that is psychotic, inhibited, bizarre, isolated, non-accessible, insecure, covered-up and frozen, towards a functioning that is experiential, anchored, in-touch, shared, decided, active, creative, varied, concentrated, enjoyed and in process.

The treatment of choice is to look for contact and work with that part of a person's functioning that seems (still or already) rooted and operative, however small that part may be. We ally ourselves with that part that can congruently deal with the situation or that still has some strength left. As a psychotherapist or contact facilitator, we try to make contact, thus strengthening the anchorage, resulting in the person gradually mastering the situation again by his own force. The reasoning is that 'when contact increases, symptoms decrease'. We strive to communicate with patients and their families about how we think and what we do and why: to explain, for example, to clients why participating in all kinds of therapies is important – it helps them to strengthen their contact functioning and thus indirectly reduces psychosis as well.

Sometimes it is hard to grasp the pattern of change in a patient. Maybe at a given moment, the patient suffers more chaos and is threatening to the ward structure; because old psychological patterns are challenged, then a process of problematic experiencing starts up again and, consequently, a new personal equilibrium has to be found. Working on the strengthening of the contact functions, however, does not mean that we lose sight of our responsibilities for managing the individual patient and the ward as a whole. Reality is presented and is worked with, even when this means confronting or temporarily restricting the patient. Pre-therapy and contact work in general do help to bridge these two interests. As a matter of fact, and as previously stated, when contact increases, symptoms decrease, and the patient as a consequence 'fits' the structure better.

Basic in all this thinking about the translation of the contact paradigm into establishing a person-centred milieu is that we try not to deny psychosis, or hide it, or patronise the client. In line with the thoughts of Garry Prouty, we see psychotic behaviour as pre-expressive behaviour. That means that we look at such behaviour as a way of the client expressing meanings that are there, but not yet fully in process or available to the person himself. Thinking in terms of 'contact' and using the pre-therapy reflections when indicated serves as an overall source of inspiration and a vehicle for concrete staff–patient interactions. Our interventions can be aimed at either restoring absent contact, or at strengthening the newly recovered but still fragile contact. It is interesting to note that these efforts can be made without neglecting the other tasks that have to be done on the ward. It also helps to make more appropriate observations from within a phenomenological attitude (meaning without immediate labelling, interpreting or judging patients and their behaviour). It becomes a natural way of looking at, thinking about, interacting and working with the patients.

Bringing all this together in the multidisciplinary setting of a ward milieu can be considered – as Garry Prouty stated (personal communication) – an advancement in the person-centred method and as an expansion of pre-therapy practice.

References

Coffeng T (2001). Contact in the therapy of trauma and dissociation. In: Wyatt G, Sanders P (eds). *Rogers' Therapeutic Conditions: evolution, theory and practice. Volume 4: Contact and perception.* Ross-on-Wye: PCCS Books (pp153–167).

Dekeyser M, Prouty G, Elliott, R (2008). Pre-therapy process and outcome: a review of research instruments and findings. *Person-Centered and Experiential Psychotherapies* 7: 37–55.

Krietemeyer B, Prouty G (2003). The art of psychological contact: the psychotherapy of a mentally retarded psychotic client. *Person-Centered and Experiential Psychotherapies 2*: 151–161.

Lietaer G (1990). The client-centered approach after the Wisconsin project: a personal view on its evolution. In: Lietaer G, Rombauts J, Van Balen R (eds). *Client-Centered and Experiential Psychotherapy in the Nineties.* Leuven: Leuven University Press (pp19–45).

Peters H (1999). Pre-therapy: a client-centered experiential approach to mentally handicapped people. *Journal of Humanistic Psychology 39*: 8–29.

Pörtner M (2000). *Trust and Understanding: the person-centered approach to everyday care for people with special needs.* Ross-on-Wye: PCCS Books.

Prouty G (1976). Pre-therapy – a method of treating pre-expressive psychotic and retarded patients. *Psychotherapy: Theory, Research and Practice 13*: 290–295.

Prouty G (1994). *Theoretical Evolutions in Person-Centered/Experiential Therapy. Applications to schizophrenic and retarded psychoses.* New York: Praeger.

Prouty G (1998). Pre-therapy and the pre-expressive self. *Person-Centered Practice 6*: 80–88.

Prouty G (ed) (2008). *Emerging Developments in Pre-Therapy: a pre-therapy reader.* Ross-on-Wye: PCCS Books.

Prouty G, Van Werde D, Pörtner M (2002). *Pre-Therapy: reaching contact-impaired clients.* Ross-on-Wye: PCCS Books.

Rogers C (1957). The necessary and sufficient conditions of therapeutic personality change. *Journal of Consulting Psychology 2*: 95–103.

Sommerbeck L (2003). *The Client-Centred Therapist in Psychiatric Contexts: a therapists' guide to the psychiatric landscape and its inhabitants.* Ross-on-Wye: PCCS Books.

Sanders P (ed) (2007). *The Contact Work Primer.* Ross-on-Wye: PCCS Books.

Van Werde D (2002a). Prouty's pre-therapy and contact-work with a broad range of persons' pre-expressive functioning. In: Wyatt G, Sanders P (eds). *Rogers' Therapeutic Conditions: evolution, theory and practice. Volume 4: Contact and perception.* Ross-on-Wye: PCCS Books (pp168–181).

Van Werde D (2002b). The falling man: pre-therapy applied to somatic hallucinating. *Person-Centred Practice 10*: 101–107.

Van Werde D (2002c). Pre-therapy applied on a psychiatric ward. In: Prouty G, Van Werde D, Pörtner M (eds). *Pre-Therapy: reaching contact-impaired clients*. Ross-on-Wye: PCCS Books (pp61–120).

Van Werde D (2004). Cliëntgericht werken met psychotisch functioneren. In: Leijssen M, Stinckens N (eds). *Wijsheid in Gesprekstherapie*. Leuven: Universitaire Pers Leuven (pp209–224).

Van Werde D (2007). Contact work in a residential psychiatric setting: bridging person, team and context. In: Sanders P (ed). *The contact work primer*. Ross-on-Wye: PCCS (pp60-71).

Van Werde D (2014). Pre-therapy at its edges: from palliative care to exercising newly recovered contact functioning. In: Pearce P, Sommerbeck L (eds). *Person Centred Practice at the Difficult Edge*. Ross-on-Wye: PCCS Books (pp54–66).

Van Werde D (2016). Pre-therapy and working on contact. In: Lago C, Charura D (eds). *The Person-Centred Counselling and Psychotherapy Handbook: origins, developments and current applications*. Maidenhead: Open University Press (pp179–187).

Van Werde D, Morton I (1999). The relevance of Prouty's pre-therapy to dementia care. In: Morton I (ed). *Person-Centred Approaches to Dementia Care*. Bicester: Winslow Press (pp139–166).

Van Werde D, Prouty G (2013). Clients with contact-impaired functioning: pre-therapy. In: Cooper M, O'Hara M, Schmid P, Bohart A (eds). *The Handbook of Person-Centered Therapy* (2nd ed). Basingstoke: Palgrave (pp327–342).

Van Werde D, Sommerbeck L, Sanders P (2015). Introduction to the special issue on pre-therapy. *Person-Centered and Experiential Psychotherapies 14*(4): 263–267.

From patient to person: how person-centred theory values and understands unusual experiences

13

Kirshen Rundle

Some behaviour and distress appears so extreme or bizarre that it can be difficult for a person-centred therapist to enter fully into a client's frame of reference, particularly when there is no consensual reality. Such experiences and behaviours are commonly described in current western culture as 'psychotic', and are seen as signs or symptoms of mental illness. This medical metaphor is powerful, but also hotly contested by those who believe that theories about illness vary across history and culture.

Work with clients diagnosed as 'psychotic' is likely to bring a person-centred therapist into contact with other professionals who believe fervently that the way to help is by understanding their patients in medical terms. Indeed, clients themselves often believe this, equating their experiences with physical symptoms that are markers of physical illness, disorder or disease. Emphasis is placed on eliminating, or at least minimising, 'symptoms', often through use of medication, and sometimes through hospital admission. Some researchers, however, including some within the person-centred approach, question the rationale behind the medical metaphor and the usefulness of the consequent pathologising of unusual experience, and tend also to privilege individual meanings and views about what might help alleviate associated distress.

The first section of this chapter will explore different ideas about why people might start to have so-called psychotic experiences. A discussion of the medical model will be followed by examples of evidence that suggest unusual experiences can be better understood in non-medical terms. I will also outline how person-centred theory might explain such experiences. I will then describe some of the help currently offered to people who suffer distress associated with their unusual experiences, and evaluate the effectiveness of those methods in the light of evidence that demonstrates the value of attending to individual understandings. The effects of negative public attitudes towards 'mental illness' will be acknowledged. Finally, I will summarise arguments for the inclusion of person-centred therapy as an option for this client group, noting also the potential problems with achieving this goal.

Why do people develop 'psychotic' or unusual experiences?

There are various ways in which unusual experiences are explained or understood. This section will consider, first, the mainstream medical model, then evidence that challenges the medical explanation, and then how person-centred theory might explain these experiences.

1. Understanding 'psychotic' experiences as symptoms of mental illness or disorder

Mental distress and experiences that lie outside commonly accepted societal norms are often diagnosed as 'mental illnesses' when psychiatrists or psychologists become involved. People who, for example, hear voices, or see things that others do not, or hold unusual beliefs, or have unusual thought patterns would be described, respectively, as having auditory or visual hallucinations, delusions or being thought disordered. They are then positioned as 'mentally ill' or 'disordered'. The consequent prognosis is often poor, the treatments unpleasant, the implications far reaching and hope of recovery extinguished (Boyle, 2002).

Psychiatric classification does not always, however, connect with what the person is experiencing, and presents a stereotype of what is regarded as a concrete 'brain disease', despite a lack of reliable evidence for its existence (Boyle, 2002; van Os, 2014; Newnes, Holmes & Dunn, 1999, 2001). Some dispute the facticity of the medical model of mental distress, and claim that psychiatric diagnoses are representations that are conceptually weak and tautological, where symptoms are used to warrant a diagnosis and symptoms are explained by the diagnosis (Pilgrim, 2005). Attempts are then necessary to find evidence of their existence (Linscott & van Os, 2013; van Os et al, 2009).

The National Institute for Health and Care Excellence (NICE) has produced guidelines (most recently in 2014) that outline current recommendations for best practice in the diagnosis and treatment of psychosis and schizophrenia. It summarises evidence that theorises various biological, genetic and psychological factors that locate the genesis of the experiences described as 'psychosis' within the affected individual (NICE, 2014: 24–26). It concludes that these so-called mental illnesses are likely to be caused by an interaction between different factors, but acknowledges that the mechanisms behind such interactions have not yet been identified (Tandon, Keshavan & Nasrallah, 2008).

Genetic factors
Attempts to identify specific genetic factors involved in psychosis have, as yet, suggested only the likelihood that a range of genes are involved to varying degrees

(Sullivan, 2008). But this does not explain why any particular individual develops psychosis, as most people so diagnosed have no other affected relative (Harrison et al, 2001).

Biological factors

Various studies have found associations between the prevalence of schizophrenia and biological factors, including toxins, parental health and age, and problems at birth. But it has proved difficult to replicate results with any consistency (NICE, 2014: 24).

Neurotransmitter factors

The 'dopamine hypothesis' (Kapur & Mamo, 2003) suggests that psychotic experience might be caused by over-activity in the dopamine neurotransmitter system. But this suggestion is founded on the effects of antipsychotic medication on the 'symptoms', which, as Moncrieff (2009) has pointed out, does not imply causality, or even a connection. It merely means that these strong chemicals have a general flattening effect on every aspect of experience.

Psychological factors

There is some evidence that psychological factors, such as cognitive, emotional and reasoning functioning, are implicated in the development of psychosis (Garety et al, 2007; Gray et al, 1991; Hemsley, 1993), but nothing conclusive has yet been identified.

Psychosocial factors

Psychosocial issues to do with childhood trauma, poverty, lack of education and adversity are noted as contributing to the manifestation of 'psychotic illness' (NICE, 2014: 24). Such issues are discussed in the NICE guideline as factors that might increase an existing vulnerability to disease, rather than as causes in and of themselves. The same issues have been studied and reported on differently by other researchers (see, for example, Read & Dillon, 2013 below).

It is acknowledged, however, that no one theory captures completely the complexity of what is involved in the onset of these unusual experiences (van Os, 2010). Yet, those who accept and work within the medical model do not question whether such 'diseases' actually exist in the first place (Boyle, 2002). When people who have these experiences then seek advice or understanding from, for example, the NHS (2015) or mental health charities such as Mind (2016), the information available confirms they are suffering from an illness but offers no conclusive reasons for why they might have it. Arguably, being told your illness appears to be caused by a number of interdependent psychological, biological and environmental factors offers nothing of use in alleviating the associated distress or explaining why these experiences are happening.

These sources of advice and support also fail to explain why such 'psychotic experiences' are best understood as medical problems in the first place. The experience is problematised as 'medical' and treatment recommendations are made, based on such understanding. This is then accepted by society in general without question.

It is clear that the experience of hearing voices, or believing things that others do not, can often cause distress and make it difficult for a person to manage her life. This can be exacerbated when she applies stigmatising public attitudes to herself because of an awareness that her experiences might mean she is 'mad'. When this happens, there can be relief and comfort in being told you are ill by an expert who appears to have had experience of other people with such 'illnesses'. Hemmings (2008), citing Yalom (1995), suggests '"naming the beast", universality and hope' are positive effects that can come from reifying distress. People may start to feel supported and that they are not the only one suffering in this way. They can hope for treatment that will ameliorate their distress or confusion and put an end to their struggles. They might well describe themselves as 'ill' and want to get rid of what they see as the 'symptoms' that are causing the problem (Barham, 1997; Chadwick, 1997; Pitt et al, 2007).

2. Can unusual experiences be explained in a non-medical way?

Other research challenges the helpfulness of pathologising people on the basis of such experience (Boyle, 2002; Read & Dillon, 2013; Romme et al, 2009). Trauma and adversity have frequently been linked with the development of unusual experiences commonly described as psychotic (Geekie & Read, 2009; Longden et al, 2015; Read & Dillon, 2013).

This has major implications for treatment options, and for public and individual attitudes and understandings. Rather than asking, 'What is wrong with you?', with the emphasis indicating some deficit in the individual, it might be more appropriate to ask, 'What has happened to you?" (Dillon, 2011: 155). This response acknowledges that something other than disease or deficit might explain why the individual is having these unusual experiences. This approach might be described as a potentiality model, where, at worst, the experience is understood as an individual's struggle to make sense of their world in difficult circumstances (Laing, 1960; McCarthy-Jones, 2012; Romme et al, 2009), and at best is viewed as enhancing or developing an individual's life-world and psychological wellbeing (Grof & Grof, 1986; Laing, 1967; McCarthy-Jones et al, 2013).

Furthermore, these positions privilege meanings and understandings that 'experts by experience' themselves use, rather than those ascribed by a professional. Indeed, McCarthy-Jones and Longden (2015) found the phenomenology of hearing voices to be similar across diagnostic categories (specifically, post-traumatic stress disorder and schizophrenia). The origin and meaning of such experience might, therefore, be more usefully understood from the perspective of the person who is going through it. Help for any associated distress can then be tailored to what is needed, rather than offered in a standardised diagnostic treatment plan.

These arguments are also supported by evidence from cross-cultural (Larøi et al, 2014; Luhrmann et al, 2015) and historical studies (Leudar & Thomas, 2000). For instance, it appears that many people across the world hear voices without being diagnosed as mentally ill, and they live quite happily with their unusual experiences (Linscott & van Os, 2013; McGrath et al, 2015; Romme & Escher, 1993).

Such research shows the 'technological paradigm' (Thomas, 2014) is a relatively recent introduction into western thinking, and makes redundant any notion of 'psychotic' or 'non-psychotic', and 'abnormal' or 'normal' behaviour, so removing the relevance of pathologising unusual experience (Boyle, 2002; Newnes, Holmes & Dunn, 1999, 2001; Szasz, 1960). It accepts that understanding experiences as reactions to context and events is enough in itself. It also privileges individual meaning, which has implications for the help offered to those in distress or in need of support to function because of their experiences.

3: Person-centred ideas about how distress arises

Rogers did not concentrate on the mechanisms behind the development of different disturbances, or on classifying those disturbances; he was more interested in what those experiences might mean to the person and in facilitating individually tailored ways of alleviating associated distress (1961). Nor is there much person-centred theory since then that offers insight into why people might develop the particular experiences being discussed in this chapter.

A widely held view suggests that there is a fluid continuum of experience, with no need for arbitrary, culturally and historically determined categories of 'normal' and 'abnormal', or 'sane' and 'mad' (eg. McCarthy-Jones, Waegeli & Watkins, 2013: 255). This seems to concur with the person-centred approach, which views idiosyncratic responses to experience as part of what it is to be human. We do not, then, need to seek general causes for why people might start to hear voices, hold unusual beliefs or have disordered thought patterns. Instead, we must take account of the individual client's understanding. She might be suffering from an illness, or has experienced some trauma or adversity, but she might not. Support for this view comes from evidence showing a significant number of people hear voices and are not diagnosed as mentally ill (Linscott & van Os, 2013; McGrath et al, 2015), as well as from studies into experiences that could be defined as psychotic in different cultures and times (Leudar & Thomas, 2000). Any co-existing distress may, therefore, be linked to factors other than the experience itself – for instance, stigmatising public attitudes towards mental illness, which might also be internalised.

Building also on evidence that shows associations between psychotic experience and childhood trauma or adversity (eg. Varese et al, 2012), person-centred theory can account for the development of distress that leads to the experiences discussed in that research. This then has implications for the ways help is offered to those in distress. That theorising will now be explored.

Incongruence between experiencing and self-concept

Person-centred theory is founded on the principle of an actualising tendency that is always in operation to optimise the development of the organism. Ideally, we would always be open to the flow of our experiencing and be able to act according to our actualising tendency. In reality, however, we are constrained by the need to maintain the picture of ourselves we have developed over the course of our lives – the 'self-concept'. This invariably includes what Rogers called 'conditions of worth', which start to arise when we are children. He explains these conditions as denials or distortions of our experiencing made necessary in order to ensure we remain 'lovable' and, therefore, can retain the positive regard necessary from significant caregivers before we are old enough to care for ourselves (Rogers, 1951). Rogers argued that distress arose when the incongruence between the self-concept and organismic experiencing became too great to manage (1961).

Disruption of the actualising process

Mearns and Thorne (2000) developed Rogers' concept of the actualising tendency, proposing instead an actualising process. They suggest that distress is only experienced when the balance is lost between the drive of the actualising tendency and the counterforce of 'social mediation' (the interaction with the individual's social contexts) (Mearns & Thorne, 2000: 184), in either direction. This acknowledges that, despite the actualising tendency's drive to optimise organismic potential, it cannot operate successfully without taking account of context if humans are, as Rogers claimed, essentially prosocial. It is important, therefore, to maintain a balance that satisfies both individual and social needs. This might, to some extent, explain the power that 'experts' have over people who seek help. There is a basic need to balance our own needs with those laid down by society. This would explain not just our own disquiet at being different from the norm, but also our going along with treatments imposed by so-called experts who claim to know best how to return us to 'normal'.

Alienation and inauthenticity

Schmid (2005, also Chapter 5, this volume) similarly emphasises the need to be successful in relationship – with ourselves and with others. He suggests that people can live contentedly in an inauthentic way and that distress is only experienced if they also feel alienated from others or themselves. In current western societies, where 'psychotic experience' is considered so negatively and as a disorder, it makes sense that a person would find it difficult to accept the experience without negative judgement – and hence, alienation from themselves. In an attempt to comply with the force of social mediation and their self-concept, they might try to deny, distort or externalise the experience. When this inauthenticity becomes too difficult to sustain, distress might occur. Distress might also occur due to alienation from those who do not share the same reality. Schmid notes that psychological suffering is experienced as real, but an understanding of *order* and *disorder* may also be understood as real, despite those notions being social constructions (2005: 34). The individual is then faced with a dilemma about whether to live authentically but isolated and ostracised, or to live inauthentically and deny self or experiencing.

Thwarting of effective processing

Warner (2009, also Chapter 6, this volume) suggests there is a universal drive towards processing information that can be interrupted or hampered if adversities such as childhood trauma occur. She offers a framework for why and how things that happen to us affect how we are and our potential for change. For instance, people who labour under 'psychotic process' (Warner, 2002) find it difficult to construct a narrative about their lives that offers the possibility of coherent acceptance into the prevailing culture. Warner argues that such people sometimes experience hallucinations or delusions that are difficult to understand and process, especially given cultural norms. This then adds to the stress and isolation they are experiencing and they find it difficult to connect with themselves and others in any meaningful way. 'Dissociated process' (Warner, 2000) means people struggle to 'understand or moderate the intensity' (Warner, 2005: 92) of early traumatic experiences. They have, therefore, dissociated, or separated themselves, from the trauma as a way of dealing with it. 'Fragile process' (Warner, 2000) again arises because of inconsistent or neglectful experiences of early relationships with caregivers. People are unable to predict the types of behaviour likely to elicit positive responses. They are therefore emotionally labile and hold things at very low or very high levels of intensity. Finally, 'metaphact process' (Warner, 2007) is a form of understanding and communicating that can seem odd to others. Warner describes it as combination of fact and metaphor that is meaningful to the individual and is used by them in a fairly stable way to convey certain feelings or meanings. Such communication can give the impression of 'thought disorder', and if, as is likely, the person is misunderstood, their distress and isolation is likely to increase even more.

This notion of processing offers a way of understanding how and why people may come to behave in certain ways. It also reinforces ideas about agency through its reliance on the actualising process, which proposes that the individual seeks to find the optimal way of coping at all times. Warner's ideas are supported by other work on trauma (Longden et al, 2015; Read & Dillon, 2013), and by studies specifically into voice hearing (Romme & Escher, 1993, 2000; Romme et al, 2009).

Unusual experiences as authentic experiencing and potential for healing

My PhD research on person-centred therapy with people who hear voices leads me to speculate that 'psychotic' experience might not be evidence of a problem with the actualising tendency at all. Staying with a potentiality model, I suggest it is more likely to be a positive manifestation of the actualising tendency breaking through the self-concept and the constraints of the prevailing cultural and social mores; that it is, therefore, a most authentic form of processing and experiencing that highlights what needs to be attended to in order for progress to be made towards more positive functioning. This proposition might equally apply to other forms of 'psychotic experiencing'. For example, the concept of spiritual emergency as 'breakthrough' (Spiritual Crisis Network, 2016) and Schmid's (2005) views on alienation and authenticity seem relevant here. If this is so, the voices might be a very accurate symbolisation of experiencing and affect and may offer valuable clues for the client to use as the basis for work to be done in therapy. Hearing voices could then be the start of becoming more open to the flow of experiencing, as Rogers advocates in his process conception of therapy.

It is up to the therapist to follow the client's lead in working out what the experience signifies, and this might, at times, be difficult to do. But, as Warner argues in her discussion of 'metaphact process' (2007), it is not the client's job to speak the language of the therapist but the therapist's duty to try to understand the way the client is communicating.

While the above perspectives can offer a way of understanding why people might become distressed and why they might act in certain ways, none of them account specifically for the mechanisms responsible for the development of 'hallucinations', 'delusions' or 'thought disorder'. We are left, I propose, with the notion that these experiences are just that – some people's experiences. The responsibility of a therapist is to work with people in distress according to their unique frame of reference. It might even be that the mechanisms are idiosyncratic and the experience itself is a manifestation of the unique person and her context. This answers the question why some people who have experienced trauma start to have 'psychotic experiences' and others do not.

Ways of helping people who have unusual experiences and are suffering distress

The next section will explore various kinds of help offered to people who have unusual experiences and are in distress. Similarities with the person-centred approach will be noted.

Medication

Antipsychotic medication can affect 'psychotic symptoms' in about 33 per cent of cases (Moncrieff, 2009). This does not mean the 'symptoms' have been 'cured'. These drugs are very powerful chemicals and will flatten or mask emotional responses so that an individual no longer minds so much about what they are experiencing, or is not so acutely aware of it in such a vivid way (Moncrieff, 2013). This might offer some welcome respite when someone has been overwhelmed by such strange experiences. The decrease in agitation might also be seen as a relief to those around them.

Unfortunately, these chemicals can have very unpleasant side effects and do not always have the desired result. Nor do they tackle the root cause or meaning of the experiences. Furthermore, the sedative effects are such that a person is unable sometimes to continue functioning in their daily life, which obviously has implications for work, family and practical issues.

This medical treatment is chosen and administered by medical professionals. Once a person has described their experiences, any subsequent input from the 'patient' is dismissed as of little value. Personal meaning is not explored and, indeed, such reflections are discouraged. The view is that discussion of such experience is 'colluding' in madness and is, therefore, unhelpful, or even dangerous. There is little here in common with the person-centred approach.

Hospitalisation

People can sometimes feel overwhelmed, distressed, confused or scared by what is happening to them, and may decide they need hospital treatment. Occasionally, people's behaviour can seem so odd or be so disruptive to others that they are deemed to be at risk of hurting themselves or others. Under the Mental Health Act (1983), they can then be detained and treated against their will in a psychiatric hospital.

This can provide a much-needed rest from the stresses and strains of the world and they can feel supported in their struggles to recover. They are likely to be given medication that, as mentioned above, can have a calming effect. The treatment and medication can be given without their consent if they are detained under a section of the Mental Health Act 1983, but consent is needed if someone is admitted as a voluntary patient.

Fewer inpatient beds are available than in the past, and the era of the long-stay asylum is over. The negative effects of institutionalisation are, therefore, less than they once were. The emphasis now is on short hospital stays for acute treatment, and ongoing support in the community. Availability of mental health services is variable, and there are campaigns to increase funding for the mental health sector in the UK, to avoid people being sent to hospitals many miles from their homes and families, and to ensure those in need can access appropriate care when it is needed (Cooke, 2014).

There are still some people, however, who are considered sufficiently disturbed, vulnerable or at risk of harm to themselves or others to need long-term inpatient care. These people often live in 'secure units', where they have little freedom to do as they please, and where many everyday decisions are made for them. Hospitals are run by medical professionals. Decisions about patients are often made for them, although I have experience of a secure unit where patients are actively involved in discussions about their care. In the main, though, patients are regarded as mentally ill, with little capacity to contribute to their care plans. Exploration of personal meaning behind their experiences is also avoided and, if their 'psychotic experiences' become apparent, the 'patients' are described as being 'unsettled' and efforts are made to sedate them. This kind of treatment often has little in common with a person-centred approach.

Self-help and peer support

Many self-help and peer support groups are led by 'experts-by-experience' – service users who have had unusual experiences themselves. Individual understandings of experience are valued, widespread stigma is challenged, and hope of recovery is offered.

An example is the Hearing Voices Network (HVN). This was set up following research by Marius Romme and Sandra Escher (1993, 2000), who found that many people live quite happily with hearing voices and that there is no need to regard the experience as evidence of mental illness. They also found that paying attention to what the voices were saying helped people uncover personal meaning or significance. Voice hearers could often then develop different, even positive, relationships with those voices, or the voices would disappear entirely.

HVN groups exist worldwide. They are all run by voice hearers, and offer an accepting, supportive space to explore experience, as well as information and access to therapy, or other support, if required. An approach to therapy and self-help has also been developed that offers a structured way of trying to discover what voices mean and how they might be assimilated positively into a person's life (Romme & Escher, 2000).

The Paranoia Network is a similar organisation, set up to help people who have unusual beliefs, which also values and works with individual meaning. Some UK mental health trusts and charities also run more informal peer support or service user-led groups that are not necessarily linked to any one particular unusual experience.

Alongside arguing for recognition of the right to be heard and for idiosyncratic meaning to be accepted, service user organisations are actively challenging stigmatising public attitudes towards unusual experiences and the people who have them. For instance, Mad Pride, Mad Hatters of Bath and the Asylum Network advocate for the rights of those who have unusual experiences to be treated in the same way as others. This campaign has been described as 'the last great civil rights movement' (Dillon et al, 2013: 315).

That such groups are interested in facilitating the exploration of personal meaning is a link with the person-centred approach. It also appears that the therapeutic conditions of acceptance, understanding and genuineness are key to the attitudes important to these groups. These attitudes and the egalitarian nature of the groups, where experts do not take the lead or impose agendas, are indicative of good person-centred therapy. Studies into the HVN, in particular, demonstrate the empowering effect of the groups, as well as their offer of hope that a fulfilling life is possible after having, or even with, unusual experiences (Dillon & Hornstein, 2013).

Other organisations operate from within the medical model but argue that mental illness should be regarded without stigma, in the same way as physical illness. Examples include Rethink and Mind.

Cognitive behavioural therapy

Cognitive behavioural therapy (CBT), and specifically cognitive behavioural therapy for psychosis (CBTp), is the most widely researched talking therapy for people who have experiences described as symptoms of psychosis. The model assumes that there is some state of normality, and that variations from it are necessarily disordered.

Early approaches challenged and dismissed individual perceptions of reality as evidence of a dysfunction, and distraction techniques were widely used as a way of teaching the patient not to engage with the voices they heard or their delusional thoughts (Tarrier, 2010). More recent approaches advocate the exploration of clients' own understandings of the experience (Bentall, 2009; Turkington et al, 2004, 2006) and the involvement of clients in developing their own formulation of problems (Chadwick, 2006; Johnstone & Dallos, 2014).

These researchers are, however, clear on the need to return patients to 'normality', and also argue that the therapy is not suitable for some people who are very thought disordered or paranoid. They support the use of antipsychotic medication as a way of ensuring people are calmed enough to enter treatment, and suggest that CBT is of limited use for those who refuse this medication (Turkington et al, 2006: 369). CBTp practitioners seem, thus, still to be entrenched in a biomedical and deficit model, despite their claims to accept the patient's formulation, use normalisation techniques, emphasise personal meaning and adopt the stress-vulnerability model, all of which regard behaviour, thoughts and feelings as part of a continuum (Kingdon, 2012).

Rogerian principles (Rogers, 1957, 1961) acknowledging the centrality of the therapeutic alliance and the importance of working from the patient's (client's) framework are often noted as vital aspects of talking therapy (Bentall, 2009; Cooke, 2014; Johnstone & Dallos, 2014). Chadwick (2006) explicitly cites the influence of Rogers (1961), acknowledging it is not just the quality of a warm and understanding alliance with the therapist that is important, but also the active collaboration between therapist and client in the search for personal solutions.

Family and systemic interventions

The circle of people around a person having unusual experiences can also be affected. Approaches that involve the whole family have tried to work out what behaviours or 'systems' might be adapted to bring about changes in the 'abnormal' experiences and what others in the family can do to help the person in distress

(Grácio, Gonçalves-Pereira & Leff, 2016; Leff et al, 1989, 1990; Pilling et al, 2002). NICE (2014) recommends use of practical family interventions, and it seems logical that this approach might help if other family members find it difficult to cope with any detrimental effects of unusual behaviours and experiences.

Family therapy has parallels with a person-centred approach to working with configurations of self, in that it values all voices. But it also imposes a structure based on a presumption of faulty or unhelpful systems in operation within a family. Furthermore, the therapist is seen as the expert in charge of directing the correction of such failings in order to minimise the disruption caused by an individual's psychosis.

Other talking therapies

There are other talking therapies that have demonstrated some success in helping people diagnosed with psychosis. But there is not, as yet, sufficient evidence to justify their inclusion in the NICE guidelines. They include:

- trauma-focused therapy (Herman, 1997; Larkin & Morrison, 2006). Adaptations from this model have been developed to deal with psychotic experiences
- interpersonal relating therapy (Hayward, Berry & Ashton, 2011; Hayward et al, 2009). Voice hearers are encouraged to develop relationships with their voices, on the basis that associated distress will diminish and they will develop more understanding of what the voices signify
- voice dialoguing (Corstens, Longden & May, 2012). This approach is based on the assumption that voices described as hallucinations can be related to in the same way as other parts of the self, and that this form of relating can uncover meaning and decrease distress
- Open Dialogue (Seikkula et al, 2006; Seikkula & Arnkil, 2006). People who have taken part in this family and community-based intervention have needed significantly less medication, have much improved levels of social functioning and have required fewer hospital admissions (Seikkula et al, 2006; Seikkula & Arnkil, 2006). At the time of writing, Open Dialogue is being piloted in four NHS trusts in the UK.

Person-centred therapy

There is some recent evidence that person-centred therapy is experienced as helpful by people who have unusual experiences (eg. Sommerbeck, 2003; Traynor, Elliott & Cooper, 2011; Warner, 2005, 2007). There is also support from other researchers who do not directly identify as working in a person-centred way (eg. Chadwick, 2006; Bentall, 2009). An example of a discrete person-centred method that has been developed with some success for helping 'contact-impaired' clients is the work carried out by Garry Prouty and colleagues (Prouty, Van Werde & Pörtner, 2002), which is explained below.

Pre-therapy

Prouty and his colleagues discovered that people given a diagnosis of schizophrenia found it difficult to accept empathy and to engage in reflection (Prouty, Van Werde & Pörtner, 2002). This is supported by evidence from research into CBTp (Turkington et al, 2006). Working from the premise that therapy could only begin to happen if two people were in psychological contact (Rogers' first condition of therapy (1957)), Prouty focused on using concrete reflections as a way of establishing contact with clients who were described as 'contact impaired' (Prouty, Van Werde & Pörtner, 2002). These participants struggled to receive empathy, frequently experiencing a crossover from encounter into invasion (Mearns & Cooper, 2005); they also found it easier to understand and respond to reflections that were more concrete, such as 'You are smiling'. Rogers et al (1967) also found that people diagnosed with schizophrenia regarded empathy as less important than acceptance and genuineness in a therapeutic relationship. This might be connected with the participants having been institutionalised for some time and being unused to anyone offering understanding of their situations or worldviews, making it hard for them to receive someone else's attempts to empathise with them.

Similarly, Van Werde (1998; 2005) argues that a therapist who acknowledges her separateness and different reality from psychotic clients can act as a helpful 'anchor' to a consensual reality for those fearful of being alone in their own confusing world. These elements of the therapeutic alliance are also supported by evidence from other approaches that respect and work with alternative views of reality and individual meaning (Chadwick, 2006; Johnstone & Dallos, 2014; Romme & Escher, 1993, 2000).

One treatment for all cases?

There have been debates within the person-centred world about how best to work with clients 'at the difficult edge' (Warner, 2000), who might be diagnosed by other professionals as having a mental illness or disorder. Some person-centred therapists consider it unnecessary to include anything else or different in a therapy that claims not to rely on tools and techniques, maintaining 'there is only one treatment for all cases' (Levant & Shlien, 1984; Shlien, 1989: 160). The idea that there might be specific treatment needed for specific problems has been called a 'myth' (Glauser & Bozarth, 2001: 142).[1]

Warner's work on difficult process (2005, 2007) does offer a way of understanding unusual phenomena that frames the experience in non-medical

1. Rogers' emphasis on the attitudes necessary in a therapist might be considered techniques, even though some person-centred practitioners might argue that they are ways of being rather than things therapist do.

terms. This is more in line with other research that is positioned outside the medical model. But I worry about developing a new discourse that is still rooted in pathology, even though it uses different terms from those used by the medical establishment. Margaret Warner has stressed that her difficult process theory is meant only as an aid to empathy and that, if it gets in the way, a therapist is best advised to leave it alone (personal communication, 2008).

Specificity myth or aids to empathy?

My view is that this person-centred re-framing of unusual experience may offer a 'security blanket' (Shlien, 1989) to therapists but that it can only get in the way of being present to the unique individual with whom we are working. It is more helpful to accept that some people have experiences that seem unusual to us, but that they have as much value as any other. Associated distress cannot then be assumed to be caused by a problem in the individual; it is perhaps more likely to be introjected from the public attitudes around us because the particular behaviour – eg. hearing voices – is unacceptable or inconsistent with the culture or society the person lives in. Nevertheless, if the client herself has a worldview encompassing a belief that she is suffering from symptoms of illness, an awareness of that discourse might be of use, in the same way as awareness of cultural differences might be helpful with clients from different cultures.

It is important to note, for example, that two participants in my study reported that they did not experience any long-term change in the voices they heard or how they felt about them. They also said that they would have preferred a more directive therapy that focused on ways to get rid of their voices, and that nothing could help as they were 'mentally ill'. Conversely, they valued the chance to talk and be heard, which offered brief respite from the ongoing difficulties of living with voices. These people were long-stay, psychiatric inpatients who were used to decisions being made for them. Perhaps, at that moment, the freedom to set and run the agenda in therapy was too big a change for them, and they found the lack of structure threatening and difficult to manage. This suggests that different types of therapy work for different people and confirms that therapists need to take full account of individual clients' own worldviews.

Furthermore, person-centred practitioners have to work and liaise with professionals in other disciplines. If we are to increase availability and opportunities for person-centred therapy, we must demonstrate our understanding of 'severe and enduring mental illness', as well as demonstrate that our approach to alleviating distress can be effective. As therapists, we do not necessarily accept a client's reality as our own. Nor, then, do we need to accept the medical model of mental distress. We simply have to find a way of communicating successfully with those that do, as well as with those who might have other non-medical, but not person-centred, understandings (Sommerbeck, 2003).

Discussion

The medical metaphor of mental distress has a powerful hold on the consciousness of western society. Despite a lack of consistent evidence of aetiology, disorders and diseases are still assumed to exist, along with the consequent pathologisation of supposedly symptomatic human experience (Boyle, 2002; Cooke, 2014; Newnes, 2004; Newnes, Holmes & Dunn, 1999, 2001; Sanders & Tudor, 2001). This medical discourse requires a trust in psychiatrists as holders of expert knowledge and dispensers of treatments and cures (Thomas, 2014), despite limited proof of success (Hansen, McHoul & Rapley, 2003; Newnes, Holmes & Dunn, 1999, 2001; Sanders & Tudor, 2001) and some evidence of harm (Moncrieff, 2009).

Sadly, however, the treatments on offer, the public attitudes towards those described as 'mentally ill' and the enduring problems with social functioning mean that hope of a 'cure' or 'treatment' are often misplaced. Furthermore, the absence of symptoms does not always lead to an improved quality of life (Barham, 1997).

By removing the emphasis on symptoms and deficit, person-centred therapy creates space to consider more broadly the elements that comprise a positive quality of life. These include being in relationship, living authentically, development of the capacity to explore and make sense of unsettling or confusing experiences, and positive self-regard. It might not be regarded as a medical 'treatment' for an 'illness', because it does not attempt to eliminate 'symptoms'. It can, however, still be healing because of its impact on the person's overall functioning, actualisation and ability to live authentically. As with other research that works with personal meaning (eg. Romme & Escher, 2012), participants in my doctoral study showed a number of different positive outcomes. Most people found ways of living in harmony with the voices they heard; some no longer felt scared or controlled by their voices, and some found that the voices disappeared completely.

Ongoing changes in classification and the unreliability of diagnosis across culture and time, and even between clinicians, indicate that the language of medicine may be of limited use. It restricts the ways in which experience can be understood because 'symptoms' are placed in discrete categories, with specific treatments and rigid explanations. It also perpetuates a model that positions the clinician as expert and the patient as deficient. This discourse is evidently so powerful that it has become accepted as 'truth', even to the extent that some people can conceive of no other explanation or understanding for their experiences (Barham, Hayward & Barham, 1995; Rundle, 2012; Wise & Rapley, 2009).

The location of the 'problem' of unusual experiences within the individual also stops us looking at the underlying social issues of inequality, poverty, discrimination and lack of education (eg. Read & Dillon, 2013; Smail, 2005) that are linked with unusual experiences. These issues are mentioned by NICE (2014) as factors that might exacerbate the underlying or pre-existing 'illnesses' but they are not considered to be causative, except insofar as a person subjected to these factors might have a 'vulnerability' to developing the putative 'illness' in the first place.

The importance of individual understandings and contexts is often disregarded in the medical model. Bentall (2009), however, sees merit in asking individuals about what they understand their experiences might mean and, if they are in distress, listening to what they believe might help them feel better. In discussing CBTp, he stresses the value of trying to work out the meaning of 'psychotic experience' when he concludes that a well-trained therapist will make:

> … every effort to treat the patient's beliefs, no matter how implausible, as if they might just be true. Not surprisingly… it often becomes obvious that there is a nugget of truth in even the most paranoid systems. (Bentall, 2009: 253)

Along with others (Romme et al, 2009; Sanders & Tudor, 2001), he argues for greater involvement of service users in research into mental distress and delivery of services to those who need help (2009: 287). For example, people do not always want to lose the voices they hear. Some develop positive relationships with them and value them as an important part of their coming to terms with the dreadful events that damaged them so badly (Romme et al, 2009). Other people find ways of negotiating with the voices and thereby re-establishing control over them and their lives (Romme & Escher, 2012; Romme et al, 2009).

Similarly, those who experience a spiritual crisis are often clear that it is not helpful to call it a mental illness, even though it can feel chaotic and intense (Spiritual Crisis Network, 2016). Conversely, others may fear the prospect of being under the control of such a supernatural force and of not being offered opportunities for help (McCarthy-Jones, Waegeli & Watkins, 2013: 247). McCarthy-Jones and colleagues (2013: 255) suggest there is a fluidity between what are described variously as psychotic and spiritual voice-hearing. If this is so, then it supports the evidence for idiosyncratic understandings of experience so that approaches to alleviate any associated distress can be tailored to the individual.

While it is still important to accept that a medical understanding might feel more comfortable for some, alternative researchers make it possible to refute the medical model's assumption that a psychiatric diagnosis is a life sentence with no reprieve. Evidence for a 'recovery model' from service users' viewpoints (eg. Coleman & Smith, 2006; Newnes, Holmes & Dunn, 1999, 2001) concurs with this position of hope and potential for change. It is also more in line with a person-centred approach to understanding distress and offering help.

Conclusion

The person-centred approach is at risk of continuing to be excluded from consideration as a useful therapy for people who have unusual experiences. This is partly because of the dearth of recent research into the approach that satisfies the requirements of policy-makers and funders. The apparent reluctance to offer the outcome-based evidence required (Cooper, 2011; Wilkins, 2003) seems at odds with Rogers, who embraced mechanical and quantitative research as necessary to identify the elements of successful (and unsuccessful) therapy.

It is already difficult for person-centred practitioners to find work in psychiatric settings in the UK, partly because person-centred therapy is not a recommended treatment for people 'with psychosis'. Only by contributing through rigorous research to the debate about how best to help people in distress can we hope to be taken seriously by those responsible for recommending services and allocating resources.

The evidence presented here suggests that person-centred theory can help us understand how the experience of distress might result in a person having unusual experiences. It also suggests that positing explanatory mechanisms for specific behaviours might not be relevant if we accept that experience lies along a continuum and that 'madness' might be culturally determined. Importantly, person-centred therapy can alleviate distress suffered by those who have unusual experiences in ways that are not always related to features of, or the elimination of, the unusual experience itself. While it might not be regarded as a 'treatment' for an 'illness' in a medical sense, person-centred therapy can still be healing in a wider sense because of its impact on the person's overall functioning, actualisation and ability to live authentically.

If we can communicate our theoretical perspective and back it up with evidence that policy-makers regard as valid, we might be in a better position to play a greater role in helping alleviate the distress of those who have unusual experiences.

References

Barham P (1997). *Closing the Asylum: the mental patient in modern society* (2nd ed). London: Penguin.

Barham P, Hayward R, Barham PF (1995). *Relocating Madness: from the mental patient to the person.* London: Free Association Books.

Bentall RP (2009). *Doctoring the Mind: why psychiatric treatments fail.* London: Allen Lane.

Boyle M (2002). *Schizophrenia: a scientific delusion?* (2nd ed). London: Routledge.

Corstens D, Longden E, May R (2012).Talking with voices: exploring what is expressed by the voices people hear. *Psychosis: Psychological, Social and Integrative Approaches* 4(2): 95–104.

Chadwick P (2006). *Person-Based Cognitive Therapy for Distressing Psychosis.* Chichester: John Wiley & Sons.

Coleman R, Smith M (2006). *Working With Voices: victim to victor* (2nd ed). Fife: P&P Press Ltd.

Cooke A (2014). *Understanding Psychosis and Schizophrenia: why people sometimes hear voices, believe things that others find strange, or appear out of touch with reality... and what can help.* Leicester: BPS Division of Clinical Psychology.

Dillon J (2011). The personal is the political. In: Rapley M, Moncrieff J, Dillon J (eds). *De-medicalizing Misery: psychiatry, psychology and the human condition*. Basingstoke: Palgrave Macmillan (pp141–157).

Dillon J, Bullimore P, Lampshire D, Chamberlin J (2013). The work of experience-based experts. In: Read J, Dillon J (eds). *Models of Madness: psychological, social and biological approaches to psychosis* (2nd ed). New York: Routledge/Taylor & Francis Group (pp305–318).

Dillon J, Hornstein GA (2013). Hearing voices peer support groups: a powerful alternative for people in distress. *Psychosis 5*(3): 286–295.

Garety PA, Bebbington P, Fowler D, Freeman D, Kuipers E (2007). Implications for neurobiological research of cognitive models of psychosis: a theoretical paper. *Psychological Medicine 37*(10): 1377–1391.

Geekie J (2012). *Experiencing Psychosis: personal and professional perspectives*. London: Routledge.

Geekie J (2013). Listening to the voices we hear: clients' understandings of psychotic experiences. In: Read J, Dillon J (eds). *Models of Madness: psychological, social and biological approaches to psychosis* (2nd ed). London/New York: Routledge (pp178–190).

Geekie J, Read J (2009). *Making Sense of Madness: contesting the meaning of schizophrenia*. London/New York: Routledge.

Glauser AS, Bozarth JD (2001). Person-centered counseling: the culture within. *Journal of Counseling & Development 79*(2): 142–147.

Grácio J, Gonçalves-Pereira M, Leff J (2016). What do we know about family interventions for psychosis at the process level? A systematic review. *Family Process 55*(1): 79–90.

Gray JA, Feldon J, Rawlins JNP, Hemsley DR, Smith AD (1991). The neuropsychology of schizophrenia. *Behavioral and Brain Sciences 14*(01): 1–20.

Grof C, Grof S (1986). Spiritual emergency: the understanding and treatment of transpersonal crises. *ReVISION 8*(2): 7–20.

Hansen S, McHoul A, Rapley M (2003). *Beyond Help: a consumers' guide to psychology*. Ross-on-Wye: PCCS Books.

Harrison G, Gunnell D, Glazebrook C, Page K, Kwiecinski R (2001). Association between schizophrenia and social inequality at birth: case-control study. *British Journal of Psychiatry 179*(4): 346–350.

Hayward M, Berry K, Ashton A (2011). Applying interpersonal theories to the understanding of and therapy for auditory hallucinations: a review of the literature and directions for further research. *Clinical Psychology Review 31*(8): 1313–1323.

Hayward M, Overton J, Dorey T, Denney J (2009). Relating therapy for people who hear voices: a case series. *Clinical Psychology & Psychotherapy 16*(3): 216–227.

Hemmings A (2008). A response to the chapters in *Against and for CBT*. In: House R, Loewenthal D (eds). *Against and for CBT: towards a constructive dialogue?* Ross-on-Wye: PCCS Books (pp42–51).

Hemsley DR (1993). A simple (or simplistic?) cognitive model for schizophrenia. *Behaviour Research and Therapy 31*(7): 633–645.

Herman J (1997). *Trauma and Recovery: the aftermath of violence – from domestic abuse to political terror* (new ed). New York: Basic Books.

Johnstone L, Dallos R (2014). *Formulation in Psychology and Psychotherapy: making sense of people's problems* (2nd ed). London/New York: Routledge.

Kapur S, Mamo D (2003). Half a century of antipsychotics and still a central role for dopamine D2 receptors. *Progress in Neuro-Psychopharmacology & Biological Psychiatry 27*(7): 1081–1090.

Kingdon D (2012). Understanding psychosis and cognitive therapy. In: Romme M, Escher S (eds). *Psychosis as a Personal Crisis: an experience-based approach*. London/New York: Routledge (pp179–184).

Laing RD (1960). *The Divided Self: a study of sanity and madness*. London: Tavistock Publications.

Laing RD (1967). *The Politics of Experience and the Bird of Paradise*. Harmondsworth: Penguin Books.

Larkin W, Morrison A (eds) (2006). *Trauma and Psychosis: new directions for theory and therapy*. London: Routledge.

Larøi F, Luhrmann TM, Bell V, Christian WA, Deshpande S, Fernyhough C, Jenkins J, Woods A (2014). Culture and hallucinations: overview and future directions. *Schizophrenia Bulletin 40*(Suppl 4): S213–S220.

Leff J, Berkowitz R, Shavit N, Strachan A, Glass I, Vaughn C (1989). A trial of family therapy v a relatives group for schizophrenia. *British Journal of Psychiatry 154*(1): 58–66.

Leff J, Berkowitz R, Shavit N, Strachan A, Glass I, Vaughn C (1990). A trial of family therapy versus a relatives' group for schizophrenia. Two-year follow-up. *British Journal of Psychiatry 157*(4): 571–577.

Mental Health Act (1983). www.legislation.gov.uk/ukpga/1983/20/contents (accessed 9 November, 2016).

Leudar I, Thomas P (2000). *Voices of Reason, Voices of Insanity: studies of verbal hallucinations*. London: Routledge.

Levant RF, Shlien JM (1984). *Client-Centered Therapy and the Person-Centered Approach: new directions in theory, research, and practice*. Westport, CT: Praeger Publishers/Greenwood Publishing Group.

Linscott RJ, van Os J (2013). An updated and conservative systematic review and meta-analysis of epidemiological evidence on psychotic experiences in children and adults: on the pathway from proneness to persistence to dimensional expression across mental disorders. *Psychological Medicine 43*(6): 1133–1149.

Luhrmann TM, Padmavati R, Tharoor H, Osei A (2015). Differences in voice-hearing experiences of people with psychosis in the USA, India and Ghana: interview-based study. *British Journal of Psychiatry 206*(1): 41–44.

McCarthy-Jones S (2012). *Hearing Voices: the histories, causes, and meanings of auditory verbal hallucinations*. Cambridge: Cambridge University Press.

McCarthy-Jones S, Longden E (2015). Auditory verbal hallucinations in schizophrenia and post-traumatic stress disorder: common phenomenology, common cause, common interventions? *Frontiers in Psychology 6*: 1071.

McCarthy-Jones S, Waegeli A, Watkins J (2013). Spirituality and hearing voices: considering the relation. *Psychosis 5*(3): 247–258.

McGrath JJ, Saha S, Al-Hamzawi A, Alonso J, Bromet EJ, Bruffaerts R et al (2015). Psychotic experiences in the general population: a cross-national analysis based on 31,261 respondents from 18 Countries. *JAMA Psychiatry 72*(7): 697–705.

Mearns D, Cooper M (2005). *Working at Relational Depth in Counselling and Psychotherapy*. London: Sage.

Mearns D, Thorne B (2000). *Person-Centred Therapy Today: new frontiers in theory and practice*. London: Sage.

Mind (2016). *Psychotic Experiences*. [Online.] London: Mind. www.mind.org.uk/information-support/types-of-mental-health-problems/psychosis/ (accessed 15 March, 2016).

Moncrieff J (2009). *The Myth of the Chemical Cure* (revised ed). London: Palgrave.

Moncrieff J (2013). *The Bitterest Pills: the troubling story of antipsychotic drugs*. Basingstoke: Palgrave Macmillan.

Newnes C (2004). Psychology and psychotherapy's potential for countering the medicalization of everything. *Journal of Humanistic Psychology 44*(3): 358–376. doi:10.1177/0022167804266180

Newnes C, Holmes G, Dunn C (1999). *This is Madness: a critical look at psychiatry and the future of mental health services*. Ross-on-Wye: PCCS Books.

Newnes C, Holmes G, Dunn C (2001). *This is Madness Too: critical perspectives on mental health services*. Ross-on-Wye: PCCS Books.

NHS UK (2015). *NHS Choices, Psychosis*. [Online.] www.nhs.uk/Conditions/Psychosis/Pages/Introduction.aspx (accessed 15 March, 2016).

NICE (2014). *Psychosis and Schizophrenia in Adults: treatment and management*. Clinical guideline 178. London: National Institute for Health and Care Excellence.

Pilgrim D (2005). Defining mental disorder: tautology in the service of sanity in British mental health legislation. *Journal of Mental Health 14*(5): 435–443.

Pilling S, Bebbington P, Kuipers E, Garety P, Geddes J, Orbach G, Morgan C (2002). Psychological treatments in schizophrenia: I. meta-analysis of family intervention and cognitive behaviour therapy. *Psychological Medicine 32*(05): 763–782.

Pitt L, Kilbride M, Nothard S, Welford M, Morrison AP (2007). Researching recovery from psychosis: a user-led project. *The Psychiatrist 31*(2): 55–60.

Prouty G, Van Werde D, Portner M (2002). *Pre-Therapy: reaching contact-impaired clients*. Ross-on-Wye: PCCS Books.

Read J, Dillon J (eds) (2013). *Models of Madness: psychological, social and biological approaches to psychosis* (2nd ed). New York: Routledge/Taylor & Francis Group.

Rogers CR (1951). *Client-Centred Therapy: its current practices implications and theory*. London: Constable and Company Ltd.

Rogers CR (1957). The necessary and sufficient conditions of therapeutic personality change. *Journal of Consulting Psychology 21*(2): 95–103.

Rogers CR (1961). *On Becoming a Person: a therapist's view of psychotherapy*. London: Constable & Co.

Rogers CR, Gendlin ET, Kiesler D, Truax CB (1967). *The Therapeutic Relationship and its Impact: a study of psychotherapy with schizophrenics*. Madison, WI: University of Wisconsin Press.

Romme M, Escher S (1993). *Accepting Voices*. London: Mind Publications.

Romme M, Escher S (2000). *Making Sense of Voices: the mental health professional's guide to working with voice-hearers*: London: Mind Publications.

Romme M, Escher S (2012). *Psychosis as a Personal Crisis: an experience-based approach*. London/New York: Routledge.

Romme M, Escher S, Dillon J, Corstens D, Morris M (2009). *Living with Voices: 50 stories of recovery*. Ross-on-Wye: PCCS Books.

Rundle K (2012). 'Though this be madness, yet there is method in't': person-centred approaches to different realities. In: Wilkins P, Tolan J (eds). *Client Issues in Person-Centred Counselling and Psychotherapy*. London: Sage (pp97–112).

Sanders P, Tudor K (2001). This is therapy: a person-centred critique of the contemporary psychiatric system. In: Newnes C, Holmes G, Dunn C (eds). *This is Madness Too: critical perspectives on mental health services*. Ross-on-Wye: PCCS Books (pp147–160).

Schmid PF (2005). Authenticity and alienation: towards an understanding of the person beyond the categories of order and disorder. In: Joseph S, Worsley R (eds). *Person-Centred Psychopathology: a positive psychology of mental health*. Ross-on-Wye: PCCS Books (pp75–90).

Seikkula J, Aaltonen J, Alakare B, Haarakangas K, Keränen J, Lehtinen K (2006). Five-year experience of first-episode nonaffective psychosis in open-dialogue approach: treatment principles, follow-up outcomes, and two case studies. *Psychotherapy Research 16*(02): 214–228.

Seikkula J, Arnkil TE (2006). *Dialogical Meetings in Social Networks.* London: Karnac Books.

Shlien JM (1989). Response to Boy's symposium on psychodiagnosis. *Person-Centered Review 4*(2): 157–162.

Smail D (2005). *Power, Interest and Psychology: elements of a social materialist understanding of distress.* Ross-on-Wye: PCCS Books.

Sommerbeck L (2003). *The Client-Centred Therapist in Psychiatric Contexts: a therapist's guide to the psychiatric landscape and its inhabitants.* Ross-on-Wye: PCCS.

Spiritual Crisis Network (2016). What is Spiritual Crisis? Our description. [Online.] http://spiritualcrisisnetwork.uk/what-is-sc/our-description/ (accessed 16 March, 2016).

Sullivan PF (2008). Schizophrenia genetics: the search for a hard lead. *Current Opinion in Psychiatry 21*(2): 157–160.

Szasz TS (1960). *The Myth of Mental Illness.* New York: Hoeber-Harper.

Tandon R, Keshavan MS, Nasrallah HA (2008). Schizophrenia, 'just the facts': what we know in 2008. Part 1: overview. *Schizophrenia Research 100*(1–3): 4–19.

Tarrier N (2010). Cognitive behavior therapy for schizophrenia and psychosis: current status and future directions. *Clinical Schizophrenia & Related Psychoses 4*(3): 176–184.

Thomas P (2014). *Psychiatry in Context: experience, meaning and communities.* Ross-on-Wye: PCCS Books.

Traynor W, Elliott R, Cooper M (2011). Helpful factors and outcomes in person-centered therapy with clients who experience psychotic processes: therapists' perspectives. *Person-Centered and Experiential Psychotherapies 10*(2): 89–104.

Turkington D, Dudley R, Warman DM, Beck AT (2004). Cognitive-behavioral therapy for schizophrenia: a review. *Journal of Psychiatric Practice 10*(1): 5–16.

Turkington D, Kingdon D, Weiden PJ (2006). Cognitive behavior therapy for schizophrenia. *American Journal of Psychiatry 163*(3): 365–373.

van Os J, Linscott RJ, Myin-Germeys I, Delespaul P, Krabbendam L (2009). A systematic review and meta-analysis of the psychosis continuum: evidence for a psychosis proneness–persistence–impairment model of psychotic disorder. *Psychological Medicine 39*(2): 179–195.

van Os J (2010). Are psychiatric diagnoses of psychosis scientifically useful? The case of schizophrenia. *Journal of Mental Health 19*: 305–317.

van Os J (2014). *Connecting to Madness.* TEDxMaastricht. [Online.] https://www.youtube.com/watch?v=sE3gxX5CiW0 (accessed 10 January, 2016).

Van Werde D (1998). Anchorage as a core concept in working with psychotic people. In: Thorne B, Lambers E (eds). *Person-Centred Therapy: a European perspective.* London: Sage (pp195–205).

Van Werde D (2005). Facing psychotic functioning: person-centred contact work in residential psychiatric care. In: Joseph S, Worsley R (eds). *Person-Centred Psychopathology: a positive psychology of mental health.* Ross-on-Wye: PCCS Books (pp158–168).

Varese F, Smeets F, Drukker M, Lieverse R, Lataster T, Viechtbauer W, Read J, van Os J, Bentall RP (2012). Childhood adversities increase the risk of psychosis: a meta-analysis of patient-control, prospective- and cross-sectional cohort studies. *Schizophrenia Bulletin 38*(4): 661–671.

Warner MS (2000). Person-centred therapy at the difficult edge: a developmentally based model of fragile and dissociated process. In: Mearns D, Thorne B. *Person-Centred Therapy Today: new frontiers in theory and practice.* London: Sage (pp144–171).

Warner MS (2002). Luke's dilemma: a client-centred experiential model of processing with a schizophrenic thought disorder. In: Watson JC, Goldman RN, Warner MS (eds). *Client-Centred and Experiential Psychotherapy in the 21st Century: advances in theory, research and practice.* Ross-on-Wye: PCCS Books (pp459–472).

Warner MS (2005). A person-centered view of human nature, wellness and psychopathology. In: Joseph S, Worsley SR (eds). *Person-Centred Psychopathology.* Ross-on-Wye: PCCS Books (pp91–109).

Warner MS (2007). Luke's process. In: Worsley R, Joseph S (eds). *Person-Centred Practice: case studies in positive psychology.* Ross-on-Wye: PCCS Books (pp142–155).

Warner MS (2009). Defense or actualization? Reconsidering the role of processing, self and agency within Rogers' theory of personality. *Person-Centered & Experiential Psychotherapies* 8(2): 109–126.

Wilkins P (2003). *Person-centred therapy in focus.* London: Sage.

Wise MJ, Rapley M (2009). Cognitive behaviour therapy, psychosis and attributions of irrationality. Or, how to produce cognitions as 'faulty'. *The Journal of Critical Psychology, Counselling and Psychotherapy* 9(4): 177–196.

Yalom ID (1995). *The Theory and Practice of Group Psychotherapy* (4th ed). New York: Basic Books.

14 Understanding post-traumatic stress from the person-centred perspective

Stephen Joseph

Since the term post-traumatic stress was first introduced, there has been a huge research effort to understand the effects of trauma and how to help people cope. But, more recently, researchers have also begun to note that sometimes in their struggle with adversity people are able to find new meaning and purpose in life, and are able to look back on their tragedies and misfortunes as having provided a trigger towards a more enriched and fulfilled life – a phenomenon that has been called post-traumatic growth.

Major texts on post-traumatic stress disorder (PTSD) do not reference person-centred theory or client-centred therapy (CCT). This is not surprising, given that client-centred therapists have tended not to adopt the language of the medical model and do not make the assumption that specific conditions require specific treatments. However, over the past decade there has been much work on providing a person-centred understanding of the experiences associated with PTSD. In this chapter I will discuss this work and how the person-centred approach provides an understanding of growth processes and encourages us, as therapists, to adopt a more positive psychological perspective in our understanding of how people adjust to stressful and traumatic events. I will also show how person-centred theory provides an explanation not only for post-traumatic growth processes but also for the phenomena characteristic of the diagnostic category of PTSD (American Psychiatric Association, 2013).

Post-traumatic stress disorder

PTSD is the term used by mental health professionals to describe reactions that cause clinically significant distress or impairment in social, occupational or other important areas of functioning in people who have experienced a traumatic event. The term PTSD refers to a familiar constellation of psychological reactions often experienced by people in the aftermath of a traumatic event. PTSD can result from events that involve some form of confrontation with death and injury, such as major disasters, technological accidents, road traffic accidents, criminal victimisation, sexual assault, war experiences, disease and illness and political violence.

Typically, people with a diagnosis of PTSD are highly aroused and anxious and suffer from various intrusive and avoidance experiences. The person is likely to be experiencing highly distressing thoughts, images and dreams, while simultaneously trying to avoid anything that arouses recollections of what happened to them (American Psychiatric Association, 2013).

PTSD consists of four symptom clusters. First, people experience distressing recollections, including images, thoughts and distressing dreams. It may even seem as if the event were happening again. Many often describe 'flashbacks'. Flashbacks are when the person re-experiences the event as if it were happening again: they *feel* as though they are back in the burning car, or can *actually smell* the body odour of their assailant. Second, people experience problems with avoidance. Reminders of the event can leave people feeling distressed and shaken up. As a result, people often try to avoid reminders, such as thoughts, feelings and conversations associated with the trauma, or activities, places and other people that bring back memories. Third, there are negative cognitions and disturbances in mood. People with PTSD may experience changes in their beliefs about themselves, others and the world, leading them to feel that others cannot be trusted or that the world is a dangerous place. Fourth, there are problems of arousal; they may have difficulties falling or staying asleep, or episodes of reckless or self-harming behaviour; they may have periods of intense irritability or outbursts of anger, hyper-alertness, an exaggerated startle response or difficulty concentrating. When these problems last for more than a month, a diagnosis of PTSD can be made.

Person-centred therapists tend to avoid using psychiatric terms because of their theoretical position in relation to the medical model. So they are unlikely to use the term PTSD, and certainly not in a diagnostic way. Nevertheless, it is likely that many person-centred therapists work with clients who have experienced trauma and who would be diagnosed as suffering from PTSD if they were to consult a different kind of health professional.

For example, John was recently severely physically assaulted outside a nightclub. Although it is now two months later and he has made a good recovery physically, his daytime thoughts often turn uncontrollably to that evening, and at night he often has nightmares about the experience and wakes up in terror.

Jill was driving to a late morning meeting at work when another car unexpectedly veered off the road and crashed into her, sending her vehicle across the carriageway. Several other cars were involved in the resulting horrific accident, and one person died. Jill escaped with her life but sustained severe injuries. Now, almost three years later, she can't get back into a car and is haunted by thoughts of that day and of how she could have avoided the accident. Although a careful driver, she blames herself for not paying enough attention that day.

Ahmed had a minor heart attack three months previously and, although the doctors tell him his prognosis is good, he remains frightened that he will have another one. His thoughts keep returning to the heart attack – the shortness of breath, the tightness in his chest, the intense fear, the look of fear on his wife's face – and as he talks about it he feels a sense of rising panic.

It is not unusual for people to seek therapy to help them cope with the experience of loss or the psychological aftermath of an accident or illness. The experiences of John, Jill and Ahmed are typical of people who may meet the diagnostic criteria for PTSD. The point is that PTSD is a term used by psychologists and psychiatrists to simply describe a set of reactions people often have to horrific and tragic events in their lives – for example, upsetting thoughts and images that come into their mind, and attempts to avoid circumstances that trigger these distressing thoughts and images. All therapists will have come across clients with these presenting problems, but whether or not they use the term PTSD depends on their theoretical stance.

Psychopathology in the person-centred approach is usually explained as what happens when the actualising tendency is thwarted by adverse social-environmental conditions. But, although thwarting of the actualising tendency can explain a variety of psychological problems, it is not immediately obvious how person-centred theory is able to provide an account of PTSD. Clearly, PTSD does not directly result from an internalisation of conditions of worth in childhood, but from exposure to a traumatic event. However, I would argue that a more detailed exploration of person-centred theory is able to provide us with an adequate understanding of PTSD. This chapter is an adaptation of two previous articles in which I have explored this topic in different professional contexts (Joseph, 2003, 2004).

Breakdown and disorganisation of the self-structure

Although he was writing well before the introduction of the term PTSD, Carl Rogers provided a theory of therapy and personality that contains an account of threat-related psychological processes that is consistent with contemporary trauma theory, and that provides the conceptual underpinnings to client-centred and experiential ways of working with traumatised people. In person-centred terminology, PTSD symptoms are simply another way of talking about what Rogers (1959) described as the breakdown and disorganisation of the self-structure.

Self-structure

Carl Rogers' most detailed theoretical paper was 'A theory of therapy, personality and interpersonal relationships, as developed in the client-centered framework', published in 1959. The first important concept Rogers introduces in this paper is what he calls the self-structure. I suggest that PTSD can be understood as representing the normal psychological manifestation of a process that is instigated when the self-structure comes under threat. Self-structure refers to:

> ... the organized, consistent conceptual gestalt composed of perceptions of
> the characteristics of the 'I' or 'me' and the perceptions of the relationships of
> the 'I' or 'me' to others and to various aspects of life, together with the values
> attached to these perceptions. (Rogers, 1959: 200)

Rogers (1959) goes on to discuss the process of breakdown and disorganisation of the self-structure. We 'subceive' as threatening experiences that are incongruent with the self-structure, Rogers writes, and do not allow them to be accurately symbolised in awareness. The denial of awareness of the experience is an attempt to keep its perception consistent with the self-structure. This is true, Rogers wrote, of every person, to a greater or lesser extent. Only in the fully functioning person is the self-structure congruent with experience and always in the process of changing with new experience.

Threat to self-structure

Of course, the fully functioning person is an ideal, and at least some degree of incongruence between self and experience is usual; people differ widely in their degree of incongruence. This is the usual state of affairs: we maintain our self-structure with a process of defence until we experience a threat that is overwhelmingly incongruent with our self-structure – at which point, the process of breakdown and disorganisation of the self-structure described by Rogers (1959) is instigated. Rogers writes:

> 1. If the individual has a large or significant degree of *incongruence between
> self and experience* and if a significant experience demonstrating this
> *incongruence* occurs suddenly, or with a high degree of obviousness, then the
> organism's process of *defense* is unable to operate successfully.
>
> 2. As a result *anxiety* is *experienced* as the *incongruence* is subceived. The
> degree of *anxiety* is dependent upon the extent of the *self-structure* which is
> threatened.
>
> 3. The process of *defense* being unsuccessful, the *experience* is *accurately
> symbolized in awareness*, and the gestalt of the *self-structure* is broken by this
> *experience* of the *incongruence in awareness*. A state of disorganization results.
>
> 4. In such a state of disorganization the organism behaves at times in ways
> which are openly consistent with experiences which have hitherto been
> distorted or denied to awareness. At other times the self may temporarily
> regain regnancy, and the organism may behave in ways consistent with it.
> (Rogers, 1959: 228–229)

Rogers' 1959 theory is generic; the process of breakdown and disorganisation of the self-structure is usually considered within the context of more everyday events. What I would argue, however, is that the statement on breakdown and disorganisation of the self-structure applies equally well to traumatic events. Although Rogers was probably not thinking of traumatic events per se when he formulated his statement on the breakdown and disorganisation of the self-structure, and he was writing well before the term PTSD was introduced, it should be remembered that Rogers was experienced in working with World War 2 veterans and was aware of the psychological impact of trauma (Rogers, 1942; Rogers & Wallen, 1946). Traumatic events most certainly present us with information that demonstrates incongruence between self and experience.

Shattered assumptions

The nature of traumatic events is that they will demonstrate incongruence to most people because there are common distortions in the self-structure. One aspect of self-structure in which there is a high degree of discrepancy between self and experience is the denial of awareness of existential experiences: for example, that we are fragile, that the future is uncertain, and that life is not fair. Although many people will say they know these to be truths, when it comes to how we actually lead our lives, most of us go from day to day as if we were invulnerable, that tomorrow will certainly come as expected, and that we will be rewarded for good deeds and punished for bad ones. Traumatic events abruptly and obviously present us with experience that leads to a breakdown of these aspects of self-structure. Trauma shows us the limits of the human condition and brings into question our values and assumptions about ourselves and how we lead our lives.

To those familiar with the PTSD literature, this is not saying anything new. Rogers' description is simply consistent with the current social cognitive theories of post-traumatic stress. For example, one of the most influential theorists of recent years has been the social psychologist Janoff-Bulman (1989, 1992), who has discussed how the experience of trauma has a shattering effect on people's assumptive world. She describes how individuals possess a schema of the self and the world, and suggests that victims who have experienced a wide range of traumatic situations share common psychological experiences. She proposes that post-traumatic stress following victimisation is largely due to the shattering of basic assumptions that the victims hold about themselves and the world.

Importantly, Rogers' description in his 1959 paper accounts for the phenomenology of PTSD. Certainly he does not use the term PTSD, as he was writing well before this term was introduced, but his description of the process of breakdown and disorganisation shows how the phenomenology of PTSD arises. Rogers talks about the anxiety that is experienced as the incongruence is subceived. However, the hallmark signs of PTSD are the re-experiencing and avoidance phenomena, and any theory must be able to account for these. Rogers does account for the intrusive and avoidant features when he goes on to describe the disorganisation that results when the self-structure breaks down. He says that the person attempts, on the one hand, to accurately symbolise in awareness their experience (intrusion) and, on the other, to deny their experiences and hold onto their pre-existing self-structure (avoidance). This account of the phases of intrusion and avoidance is similar to that of the information-processing theory proposed by Horowitz (1986), a leading theorist in the field of trauma. Horowitz (1986) also describes how people work through their experiences in terms of a tension between intrusive and avoidant states.

Horowitz's (1986) information-processing approach is based on the idea that individuals have mental models, or schemata, of the world and of themselves, which they use to interpret incoming information. He also proposes that there is an inherent drive to make our mental models coherent with current information, which he refers to as the *completion tendency*. A traumatic event presents information that is incompatible with existing schemas. This incongruity gives rise to a stress response, requiring reappraisal and revision of the schema. As traumatic events generally require massive schematic changes, complete integration and cognitive processing take some time to occur. During this time, active memory tends to repeat its representations of the traumatic event, causing emotional distress. However, to prevent emotional exhaustion, there is a process of inhibition and facilitation that acts as a feedback system, modulating the flow of information. The symptoms observed during stress responses, which Horowitz categorises as involving denials and intrusion, occur as a result of opposite actions of a control system that regulates the incoming information to tolerable doses. If inhibitory control is not strong enough, intrusive symptoms such as nightmares and flashbacks emerge. When inhibitory efforts are too strong in relation to active memory, symptoms indicative of the avoidance phase occur. Typically, avoidance and intrusion symptoms fluctuate in a way that is particular to the individual, so as not to cause flooding or exhaustion that would prevent adaptation. The person oscillates between the states of avoidance and intrusion until a relative equilibrium is reached and the person is said to have worked through the experience.

Individual differences in vulnerability

Contemporary theory in PTSD recognises that not everyone who experiences a traumatic event goes on to develop PTSD, and therefore any theory needs to be able to account for this observation. The above extract from Rogers' theoretical account is also able to account for individual differences. Rogers' theory provides a similar perspective to Horowitz (1986), who provides an account of cognitive processes involved in adaptation to trauma. Recovery from trauma is explained as resulting from cognitive assimilation of the traumatic memory or a revision of existing schemas to accommodate new information. Horowitz's (1986) theory explains individual differences in trauma response in terms of the degree of disparity between the trauma and pre-existing expectations and beliefs, or, in Rogers' terminology, the extent of incongruence between self and experience. The pivotal part of Rogers' description of breakdown is that the event demonstrates incongruence between self and experience. Here is the notion that it is the person's perception of the event that is important. It is in the nature of incongruence between self and experience that it will always be idiosyncratic to the person. We all have different experiences in life; consequently, an event that is experienced as incongruent by one person may not be so experienced by another. In Rogers' theory, cognitive appraisal processes are central.

Also, Rogers suggests that the more obvious and sudden the threat, the greater the degree of anxiety it engenders. Rogers uses the term 'obviousness' to describe the characteristics of an event that lead to difficulties in emotional processing. Although this term lacks the more fine-grained analysis provided by, for example, the behavioural psychologist Rachman (1980), it does capture the essence of those characteristics necessary to understand which events might be most likely to lead to PTSD. Rachman listed other stimulus characteristics that would constitute obviousness: for example, suddenness, intensity and dangerousness. Of course, trauma theorists will have paid particular attention to event factors, individual difference factors and so on that Rogers' generic theory from over 40 years ago does not explicitly address; what is important is that Rogers' theory provides us with sufficient understanding of trauma consistent with contemporary trauma theory and within which we can understand the operation of various vulnerability factors as expressions of incongruence.

The process of reintegration

Rogers (1959) goes on to suggest that accurate symbolisation in awareness of experience is necessary for reintegration of self and experience to take place. Similarly, current thinking on the most effective ways of helping people with post-traumatic stress integrate their experiences emphasises therapies that use exposure (for example, Foa & Kozak, 1986; Foa & Rothbaum, 1998). Certainly, the evidence shows that therapies that help the person to accurately symbolise their experiences, to use Rogers' terminology, are effective in helping people with PTSD. Person-centred theorists would, therefore, not disagree about the importance of exposure. Biermann-Ratjen (1998), for example, writes:

> As well as knowing that self-experience can only be integrated by accepting it, we also know nowadays that the best way of treating post-traumatic disorders is to help the traumatised person to remember the traumatic experience in the safety of a therapeutic relationship marked by empathic unconditionally [sic] positive regard. In this frame the experience which has been repeatedly driven out of consciousness can be retrieved piece by piece and reach awareness and the person can come to accept and understand his/her behaviour and feelings in reaction to the traumatic experience as a form of self-defence. (Biermann-Ratjen, 1998: 125)

What is key to the practice of psychotherapy is the way in which the therapist engages with the client in facilitating the process of exposure. The notion that the client should lead the process is not confined to writers from the client-centred tradition, however; others have also commented on the importance of not pushing the client. In writing about exposure, Meichenbaum (1994) states:

> … some clients may be reluctant to mentally 'relive' and 're-experience' the trauma-related events in the course of treatment. Clients may resist doing so-called 'memory work' of traumatic events. There is a danger of the therapist 'pushing' his/her agenda of the way to conduct treatment without 'spelling out' the options for the client… this therapeutic process needs to be collaborative with the clients being 'informed' and 'in-charge' throughout. (Meichenbaum, 1994: 303)

It is important to understand that the process of accurate symbolisation is what exposure therapies set out to achieve; what person-centred theory adds is the idea that there is no need for the therapist to push the client, because the client will be intrinsically motivated to increase congruence between self and experience and to accurately symbolise their experiences in awareness when the right social environmental conditions are present. This is what makes person-centred therapy different – the belief that the actualising tendency will, when the social environment is supportive, lead the person to accurately symbolise their experience. Thus there is no need to direct the client towards engaging in various cognitive-behavioural exercises, as the client will find their own best way to engage in retrieving, remembering and re-evaluating their experiences. Person-centred theory states that, if the client is not engaging in this process, it must be because the social environment is not supportive enough for them to feel unconditionally accepted and thus able to drop their defences and listen to their own inner voice.

Post-traumatic growth

As mentioned, one of the most important features of the person-centred conceptualisation of traumatic stress reactions is that it allows for a theoretical understanding not only of PTSD but also of post-traumatic growth. Post-traumatic growth refers to the positive psychological changes often observed in people following trauma, such as their enhanced appreciation of life, their shifts in priorities about what is important to them, their ability to form deeper and more intimate relationships, and their recognition of the development of new strengths (Joseph, 2011). Post-traumatic growth is explained by Rogers' theory that, when the client develops a self-structure that is congruent between self and experience, they also become more able to engage in organismic valuing. The 19th of Rogers' (1951) propositions sums this up:

> As the individual perceives and accepts into his self-structure more of his
> organic experiences, he finds that he is replacing his present value *system* –
> based so largely upon introjections which have been distortedly symbolized
> – with a continuing organismic valuing *process*. (Rogers, 1951: 522)

Thus, congruent reintegration of self with experience is not about the client returning to their pre-trauma levels of functioning, but about the client going beyond their previous levels of functioning to become more fully functioning. Rogers' (1959) description of the fully functioning person is of someone who, for example, is open to experience, perceives him or herself as the locus of evaluation, and has no conditions of worth. Such movement in traumatised clients towards becoming fully functioning might be described as post-traumatic growth (see Linley & Joseph, 2004; Tedeschi, Park & Calhoun, 1998).[1]

The focus on the fully functioning person is what makes the person-centred approach to understanding trauma very different from other social cognitive approaches. All psychological theories draw attention to the fact that the person must somehow integrate the new trauma-related information with pre-existing schemas, but what person-centred theory does is draw the distinction between the two ways in which trauma-related experience can be accommodated. Those aspects of self-structure that have broken down can be rebuilt in the direction of the person's conditions of worth, or the self-structure can be rebuilt in the direction of the person's actualising tendency.

Person-centred theory offers a powerful explanatory framework for understanding both post-traumatic stress reactions and growth through adversity. Person-centred therapy is a way of working with people founded on the alternative paradigm that people have an innate tendency towards the actualisation of their potentialities.

Client-centred therapy

The concept of the actualising tendency is unique to the person-centred way of working, and has profound significance for therapeutic practice. What client-centred therapy can offer traumatised clients is an unconditionally accepting relationship in which the client does not feel pushed to move in any direction other than their own. As Kennedy-Moore and Watson (1999: 253) write:

> In working with trauma survivors, it is essential to bear in mind that emotional
> expression rarely proceeds in an orderly fashion. Clients may express a little,
> then retreat from their feelings, then express a little more, then need to return
> to laying the groundwork for expression. Therapists need to be sensitive to

---

1. A more detailed account of integration of organismic theory within mainstream psychological approaches to trauma is available in Joseph & Linley (2005).

these fluctuations and to let clients take the lead in determining how much they can handle and how fast. Forcing clients to express their feelings before they are ready to do so can lead to emotional flooding and can compound clients' sense of victimisation. On the other hand, helping trauma survivors achieve a sense of mastery in their ability to articulate and manage their feelings can counter the sense of vulnerability and lack of control that traumatic events evoke.

In offering the conditions of empathy, congruence and unconditional positive regard to their client, the client-centred therapist is able to offer a social environment that serves to slowly dissolve the conditions of worth. The consequence is that the self-structure is gradually broken down and the self is reintegrated with experience to rebuild a new self-structure consistent with the actualising tendency. In working with traumatised clients, however, aspects of the self-structure have already been abruptly shattered. The task of the client-centred therapist is therefore to help the client rebuild their self-structure by reintegrating self with experience. As noted above, person-centred theory suggests that, as the client comes to develop a self-structure that is more congruent between self and experience, they should also become more fully functioning, and that such movement in traumatised clients might be described in current terminology as post-traumatic growth (Linley & Joseph, 2004; Tedeschi, Park & Calhoun, 1998).

Person-centred personality theory provides a framework to explain the development of post-traumatic growth, while simultaneously accounting for the phenomenology characteristic of PTSD. Having set out how person-centred theory is able to account for trauma, the task now for the person-centred community is to provide the research evidence to support it.

Person-centred theory suggests that, as clients gain in unconditional positive self-regard (UPSR), they are able to integrate self and experience. It would be expected, therefore, that UPSR is a predictor of post-traumatic growth. Two studies have investigated this. In the first, 143 participants completed an online questionnaire to assess the experience of traumatic life events, UPSR and post-traumatic growth at two points in time. Results showed that higher UPSR at the first point in time was associated with higher post-traumatic growth at the second point in time (Flanagan et al, 2015). In the second, the mediating effect of intrinsic aspirations on the association between UPSR and post-traumatic growth was investigated in a sample of 99 participants. It was found that greater UPSR was associated with post-traumatic growth and that the association between UPSR and post-traumatic growth was mediated by intrinsic aspirations (Murphy, Demetriou & Joseph, 2015). These two studies point to the importance of a self-accepting attitude and how it may contribute to the development of post-traumatic growth. It is likely that, when a person is self-accepting, they will behave in ways more in keeping with their intrinsic aspirations. Intrinsic aspiration, in turn, is linked to and energises significant growth-oriented behaviours, such as seeking out new challenges, pursuing one's interests and exercising skills.

However, empirical research on client-centred therapy for PTSD that uses well-controlled studies has not been conducted. We now need empirical evidence that client-centred therapy not only helps to alleviate the so-called symptoms of PTSD but also facilitates post-traumatic growth. This is what sets person-centred theory and client-centred therapy apart from other approaches: namely, the theoretical stance that the client will be motivated by the actualising tendency to accurately symbolise their experience and, with the right therapeutic conditions, will be able to do so. The implication of this is that there is no need to direct the client to engage in exposure-based exercises, because the theory holds that the traumatised client will be intrinsically motivated to do this for themselves, in their own way and at their own pace, when the therapist is providing the appropriate social-environmental conditions (Rogers, 1957). However, the assumption that clients will be intrinsically motivated to accurately symbolise their experiences is one that many therapists from other traditions might question, and there is a need now for research to test out whether this is indeed the case.

Conclusion

In conclusion, the most significant feature of person-centred theory as it applies to understanding trauma is the fact that the theory accounts not only for the development of the experiences characteristic of PTSD but also for the development of post-traumatic growth.

References

American Psychiatric Association (2013). *Diagnostic and Statistical Manual of Mental Disorders* (5th ed). Washington, DC: American Psychiatric Press.

Biermann-Ratjen EM (1998). Incongruence and psychopathology. In: Thorne B, Lambers E (eds). *Person-Centred Therapy: a European perspective*. London: Sage (pp106–118).

Flanagan S, Patterson TG, Hume IR, Joseph S (2015). A longitudinal investigation of the relationship between unconditional positive self-regard and posttraumatic growth. *Person-Centered & Experiential Psychotherapies* 14: 191–200.

Foa EB, Kozak MJ (1986). Emotional processing of fear: exposure to corrective information. *Psychological Bulletin* 99: 20–35.

Foa EB, Rothbaum BO (1998). *Treating the Trauma of Rape: cognitive behavioral therapy for PTSD*. New York: Guilford.

Horowitz M (1986). *Stress Response Syndromes*. Northville, NJ: Jason Aronson.

Janoff-Bulman R (1989). Assumptive worlds and the stress of traumatic events: applications of the schema construct. *Social Cognition* 7: 113–136.

Janoff-Bulman R (1992). *Shattered Assumptions: toward a new psychology of trauma*. New York: The Free Press.

Joseph S (2011). *What Doesn't Kill Us: the new psychology of posttraumatic growth*. Basic Books: New York.

Joseph S (2003). Person-centred approach to understanding posttraumatic stress. *Person-Centred Practice 11*: 70–75.

Joseph S (2004). Client-centred therapy, posttraumatic stress disorder and posttraumatic growth. Theory and practice. *Psychology and Psychotherapy: Theory, Research and Practice 77*: 101–120.

Joseph S, Linley PA (2005). Positive adjustment to threatening events: an organismic valuing theory of growth through adversity. *Review of General Psychology 9*: 262–280.

Kennedy-Moore E, Watson JC (1999). *Expressing Emotion: myths, realities and therapeutic strategies*. New York: Guilford Press.

Linley PA, Joseph S (2004). Positive changes following trauma and adversity: a review. *Journal of Traumatic Stress 17*: 11–21.

Meichenbaum D (1994). *Treating Post-Traumatic Stress Disorder: a handbook and practice manual for therapy*. Chichester: Wiley.

Murphy D, Demetriou E, Joseph S (2015). A cross-sectional study to explore the mediating effect of intrinsic aspiration on the association between unconditional positive self-regard and posttraumatic growth. *Person-Centered & Experiential Psychotherapies 14*: 201–213.

Rachman S (1980). Emotional processing. *Behaviour Research and Therapy 18*: 51–60.

Rogers CR (1942). *Counseling and Psychotherapy: newer concepts in practice*. Boston: Houghton Mifflin.

Rogers CR (1951). *Client-Centered Therapy: its current practice, implications and theory*. Boston: Houghton Mifflin.

Rogers CR (1957). The necessary and sufficient conditions of therapeutic personality change. *Journal of Consulting Psychology 21*: 95–103.

Rogers CR (1959). A theory of therapy, personality and interpersonal relationships, as developed in the client-centered framework. In: Koch S (ed). *Psychology: a study of a science. Vol 3: Formulations of the person and the social context*. New York: McGraw-Hill (pp184–256).

Rogers CR, Wallen JL (1946). *Counseling with Returned Servicemen*. New York: McGraw-Hill.

Tedeschi RG, Park CL, Calhoun LG (eds) (1998). *Posttraumatic Growth: positive changes in the aftermath of crisis*. Mahwah: Lawrence Erlbaum.

15 Working with maternal depression: person-centred therapy as part of a multi-agency approach

Elaine Catterall

My intention in this chapter is to write about maternal depression, by first referring to the psychiatric and psychotherapeutic evidence base, to provide the reader with an overview of the current thinking and practice. Against this clinical background, I will then consider maternal depression from a person-centred theoretical perspective and what person-centred therapy has to offer mothers experiencing psychological distress. The discussion would be incomplete, though, without including a brief overview of western social-cultural perspectives surrounding motherhood and maternal depression, as I believe this will provide the therapeutic relationship with the necessary context in which to engage with this client group in a more meaningful way.

There is also an autobiographical element to this chapter, which inevitably introduces subjective personal bias. I make no apologies for this. At one time, I might have considered personal reference 'unprofessional' in a text of this kind, yet without it there would be a denial of the influence that phenomenological experience has on all of our work. Indeed, it is unlikely that I would be writing this chapter if I had not personally experienced postnatal depression. I make no pretence to original thought in what follows, but I hope to bring together a range of ideas about maternal psychological distress that are already 'out there', and to present them in a way that health professionals and psychotherapists may not have come across before. I also acknowledge that I am only presenting one cultural perspective.

Personal background

I have three daughters, and my interest in maternal depression started when I experienced severe psychological distress after my second daughter was born, in 1992. The journey to recovery was a long and seemingly *ad hoc* affair, with family and friends at its core, but also involving primary care and psychiatric treatment interventions (including inpatient care), as well as private, long-term psychotherapy, alternative therapies and invaluable support from other women through voluntary support agencies. (See the appendix for details of UK-based organisations offering support for postnatal depression.)

Psychiatric opinion and interpretation did not provide a complete explanation of my experience; nor did it provide a 'cure'. It was this discrepancy between internal experiencing and external, expert opinion that inspired me to want to know more, not only about myself but also about the label 'postnatal depression' and its relevance and meaning in society.

My subsequent involvement in voluntary support agencies, offering individual and group support to other new mothers, led to formal counselling training. At this point I began to realise that much of what had helped my recovery – and, indeed, what I was now trying to communicate to others – could be explained by person-centred theory. For the last 17 years, I have worked therapeutically with adolescents and adults, and more recently with children. This has included specific therapeutic work relating to maternal depression and motherhood, through projects such as Surestart and NHS-sponsored postnatal support groups. Counselling younger children in schools also involves meeting and supporting parents, and maternal depression is all too often a part of the family story.

The countless conversations I have had in the last two decades with mothers experiencing maternal depression have all, in some way, informed and influenced the ideas set out in this chapter. For them all, I am eternally grateful.

Social-cultural influences on the experience of motherhood and maternal depression

Childbirth and motherhood are more than a set of instinctual urges and natural behaviours. They are profoundly shaped by the cultural norms of the societies we live in. Different societies and different historical periods reveal wide variations in the beliefs, values and practices surrounding motherhood and raising children. This has a significant impact on a woman's mental wellbeing and sense of self as a mother. I can only provide a very brief summary of a few key themes here, but for the interested reader, Kitzinger (1992) provides a fascinating account of the comparative sociology of birth and motherhood across a diverse range of cultures.

Maternal and infant mortality

Until the early part of the 20th century, childbirth was a leading cause of death, second to tuberculosis (Figes, 1998), and women would have known others in their families and communities who died or sustained serious injury during childbirth. Fears for their own life, and for that of their infant, as well as mourning for the loss of others, are likely to have been the primary psychological focus for many women, and thus any psychological changes associated with the transition to motherhood were likely to have been overshadowed. Except for the work of the French doctors JED Esquirol and Louis Marcé in the 1850s, the notion of a specific 'mental illness' associated with childbirth had not yet emerged.

Increasing focus on child development and welfare

As obstetric and medical procedures improved maternal mortality and health during the early part of the 20th century, the focus of care quickly shifted away from the mother to the infant's health and welfare. By the 1940s and 50s, ideas from humanistic psychology and psychoanalysis relating to child development were becoming increasingly influential. The theories of Bowlby (1988) and Winnicott (1986) highlighted the importance of a good mother–infant relationship to the emotional wellbeing of the child, and their ideas informed doctors, teachers and social workers about good childcare practice. Rogers' work was also influential at this time (particularly in the US), and person-centred theoretical concepts have also been assimilated into the social discourse around motherhood and raising children. When I ask women what it means to them to be a 'good' mother, they often describe one aspect as being able to give 'unconditional love', and expect themselves to be able to do this, but without having given much thought to what 'unconditional' might mean.

By implication, therefore, it is 'mother's love' and 'mother's care' that produces a secure and emotionally stable child. But what is also becoming clear is that influences on the child's psychological wellbeing are far more complicated than the quality of the mother–infant relationship alone. Bowlby's early work on attachment theory has been criticised as too simplistic and methodologically flawed (Holmes, 1993; Parker, 1995; Figes, 1998; Blaffer Hrdy, 2009), and it is now known that other significant attachment relationships in the baby's life are just as important: for example, the father's relationship with the baby (eg. Cox & Holden, 1994; Lamb, cited in Blaffer Hrdy, 2009: 126), shared childcare, and maternal grandmothers, as well as social support (Blaffer Hrdy, 2009; Cree, 2015). Despite this knowledge, there still remains a commonly held belief in society that babies and young children are best cared for solely by their mother.

A change in emphasis from illness to health

In the western pre-industrial era, newly delivered mothers were considered to be 'ill', and an enforced 'lying-in' period followed delivery. The woman was considered to be in social and physical transition, and remained in the house while other women took over her chores. With the arrival of the industrial era in the mid-18th century, this lying-in period started to reduce, especially for working-class women. Even so, the benefits of bed rest were still considered to be important, even if women couldn't stick to it (Figes, 1998).

Western medical and childbirth experts have moved away from this notion of 'illness', and now define a newly delivered mother as 'healthy'. While this is more in line with the anthropological view that becoming a mother is a natural experience (Kitzinger, 1992), it doesn't describe those childbirth experiences where a woman's physical and psychological state leave her feeling anything but healthy.

In her book critiquing the traditional explanations of maternal depression, Paula Nicholson reminds us that, despite this notion of 'health', childbirth still remains a medical event in the UK and US, and that medical and surgical interventions are increasingly common during childbirth and delivery (Nicholson, 1998: 86). Ellie Lee also writes extensively on the increasing medicalisation of experiences relating to motherhood (Lee, 2003), and both authors point to the contradictions that exist within society about the experience of women becoming mothers. On the one hand, it is described as a natural, healthy and happy experience, but on the other, it is a medically 'monitored and managed' experience, making it almost impossible for a woman to follow any instinctive feelings she may have. Within this context of 'health', it may be possible to see why the medical discourse relating to childbirth describes anything outside of this 'norm' as pathology, and why a specific branch of psychiatry specialising in maternal mental illness, known as perinatal psychiatry, has emerged.

Maternal depression and current psychiatric classification

Before describing the psychiatric classification of maternal depression, a brief description is needed of the commonly used language and terminology within the field of maternal mental health. Postnatal depression and the baby blues are still the commonly used terms with which many people will be familiar (they are used by women and their families, as well as by health professionals). Postpartum, puerperium and puerperal are the clinical terms used to refer to the period following childbirth (usually the first six weeks). Perinatal is the latest addition to the medical and health literature and describes the period from conception to one year after the birth, as it is now understood that maternal distress is not exclusive to the postpartum period: it can start in pregnancy and go well beyond the first six weeks postpartum. Perinatal psychiatry specialises in the treatment of antenatal and postnatal mental disorders.

For simplicity, I use 'maternal depression' and 'maternal distress' generically to refer to the range of psychologically distressing experiences described by pregnant and new mothers. However, where I refer to the research and ideas from other authors, I use their terminology. (Throughout the chapter, I use the term 'new mother' and 'mother' interchangeably to describe women in the perinatal period, and this is not restricted to first-time mothers.) I want to acknowledge at this point that puerperal psychosis deserves a separate discussion in terms of treatment and support, but there is not the space in this chapter to give it the attention it also deserves. However, my conversations and friendships with a handful of women who have experienced puerperal psychosis have also influenced the thinking behind this chapter.

Psychiatric classification

In the 1960s, Professor Brice Pitt was one of the first British psychiatrists to describe depression following childbirth as atypical and different from depression experienced at other times (Pitt, 1968). By the 1980s, health professionals with a particular interest in perinatal mental health had formed the Marcé Society to counter the lack of information about maternal distress. More recently, the Maternity Mental Health Alliance (MMHA) was formed, to raise awareness and campaign for better services. (Details of these organisations and the MMHA 2014 campaign #everyonesbusiness are included in the Appendix.)

Until recently, the medical literature commonly described three disorders associated with maternal mental illness: postpartum blues, postpartum psychosis and postpartum depression. Their relevance to medical professionals is that each term conveys something about the timing of onset and relative severity of the mental disorder. There are now no formal diagnostic categories for perinatal mental disorders in the latest, fifth edition of the *Diagnostic and Statistical Manual* (American Psychiatric Association, 2013). The only exception is mention of the increased risk of psychosis in the postnatal period, and childbirth is said to be a specific trigger for a 'hypomanic episode'. The 10th edition of the *International Classification of Diseases* (ICD-10) does have a specific classification (F53) for 'mental and behavioural disorders associated with the puerperium, not elsewhere classified' (WHO, 1992), but clinicians are encouraged to use other diagnostic categories where possible. The latest NICE guidelines on perinatal mental health acknowledge that, while many symptoms are similar in nature to mental disorders experienced at other times, their management and treatment is different because of the potential impact on the woman and the baby (NICE, 2014).

Postpartum (baby) blues was the term traditionally used to describe the transient low mood, tearfulness and irritability commonly experienced by 50 to 80 per cent of new mothers within the first few days following delivery. It was considered to be a normal part of the transition to motherhood. Evidence now suggests that the severity and duration of the blues may be an indicator of the onset of more severe depression (Green & Murray, 1994; Henshaw et al, 2004, cited in Hanley 2015: 7).

Postpartum or puerperal psychosis affects between one and two women per 1000 births, and 80 per cent of cases develop within 14 days after delivery. Postpartum psychosis is, by definition, severe, and may persist for a considerable period. Despite reported symptom differences between puerperal and non-puerperal psychoses (for example, puerperal psychosis has been described as 'being more bizarre or extreme pathologically, with greater perplexity or confusion, yet women recover more quickly and "completely"' (Cox, 1994: 4)), puerperal psychosis is increasingly considered a variant of bipolar disorder (Oates, 1994; Brockington, 1996; NICE, 2014).

Postpartum depression was the commonly used term. However, it is now recognised that women commonly experience depression and/or anxiety during pregnancy and the first postnatal year. According to NICE, between 12 and 13 per cent of women are affected antenatally and 15 to 20 per cent postnatally (NICE, 2014). The Royal College of Midwives states that as many as 20 per cent of women are affected during pregnancy (2015), and this has implications for detection and early intervention. A report from the National Perinatal Epidemiology Unit (Knight et al, 2015) warns that maternal psychological distress can deteriorate quickly and gives a 'red flag' list of symptoms that all practitioners who come into contact with new mothers need to be aware of.

Problems of labelling

Many psychiatrists involved in perinatal mental health consider postnatal depression to be a 'relatively minor disturbance (in psychiatric terms), which tends to remit spontaneously within a few months' (Brockington, 2004; Cooper & Murray, 1997; O'Hara, 1997) and therefore does not warrant a separate classification. Indeed, a review of the research suggests that the symptoms and duration of postnatal depression are not noticeably different from depression occurring at other times (see, for example, O'Hara, 1997; Brockington, 2004).

Other perinatal specialists argue that, despite this clinical picture, women experience postnatal mental disorders as 'distressing and unexpected and not as a time of personal growth, or purposive suffering' (Holden, 1991, cited in Cox & Holden, 1994: 5). Cox states that many women regard postnatal depression as 'different from depression at other times' (Cox, 1994: 5).

Few of the women I've listened to have described their experience as a 'minor disturbance' that disappears after a few months. While some find meaning in the experience, many do not. It is often shocking and frightening; many women fear they 'are going mad'. Women are therefore often relieved to be given the label of 'postnatal depression', as it provides an explanation for their experience. However, it can also feel stigmatising. Elliott points out that labelling can inhibit or delay the process of change that the 'depressed mood should be heralding' (Elliott, 1994: 223) – a phenomenon I have sometimes observed in peer support groups. A clinical label aligns the experience to a physical illness, often disconnecting the woman from any personal meaning in it. This can also turn the experience into something that is not 'a part of me' but something that is 'happening to me', something to get 'rid of', 'out of my control'. This disconnection or sense of helplessness is heard sometimes when women describe their experience as 'the illness', or refer to it as 'when I had PND'.

Yet, dismissing the idea of maternal depression as an illness may deny the experiences of some mothers who are severely depressed and describe feeling physically 'very ill' (often in terms of overwhelming exhaustion and tiredness, not eating or sleeping), in addition to their psychological distress. For these women, 'the label may point the way out and bring in some badly needed care and attention' (Elliott, 1994: 223).

Postnatal depression – an oversimplification?

The traditional view of the blues, postnatal depression and psychosis is, in fact, considered an oversimplification by the psychiatric profession, which now sees the range of disorders that women experience in the perinatal period as much wider (Brockington, 2004: 303). Post-traumatic stress disorder, fears and obsessions about child-harm, serious disturbances in the mother–infant relationship, and a range of anxiety disorders are just some of the 'disorders' identified in NICE guidelines, which now describe specific care pathways for each disorder (2014).

What becomes clear from this debate is that the experience of maternal psychological distress is not a uniform experience and is too complex to be captured in a single clinical diagnosis of postpartum depression. Women describe a wide range of symptoms that they associate with maternal distress and that do not fit neatly into the psychiatric list of clinical symptoms of depression. Excessive and constant anxiety is commonly the main presenting symptom, rather than depressed mood (Dion, 2002; Hogg, 2013), and is frequently accompanied by obsessional thoughts, often relating to fears about the infant's or mother's health. But are these 'separate disorders', or all part of the same experience?

Traumatic experiences during pregnancy and birth do leave some women describing symptoms that warrant a diagnosis of PTSD associated with childbirth (Bailham & Joseph, 2003), and disturbances in the mother–infant relationship, for example, can occur in the absence of maternal depression (Cramer, 1997). Some mothers may also have an existing psychiatric diagnosis of a mental illness and/or a history of past trauma, including childhood abuse and domestic abuse (which may be ongoing), all of which are likely to trigger and contribute to psychological distress in the perinatal period (Catterall, 2007).

But is it any more helpful to new mothers to have their experiences described as a range of separate 'disorders' that require the 'correct' diagnosis in order to receive the 'correct' treatment?

Aetiology

Research has been unable to confirm a specific aetiology for perinatal anxiety and depression. Risk factors have been identified, and health professionals need to be aware of them, to aid prevention and early detection (Hogg, 2013). But it is generally accepted that maternal psychological distress has multiple causes and affects women of all ages and from all social and ethnic backgrounds (Cox & Holden, 1994; Hogg, 2013; Russell & Lang, 2013).

Despite a lack of aetiology, the medical profession continues to classify maternal psychological distress in terms of perinatal mental health disorders and perinatal mental illnesses, in order to ensure that service providers are aware of the particular needs of new mothers and infants, which may otherwise be missed (Riecher-Rossler & Hofecker-Fallahpour, 2003; NICE, 2014). This recommendation implies that maternal distress needs to be pathologised in order to allocate resources. This line of reasoning feels ethically wrong to me, as many of the risk factors are connected with how we live, relate and function in and with society. Sadly, however, I believe this will remain the prominent discourse in societies where diagnoses and 'treatments' for psychological distress are dominated by the medical model (Lee, 2003), and where health outcomes are measured in terms of economic, rather than human, cost (Bauer et al, 2014; Catterall, 2014; Herman, 2015).

Current approaches to treatment and support

Maternal depression is now considered to be a very distressing experience, occurring at a time when a woman is already highly vulnerable emotionally, and has an infant to care for who is, for the most part, totally dependent on her for his/ her needs. A wealth of research studies reveals the longer-term negative impact of untreated maternal depression on the whole family, in addition to the woman's distress. These include chronic mental health problems for the woman, higher risk of adverse emotional, behavioural and development effects on the child (Murray, 1992; Siegel, 2012), negative effects on the couple's relationship, and increased risk of paternal depression (Watson & Foreman, 1994; Hanley, 2015). Shockingly, suicide remains one of the leading causes of maternal death (Hanley, 2015: 19, 45) and women remain at high risk of suicide due to mental distress throughout the first year after giving birth (Knight et al, 2015).

The Edinburgh Postnatal Depression screening questionnaire and the role of the health visitor

The above issues highlight the importance of early detection and treatment of perinatal depression (Cox & Holden, 1994), and have stimulated further research into the issue. Several key studies from the 1980s have been influential in this area: most notably, the development of a 10-item self-report mental health questionnaire known as the Edinburgh Postnatal Depression Scale (EPDS) (Cox, Holden & Sagovsky, 1987) and a controlled trial to investigate the effectiveness of health visitor 'listening' visits (Holden et al, 1989).

Holden and colleagues' 1989 study demonstrated a reduction in the duration and severity of depression in 69 per cent of women who received listening visits, compared with 38 per cent in the control group. The study thus highlighted the benefits of a listening, non-judgmental relationship, and that such a relationship can be provided by health visitors (in particular), but also by midwives, the voluntary sector and peer support groups (Holden, Sagovsky & Cox, 1989; Seeley, Murray & Cooper, 1996; Clement, 1995; Mauthner, 1997; Hanley, 2015). Holden and colleagues (1989) recommended six to eight health visitor listening visits for women scoring above 10 on the EPDS, as an early intervention for postnatal depression.

The EPDS remains the most validated and well-used self-report measurement tool worldwide (Hanley, 2015), and in the UK health visitors are still trained in the use of the EPDS and listening visits. Since 2013, over 10,000 health visitor and public health practitioners have received this training, and the development of regional networks is proposed, to integrate and promote best practice in multidisciplinary care (Walker, 2015; personal communication). In Scotland, health guidelines also recognise the importance of additional psychosocial support, alongside listening visits (SIGN, 2012).

Despite the known benefits and efficacy of this type of intervention and substantial ongoing investment in training, health professionals report that, even when they are adequately trained, they do not have the time to explore a woman's mental wellbeing properly (Elliott & Leverton, 2000; Shakespeare, 2002; Rowley & Dixon, 2002; Russell & Lang, 2013: 22). Meanwhile, NICE no longer recommends routine use of the EPDS because of resource implications, and recommends instead the use of the two Whooley questions (Aroll, Khin & Kerse, 2003), designed for detection of general depression. Health visitors are already noticing that the latter, when used outside of a relational, holistic assessment, are not reliable in detecting perinatal mental health problems (Littlewood et al, 2016; Russell & Lang, 2013; Hanley, 2015: 31).

Listening visits confused with person-centred counselling

Some mothers do not find health visitor listening visits sufficient to alleviate their depression (Alder & Truman, 2002). Health visitors also report that use of non-directive counselling skills is not enough, and some women find it unhelpful to keep talking 'over and over' the same issues. This has led to some practitioners using cognitive behavioural therapy (CBT) and solution-focused skills instead (Seeley, 2004; personal communication). It is worth noting that, in some of the literature, the terms 'listening visits' and 'health visitor intervention' have become synonymous with non-directive or person-centred counselling (see, for example, Watson & Foreman, 1994). By implication, then, based on the experiences of some health visitors, person-centred counselling might not be an effective psychological intervention for this client group.

The key issue seems to be a misunderstanding of person-centred therapy, which has been reduced here to a set of mechanistic *skills* used to facilitate listening. If we refer back to person-centred theory (Rogers, 1957; 1959), Rogers proposed that it is the *quality* of the relationship that matters most, and that it is this that determines the extent to which the relationship is an experience that 'releases or promotes development and growth' (Rogers & Stevens, 1967: 89). Recent studies examining the effectiveness of different psychotherapies confirm that relationship factors (for both client and therapist) are stronger predictors of treatment outcome than therapeutic modality (Watson, Greenberg & Lietaer, 2010). However, Elliott and Friere's (2010:11) review of six meta-analyses on the outcome of person-centred/experiential therapies in general adult populations also identified that 'supportive' or 'non-directive' therapies (which are not the same as bona fide person-centred therapy) are not quite as effective, which supports these reports of the limited effectiveness of health visitor listening visits.

This would suggest, therefore, that the attitudinal qualities first described by Rogers (ie. unconditional positive regard, empathy and congruence) as necessary for therapeutic change (Rogers, 1957) are not always present in the relationship between mother and health visitor. In her guide to listening visits for health professionals, Hanley (2015) does highlight the complexities of 'listening well' and the frustrations and potential role conflicts that many health visitors may experience when working with mothers experiencing maternal depression.

Listening visits are also a short-term intervention, and only permit a superficial exploration of the woman's experience, which may not be enough for those women whose distress seems 'inexplicable' or is extreme. Also, the role of the health visitor is to look after the welfare of the woman and the baby, and this dual role can make it extremely difficult for some women to reveal their true thoughts and feelings, for fear that they will be seen as inadequate or that the baby will be taken away from them (Russell & Lang, 2013; Catterall, 1995). In Russell and Lang's study (2013), seven in 10 new mothers experiencing postnatal depression were found to have hidden or minimised the severity of their symptoms. This common fear may in part explain why relatively few new mothers seek help for mental distress (Whitton, Warner & Appleby, 1996).

Further treatment interventions

If listening visits are not available, or make little difference to the mother's mental health, referral to Improving Access to Psychological Therapies (IAPT) services is the next option for women living in England, and to primary care counselling in the other three countries of the UK. Because of the potential negative impact of maternal distress, NICE (2014) recommends fast-tracking new mothers to IAPT. Antidepressants are still likely to be a common treatment option for women seeking help from their GP. However, Appleby and colleagues (1997) found cognitive behavioural counselling to be equally effective as the antidepressant fluoxetine (Prozac) in the treatment of postnatal depression, potentially offering women an alternative to medication. This is an important choice because, as Cooper and Murray (1997) point out, while antidepressants may be as effective as psychological therapy, in practice, medication is not usually the preferred choice of new mothers, especially if they are breastfeeding. In fact, Cooper and Murray go on to say that 'non-directive counselling is highly acceptable to women' (Cooper & Murray, 1997).

Other counselling and psychotherapy options

Several other studies have evaluated the effectiveness of psychological therapies for maternal depression (Holden, Sagovsky & Cox, 1989; Alder & Truman, 2002;

Cooper & Murray, 1997; O'Hara et al, 2000). Although O'Hara and colleagues (2000) have highlighted methodological limitations in some of these studies, their overall conclusion is that individual and group work, as well as different therapeutic approaches (including person-centred, psychodrama, gestalt, psychodynamic, cognitive behavioural and interpersonal therapy) are equally effective. Although not specific to maternal depression, Elliott and Friere's (2010: 10) review of the meta-analyses showing the effectiveness of person-centred/experiential psychotherapies corroborates these findings.

There are also plenty of recent examples of successful therapeutic programmes to support new mothers, but these are local schemes and tend to be dependent on individuals and clinicians with a passionate interest in perinatal mental health (eg. Cree, 2015; Bertrum, 2008).

Despite the available evidence, women will not routinely be offered any form of psychological support other than CBT, which is currently offered through IAPT. In practice, a lack of resources within NHS mental health services means that IAPT is not easily accessed. And provision of specialist perinatal services across the UK remains patchy, falling woefully short of the Royal College of Psychiatrists' recommendations (Oates, 2015) and NICE (2014) guidelines. (The Maternal Mental Health Alliance campaign *#everyonesbusiness*, maps the availability of perinatal services nationwide, and is available to view on their website. See Appendix for details.)

An explanation of maternal distress from the person-centred theoretical perspective

Rogers' theory in relation to personality development (or self-theory) and emotional disturbance requires an acceptance that, from infancy, the person develops a self-concept introjected with the values and judgments of significant others. The child accepts these external values, or conditions of worth, as her own, in order to gain the positive approval of others that she requires to maintain her own sense of self-worth (Rogers, 1959; Mearns, 1994; Merry, 2004). It is the self-concept and associated conditions of worth that inform a person's way of being in the world and in future relationships with self and other. With respect to a woman becoming a mother (either for the first or subsequent time), I believe that her existing self-regard and self-concept will be challenged in a way not previously experienced by having to adapt to incorporate a new sense of self as a 'mother'. It is helpful to think of this occurring at three levels:

1. the *intrapersonal or dialogical level*. The person-centred theoretical proposal of a *plural self* (Rowan & Cooper, 1999), described as 'configurations of self' by Mearns and Thorne (2000; Mearns, 2002), is a useful way to conceptualise a woman's emerging identity as a mother and the processes and conflicts involved in integrating this 'part', or 'configuration', with other aspects of

herself, including existing beliefs about and attitudes towards herself as a 'mother' that she may have held since childhood. (This theoretical concept is discussed in more detail later)

2. the *interpersonal level*, in terms of the mother's newly developing relationship with the baby and changing relationships with the other significant people in her life

3. the *familial and societal level*, with respect to how the mother sees herself as fitting in with familial and cultural norms and expectations associated with motherhood. (I discuss the impact of society's expectations more fully in the section describing the cultural context for person-centred theory and therapy.)

With respect to the woman's relationship with her baby (particularly her first-born), her existing self-concept will be confronted with a totally new set of experiences, quite unique from anything that has gone before, especially in terms of her feelings and expectations in relation to the unborn baby and then to the new-born infant. The mother has to perceive and relate to the baby's needs primarily through non-verbal cues and empathic engagement (Warner, 1997; Siegel, 2012). If the mother's sense of self-worth is low, and her internal locus of evaluation is fragile, she may be constantly preoccupied with her 'performance' as a 'good enough' mother and, in the first instance, will only have feedback about her 'performance' from the baby's behaviour and levels of contentment.

If a woman has a highly externalised locus of evaluation, and relies heavily on the values and judgments of others, she will be particularly vulnerable to any perceived negative value judgments, such as a crying or fretful baby. This may then fuel any beliefs she may have about being an inadequate mother and increase her self-preoccupation and anxieties about her abilities. A woman may then begin to experience shame as she loses her self-confidence, and this in turn will make it more difficult for her to seek support and isolate her further in her experience.

Dissonance between self-concept as 'mother' and actual experience as 'mother'

Maternal distress may not, however, specifically be about difficulties in the mother–infant relationship. In terms of her existing relationships, new conflicts may arise, either for the woman personally if she is determined that the baby will not change her existing relationships, or with those around her (especially her partner, other children and close family) if they expect her to behave as she has always done. If this conflict between self-concept as a mother and the actual experience of mothering is too great, then psychological distress is likely to result. Mearns proposes that:

> ... if the threat (to the self-concept) has caused serious damage to the self-regard, disorder may result. The threat has invaded the person's fundamental

existential process to create damage that can range from self-doubt to self-annihilation. (Mearns, 2002: 24)

As a simple example, some women who experience maternal distress describe themselves as previously being organised and capable, and expect that, as in other life situations, they should be able to cope with a new baby. If the reality is that they feel out of control, or overwhelmed by the responsibility of mothering, or they are simply exhausted and need sleep, then asking for help may threaten their existing self-concept (that they can cope alone), as they now perceive themselves as 'not coping'. Thus, the development of maternal distress may be explained from a person-centred perspective.

Person-centred 'configurations of self as mother' vs psychoanalytical 'motherhood constellation' – same or different?

As a new mother makes the psychological transition into motherhood, a new role or identity emerges, and existing ones may change or disappear. Rogers recognised the importance of the mother–infant relationship, but it was Winnicott (1986) who first described how new mothers enter a different psychological state as they relate and attune to the emotional needs of the baby, which he called 'primary maternal preoccupation' (Winnicott, 1986). Stern added to Winnicott's ideas with his theory of the motherhood constellation – a newly created psychic organisation or construct that is 'a unique, independent construct in its own right, of great magnitude in the life of most mothers' (1995: 173) and 'entirely normal' (1995: 170). Stern goes on to state that new mothers require a different kind of therapeutic input that doesn't fit with a classical psychoanalytical approach:

> ... mothers in therapy have known this all along... they know full well that they have entered into a different psychic zone that has largely escaped psychiatry's official systematic theorising but is perfectly evident to them. And they have most often, when in psychodynamic-type therapies, tolerated the traditional psychodynamic interpretations without giving them too much weight, *in order to benefit from other aspects of the therapeutic relationship.* (1995: 198; my emphasis)

Stern's observations about the importance of relational factors will of course come as no surprise to person-centred therapists. With respect to the proposition of a specific 'motherhood constellation', though, is Stern proposing something that is a universal set of experiences, or the same phenomenon that a person-centred therapist might refer to as a 'configuration of self as mother'? Mearns and Thorne have provided a working definition for this concept:

> A configuration is a hypothetical construct denoting a coherent pattern of feelings, thoughts and preferred behavioural responses symbolised or pre-symbolised by the person as reflective of a dimension of existence within the Self. (2000: 102)

From my own experience, and from listening to others, there do appear to be some common themes and experiences that weave through the narrative of motherhood and maternal distress and are similar to those described by Stern (1995: 173) – and this makes sense to me when I think about motherhood being a transitional or developmental stage through which all new mothers journey. While this theoretical knowledge may be deemed interpretative and therefore counter to person-centred theory, some therapists may find it helps inform their personal understanding of psychological processes that are specific to motherhood. Alongside this, the theory of configurations of self provides a useful framework for person-centred therapists to listen to a woman's 'mother' configuration, but with the all-important distinction that the mother will use her own language and perceptions to describe her experience of 'self as mother' and not be conditionally accepted solely on the assumptions set out in a theory.

A cultural context for person-centred theory and therapy

The development of maternal psychological distress, as outlined above, narrowly focuses on the conditions of worth experienced in childhood. However, I believe this does not adequately account for the wider influence of society's values and expectations on a woman's identity as a mother. Therefore, a consideration of person-centred theory within the cultural context of motherhood may be helpful.

Phenomenologically, the experience of pregnancy, childbirth and caring for a new-born baby is likely to trigger wide-ranging emotions, sensations and experiencing that may not necessarily fit idealised cultural images of motherhood. These commonly describe the experience as 'natural and instinctive' and expect mothers to 'bond' with their babies immediately. A woman can feel she has 'failed' as a mother if her experience does not match these cultural messages.

Societal expectations and conditions of worth

In industrialised western societies, at least (with the possible exception of ethnic minority communities that maintain their non-western cultural traditions), when a woman is handed her baby, it seems that any (childlike) dependency needs she may have must be put aside. She is an adult now, a mother. Mothers are expected to 'get on with it', largely unaided and often with very little experience of new-born babies. Paradoxically, a new mother will be inundated with advice and opinions from almost everyone she meets. It seems that everyone (parent or not) has something to say on the subject of motherhood and raising children. It is such a fundamental part of our existence, and yet it seems that most people only want to consider the brighter, more idealised aspects of mothering. The less than ideal aspects are too shadowy, too dark to contemplate, and so remain hidden (Price, 1988; Littlewood & McHugh, 1997; Nicholson, 1998). If they do appear, it is often in relation to the negative impact on children of 'deficient' mothering, leading to an attitude of blaming rather than compassion – an attitude that Lee (2003) believes is the result of a child-centred culture within which most parents are left feeling anxious and inadequate, rather than affirmed and supported. It will be interesting to see whether public perception of parenting starts to change and becomes less conditional and more accepting in response to national campaigns to raise awareness of the wider support needs of women and their families in the perinatal period (for example, the Maternal Mental Health Alliance's #everyonesbusiness campaign (see Appendix for details)).

Client expectations of self

Within the therapeutic relationship, the new mother will be unused to having her vulnerabilities and negative feelings really heard and explored without judgment and with empathic understanding. This experience is likely to feel very unfamiliar and in stark contrast to the usual advice or sympathy she receives. In addition, the woman herself will bring her own cultural prejudices and beliefs about motherhood to her experience. Therefore, to face those aspects within herself that feel unacceptable in societal, familial or individual terms is likely to threaten her self-concept as a woman and a mother. Feminist authors often describe the negative thoughts and feelings about motherhood as being a 'big taboo' that rarely gets talked about in an honest, open way, even between mothers. The title of Kate Figes' book, for example, echoes this: *Life after Birth: what even your friends won't tell you about motherhood* (1998). Some feminist writers argue that it is the patriarchal nature of our society that maintains the myth of perfect motherhood, and that to challenge that view risks being branded a bad mother (Ussher, 1991; Choderow, 1978; Walker, 1990; Price, 1988; Nicholson, 1998; Figes, 1998).

Self-theory and society

In countless conversations with new mothers over many years, women have told me that they know that the idea of perfect motherhood is a myth and, contrary to the feminist argument above, will talk about it and support each other in being less than perfect, and even celebrate each other's successes – an aspect of mothers' groups that Stadlen also highlights (2004a). (It needs to be recognised that many depressed women find general mother and baby groups isolating because their experience of being a mother does not match what they see in these groups. Support groups specifically for maternal depression can help counteract this sense of isolation.)

Knowing that perfect motherhood is a myth makes little difference to the distorted view of motherhood that persists in some parts of society, and many women still feel guilty when they see their attempts as not matching society's expectations of what constitutes 'good' mothering. Self-theory may help to shed some light on this difficulty.

Mearns (1994) argues that to change a person's self-concept requires more than naïve attempts to change their attitude. The self-concept consists of cognitive, affective and behavioural components that tend to be consistent with each other. Therefore, trying to change one aspect of the self-concept in isolation is unlikely to be successful (Mearns, 1994). That mothers cognitively *know* there is a discrepancy between the ideal and the reality of mothering may not be enough to make a lasting difference to their self-concept as mothers.

The relevance of the core conditions of person-centred therapy to maternal depression

The discussion so far has highlighted how Rogers' theory of personality development (1951) adequately describes how internalised conditions of worth, as well as societal conditional value judgments of women as mothers, may lead to psychological distress. For a woman to integrate her experiences as a mother into her self-concept, the attitudinal qualities that are at the core of a person-centred therapeutic relationship are highly pertinent, and some aspects of the core conditions are worth considering in more detail.

Being authentic

I propose that being in a state of *incongruence* becomes the inevitable starting point for many new mothers, because of the many contradictions that are a part of the experience of motherhood. (I do not mean that this 'incongruence' equates directly to maternal depression, only that it highlights the vulnerability of all new mothers in terms of the fragility of their self-valuing process at this time.) That the therapist is able to be real and genuine and committed to the woman and her experience is vital, both in terms of the woman feeling understood and accepted and also in providing a role model (especially for female therapists). If a new mother can really get in touch with and express her own inner feelings and beliefs in a therapeutic relationship, it may provide her with an experience of the value of authentic relating and intimacy. This is then likely to be helpful in other relationships, especially with her baby (Raphael-Leff, 1991; Holden, Sagovsky & Cox, 1989).

The importance of empathy

At this point, empathy deserves a special mention. As described earlier, empathic engagement and affect attunement are fundamental to the new baby's survival and developing sense of self, and maternal distress can interfere with this process. For me, Jordan's work (1997) on the importance of mutual empathy in the therapeutic relationship is helpful in understanding the relational significance of the new mother developing empathy towards self as a pre-requisite to increasing empathic attunement with the baby. Jordan describes this 'empathic expansion' as 'moving out of a certain kind of self-centredness into an understanding of the growth of the self and other, and of relational awareness' (1997: 344). Jordan describes the state of mutual empathy as '[getting] to experience oneself as affecting and being affected by another' (1997: 343). This includes both the client and the therapist.

Jordan's description of mutual empathy may not, at first glance, fit within the framework of Rogers' more neutral 'as if' requirement of therapist empathy (Rogers, 1959); yet, as a concept, mutual empathy is central to existential relational encounter. It is described by Buber's philosophy of the 'I-Thou' relationship (Buber, 1958), and resonates with current person-centred theory about working at relational depth, where the therapist is relating to the client at their deepest existential level (Mearns, 2002; Knox et al, 2013). Mearns and Cooper (2005) describe how this process relates to the inter-subjective aspects of child development and the important implications this has for the practice of psychotherapy:

> If humans come into the world fundamentally oriented towards others, this suggests that the client/therapist relationship is of paramount importance in the therapy because it is the arena or 'crucible' in which the client can explore, revise and heal that which is most central to who we are. (2005: 12)

Relating at this profound level is also significant with regard to reducing the experience of shame, which is often a prominent feature of maternal depression. Jordan describes how 'in shame we lose the sense of empathic possibility… when ashamed we have great difficulty trusting that another will accept the rejected aspects within ourselves. Fearing exposure, we contract and withdraw' (1997: 346). If, as therapists, we offer 'acceptance' and reflective empathic understanding but without ever really 'meeting' a mother at this deeper, relational level, those shameful aspects of her experiencing are less likely to be revealed.

There is not the space here to explore empathy more fully. However, I think it is a key process to reflect on, because of the significance of reciprocity in empathic attunement in promoting psychological growth and healing (see, for example, Warner, 1997; Siegel, 2012).

Conditional acceptance and blocks to empathy

Factors contributing to blocks in empathy in the therapeutic relationship have been described by several authors (see, for example, Mearns & Thorne, 1988; Fairhurst, 1999). I will discuss Fairhurst's work briefly, as I feel her ideas about unconscious therapist prejudice are relevant to motherhood. Fairhurst argues that the 'holding of *positive or negative beliefs* towards members of a group or "types" of people *without prior experience* constitutes prejudice' (Fairhurst, 1999: 28; my italics). She describes the 'unconscious' aspect of prejudice as deriving from the introjected, learned messages from significant others that signify conditional acceptance, and that good training, personal therapy and sound supervision should all provide the person-centred therapist with an opportunity to allow personal prejudices into awareness.

I am not convinced, however, that the attitudes towards motherhood of person-centred therapists have been sufficiently explored and challenged in training – an issue that has also been highlighted by Stadlen (2004b). While we may be aware of our prejudices about certain 'types' of mothers, Fairhurst's statement, by definition, implies that we cannot be prejudiced against 'motherhood' because we all have experience of it – not necessarily in our work as therapists, but certainly in our roles as sons or daughters and mothers or fathers.

The concept of unconscious prejudice may help to explain why motherhood as a general concept is unlikely to be a topic for discussion in psychotherapy trainings beyond the traditional theoretical narratives about the mother–infant relationship and child development. It would be helpful, therefore, if therapists – and, indeed, anyone working with new mothers – were to devote some time to exploring their own attitudes and values towards women as mothers. Motherhood has a central role in society and is fundamental to our existence; it seems crucial, therefore, that the therapist becomes aware of how his/her own views and experiences of 'mother' and motherhood influence or interrupt the therapeutic process with a client experiencing maternal distress. Questions we may ask ourselves include, for example:

- What was your mother like and how has that informed your views about the role of mothers?
- What assumptions might you be holding about single, older, adolescent or lesbian mothers? What about mothers with many children, or mothers' reactions to their screaming children? Mothers who work, mothers who stay at home? Mothers with different cultural beliefs about parenting?
- If you are a parent, how do your own parenting styles differ from those of your client?
- Which child development theories inform your practice and how do they affect your ability to offer the core conditions to clients experiencing maternal distress? Are you able to hold your concerns about the potential impact of the mother's distress on her baby? (Psychological disturbance in children and adults is linked to poor parenting and maternal depression is a risk factor in poor outcomes for children (Hogg, 2014).)

Motherhood, depression and loss

Nicolson (1998) makes an important contribution to the theme of loss in relation to maternal depression when she highlights how the psychological concepts normally used to describe the relationship between depression and loss are not usually applied to new mothers and are rarely described in the medical literature on childbirth. Nicholson argues that women are not allowed to grieve or mourn at this point in life, and if they do, they are pathologised: 'So strong is this taboo that women themselves frequently fail to admit their sense of loss in a conscious way' (1998: 88).

Many new parents will have thought about the losses that accompany the arrival of a new baby. External losses relating to work, money, independence and leisure time, for instance, may cause difficulty for some mothers. However, losses associated with status and identity are often less tangible (and even more complex for adolescent mothers). It seems paradoxical to think about motherhood in terms of loss when everyone's main focus is the *gaining* of a baby and *becoming* a mother. Surely the happiness surrounding the baby's arrival more than compensates for any feelings of loss or sadness? A reluctance to dwell on this issue often occurred in postnatal support groups that I facilitated, because of the uncomfortable feelings it stirs up, even in an atmosphere of acceptance. The idea of grieving the loss of their old self is too far removed from and doesn't fit with images of motherhood as being 'happy' and fulfilling.

I did not experience a loss of my former, or 'non-mother', self when my first daughter was born. However, within days of my second daughter's birth, I was overwhelmed and distressed by feelings of grief and loss. I felt as though someone had indeed died, but this remained inexplicable to me and those around me, including other mothers and health professionals. My experiencing did not fit with my image of motherhood, and so I tried to push it away; other symptoms rushed in to fill its place, and in six weeks what started out as grief for many things lost (including my sense of self as a capable adult, but also my fantasies surrounding pregnancy, birth and being a 'mother of two') was given a diagnosis of 'postnatal depression'. This label then described my way of being in the world for the next two years. I wonder what this journey into self-disintegration would have been like if someone had really understood and accepted my reaction and feelings of loss and grief in those early weeks, and not tried to hurry me back on to the road of maternal 'happiness'?

Nicolson focuses particularly on loss relating to identity but, listening to the experiences of others, I feel that grief reactions can be just as acute around losses associated with the pregnancy or birth experiences, leaving a woman shocked, traumatised or disappointed. A client, describing her second, traumatic, caesarean birth, recounted how she felt that her feelings of panic, disappointment, sadness and anger about the birth were 'hurried' along by the midwives in hospital, with the well-meaning but unhelpful encouragement to 'focus' on the baby and put the birth behind her. (This client's experience was described 10 years ago; I hope that midwives today have a better awareness of the psychological impact of birth trauma and respond more sensitively to this experience.)

Do the needs of women experiencing maternal depression set them apart from other clients?

When person-centred therapy is framed within the classical proposition that it is *the relationship* between client and counsellor that is therapeutic, 'aside from anything that may be said or done within it' (Merry, 2004), then I believe the relational experience of being unconditionally accepted, valued and understood within the context of the 'six necessary and sufficient conditions', as first proposed by Rogers in 1957, will be therapeutic to women experiencing maternal depression. However, I propose that there are some special considerations relating to this time in a woman's life that may impact on the 'sufficiency' of individual person-centred therapy.

The need for reassurance, the need to belong

Mauthner, reporting on her qualitative research into the types of support women found helpful in their recovery from postnatal depression, concluded:

> Mothers experiencing postnatal depression also wanted... reassurance that other mothers experience similar feelings and that they would get better.
> (1997: 168)

Offering such reassurances may be seen as failure to trust the client's own valuing process by relating to the client outside of their frame of reference (Mearns & Thorne, 1988). Yet, from my own experience and from talking to others, women do want reassurance that they are not going mad, that they are not alone in their experience and they will get better.

Many women feel isolated from other mothers by their experience of maternal distress, and meeting others who can understand this experience is likely to mitigate this. Watson and Foreman's (1994) work with postnatally depressed women acknowledges the role of support groups and group therapy in bringing together women with similar experiences, which often provides this sense of belonging. Several other professionals working with depressed mothers have also demonstrated the benefits of various types of group therapy and support (for example, Field, 1997; Russell & Lang, 2013; Bertrum, 2008; Cree, 2015).

Learning to be a mother

A related theme to belonging and reassurance is the issue of instruction and learning, which all new mothers need and are only likely to take from other women (preferably mothers) whom they trust and respect (Raphael-Leff, 1991;

Blaffer Hrdy, 2009; Cree 2015). Traditionally, the extended female family network would have provided this. For many women today, however, this network has diminished. Instead, midwives and health visitors provide instruction in the early days and weeks following the birth, and the woman's partner is often their primary source of support and reassurance. (The support network of single mothers may be very different.) While a father's involvement is very important, their relationship with the mother is different from that provided by other mothers. If the latter is not available, or other significant relationships are lacking in some practical or psychological way (especially between the baby's grandmother and mother), a woman may feel alone or abandoned in learning the job of mothering (Price, 1988; Cree, 2015). Therefore, the counsellor needs to be sensitive to this possible gap in a new mother's experience, and to explore with her what other support and help might be available in addition to therapy (see the Appendix for sources of support).

Mothers need mothering too?

A woman's own need for nurture and support at this time is greatly heightened, leaving her vulnerable and dependent on those around her (Price, 1988; Raphael-Leff, 1991; Blaffer Hrdy, 2009). This is likely to impact on the therapeutic relationship as well. The ethical issue of dependency in therapy continues to be a topic for debate; within the humanistic philosophies, it seems to contradict theories of separation, autonomy and the notion of self-sufficiency.

Several person-centred practitioners (for example, Warner, 2000, Mearns & Thorne, 2000; Hawkins, 2005) do address the issue of client dependency and embrace its therapeutic importance, but they also emphasise the need for counsellor awareness around relationship boundaries. I would argue, from the perspective both of client and therapist, that it is important to acknowledge, explore and experience the strong dependency needs that motherhood evokes. However, the dependency issue with this client group feels different to that experienced with other clients, and the phrase that persistently comes to my mind is that 'mothers need mothering too'. By this I mean that, when new mothers are cared for or 'mothered' by others, this allows them to focus on establishing a relationship with their new baby and their developing selves as mothers. This phenomenon of new mothers 'yearning' to have their own mothers close by, both for emotional support and instruction, has also been highlighted by Cree (2015: 13).

Person-centred theory does not adequately explain this unique phenomenon of motherhood. I have therefore found it personally helpful to reflect on the purpose and meanings of motherhood beyond the psychological frame. Diverse disciplines such as human ecology (for example, Brofenbrenner, 1979) and social anthropology (for example, Blaffer Hrdy, 2009) have helped me to relate and respond to this process of 'dependency' or 'yearning' with greater understanding and compassion.

The challenge to person-centred therapists, therefore, is to find a respectful way to work with this need, so that the woman feels nurtured and supported, but not disempowered.

And baby comes too?

Compared with other clients, a new mother is in a unique relational situation. Her infant is primarily dependent on her and will take up much of her psychological and physical space. I am not sure that any special consideration would be given to the significance of this relationship by the person-centred therapist, in terms of how it affects the woman's ability to think and live as an autonomous person at this point in her life. The mother–infant relationship also raises practical issues about what happens to the baby during sessions and how the woman feels about leaving the baby, opening up the whole question of where, when and how therapy sessions are set up.

Within the different psychotherapeutic models, however, the person-centred therapist is well placed to acknowledge and consider ways of working creatively with such issues. For instance, a few clients have, on occasion, brought their babies to sessions (Catterall, 2007). This has been for a variety of reasons, ranging from cancelled childcare to fears about being separated from the baby. When a long-term client came to see me with her two-week-old second baby, it was because she wanted the opportunity to share her difficult birth experience soon after the birth. It was something this client felt she really needed to do. It also gave me the opportunity to genuinely celebrate with the client the arrival of her second baby, who had been so much a part of our sessions during her pregnancy. Far from being a distraction, a baby's presence has often stimulated discussion about the woman's relationship with and feelings towards the baby. This has allowed me to be more real, because I am responding to what I see, rather than what I assume. I do acknowledge, though, that the baby can distract both client and therapist from more difficult aspects of the work, and this possibility also needs to be explored within the therapy.

For me, Mauthner's conclusion from her in-depth interviews summarises beautifully the important role that person-centred therapy could have in helping women with maternal depression:

> Once their feelings had been identified, the women I interviewed wanted to be given permission to talk in-depth about their feelings, including ambivalent and difficult feelings; they wanted to talk to a non-judgemental person who would spend time listening to them, take them seriously, and understand and accept them for who they were; they wanted recognition that there was a problem, and reassurance that other mothers experience similar feelings and that they would get better... These were the essential types of support that mothers wanted and that helped them begin the recovery process. In a sense, the source of the support was less important... (1997: 168)

Person-centred therapy as part of a multi-agency approach

My intention in this chapter has been to provide the reader with a greater understanding of maternal distress (in its broadest sense) and some of the unique issues relating to the experience of new motherhood. Unlike many other clients seeking counselling, women experiencing maternal depression are in most cases in contact with other health professionals, either directly because of the depression or indirectly through the contacts and check-ups associated with the welfare of the baby and any other children. Therefore, it is prudent to be aware of the responsibilities of others involved in the mother's care, and I hope the information provided in this chapter goes some way to highlight these.

If the new mother seeks therapy privately, the therapist should still see their role as part of a team. Ethical practice and safeguarding legislation requires all of us to take into account the best interests of the mother and the baby. If it becomes apparent in the initial sessions that others are not aware of the mother's distress, the therapist needs to discuss with the client her feelings about the involvement of the GP or health visitor and consider what additional help she may need. Exploring suicide risk is also important, as depressed mothers are at high risk of suicide throughout the first year after giving birth (Knight et al, 2015). In addition to medical help, providing information about other sources of support (for example, voluntary agencies, mothers' groups etc) may also be helpful, especially if the woman is feeling isolated (physically or psychologically) from other mothers.

I know from my own experience that personal therapy alone would not have been enough. The help and support I (and my daughters) received from a variety of sources, including family, friends and medical professionals, as well as group support and couples counselling, were all important elements. In many ways, these other aspects provided the safety net and space for me to undertake personal counselling.

We can never know, as psychotherapists and counsellors, what a woman's experience of maternal depression will be. However, I feel there is one aspect that is clear, and is an important part of the therapeutic relationship: that the client's role as a mother can be affirmed by us as therapists as it is unlikely that the woman has received that affirmation sufficiently from anyone else. (This point is illustrated in the therapeutic work I did with my client 'Josie' (Catterall, 2007).)

Conclusion

Psychiatry considers the clinical presentation of perinatal anxiety and depression to be the same as anxiety and depression occurring at other times of life, and has not created a specific aetiology for it. Despite this clinical picture, many health professionals and mothers argue that maternal depression is completely different, in that its effects are experienced at a time when exceptional physical, psychological and emotional demands are also present.

The mother–infant relationship and the consequences of maternal distress must be one of the most well-researched issues of the 20th and 21st centuries. Research studies are available that confirm the benefits of psychotherapeutic interventions, including person-centred therapy, to new mothers. These findings are supported by recent, larger-scale studies of general adult client populations that clearly demonstrate the effectiveness of therapies from the person-centred approach (Cooper, Watson & Hölldampf, 2010). Advances in neuroscience and attachment research also show '*how*' the relational factors first described by Rogers facilitate psychological and emotional wellbeing – albeit using a different language (Siegel, 2012). With such a rich research base on which to draw, therapists can confidently argue the case for offering person-centred therapy to this client group. Importantly, when the unique relational situation of the mother and infant and the social-cultural context of motherhood are also taken into account, it is clear that the person-centred therapist is well-placed to provide the warm, caring and compassionate therapeutic relationship (as part of a multi-agency approach) that a distressed mother needs.

The evidence base is not lacking to support the suitability and efficacy of person-centred therapy when working with maternal distress. Nor is there an absence of dedication, passion and belief shown by many health professionals and therapists working with mothers and families. For me, it is a lack of political will and courage to face the challenges of how we live well together as a society and support each other in meaningful and compassionate ways.

References

American Psychiatric Association (APA) (2013). *Diagnostic and Statistical Manual of Mental Disorders* (5th Ed). Washington, DC: American Psychiatric Press.

Alder E, Truman J (2002). Counselling for postnatal depression in the voluntary sector. *Psychology and Psychotherapy 75*: 207–220.

Appleby L, Warner R, Whitton A, Faraghar B (1997). A controlled study of fluoxetine and cognitive-behavioural counselling in the treatment of postnatal depression. *British Medical Journal 314*: 932–936.

Arroll B, Khin N, Kerse N (2003). Two verbally asked questions are simple and valid. British Medical Journal *327*: 1144–1146.

Bailham D, Joseph S (2003). Post-traumatic stress following childbirth: a review of the emerging literature and directions for research and practice. *Psychology, Health and Medicine 8*: 159–168.

Blaffer Hrdy S (2009). *Mothers and Others: the evolutionary origins of mutual understanding.* Cambridge, MA: Harvard University Press.

Bauer A, Parsonage M, Knapp M, Lemmi V, Adelaja B (2014). *Costs of perinatal mental health problems.* London: LSE/Centre for Mental Health.

Bertrum L (2008). *Supporting postnatal women into motherhood: a guide to therapeutic group work for health professionals*. Oxford: Radcliffe Press.

Bowlby J (1988). A *Secure Base: clinical applications of attachment theory*. London: Routledge.

Brockington I (1996). *Motherhood and Mental Health*. Oxford: Oxford University Press.

Brockington I (2004). Postpartum psychiatric disorders. *The Lancet 363*: 303–310.

Brofenbrenner U (1979). *The Ecology of Human Development*. Cambridge, MA: Harvard University Press.

Buber M (1958). *I and Thou* (2nd ed) (Trans RG Smith.) Edinburgh: T & T Clark.

Catterall E (1995). *Support and Treatment Offered to Women with Postnatal Illness (PNI): are the needs of these women being met?* Unpublished report, available from the author.

Catterall E (2007). Love, loss and maternal distress. In: Worsley R, Joseph S (eds). *Person-Centred Practice: case studies in positive psychology*. Ross-on-Wye: PCCS Books (pp53-67).

Catterall E (2014). Postnatal therapy. Letter to the Editor. *Therapy Today* 25(10): 45.

Choderow N (1978). *The Reproduction of Mothering: psychoanalysis and sociology of gender*. Berkeley, CA: University of California Press.

Clement S (1995). 'Listening visits' in pregnancy: a strategy for preventing postnatal depression? *Midwifery 11*: 75–80.

Cooper M, Watson JC, Hölldampf D (2010). *Person-Centred and Experiential Therapies Work: a review of the research on counselling, psychotherapy and related practices*. Ross-on-Wye: PCCS Books.

Cooper PJ, Murray L (1997). The impact of psychological treatments of postpartum depression on maternal mood and infant development. In: Murray L, Cooper PJ (eds). *Postpartum Depression and Child Development*. London/New York: Guilford Press (pp201–220).

Cox JL (1994). Introduction and classification dilemmas. In: Cox JL, Holden JM (eds). *Perinatal Psychiatry: use and misuses of the Edinburgh Postnatal Depression Scale*. London: Gaskell (pp3–7).

Cox JL, Holden JM (eds) (1994). *Perinatal Psychiatry: use and misuses of the Edinburgh Postnatal Depression Scale*. London: Gaskell.

Cox JL, Holden JM, Sagovsky R (1987). Detection of postnatal depression: development of the 10-item Edinburgh Postnatal Depression Scale. *British Journal of Psychiatry 150*: 782–786.

Cramer B (1997). Psychodynamic perspectives on the treatment of Postpartum Depression. In: Murray L, Cooper PJ (eds). *Postpartum Depression and Child Development*. London/New York: Guilford Press (pp237–264).

Cree M (2015). *Postnatal Depression: using compassion focused therapy to enhance mood, confidence and bonding*. London: Robinson.

Dion X (2002). Anxiety: a terrifying facet of postnatal depression. *Community Practitioner 75*: 376–380.

Elliott SA (1994). Uses and misuses of the Edinburgh Postnatal Depression Scale in primary care: a comparison of models developed in health visiting. In: Cox JL, Holden JM (eds). *Perinatal Psychiatry: use and misuses of the Edinburgh Postnatal Depression Scale*. London: Gaskell (pp221–232).

Elliott R, Freire E (2010). The effectiveness of person-centred and experiential therapies: a review of the meta-analyses. In: Cooper M, Watson JC, Hölldampf D (2010). *Person-Centred and Experiential Therapies Work: a review of the research on counselling, psychotherapy and related practices*. Ross-on-Wye: PCCS Books (pp1–15).

Elliott SA, Leverton TJ (2000). Is the EPDS a magic wand? 'Myths' and the evidence base. *Journal of Reproductive and Infant Psychology 18*: 298–307.

Fairhurst I (1999). Empathy at the core of the therapeutic relationship: contaminators of empathic understanding. In: Fairhurst I (ed). *Women Writing in the Person-Centred Approach*. Ross-on-Wye: PCCS Books. (pp19–36).

Field T (1997). The treatment of depressed mothers and their infants. In: Murray L, Cooper PJ (eds). *Postpartum Depression and Child Development*. London/New York: Guilford Press (pp221–236).

Figes K (1998). *Life After Birth: what even your friends won't tell you about motherhood*. London: Viking.

Green MJ, Murray D (1994). The use of the EPDS in research to explore the relationship between antenatal and postnatal dysphoria. In: Cox JL, Holden JM (eds). *Perinatal Psychiatry: use and misuses of the Edinburgh Postnatal Depression Scale*. London: Gaskell (pp180–198).

Hanley J (2015). *Listening Visits in Perinatal Mental Health: a guide for health professionals and support workers*. Oxford: Routledge.

Hawkins J (2005). Living with pain. In: Joseph S, Worsley R (eds). *Person-Centred Psychopathology: a positive psychology of mental health*. Ross-on-Wye: PCCS Books (pp226–241).

Herman J (2015). *Trauma and Recovery: the aftermath of violence – from domestic abuse to political terror*. New York: Basic Books.

Hogg S (2013). *Prevention in Mind: all babies count – spotlight on perinatal mental health*. London: NSPCC.

Holden JM, Sagovsky R, Cox JL (1989). Counselling in a general practice setting: controlled study of health visitor intervention in treatment of postnatal depression. *British Medical Journal 289*: 223–226.

Holmes J (1993). *John Bowlby and Attachment Theory*. London: Routledge.

Jordan, JV (1997) Relational development through mutual empathy. In AC Bohart and LS Greenberg (eds) *Empathy Reconsidered. New directions in psychotherapy*. Washington DC: American Psychological Association (pp343–350).

Kitzinger S (1992). *Ourselves as Mothers*. London: Doubleday.

Knight M, Tuffnell D, Kenyon S, Shakespeare J, Gray R, Kurinczuk JJ (eds) (2015) on behalf of MBRRACE-UK. Saving Lives, Improving Mothers' Care: surveillance of maternal deaths in the UK 2011-13 and lessons learned to inform maternity care from the UK and Ireland Confidential Enquiries into Maternal Deaths and Morbidity 2009-13. Oxford: National Perinatal Epidemiology Unit, University of Oxford. www.npeu. ox.ac.uk/downloads/files/mbrrace-uk/reports/MBRRACE-UK%20Maternal%20Report%202015.pdf (accessed 28 November, 2016).

Knox R, Murphy D, Wiggins S, Cooper M (2013). *Relational Depth: new perspectives and developments*. Basingstoke: Palgrave Macmillan.

Lee E (2003). *Abortion, Motherhood and Mental Health*. New York: Aldine de Gruyter.

Littlewood E, Ali S, Ansell P, Dyson L, Gascoyne S, Hewitt C et al, on behalf of the BaBY PaNDA study team (2016). Identification of depression in women during pregnancy and the early postnatal period using the Whooley questions and the Edinburgh Postnatal Depression Scale: protocol for the Born and Bred in Yorkshire: PeriNatal Depression Diagnostic Accuracy (BaBY PaNDA) study. *BMJ Open* 6: e011223. doi:10.1136/bmjopen-2016-011223. http://bmjopen.bmj.com/content/6/6/e011223.full (accessed 28 October, 2016).

Littlewood J, McHugh N (1997). *Maternal Distress and Postnatal Depression*. London: MacMillan Press Ltd.

Mauthner NS (1997). Postnatal depression: how can midwives help? *Midwifery 13*: 163–171.

Mearns D (1994). *Developing Person-Centred Counselling*. London: Sage.

Mearns D (2002). Further theoretical propositions in regard to self theory within person-centred therapy.

Person-Centered and Experiential Psychotherapies 1: 14–27.

Mearns D, Cooper M (2005). *Working at Relational Depth in Counselling and Psychotherapy.* London: Sage.

Mearns D, Thorne, B (1988). *Person-Centred Counselling in Action.* London: Sage.

Mearns D, Thorne B (2000). *Person-Centred Therapy Today: new frontiers in theory and practice.* London: Sage.

Merry T (2004). Classical client-centred therapy. In: Sanders P (ed). *TheTribes of the Person-Centred Nation.* Ross-on-Wye: PCCS Books (pp21–44).

Murray L (1992). The impact of postnatal depression on infant development. *Journal of Child Psychology and Psychiatry 33*: 543–561.

Murray L, Cooper PJ (1997). *Postpartum Depression and Child Development.* New York: Guilford Press.

Nicolson P (1998). *Post-Natal Depression: psychology, science and the transition to motherhood.* London: Routledge.

Oates M (1994). Postnatal mental illness: organisation and function of services. In: Cox JL, Holden JM (eds). *Perinatal Psychiatry: use and misuses of the Edinburgh Postnatal Depression Scale.* London: Gaskell (pp180–198).

Oates, M (2015). Perinatal mental health services: recommendations for the provision of services for childbearing women. College Report CR197. London: Royal College of Psychiatrists. Available from http://maternalmentalhealthalliance.org.uk (accessed 28 November, 2016).

O'Hara M (1997). The nature of postpartum depressive disorders. In: Murray L, Cooper PJ (eds). *Postpartum Depression and Child Development.* New York: Guilford Press (pp3–26).

O'Hara M, Stuart S, Gorman L, Wenzel A (2000). Efficacy of interpersonal psychotherapy for postnatal depression. *Archives of General Psychiatry 57*: 1039–1045.

Parker R (1995). *Torn in Two: the experience of maternal ambivalence.* London: Virago Press.

Pitt B (1968). 'Atypical' depression following childbirth. *British Journal of Psychiatry 114*: 1325–1335.

Price J (1988). *Motherhood: what it does to your mind.* London: Pandora.

Raphael-Leff J (1991). *Psychological Processes of Childbearing.* London: Chapman and Hall.

Riecher-Rossler A, Hofecker-Fallahpour M (2003). Postpartum depression: do we still need this diagnostic term? *Acta Psychiatrica Scandinavica; supplement 418*: 51–56.

Rogers CR (1957). The necessary and sufficient conditions of therapeutic personality change. *Journal of Consulting Psychology 2*: 95–103.

Rogers CR (1959). A theory of therapy, personality, and interpersonal relationships, as developed in the client-centred framework. In: Koch S (ed). *Psychology: a study of a science. Vol. 3: Formulations of the person and the social contract.* New York: McGraw-Hill (pp184–256).

Rogers CR, Stevens B (1967). *Person to Person.* London: Souvenir Press Ltd.

Rowan J, Cooper M (eds) (1999). *The Plural Self: multiplicity in everyday life.* London: Sage.

Rowley C, Dixon L (2002). The utility of the EPDS for health visiting practice. *Community Practitioner 75*: 385–389.

Russell S, Lang B (2013). *Perinatal Mental Health: experiences of women and health professionals.* London: Boots Family Trust Alliance. Available at http://everyonesbusiness.org.uk/ (accessed 28 November, 2016).

Seeley S, Murray L, Cooper PJ (1996). The outcome for mothers and babies of health visitor intervention. *Health Visitor 69*: 135–138.

Shakespeare J (2002). Health visitor screening for PND using the EPDS: a process study. *Community Practitioner 75*: 381–384.

Siegel DJ (2012). *The Developing Mind* (2nd ed). New York: Guilford Press.

SIGN (2012). *Management of perinatal mood disorders.* SIGN guideline 127 Edinburgh: Scottish Intercollegiate Guidelines Network.

Stadlen N (2004a). *What Mothers Do: especially when it looks like nothing.* London: Piatkus.

Stadlen N (2004b). Mothers at the cutting edge of science. *Counselling and Psychotherapy Journal 15*: 5–7.

Stern DN (1985). *The Interpersonal World of the Infant: a view from psychoanalysis and developmental psychology.* New York: Basic Books.

Stern DN (1995). *The Motherhood Constellation.* New York: Basic Books.

Ussher J (1991). *Women's Madness: misogyny or mental illness?* London: Wheatsheaf and Harvester.

Walker M (1990). *Women in Therapy and Counselling: out of the shadows.* Maidenhead: Open University Press.

Warner MS (1997). Does empathy cure? A theoretical consideration of empathy, processing, and personal narrative. In: Bohart AC, Greenberg LS (eds). *Empathy Reconsidered: new directions in psychotherapy.* Washington, DC: American Psychological Association (pp124–140).

Warner M (2000). Person-Centred Therapy at the Difficult Edge: a developmentally based model of fragile and dissociated process. In: Mearns D, Thorne B (eds). *Person-Centred Therapy Today: new frontiers in theory and practice.* London: Sage (pp144–171).

Watson M, Foreman D (1994). Diminishing the impact of puerperal neuroses: towards an expressive psychotherapy useful in a community setting. In: Cox JL, Holden JM (eds). *Perinatal Psychiatry: Use and misuses of the Edinburgh Postnatal Depression Scale.* London: Gaskell (pp233–247).

Watson JC, Greenberg LS, Lietaer G (2010). Relating process to outcome in person-centred and experiential psychotherapies. In: Cooper M, Watson JC, Hölldampf D (eds). *Person-Centred and Existential Psychotherapies Work: a review of the research on counselling, psychotherapy and related practices.* Ross-on-Wye: PCCS Books (pp132–163).

Whitton A, Warner R, Appleby L (1996). The pathway to care in postnatal depression: women's attitudes to postnatal depression and its treatment. *British Journal of General Practice 46*: 427.

Winnicott DW (1986). *Home is Where We Start From: essays by a psychoanalyst.* London: Penguin.

World Health Organization (WHO) (1992). *International Classification of Diseases* (10th ed) (*ICD-10*). Geneva: World Health Organization.

Appendix

The Maternal Mental Health Alliance (MMHA)
http://maternalmentalhealthalliance.org.uk
A coalition of UK organisations committed to improving the mental health and wellbeing of women and their children in pregnancy and the first postnatal year. The MMHA *#everyonesbusiness* campaign provides key information and tools to support commissioners and service providers to make the necessary improvements to services. Maps highlighting the gaps in service provision are available to view at http://everyonesbusiness.org.uk/wp-content/uploads/2015/12/UK-Specialist-Community-Perinatal-Mental-Health-Teams-current-provision_2015.pdf

The Royal College of Midwives
www.rcm.org.uk
Monitors the cross-party manifesto 'The 1001 Critical Days' – a key government policy commitment to achieving better perinatal mental health and stronger attachment between babies and their parents from conception to two years. *www.1001criticaldays.co.uk*

The Association for Postnatal Illness (APNI)
http://apni.org.uk
Helpline: 0207 386 0868 10am – 2pm
A national voluntary organisation with strong links to the medical profession, providing leaflets, information and one-to-one support to depressed mothers from other women who have recovered from maternal depression.

PANDAS Pre- and postnatal Depression Advice and Support
www.pandasfoundation.org.uk/
Helpline: 0843 289 8401, 9am – 8pm, every day.
Provides information and support groups.

Action on Postpartum Psychosis
www.app-network.org/
Tel: 020 3322 9900
APP is a network of people who have been affected by postpartum psychosis. Provides an online support forum (*https://healthunlocked.com/app-network*), information and one-to-one email support.

Netmums
www.netmums.com
Covers a variety of parenting topics, an online 'drop-in clinic' staffed by parent supporters, a round-the-clock support forum and an online postnatal depression course.

The National Childbirth Trust (NCT)
www.nct.org.uk
Helpline: 0300 330 0700
Offers support and information to all new parents on issues and experiences relating to pregnancy, childbirth and early parenting. Some local branches run postnatal depression support groups.

Homestart UK
www.homestart.org.uk
Tel: 0116 258 7900
A voluntary organisation with local branches throughout the UK, offering home support, friendship and practical help to families under stress with pre-school children.

16 Living with pain: mental health and the legacy of childhood abuse

Jan Hawkins

And must I then, indeed, Pain, live with you
All through my life? – sharing my fire, my bed,
Sharing – oh, worst of all things! – the same head? –
And, when I feed myself, feeding you, too?
(Edna St Vincent Millay)

The person-centred approach (PCA) has much to offer in the understanding and recovery of those who have suffered abuse as children and developed psychiatric illnesses as a result. This chapter seeks to encourage more collaboration between those who see the nature of human distress in pathological terms and those who see it in more adaptive terms.

In the years since the first edition of this book was published, new evidence has emerged that expands our understanding of the effects of childhood sexual abuse and how we respond. Evidence from neuropsychological research has added to our understanding of the long-term difficulties faced by survivors of childhood abuse. In particular, the inclusion of complex post-traumatic stress disorder (C-PTSD) in the *Diagnostic and Statistical Manual of Mental Disorders* (*DSM-5*) (American Psychiatric Association, 2013) shows a recognition in psychiatric circles of the cluster of symptoms and effects that survivors may have experienced throughout their lives.

Joseph (2003, 2004, 2005) has demonstrated how person-centred theory can explain PTSD as a process of breakdown and disintegration of self, as well as recovery, adjustment and post-traumatic growth. This chapter argues that the reparative relationship provided by the person-centred approach creates an environment in which the survivor's natural actualising tendency can emerge. Within the trusting relationship, guided by his/her own inner promptings, and accompanied by a therapist who is able to bear to hear such painful material, the client is able to process and integrate the memories, as well as begin to find the self they can own.

Different selves

'If anyone were to see me when I am at my most distressed, they would send for the men in white coats, lock me up and throw away the key' (Maria's 'Reporter'). The 'Reporter' is one aspect of Maria; the Reporter's function is to report what is happening. The Reporter does not have feelings, but is good at the facts. The Reporter has been the part of Maria who has attended most of her therapy, and has frequently mentioned this fear of being locked up. At other times, Maria has longed to be able to give up, crawl into a foetal position and be left in a quiet, tiny, padded cell until death releases her.

There are many other selves within Maria, including the Teenager, the Youngest, the Tinies and the Performer. Her perceptions and fantasies of what a psychiatric system might be like have never been tested in reality. Maria is a survivor of multiple sexual abusers; she had a violently sadistic mother and a lifetime of abject emotional and physical deprivation. Yet she functions in the world, has managed to survive, has learned to overcome severe debilitating panic attacks, nightmares, agoraphobia, social phobia, numerous physical illnesses and bouts of unrelenting depression, and is still capable of feeling joy.

Maria has a sense of having achieved something by avoiding psychiatric institutions and sees her two brief spells of a few months on antidepressants as temporary failures. She has contact with what she identifies as her 'core self', the part of her that was not damaged by the abuse, and she clings onto that, fearing that any pharmaceutical intervention might threaten it. In person-centred terms, this could be described as her 'directional organismic processes' (Rogers, 1963: 20–21) or 'organismic valuing process' (Mearns & Thorne, 1999: 9) – the means by which the organism knows what it needs. She has reclaimed her organismic valuing process (or, in her terms, 'self'), and knows how fragile other parts of her are. Her feeling is that she must, at all costs, keep her selves away from situations that might evoke memories of her abuse – any situation where another has power over her; any situation where chaos abounds; any situation where human distress is not heard or understood; any situation where only her 'madness' might be seen and her grounded, sane self might be missed. Her fantasy of psychiatric institutions includes all those threats. However desperate she has been, she has never let this be known to those who might try to fast-track her into the psychiatric system, for fear of losing herself completely.

Maria's survival is due to her ability to dissociate, so taking herself away from where the pain is too great or too confusing. This ability may well have protected her from developing other, more dangerous survival strategies, such as self-harm, addictions or eating disorders, or other devastating psychiatric problems. But Maria feels that her recovery from her abuse would have cost her less in terms of her energies had there been the possibility much earlier of a relationship with a therapist who understood what was happening for her. She will never know if, had her brief encounters with general practitioners (GPs), and even briefer ones with psychiatrists, brought understanding and compassion, she might have recovered better, and sooner. But she does know now that she always had the potential for healing. She knows this because she has a relationship with a therapist who is able to meet every one of her; a therapist who offers a real relationship and is steadfast and safe; a therapist who never diagnoses or labels her, but seeks to truly understand how life and her inner lives are for Maria. Whatever distress she is feeling, and whatever the challenges this relationship poses, it also offers hope. Sadly, the kind of relationship she needed to heal the damage earlier in her life is still not readily available from the NHS.

An incongruent infancy

Babies are capable of learning from their very first breath, at least, and will demonstrate preferences for sounds, tastes and sensations. The infant's cries need to be met with warmth and empathy: is the baby hungry, or too hot or cold? Is she wet and uncomfortable, or lonely and wanting a soothing voice? In a good-enough environment, where the mother (usually, but not exclusively) is able to attune herself to the infant in this way, the infant will grow to trust that she is capable of communicating her needs, and that they will be met. In this sense, the infant is born with the ability to be congruent (real or genuine).

This 'lyrical duet' (Cozolino, 2006: 97) between infant and parent shapes and changes the brains of both. Not only does the process release the bonding and pleasure chemicals oxytocin and endorphins; it contributes to the healthy development of the infant's brain structure as well. Attuned connections with caregivers – so-called 'dyadic regulation' – allow the child's brain to develop the neural structures necessary to move in time to more autonomous forms of self-regulation (Siegel & Hartzell, 2003: 215). Children whose development is not distorted by other people's conditions of worth – that is, children who do not have to find ways of being that fit with others' needs or expectations – are equipped to recognise what is not safe or appropriate behaviour in others. These children are more likely to seek help and understanding if things happen to them that are confusing or frightening. They are more likely to have developed self-protective skills that may help them get away if they perceive danger.

The youngest of babies are capable, too, of being very angry when their needs are not met. This is a very healthy sign, because anger is a signal that something is wrong (Averill, 1982). For infants who do not receive this empathic and accepting caregiving, their learning takes a different direction. The infant quickly understands that their cries can bring a very angry or harmful reaction, and they will take in the 'condition of worth' that says, 'I am only acceptable if I am quiet.' If an infant's healthy anger and rage at not having his needs met are continually ignored or met with hostility, the child may lose touch altogether with that anger and rage and slip into despair.

It is easy to see how infants whose most basic organismic needs are not met with love, acceptance and empathic understanding will be vulnerable to learning not only that their needs are not important but that having needs and feelings is, in fact, dangerous and not to be trusted. Conditions of worth that teach a child that they are only acceptable if they meet an adult's needs create further vulnerability; such a child has not learned how to protect or defend himself. Children who are clearly not being protected and supervised, and who demonstrate a lack of ability to protect themselves, are the easy targets of those who seek to abuse (Finkelhor, 1986).

> One of the first and most important aspects of the self-experience of the ordinary child is that he is loved by his parents. He perceives himself as loveable, worthy of love and his relationship to his parents is one of affection. He experiences all this with satisfaction. (Rogers, 1951: 499)

Such children develop a self-concept that includes the need and willingness to meet the other's needs without question. A child who lives with the continual possibility of being required to do things that are confusing, humiliating, strangely and confusingly pleasurable or brutal and painful develops a sense of self that includes the notion that 'I do not matter' and 'I am always at risk', and possibly also, 'My very life depends on me figuring out what the other wants and doing it without question.' In this way, they move further and further away from any sense of 'who I am', or 'what I want' to a position where they lose contact altogether with what satisfies the organism or core self. In situations where the child is repeatedly sexually and/ or physically abused, they may learn to survive by dissociating, taking themselves further away from the core of themselves to mitigate pain that is too great or too confusing. For Maria, this meant that each dissociated self stopped or 'died', and a new, even more compliant and need-less self emerged to take over, until that self had to die. As an adult, these selves each have their own memories, feelings, terrors and abilities. Finding her own, undamaged, core self has been Maria's life's work – who might she have been had she not been continually traumatised?

Survival strategies

Dissociation

Adults who were abused as children have been disempowered. Children in homes where there is persistent threat in the form of violence, sexual abuse, verbal denigration and assault – where there is chronic trauma – develop coping strategies that help them survive. These strategies can become so habitual that it is impossible in adulthood to let go of them when the threat has passed. Some children survive by becoming 'good girls/boys' who never complain, never make demands and attempt to anticipate the adults' every need, having received the idea that their existence depends on being 'good'. Some children survive by lashing out at others or getting involved in criminal behaviour – these children are the visible ones, although, sadly, their self-esteem is further damaged because of the negative attention they draw to themselves. Some children survive by squashing their feelings: commonly either by denying themselves food (what is anorexia saying? 'I have no needs'), by developing a binge-vomit cycle (swinging between 'I have overwhelming needs', and 'I have no needs'), by overeating in vain attempts at comfort, or by anaesthetising themselves with alcohol or other drugs.

Some children develop a creative coping strategy of dissociation. This is often pathologised but, of all coping strategies, it is the one that is the most invisible. Clients will describe their dissociative behaviours in terms of, for example, 'leaving my body', 'hiding in the plug socket', 'going numb', 'it all goes black', 'watching from the ceiling', 'it happened to that child there, not me', 'I wasn't real anymore, I dissolved.' Many and various descriptions show that the person has split away from the experience. All these coping strategies can be viewed as distress flares but, far from summoning the rescue services, they distance the individual further from potential sources of comfort for their pain. People for whom dissociation is a survival tactic confuse others, including therapists, GPs and psychiatrists, by talking about very traumatic material in a totally flat voice. Divorced from the affect, the person is vulnerable to a whole variety of judgments, and also to isolation in the confusion of their traumatised inner world.

> 'Dissociated' process is a style of process in which aspects of the person's experience are separated into 'parts'… allowing the person to alter perceptions, to alter physiological states and to hold contradictory beliefs without discomfort. Such parts seem to have been created in early childhood as a way to keep the person from being overwhelmed by experiences of incest or other abuse… They may come into the person's consciousness as 'others' whose images and voices have an impact… they may emerge as temporarily dominant personalities. (Warner, 2000: 145)

Self-harm

Survivors who self-harm to the point where they need emergency treatment in hospital are often punished because they are thought by healthcare providers to be attention-seeking. Some clients report having been made to wait far longer for treatment in casualty departments than others with 'legitimate' injuries. They have been treated with contempt and rudeness and told that their self-inflicted injuries are a waste of NHS resources. I have met more than one survivor who was not given a local anaesthetic while their wounds were being stitched, and were told they did not deserve it because they caused the injury. There are various reasons why people find self-harming to be the only option. Research suggests that most self-harming occurs when the person is in a dissociated state (for example, Herman, 1992a; 1992b). People who self-harm are sometimes trying to get back into their body after having dissociated – the cutting makes them feel real again. Some do it to release some of the pent-up pain and frustration. Some do it to punish themselves.

Long-term depression

Most authors consider there is a relationship between environmental factors (including life stress) and a genetic predisposition and possibly organic and/or biochemical disorders. For survivors of abuse, depression can be seen as resulting from persistent and total disempowerment. Where a child is not allowed to have needs, to be angry about being hurt, to say no and have their 'no' attended to if they do say it, or to have comfort for their confusion and pain, what alternative exists? That the person has developed with no other experience than that of being the victim of others' violence and/or sexual attentions seems to be ignored. And the more that pain is denied, ignored, judged or expressed in sublimated or distorted form, the more the person has to suppress to survive – and all this reinforces the depression.

Complex post-traumatic stress disorder

For many survivors of childhood sexual abuse, the diagnosis of post-traumatic stress disorder (PTSD) has seemed appropriate. This is because the symptoms that have caused them distress and brought them to the attention of the psychiatrist meet the criteria for PTSD. However, some do not receive this diagnosis, because their symptoms do not fit the one-off, life threatening experience expected for PTSD. It is only very recently that the fifth edition of the *DSM* (American Psychiatric Association, 2013) has included the more relevant diagnosis of complex PTSD (C-PTSD), which Judith Herman first suggested in 1992 (Herman 1992a; 1992b) to describe the long-term sequelae of repeated trauma in early life. This diagnosis, now legitimised in *DSM-5*, may save survivors from attracting unhelpful and less relevant diagnoses.

> 'Renowned traumatologist, John Briere, is said to have quipped that if Complex PTSD were ever given its due – that is, if the role of dysfunctional parenting in adult psychological disorders was ever fully recognized – the *DSM*… would shrink to the size of a thin pamphlet.' (Walker, 2015)

C-PTSD describes the experience of so many survivors for whom flashbacks, nightmares, anxiety, sleep disorders, intrusive thoughts and imagery and so on are so familiar to them that they don't even think to mention them. Recognition of the prevalence of C-PTSD and, more importantly, the treatment possibilities (for example, Walker, 2013) is a welcome development. It supports healing and recovery rather than management of symptoms. While person-centred therapists tend to avoid using diagnostic terms, it can be helpful to have a working knowledge of them. This does not mean behaving in any different way with clients who may be experiencing C-PTSD; rather, the therapist may notice in a slightly different way what a client is struggling to describe. It may even feel appropriate to suggest some resources that the client might find helpful in their recovery. The mere fact that the therapist does recognise the experience of C-PTSD can be reassuring to those clients who have been diagnosed with it (or with PTSD). It indicates that their therapist accepts the reality of the experience, while also seeing it as something that can be overcome. I have been asked by more than one survivor with a diagnosis of PTSD (few so far have been diagnosed with the more relevant C-PTSD) whether recovery is possible. It has been helpful to have an understanding of the condition and the process of recovery from a person-centred perspective, so that my congruent response is affirmative.

Neuropsychological effects

In recent years, evidence from neuropsychological research has given a new appreciation of the long-term harm caused by trauma and neglect in childhood. Sue Gerhardt has described the research showing that:

> Romanian orphans… who were cut off from close bonds with an adult by being left in their cots all day, unable to make relationships, had a virtual black hole where their orbitofrontal cortex should be. (Gerhardt, 2004: 38–39).

She goes on to report:

> When social relationships are denied during the period in which this part of the brain normally develops (up to the age of 3), there is little hope of fully recovering these lost social abilities or of developing this part of the brain adequately. A baby can't develop an orbitofrontal cortex on his or her own. It depends on the relationships with other people that are available. (Gerhardt, 2004: 39)

And later, citing Joseph LeDouz (2002):

> Early experience can alter the biochemistry of the brain. As Joseph LeDoux put it, 'A few extra connections here, a little more or a little less neurotransmitter there, and animals begin to act differently.' (Gerhardt, 2004: 211)

In order to feel safe in the world, we all need the ability to react to threat and to calm down when the threat has passed. For infants and children living with the constant threat of sexual abuse, as well as the potential emotional and psychological harms that accompany it, there is so much activity in the sympathetic nervous system that the brain can become stuck in hyperarousal (Scaer, 2014). Thus, the individual may be almost constantly flooded with stress hormones, resulting in increased heart rate and blood pressure. This explains why so many children who lived with repeated sexual abuse grow into adults with chronic illnesses (Scaer, 2014). To have a healthy immune system, we need the homeostatic balance of the two branches of the central nervous system, the sympathetic and parasympathetic, to be working smoothly. When the sympathetic branch is in constant overdrive, the parasympathetic drive (which brings rest, sleep and repair) is not activated in a regular way. Sleep disorders and exhaustion may be a constant from childhood throughout life.

> ...without effective internalised parental strategies for soothing and calming high arousal in the right brain, the individual is vulnerable to stress, which can more easily escalate into overwhelming distress. (Gerhardt, 2004: 47)

> Anything that threatens this regulation is very stressful because it puts survival at risk. It does not make much difference whether the lack of regulation is caused by being emotionally isolated from the caregiver or physically isolated by separation. What a small child needs is an adult who is emotionally available and tuned in enough to help regulate his states. (Gerhardt, 2004: 48)

These studies highlight the very real harm that trauma causes to the developing brain. Gerhardt points out how even the looks given by parents to young children can have a negative effect:

> These disapproving or rejecting looks produce a sudden lurch from sympathetic arousal to parasympathetic arousal, creating the effects we experience in shame – a sudden drop in blood pressure and shallow breathing... Shame is an important dimension of socialisation. But what matters equally is recovery from shame. (Gerhardt, 2004: 49)

From the new understandings of the structural effects of early trauma on the developing brain, it would be easy to conclude that the long-term effects can never be healed. However, hope comes from research into the neuropsychological impact of relationship-based therapy, which shows that new neural pathways can develop where previously they were absent. This evidence lends weight to what relationship-based therapists have witnessed – real, positive changes and healing, even in the most traumatised individual (for example, Kandel, 1998, 2005; Cozolino, 2010; Siegel, 1999, 2010, 2013; Hanson, 2013). Kandel's (1998, 2005) principles emphasised the neuroplasticity of the human brain, and that a central component of psychotherapy is that it affects clients' brains. The term *neuroplasticity* refers to the brain's ability to change and adapt as a result of life experiences (Butz, Worgotter & van Ooyen, 2009; Holtmaat & Svoboda, 2009). In psychological terms, these findings fit with Rogers' (1959) description of the breakdown and disorganisation that occurs when experiences that are incongruent with the self-structure are subceived as threatening, and therefore cannot be accurately symbolised into awareness:

> Rogers (1959) goes on to suggest that accurate symbolization in awareness
> of experience was necessary for reintegration of self and experience to take
> place. (Cited in Joseph, 2005).

Research consistently demonstrates that exposure to childhood sexual abuse appears to increase the risk of psychiatric disorders by about two to four times, in comparison with people not exposed to such abuse (for a review of studies, see Fergusson & Mullen, 1999). Increasing numbers of studies since the 1990s have shown evidence of an association between childhood sexual abuse and a wide range of problems in adulthood, including:

- depressive disorders (for example, Fergusson, Horwood & Lynskey, 1996; Mullen et al, 1993; Silverman, Reinherz & Giaconia, 1996)
- anxiety disorders (for example, Fergusson, Horwood & Lynskey, 1996; Mullen et al, 1993)
- antisocial behaviours (for example, Fergusson, Horwood & Lynskey, 1996; Scott, 1992)
- substance abuse disorders (for example, Fergusson, Horwood & Lynskey, 1996; Mullen et al, 1993; Scott, 1992)
- eating disorders (for example, Miller & McCluskey-Fawcett, 1993; Romans et al, 1995; Wonderlich et al, 1997)
- suicidal and self-damaging behaviours (for example, Fergusson, Horwood & Lynskey, 1996; Mullen et al, 1993; Peters & Range, 1995)
- post-traumatic stress disorders (Silverman, Reinherz & Giaconia, 1996) or dissociative disorders, including dissociative identity disorder (Putnam et al, 1986)
- problems with sexual adjustment (for example, Fergusson, Horwood & Lynskey, 1997; Mullen et al, 1994).

With traumatic experiences in which the person is blocked from fight or flight, as in sexual abuse, the brain and the body are unable to do their work in response to threat (van der Kolk, 1984). Post-traumatic stress disorder (PTSD) is considered a physical reliving of the trauma, with all the attendant hormonal activation. In flashbacks, the amygdala is overactive and the prefrontal cortex is temporarily disabled. Individuals with PTSD are very sensitively tuned to pick up threat and may respond to minor stimuli as if their life were in danger (van der Kolk, 2006).

Carmen and colleagues in 1984 found that 50 per cent of psychiatric inpatients report histories of physical or sexual abuse. One of the difficulties in extrapolating from studies is that there is no consistency in what the researchers define as 'abuse'. For example, some prevalence studies on childhood sexual abuse include only penetrative sex, whereas others include covert (non-touch) sexual abuse, and other forms of non-penetrative sex. From a person-centred perspective, the focus is on the experience of the person, rather than on any external judgment that something is or is not abuse.

It is helpful to have knowledge of the research, as clients often have questions about the impact of abuse. It is striking how often a client will ask, 'Does what happened to me count as abuse?' or will say, 'It must have been me attracting them, mustn't it?' Often these questions seem to be coming from someone far younger than the person in front of me. The tone or timbre of their voice and their appearance and posture may change too. Even people who, at other times, are utterly clear and sometimes very angry about what happened to them will ask these kinds of questions. What is in the forefront of my mind at these times is to meet the person empathically in that moment when the questions are being asked. I might share my sensing of the different quality of the question, occasionally going as far as to say, 'How old are you feeling as you wonder if you attracted the abuse?' This question is put in the most tentative of terms, yet what draws this question from me is the change in the energy between me and the client in the moment – a sense that the person has shifted gear, has shifted into another part of herself. Mearns and Thorne (2000) refer to 'configurations of self' to describe the different parts of self to which many clients refer. For those who have been abused, these parts of self may be separated by deeper fissures. Certainly, in my own experience, it is deeply healing when the different selves or parts of self are recognised. For clients who really want answers, and feel empowered by knowing these answers, their therapists' ability to point them in the direction of useful books or resources can be experienced as normalising ('I can't be that bonkers or you wouldn't know about this stuff!'), grounding and valuing ('I must be of some worth if my therapist is bothering to read about this stuff I'm dealing with'). More recent findings from neuroscience can be perceived as liberating when a survivor of childhood sexual abuse learns that their trauma has shaped how their brain works, and that rewiring is possible (see, for example, Siegel, 2010): 'Knowing about the brain can allow someone to move from self-judgement to self-acceptance' (Siegel & Hartzell, 2003:169, cited in Fishbane, 2007).

The effectiveness of therapies

Survivors of abuse rarely seek help for the legacy of their abuse. Many will initially seek help from their GP for depression or anxiety and panic attacks. GPs, often lacking alternatives, still reach first for the prescription pad to offer antidepressants. Sadly, for many people given such prescriptions, this is just further evidence of their inadequacy. Depression is the most commonly reported symptom of past abuse. Adult survivors have a four times greater lifetime risk for a major depressive episode than do those who were not abused or neglected (Johnson et al, 1999; Widom, DuMont & Czaja, 2007; Sugaya et al, 2012; Maniglio, 2012). Some of this vulnerability to depression can be the result of changes to the way the brain manages stressful events, due to severe or chronic exposure to stressors (Weiss, Longhurst & Mazure, 1999). Treatment with medication for depression and/or anxiety can give some relief for symptoms, but can also block potential for healing. Survivors may also present with an eating disorder, an alcohol problem, self-harm, sexual dysfunction, difficulties concentrating or a sense of not knowing who they are, of unreality. These and other symptoms then become the pathology, and survivors of abuse become trapped in the revolving door of mental health services, because the treatments attend only to the symptoms, not the cause.

In mental health services the significance of abuse is often minimised and trivialised, and survivors are held responsible for their own trauma (Watson et al, 1996). Where diagnoses of 'borderline personality disorder', 'psychosis' and 'postnatal depression' are treated with familiar but ineffectual and punitive treatment responses (Williams et al, 1998), the survivor has little chance of finding a new sense of worth that will play a part in healing from abuse. Williams (1999: 34) notes: 'Given these difficulties, it is unsurprising that, with a few exceptions (eg. Watson et al, 1996) most of the development in service provision for women survivors of abuse and violence has been in the independent and voluntary sector.'

For women and men who were abused as children, either within the home or outside it by strangers or family friends, there can be major difficulties and retraumatisation when they feel disempowered again by authority figures like doctors, nurses and social workers, and any professional seeking, with the best will in the world, to help them. The very fact that psychiatric services tend to be clinical in appearance can act as a trigger to people who have been abused. Institutionalisation can very often reinforce feelings of powerlessness, failure and self-loathing. Men and women who have been abused are at risk of revictimisation because they have not developed self-defence systems, and can be triggered into feeling (and being) the age they were when they were abused as a child. In these dissociated states, survivors will often revert to passive compliance, making them highly vulnerable to revictimisation. Survivors, overwhelmed by responsibility and feelings they cannot comprehend, often yearn for the sanctuary of a place where they are looked after. Their actual experience of asylum, however, is unlikely to meet these needs.

Children learn to protect themselves by being protected; they learn to defend themselves by being defended; they learn that they are worthy human beings because that is demonstrated to them. Adults with histories of chronic abuse were not protected, defended or shown they were worthy of love, comfort and support. So they simply do not learn the prerequisites for keeping safe in the world. Even when they do, they are at risk of being triggered to an earlier state.

Mental health professionals are under massive pressure, and it is understandable that treatment modalities offering readily measurable outcomes very quickly become the order of the day. Many people who are given short-term therapies like cognitive behavioural therapy (CBT), solution-focused therapy (SFT), or brief focal therapy seem to improve, but may return later for further treatment, with the same symptoms, or others. Statistically, the short-term results can look very attractive. But do we really know if patient X in one set of statistics isn't also patient Y with another set of symptoms?

Often, too, the creative survival skill of dissociation is perceived as psychosis, so that people experiencing terrifying flashbacks or regressing to traumatic events are retraumatised by the treatment intended to help them. In extreme cases, a survivor could, through a trigger event, dissociate, lose herself in the terrors of the past, and find herself in the power of people who are able to place her in a hospital ward with other people who may in fact be experiencing a loss of shared reality. This will only increase the terror, powerlessness and triggering problems with which she is already struggling. Diagnoses of various pathologies can contribute to a continually developing negative self-concept that pushes the person further away from the healthy relationships they might otherwise find, and which could demonstrate to them that they are able to relate positively with others. As Rogers writes:

> If I accept the other person as something fixed, already diagnosed and classified, already shaped by his past, then I am doing my part to confirm this limited hypothesis. If I accept him as a process of becoming, then I am doing what I can to confirm or make real his potentialities. (Rogers, 1967)

For me, the key word here is 'fixed'. Of course, people who are traumatised as children are shaped by that experience – our sense of who we are and what we are worth is defined by our experiences. But childhood abuse survivors are not fixed; they are in a process of becoming that can be mediated by their continued experiences. As Joseph writes, in relation to post-traumatic growth:

> … congruent reintegration of self with experience is not about the client returning to their pre-trauma levels of functioning, but about the client going beyond their previous levels of functioning, to become more fully functioning. (Joseph, 2005: 197)

If these continued experiences label them, squeeze them into services that focus on the label, subject them to unpleasant and unhelpful treatments and refuse to regard them as a person in the process of becoming, then the damage is continued.

One of the problems facing anyone experiencing emotional distress of any kind is that there are continual arguments about which kind of therapy is the most effective. Because the NHS currently favours CBT and SFT (NICE, 2005, 2009, 2014), the implication is that those are the most effective treatments. In fact, research repeatedly demonstrates that no particular model of therapy is more effective than any other (Horvath & Bedi, 2002; Wampold, 2001; Martin, Garske & Davis, 2000; Krupnick et al, 1996; Horvath & Symonds, 1991; Gaston, 1990). Well over 100 studies and meta-analyses find a significant, consistent relationship between the therapeutic alliance and successful outcome. The therapeutic alliance is defined as the personal bond between therapist and client, and collaborative commitment to the mutual work and goals of therapy. The qualities of the therapist that promote such an alliance are an ability to instil confidence and trust, dependability, benevolence, responsiveness, empathy, and responsive, collaborative application of techniques (Ackerman & Hilsentroth, 2003).

This finding holds across all therapy approaches studied (Horvath & Bedi, 2002; Wampold, 2001; Martin, Garske & Davis, 2000; Krupnick et al, 1996; Horvath & Symonds, 1991; Gaston, 1990). Castonguay and colleagues (1996: 497) studied cognitive therapy with or without medication:

> Improvement was found to be predicted by... the therapeutic alliance and the client's emotional involvement... However... therapists' focus on the impact of distorted cognitions on depressive symptoms correlated negatively with outcome... Descriptive analyses [suggested] that therapists sometimes increased their adherence to cognitive rationales and techniques to correct problems in the therapeutic alliance. Such increased focus, however, seems to worsen alliance strains, thereby interfering with therapeutic change.

> ... the particular treatment that the therapist delivers does not affect outcomes... Clearly, the person of the therapist is a critical factor in the success of therapy. (ibid: 202)

These findings support the assertion that the core attitudinal qualities of the person-centred approach are both necessary and sufficient for growth to occur.

Some therapists do damage, primarily through destructive relationship behaviours. Research by Hovarth & Bedi (2002) and Mohr (1995) suggest such therapists include those who:

- seek to 'take charge' early in the therapy
- are 'cold', argumentative or irritable, or generally lack empathy
- prematurely offer insight or interpretations
- make high use of transference interpretations or negative countertransference
- adopt 'aggressive stimulator' approaches – intrusive, confrontational, caring, self-revealing, charismatic, authoritarian
- place a high focus on the client-therapist relationship, yet lack empathy, genuineness and warmth.

These behaviours are damaging to any therapeutic relationship but they could also replicate those of abusing parents, triggering distress and prompting the client to resort to their survival strategies, such as alcohol, drugs, eating disorders, or self-harm, which will only reinforce the trauma.

Treatments developed from the findings of neuropsychological research include EMDR (Shapiro, 1995; 2001), coherence therapy (Ecker, Ticic & Hulley, 2012), and brainspotting therapy (Grand, 2013). Finding accurate data on outcomes from specific therapies with survivors of childhood abuse is complicated by the fact that the research tends to focus on the condition for which the person is being treated, such as depression, anxiety disorders, PTSD and other conditions, making it hard to identify those who are survivors of sexual abuse. Schottenbauer and colleagues' (2008) review of 55 studies of CBT and EMDR for PTSD found that drop-out rates varied widely and that non-response rates of up to 50 per cent were not uncommon.

My concern about some of the more technique-based approaches is that, from my experience of working with survivors and what they have told me, the directive nature of these approaches can trigger the same feelings of powerlessness that the person experienced as a child, which makes them counterproductive as healing possibilities. Person-centred therapy offers the client a safe, facilitative relationship in which they lead their own process and are not pushed to expose and experience more than they feel ready for. Such pushing can result in retraumatisation. Trusting the client to direct their own process provides a new experience; the client's actualising tendency will allow them to accurately symbolise their experience and, because they have led, they can more fully trust themselves.

Some psychiatrists hold to the view that talking about abuse issues will make matters worse, and that control of symptoms is the best treatment. However, there is an equally strong opposing view in the psychotherapeutic community that 'the efficacy of psychotherapy has now been firmly established and is no longer a subject of debate' (Wampold, 2001: 59) and that '[p]sychotherapy is successful in general, and the average treated client is better off than 80% of untreated subjects' (Lambert & Barley, 2002: 26). There is much evidence that demonstrates that relationship-based therapy provides the best chance of positive outcomes regardless of technique or orientation. The person-centred approach, with its focus on the relationship, provides the survivor of abuse with something they may never have experienced:

> Recently, for example, I was awestruck as I read the account of the relationship one of my trainees is currently forging with a woman who experienced sexual abuse from her father and her brother throughout most of her adolescence. My awe springs from the realisation of the healing that is being wrought in and through this relationship and almost as a matter of course in both the client and in the trainee therapist who is seeking to be with her in her pain... (Thorne, 1998: 32)

> The therapist's task is thus formidable, for he or she has somehow to rekindle hope in the client's heart and that is impossible without the rediscovery of trust... Psychological skills, therapeutic insights, sophisticated medication may all have their part to play in the process of healing but, as St Paul put it

in another context, without love they are likely in the end to profit nothing.
(Thorne, 1998: 108)

Findings from neuroscience over the past decade have shown the neurophysiological basis for empathy. When a client is expressing her/himself, mirror neurons in the therapist's brain are also firing, enabling the therapist to more fully understand the client's world from the client's perspective. Neurological mirroring is facilitated when the interpersonal interactions between therapist and client are experienced as being non-judgmental, positively regarding, respectful, accepting and empathic in nature (Schulte-Ruther et al, 2007). The more accurately that therapists can mirror the neural activity in their client's brain, the more likely is it that they will be able to understand them (Newberg & Waldman, 2013). When therapists are able to accurately mirror their client's feelings, they create neural resonance between them (Gerhardt, 2004; Siegel, 2010).

So, what therapists have observed in their clients is now supported by neuroscientific evidence showing that 'talking therapies' change the behaviour of the brain, its chemical operations, and its structure (Linden, 2006; Rossouw, 2013). For survivors of early childhood trauma, these findings offer real, concrete evidence that change is possible. Person-centred therapists focus on providing a safe and facilitative environment, and, as Allison and Rossouw (2013) have observed, this can help a client to down-regulate his or her stress response so they can change their behaviour from a pattern of avoidance and protection to one of approach and connection. A genuine, supportive relationship with a therapist provides reparation, as our need for secure attachments and our vulnerability to the ups and downs of our relational lives continue throughout adulthood. Whereas distressed adult relationships are correlated with increased secretion of stress hormones and lowered immune functioning, nurturing relationships are correlated with better physical health, including improved heart and immune function and resistance to stress (Cozolino, 2006). As Lewis, Amini and Lannon (2000: 86) put it: 'Stability means finding people who regulate you well and staying near them.' Healthy interdependence in adulthood entails a balance between self-regulation and looking to others for resonance and soothing in intimate relationships. These very necessary experiences can begin in a healthy therapeutic alliance.

Going forward

Survivors of childhood abuse need understanding; they need to be allowed to talk about what has happened. The damage was done within relationships; it makes sense that healing can only really take place within relationships. Survivors need to be able to choose their therapist, and to be allowed to set the pace of therapy. It may take a long time to establish a healthy therapeutic alliance that will allow the survivor to do the work necessary to reclaim her/his life and move into positive and healthy ways of being in the world.

At times of crisis, survivors need to know that there are safe places to go to for support and help, where there is an understanding of the legacy of abuse. These places of safety may offer residential care for a period. There are some therapeutic communities where re-parenting is offered; where people can come when they are in what RD Laing (1965) referred to as the 'authentic state of madness'; where therapeutic support is available 24 hours a day. More such places are needed. Fears that people will become dependent on this are unfounded. Dependency may be a phase, but in healthy, boundaried homes, children do not usually get stuck there; they move on and outgrow the safe home container, and so do people who are allowed to work on their healing. And it is hard work, involving commitment to taking responsibility for one's own actions and putting responsibility for abuse where it belongs – on the perpetrator of that abuse. It involves learning new skills in self-care and communication and developing healthy boundaries. A place of safety needs to look like a place of safety – and needs to feel like a place of safety, or it will retraumatise and reinforce anxiety, fear and unhealthy ways of coping.

Such places need to be staffed by people who understand about the legacy of abuse and about the fears so many have about repeating that abuse on their children. Such places would not judge the survivor when they just need time out, when they just need to talk, when they need someone to give some attention to the children because they can't do it. Such support would encourage survivors to take care of themselves, to receive care in the same nurturing environment where their children are being cared for. A couple of hours may be all that is needed.

The companionship of other survivors who are working on their healing can make a very big difference. Groupwork and drop-in provision may provide a sense of home and care that men and women who have suffered childhood abuse may never have experienced. Such nurturing and acceptance are healing in themselves. Support workers would need a thorough understanding of the legacy of abuse, and the opportunity to experience in their own professional development the core attitudinal qualities of the person-centred approach. They need to feel valued and supported if they are to offer those same qualities to clients. An emphasis on real relationships, where empathy and acceptance are givens, would offer real hope of healing.

> Abused people desperately require the corrective experience of an affirming, deeply committed, non-abusive relationship in which they can find healing and discover hope for living. So profound is the woundedness in some cases, however, that the offering of such a relationship may well uncover an ocean of pain or provoke in the client a fear of seduction. The therapist who is prepared to accompany such pain or fear and even face being falsely accused will need exceptional courage and absolute trust in his or her own integrity.
> (Thorne, 2002: 65–66)

Positive reinforcement, including validating the truth of the experience and that it was not the child's fault, is like making a 'deposit in [a survivor's] psychic savings bank' (Sanford, 1999: 129). Anyone supporting individuals who are healing from the legacy of abuse would benefit from being given the space and time to explore their own attitudes, feelings and needs so that they can develop within themselves the capacity to hear the truth behind the symptoms.

> The repression of our suffering destroys our empathy for the suffering of others. (Miller, 1991: 10)

Women and men who have suffered abuse as children and have the courage to challenge their legacy need fearless companions. As I have asserted elsewhere (Hawkins, 2002), healing from abuse is not going mad – it's going sane!

References

Ackerman SJ, Hilsentroth MJ (2003). A review of therapist characteristics and techniques positively impacting the therapeutic alliance. *Clinical Psychology Review 23*: 1–33.

Allison KL, Rossouw PJ (2013). The therapeutic alliance: exploring the concept of 'safety' from a neuropsychotherapeutic perspective. *International Journal of Neuropsychotherapy 1*: 21–29.

American Psychiatric Association (2013). *Diagnostic and Statistical Manual of Mental Disorders* (5th ed). Washington, DC: American Psychiatric Association.

Averill JR (1982). *Anger and Aggression*. New York: Springer-Verlag.

Butz M, Worgotter F, van Ooyen A (2009). Activity-dependent structural plasticity. *Brain Research Reviews 60*(2): 287–305.

Carmen EH, Ricker RP, Mills T (1984). Victims of violence and psychiatric illness. *American Journal of Psychiatry 141*: 378–383.

Castonguay LG, Goldfried MR, Wiser S, Raue PJ (1996). Predicting the effect of cognitive therapy for depression: a study of unique common factors. *Journal of Consulting and Clinical Psychology 64*: 497–504.

Cozolino L (2006). *The Neuroscience of Human Relationships: attachment and the developing social brain*. New York: WW Norton & Co.

Cozolino L (2010). *The Neuroscience of Psychotherapy: healing the social brain* (2nd ed). New York: WW Norton & Company.

Ecker B, Ticic R, Hulley L (2012). *Unlocking the Emotional Brain: eliminating symptoms at their roots using memory reconsolidation*. New York/Hove: Routledge.

Fergusson DM, Mullen PE (1999). *Childhood sexual abuse: an evidence-based perspective*. Developmental Clinical Psychology and Psychiatry Series, vol 40. London: Sage.

Fergusson DM, Horwood LJ, Lynskey MT (1996). Childhood sexual abuse and psychiatric disorders in young adulthood. Part II: psychiatric outcomes of sexual abuse. *Journal of the American Academy of Child and Adolescent Psychiatry 35*: 1365–1374.

Fergusson DM, Horwood LJ, Lynskey MT (1997). Childhood sexual abuse, adolescent sexual behaviours and sexual revictimisation. *Child Abuse and Neglect 21*: 789–803.

Finkelhor D (1986). *A Sourcebook on Child Sexual Abuse*. Beverly Hills, CA: Sage.

Fishbane MD (2007). Wired to connect: neuroscience, relationships and therapy. *Family Process 46*: 395–412.

Gaston L (1990). The concept of alliance and its role in psychotherapy: theoretical and empirical considerations. *Psychotherapy 27*: 143–153.

Gerhardt S (2004). *Why Love Matters: how affection shapes a baby's brain*. London/New York Routledge.

Grand D (2013). *Brainspotting: the revolutionary new therapy for rapid and effective change*. Boulder, CO: Sounds True Inc.

Hanson R (2013). *Hardwiring Happiness: the new brain science of contentment, calm, and confidence*. New York: Harmony.

Hawkins J (2002). Paradoxical safety: barriers to the actualising tendency, and beyond. *Person-Centred Practice 10*: 21–26.

Herman JL (1992a). *Trauma and Recovery: the aftermath of violence – from domestic abuse to political terror*. New York: Basic Books.

Herman JL (1992b). Complex PTSD: a syndrome in survivors of prolonged and repeated trauma. *Journal of Traumatic Stress 5*(3): 377–391.

Holtmaat A, Svoboda K (2009). Experience-dependent structural synaptic plasticity in the mammalian brain. *Nature Reviews Neuroscience 10*: 647–658.

Horvath AO, Bedi RP (2002). The Alliance. In: Norcross JC (ed). *Psychotherapy Relationships that Work*. New York: Oxford University Press (pp37–69).

Horvath AO, Symonds BE (1991). Relation between working alliance and outcome in psychotherapy: a meta-analysis. *Journal of Counselling Psychology 38*: 139–149.

Johnson JG, Cohen P, Brown J, Smailes EM, Bernstein DP (1999). Childhood maltreatment increases the risk for personality disorders during early adulthood. *Archives of General Psychiatry 56*(7): 600–606.

Joseph S (2003). Person-centred approach to understanding posttraumatic stress. *Person-Centred Practice 11: 70–75.*

Joseph S (2004). Client-centred therapy, posttraumatic stress disorder and posttraumatic growth. Theory and practice. *Psychology and Psychotherapy: Theory, Research and Practice 77: 101–120.*

Joseph S (2005). Understanding post-traumatic stress from the person-centred perspective. In: Joseph S, Worsley R (eds). *Person-centred Psychopathology: a positive psychology of mental health*. Ross-on-Wye: PCCS Books.

Kandel E (1998). A new intellectual framework for psychiatry. *The American Journal of Psychiatry 155: 457–469.*

Kandel E (2005). *Psychiatry, Psychoanalysis, and the New Biology of Mind*. Arlington, VA: American Psychiatric Association Publishing.

Krupnick JL, Sotsky SM, Simmens A, Moyer J, Elkin I, Watkins J, Pilkonis PA (1996). The role of the alliance in psychotherapy and pharmacotherapy outcome: findings in the National Institute of Mental Health treatment of depression collaborative research program. *Journal of Consulting and Clinical Psychology 6*: 532–539.

Laing RD (1965). *The Divided Self*. London: Pelican Books.

Lambert MJ, Barley DE (2002). Research summary on the therapeutic relationship and psychiatric outcome. In: Norcross JC (ed). *Psychotherapy Relationships that Work*. New York: Oxford University Press (pp17–32).

LeDoux JE (2002). *Synaptic Self: how our brains become who we are*. New York: Viking. Cited in Gerhardt S (2004). *Why Love Matters: how affection shapes a baby's brain*. London/New York: Routledge.

Lewis T, Amini F, Lannon R (2000). *A General Theory of Love*. New York: Random House.

Linden DEJ (2006). How psychotherapy changes the brain – the contribution of functional neuroimaging *Molecular Psychiatry 11*: 528–538.

Maniglio R (2012). Child sexual abuse in the etiology of anxiety disorders: a systematic review of reviews. *Trauma, Violence & Abuse 14*(2): 96–112.

Martin DJ, Garske JP, Davis MK (2000). Relation of the therapeutic alliance with outcome and other variables: a meta-analytic review. *Journal of Consulting and Clinical Psychology 68*: 438–450.

Mearns D, Thorne B (1999). *Person-Centred Counselling in Action* (2nd ed). London: Sage.

Mearns D, Thorne B (2000). *Person-Centred Therapy Today: new frontiers in theory and practice*. London: Sage.

Miller A (1991). *Banished Knowledge*. London: Virago.

Miller DAF, McCluskey-Fawcett K (1993). The relationship between childhood sexual abuse and subsequent onset of bulimia nervosa. *Child Abuse and Neglect 17*: 305–314.

Mohr DC (1995). Negative outcomes in psychotherapy: a critical review. *Clinical Psychology: Science and Practice 2*: 1–27.

Mullen PE, Martin JL, Anderson JC, Romans SE, Herbison GP (1993). Childhood sexual abuse and mental health in adult life. *British Journal of Psychiatry 163*: 721–732.

Mullen PE, Martin JL, Anderson JC, Romans SE, Herbison GP (1994). The effects of child sexual abuse on social, interpersonal and sexual function in adult life. *British Journal of Psychiatry 165*: 35–47.

Newberg A, Waldman MR (2013). *Words Can Change Your Brain: 12 conversation strategies to build trust, resolve conflict and increase intimacy*. New York: Plume/Penguin Group.

National Institute for Health and Clinical Excellence (NICE) (2005). *Post-Traumatic Stress Disorder: management*. Clinical guideline CG26. London: NICE.

National Institute for Health and Clinical Excellence (NICE) (2011). *Depression in Adults*. Quality standard QS8. London: NICE.

National Institute for Health and Care Excellence (NICE) (2014). *Anxiety Disorders*. Quality standard QS53. London: NICE.

Peters DK, Range LM (1995). Childhood sexual abuse and current suicidality in college women and men. *Child Abuse and Neglect 19*: 335–341.

Putnam FW, Guroff JJ, Silberman EK, Barvan L, Post RM (1986). The clinical phenomenology of multiple personality disorder: review of 100 recent cases. *Journal of Clinical Psychiatry 47*: 285–293.

Rogers CR (1951). *Client-Centered Therapy*. London: Constable.

Rogers CR (1959). A theory of therapy, personality and interpersonal relationships, as developed in the client-centered framework. In: Koch S (ed). *Psychology: a study of a science. Vol. 3: Formulations of the person and the social context*. New York: McGraw-Hill (pp184–256).

Rogers CR (1963). The actualizing tendency in relation to 'motives' and to consciousness. In: Jones M (ed). *Nebraska Symposium on Motivation*. Lincoln, NE: University of Nebraska Press (pp1–24).

Rogers CR (1967). *On Becoming a Person*. London: Constable.

Romans SE, Martin JL, Anderson JC, O'Shea ML, Mullen PF (1995). Factors that mediate between child sexual abuse and adult psychological outcome. *Psychological Medicine 25*: 127–142.

Rossouw PJ (2013). The neuroscience of talking therapies: implications for therapeutic practice. *The Australian Journal of Counselling Psychology 13*(1): 40–50.

St Vincent Millay E (1988). Mine the harvest. In: St Vincent Millay E. *Collected Sonnets*. New York: Harper & Row (p159).

Sanford L (1999). *Strong at the Broken Places: overcoming the trauma of childhood abuse*. London: Virago.

Scaer R (2014). *The Body Bears the Burden: trauma, dissociation and disease* (3rd ed). New York/Hove: Routledge.

Scott KD (1992). Childhood sexual abuse: impact on a community's mental health status. *Child Abuse and Neglect 16*: 285–295.

Shapiro F (1995). *Eye Movement Desensitization and Reprocessing: basic principles, protocols and procedures*. New York: Guilford Press.

Shapiro F (2001). *Eye Movement Desensitization and Reprocessing (EMDR): basic principles, protocols and procedures* (2nd ed). New York/London: Guilford Press.

Schottenbauer MA, Glass CR, Arnkoff DB, Tendick V, Gray SH (2008). Nonresponse and dropout rates in outcome studies on PTSD: review and methodological considerations. *Interpersonal and Biological Processes 71*(2): 134–168. doi: 10.1521/psyc.2008.71.2.134

Siegel DJ (1999). *The Developing Mind: toward a neurobiology of interpersonal experience*. New York: Guilford Press.

Siegel DJ, Hartzell M (2003). *Parenting from the Inside Out: how a deeper self understanding can help you raise children who thrive*. New York: Jeremy P Tarcher/Penguin.

Siegel DJ (2010). *The Mindful Therapist: a clinician's guide to mindsight and neural integration*. New York: WW Norton & Co.

Siegel DJ (2013). *Brainstorm: The power and purpose of the teenage brain*. New York: Penguin Putnam.

Schulte-Ruther M, Markowitsch HJ, Fink GR, Piefke M (2007). Mirror neuron and theory of mind mechanisms involved in face-to-face interactions: a functional magnetic resonance imaging approach to empathy. *Journal of Cognitive Neuroscience 19*(8): 1354–1372.

Silverman AB, Reinherz HZ, Giaconia RM (1996). The long-term sequelae of child and adolescent abuse: a longitudinal community study. *Child Abuse & Neglect 20*(8): 709–723.

Sugaya L, Hasin DS, Olfson M, Lin K-H, Grant BF, Blanco C (2012). Child physical abuse and adult mental health: a national study. *Journal of Traumatic Stress 25*: 384–392.

Thorne B (1998). *Person-Centred Therapy and Christian Spirituality: the secular and the holy*. London: Whurr.

Thorne B (2002). *Mystical Power of the Person-Centred Approach: hope beyond despair*. London: Whurr.

Van Der Kolk BA (1984). *Post-Traumatic Stress Disorder: psychological and biological sequelae*. Washington, DC: American Psychiatric Press.

Van Der Kolk BA, McFarlane MC, Weisaeth L (eds) (2006). *Traumatic Stress: the effects of overwhelming experience on mind, body, and society*. New York: Guilford Press.

Walker P (2013). *Complex PTSD: from surviving to thriving: a guide and map for recovering from childhood trauma*. Lafayette, CA: Azure Coyote.

Walker P (2015). *Frequently Asked Questions about Complex PTSD.* [Blog.] pete-walker.com/fAQsComplexPTSD.html (accessed 30 November, 2016)

Wampold BE (2001). *The Great Psychotherapy Debate.* Mahwah, NJ: Lawrence Erlbaum Associates.

Warner MS (2000). Person-centred therapy at the difficult edge: a developmentally based model of fragile and dissociated process. In: Mearns D, Thorne B (eds). *Person-Centred Therapy Today.* London: Sage (pp144–171).

Watson G, Scott C, Ragalsky S (1996). Refusing to be marginalised: groupwork in mental health services for women survivors of childhood sexual abuse. *Journal of Community and Applied Social Psychology 6:* 341–354.

Weiss EL, Longhurst JG, Mazure CM (1999). Childhood sexual abuse as a risk factor for depression in women: psychosocial and neurobiological correlates. *American Journal of Psychiatry 156*(6): 816–828.

Widom C, DuMont K, Czaja S (2007). A prospective investigation of major depressive disorder and comorbidity in abused and neglected children grown up. *Archives of General Psychiatry 64:* 49–56.

Williams J (1999). Social inequalities and mental health. In: Newnes C, Holmes G, Dunn C (eds). *This is Madness: a critical look at psychiatry and the future of the mental health services.* Ross-on-Wye: PCCS Books (pp29–50).

Williams J, Liebling H, Lovelock C, Chipchase H, Herbert Y (1998). Working with women in special hospitals. *Feminism and Psychology 8:* 357–369.

Wonderlich SA, Brewerton TD, Jocic Z, Dansky BS, Abbott DW (1997). Relationship of childhood sexual abuse and eating disorders. *Journal of the American Academy of Child and Adolescent Psychiatry 36:* 1107–1115.

17 | Nine considerations concerning psychotherapy and care for people 'with special needs'

Marlis Pörtner

This chapter will consider the question if psychotherapy – and, in particular, person-centred psychotherapy – for people 'with special needs' is useful or possible at all. First, I will point out the variety of persons embraced by this term and describe how paradigms relating to them have changed over the last decades. I shall talk about my own experience (of more than 30 years) with person-centred psychotherapy for clients with special needs, and highlight some specific aspects of this work, such as particular conditions, main issues in the therapeutic process etc. I shall indicate two negative side effects of normalisation that – without belittling its invaluable merits and the unquestionable improvements it brings about – need to be looked out for. Furthermore, the influence of the environment will be pointed out, and the need for carers as well as for psychotherapists to find a disabled person's – verbal or non-verbal – language. Examples from practice illustrate the complexity of working in this field.

My conclusion is that a person-centred attitude is indispensable particularly with these clients, and that psychodiagnostic knowledge is helpful as long as it is used to *understand* and not to label individuals. Cooperation and exchange of experience between psychotherapists, carers and professionals of different backgrounds working in this field is considered useful and necessary.

1. Who are 'people with special needs'?

The use of 'politically correct' language sometimes makes it difficult to make clear who exactly we are talking about, especially when one term after another comes to be considered as disparaging and the 'correct' words to describe them are constantly changed. So 'retarded' was first replaced by 'mentally handicapped', which was replaced by 'mentally disabled', then by 'people "with" handicaps or disabilities'. Later on, the correct way was to talk about 'special needs', whereas for a certain time anything but 'learning disabilities' seemed to be taboo. The trouble is that these changing 'politically correct' terms in no way cover the variety of persons we are talking about. Despite the undoubtedly honourable original intentions, this evolution has not only caused a regrettable impoverishment of language but also holds the danger that existing handicaps are not properly recognised and the persons concerned do not get the support they need. Moreover, to my surprise, I found that the scale of what is estimated 'correct' is in parts diametrically opposed to the original meaning of the words. For example, 'retarded' (meaning 'slow') is much less judgmental and determinate than 'disabled' (meaning 'incapable', 'incapacitated') (Pörtner 2000: 2–3).

Not that the words themselves are derogatory: it is the attitude behind the words. And as long as the attitude towards mentally handicapped or disabled or retarded persons or people with special needs is disparaging, any word that is used, after a time, will become disparaging too. What we need is to accept and respect persons with mental disabilities as equal human beings. With such an attitude, I think there is no need to avoid words that indicate their existential condition. Therefore, depending on the context, I shall use the more neutral 'special needs', as well as other terms – thus taking into account that it is in no way a homogenous group we are talking about, and that frequently we do not know much about how a person came to be labelled as having 'special needs'.

The confusion about using the correct term is not just a language problem; it also reflects the difficulty of doing justice to the wide variety of individuals who live or work in communities and organisations for persons with disabilities. They are impaired in most different ways: learning disabilities, psychological disorders, genetic deficiencies, congenital or developmental brain defects, physical disabilities combined with not having been offered adequate opportunities for education – and sometimes we see persons who give the impression that their continued presence in these communities is more due to bad luck than to anything else. So, who are people with special needs?

2. Changing paradigms

For many years, persons with mental disabilities were not considered capable of further development and were kept either hidden in their families or – particularly those with severe behaviour disorders – in psychiatric hospitals. They were provided for in a very basic way, but neither did they get proper treatment nor the necessary opportunities to learn and develop. It was commonly agreed that behaviour disorders of persons with mental disabilities were exclusively due to organic brain deficiencies and could neither be understood nor altered.

However, since the 1960s/1970s, it has gradually come to be understood that behaviour disorders might as well be caused by unfavourable circumstances. A movement developed to get persons with mental disabilities out of the hospitals and to normalise their life conditions. It was the beginning of an evolution that brought considerable improvements for people with special needs and created new prospects for growth and development. Mental disabilities were no longer seen 'as a disease but as one possible way to cope with the world'[1] (Hennicke & Rotthaus, 1993: 9) and as 'one possible mode of existence' (Hennicke & Rotthaus, 1993: 10). Deficiency-oriented views were replaced by growth-oriented concepts. A shift in thinking began 'from typology and classification towards individualization' that asked for a shift 'from a psychology from outside to a psychology from inside' (Eggert, 1993: 205). Even in a recent clinical textbook about mental handicaps, we can find the following statement: 'We understand mental disability of a person as a complex condition that, influenced by manifold social factors, developed from medically defined disorders. Diagnosed pre-, peri- and postnatal deficiencies do not allow a statement about a person's mental disability, which is determined by the interaction between his/her potential abilities and the demands of his/her concrete environment' (Thimm, 1999: 10).

In this relatively new and, in many aspects, still little-explored field, there is not such a clear dividing line between psychiatry/psychopathology on the one hand and humanistic approaches on the other. The borderline is much more between progressive and backward or uninformed views on both sides. There were unrecognised early pioneers among classic clinicians, and there are to this day professionals of different backgrounds (educators, carers, psychologists, physicians, nurses) with alarmingly outdated or uneducated opinions about people with special needs. Often the humanistic approach is limited to fine ideals that fail to be concretised in everyday practice. Moreover, there is a tendency to pervert humanistic intentions into the opposite by denying or not recognising existing handicaps, thus depriving individuals of necessary support. And sometimes, in institutions, we find – depending on which person we come across – a confusingly inconsistent mix of attitudes and approaches, which certainly is not beneficial to the mental health and personal growth of those who have to live there.

The pioneers' assumption that the organism would react positively to favourable circumstances, and that behaviour disorders would automatically disappear, proved to be wrong. Not all behaviour disorders disappeared just by normalising people's life conditions. Sometimes they became even more apparent, because the new concepts allowed people's individuality to manifest itself more distinctly. It turned out that mental health problems were more frequent among mentally disabled people than among the average population (Gaedt, 1987; Lotz & Koch, 1994).

Despite the considerable improvements due to normalisation, these findings are not surprising when we look at the biographies and life conditions of many people with special needs. The German psychologist Barbara Senckel explains quite plausibly why these persons are 'particularly vulnerable and wounded' (Senckel, 1998). She states that, 'in addition to limitations due to disabilities', the reasons are

---

1. Original German quotations in this chapter have been translated by Marlis Pörtner.

traumatic experiences such as 'fundamental lack of acceptance and esteem; repeated experiences of being abandoned and of separation; disparagement, neglect, isolation; heteronomy, pressure to conform; control, lack of self-determination (even where it would be possible) and no real prospects for the future' (Senckel, 1998: 37). In the biographies of people with mental disabilities, again and again we come across such experiences that shape their behaviours in a way other people find strange and incomprehensible and that often are at the roots of psychological disorders.

In addition, Valerie Sinason, a British psychoanalyst and author, who for many years worked at the Tavistock Institute as a psychotherapist for mentally disabled persons, points to another aspect. She describes the 'handicapped smile' as a 'defence against trauma' (Sinason 1992: 136), and states: ' My own clinical work and that of colleagues has clarified instances where mental handicap is actually caused by abuse. Sometimes, trauma evokes handicap as a defence about the memory of physical and sexual abuse' (Sinason, 1992: 137). She refers to J Oliver, who confirms her opinion and, as a result, based on his own research studies, speaks of 'VIMH = violence-induced mental handicap'. (Oliver, 1988, quoted in Sinason, 1992: 137). Moreover, 'the environment in itself can be traumatogenic' (Sinason, 1992: 138), and she thinks that: 'If knowing and seeing involve knowing and seeing terrible things, it is not surprising that not-knowing, becoming stupid, becomes a defence' (Sinason, 1992: 137). More than once during therapy sessions she observed a client, suddenly, and for a varying length of time, express him or herself in an understandable and realistic way. Prouty refers to a similar experience with his disabled brother (Van Werde & Morton, 1999).

The Brisbane Study (Berry, Gunn & Andrews, 1984), which followed the development of children with Down syndrome (trisomy-21) from birth to the age of five, is particularly interesting because its comparison of a group of children with the same clearly defined genetic deficiency proves that the differences in how these children developed was much more determined by their environment than by the deficiency. This was a real breakthrough as, for years, people with Down syndrome had been considered incapable of further development.

From all this it becomes clear that:

- the degree of mental disabilities and of the impact they have on a person cannot just be defined by psychopathological diagnostics, but is influenced as well by social factors
- psychotherapy must be available for people with special needs
- an environment that fosters mental health and personal growth is of crucial importance.

For all three aspects, the person-centred approach offers valuable concepts and represents a helpful – and, in my experience, necessary – completion to psychopathological knowledge.

3. My experience with the person-centred approach and clients with special needs

It was by pure coincidence that I came to work with these clients. I didn't have any previous experience in this field when, more than 30 years ago, as a beginning psychotherapist and still a trainee in client-centred psychotherapy, I was asked to take a client with special needs. I was doubtful. Was there any point in psychotherapy for these people? Was it possible at all? This, at the time, was in no ways certain. It meant breaking new ground, not only for me, but also for my supervision group and our trainers. They shared my doubts, as we had learned that Rogers considered an average level of intelligence as a necessary condition for psychotherapy (Rogers, 1942). The general opinion at that time – with a few exceptions – regarded psychotherapy with mentally disabled persons as impossible. However, I decided to try – a decision I never regretted, as I owe to it most precious insights for my work as a psychotherapist.

The first experiences with two women with special needs (Pörtner, 1984, 1990) were crucial for my development as a client-centred psychotherapist, as well as for my understanding of psychotherapy in general and of the person-centred approach in particular. Since these beginnings, I have always worked with (among other clients) more and less severely mentally disabled persons. The insights I owe them were meaningful for my whole therapeutic practice. With them I learned, even more than with other clients, that a therapist's work is not about 'doing', but about 'enabling', and that its most fundamental factor is to empathically and congruently enter the other person's world. No other clients have ever reacted as sensitively as those with special needs, or given me such immediate and open feedback when, for a tiny moment, I was not completely attentive or when I did not accurately understand them.

It was an important completion of my experience not only to do psychotherapy with individuals, but also to consult and supervise carers, staff and organisations. It highlighted the environment's crucial influence on the mental health and wellbeing of people with special needs and the significance of person-centred concepts for everyday care. I discovered that carers, who didn't know anything about the person-centred approach, when everything else had failed, sometimes intuitively found solutions that to a large extent conformed to its principles. These experiences led me to develop a person-centred concept specifically designed for everyday care (Pörtner, 1996a, 1996b, 2000).

It was encouraging, in 1981, to meet Garry Prouty at a Gendlin workshop in Chicago, and to realise I was not alone: there were other client-centred psychotherapists working with this group of clients. Later on, I got to know Isolde Badelt's pioneering work in Heidelberg (Badelt, 1984, 1990, 1994) and, with time, that of other colleagues in different countries, such as Hans Peters in Holland (Peters, 1992/2001). The circle slowly expanded. Yet, all in all, to this day, there are still only a few practitioners who work in this field. This is highly regrettable, not only for the potential clients but also for the psychotherapists themselves, because entering the world of a person with a mental disability offers invaluable opportunities to expand the psychotherapist's horizons in ways that will benefit the whole of their therapeutic work.

4. Why person-centred?

Since the 1980s, increasing attention has been paid to psychotherapy for people with special needs, at least at conferences and in literature. The question was: is psychotherapy with people suffering from mental disabilities possible and useful at all, and how can it cope with their specific conditions and needs? Psychotherapists of different orientations have dealt with the issue and proposed their ideas (Lotz, Koch & Stahl, 1994; Lotz, Stahl & Irblich, 1996). Interestingly, the necessary conditions many of these authors describe correspond precisely with person-centred principles.

Sylvia Görres, an author of psychoanalytic orientation, writes on behalf of people with special needs: 'For them psychotherapy might be the first experience of an accepting, non-judgmental relation with another person who takes them seriously' (Görres, 1996: 30). This corresponds exactly with what in client-centred psychotherapy is seen as an essential element of the therapeutic process. And her statement, 'People with mental disabilities are more helpless in the face of authoritarian power than we are, and not in a position to protect themselves against uncontrolled emotional infringements like, for example, in a negative transference' (Görres, 1996: 34) should be taken to heart not only by psychotherapists of any orientation but by anybody who, in some way or other, has to do with people with special needs. It remains a basic principle of the person-centred approach, which makes it explicit that empathy, acceptance and a non-judgmental attitude are essential in psychotherapy, as well as in everyday care – also and particularly – with persons suffering from mental disabilities. It is essential to be willing to enter their world, as unapproachable and incomprehensible as it may appear.

With good reason, some authors also express reservations against psychotherapy, arguing that people with special needs should be 'accepted, not treated' (Stahl, 1996: 20). Yet, from a person-centred viewpoint, psychotherapy and an accepting attitude are not contradictory. On the contrary, in client-centred psychotherapy, accepting human beings as they are is seen as a basic condition for facilitating personal growth. However, to accept a disabled person as she is does not imply that we do not believe her capable of further development. Both are needed: on the one hand, accepting individuals as they are, and on the other hand, believing them capable of taking steps of growth. We have to be carefully aware of where such steps seem to emerge and empathically support them. Therefore, my statement is: *We have to accept disabled persons as they are and not try to change them, but offer conditions that make changes possible.*

This, at the same time, describes a fundamental aspect of the person-centred approach, where psychotherapy is not seen as something to be 'done' with clients but as opening a space where they may discover their own resources – resources that they previously could not access.

Another point in favour of the person-centred approach: it is often hard to discern if a specific behaviour is due to mental disability or has to be seen as a symptom of a psychological disease. For many symptoms, 'it is not clear if they allow the same conclusions with a mentally disabled person as with one who is not disabled' (Senckel, 1998: 21). Traditional diagnostic categories therefore only partly apply. In this context, it is an advantage of the person-centred approach that it does not primarily focus on diagnostics but on trying *to understand the client's subjective world.* This is particularly important for people with special needs, as 'they have only a limited range of behaviours and reactions to express all kinds of states of mind' (Senckel, 1998: 21). The notion of a 'pre-expressive' level (Prouty, 1994; Prouty, Van Werde & Pörtner, 1998), where something struggles to express itself, allows a deeper understanding of ways to behave or express things which at first do not seem comprehensible.

The 'diagnostic eye', exclusively focused on deficiencies, fixates a person with special needs on what she is not able to do, thus blurring the view of what she can do. Therefore, the 'person-centred eye', focused on resources, is a helpful – and, in my opinion, necessary – complement. Yet, on the other hand, we are of no help to a person with special needs if we are blind to the concrete limitations a specific handicap imposes on her. We then will ask too much of her and make her repeat once again the experience of failure. We must know about the nature of different disabilities, because ignorance of what people have to live with leads to inadequate support and inadequate care. This is a dark side of normalisation.

5. The light and dark side of normalisation

The principle of normalisation, calling for empowerment and self-advocacy, brought significant improvements in care and education of people with special needs. Their range of activity has considerably expanded, and they are offered many more opportunities to participate in what is considered normal life. No longer do they live out of the public eye, but can be seen anywhere: on trains and buses, at the zoo, at the shopping mall, at the restaurant, at museums, on the beach. Compared to former times, their quality of life, without any doubt, has considerably improved.

Yet, there is also a dark side to normalisation (Pörtner, 2003: 62–71). To recognise it in no way means to condemn or give up on normalisation, or to belittle its merits, but helps to clearly discriminate between where it really serves its purpose and where it risks turning into the opposite. Two tendencies are particularly pernicious:

- trying to adjust mentally disabled persons to 'the' normal
- ignoring existing handicaps.

It is a misunderstanding that normalisation should, at all costs, try to adjust people with mental disabilities to what is considered 'normal'. Normalisation is not about creating 'normality' by hiding or denying handicaps. Normalisation means: it is as normal to be handicapped as it is normal to have blue or brown eyes, white or black skin, long or short legs or to need glasses. Normalisation is about accepting a broader range of modes of existence, including mental disabilities. Normalisation is about offering persons with special needs conditions that, according to their capabilities, facilitate their autonomy and personal growth and let them find *their own* best way to cope with the world they have to live in.

It is certainly positive not to stigmatise individuals with the label 'handicapped' and to respond to them as normally as possible. However, it must not result in ignoring a person's disability and withholding from her the support she needs. Unfortunately, this happens quite frequently, and the earlier mentioned impoverishment of language contributes to it. Even more harmful, though, is the widely-held black-and-white thinking that leads to either treating a person as 'disabled' and overlooking her capabilities (thus impeding her potential development), or treating her as 'normal' and overlooking her disabilities (thus depriving her of adequate care). What we badly need is *differentiation* – its increasing lack is one of the most disastrous tendencies of our time, not only in care for mentally handicapped people but in many other social and political spheres as well.

We should not, from the perspective 'disabled', create differences where there are none, but we have to recognise and accept differences that really exist. To blur differences is just another way of discrimination. To only accept what is like us is no real integration. Integration is *not* about *making disabled persons equal* but about *accepting them as equal*. To respect the 'otherness' in other people is a basic principle of the person-centred attitude. Therefore, knowledge about the nature of different handicaps and psychological disorders is necessary for psychotherapists as well as for carers, in order to better understand differences and be able to more adequately meet the needs of those who must live with such handicaps.

6. What is different in comparison with 'normal' psychotherapies?

The therapist's basic attitude of empathy, acceptance and congruence is precisely the same as with any other client. However, concerning the circumstances as well as the main focus in the therapeutic process, there are some differences when working with disabled clients.

- As a rule, these clients do not see a psychotherapist on their own initiative. Others – who usually have quite concrete ideas about the effect of what psychotherapy should achieve – decide that it is necessary for them.

- Language disorders, being non-verbal and bizarre behaviours are barriers to understanding that therapists have to overcome. Many people with special needs have only very poor language available, or even none at all. The therapeutic relationship then develops at a very subtle non-verbal or pre-verbal level, which therapists first have to discover.

- The setting may be very different from what psychotherapists are used to, and from what would be desirable. Often there is no proper room to work in, and they have to make do with the entrance hall, the cafeteria or the living room, and all the disturbances that implies.

- Persons with special needs are only very rarely in a position to consciously deal with, talk about or work on their problems.

- Cooperation and exchange with the carers in most cases is necessary.

For therapists, it means not letting themselves be used to carry out the instructions of carers, but staying completely open to the concerns of the clients. Only in this way is there a chance that trust will build up and a therapeutic relationship can develop. Moreover, therapists must be flexible in terms of the setting and – this is perhaps the most difficult – lower their expectations with regard to what psychotherapy can achieve.

Phases where nothing seems to move are much more pronounced than in psychotherapy with other clients. All the more, the therapist has to be carefully aware of the *small, sometimes even tiny steps* that nevertheless do happen. Therefore, it is helpful from time to time to look back. From a distance, the – sometimes considerable – stretch of road that the client has covered, despite the apparent standstill, becomes visible. Also, what had seemed to turn in circles, on reflection might reveal itself as a spiral that imperceptibly but steadily is opening up. It is a matter of nuances: the client still may be overcome by rage about the behaviour of one of her roommates, but she now recovers more quickly; the client who used to frighten his group with his aggression might still get angry, but now for the most part expresses it verbally, and only very rarely through physical attacks. Such changes *do count*, even if they represent only small steps. The importance of small steps in client-centred psychotherapy, as well as in everyday care for people with special needs, has been emphasised and described in several publications (Pörtner, 1994, 1996, 2000, 2003).

Mildly disabled persons frequently suffer from various kinds of language disorders that make empathic understanding difficult for the therapist. With them, an old methodical element of client-centred psychotherapy proves to be helpful again: *to reflect what has been understood.* People who have difficulties in expressing themselves verbally experience again and again that others respond with 'mhm' or 'sure', without having understood anything of what they have tried to express. Such experiences increase the isolation of a person with special needs, whereas to experience – perhaps for the first time – that somebody does not give up until she or he does really understand brings about deep release. (The person often expresses that by taking a deep breath.) I learned from one of my first clients with special needs how important this experience is. Despite my coming to understand her way of expressing herself quite well, and no longer feeling it necessary to reflect everything, she stubbornly insisted on my repeating each sentence she said. Obviously, she needed it to make sure that I had really understood (Pörtner, 1984, 1990).

Another difficulty is that clients who are verbal and seem quite able to express themselves often do so in 'ready-made' stereotypes picked up from the 'normal people' they so much want to resemble. They are not used to talking about what they feel and experience, and refer perhaps only to apparently 'banal' events of their daily life. The therapist has to be sensitively aware of the perhaps only very indirectly expressed *experiencing quality* in what on the surface seems to be banal or stereotyped. She needs patience and staying power to slowly and carefully help clients get more in contact with their experiencing, by again and again *reflecting the experiencing quality and emotional content* of what the person is expressing – another well-proven methodical element of client-centred psychotherapy.

It is even more difficult with people who do not speak at all, or barely speak. An impressive example is the experience of the German psychologist Barbara Krietemeyer with a severely disabled non-verbal woman (Krietemeyer, 2000; Krietemeyer & Prouty, 2003), described in the chapter 'A hopeless case?' (Pörtner 2000: 105–113). Prouty's pre-therapy is an invaluable support in approaching persons 'without language' (Prouty, 1994; Prouty, Van Werde & Pörtner, 1998, 2002). Verbal or not, psychotherapists have to *find the 'language' of the other person* – and, whenever they succeed, it will be a precious experience, expanding their human understanding as well as their therapeutic competence.

The necessary cooperation and exchange with carers and, at the same time – as with any other client – the obligation to strictly respect *confidentiality of the therapy session* is a delicate balance requiring subtlety, transparency and clear thinking on the part of the therapist. He may, for example, add to the carers' understanding by telling *his view* of where the client is at the moment, without giving away any of the contents the client has entrusted him with. Psychotherapists have to keep in mind this principle: *Psychotherapy is never about remodelling disabled persons to the wishes of their carers.* So, what is the purpose of psychotherapy for people with special needs if it is not to deliberately change undesirable behaviours, and particularly when it is not possible to systematically and consciously work on their problems?

7. Main issues in the therapeutic process

There are two main issues in psychotherapy for people with special needs:

- changes in the self-concept
- development of contact functions.

Facilitating changes in the self-concept is what psychotherapy basically is about. For most people with mental disabilities (and other clients as well), the crucial first step is to restore self-esteem and find *a more accepting and more positive attitude towards themselves,* in order that further changes become possible at all. This is particularly important for people with special needs. As they are constantly confronted with their incompetence and inadequacy, they usually find it hard to accept themselves. They suffer from 'being different', and judge themselves by what they think is 'normal'. Their self-esteem, in general, is very low – the unrealistic overestimation of some of them is just the other side of the same coin. On the one hand, to *develop more self-confidence* and, on the other, to *better recognise one's own limits* – these are issues psychotherapy can help with, and the person-centred attitude is a crucial factor. To be accepted by the therapist helps clients to accept themselves – including their inadequacies. This in itself represents a change. Awareness of life improves, and energies are set free that may open new prospects and facilitate further steps of growth.

Another essential aspect of psychotherapy with these clients is to *establish, restore and reinforce contact functions,* defined by Prouty as reality contact, emotional contact and communicative contact (Prouty, 1994; Prouty, Van Werde & Pörtner, 1998, 2002). In the majority of people with special needs, these contact functions are impaired or not sufficiently developed. Here Prouty's concept of pre-therapy, built on client-centred fundamentals, offers precious support. It is not only helpful in psychotherapy but can also be transferred to everyday situations (Prouty, 1994; Prouty, Van Werde & Pörtner, 1998, 2002; Van Werde, 1998). Dion Van Werde's work at the psychiatric hospital Sint-Camillus in Gent is exemplary in this respect, and well transferable to organisations for people with special needs.

For them to be more able to accept themselves, to be more in contact with reality, with their own feeling and experiencing, as well as with other people, inevitably has consequences on their behaviours and expands their radius of action. Even though we do not specifically aim at changing behaviours, it will happen when the self-concept changes and self-esteem improves. And it makes a crucial difference for a person to discover fallow resources in herself and take her own steps – even though, perhaps, not those the carers are expecting – rather than be pushed in a specific direction. This too is an essential element of the person-centred approach, not restricted to people with special needs but particularly important for them.

Many persons with special needs are well able to verbalise changes in their self-concept, sometimes using amazingly expressive images. But, above all, it shows in their behaviour: more self-assurance, more self-confidence, more trusting of their own ways and opinions – in daily life as well as in relation to the therapist.

8. The crucial importance of the environment

The most important happens outside the therapy session is a truism that psychotherapists can never keep in mind enough. The most exciting experiences during a therapy session will not be of much use for the clients if they cannot create new and different experiences with themselves and with others in their daily life. This is particularly true for people with special needs. They usually cannot, without support, transfer their experiences from the therapy session into daily life. They get stressed if there is too big a discrepancy between what is developing in psychotherapy and what is required or tolerated by their environment. The therapist and the carers must not work against each other, as it will always be the disabled person who has to suffer the consequences. That is why cooperation is necessary.

Carers should be in a position to understand when a psychological process is in the offing, in order that it will not be impeded in daily routine but be encouraged. Behaviours that might be seen as disturbing often are the first indications of a significant step of growth. If carers are sensitive to that, they will be able to respond more adequately. Much psychotherapy for people with special needs would not be necessary if some basic person-centred principles were followed in everyday care. A detailed concept of what this means concretely is to be found in *Trust and Understanding* (Pörtner, 2000).

It is essential for the mental health and quality of life of people with special needs that in daily life too, wherever possible, their autonomy is fostered and respected and they are offered choices, be it in even tiny issues that may appear of no importance to people who aren't disabled. For individuals whose lives are to a large extent determined by others, they mean a lot. It makes a crucial difference for a person not able to move to choose where she wants the wheelchair to be put, rather than have it decided by the carer. To respect human dignity means to *ask* a person who is not able to use the toilet by herself if it is ok to take her to the toilet now. It matters for somebody who cannot eat by himself to be given a chance to open his mouth, or to indicate in some other way that he is ready, before the spoon is put between his lips. With severely disabled persons, respect for human dignity and allowing self-advocacy is not about big words but about these tiny issues that, because of their apparent triviality, are much too often neglected.

It matters for a person who does not speak that carers in her presence talk *with her and not about her*. Being asked means something to non-verbal persons too, as they will sense the attitude behind the words and realise that they are being taken seriously, instead of just ignored. And with the very few who are not reachable by language at all, a question, or the offer of an opportunity to decide about something themselves, can be communicated non-verbally as well.

Not concentrating on deficiencies but being aware of and fostering resources, as well as supporting every tiny step that a person succeeds in making, is at least as important in everyday care as in psychotherapy. It improves the quality of life not only for people with special needs but for carers as well, as their work then becomes more interesting and satisfying. Just as in psychotherapy, focusing on resources does not mean that carers must ignore or deny existing handicaps and their possible impact on a person – on the contrary.

9. How can person-centred principles and knowledge of psychodiagnostics and the nature of specific handicaps complement each other?

In order to discover a person's resources, her disabilities have to be recognised. This is vital in order to be able to provide adequate care and foster individual potential instead of causing stress to disabled persons with unrealistic demands. In this respect, knowledge of psychodiagnostics can be helpful – on condition that it serves *to understand,* and *not to label* a person. To know basic facts about different disabilities is useful – on condition that one is aware that these facts do not explain anything about how a person experiences and copes with their disability. Only from how a person experiences and copes with his or her disability can we learn how the handicap affects her and find the best way to offer her adequate support. What we always have to keep in mind is that diagnostics are categories that help *us,* the observers, to get some orientation about and put in an order the multiple phenomena we come across. Diagnostics can *never* establish the reality of how this person is. This is only to be learned from the person herself. We have to carefully explore an individual's specific experience of and reaction to the disability, as well as her attempts to cope with it. For this, as I mentioned before, the 'diagnostic eye' is not sufficient, but needs to be complemented by the 'person-centred eye'. Both eyes together may help carers, as well as psychotherapists, to more clearly see the meaning of a person's strange behaviour, and to discover – in their different ways and in relation to their different tasks – adequate ways to respond.

Yet, knowledge of diagnostics and psychopathology can also be treacherous if it entices carers (and sometimes also psychotherapists) to see symptoms everywhere and pathologise any behaviour or reaction that they have difficulty in understanding. The purpose of knowledge is not to set limits for disabled persons, but to *acknowledge* their limitations where they arise, and to help them find their own best ways to live and cope with these limitations. Knowledge must serve to *recognise* symptoms when they occur, but not to persistently look out for and attach them to disabled persons. The trouble is that, if we are sufficiently determined, we will always find what we are looking for. We have to keep in mind that, through our interactions and expectations, we influence another person more than we may imagine. Interestingly, the considerable impact of interaction on development and behaviours of individuals has been affirmed by scientists doing research into brain functions (Koukkou & Lehman, 1998). The viewpoint we hold plays a powerful role in terms of self-fulfilling prophecy, on the personal as well as on the scientific level.

So, we need to keep knowledge in the background, in order to refer to it when reaching the limits of our empathic understanding. We also need to recognise the limits of our own professional background and enhance it by co-operating with other professionals. Educators, psychotherapists, physicians, psychiatrists and carers, they all can learn from each other – on condition that they share the same basic attitude of accepting and respecting the individuality and 'otherness' in a person with special needs.

As we all well know, there is no formula in the mode of 'if... then'. In practice, the different points that have been described do not occur in isolation, but are interwoven, interdependent, and in various combinations. To conclude my considerations, this complexity is illustrated by the following examples.

Brian

Brian, 20, suffers from a rare chromosome aberration. He recently moved from his parents' house to a supported-living unit. On one of his first Friday evenings there, the carers let him go to the pub by himself, and with more money in his pocket than he could handle. Brian could not cope with the situation; he did what he saw the other men doing there: drinking one beer after the other. He ended up totally drunk, at the police station. When Brian's parents reproached the carers, saying that they were irresponsible to let Brian get into a situation that he was not capable of handling adequately, the answer was: 'We are a learning unit, not a behaviour unit.' With justification, the parents were upset: 'It is wrong to split a person up in this way. Intellect, feeling and environment are interconnected and come together as a whole, which is expressed as behaviour. When carers only consider one aspect of the personality, they create a real problem.'

Fred

The fact that many persons with Down syndrome tend to suffer from fatigability is, unfortunately, not always sufficiently known to carers. Fred, 22, has Down syndrome, and during the psychotherapy session frequently has to fight against falling asleep. Yet he refuses the therapist's suggestion to relax for a minute and close his eyes. 'No,' he says resolutely, 'It's okay, I can pull myself together.' That's what he is always told, when the same happens to him at work or in his residential facility. The psychotherapist is perplexed to hear about Fred's schedule for this day: therapy session, a meeting with the staff, music lesson – all this after a full working day. Obviously, the carers do not realise that they should consider Fred's fatigability when planning his schedule. Moreover, at work or during group activities, he should be allowed to relax for a few minutes when he is about to fall asleep. The staff should show him how to do that, instead of telling him to pull himself together. It would be to everybody's benefit, as this way Fred could certainly work more efficiently than if he is using all his energy to fight drowsiness. Hopefully the psychotherapist will find a good way to communicate with the staff about Fred's problem and to convince them to handle it more satisfactorily by helping him to adequately deal with it, instead of fighting it. In situations like this, it is important that the therapist does not come from a position of 'I know better', but shows empathy and understanding for the carers also.

Kerstin

Kerstin, 35, lives in a supported-living apartment. She has learning disabilities (but there is no information about when and why this was first diagnosed) and serious psychological disorders. She hears voices that persistently derogate her in a most painful way. About a year ago, she felt suicidal and, at her own wish, was hospitalised for some weeks at a psychiatric clinic. Since then she has medication, and for that is seeing a psychiatrist every two or three months. She also has taken up seeing her former psychotherapist again every two weeks. She still hears voices but, due to medication, they are no longer as loud and persistent as they had been. This is a relief. But, on the other hand, medication makes her very tired, passive, and even depressive sometimes. She is too intimidated to tell the psychiatrist about it, even though he asked her and seems really interested to know. In this situation, it is helpful that the psychotherapist, with Kerstin's consent, communicates with the psychiatrist so that he can decide about changing either the medication or its dosage. After a while, Kerstin feels better, if still somehow subdued. The voices are more persistent again, but it seems to a tolerable extent.

Kerstin (at least up until now) is neither intellectually nor emotionally in a position to work on these voices and perhaps discover what they mean. But at least she is able to talk about how they belittle her and are sometimes more, sometimes less, troublesome. The therapist encourages Kerstin to not just listen to the voices, but also to address them when they get too bad: for example, to try to contradict them or tell them to shut up. Though this will not stop the voices, it fosters the client's contact with herself and makes her discover that she has a little influence on them too. Sometimes they take it with humour. 'How are they behaving this week?' the therapist asks. The client smiles. 'More or less,' she says, 'but it is ok. Mostly I manage to just not listen.' It is a small, yet very important step for the client to be aware that she has some power over the voices, be it only to smile at them from time to time and not listen. She no longer feels entirely at their mercy but has gained a little more scope of action; this makes her feel a lot better.

Thomas

Thomas, 40, lives in a supported-living facility and works in a sheltered workshop. His psychological disorders are obvious, but with him too, nothing is known about when and why he was originally diagnosed as 'mentally handicapped'. He seems rather intelligent, but has a speech defect (probably due to his operated-on harelip). It had been the carers' idea that Thomas should see a psychotherapist. They were worried about his psychological problems and his sometimes extremely strange behaviour, and felt it to be too much for them to deal with. The first time Thomas came to the psychotherapist, he just sat there, completely withdrawn and breathing heavily. He did not say anything and did not look at the therapist once. To the few questions she asked, he answered: 'I don't know.' However, to her surprise, he came back, and, despite the next sessions being not much different from the first, gradually a therapeutic relationship began to develop. Thomas started to sometimes say something, never about himself, but perhaps about the weather or something he had heard on the news. He often asked the therapist questions. With him, she felt it more necessary to respond than is usual in a therapeutic setting. At that time, it was, for Thomas, the only possible way to gradually establish contact and trust. Moreover, by the therapist telling him something about herself, a bridge was built over which he could be encouraged to talk about how he thought or felt as well. So, very slowly and in tiny steps, he came more into contact with his own experience and feelings.

It soon became obvious that Thomas suffered from the so-called bipolar disorder (formerly known as manic-depressive disorder). His depressive phases were so extreme, and he was suffering so much, that nothing could really reach him in those times. When it got too bad, he even skipped the therapy session. Nevertheless, he went to work, but in the evening and at the weekend locked himself up in his room and remained inaccessible to the carers.

With time, he could at least afterwards tell the therapist a little about how he had felt and that he had been 'in a deep black hole'. More was not possible. The therapist could only be there, and feel and bear the black hole with him. The manic phases were less extreme; he was just quite vivid and talked a lot. With time, the depressive phases seemed to become a little less severe. 'I was in a hole, but not that deep,' he said. Once, in a phase when he was talking a lot, he observed at the end of the session: 'Today I did not say anything about myself,' and seemed to regret it. And another time, after having talked – very briefly – about something that bothered him, he said: 'This was a good conversation, don't you think so?' Obviously, there was some progress.

Yet, even as the depressive phases became less pronounced, he still sometimes suffered terribly. He took it bravely, saying: 'I shall come through, I always have.' The therapist felt that medication might help him over the worst periods, and suggested that he should see a psychiatrist, who had experience with mentally disabled patients and was known for his subtly differentiated way to prescribe medication. But Thomas refused. He had once had a bad experience with a psychiatrist and medication, and had been determined ever since to never see one again. So, unfortunately, he still suffers terribly from time to time, even though 'the hole is not as dark and deep anymore.'

Conclusion

There is a need for psychotherapists who are willing and able to work with persons with special needs because many of them suffer from psychological disorders. The large variety of very different persons embraced by the term 'special needs' calls for a *subtly differentiated, individual approach* in psychotherapy, as well as in everyday care. Particularly with these clients, a person-centred attitude is needed, as their strange and apparently inaccessible inner world can be approached only by empathically trying to understand their individual way of experiencing. The therapist has to be perceptive for *changes in the self-concept* and *development of the contact functions* along the therapeutic process, and to take into account some conditions that are different than for 'normal' clients. Cooperation with carers is useful and necessary because psychotherapy will not work for the clients if it is not supported by their environment.

It is crucial that psychotherapists, as well as carers, do not stress a person with special needs (and themselves) by overly high expectations, yet at the same time remain open to surprises and the possibility that a person might develop more than she is credited for, given her disability. It is necessary to be sensitively aware of, *to acknowledge and encourage even very small steps* that a disabled person succeeds in taking, in order to reinforce her self-confidence and possibly facilitate further steps.

Knowledge of psychopathology and the nature of different handicaps is useful, however, with the purpose not to pathologise people with special needs or to define limits for them but to be able to *recognise and understand existing* impairments and limitations of an individual and respond adequately. The extent, level and main focus of knowledge will, of course, differ according to different tasks and professional backgrounds. For *all* professionals working in this field, it is important to be aware of their own specific limitations and be willing to turn to and co-operate with others when at their wits' end. Instead of competing and mistrusting each other, different disciplines could learn from and complement each other – not only for the benefit of clients but also for their own. Cooperation between different professionals in this field is necessary and helpful – on condition that there is common agreement *not to aim at remodelling* persons with special needs along concepts of what is 'normal', but at improving their wellbeing and quality of life and *enabling them to be themselves* and find *their* best way to cope with reality.

References

Badelt I (1984). Selbsterfahrungsgruppen geistig behinderter erwachsener. *Geistige Behinderung 23*: 243–253.

Badelt I (1990). Client-centered psychotherapy with mentally handicapped adults. In: Lietaer G, Rombauts J, van Balen R (eds). *Client-Centered and Experiential Psychotherapy in the Nineties.* Leuven: Leuven University Press (pp671–681).

Badelt I (1994). Die klientenzentrierte psychotherapie mit geistig behinderten menschen. In: Lotz W, Koch U, Stahl B (eds). *Psychotherapeutische Behandlung Geistig Behinderter Menschen. Bedarf, rahmenbedingungen, konzepte.* Bern: Hans Huber (pp141–152).

Eggert D (1993). Veränderungen im bild von der geistigen behinderung in der psychologie. In: Hennicke K, Rotthaus W (eds). *Psychotherapie und Geistige Behinderung*. Dortmund: verlag modernes lernen (pp204–218).

Gaedt C (ed) (1987). *Psychotherapie bei geistig Behinderten*. 2. Neuerkeröder Forum. Neuerkeröder Anstalten. Eigenverlag.

Görres S (1996). Ethische Fragen in der Psychotherapie mit geistig behinderten Menschen. In: Lotz W, Stahl B, Irblich D (eds). *Wege zur seelischen Gesundheit für Menschen mit geistiger Behinderung – Psychotherapie und Persönlichkeitsentwicklung*. Bern: Hans Huber (pp29–39).

Berry P, Gunn VP, Andrews RJ (1984). The development of Down syndrome children from birth to five years. In: Berg JM (ed). *Perspectives and Progress in Mental Retardation. Vol 1: Social, psychological and educational aspects*. Baltimore: University Press (pp167–177).

Hennicke K, Rotthaus W (eds) (1993). *Psychotherapie und Geistige Behinderung*. Dortmund: verlag modernes lernen.

Irblich D (1999). Gewalt und geistige Behinderung. *Geistige Behinderung 2*: 132–145.

Koukkou M, Lehmann D (1998). Ein systemtheoretisch orientiertes modell der funktionen des menschlichen gehirns und die ontogenese des verhaltens. In: Koukkou M, Leuzinger-Bohleber M, Mertens W (eds). *Erinnerung von Wirklichkeiten. Psychoanalyse und neurowissenschaften im dialog. Vol. 1*. Stuttgart: Verlag Internationale Psychoanalyse (pp287–415).

Krietemeyer B (2000). Wege aus der inneren Isolation. *Kerbe 2*: 21–22.

Krietemeyer B, Prouty G (2003). The art of psychological contact: the psychotherapy of a retarded psychotic client. *Person-Centered and Experiential Psychotherapies 2*: 151–161.

Lotz W, Koch U (1994). Zum Vorkommen psychischer Störungen bei Personen mit geistiger Behinderung. In: Lotz W, Koch U, Stahl B (eds). *Psychotherapeutische Behandlung geistig behinderter Menschen – Bedarf, Rahmenbedingungen, Konzepte*. Bern: Hans Huber (pp13–39).

Lotz W, Koch U, Stahl B (eds) (1994). *Psychotherapeutische Behandlung geistig behinderter Menschen – Bedarf, Rahmenbedingungen, Konzepte*. Bern: Hans Huber.

Lotz W, Stahl B, Irblich D (eds) (1996). *Wege zur Seelischen Gesundheit für Menschen mit geistiger Behinderung – Psychotherapie und Persönlichkeitsentwicklung*. Bern: Hans Huber.

Peters H (1992). *Psychotherapie bij geestelijk gehandicapten*. Amsterdam/Lisse: Swets, Zeitlinger. German edition (2001). *Psychotherapeutische Zugänge zu Menschen mit Geistiger Behinderung*. Stuttgart: Klett-Cotta.

Pörtner M (1984). Gesprächstherapie mit geistig behinderten Klienten. *Brennpunkt 18*: 6–23 und in *GwG-info 56*: 20–30.

Pörtner M (1990). Client-centered therapy with mentally retarded people: Catherine and Ruth. In: Lietaer G, Rombauts J, van Balen R (eds). *Client-Centered and Experiential Psychotherapy in the Nineties*. Leuven: Leuven University Press (pp659–669).

Pörtner M (1994). *Praxis der Gesprächspsychotherapie. Interviews mit Therapeuten*. Stuttgart: Klett-Cotta.

Pörtner M (1996a). *Ernstnehmen, Zutrauen, Verstehen – Personzentrierte Haltung im Umgang mit geistig behinderten und pflegebedürftigen Menschen* (11th ed 2017). Stuttgart: Klett-Cotta. Dutch edition (1998). *Serieus Nemen, Vertrouwen, Begrijpen*. Maarssen: Elsevier/De Tijdstroom. English edition (2000 see below). Danish edition (2003). *Den Personcentrerede Metode i Arbejdet med Sindslidende, Undviklingshaemmende og Demente Mennesker*. Kopenhagen: Reitzels. French edition (2010) *Écouter, Comprendre, Encourager. L'approche centrée sur la personne*. Lyon: Chronique Sociale.

Pörtner M (1996b). Working with the mentally handicapped in a person-centered way – is it possible, is it appropriate and what does it mean in practice? In: Hutterer R, Pawlowsky G, Schmid PF, Stipsits R (eds).

Client-Centered and Experiential Psychotherapy: a paradigm in motion. Frankfurt am Main: Peter Lang, Europäischer Verlag der Wissenschaften (pp513–527).

Pörtner M (2000). *Trust and Understanding: the person-centred approach to everyday care for people with special needs* (2nd revised and extended edition 2007). Ross-on-Wye: PCCS Books.

Pörtner M (2001). The person-centred approach in working with people with special needs. *Person-Centred Practice 9*: 18–30.

Pörtner M (2002a). Der personzentrierte Ansatz in der Arbeit mit geistig behinderten Menschen. In: Keil W, Stumm G (hrsg). *Der Personzentrierte Ansatz in der Psychotherapie. Die vielen Gesichter der klientenzentrierten Psychotherapie.* Wien: Springer (pp511–532).

Pörtner, M (2002b). Psychotherapy for people with special needs: a challenge for client-centered psychotherapists. In: Watson JC, Goldman RN, Warner MS (eds). *Client-Centered and Experiential Psychotherapy in the 21st Century: advances in theory, research and practice.* Ross-on-Wye: PCCS Books (pp380–386).

Pörtner M (2003). *Brücken Bauen. Menschen mit geistiger behinderung verstehen und begleiten* (3rd ed 2015). Stuttgart: Klett-Cotta.

Pörtner M (2005). *Alt sein ist anders. Personzentrierte Betreuung von alten Menschen.* (4th ed 2016). Stuttgart: Klett-Cotta. English edition (2008 see below). French edition (2012) *Accompangnement des Personnes Agées avec L'approche Centrée sur la Personne.* Lyon: Chronique Sociale.

Pörtner M (2008). *Being Old is Different. Person-centred care for old people.* Ross-on-Wye: PCCS Books.

Prouty G (1994). *Theoretical Evolutions in Person-Centered/Experiential Therapy – applications to schizophrenic and retarded psychoses.* Westport: Praeger.

Prouty G (1998). Pre-therapy and the pre-expressive self. *Person Centred Practice 6:* 80–88.

Prouty G, Van Werde D, Pörtner M (1998). *Prä-Therapie.* Stuttgart: Klett-Cotta. English edition (2002) *Pre-Therapy: reaching contact-impaired clients.* Ross-on-Wye: PCCS Books.

Rogers CR (1942). *Counseling and Psychotherapy.* Boston: Houghton Mifflin.

Rotthaus W (1993). *Menschenbild und psychische krankheit des geistigbehinderten aus systemischer sicht.* In: Hennicke K, Rotthaus W (hrsg) (1993). *Psychotherapie und Geistige Behinderung.* Dortmund: verlag modernes lernen (pp195–203).

Senckel B (1998). *Du bist ein weiter Baum – Entwicklungschancen für geistig behinderte Menschen durch Beziehung.* München: Beck.

Sinason V (1992). *Mental Handicap and the Human Condition.* London: Free Association Books.

Stahl B (1996). Zum Stand der Entwicklung in der Psychotherapie mit geistig behinderten Menschen. In: Lotz W, Stahl B, Irblich D, (hrsg) (1996). *Wege zur seelischen Gesundheit für Menschen mit geistiger Behinderung – Psychotherapie und Persönlichkeitsentwicklung.* Bern: Hans Huber (pp14–28).

Thimm W (1999). Epidemologie und soziokulturelle Faktoren. In: Neuhäuser G, Steinhausen H-C. *Geistige Behinderung. Grundlagen. Klinische Syndrome. Behandlung und Rehabilitation.* 2. überarbeitete und erweiterte Auflage. Stuttgart: W Kohlhammer (pp9–25).

Van Werde D (1998). Anchorage as a core concept in working with psychotic people. In: Thorne B, Mearns D, Lambers E (eds). *Person-Centred Therapy: a European perspective.* London: Sage.

Van Werde D, Morton I (1999). The relevance of Prouty's pre-therapy to dementia care. In: Morton I (ed). *Person-Centred Approaches to Dementia Care.* Bicester: Winslow Press (pp139–166).

18 | Children and the autism spectrum: person-centred approaches

Jacky Knibbs and Anja Rutten

This chapter will consider some of the fundamental tenets of person-centred thinking in relation to autism and children. While client-centred psychotherapists do not routinely take developmental histories or assess or diagnose clients, we will argue here that these aspects of professional practice have a particularly important function with people on the autism spectrum. Having a framework for shared understanding, and access to others with similar experiences, may provide opportunities both for clients' growth and for congruence, empathic understanding and unconditional positive regard from therapists and surrounding systems.

In appropriately informed advocacy for children and their families, particularly in the educational system, assessment drawn from the clinical and research evidence base helps the systems around the child appreciate and convey the complexity of their internal frames of reference. The person-centred perspective is central in recognising each individual's uniqueness, and in achieving true empathic understanding (Rogers, 1957). It also provides a model for considering the complex conditions of worth and accompanying challenges for individuals with social learning difficulties. While autism does not have, or need, a 'cure', optimal recognition may contribute to preventing or ameliorating additional mental health difficulties, and help individuals realise their social potential. The essential aim of our work is to achieve conditions where clients feel accepted and valued, listened to and understood, not judged or required to conform to inappropriate expectations.

Autism and Asperger syndrome

Aetiology

The autism spectrum is continuing to receive growing popular (Haddon, 2003; Hoopmann, 2001; Ryan, 2015; Simsion, 2014), clinical and research attention.

Evidence relating to the aetiology of autism has shifted considerably over time, with Bruno Bettelheim's notion of 'refrigerator mothers' (Bettelheim, 1967) now supplanted by neurodevelopmental findings. Strong evidence suggests that the autism spectrum is biological in origin, and not caused by parenting or other psychosocial, environmental causes (Boucher, 2009).

Some psychoanalytic authors (eg. Tustin, 1991) have argued that impoverishment in emotional nurturing (whether environmentally or constitutionally determined) is a precursor to the development of autism as a 'sensation-dominated' state of being. It is possible that, in a minority of cases, extreme environmental events (for example, significant early abuse) impact on the developing baby's brain to create or exacerbate the neurodevelopmental conditions for autism (Glaser, 2000; Rutter et al, 1999). Three typical potential biological causes have been identified (Attwood, 2007): namely, unfavourable obstetric events, infections during pregnancy or early infancy that affect the brain, and genetic factors. Differences have been found in the size and organisation of the brain, as well as how it works in people on the autism spectrum in comparison with 'neurotypical' individuals. There is increasing evidence from neuropsychological assessment and brain imaging (Brothers, 1997; Frith & Frith 2003) that the frontal and temporal lobes are implicated in the processing of social and emotional information. There may be quite precise areas of unusual functioning in the frontal lobes that produce the pattern of behaviour and abilities associated with the autism spectrum (Frith, 2003; 2004; Happé et al, 1996; Volkmar et al, 2004).

Early research involving the study of twin pairs has demonstrated a genetic predisposition to autism: if one twin has autism, the likelihood of the other twin having autism is far higher for identical (monozygotic) twins than for non-identical (dizygotic) twins (Folstein & Rutter, 1977). It has also been found that autism is 50 times more common in the siblings of people with autism (Smalley, Asarnow & Spence, 1988). The precise means of genetic transmission have not been identified (Pickles et al, 1995; Volkmar et al, 2004). What appears to be transmitted is not autism per se, but a distinctive process: ie. a style of thinking, relating and reacting to the world that brings with it limitations and strengths (Baron-Cohen, 2003; Dorris et al, 2004). To date, however, no signature pattern – one that is universal and specific to the autism spectrum – has been found. This is not surprising, given the very wide diversity of people so described (Waterhouse & Gillberg, 2014). In any event, what causes autism does not affect the daily living experiences of those who are on the autism spectrum and their families, and it may be argued that 'autism process' is a more helpful construct than more conventional diagnostic endeavours (Rutten, 2014). We think that the distinctive way of thinking in autism is best understood through the lens of neurodevelopmental process. While person-centred approaches are not able to account for the aetiology of these core difficulties, we will argue that people on the autism spectrum are subject to heightened conditions of worth, which lead to a range of associated difficulties in living. This is where the person-centred perspective has an important contribution to make in helping the person find self-acceptance, value their differences, and develop their strengths.

Difficulties associated with autism

There is evidence that a core difficulty for individuals on the autism spectrum is related to the development of their theory of mind (Baron-Cohen, 1995; Scheeren et al, 2013), although there are also critics of this position (Timimi, Gardner & McCabe, 2011; Waterhouse & Gillberg, 2014). Autism is seen as a specific social and emotional learning style, where understanding the perspectives, emotions and worlds of others may not develop spontaneously. From the age of around four years, children understand that other people have thoughts, knowledge, beliefs and desires that will influence their behaviour. Children on the autism spectrum appear to have some difficulties in conceptualising and appreciating the thoughts and feelings of another person. They may not realise that their comments may cause offence or embarrassment, or that an apology would help to remedy a mistake (Attwood, 2007). This is often accompanied by problems in making sense of their own experiences and emotional states (Hill, Berthoz & Frith, 2004), and in seeking out ways of developing understanding. Temple Grandin has explained:

> I prefer factual, non-fictional reading materials. I have little interest in novels with complicated interpersonal relationships. When I do read novels, I prefer straightforward stories that occur in interesting places with lots of description. (1992: 123)

There is also research and clinical evidence that people on the autism spectrum may be aware of other people's thoughts and feelings but struggle to apply this knowledge effectively (Bowler, 1992; Scheeren et al, 2013). It is possible to appreciate at an intellectual level what a person may be thinking or feeling, but not recognise readily what behaviour is appropriate to the situation. This has been described as problems with a central drive for coherence (selecting focus on gist or detail) and of executive function (which includes flexible shifting of attention) – in this context, seeing the relevance of different types of knowledge to a particular problem (Frith & Happé, 1994; Hoy, Hatton & Hare, 2004). Attwood (2007) cites an example of how a child on the autism spectrum who has taken the favourite toy of another child without permission, when asked how they think the other child will feel, may give an appropriate answer, yet this awareness seemed not to be in their mind when they took the toy. Thus, knowledge may be available but not recognised as relevant. This is where psychoeducation – for example, in the form of social stories that make social rules explicit – has been found helpful (Gray, 1998; Gray & White, 2002).

There are also particular vulnerabilities associated with the autism spectrum (Berney, 2004; Eriksson et al, 2013). People on the spectrum are more likely to have a range of accompanying difficulties, some of which may be also neurodevelopmentally determined, such as epilepsy (Levisohn, 2007), dyspraxia, and attention deficit hyperactivity disorder (Goldstein & Schwebach, 2004; Rao & Landa, 2014; Tantam, 2000, 2003). Also, some problems may be exacerbated by the incongruence between individuals and their surroundings. High anxiety (Dubin, Liebermann-Betz & Lease, 2015; Gillott, Furniss & Walter, 2001; Kim et al, 2000), depression (Ghaziuddin & Greden, 1998; Salazar et al, 2015) and obsessive compulsive disorders (Baron-Cohen, 1989; Hollander et al, 2003) are common. Finally, people on the autism spectrum are more likely to experience exclusion or victimisation (Dubin, 2006). David Andrews has a diagnosis of Asperger syndrome, and writes:

> It is supremely important to value the Asperger autistic client and his or her experience and to realise that this experience will (in most cases) have been particularly nasty at some point. So, when such a client is showing signs of anxiety or depression, it is important that these problems not be attributed to 'the biochemistry of autism' or even to the autism itself. The problems come from how the client is experiencing society. (Andrews, 2004: 27)

Diffability rather than disability

While the autism spectrum is now considered to be a much broader phenomenon (Volkmar et al, 2004; Wing, 2002), than when first described (Asperger, 1944; Kanner, 1943), the language associated with diagnosis in the medical and psychoanalytical models often continues to be essentially deficit driven (Alvarez, 1996; Baird, Cass & Slonims, 2003). A dyad of impairments is now outlined as diagnostic criteria for autism in the current edition of the *Diagnostic and Statistical Manual of Mental Disorders* (*DSM-5*) (American Psychiatric Association, 2013; Smith, Reichow & Volkmar, 2015). In the UK, the *International Classification of Mental and Behavioural Disorders* (*ICD-10*; *CD-11* is expected to be out in 2017) (World Health Organization, 1992) includes the more traditionally recognised triad of impairment: namely, qualitative impairments in social communication, social interaction and social imagination, with a restricted range of interests and often stereotyped repetitive behaviours and mannerisms (Baird, Cass & Slonims, 2003).

Asperger syndrome is currently under review as a diagnosis; it has historically been used to describe people presenting with the same pattern of development without an accompanying clinically significant general cognitive or language disorder (Wing, 1981). *DSM-5* does not now include Asperger syndrome as a diagnosis, but there is a both a wealth of research and literature on Asperger syndrome and a significant group of individuals and groups who have assimilated this descriptor as part of their identity. Recent evidence of the broader phenotypes of the autism spectrum proposes that aspects and degrees of autism are experienced by many people (Baron-Cohen, 2003; Dorris et al, 2004). It could be argued that these controversies help to underscore the fundamental lack of usefulness of these diagnostic categorisations. The argument in this chapter is that, by linking with the clinical, educational, research and advocacy worlds of those described as being on the autism spectrum, therapists working in this field are much better equipped to experience empathic understanding; to appreciate and respond appropriately to the client's very individual internal frame of reference, and to facilitate their potential for personal growth.

There is a growing range of first-hand accounts from individuals on the autism spectrum (Grandin, 1992, 1995; Olinkiewicz, 2012; O'Neill, 1998a; Schneider, 1999) and accompanying pleas to be considered different rather than impaired (Baron-Cohen, 2000). Wenn Lawson argues for recognition of the autism spectrum as a 'diffability' rather than disability (Lawson, 2001). References to the worlds of people with autism as being very distinct from that of the 'neurotypical' population presumes an 'us and them' dichotomy that may not in itself be helpful. Wenn Lawson's experience is of being chronically misunderstood and misdiagnosed (treated with powerful antipsychotics for schizophrenia for 25 years, with debilitating side effects). This, and the more recent acknowledgement of gender dysphoria, perhaps allow a better understanding of what it is to feel essentially different. In his book introducing a humanistic approach to autism, Stillman (2003) seeks to 'demystify the autistic experience'. He describes clearly the process of discovery of his own Asperger syndrome and his very particular, all-consuming enthusiasm as a child for *The Wizard of Oz*. He now acts as a consultant, helping to present an autism spectrum perspective. Although the generalisability of autobiographical accounts has to be considered carefully (Happé, 1991), these texts provide invaluable insights into others' diverse internal frames of reference (Hale, 1998; Hall, 2001; Hoy, 2007; Jackson, 2002). While there are times when receipt of a diagnosis is devastating for families and individuals, there are also many instances when it is described as a relief, and even life-enhancing and affirming. The thrust of most of these personal accounts is that we do not abandon identification or diagnosis, but that we aim for a much more widespread understanding of the complexity, interest and challenge of atypical worlds (Armstrong, 2010), as demonstrated here:

> I tried asking questions to find out if there was anything tangibly the matter with me. I had this vague, insistent idea all the time – that there was something wrong with me. But questions that to me were deeply serious were answered in amused voices: 'Oh, no, there's nothing wrong with you, dear.' (Gerland, 1997: 127)

Claire Sainsbury (2009) writes powerfully about her experiences, and argues for honesty and acceptance:

> Because of our great difficulties in deciphering the social world by ourselves, we are particularly dependent on receiving accurate information from adults.

Any child with Asperger's who is old enough to understand a simple verbal explanation of their condition is also old enough, if they don't get such an explanation, to notice that they are different from their 'normal' peers, and that they have difficulty doing things which seem to be easy for 'normal' children. Often they will infer that there must be something wrong with them. Many people with Asperger's concluded as children that they must be 'stupid', 'crazy', 'retarded', 'brain-damaged', or that what was wrong with them must be so awful that no one would talk about it. A label is the key to self-understanding. A label lets a child know that their disability is not their fault; it lets them know that their problem has a name; and it lets them know that there are others out there like them. Accurate self-understanding is vital if a child is to take control and learn how to manage and work around their problems and make the best use of their strengths. Becoming aware of how one functions and of how others may perceive one's behaviour is essential if a child is to be able to begin to develop their own creative solutions of the problems they may come across, instead of being perpetually dependent on others for help. Knowledge, as Francis Bacon pointed out, is power... It is important not to give the impression that everything about Asperger syndrome is known, or that one knows the child better than they know themselves, but to recognize and help a child to articulate their own knowledge of how they function – to empower them to become experts on their own condition. (Sainsbury, 2009: 125–128)

Gunilla Gerland too makes a plea for a person-centred perspective in this process:

... you are not best helped if the people around you... act as experts telling you that they know exactly what your condition is. What you need is guiding from them to come to your own truth, and to develop your personal approach to your condition. (Gerland, 2000: 4)

As described in detail elsewhere, person-centred theory presents the core belief that the client is expert (Joseph, 2003; Rogers, 1957); this maps neatly on what people on the autism spectrum say they need from practitioners.

Identification

The initial challenge in work with children on the autism spectrum is identifying clearly those for whom this is an appropriate description (Noland & Gabriels, 2004). Children may present in a range of different ways and to different services; one of the significant advances outlined in Lorna Wing's seminal paper (Wing, 1981) is the emphasis on the diversity of individuals affected and the importance of the concept of a spectrum of difference (Armstrong, 2010; Silberman, 2015). A key question in person-centred thinking is whether it is in the child's best interests to be identified, labelled and diagnosed. Parents often struggle with the dilemma of whether they are creating more harm by presenting their child to professionals or 'specialists' and highlighting their difference. Where a child has accompanying, evident physical or learning difficulties, it may be recognised early on that different expectations and demands are required. However, particularly in high-functioning people (often described as having Asperger syndrome), distinctive patterns of development are often misunderstood; Peacock and colleagues (1996) refer to the autism spectrum as the 'invisible handicap'. As a consequence, individuals may be exposed to a more than usual extent to social conditions of worth. In social environments that demand compliance and cooperation, such as schools, youngsters with distinctive social learning styles are immediately significantly disadvantaged (Marshall & Goodall, 2015; O'Connor & Kirk, 2008; Tierney, Burns & Kilby, 2011). At the same time, their behaviour is often misinterpreted as bloody-mindedness, or a consequence of poor parenting. In extreme cases, unusual or bizarre behaviours may be misattributed to child abuse, particularly where there are complex family circumstances.

It is sometimes possible in very child-centred environments for children on the autism spectrum to thrive, and for any differences to be acceptable and, indeed, applauded (Holliday Willey, 1999, 2001; Weiss & Riosa, 2015). Unfortunately, it is rare that both home and school are able to provide these optimal conditions. Children may respond well to high levels of structure and predictability at school, but struggle with the more emotionally-laden climate of home life – particularly when there are demanding younger siblings (Wood Rivers & Stoneman, 2003). Alternatively, home may provide a sanctuary, and school a setting where the child feels overwhelmed (Carrington & Graham, 2001). While a utopian position is clearly that each person's individuality is respected, current reality is that the social, communicative and behavioural characteristics of the autism spectrum often differentiate children and adults very explicitly (Winters-Messiers, 2007). The argument here for working within the model we currently have is that early identification may encourage a better understanding of the complex inner worlds of vulnerable children, along with the unconditional positive regard that grows from enhanced appreciation of other people's positions and strengths.

Assessment

One of the key features of the autism spectrum is the complexity and diversity of individuals so described. It has been suggested that this is potentially the most severe of all child mental health presentations (Baron-Cohen, 2000). It could be argued that the concept of a broad spectrum is so over-inclusive as to limit significantly its usefulness. The crucial task of assessment here is to reflect the client's individuality. Evidence suggests that autism may include a range of complex and subtle neuropsychological presentations (Liss et al, 2001; Manjiviona & Prior, 1999). Unusual sensory experiences are poorly researched (Schaaf &

Lane, 2015), but feature largely in first-hand and anecdotal accounts of living with the autism spectrum (Grandin, 1992). For non-verbal people, or those who are unable to articulate their experiences, it is likely that aversive sensory stimulation is contributing to clients' distress, which may then be translated into challenging behaviour (Clements & Zarkowska, 2000).

A central requirement of practice from the person-centred perspective is to have an empathic understanding of the client's unique frame of reference. We argue that to understand as fully as possible each child's unique presentation (Jacobsen, 2003), different sources of evidence should be accessed. Direct contact with the child may be supplemented with parent, sibling, teacher and significant other accounts, and observations of the child in different settings may yield a range of clues to their very specific profile. While this assumption of others' expertise may not sit comfortably with a traditional person-centred view, one important aspect of the autism spectrum is the challenge of effective communication. It may be possible to build an empathic understanding of the client's internal world by experience, trial and error, but this may be undervaluing the real complexity of some clients' developmental profiles (McKelvey et al, 1995). Indeed, in more extreme instances where the child experiences social contact as highly aversive, an appropriate empathic perspective may be best achieved initially by less direct means than face-to-face contact. Howlin (2000) and Le Couteur and Baird (2003) describe some of the assessment options currently available, as do the most recent NICE guidelines (2011).

Impact of diagnosis

The diagnosis of autism is both much more widespread currently, and generally more acceptable than it once was. The latter is likely to be a result of high-profile media debate, a general demystifying of the condition, pioneering work of advocacy groups and the first-hand account literature, which is beginning to celebrate autism (Elder, 2005). Berney (2004) provides a useful discussion of some of the issues to consider, particularly for high-functioning individuals. The professional world abounds with confusing and unhelpful diagnostic terms – pervasive developmental disorders, semantic-pragmatic language disorder (Bishop, 1989), pathological demand avoidance syndrome (Newson, Marechal & David, 2003), and schizotypal personality disorder, to name but a few. While some parents may be able to understand these more esoteric descriptions and their children may benefit from an enhanced understanding, many don't find them helpful. The crucial task is to find a shared language that promotes access to appropriate conditions, expectations and resources (Armstrong, 2010; Jackson, 2003; Silberman, 2015). We have an additional responsibility to be open and clear with children and young people themselves, and to use language that is comprehensible and acceptable (Durà-Vilà & Levi, 2013; Ives, 1999; Vermeulen, 2000). When diagnoses are explained to clients appropriately (Jackson, 2002; Jones, 2001), it can be liberating – as outlined by Sainsbury (2009) above. Equally, some youngsters find this process highly aversive and are overwhelmed by their need for acceptance and their struggles with difference. The following examples illustrate the range of difficulties that may be experienced and the potential impact of diagnosis for the child and family.

> Claire was aged 16 at diagnosis. She was a bright young person who was failing badly in school, in spite of her clear intellectual ability. She came from a somewhat alternative family, with intellectual interests. Claire had a very intense interest in science and a love of philosophy and war games. At home, her interests were accepted and encouraged. However, she had been severely bullied in school because of her difference from her teenage peers. Claire greeted the diagnosis with relief, explaining that she was very tired of trying to fit in with others her age, and that she was angry about the lack of acceptance of her right to be different. Within the family, the diagnosis was less acceptable because difference was not a problem. After diagnosis, Claire moved on to college to study for GCSEs and was provided with a package of support to help her organise and complete her academic work.

> Robert was aged 12 at diagnosis. He had been diagnosed with dyslexia in primary school and his unusual behaviour was accommodated in a school that had many children with behavioural problems. Robert had been excluded from secondary school in his first term and had not attended since. He had become reclusive, barely leaving the house and finding it impossible to tolerate any visitors. Even family members were unwelcome if they called at the wrong time or on the wrong day. Robert's siblings had moulded around him, frustrated by his aggressive and intolerant behaviour and embarrassed by his behaviour in public, but very aware that he could not manage without their support. His behaviour was understood in terms of a stress reaction and his family began to accept that the adjustments they had made instinctively were necessary for Robert, rather than an indication of their failure to help him socialise.

> Craig was diagnosed at nine years. He relied heavily on his younger sister to help him socialise and look after him in the playground at school. When he moved into a different area of the school and she could no longer do this, Craig's social difficulties became much more evident. His family were accepting of the diagnosis, feeling that their son's intellectual ability far outstripped his social problem-solving skills. They were able to help him to develop more independence and tried to relieve his sister of some of the responsibility she had taken for him.

Person-centred systems and support

Rogers (1957) emphasises that it is how the individual perceives reality that is important, and that the best vantage point for understanding a person is that person. The perception of reality argument is a potent one here, given the awareness that it is precisely their unique and distinctive perceptions of reality that differentiate individuals on the autism spectrum (Jackson, 2002). Crucial to this is the therapist's readiness to be sensitive to and follow the client's agenda. Children as young as three years old are frequently observed to be very strongly pursuing their own preferences, with apparent disregard or avoidance of the wishes of those around them (Newson, Marechal & David, 2003). The challenge for others is to find ways to communicate effectively with a child who may have a particularly limited sense of how other people function.

The Autism Education Trust (2011) emphasises, as one of the fundamentals of person-centred planning (Mount, 2000), the need to see people in the context of their local community. It could therefore be argued that the necessary and sufficient conditions of constructive personality growth described by Rogers (1957) might be extended to encompass systems surrounding the child with autism, as follows:

- the child is in psychological contact with siblings and parents at home and peers and adults at school
- the child is in a state of incongruence, being vulnerable or anxious
- home and school systems are congruent or integrated in the relationship
- siblings, parents, peers and teachers experience unconditional positive regard for the child
- individuals around the child experience an empathic understanding of the child's internal frame of reference and endeavour to communicate this experience to the child
- the communication to the child of the above is to a minimal degree achieved.

Using this systemic extension of the client-centred position helps to focus on key areas for development. The experience of the person with autism is very typically that of being misunderstood, alienated or marginalised. The titles of relevant accounts reflect this: *My World is Not Your World* (Hale, 1998); *Martian in the Playground* (Sainsbury, 2009); *Through the Eyes of Aliens* (O'Neill, 1998b), and accounts of bullying and peer difficulties are widespread (Bauminger & Kasari, 2000; Little, 2001). Appropriate psychoeducational interventions may be targeted at addressing these 'system deficits' by attempting to represent and describe what life is like for people with autism. This typically may involve advocacy in schools, aimed at peers and staff (Barron & Barron, 1992; Bozic, Croft & Mason-Williams, 2002; Dubin, 2006; Jackson, 2002; Lord, 1995; Stillman, 2003). Stillman writes:

> In my work as a consultant, I'm certain that initially I bewilder and disappoint those who are under the impression that my purpose is to 'fix' the person. Nothing could be further than the truth. My presence is as an agent of

transformation to shift the team's perceptions of the person in a kind and gentle manner. When this occurs truly, the person cannot help but to respond positively to the new ways in which others are demonstrating respect and interacting differently. This is when the seeds of change for all concerned may begin to bud and blossom. (Stillman, 2003: 9)

Families also often ask for help to support siblings (Pilowsky et al, 2004). Here, again, information about the complex worlds and challenges facing youngsters on the autism spectrum may be very helpful (Davies, 1994; Gorrod, 1997; Harris, 1996; Walton & Ingersoll, 2015).

Groups

Psychoeducational groups for siblings help children to understand their sibling's differences and needs, using approaches based on play, drama and relationships. At one local child and adolescent mental health service, person-centred groups are offered for children aged 10–16 years who have been diagnosed on the autism spectrum. Most of these youngsters are in mainstream school, but few have friends and even fewer have mutually supportive friendships. There are two groups, for children aged 10–13 and 13–15, each with five to eight youngsters. The aims of the groups are to reduce social isolation by providing a place where the young person is accepted and welcomed. This is in stark contrast to the life experiences these young people often report. The group provides a regular meeting place for youngsters who know their diagnosis. There is a simple structure: sharing refreshments, taking turns to give news from the previous week, and playing a game. All the children and young people are listened to in turn, and their news is valued, whatever the topic. Often issues of family and school life are raised, but so are computer games, pets and special interests. The shared social events of refreshments and a game provide a connection between group members. It also provides an opportunity to develop social and relationship skills in a naturalistic setting.

In their final school year, the young people transfer to a youth club for young adults (16–21 years), which is run by a voluntary agency. This group was designed by consulting young people with autism who were attending the groups at the child and adolescent mental health service. Their parents and the professionals working with them were also consulted about the needs of these young adults. The group is open to young people with mental health needs, but is suitable for young adults with autism because it provides a calm atmosphere and a high staffing ratio. This allows staff sufficient time to talk with young people who might take a long time to express themselves clearly. It is a place where young people can meet and feel accepted. It is accessible to those who need support and encouragement to socialise but who do want to mix with other people. One advantage of attending these groups is that young people have had an opportunity to ask questions about their diagnosis and what it means. Many myths and issues (for example, will I die from it? Will it change things at school?) have been addressed through group discussions. The questions raised have been used to develop a leaflet for young people to help them understand their diagnosis.

Strategic thinking

Service developments for people with complex needs emphasise the experience and wishes of the individual (NICE, 2011). 'The active involvement of children and parents in decisions regarding their treatment, care and service planning is seen as key to service improvement' (Department of Health, 2003: 29). 'A person-centred approach to planning means that planning should start with the individual (not with services) and take into account their wishes and aspirations' (Department of Health, 2001: 49).

Person-centred planning (Mount, 2000; Autism Education Trust, 2011) is now gaining a strong following in the development of high quality services. Sanderson et al (1997) and Sanderson, Lunt and the National Autistic Society (2009) describe five key features: the person is at the centre; family members and friends are partners in planning; the plan reflects what is important to the person, their capacities and what support they require; the plan results in actions that are about life, not just services, and that reflect what is possible, not just what is available; and, finally, the plan results in ongoing listening, learning, and further action.

Conclusions

It is argued here that it is unhelpful to discard comprehensive assessment and identification/diagnosis of people on the autism spectrum. While the diagnoses currently available are crude and incorporate unhelpful medical terminology, and while it may be difficult at times to achieve consensus, there is potentially a significant advantage to the person and their family if they are identified and understood. A person-centred perspective rejects the language of deficit, and integrates an acknowledgement and, where appropriate, celebration of difference. While the distinctive personality profile of the autism spectrum is lifelong and there are specific cognitive aspects that appear to have a genetic component, the vulnerabilities and associated difficulties that result from the heightened social conditions of worth experienced by these people may be ameliorated by a person-centred approach. A clear and comprehensive understanding of their uniqueness and its communication to them and those around them are the best way to manifest empathy and unconditional positive regard and so open the way for clients to achieve self-acceptance and positive growth.

References

Alvarez A (1996). Addressing the element of deficit in children with autism: psychotherapy which is both psychoanalytically and developmentally informed. *Clinical Psychology and Psychiatry 1*: 525–538.

American Psychiatric Association (2013). *Diagnostic and Statistical Manual of Mental Disorders* (5th ed). Washington DC: American Psychiatric Association.

Andrews D (2004). Mental health issues in Asperger syndrome: preventive mental health work in good autism practice. *Good Autism Practice 3*: 22–28.

Armstrong T (2010). *The Power of Neurodiversity: unleashing the advantages of your differently wired brain.* Cambridge, MA: Da Capo Lifelong Books.

Asperger H (1944). Die 'autistischen psychopathien' im kindesalter. *Archiv fur Psychiatrie und Nervenkrankheiten 117*: 76–136.

Attwood T (2007). *The Complete Guide to Asperger's Syndrome.* London: Jessica Kingsley Publishers.

Autism Education Trust (2011). *Person-Centred Planning.* London: Autism Education Trust.

Baird G, Cass H, Slonims V (2003). Diagnosis of autism. *British Medical Journal 327*: 488–493.

Baron-Cohen S (1989). Do autistic children have obsessions and compulsions? *British Journal of Clinical Psychology 28*: 193–200.

Baron-Cohen S (1995). *Mindblindness: an essay on autism and theory of mind.* London: MIT Press.

Baron-Cohen S (2000). Is Asperger syndrome/high-functioning autism necessarily a disability? *Development and Psychopathology 12*: 489–500.

Baron-Cohen S (2003). *The Essential Difference: men and women and the extreme male brain.* London: Allen Lane, Penguin Books.

Barron J, Barron S (1992). *There's a Boy in Here.* New York: Simon & Schuster.

Bauminger N, Kasari C (2000). Loneliness and friendship in high-functioning children with autism. *Child Development 71*: 447–456.

Berney T (2004). Asperger syndrome from childhood into adulthood. *Advances in Psychiatric Treatment 10*: 341–351.

Bettelheim B (1967). *The Empty Fortress.* New York: Free Press.

Bishop DVM (1989). Autism, Asperger's syndrome and semantic-pragmatic disorder: where are the boundaries? *British Journal of Disorders of Communication 24*: 107–121.

Boucher J (2009). *The Autistic Spectrum: characteristics, causes and practical issues.* London: Sage.

Bowler DM (1992). 'Theory of mind' in Asperger's syndrome. *Journal of Child Psychology and Psychiatry 33*: 877–893.

Bozic N, Croft A, Mason-Williams T (2002). A peer support project for an eight-year-old boy with an autistic spectrum disorder: an adaptation and extension of the Circle of Friends approach. *Good Autism Practice 3*: 22.

Brothers L (1997). *Friday's Footprint: how society shapes the human mind.* Oxford: Oxford University Press.

Carrington S, Graham L (2001). Perceptions of school by two teenage boys with Asperger syndrome and their mothers: a qualitative study. *Autism 5*: 37–48.

Clements J, Zarkowska E (2000). *Behavioural Concerns and Autistic Spectrum Disorders.* London: Jessica Kingsley Publishers.

Davies J (1994). *Children with Autism* and *Able Autistic Children – Children with Asperger's Syndrome: 2 booklets for brothers and sisters*. Nottingham: Early Years Centre.

Department of Health (2001). *Valuing People: a new strategy for learning disability in the 21st century*. London: Department of Health.

Department of Health (2003). *Getting the Right Start. National service framework for children: emerging findings*. London: Department of Health.

Dorris L, Espie CAE, Knott F, Salt J (2004). Mind-reading difficulties in siblings of people with Asperger's syndrome: evidence for a genetic influence in the abnormal development of a specific cognitive domain. *Journal of Child Psychology and Psychiatry 45*: 412–419.

Dubin AH, Lieberman-Betz R, Lease M (2015). Investigation of individual factors associated with anxiety in youth with ASD. *Journal of Autism and Developmental Disorders 45(9)*: 2947–2960.

Dubin N (2006). *Being Bullied; strategies and solutions for people with Asperger syndrome*. London: Jessica Kingsley Publishers.

Durà-Vilà G, Levi T (2013). *My Autism Book: a child's guide to their autism spectrum diagnosis*. London: Jessica Kingsley Publishers.

Elder J (2005). *Different Like Me: my book of autism heroes*. London: Jessica Kingsley Publishers.

Eriksson MA, Westerlund J, Hedvall A, Amark P, Gillberg C, Fernell E (2013). Medical conditions affect the outcome of early intervention in preschool children with ASD. *European Child and Adolescent Psychiatry 22*: 23–33

Folstein S, Folstein S, Rutter M (1977). Infantile autism: a genetic study of 21 twin pairs. *Journal of Child Psychology and Psychiatry 18*: 297–321.

Frith U (2003). *Autism: explaining the enigma*. Oxford: Blackwell.

Frith U (2004). Emmanuel Miller Lecture: confusions and controversies about Asperger syndrome. *Journal of Child Psychology and Psychiatry 45*: 659–671.

Frith U, Frith CD (2003). Development and neurophysiology of mentalising. *Philosophical Transactions of the Royal Society: biological sciences 358*: 459–473.

Frith U, Happé F (1994). Autism: beyond theory of mind. *Cognition 50*: 115–132.

Gerland G (1997). *A Real Person: life on the outside*. London: Souvenir Press.

Gerland G (2000). *Normality vs self-esteem: the road to increased independence and reflective thinking in children and young people with Asperger syndrome*. Presented at Autism Europe Congress, Glasgow, May 2000.

Ghaziuddin M, Greden J (1998). Depression in children with autism/pervasive developmental disorders: a case-control family history study. *Journal of Autism and Developmental Disorders 28*: 111–115.

Gillott A, Furniss F, Walter A (2001). Anxiety in high-functioning children with autism. *Autism 5*: 277–286.

Glaser D (2000). Child abuse and neglect and the brain – a review. *Journal of Child Psychology and Psychiatry 41*: 97–116.

Goldstein S, Schwebach AJ (2004). The comorbidity of pervasive developmental disorder and attention deficit disorder: results of a retrospective chart review. *Journal of Autism and Developmental Disorders 34*: 329–339.

Gorrod L (1997). *My Brother is Different*. London: National Autistic Society.

Grandin T (1992). An inside view of autism. In: Schopler E, Mesibov GB (eds). *High-Functioning Individuals with Autism*. New York: Plenum (pp105–126).

Grandin T (1995). *Thinking in Pictures and Other Reports from My Life with Autism*. New York: Doubleday.

Gray C (1998). Social stories and comic strip conversations with students with Asperger syndrome and high-functioning autism. In: Schopler G, Mesibov G, Kunce LJ (eds). *Asperger Syndrome or High-Functioning Autism?* New York: Plenum (pp167–198).

Gray C, White AL (eds) (2002). *My Social Stories Book*. London: Jessica Kingsley Publishers.

Haddon M (2003). *The Curious Incident of the Dog in the Night-Time*. London: Jonathan Cape.

Hale A (1998). *My World is Not Your World*. New York: Archimedes.

Hall K (2001). *Asperger's Syndrome, the Universe and Everything*. London: Jessica Kingsley Publishers.

Happé F (1991). The autobiographical writings of three Asperger syndrome adults: problems of interpretation and implications for theory. In: Frith U (ed). *Autism and Asperger Syndrome*. Cambridge: Cambridge University Press (pp207–242).

Happé F, Ehlers S, Fletcher P, Frith U, Johansson M, Gillberg C, Dolan R, Frackowiak R, Frith C (1996). 'Theory of mind' in the brain. Evidence from a PET-scan study of Asperger's syndrome. *Clinical Neuroscience and Neuropathology 8*: 197–201.

Harris SL (1996). *Siblings of Children with Autism; a guide for families*. London: National Autistic Society.

Hill E, Berthoz S, Frith U (2004). Brief report: cognitive processing of own emotions in individuals with autistic spectrum disorder and in their relatives. *Journal of Autism and Developmental Disorders 34*: 229–236.

Hollander E, King A, Delaney K, Smith CJ, Silverman JM (2003). Obsessive-compulsive behaviours in parents of multiplex autism families. *Psychiatry Research 117*: 11–16.

Holliday Willey L (1999). *Pretending to be Normal: living with Asperger's*. London: Jessica Kingsley Publishers.

Holliday Willey L (2001). *Asperger's Syndrome in the Family: redefining normal*. London: Jessica Kingsley Publishers.

Hoopmann K (2001). *The Bluebottle Mystery: an Asperger adventure*. London: Jessica Kingsley Publishers.

Howlin P (2000). Assessment instruments for Asperger syndrome. *Child Psychology and Psychiatry Review 5*: 120–129.

Hoy R (2007). Autism and me. [DVD.] London: Jessica Kingsley.

Hoy JA, Hatton C, Hare DJ (2004). Weak central coherence: a cross-domain phenomenon specific to autism? *Autism 8*: 267–281.

Ives M (1999). *What is Asperger Syndrome and How will it Affect Me?* London: National Autistic Society.

Jackson L (2002). *Freaks, Geeks and Asperger's Syndrome*. London: Jessica Kingsley Publishers.

Jackson J (2003). *Multicoloured Mayhem: parenting the many shades of adolescents and children with autism, Asperger syndrome and AD/HD*. London: Jessica Kingsley Publishers.

Jacobsen P (2003). *Asperger Syndrome and Psychotherapy: understanding Asperger perspectives*. London: Jessica Kingsley Publishers.

Jones G (2001). Giving the diagnosis to the young person with Asperger syndrome or high functioning autism: issues and strategies. *Good Autism Practice. 2*: 65–74.

Joseph S (2003). Why the client knows best. *The Psychologist 16*: 304–307.

Kanner L (1943). Autistic disturbances of affective contact. *Nervous Child 2*: 217–250.

Kim J, Szatmari P, Bryson S, Steiner D, Wilson F (2000). The prevalence of anxiety and mood problems among children with autism and Asperger syndrome. *Autism 4*: 117–132.

Lawson W (2001). *Understanding and Working with the Spectrum of Autism: an insider's view.* London: Jessica Kingsley Publishers.

Le Couteur A, Baird G (2003). National Initiative for Autism: Screening and Assessment (NIASA). *National Autism Plan for Children.* London: National Autistic Society.

Levisohn PM (2007). The autism-epilepsy connection. *Epilepsia 48* (9): 33–35.

Liss M, Fein D, Allen D, Dunn M, Feinstein C, Morris R, Waterhouse L, Rapin I (2001). Executive functioning in high-functioning children with autism. *Journal of Child Psychology and Psychiatry 42*: 261–271.

Little L (2001). Peer victimization of children with Asperger spectrum disorders. *Journal of the American Academy of Child and Adolescent Psychiatry 40*: 995–996.

Lord C (1995). Facilitating social inclusion. Examples from peer intervention programmes. In: Schopler E, Mesibov GB (eds). *Learning and Cognition in Autism.* New York: Plenum Press (pp221–240).

Manjiviona J, Prior M (1999). Neuropsychological profiles of children with Asperger syndrome and autism. *Autism 3*: 327–356.

Marshall D, Goodall C (2015). The right to appropriate and meaningful education for children with ASD. *Journal of Autism and Developmental Disorders 45*(10): 3159–3167.

McKelvey JR, Lambert R, Mottson L, Shevell MI (1995). Right hemisphere dysfunction in Asperger's syndrome. *Journal of Child Neurology 10*: 310–314.

Mount B (2000). *Person-Centered Planning; finding directions for change using personal futures planning.* New York: Capacity Works.

Newson E, Marechal KL, David C (2003). Pathological demand avoidance syndrome: a necessary distinction within the pervasive developmental disorders. *Archives of Disease in Childhood 88*: 595–600.

National Institute for Health and Clinical Excellence (NICE) (2011). Autism in under 19s: recognition, referral and diagnosis. NICE guideline CG128. London: NICE.

Noland RM, Gabriels RL (2004). Screening and identifying children with autism spectrum disorders in the public school system: the development of a model process. *Journal of Autism and Developmental Disorders 34*: 265–278.

O'Connor K, Kirk I (2008). Brief report: atypical social cognition and social behaviours in ASD: a different way of processing rather than an impairment. *Journal of Autism and Developmental Disorders 38*(10): 1989–1997.

Olinkiewicz A (2012). *In My Mind: a journey through my life with Asperger's/autism.* Charleston: Createspace.

O'Neill J (1998a). Autism: isolation not desolation – a personal account. *Autism 2*: 199–204.

O'Neill J (1998b). *Through the Eyes of Aliens.* London: Jessica Kingsley Publishers.

Peacock G, Mills R, Forrest A (1996). *Autism–The Invisible Children? Agenda for action.* London: National Autistic Society.

Pickles A, Bolton P, Macdonald H, Bailey A, Le Couteur A, Sim CH, Rutter M (1995). Latent-class analysis of recurrence risks for complex phenotypes with selection and measurement error: a twin and family history study of autism. *American Journal of Human Genetics 57*: 717–726.

Pilowsky T, Yirmiya N, Doppelt O, Gross-Tsur V, Shalev RS (2004). Social and emotional adjustment of siblings of children with autism. *Journal of Child Psychology and Psychiatry 45*: 855–865.

Rao PA, Landa RJ (2014). Association between severity of behavioural phenotype and comorbid attention deficit hyperactivity disorder symptoms in children with ASD. *Autism: The International Journal of Research and Practice 18*: 272–280.

Rogers CR (1957). The necessary and sufficient conditions of therapeutic personality change. *Journal of Consulting Psychology 21*: 95–103.

Rutten A (2014). A person-centred approach to counselling clients with autistic process. In: Pearce P, Sommerbeck L (eds). *Person-Centred Practice at the Difficult Edge*. Ross-on Wye: PCCS Books (pp74–87).

Rutter M, Anderson-Wood L, Beckett C, Bredenkamp D, Castle J, Groothues C, Kreppner J, Keaveney L, Lord C, O'Connor TG, the ERA Study Team (1999). Quasi-autistic patterns following severe early global privation. *Journal of Child Psychology and Psychiatry 40*: 537–550.

Ryan E (2015). *The Morisot Connection (Book 8) (Genevieve Lenard)*. Charleston: Createspace.

Sainsbury C (2009). *Martian in the Playground* (2nd ed). Bristol: Lucky Duck Publishers.

Salazar F, Baird G, Chandler S, Tseng E, O'Sullivan T, Howlin P, Pickles A, Simonoff E (2015). Co-occurring psychiatric disorders in preschool and elementary school-aged children with ASD. *Journal of Autism and Developmental Disorders 45*(8): 2283–2294.

Sanderson H, Kennedy J, Ritchie P, Goodwin G (1997). *People, Plans and Possibilities – exploring person-centred planning*. Edinburgh: SHS.

Sanderson H, Lunt J, National Autistic Society (2009). *Person-Centred Thinking for People who have Autism*. Stockport: The Learning Community for Person-Centred Planning.

Schaaf RC, Lane AE (2015). Toward a best-practice protocol for assessment of sensory features in ASD. *Journal of Autism and Developmental Disorders 45*(5): 1380–1395.

Scheeren AM, Rosnay MD, Koot HM, Begeer S (2013). Rethinking theory of mind in high-functioning ASD. *Journal of Child Psychology and Psychiatry 54*: 628–635.

Schneider E (1999). *Discovering My Autism*. London: Jessica Kingsley Publishers.

Silberman S (2015). *Neurotribes: the legacy of autism and how to think smarter about people who think differently*. London: Allen & Unwin.

Simsion G (2014). *The Rosie Project*. London: Penguin Books.

Smalley SL, Asarnow RF, Spence A (1988). Autism and genetics: a decade of research. *Archives of General Psychiatry 45*: 953–961.

Smith IC, Reichow B, Volkmar FR (2015). The effects of DSM-5 criteria on number of individuals diagnosed with ASD: a systematic review. *Journal of Autism and Developmental Disorders 45*(8): 2541–2552.

Stillman W (2003). *Demystifying the Autistic Experience: a humanistic introduction for parents, caregivers and educators*. London: Jessica Kingsley Publishers.

Tantam D (2000). Psychological disorder in adolescents and adults with Asperger syndrome. *Autism 4*: 47–62.

Tantam D (2003). The challenge of adolescents and adults with Asperger syndrome. *Child and Adolescent Psychiatric Clinics of North America 12*: 143–163.

Tierney S, Burns J, Kilbey E (2011). Looking behind the mask: social coping strategies of girls on the autism spectrum. *Research in Autism Spectrum Disorders 23*: 73–83.

Timimi S, Gardner N, McCabe B (2011). *An Alternative Voice: the myth of autism*. London: Palgrave Macmillan.

Tustin F (1991). What autism is and what it is not. In: Szur R, Miller S (eds). *Extending Horizons: psychoanalytic psychotherapy with children, adolescents and families*. London: Karnac (pp243–266).

Vermeulen P (2000). *I am Special; introducing children and young people to their autistic spectrum disorder*. London: Jessica Kingsley Publishers.

Volkmar FR, Lord C, Bailey A, Schultz RT, Klin A (2004). Autism and pervasive developmental disorders. *Journal of Child Psychology and Psychiatry 45*: 135–170.

Walton KM, Ingersoll BR (2015). Psychosocial adjustment and sibling relationships in siblings of children with ASD: risk and protective factors. *Journal of Autism and Developmental Disorders 45*(9): 2764–2778.

Waterhouse L, Gillberg C (2014). Why autism must be taken apart. *Journal of Autism and Developmental Disorders 44*(7): 1788–1792.

Weiss JA, Riosa PB (2015). Thriving in youth with ASD and intellectual disability. *Journal of Autism and Developmental Disorders 45*(8): 2474–2486.

Wing L (1981). Asperger's syndrome: a clinical account. *Psychological Medicine 11*: 115–129.

Wing L (2002). *The Autism Spectrum: a guide for parents and professionals*. London: Constable & Robinson.

Winters-Messiers MA (2007). From toilet brushes to tarantulas: understanding the special interest areas of children and youth with Asperger syndrome. *Remedial and Special Education 28*(3): 140–152.

Wood Rivers J, Stoneman Z (2003). Sibling relationships when a child has autism: marital stress and support in coping. *Journal of Autism and Developmental Disorders 33*: 383–394.

World Health Organization (1992). *The ICD-10 Classification of Mental and Behavioural Disorders: clinical descriptions and diagnostic guidelines* (10th ed) (*ICD-10*). Geneva: World Health Organization.

19 Clinical psychology and the person-centred approach: an uncomfortable fit?

Gillian Proctor

In this chapter, I am exploring my unusual dual position. I worked as a clinical psychologist for 17 years in NHS adult mental health, forensic and primary care mental health services, using the person-centred approach. These dual positions, roles or approaches have many points of conflict in theory and practice. Clinical psychology adopts fundamentally a technical position, in which the idea of psychologist as applied scientist is central. In contrast, the person-centred approach is philosophically based on an ethical and relational foundation. I aim to discuss how each of these approaches influences me and the drawbacks of each. I hope to clarify how I deal with the conflicts and integrate the two in theory and practice.

The main therapy model taught in clinical psychology training is cognitive behaviour therapy (CBT), although all courses must provide teaching about a variety of therapy models. Although most clinical psychologists describe themselves as integrative therapists, drawing from several models, there are very few who would claim to be person-centred. I ended up in this position after struggling with the clinical psychology training and finding the position of expert inherent in the CBT approach ethically uncomfortable, and the psychodynamic approach no better (see Proctor, 2002a). During my training, I discovered the person-centred approach from an introduction to counselling training, and was reassured that I could be a therapist in a way I found compatible with my personal ethics and politics. I completed the clinical psychology training using classical person-centred therapy (see Sanders, 2004 for an explanation of the various person-centred therapies) and have practised this way in therapy ever since, devising my own further training in the person-centred approach through a combination of supervision, extensive reading, group experiences and conferences.

I will present a brief history and the current context of the profession of clinical psychology. I will then critique the concept of the 'scientist-practitioner' and the psychologist as objective scientist, and how clinical psychology uses these ideas politically to ensure its status. I will use Foucault to examine the psychologist's role as an agent of social control, following Foucault's critique of psychiatry. I will then turn to the person-centred approach and explain its foundations in science and research and its subsequent development. I will elaborate the principles and ethics behind the person-centred approach, and my critiques of it. I will contrast the principles of the person-centred approach with those used by clinical psychology and identify the main areas of incompatibilities: in particular, the idea of assessment, formulation and the 'expert' professional. I will then endeavour to describe how I bridge these two worlds, or, more accurately, how I continue to uphold person-centred principles and ethics within the world of clinical psychology. I will use the concept of the 'reflective practitioner' to identify some hope for the future of clinical psychology, but remain cynical that this concept truly challenges the superior positioning of the profession and its expertise. I will further conclude that practitioners of the person-centred approach and clinical psychologists would both benefit from using the concept of the 'critical practitioner' to continually interrogate any professional practices involving power.

What is clinical psychology?

Marzillier and Hall (1992: 1) describe the profession of clinical psychology and the main activities of clinical psychologists. They list the three main activities of clinical psychologists as:

1. *assessment* ('the use of psychological methods and principles to gain better understanding of psychological attributes and problems')
2. *treatment* ('the use of psychological procedures and principles to help others to bring about change')
3. *evaluation* ('the use of psychological principles to evaluate the effectiveness of treatments or other forms of intervention').

They also list training, research and involvement in service policies as other possible activities of the clinical psychologist. Little has changed since then.

It is useful to examine the rhetoric of clinical psychology, how it is talked about within the profession and how the profession has marketed itself. The focus of this rhetoric since the Manpower Advisory Group of the Department of Health (MPAG) report (Mowbray, 1989), and still, today, is on being a 'scientist-practitioner'. Marzillier and Hall explain (1992: 9): 'The clinical psychologist is first and foremost an "applied scientist" or "scientist-practitioner" who seeks to use scientific knowledge to a beneficial end.'

Another growing focus within clinical psychology is the clinical psychologist's ability to 'formulate' problems. This is often presented as the hallmark of the profession, The Division of Clinical Psychology within the British Psychological Society (BPS) explains:

> Formulation is the summation and integration of the knowledge that is acquired by the assessment process (which may involve a number of different procedures). This will draw on psychological theory and data to provide a framework for describing a problem, how it developed and is being maintained. (Division of Clinical Psychology, 2001: 3)

Unlike diagnosis, formulation is a 'complex' understanding of the client's problems, putting together many factors, and is open to further clarification and adjustment as understanding of the client progresses (see Johnstone, 2006). Here the clinical psychologist is in their element, able to apply their complex understanding of a variety of theories to the uniqueness of a particular client's life and present hypotheses to the client of how their problems can be fitted within the theoretical frameworks of their psychological theories. Of course, if one theory does not quite fit, no worries – there is a plethora of other theories from which to choose.

How did this profession come about with such a focus? It is useful to examine the history of the development of clinical psychology as a profession to contextualise the current ways of talking about it.

The history of the profession of clinical psychology

Clinical psychologists were used to recruit and select service personnel during World War 2. In 1948, when the NHS was formed, a few clinical psychologists worked in psychiatric hospitals (see Cheshire & Pilgrim 2004; Hall, Pilgrim & Turpin, 2015 for more detailed accounts of this history). From 1948 to 1960, clinical psychologists carried out psychometric tests. Lavender (2003) explains the role of Eysenck in determining the early direction of clinical psychology in the UK. Eysenck was involved in the development of the first clinical psychology course at the Institute of Psychiatry, and went to the US to look at how clinical psychology had developed there. He was clear that clinical psychologists should have nothing to do with therapy (which was primarily psychoanalytic at the time), as he considered psychoanalysis to be 'pseudoscientific'. Instead, he focused on the role of the clinical psychologist as scientist and researcher. However, Cheshire and Pilgrim (2004) argue that the early professionalisation of psychology grew in tandem with early popularisation of psychology, influencing each other, and that professional psychology tried to both distinguish itself from popular psychology by appealing to its scientific base and jump on the back of lay psychology to appeal to a wider audience.

By the end of the 1960s, clinical psychologists had established themselves as practitioners using behaviour therapy. By the 1970s, pluralism, or an eclectic approach to therapy, was common in clinical psychology departments (see

Parry 2015). In the 1980s, demand for clinical psychologists outstripped supply, so the government commissioned a review of their special function. The result was the MPAG report (Mowbray, 1989), which suggested the way forward for clinical psychologists was as consultants in psychological knowledge and skills to other professionals. The report claimed that, among health professionals, only clinical psychologists could offer level-3 skills and provide complex psychological formulations and interventions in particular person-situation contexts. According to this report, clinical psychologists have 'an ability to form alternative hypotheses to help explain a given set of behaviours' and 'a variety of theoretical models for interpreting and understanding behaviour'; their practice is 'determined by scientific method and systematic enquiry', and they have a 'sophisticated and eclectic grasp of treatment models'. From this developed formulation, the unique selling point for the profession.

As is evident, the profession of clinical psychology has relied on the concept of science to argue for its status and expertise in healthcare, with a 'core orthodoxy of psychometrics and elaborated methodological behaviourism' (Cheshire & Pilgrim, 2004: 20). However, the objectivity of science has been problematised in most areas of academia in the last 30 years, by feminists, post-structuralists and social constructivists. These critiques have variously exposed and deconstructed the value-base and subjectivity behind what has been presented as 'scientific fact'.

Critiques of science as 'truth'

The main foundations of post-structuralist critiques of science, and in particular of psychiatry and psychology, are the critiques presented by Foucault (1977a, 1977b, 1979, 1980). He provides a counter-history of madness to that sanctioned by psychiatry.

The history of psychiatry

Foucault challenges the conventional conception of the history of madness: the march of reason and progress to the final recognition of madness as mental illness and growth of knowledge of psychiatry. Instead, he contends that the conception of madness as mental illness is a result of the convergence of internment and medicine, not objective truth.

Foucault also focuses on the 'regimes of truth': 'the ensemble of rules according to which true and false are separated and specific effects of power attached to truth' (1980: 132). These regimes are that scientific discourses are truth; that there is a 'will to truth', and that truth is a battleground. He suggests that scientific discourses are only one way of talking about the world, but that the power attached to these discourses establishes science as 'fact'. Of course, within this, what is defined as 'science' or 'fact' is determined by those in a position of power to identify this. Foucault emphasises that there have always been alternative discourses, or resisting discourses, but they are ways of talking about the world that do not serve the interests of those with power.

Thus, by bringing in science to justify the discipline of psychiatry, psychiatrists have the power to define people as 'mad', leaving the objects of this discourse relatively powerless to resist or define themselves.

The context of therapy

Foucault's analyses of the human sciences, of the history of madness and of the history of sexuality all provide an analysis of the context in which therapy takes place (see Foucault, 1977a, 1977b, 1979, 1980). He describes the idea of the 'confession' as a 'disciplinary technique' – that is, a tactic of social control – and questions the objectivity of 'madness' as a condition requiring treatment. His analyses force us to investigate how psychotherapy can be a context for surveillance and the application of disciplinary techniques of the self – of normalisation. He describes the ways in which power can be observed in psychiatric and psychotherapeutic practices that normalise people by defining expectations of 'sanity' or 'normality'.

Clinical psychology and social control

Rose (1985), following Foucault, deconstructs the history of psychology. He notes that, far from psychology developing a science of the 'normal' that was then applied to the pathological or 'abnormal', psychological knowledge of the individual was constituted around the pole of abnormality. In fact, psychology specifically set itself up to deal with the problems posed for social apparatuses by dysfunctional conduct. From the origins of psychology, the pole of 'normal–abnormal' was set around social efficiency and need for social regulation. In other words, psychology only got off the ground as an accepted discipline when it abandoned its theories of cognitive function and produced instead norms of social behaviour that would permit its regulation. Pilgrim and Treacher (1992: 190) further explain:

> During the twentieth century, with the decline of control by segregation in institutions, coercive power has become less and less relevant. Within this analysis, psychological therapies, counselling and health education are examples par excellence of a new type of moral regulation favoured by government and public.

Thus, from its conception, psychology has acquired status as a regulator of social behaviour: an agent of the state. Pilgrim, Turpin and Hall (2016: 369) note the place of clinical psychology within the 'psy complex' and how this 'raises complex ethical and political questions for the profession about the relationship between care and control'.

Science as justification

Pilgrim and Treacher (1992) follow the same theme as Rose (1985) with respect to psychology as an agent of control, pointing to the scientificism of psychology as a defence against accusations of performing the function of social control. They explain that (p30) 'psychologists… could play out a highly political role in terms of the management of the population, whilst at the same time disowning such a role by pointing to their "disinterested" scientific training and credentials'. They further contend that (p31): 'Scientificism as a justificatory ideology is still a dominant strand in the profession today.'

Ignoring social and environmental causes of distress

This strategy of scientificism, in addition to removing the person of the clinical psychologist from their training and their work, also serves to distract attention from environmental causes of distress. As with the medicalisation of distress, the psychologisation of distress firmly places the responsibility for psychological ill health within the individual. This is reflected by the dominant model of cognitive behavioural therapy (CBT) within clinical psychology, where the client's distorted thinking is blamed for their problems. Thus, deprivation, abuse, oppression and the social and political context of distress can largely be ignored, and the practice of clinical psychology can continue to try to mop up problems caused by a sick society, while preserving their status, power and the inequality status quo, which in turn creates more distressed people. Madsen (2014: 164) critiques the individualising focus of psychology, saying: 'Clinical psychology is often critical of mainstream psychology for unilaterally emphasising the individual psyche and neglecting surrounding factors and structures, while it seeks to apply psychology progressively with an eye towards social change to reduce the incidence of psychopathology in society.' He argues (2014: 150) that this is political: 'The social sciences such as psychology can therefore never be neutral because they must contribute to either social reproduction or social transformation.' Newnes (2014: 40) concurs, saying: 'As in all scientific endeavour, psychology is a socially embedded activity which must be understood as a social phenomenon, at times serving as a mirror of social movements.' The individualisation of psychology, increasingly popularised in self-help books, on the internet and in the media, creates a language of distress and a culture that encourages the consumers of psychology to define themselves as in distress and in need of help, thereby perpetuating its own market. It also provides a discourse that serves the invaluable political purpose of blaming those who suffer from inequalities for their own position and distress.

Status of the profession

The appeal to science by clinical psychology has always been an important tool in the profession's fight for status. Pilgrim and Treacher (1992) argue that among the consequences of clinical psychology's fight for status based on elitism have been the insecurity of the profession within the NHS and the marginalisation of women, working-class people and black people within the profession. Newnes (2014:13) argues that 'clinical psychology, as a profession, began as a mixture of scientific pretension, ambition and a willingness to support the dominant medical discourse for personal gain and professional standing'.

Thus, to maintain its professional status, clinical psychology has presented itself as a useful adjunct to the medical model, rather than a direct threat, despite the fundamental ontological understandings of psychological distress. CBT has developed with this aim in mind, and most research into the effectiveness of CBT presents it as an adjunct to medication. Thus, a psychological understanding to distress is positioned as complementary rather than as a challenge to the medical model. In May 2013, the BPS Division of Clinical Psychology, for the very first time, issued a position statement directly condemning psychiatric diagnosis, as manifested in the latest, fifth edition of the *Diagnostic and Statistical Manual of Mental Disorders* (DSM-5). Some have hailed this as a victory in a new era of critical clinical psychology (Johnstone, 2015), but others are more cynical: Newnes (2014) positions this statement as a move to further the status of clinical psychology's unique selling point of 'formulation'.

A social constructionist perspective (for example, McNamee, 2003) would see scientific discourse as one way of talking about the world and about mental health. However, clinical psychology has used the power accorded science in our society to argue that the results of scientific research that serve the interest of the profession make clinical psychologists experts in such matters. Thus, other ways of understanding 'mental health', such as spiritual understandings or reactions to and ways of coping with social and political inequalities, are dismissed as 'unscientific'. The value that society accords to science and who has access to scientific knowledge ensures the status of the profession. One consequence of this scientificism is the mystification of therapy to the general public. Throughout its history, clinical psychology has always been wary of sharing or disseminating psychological knowledge, for fear of losing this expert status.

Pilgrim, Turpin and Hall (2016) suggest that, despite the overt aim of clinical psychology to (p367) '"do good"... it has also been self-absorbed, and has created and enacted strategies of self-interest'.

This focus on science has many implications for the profession of clinical psychology. Pilgrim and Treacher (1992) point out that the conception of clinical psychologists as 'scientist-practitioners' is neither accurate (with respect to the importance of research in clinical psychology) nor useful (in that it leaves moral and epistemological questions unanswered). In particular (p97): 'Above all else, the person of the clinical psychologist never became a legitimate area of discussion within psychology'. Pilgrim, Turpin and Hall (2016) discuss the tension between scientist and therapist in clinical psychology and suggest 'scientific humanism' as a way forward, where clinical psychology is acknowledged to be a 'moral science'.

Similarly, the idea of psychologist as scientist and the neglect of the psychologist as a person has been addressed more recently in the concept of the 'reflective practitioner' in clinical psychology, which offers an alternative discourse.

Evidence

Appeals to science serve to obscure how what counts as science or 'evidence' is decided. Evidence is chosen to serve the vested interests of those who seek to gain from particular ways of thinking being seen as fact or truth. Take, for example, the emphasis on 'evidence-based practice' in mental health services today: that evidence comes from research that is funded by, and often conducted by researchers in the direct employment of, pharmaceutical companies to 'prove' that their medication, or even CBT, is effective in improving mental health, and the studies themselves are often seriously methodologically flawed (Epstein 1995). Rarely mentioned is the evidence that suggests that client factors and the quality of the therapeutic relationship are the most important factors influencing change in therapy (see Cooper, 2008), and it is equally rare for research findings on the environmental, rather than biological or genetic, causes of distress to be cited. All research questions are determined by political agendas (harmful or benign), and the research that is publicised the most and becomes the accepted 'evidence' is similarly politically determined. Goldenberg (2006) notes that the claims of science do not give rise to objectivity but instead obscure the subjective elements of all human inquiry. He proposes that we should always be suspicious of the notion of biomedicine being scientific or politically disinterested, particularly given the institutional power of medicine.

The example of IAPT

Clinical psychology involvement in the Improving Access to Psychological Therapies (IAPT) programme is a perfect illustration of many of the above points. IAPT is a government initiative launched with government funding in 2008, as a result of a proposal from the economist Professor Lord Richard Layard. He argued that investment in psychological therapies would be recouped financially by the increased numbers of people able to come off disability benefits and return to work. First, this blamed individuals for their lack of employment opportunities (as opposed to seeing poor mental health as resulting from inequalities and lack of good employment opportunities). Second, it introduced state direct involvement in the provision of therapy, and established social control as a primary purpose of therapy, in the form of getting people back into work and increasing national productivity.

By 2012, IAPT was being hailed as a huge success:[1] short-term psychological therapy had been provided to over a million people, almost exclusively in the form of CBT offered by psychological wellbeing practitioners (PWPs) with very basic

---

1. See www.iapt.nhs.uk/dil/files/iapt-3-year-report.pdf (accessed 21 January, 2017).

training. Since 2011, the IAPT offer has expanded to include a small number of other 'evidence-based' therapies that have been approved by the National Institute for Health and Care Excellence (NICE), the body responsible for drawing up guidelines for healthcare practice in England. These include Counselling for Depression (Sanders & Hill, 2014), inter-personal psychotherapy (IPT) and couples counselling, but people are still much more likely to be offered CBT and guided self-help if they seek help from their local IAPT service. The IAPT programme has been criticised for bureaucraticising therapy and using outcome scores from unvalidated and unreliable symptom-rating questionnaires to evidence its apparent success (Proctor, 2015).

However, the clinical psychology profession has, on the whole, welcomed this initiative with open arms, rushing in to offer supervision and consultation to PWPs and leading PWP training courses for IAPT practitioners, which are accredited by the BPS. The profession has notably failed to offer critiques of the medicalised model of healthcare and misuse of outcome measures. This is an example, par excellence, of the profession being uncritically involved in methods of social control while using the opportunity to attempt to further its status.

The development of the person-centred approach

I will now move on to explore the place of science in the person-centred approach right from its beginnings. Carl Rogers, the originator of the person-centred approach, was a clinical psychologist. He was certainly, at least in the early days, a keen advocate of the scientific method. Rogers' theory of therapy was based on research into what seemed to help clients in therapy. He developed it from his experiences of and experiments in helping clients, over many years. Indeed, Rogers conducted his research within an unusual framework of scientist as open-minded explorer, rather than as someone trying to confirm a strongly held belief. Rather than start with a hypothesis and then investigate its validity, Rogers began with an open mind as to what could be helpful in therapy and used the data he collected to form his hypothesis. He methodically examined hours and hours of recorded and transcribed therapy sessions to find out what the ingredients of effective therapy were. This was the first time that actual therapist–client interactions in therapy had been scrutinised using scientific research methods. Instead of relying on therapists' recollections or interpretations of what happened in therapy, he and his researchers used the transcripts of therapy sessions to systematically examine what therapists did that was helpful, and what was unhelpful. Initial findings identified that therapy progress was thwarted by therapists being directive, asking probing questions or interpreting. Therapist interventions that led to client insight and deepening or further exploration were those where the therapist 'simply recognizes and clarifies the feelings expressed' (Rogers, 1942, reprinted in Kirschenbaum & Henderson, 1989). From these direct observations of therapy, Rogers developed his theory of the six necessary and sufficient conditions (Rogers, 1959). Later, he used Q-sort methodology (where statements or characteristics are ranked and the results subjected to factor analysis) to investigate how clients' views of themselves and others changed during therapy (see Rogers & Dymond, 1954). Only from this data-generated theory did Rogers then develop his theory of personality, a hypothesis to explain the therapy theory (see Proctor, 2004a for a detailed explanation of the therapy theory and the personality theory).

Continuing research

After the development of his theory of therapy, Rogers and many others spent much time continuing to research the effectiveness of person-centred therapy. From the 1950s and continuing today, much research evidence has been produced to support the efficacy of person-centred, or client-centred, therapy for clients with many different types of difficulties, including psychotic experiences (see Cooper, 2008 for a review of the research).

In addition to specific research on the effectiveness of person-centred therapy, research to investigate the factors responsible for success in general in therapy have also added to the weight of scientific evidence for the person-centred approach. Forty years of psychotherapy research has consistently demonstrated the importance of the client's own resources and the quality of the therapy relationship for effective, good quality therapy. Lambert (1992, cited in Lambert, 2004, and Cooper 2008: 56) estimates that 40 per cent of outcome variance is accounted for by the client's external and internal resources, and 30 per cent by the quality of the therapy relationship. Bozarth (1998; Bozarth & Motomasa, Chapter 22 this volume) has discussed the implications of this research, concluding that the type of therapy, technique, training and credentials of the therapist are irrelevant, and that the most consistent relationship variables related to effectiveness are empathy, genuineness and unconditional positive regard. These research findings are consistent with the philosophy and theory of person-centred therapy, which relies directly on the client's resources and the therapy relationship. The consistency is unsurprising, given the way Rogers developed person-centred therapy from a research evidence base.

This being so, you'd expect clinical psychologists to welcome such a rigorous approach. The fact that this is not the case, and that the person-centred approach is rarely taught on clinical psychology courses, indicates that what is important for clinical psychology is something other than how 'scientific' an approach is. I suggest that the value base of the person-centred approach is inconsistent with the expert status and power sought by clinical psychologists.

Rogers himself was dubious about how science was used, and became more and more disillusioned with his own profession of clinical psychology and its focus on status and elitism. In addition to believing in the importance of the scientific method, he always regarded the ethics of his work as at least equally important as scientific claims of effectiveness. Indeed, his ethics guided his scientific research and determined the questions he sought to answer. I would argue that Rogers was unusual in his value-base; in my view, most research questions are guided by personal or political agendas.

The value-base of the person-centred approach

The fundamental ethical principle behind person-centred therapy, and specifically classical client-centred therapy (see Sanders, 2004 for an explanation of the various 'tribes' of person-centred therapy), is the autonomy of the client, as opposed to the moral principle of beneficence (doing what's deemed best for the client), which is used by many other models of therapy. Grant (2004: 157) argues that the practice of person-centred therapy is consistent with the ethics of 'respect for the right of others to determine their own ways in life'. This trust in the client's process leads to the non-directive attitude. The *non-directive attitude* is how therapists express their commitment to avoiding client disempowerment (Brodley, 1997; Brodley & Moon, 2011).

Rogers explicitly set out to change the role of the therapist from that of an expert and establish a more egalitarian therapy relationship than is typically found in psychoanalytic approaches. This notion of the equal relationship followed from the implications of the therapy theory. It also reflects the theory of personality, which can be considered the philosophy underlying person-centred therapy. Rogers argued that the premise of the actualising tendency challenges the need to control people: that is, it challenges 'the view that the nature of the individual is such that he cannot be trusted – that he must be guided, instructed, rewarded, punished, and controlled by those that are higher in status (1978: 8).

Rogers explains the implications of this philosophy and values system thus:

> The politics of the person-centered approach is a conscious renunciation and avoidance by the therapist of all control over, or decision-making for, the client. It is the facilitation of self-ownership by the client and the strategies by which this can be achieved; the placing of the locus of decision-making and the responsibility for the effects of these decisions. It is politically centered in the client. (1978: 14)

In this sense, person-centred therapy is a radical disruption of the dynamics of power in therapy. Rogers asserts that opposition to person-centred therapy emerged 'primarily because it struck such an outrageous blow to the therapist's power' (Rogers, 1978: 16). Natiello (2001: 11) explains: 'Such a stand is in radical conflict with the prevailing paradigm of authoritarian power.' I argue that the aim of the person-centred therapist is to reduce 'power-over' the client as far as possible and to maximise the 'power-from-within' of both client and therapist and the 'power-with' in the therapy relationship (Proctor, 2002a, 2002b). I suggest that this aim is contrary to the aim of the profession of clinical psychology, which is to increase the power and status of the profession.

Throughout most of its history and development, the person-centred approach has focused very clearly on its ethical base, at the expense of its scientific and research origins. In the last few decades, person-centred practitioners worldwide have realised the disadvantages of this focus in today's climate of evidence-based practice. The World Association for Person-Centered and Experiential Psychotherapies (WAPCEPC) was founded in response to this, with an academic journal. Research using traditional and accepted methods such as the randomised controlled trial (RCT) has increased (see Cooper 2008; Elliott, Greenberg & Lietaer, 2004). However, it has been more difficult to challenge the claims of science and point out how ethical and value-based decisions are imbued in the scientific method from start to finish. Grant (2004) pursues this route, arguing that ethical justification of any therapy is necessary, and these ethics determine what research, if any, is used to justify its effectiveness. The person-centred approach might achieve a more secure position by playing the game of science, but could this be at the expense of its ethical base? For example, Counselling for Depression (CfD) has secured a place in the IAPT programme by engaging in RCTs and meeting the requirements of NICE. However, many CfD practitioners have been left in positions of constant ethical conflict, trying to make the medical model and bureaucratic systems of the IAPT agenda fit with their person-centred approach to each client as a unique individual (see Proctor, 2015; Proctor & Hayes, 2017).

There is also the question of the possible naivety of the ethical position of the person-centred approach. I (and others) have criticised its claims to an 'equal' therapy relationship and lack of attention to the social and political context in which it is used (see Proctor, 2002a, 2004b, 2008, 2010a, 2010b, 2011, 2014; Proctor et al, 2006; Lago & Smith, 2010; Schmid, 2012; see also Lago, Chapter 10, this volume).

Is the ethical position of the person-centred approach naïve?

Clearly, the criticism that psychology individualises problems by focusing on the individual as the source of change applies equally to person-centred therapy. Can the person-centred approach avoid this trap and respond to distress caused by social, political and environmental factors?

Rogers clearly did a lot to challenge the perception of the therapist as 'expert' in the therapeutic relationship by his emphasis on a 'person-to-person' encounter and by demystifying the process of therapy. All the facilitative conditions work together to try to place the power with the client and minimise control by the therapist. However, in my view (Proctor, 2002a, 2002b), the focus of person-centred theorists and therapists on the therapist as a person serves to obscure the fact that the power imbalance is still present, due to the roles of therapist and client. As Lowe (1999) points out, no matter how transparent the therapist attempts to be, the institution of person-centred therapy still gives the power and authority to the person in the role of therapist and the stigma to the person in the role of client. Larner (1999: 49) summarises this point: 'Professional authority, power and social hierarchy in the therapeutic institution are real enough.'

Furthermore, the person-centred focus on 'equality' of the relationship and agency of the client allows other aspects of the dynamics of power in therapy to be ignored. Often there are differences between the therapist and client in their structural positions within society, with respect to, for example, age, gender, class, disability, sexuality and ethnicity. Also, by focusing on the therapist's provision of facilitative attitudes, there is the danger that the client's perception of these is assumed but, due to the client's potential history of powerlessness or of expectations in relationships, they do not perceive the therapist's attitudes (see Proctor, 2002a, 2002b). Rogers emphasised in the sixth necessary and sufficient condition (1959) that the client should perceive the therapist's empathic understanding and unconditional positive regard, at least to a minimal degree. However, in practice, the focus in training is often on the therapist's attitudes, and the other conditions are commonly assumed or taken for granted.

I argue that there is real, radical potential in person-centred therapy to emphasise the power and autonomy of the client and to challenge the therapist as expert. The facilitative conditions give the maximum space possible for the 'power-from-within', or 'personal power', of the client to increase, and for the client to free themselves from normative prescriptions or conditions of worth that have limited their potential. If person-centred therapists can also be aware of the power within the roles of therapist and client in the institution of therapy and the material realities of inequalities in societal structural power (see Proctor 2002a, 2004b; Proctor et al, 2006), I believe that person-centred therapy can truly be a force for personal *and* social change.

Incompatibilities

Clearly, the main foci of clinical psychology and the person-centred approach are fundamentally different. While clinical psychologists have been busy trying to prove and justify their status, based on their expert credentials, person-centred practitioners have been emphasising their lack of expert status in their relationship with clients. While clinical psychologists have been emphasising their ability to apply a variety of theoretical models to complex problems and achieve complex formulations, person-centred therapists have been keen to stress that it is the client's formulation of their problems that matters, and that applying theoretical frameworks to understanding clients prevents empathy and change, rather than promoting it.

How can these two conflicting paradigms co-exist? When I worked in forensic services for five years from 1998 to 2003 – a system that is the epitome of institutional power and coercion – I was expected to fulfil the traditional role of a clinical psychologist (see Proctor, 2004c, 2005). As well as doing therapy (where it was possible to be purely a person-centred therapist with clients who chose to see me), I was also expected to conduct psychological assessments. From 2003 to 2013, I worked in primary care mental health, where services were firmly based in a medical model of symptoms and treatment. With the introduction of IAPT, clients are increasingly seen as processes to be managed rather than distressed people needing an individualised response. Working in all these contexts requires the management of conflicts between the values and operations of these systems and the values of the person-centred approach.

Person-centred assessment?

The idea of assessment is usually anathema to a person-centred therapist, and particularly a classical client-centred therapist (see Sanders, 2004). As the therapist's aims are the same for all clients (to fulfil the necessary and sufficient conditions of therapy), assessment has no use in determining intervention. Furthermore, when the client is seen as the expert on their life and difficulties, the therapist's job is then to understand as best they can what the client presents, always keeping alongside or one step behind the client, and certainly not ahead. The idea of a therapist pronouncing on or 'formulating' the client's difficulties and talking about their client to other professionals just does not fit with the attitudes and beliefs of the person-centred approach. So how did I fulfil my role in conducting 'assessments' from a person-centred perspective?

When I was asked by a clinician from another discipline to conduct a psychological assessment of a client, what they were usually asking for was a deeper understanding of the client's thoughts and feelings and how they came to be in the position they were in. I was asked for a way to understand the client's difficulties from a psychological/phenomenological perspective, as opposed to a medical or diagnostic perspective. Sometimes clients were coerced into seeing me for assessment; at other times, clients wanted to talk to me. Often I was given a lot of information and views by other clinicians involved in their care before I met the client.

I shall illustrate this process with a hypothetical example. A client might be referred to me for assessment so I can provide other clinicians with greater insight into why he threatened his partner with a knife. The understanding the clinicians have so far is limited to 'drug-induced paranoia'. As I talk to the client, different layers of explanation for his thinking, feeling and behaviour may become clear, even though little is said about the actual incident. He may be happy for me to share with other clinicians my understanding of his story of why he took drugs, and how he is still not sure if his partner wants to kill him. He might say that he has found it useful that someone is trying to understand his explorations with drugs and might want to tell his side of the story.

I see assessments as an opportunity to try to be helpful or therapeutic to the client. This is a very different way to start a therapy relationship to the usual conditions for person-centred therapy. In private therapy, at least, a client has usually chosen to see a person-centred therapist, and has some idea of why they would like to do this.

In addition, the therapist rarely has access to other information about the client. However, in the mental health system, the therapist's clients are rarely truly free to choose therapy: all sorts of pressures and implicit or explicit coercion can be used to persuade them to talk to a therapist, and it is probably rare that a client makes this decision completely autonomously. Of course, this 'choice' to see a private therapist is also probably much more complex than we like to think; often others 'suggest' that clients come to therapy and a client is unlikely to be totally free from the influence of others. In all settings, all potential clients are unable to avoid the influence of the culture and media, which constantly give us messages about what is 'normal' and the increasing range of 'problems' that require professional help.

My primary aim in conducting assessments requested by other professionals is to be open and honest about my constraints and requirements but to nevertheless try to provide as therapeutic an environment as possible for the client. I give the client as much information as possible about what I already know about them and who the report is for and check out with them what I intend to write. I meet with the client as planned and proceed as I would in person-centred therapy, trying to understand without judgment whatever the client talks to me about and following the direction of the client. I write my report before the final, or penultimate, meeting, retelling my understanding of what the client has talked to me about, using the client's own words as much as possible. Often, clients report that they have found their time with me helpful, even if they initially did not want to see me at all. None of my clients have been unhappy about my giving my report to colleagues, and often they find the reports very helpful, and feel that I have really understood their perspective, much more than it had previously been understood. Clients often seem to perceive my taking time to write from their perspective as a way of valuing them, and they appreciate this. The referring clinicians also usually find my reports interesting and useful, and that they provide a more in-depth explanation of their client's views and ideas. Often they are surprised by how much a client has explained to me. (For more details of assessment in forensic services, including risk assessments, see Proctor, 2005, 2004a.)

In the end, I stopped working in forensic services, as the incompatibilities between the expectations of me in the system and my own and person-centred values became too great to manage. I also became increasingly dissatisfied with only being able to provide a different climate of care for the few clients I could see for individual therapy, with minimal opportunities to influence a fundamentally coercive and controlling system.

In the primary care mental health team, I worked as a person-centred therapist, and applied my role as a clinical psychologist in other areas, such as research, evaluation, supervision and service development. For some time, this was a much easier fit. For example, I developed a primary care medical service for people who self-injure; the nurses who treated the injuries were trained to offer an empathic and caring service, and service users evaluated their care very highly (see Longden & Proctor, 2012). However, as primary care trusts were amalgamated and bureaucratised and local opportunities for innovation in response to local needs were squashed, my internal ethical conflicts began to increase again. With the arrival of IAPT, even opportunities for working in concordance with my own value base with my individual clients in therapy were increasingly encroached upon, to the point where I finally left the NHS in 2013 (see Proctor, 2015 for more details on the implications of working in IAPT).

I now find it much easier to work in accordance with my person-centred values as an independent clinical psychologist in private practice and as an academic, where I am able to write about my work and comment critically on the NHS without fear of censure.

Bridging the gap

I believe there are welcome moves within the profession of clinical psychology towards some of the principles that attracted me to the person-centred approach.

The reflective practitioner

Moves have been made in the profession since the early 2000s in response to critiques of the scientist-practitioner model. The definition of clinical psychology by the BPS Division of Clinical Psychology (2001) fitted within the ethos of 'scientific humanism' (Cheshire & Pilgrim, 2004: 105), and thus showed signs of moving away slightly from the objective-scientist position. According to this statement, the philosophy of clinical psychology is as follows:

> The work of clinical psychologists is based on the fundamental acknowledgement that all people have the same human value and the right to be treated as unique individuals. Clinical psychologists will treat all people – both clients and colleagues – with dignity and respect and work with them collaboratively as equal partners towards the achievement of mutually agreed goals. (BPS Division of Clinical Psychology, 2001: 2)

However, the purpose of the profession of clinical psychology is defined as follows:

> Clinical psychology aims to reduce psychological distress and to enhance and promote psychological wellbeing by the systematic application of knowledge derived from psychological theory and data. (BPS Division of Clinical Psychology, 2001: 2)

These statements demonstrate the mixed messages within clinical psychology: between clients as human subjects to which to apply psychological theory (clinical psychologist as scientist), and clients as unique autonomous individuals to be treated with respect (clinical psychologist as humanist). Continuing in this scientific humanist vein, the accreditation criteria for clinical psychology training standards state:

> Clinical Psychologists are trained to reduce psychological distress and to enhance and promote psychological wellbeing by the systematic application of knowledge derived from psychological theory and research. Interventions aim to promote autonomy and wellbeing, minimize exclusion and inequalities and enable service users to engage in meaningful interpersonal relationships and commonly valued social activities such as education, work and leisure. (British Psychological Society, 2014: 5)

These two strands of the clinical psychology profession have been present since its inception. Stricker (1997) describes how, in the US, the 'scientist-practitioner' model was set as the template for the profession. The discussion about the compatibility or otherwise of these two strands (of science and humanism) has continued ever since. Whereas the 'scientist' was the focus for increasing the status of the profession in the 1990s, it seems that now, in the UK at least, the 'practitioner' part is back in the spotlight, with the BPS (2014) describing clinical psychologists as 'reflective scientist-practitioners'. At the same time, conceptions of 'science' have, at least in some circles, broadened to recognise the subjectivity of researchers as of relevance to the findings, in addition to purely 'objective' or experimental methods.

Lavender (2003: 15) suggests that, within clinical psychology: 'There is a growing recognition that there is a need to balance our longstanding position as scientist-practitioners with an understanding and use of the processes of reflection.' The concept of the 'reflective practitioner' is now a more central part of clinical psychology rhetoric, broadening the focus on the scientist-expert to include the practitioner who is able to reflect critically on knowledge. Stedmon and colleagues (2003: 30) suggest that, 'whereas the scientific paradigm offers a method for discovering truths, the reflective position may be best construed as a metatheoretical framework for evaluating the status of these so-called truths'.

As the cornerstone of clinical psychology, formulation usually includes the notion of the reflective practitioner. Johnstone (2006) argues that good formulation addresses all the difficulties raised by critiques of the scientist-practitioner model in clinical psychology. She suggests that all good formulations are tentative, accessible and collaborative, and are open to reconstruction. She further says that the psychologist proposing the formulation needs to be reflexive about their own beliefs and values, and that the formulation always includes the social context. This is reflected in good practice guidelines issued by the BPS Division of Clinical Psychology (2011).

Indeed, the core themes embodied in the reflective practitioner are now part of the accreditation criteria for training programmes in clinical psychology (British Psychological Society, 2014). Gillmer and Marckus (2003) reported the core themes generated by clinical psychology trainers about the idea of reflective practice. One of these was legitimising the personal in the professional; another was the recognition of the diversity of individual personal and professional development journeys. There has been an increasing focus on the socio-political context of distress and on self-care of clinical psychologists, bringing the focus back onto clinical psychologists as people. Here, parallels with training in the person-centred approach become clearer. However, the focus on self-awareness and ethics and values is limited, is often separated out as additional, rather than integrated, and is not used to challenge the scientific idea of 'evidence' by considering how the values of individual practitioners influence their choice of interventions (see Proctor, 2014).

Awareness of social context

Community psychology occupies an increasingly marginal position within clinical psychology, with its focus on socio-political causes of distress, and on community-led and collaborative interventions with socially excluded groups. Cheshire and Pilgrim (2004) argued that the commitment of the New Labour government to social inclusion and more user involvement would lead to greater involvement of clinical psychologists in community psychology. They simultaneously warned that clinical psychologists were likely to become more responsible for social control as Approved Mental Health Professionals under the proposed reforms to the Mental Health Act (the 2007 amendment to the Mental Health Act 1983), forcing them in the opposite direction. With the political shift to the right since then, this shift towards social control has escalated, and any interest in social inclusion has been diverted by increasing the weight of blame on the excluded. User involvement movements have been co-opted by the neoliberal privatisation agenda and the notion of the client as a consumer who makes choices. The discourse of 'choice' is rarely enacted in any meaningful way in NHS services.

Critical psychology

Similarly, the notion of critical psychology did gain some currency within the clinical psychology profession, particularly during the time of New Labour. Various courses focused more clearly on critiques of science and the expertise of clinicians, although still within the scientist-practitioner model. For example, the Salomons course describes its philosophy thus: 'The model adopted within Salomons conceptualises the clinical psychologist as a critical, reflective scientist-practitioner'.[2] However, I continue to sense that critical psychology is an addition to the traditional role of clinical psychology, and presents no challenge to the status and expertise of the professional clinical psychologist. Newnes (2014) is cynical about moves towards critical perspectives within the profession, such as the BPS Division of Clinical Psychology position statement about *DSM-5* (2013); indeed,

---

2. See www.leeds.ac.uk/chpccp/Clin23Salomons.html (accessed 21 January, 2017).

it can be seen from a situationist perspective as an example of resistance being co-opted by the mainstream.

Summary and conclusion

I have presented my positions as clinical psychologist and practitioner of the person-centred approach by describing the historical development of each and the methods that each approach uses to evidence their work. I have argued that clinical psychology has relied on dubious claims to scientific inquiry, and ignored the values and ethics that should determine what research questions are asked and which methods are used. I have suggested that the motive behind this focus on science is to gain and maintain status and power. In contrast, I have argued that the person-centred approach has relied fundamentally on ethical justifications, and has been explicit about how its ethical position has guided decisions on the research undertaken to demonstrate effectiveness.

While clinical psychology responds to the challenges presented by the limitations and inconsistencies inherent in the scientist-expert model, person-centred practitioners are in an ideal position to offer an alternative view of 'knowledge': one that regards people as unique and self-determining. This position is based on Rogers' view of wisdom, which challenges the notion of expert knowledge as the signifier of power, and instead regards knowledge and power as coming from congruence:

> In such an individual, functioning in a unified way, we have the best possible base for wise action. It is a process base, not a static authority base. It is a trustworthiness that does not rest on 'scientific' knowledge. (Rogers, 1978: 250)

At the same time, the person-centred approach has an opportunity to clarify its claims to science and its ethical focus on which scientific facts are most relevant. The person-centred approach can also be accused of focusing exclusively on micro-relational causes of and solutions to distress, and of ignoring overwhelming evidence for societal inequalities, deprivation and environmental causes of distress. Perhaps both clinical psychology and the person-centred approach could benefit from examining and broadening their scrutiny of relevant scientific evidence when discussing issues of effectiveness.

In the first edition of this book, I concluded my chapter (Proctor, 2005) by citing Newnes, Hagan and Cox (2000), who suggest that a sign of a mature profession is its ability to examine what it does with a critical eye. Perhaps both clinical psychology and the person-centred approach have suffered from having to defend what they do to outsiders, which creates insecurity and, in turn, makes it difficult to be self-critical. Hopefully, both now have a firm and secure enough foundation to feel able to encourage practitioners to become mature by not only advocating what they do, but also maintaining a critical focus on taken-for-granted 'truths'.

However, I am now more cynical about this possibility, having seen how both clinical psychology and the person-centred approach are more concerned to protect their own survival and status than be true to their ethics and values. Far from developing towards maturity or truth, both seem more concerned to offer whatever their political masters consider to be useful in the march towards bureaucraticisation and the relentless pursuit of economic growth. Now my only hope is that enough people with counter-cultural values can work together, wherever we are, to resist and create alternatives ways of being within the current, all-encompassing cultural hegemony.

References

Barrett-Lennard GT (1998). *Carl Rogers' Helping System: journey and substance*. London: Sage.

Barrett-Lennard GT (2002). Perceptual variables of the helping relationship: a measuring system and its fruits. In: Wyatt G, Sanders P (eds). *Rogers' Therapeutic Conditions: evolution, theory and practice. Volume 4. Contact and perception*. Ross-on-Wye: PCCS Books (pp25–50).

Bozarth JD (1998). *Person-Centred Therapy: a revolutionary paradigm*. Ross-on-Wye, UK: PCCS Books.

British Psychological Society (BPS) (2014). Standards for doctoral programmes in clinical psychology [Online] www.bps.org.uk (accessed 22 February, 2016).

Brodley BT (1997). The non-directive attitude in client-centered therapy. *The Person-Centered Journal* 4: 18–30.

Brodley BT & Moon KA (2011). *Practicing client-centered therapy: selected writings of Barbara Temaner Brodley*. Ross-on-Wye: PCCS Books.

Cheshire K, Pilgrim D (2004). *A Short Introduction to Clinical Psychology*. London: Sage.

Cooper M (2008). *Essential Research Findings in Counselling and Psychotherapy*. London: Sage.

Division of Clinical Psychology (2001). *The Core Purpose and Philosophy of the Profession*. Leicester: BPS.

Division of Clinical Psychology (2011). *Good Practice Guidelines on the Use of Psychological Formulation*. Leicester: BPS.

Elliott R, Greenberg LS, Lietaer G (2004). Research on experiential therapies. In: Lambert MJ (ed). *Bergin and Garfield's Handbook of Psychotherapy and Behavior Change* (5th ed). Chicago: John Wiley & Sons (pp493–539).

Epstein WM (1995, 2011). The illusion of psychotherapy. New Brunswick, NJ: Transaction Publishers.

Foucault M (1977a). *Madness and Civilisation*. London: Tavistock.

Foucault M (1977b). *Discipline and Punish*. London: Penguin Press.

Foucault M (1979). *The History of Sexuality, Vol 1: An introduction*. London: Penguin Press.

Foucault M (1980). *Power/Knowledge: selected interviews and other writings 1972–1977*. Brighton: Harvester Press.

Gillmer B, Marckus R (2003). Personal professional development in clinical psychology training: surveying reflective practice. *Clinical Psychology* 27: 20–23.

Goldenberg MJ (2005). Evidence-based ethics? On evidence-based practice and the 'empirical turn' from normative bioethics. *BMC Medical Ethics* 6(1): 1.

Grant B (2004). The imperative of ethical justification in psychotherapy: the special case of client-centered therapy. *Person-Centered and Experiential Psychotherapies* 3: 152–165.

Hall J, Pilgrim D, Turpin G (2015). Clinical psychology in Britain: historical perspectives. Leicester: British Psychological Society.

Johnstone L, Dallos R (2006). Introduction to formulation. In: Johnstone L, Dallos R (eds). *Formulation in Psychology and Psychotherapy: making sense of people's problems.* Hove: Routledge (pp1–16).

Kirschenbaum H, Henderson VL (1989) (eds). *The Carl Rogers Reader.* Boston: Houghton Mifflin.

Lago C, Smith B (2010). *Anti-discriminatory practice in counselling and psychotherapy.* London: Sage.

Lambert MJ (ed) (2004). *Handbook of Psychotherapy and Behavioural Change* (5th ed). New York: Wiley.

Larner G (1999). Derrida and the deconstruction of power as context and topic in therapy. In: Parker I (ed). *Deconstructing Psychotherapy.* London: Sage (pp115–131).

Lavender T (2003). Redressing the balance: the place, history and future of reflective practice in training. *Clinical Psychology* 27: 11–15.

Longden E, Proctor G (2012). A rationale for services responses to self-injury. *Journal of Mental Health* 21(1): 15–22.

Lowe R (1999). Between the 'No-longer' and the 'Not-yet': postmodernism as a context for critical therapeutic work. In: Parker I (ed). *Deconstructing Psychotherapy.* London: Sage (pp71–85).

Madden OJ (2014). *The Therapeutic Turn: how psychology altered western culture.* London: Routledge.

McNamee S (2003). Social construction as practical theory: lessons for practice and reflection in psychotherapy. In: Larner G, Pare D (eds). *Collaborative Practice in Psychology and Therapy.* US/Canada: Haworth Press Inc (pp9–21).

Marzillier J, Hall J (1992). *What is Clinical Psychology?* (2nd ed). Oxford: Oxford University Press.

Mowbray D (1989). *Review of Clinical Psychology Services.* Cheltenham: MAS.

Natiello P (2001). *The Person-Centred Approach: a passionate presence.* Ross-on-Wye: PCCS Books.

Newnes C, Hagan T, Cox R (2000). Fostering critical reflection in psychological practice. *Clinical Psychology Forum 139*: 21–24.

Newnes C (2014). Clinical psychology: a critical examination. Ross-on-Wye: PCCS Books.

Parry G (2015). Psychologists as therapists: an overview. In: Hall J, Pilgrim D, Turpin G (eds). *Clinical Psychology in Britain: historical perspectives.* London: BPS Books/Wiley (pp181–193).

Pilgrim D, Treacher A (1992). *Clinical Psychology Observed.* London: Routledge.

Pilgrim D, Turpin G, Hall J (2016). Overview: recurring themes and continuing challenges. In: Hall J, Pilgrim D, Turpin G (eds). *Clinical Psychology in Britain: historical perspectives.* London: BPS Books/Wiley (pp365–378).

Proctor G (2002a). *The Dynamics of Power in Counselling and Psychotherapy: ethics, politics and practice.* Ross-on-Wye: PCCS Books.

Proctor G (2002b). Power in person-centred therapy. In: Watson J, Goldman R, Warner M (eds). *Client-Centered and Experiential Psychotherapy in the 21st Century: advances in theory, research and practice.* Ross-on-Wye: PCCS Books (pp79–88).

Proctor G (2004a). An introduction to the person-centred approach. In: Proctor G, Napier MB (eds).

Encountering Feminism: intersections of feminism and the Person-Centred Approach. Ross-on-Wye: PCCS Books (pp26–38).

Proctor G (2004b). What can person-centred therapy learn from feminism? In: Proctor G, Napier MB (eds). *Encountering Feminism: intersections of feminism and the person-centred approach*. Ross-on-Wye: PCCS Books (pp129–140).

Proctor G (2004c). Responding to injustice: working with angry and violent clients in a person-centred way. In: Jones D (ed). *Working with Dangerous People: the psychotherapy of violence*. Oxford: Radcliffe Medical Press (pp99–116).

Proctor G (2005). Working in forensic services in a person-centered way. *Person-Centered and Experiential Psychotherapies* 4(1): 20–30.

Proctor G, Cooper M, Sanders P, Malcolm B (2006). *Politicizing the Person-Centred Approach: an agenda for social change*. Ross-on-Wye: PCCS Books.

Proctor G (2008). Gender dynamics in person-centered therapy: does gender matter? *Person-Centered and Experiential Psychotherapies* 7(2): 82–94.

Proctor G (2010a). Women-centred practice. In: Lago C, Smith B (eds). *Anti-Discriminatory Counselling Practice*. London: Sage (pp53–62).

Proctor G (2010b). Boundaries or mutuality in therapy: is mutuality really possible or is therapy doomed from the start? *Politics and Psychology* 8(1): 44–58.

Proctor G (2011). Diversity: the depoliticization of inequalities. *Person-Centered and Experiential Psychotherapies* 10(4): 231–234.

Proctor G (2014). *Ethics and Values in Counselling and Psychotherapy*. London: Sage.

Proctor G (2015). The NHS in 2015. *Therapy Today* 26(9): 18–25.

Proctor G, Hayes C (2017) *Counselling for depression: a response to counselling education in the twenty-first century*. British Journal of Guidance and Counselling. dx.doi.org/10.1080/03069885.2016.1274377 (accessed 28 January, 2017).

Rogers CR (1942). The use of electrically recorded interviews in improving psychotherapeutic techniques. *American Journal of Orthopsychiatry* 12: 429–434.

Rogers CR (1959). A theory of therapy, personality and interpersonal relationships as developed in the client-centered framework. In: Koch S (ed). *Psychology: a study of a science, vol. III: formulations of the person and the social context*. New York & London: McGraw-Hill (pp184–256).

Rogers CR (1978). *Carl Rogers on Personal Power*. Constable: London.

Rogers CR, Dymond R (eds) (1954). *Psychotherapy and Personality Change*. Chicago: University Press.

Rose N (1985). *The Psychological Complex*. London: Routledge & Kegan Paul.

Sanders P (ed) (2004). *The Tribes of the Person-Centred Nation: an introduction to the schools of therapy related to the person-centred approach*. Ross-on-Wye: PCCS Books.

Sanders P, Hill A (2014). *Counselling for Depression*. London. Sage.

Schmid P (2012). Psychotherapy is political or it is not psychotherapy: the person-centred approach as an essentially political venture. *Person-Centred and Experiential Psychotherapies* 11(2): 95–108.

Stedmon J, Mitchell A, Johnstone L, Scaife S (2003). Making reflective practice real: problems and solutions in the South West. *Clinical Psychology* 27: 30–33.

Stricker G (1997). Are science and practice commensurable? *American Psychologist* 52: 442–448.

20 | Towards a person-centred psychiatry

Rachel Freeth

Most psychiatrists, like person-centred therapists, spend a good deal of their time listening to people in mental or emotional distress. However, when considering more closely the activity they are engaged in, there appears a considerable gulf between the theory and knowledge base from which they practise, the kind of listening they are engaged in, and what their aims actually are. Indeed, a person-centred therapist and a psychiatrist seem to operate from wholly different paradigms. I have spent a lot of time thinking about and *living* the differences between these two roles because I have been a person-centred therapist for almost as long as I have worked as a psychiatrist. Furthermore, as a psychiatrist, I have made a conscious effort to be as person-centred as I can. In other words, I have endeavoured to explore, in the role of a psychiatrist, the wider applications of the person-centred approach within mental health care settings.

This chapter is in two parts. In the first, I describe my experience working as a person-centred psychiatrist within an NHS mental health service. I shall begin by reflecting on what attracted me to psychiatry and the person-centred approach, and what has motivated me to take the professional directions I have chosen. I will then describe, with the aid of some clinical vignettes, some of the ways the person-centred approach influences how I work as a psychiatrist and some of the main challenges and conflicts I have encountered working in mental health settings.

In the second part, I move from a personal perspective to considering more broadly the person-centred approach within psychiatry and mental health care organisations. I first explore Carl Rogers' relationship with psychiatry, followed by some of the most significant changes within psychiatry and the delivery of mental healthcare since his days as a therapist. Taking a historical perspective can be helpful when thinking about the relevance of the person-centred approach to modern-day psychiatry. From this, I will consider the current challenges for the person-centred approach within the field of mental healthcare, which are formidable. However, I will also sound an optimistic note by highlighting some of the movements within psychiatry and mental healthcare from which person-centred practitioners can take heart, or to which they can even align themselves.

Part one

A round peg in a square hole

A psychiatrist choosing to train as a person-centred therapist is unusual, at least in the UK, although I am not alone as a psychiatrist to hold and express person-centred values. In this section, I will describe what drew me to psychiatry, and then the person-centred approach, and why I have chosen to travel such contrasting paths.

First, I entered the medical profession, subsequently specialising in psychiatry, viewing it as fundamentally a healing profession. At the time, my conceptions of healing were fairly rudimentary, but I believed (and still do) that, at its core, healing involves thinking and practising holistically, and that it also usually involves an interpersonal relationship. It seemed to me that psychiatry, of all the medical specialties, held the most promise of being holistic and moving beyond the narrow conceptions of disease, treatment and cure (the standard medical framework). My initial (rather naïve) attraction to psychiatry was in part based on seeing its potential to be a holistic branch of medicine. The reality, however, has proved disappointing, since in my view psychiatry has sacrificed much of this potential through its preoccupation with developing and elevating its scientific status. Even its claims to work from a 'bio-psycho-social model' are often not borne out in practice.

Second, my motivation to specialise in psychiatry was shaped by a number of significant observations and experiences as a medical student. While undertaking psychiatric placements, I became aware not only of psychiatry's limitations but also of its potential to harm. I think my uneasiness with what I heard and saw of psychiatric care significantly contributed to my motivation to train and then to try to do things differently. Perhaps my motivation contained a rebellious dimension.

What was I uneasy with? Although I couldn't have fully articulated this at the time, I think it relates to the following key areas:

- how mental disturbance is conceptualised and understood
- how patients[1] are related to, or not related to
- who is considered the expert and how knowledge and power are exercised within mental health settings.

---

1. I have kept with the general convention for doctors of referring to patients, although I recognise that this term does not sit easily with many person-centred practitioners, with its implications of a power imbalance.

Elaborating on the above, I was taught as a medical student and trainee psychiatrist a way of thinking about people that emphasised their pathology, where pathology was viewed as largely residing in the individual. I was taught to *assume* (although it was rarely acknowledged as an assumption) that mentally disturbed people had something biologically wrong with them and that my task as a doctor was to discover and treat this. In order to do this, I had to learn how to extract information ('take a history') and how to examine people (perform a 'mental state examination'), with these interviewing skills being considered core skills of a psychiatrist. What is required to do this, so I was taught, is to adopt a detached and objective stance (the so-called 'scientific gaze'). Essentially, the task is to evaluate a person's story, along with their thoughts, emotions, perceptions and behaviours, with the goal of assigning that person's mental experiences to a diagnostic category according to a manualised classification system. It is a method of assessment – of 'observation and categorisation of abnormal psychological events' (Sims, 2003: 3) – that in my opinion tends to treat people as objects to be evaluated in a way that is impersonal and can be experienced as cold. This kind of process of assessing a patient's mind may seem analogous to examining parts of a machine, or to a surgical procedure where the psychiatrist acquires the skill of knowing 'where to make the incision for the psychopathological operation' (Sims, 2003: 32).

The above method of psychiatric assessment can leave little room for consideration of the therapeutic relationship, and certainly not a relationship that gives due acknowledgement to the subjective dimensions of the patient's and psychiatrist's experience. In my training, I was not encouraged to acknowledge or reflect on the subjective nature of my evaluations and judgments, nor on how I was feeling and communicating in the interaction, nor on the impact I might have on the other person by my manner and style of interviewing. I heard no suggestion that the psychiatric interview could hold within it any therapeutic potential, or how to harness this. I don't think this experience is unusual.

Underlying much of the above, and at the heart of what disturbed me most about psychiatric care, however, was my growing awareness of the power dynamics within helping relationships – particularly the power inherent to the role of the psychiatrist. History does not look kindly on how psychiatrists have wielded their power over the vulnerable. At the evil extreme are the horrific crimes committed by Nazi psychiatrists as part of Hitler's programme of eugenics. Less extreme, but all too common, is the charge that psychiatrists are agents of social control, with potentially damaging implications. But also concerning are the routine assumptions made by psychiatrists (and other mental health professionals) that we professionals know best and that our expertise is what most counts. This paternalism is built into mental health organisations (albeit sanctioned by society). It certainly seems hard-wired in the medical and psychiatric profession. It is pervasive in most aspects of clinical practice. It underpins the psychiatric assessment process outlined above. It dominates considerations of diagnosis. It frequently dictates when drugs are prescribed. It is also the basis for deciding that a patient needs to be detained in hospital and treated against their will. Of course, the underlying motivation of paternalism most of the time is to help people (which also makes it more challenging to criticise). What is too little thought about, in my opinion, is the way professional power and expertise are exercised, the power dynamics at play when we are helping people, and the effects on patients of all forms of control and coercion, whether obvious or subtle and barely recognised.

Issues of power, powerlessness, experts and expertise are areas about which I discovered the person-centred approach has a lot to say, since it is an approach that adopts a clear and radical stance on these issues. Looking back, it is easy to see why I was drawn to the writings of Carl Rogers and his associates, since they provided me with a theoretical framework, a set of values and a language that helped me to articulate my concerns and profound discomfort with psychiatry's flaws and potential to do immense harm: particularly its power to oppress and dehumanise others, albeit usually in the belief that it is doing good.

Because of the above concerns, it was therefore probably inevitable that I would pursue my interest in the person-centred approach and train as a person-centred therapist, which I was fortunate to be able to do early on in my psychiatric training by taking a year out of medical practice.

My commitment to the person-centred approach has not so far wavered. As a therapist practising outside the NHS, I remain person-centred in my orientation. What has often wavered, however, has been the degree to which I can bring the philosophy and values of the approach into my day-to-day work as a psychiatrist. The questions that have lived in me, uncomfortably, are whether it is possible to be a person-centred psychiatrist and, furthermore, what this should or could look like in practice. What I am continually brought up against is the tension between my ideals and what is possible in practice within an organisational setting such as the NHS. This statement needs further qualification, because my ideals are obviously personal and relate to my own set of values and principles and those aspects of the person-centred approach I find most meaningful. What I find possible in practice also depends on the unique set of experiences and environments I have encountered, and my own personality characteristics. Another psychiatrist might find certain aspects of the person-centred approach easier or more difficult to incorporate into practice than I have, according to their own values, situation and personality.

Person-centred psychiatry in practice

In what follows I outline, with the aid of clinical vignettes, some of the areas in which person-centred values and principles, particularly those of Carl Rogers, influence the way I work as a psychiatrist. I have also written at much greater length about the challenges of bringing the person-centred approach into mental healthcare settings (Freeth, 2007), although writing about this again now is an opportunity to distil some of my earlier writing in the light of subsequent clinical experience and reflection.

I return to my overview in the previous section of the areas of psychiatry with which I often feel uneasy and even reject. This time I will try to show how I apply the person-centred approach to my clinical practice.

Conceptualising mental disturbance

For most of us, when encountering someone who is mentally distressed, it seems natural to wonder why they are distressed – what has caused it. We may want to know whether the cause is something for which we can provide a remedy. To know how to help, we need to know what is wrong – at least that is a common assumption, certainly in healthcare settings. The medical model is one that searches for the cause in order to know what treatment to apply. The person-centred approach, in contrast, does not require a detailed theory of pathology or diagnosis in order to embody the attitudinal conditions of congruence, unconditional positive regard and empathy.

Rogers certainly thought about how and why people became disturbed, and he developed a theory of psychopathology based on the process of incongruence, albeit within an overarching growth model. Furthermore, some contemporary person-centred practitioners have developed person-centred theory in this area: for example, Margaret Warner's model of 'difficult process' (Warner, 2014, see also Chapter 6, this volume), and Stephen Joseph's understanding of post-traumatic stress (Joseph, 2011; Murphy & Joseph, 2014; see also Chapter 14, this volume). Other person-centred therapists have incorporated medical model assumptions and language into their thinking and practice: for example, Jan van Blarikom (2006) writing about a person-centred approach to schizophrenia.

What often exercises me in my clinical practice, however, concerns the very notion of pathology – the idea that there is something 'wrong' with the individual, whether described in biological or psychological language. Furthermore, psychiatry in general aims to restore or change a person's mental experiences into ones deemed to be normal, where normal is defined by the dominant culture. I regard the person-centred approach as one that challenges the pathologising nature of how illness and disturbance are understood. It invites me to think about how notions of normal and abnormal influence the way I regard other people, and also how such notions influence the way a distressed and disturbed person sees themselves (shapes their self-concept) and their place in society.

Vignette 1[2] – Peter is referred to a psychiatrist

Peter has been referred to me by his GP. I have just spent 45 minutes with him, finding out about his low mood and how this is affecting his day-to-day life and relationships. I have also enquired a bit about his family background, current personal and social circumstances and other details, to try to build up as comprehensive a picture as possible in the time allocated to us. Then

2. These vignettes are fictional but represent scenarios that typically characterise my day-to-day work.

comes the question from Peter I have been expecting – the one that hangs over most psychiatric assessment interviews, whether directly asked by the patient or not. 'What do you think is wrong with me, doctor?'

Peter knows he is not functioning as he normally does. He has been feeling distressed for some months, but only when he started to feel desperate did he consult his GP. He hoped the GP would have 'the answer', and hadn't expected a referral to a psychiatrist. It was a big deal for him to come and see me, but he remains desperate to know what is wrong with him and whether I can sort it out. The desire for an explanation is burning in him.

How do I respond to this question? Do I talk about depression in terms of an illness? Do I offer theories about the cause of depression – for example, talk about (scientifically unproven) theories of biochemical imbalances in the brain? In practice, my response is entirely dependent on and tailored to Peter. I pay attention to what theories he already brings (if any) to his situation, and how he sees himself – for example, whether as a weak person or as someone who is a failure for feeling the way he does. Will being told he is ill be a relief to him? What I generally don't do, however, is initiate talk about causes and symptoms. I try to open up discussion about how a range of things influence our mental health and wellbeing and contribute to mental distress, as well as what may help us to recover. I try to relate this to Peter's unique situation, and check with him whether what I say makes any kind of sense to him. I might say to him that what he is experiencing seems very understandable in the light of some of the things that have happened to him. I explore the understandings and meanings he has already attached to his experiences, noticing the language he uses. In other words, I try to stay as close as I can to his frame of reference, although I have also clearly brought in my own.

While psychiatry focuses predominantly on biological causes of mental illness ('correlates' would be a more useful term than 'causes'), Rogers draws our attention to environmental influences (or conditions), particularly relationships, on our *continuously* developing personalities. While not ignoring our biological reality, I am always interested to know something about a person's environment, past and present – their social world. This is because I view mental and emotional disturbances as understandable reactions or adaptations to social experiences, albeit expressed through our biology. This is very different to assessing people in a way that aims to discern their defects or an assumed underlying disease.

There are profound implications here when it comes to seeing the potential for healing and recovery. This is where I find Rogers' growth model particularly meaningful, and where, as a psychiatrist, rather than viewing what I do as treating symptoms, I am thinking about what conditions are needed to help an individual in the direction of growth and recovery. This may include psychiatric medication, but not as a treatment for disease; rather, as a psychoactive substance that may alleviate distress.

A discussion about how mental disorder is conceptualised would not be complete without considering the role of psychiatric diagnosis. As is probably already evident, I reject (in theory at least) diagnostic classification systems such as the *Diagnostic and Statistical Manual of Mental Disorders* (American Psychiatric Association, 2013). This is on many grounds, not just on their lack of reliability and scientific validity. I believe Rogers made some important remarks about classification and diagnosis. He draws attention to the labelling effects of classification and how it obscures the person, turning them into an object (Rogers, 1975: 98). I will return to the subject of psychiatric diagnosis later in this chapter, since it dominates the psychiatric landscape and how healthcare organisations operate. Suffice it to say, I try to avoid, where possible, using labels. I say 'where possible' because often it isn't possible when the NHS, other organisations (eg. welfare or criminal justice systems) or colleagues demand it. In addition, some patients also want a diagnosis, not just for practical reasons.

Vignette 2 – What is Peter's diagnosis?

When people are referred from primary care, it is typically with a request for 'clarification of diagnosis', as was the case for Peter. This request arises from many assumptions. It assumes that a specific diagnosis is necessary in order to know what the treatment should be. It also assumes that a psychiatrist is someone who can uncover what is already there, as though I only need to look in the right way, in the right place, using the diagnostic skills at my disposal, to find the 'lesion'. It assumes the existence of an actual entity, as opposed to a diagnosis simply being a construct.

Over the years, I have often been able to side-step the issue of diagnosis, but it has become harder to do this in an age where people increasingly long for certainties and the comfort of the 'known'. Furthermore, secondary care mental health services and their bureaucratic processes require it. Peter knows he has been referred for a diagnosis. He now has particular expectations, as does the referrer, that I cannot avoid. This is an area I find enormously challenging as a person-centred practitioner.

I am not anti-diagnosis when diagnosis means wanting to be clear about what a person's difficulties are and having some understanding about what might be underlying them. I am not resistant to describing Peter's experiences as low mood or anxiety, or other descriptions of mental phenomena. What I am concerned about are the potential effects of classifying his experiences with a diagnostic label arrived at using manualised operational criteria. To simply diagnose 'depressive disorder' without exploring the meaning this may have for Peter is, in my view, neglectful and potentially harmful.

Of course, depression is commonly diagnosed today and, although it does carry stigma and shame, as a diagnosis it is not as problematic as schizophrenia or personality disorder. Some diagnostic labels attract more negative stereotyping. But for all such classification, it may be more difficult to see the unique person behind the label.

Relationship and relating

As a person-centred therapist, my approach to helping is fundamentally based on relationship. As a person-centred psychiatrist, it is also based on relationship, and on trying to develop a way of relating that the other may find helpful and facilitative of growth. However, the tasks of a psychiatrist in the various NHS environments in which I have worked have placed considerable constraints on being able to develop a therapeutic relationship in the way a person-centred therapist can. I need to regularly remind myself of this and make allowances for the immense difficulties of embodying the attitudinal conditions of congruence, unconditional positive regard and empathy in my particular role and setting.

As a psychiatrist, I am expected to work according to the medical model – to assess, to diagnose, to recommend treatments, to monitor, to evaluate risk etc. That said, I have still found it possible to work in a relationally orientated way for much of the time, albeit with limitations. I certainly believe in the value and applicability of the six necessary and sufficient conditions for constructive personality change for people with more severe forms of mental disturbance. I try to be aware of the attitudes I have towards others – patients and colleagues. I think about what hinders my empathy: for example, some forms of psychosis or severe thought disorder. I notice when my positive regard is tested and when it falls well short of being unconditional: for example, when I am met with hostility, suspicion or criticism. Motivation to recover and to accept help are typical conditions of worth imposed on patients by mental health professionals, particularly when a lack of expected improvement may lead to negative judgments about their (the professional's) competence. I also know I often struggle with congruence, especially when my feelings are too painful to acknowledge or I am so overwhelmed by my workload that reflective spaces get crowded out. However, despite these limitations, I believe that at times I am able to offer a quality of listening that conveys understanding and valuing of the other and their experience, when I am not just a 'healthcare technician' but am a human being witnessing and being moved by another's distress.

Vignette 3 – How do I listen to Peter?

Peter was referred to me for assessment, a diagnosis and treatment. This task required gathering information and evaluating it – evaluating him. In this situation, I experience a lot of inner conflict, since what I would prefer to do is simply listen to whatever Peter wants and needs to talk about, enter as fully as possible into his phenomenal world (or frame of reference), and try to put aside my evaluations and judgments. I have to find a way of balancing the psychiatrist's agenda of information gathering and evaluation with my desire to provide a therapeutic space, and it often generates acute tension within me.

In the interview, I also try to be aware of the attitudes I hold towards Peter. To what degree am I able to accept him and his experiences, and what judgments of mine are getting in the way? Do I feel frustrated or irritated by his expectations of a psychiatric diagnosis or other demands, and might this be interfering with my ability to listen? Am I able to hear and stay with his despair while noticing my rising anxiety and fear that he may be at risk of suicide? How do I engage with his suicidal thoughts?

It is also worth acknowledging that, as a person-centred therapist, I have a different understanding of empathy from the more superficial and simplistic understanding taught to doctors and other healthcare professionals. Empathy is often taught to doctors as an information-gathering technique and therefore a means to an end, rather than as a principled expression of unconditional positive regard, or an end in itself.

Power and expertise

It is an inescapable fact that the role of a psychiatrist carries considerable authority and power. Of all the challenges I experience as a psychiatrist trying to bring a person-centred approach to my work, it is the use of my power, authority and expertise that is perhaps the greatest and has often created in me the most uncertainty and tension. This is an area of immense ethical complexity, where I find my own personal ethical values coming into conflict with the dominant ethics of healthcare organisations.

Again, I need to remind myself that the frequent expectations of and demands on psychiatrists (and other mental health professionals) are that they, as the experts, direct the process and management of care. Therefore, it would be quite impossible in most instances to practise with the non-directive attitude of a person-centred therapist. While saying that, what I try to bring to my psychiatric practice is an understanding of the potential harmful effects of behaviours that control and coerce, and also an awareness of how my decisions and actions (even with the best intentions) may be disempowering. What I am acutely aware of is that the machinery of NHS mental health care, with its standardised protocols and mechanistic procedures, can be experienced by too many patients as oppressive and dehumanising. I am part of this system – a system that is paternalistic and tries to pre-determine treatment outcomes.

Where does a consideration of autonomy fit into this? How does respect for a person's autonomy play out in my interactions with patients? There isn't room here to do more than raise these as questions that I take seriously but struggle with because of the many competing interests and agendas, including my own. Furthermore, autonomy is a complex concept, on which there is a range of philosophical perspectives: both about what autonomy may mean and what weight it may be given in ethical decision-making in healthcare contexts. Suffice to say, discussions about autonomy are not as routine as they should be in the clinical settings in which I have worked.

One of the heaviest responsibilities psychiatrists carry is their power to deprive people of their liberty, using the mental health legislation. In making such decisions, consideration is given not just to whether a disturbed person is putting themselves at risk, but also whether they are a danger to others. There are obvious competing agendas here, in which the psychiatrist's healthcare role may be severely compromised by a public protection one.

In my own day-to-day work, however, the kinds of challenges I more frequently encounter are around discussions I have with patients about different treatment possibilities and assessing the degree to which patients either want or are able to collaborate in and share the decision-making process. Assessment of mental capacity may be involved here, depending on the nature of a person's disturbance. But quite often I encounter a reluctance or ambivalence in patients to take responsibility and exercise choice or control of treatment decisions. It is not uncommon for patients to want me to tell them whether to take medication or not. In secondary care mental health settings, a significant proportion of patients have a poor internal locus of control. If, as a person-centred psychiatrist, I aim to facilitate the development of a person's internal locus of control, then I need to find a way to encourage collaboration in decision-making and resist attempts by patients to hand me responsibility. This is extremely difficult. Not only must I be prepared to face criticism and even hostility but I am also out of step with a system that adopts a paternalistic stance. Without the system supporting my approach, my efforts will have limited or no effect, and may be confusing for the patient. It is also the case that mental health care organisations struggle to tolerate patients making unhealthy and self-destructive choices, even if they are the result of fully autonomous choice, especially when professionals may be blamed for adverse outcomes.

Vignette 4 – Deciding how to help Peter

Peter may have felt relief that I have listened to him in an attentive and non-judgmental way, and that I have been interested in how he sees his situation (affirmed his locus of evaluation). However, he still wants to know whether he can get better and what will help him. He still expects me to know what to do and to come up with a plan (as does the referrer).

I certainly do have a few ideas about what might help him, based on my knowledge and experience of working with people with a wide range of problems in a variety of situations. I know that, for some people, their mood begins to lift after they start taking medication. Other people find it more helpful to talk through their problems and arrive at a deeper understanding of themselves, perhaps with a psychologist. Other people simply need support with practical issues – with their accommodation or finances, for example, or occupational support. Often it is a combination.

On the whole, I see my task as presenting Peter with some options and trusting him to decide which ones he thinks might work best for him. But there is still an assumption that I should know what is the best option for him and steer him towards that option. In practice, I am also likely to steer people towards what is actually available.[3] It must also be acknowledged that often medication is the easiest option and gives the patient and prescriber the satisfaction that something is being done, and straight away.

Even though Peter may still want me to tell him what to do, he is nevertheless able to engage in a discussion that explores the options, to weigh up the pros and cons, and he is able to share the decision-making process. However, in what situation might I use my power and authority to influence Peter's decision – actually recommend he starts or stops a medication? When does a recommendation become persuasion and then coercion? Would it be legitimate for me to pressure (coerce) Peter into taking medication if I did so with the aim of reducing suicide risk, even if by doing so I was overriding his autonomy? For a psychiatrist, these are daily ethical issues we face concerning the use of authority and power invested in the role.

The importance of context

I conclude this section by summarising my challenge as that of trying to be person-centred in a medical model context, with the inevitable clash of goals, methods and, ultimately, values this involves. I have come to see how the dilemmas and challenges are of an ethical nature that involves me as a person, not just as a professional. I have become more aware of how the tasks I am engaged in shape my 'way of being' and often pull me into a shape I don't want to be. Sommerbeck (2015: 65) puts it very clearly when she says that it is only possible to be 'as person-centred as the context permits'. As a psychiatrist, it seems I am not employed to offer a therapeutic relationship but 'to ensure that contractual output targets are achieved' and that the 'service operates within contractual, administrative and financial requirements', as job descriptions I have seen for psychiatry posts in the UK typically state.

While I am aware that a significant proportion of patients feel oppressed and controlled, it is also the case that many mental health professionals feel oppressed and controlled by organisational demands and expectations. This means that I have to take seriously how working in these environments impacts on my wellbeing and on my self-concept. What conditions of worth is the organisation imposing on its staff? I need to consider the effects on me when I compromise my values and my integrity, and when and where I draw the line.

As a person-centred practitioner, my use of 'self' is the foundation to what I do and how I do it. This clearly has implications for self-care, self-development and for thinking about what resources I need to work in the way I do, including my need for supervision (about which I have written in Freeth, 2004). What do I need in order to survive working in psychiatric settings while also trying to embody a person-centred 'way of being'? A common metaphor used to describe the experience of

---

3. What resources are available often influences our perception of what people need.

person-centred practitioners working in many organisations (not just healthcare) is that of 'swimming against the tide'. If I were to extend the metaphor, I need to know where the guide ropes are, how to activate a life jacket and where and when to rest and refuel.

Part two

Occasionally I have wondered what Rogers, if he were still alive, might make of my efforts to bring the person-centred approach into my role as a psychiatrist. In such an imaginative exercise, it seems too easy to call to mind my limitations and inadequacies, not that I imagine Rogers as anything but warmly understanding. I think he would acknowledge the formidable challenge presented by working in modern-day psychiatric settings dominated by discourses that run counter to the ethos of the person-centred approach. I also think that the psychiatric landscape has changed so much that it is now barely recognisable from the time when Rogers was a prominent figure in American psychology in the middle part of the last century. In the second part of this chapter, I highlight some of these changes in order to consider the place of the person-centred approach in the field of mental health today, and particularly its current challenges. However, I will begin by looking at Rogers' encounters with psychiatry, and what he had to say on aspects of mental healthcare, such as the use of psychiatric drugs and diagnostic classification systems.

Carl Rogers' relationship with psychiatry

Rogers certainly had his run-ins with psychiatry during different periods in his professional life. The most notable concerned the legitimacy of psychologists (or non-doctors) practising psychotherapy, which was originally considered a medical treatment. Non-medically trained counsellors, psychotherapists and clinical and counselling psychologists today owe something of their professional status as talking therapists to Rogers' efforts to gain credibility for himself and his co-workers as clinicians practising therapy. This is one example of the turf wars in which the professions of psychology and psychiatry have been involved (and to some extent still are). Rogers did try to bring together the psychiatric profession and his own, particularly during his period at the University of Wisconsin between 1957 and 1963, where he worked in the departments of both psychology and psychiatry, and later at the University of Wisconsin's Institute of Psychiatry.

Rogers moved to Wisconsin from the University of Chicago, attracted by the possibilities of training both psychiatrists and psychologists (described in Rogers & Russell, 2002). However, attempts to provide training where psychologists and psychiatrists learned together how to interview patients did not come to fruition. Another main ambition was to conduct research into therapy with psychotic individuals, specifically those hospitalised with a diagnosis of schizophrenia. Rogers was keen to test his hypothesis of the six necessary and sufficient conditions for constructive personality change on a group of more seriously disturbed individuals. This research was fraught with difficulties and conflicts (in part owing to its sheer complexity), as well as, in the end, producing mixed results (Rogers et al, 1967). One positive outcome, however, was the development of particular research tools. Another was Rogers' further development of the concept of congruence, as a result of his experiences working with more disturbed individuals. He involved himself much more as a person in the therapeutic work (Kirschenbaum, 2007), and it is interesting to read some of his accounts of working with individuals with psychosis (for example, in Rogers et al, 1967, and Evans, 1975).

It is commonly asserted that the person-centred approach is antithetical to the medical model. One doesn't need to look very hard for statements made by Rogers and his co-workers that would justify such an assertion. For example, in an interview in 1976 with Anthony Clare for the BBC Radio 4 programme *All in the Mind,* he describes the medical model 'as an extremely inappropriate model for dealing with psychological disturbance… We don't see them as sick and needing a diagnosis, prescription and a cure'.

It might be assumed that Rogers was against the use of psychiatric medication, but in fact he saw it as 'justified in some instances' (Rogers & Russell, 2002: 290–291), albeit also regarding it as overused and resorted to as a way of making life easier for those in caring roles. Rogers was certainly not hostile to the medical profession, and it is interesting that his son, David, became a well-known doctor, researcher and medical educator.

When it comes to psychiatric diagnosis, however, Rogers is particularly forthright in his opinions. I think this reveals the heart of Rogers' understanding and attitudes towards mental health problems and approaches to helping. He did use the broad descriptive terms 'psychosis', 'neurosis' and 'maladjustment' when differentiating forms of disturbance, but he saw the psychiatric labels generated by the main classification system (the *Diagnostic and Statistical Manual of Mental Disorders*) as potentially harmful. Rogers believed that the 'labels give a pseudoscientific sound to what is actually a very loose and unfounded categorization' (Rogers, 1975: 97). But his strongest objection seems not to be the lack of scientific validity but the objectifying nature of the process of classification. In other words, the 'object' of classification ceases to be seen 'as a real person in a relationship'. To Rogers, diagnostic classification is a process of objectification that also forecloses our attempts to understand the other and to think about the meanings of mental experiences such as psychosis. Asked whether it was possible to get beyond the 'classification wall', he acknowledged that the tradition of classification (certainly in institutions) would be hard to change (Rogers, 1975: 98). From today's perspective, this seems an understatement.

Rogers' views on psychiatric diagnosis touch on the philosophy of science, and I have found it helpful in the development of my own thinking to look at what he has to say on this subject. It is clear from his contact in his later years with individuals such as science philosopher Michael Polanyi, and his knowledge of the work of Illyn Prigogine and Fritjof Capra, that many post-modern scientific ideas came to have meaning for him: for example, the principle of complementarity in quantum physics. He questions notions of objective reality and affirms more intuitive ways of knowing. In a number of publications (for example, Rogers, 1980, and Coulson & Rogers, 1968), he explores these developments in his thinking. Rogers is moving beyond modern, positivistic, scientific methods and towards developing a more human science that sees the subjective human being. I find it disappointing that much medicine today (with the exception of complementary and alternative medicine) has not yet incorporated post-modern developments in science, where philosophical perspectives are given a rightful place. Medicine, including psychiatry, is still clinging to dualistic, reductionistic, 'cause and effect' ways of thinking. In medical circles, scientific and technological language is often afforded superiority and is largely divorced from other sources of knowledge.

The changed landscape of psychiatry and mental health care post-Rogers

I commented earlier that psychiatry today might seem barely recognisable from how it operated when Rogers was in clinical practice. In what follows, I outline some of the changes over the past 30–40 years that have profoundly influenced the way individuals are now cared for in mental health organisations such as the NHS.

Many of these changes have been driven by developments in science and technology, in which the psychiatric profession has invested its status. We have seen major developments in neuroscience as a result of technologies that now help us to understand a great deal about how the brain works. Examples include the development and now routine use of computerised tomography (CT) and magnetic resonance imaging (MRI) scans. There has also been a major revolution in psychopharmacology, to the extent that the prescription (or at least recommendation) of psychiatric drugs is now fairly routine for anyone who comes into contact with secondary care mental health services, and common for many who are simply consulting their general practitioner. It is probable that many of the individuals to whom Rogers and his associates offered counselling would today be more likely to be offered an antidepressant, or even an antipsychotic, drug.[4]

One profound consequence of the widespread use of psychiatric drugs is the way it has shaped the dominant narrative within our culture that mental and emotional distress is a medical condition requiring a medical treatment. Our understanding of mental health problems is influenced by the general discourse around neuroscience. Today we have a 'neurocentric' view of the mind, described as the 'view that human experience and behaviour can be best explained from the

---

4. Antipsychotics are now commonly prescribed for anxiety, agitation and to stabilise mood, as well as for psychosis.

predominant or even exclusive perspective of the brain' (Satal & Lilienfeld, 2013: xix). One of the major consequences of this is that less attention is paid to the environmental or social context within which mental health problems arise. This is not just an issue of what kind of knowledge is privileged. One of the scandals of the recent history of psychiatry and mental health care has been the dogmatic claims that mental disorder is the result of physical disease process, without conclusive scientific evidence to justify such claims. These claims have now been exposed as the assumptions and hypotheses they are.[5] But, despite this, their acceptance as scientific fact is still widespread. An example is the still common belief that psychiatric drugs are correcting biochemical imbalances in the brain: ie. treating underlying diseases – a misleading and grossly oversimplified message cleverly delivered by the pharmaceutical companies but swallowed by many doctors (and it is hard to tell whose vested interests are most being served). Incidentally, Rogers was asked what he thought about the physical causes of mental disorder. While not dismissive of the possibility, he declared it 'unlikely that we will discover real [biochemical] causes of mental illness' (Rogers & Russell, 2002: 292). It still seems unlikely, in my opinion.

Along with the neuroscience discourse within psychiatry and the field of mental health, another significant development has been that of psychiatric diagnosis and further editions of the *Diagnostic and Statistical Manual of Mental Disorders* (*DSM*) that have been produced since the versions with which Rogers would have been familiar. We now have the fifth edition (*DSM-5*), published in 2013 (American Psychiatric Association), but the watershed moment came in 1980, with the publication of the third edition. Earlier editions were heavily influence by psychoanalytic thinking, which viewed many mental disorders as *reactions* rather than *diseases*. The third edition heralded a new approach to psychiatric diagnosis in an attempt to improve its reliability and validity in the face of increasing attacks on the legitimacy of psychiatry as a science. *DSM-III* demonstrates the waning influence of psychoanalysis on psychiatry, and instead implies the existence of a biological foundation to mental disorder. The categorical nature of this classification system[6] suggests that mental illness is a discrete entity, and that there is a line of demarcation between normal and abnormal mental experience and behaviour. Such assumptions are pervasive within western culture, and the now vast array of diagnostic categories has profoundly influenced the organisation and delivery of mental health care and other statutory services. They also impact on the work of person-centred practitioners, who will need to consider how they personally engage with the issues raised by psychiatric diagnosis, such as the effect on a person's self-concept.

---

5. See Davies (2013) for a highly readable account of how the vested interests of psychiatrists and the pharmaceutical industry have perpetuated these ideas.

6. And also the *ICD-10 International Classification of Mental and Behavioural Disorders*, published by the World Health Organization (1992), now in its 10th edition, with the 11th in development.

Finally in this section, I consider the so-called 'anti-psychiatry movement' and key figures like RD Laing and Thomas Szasz – both psychiatrists. Psychiatry has never been without its dissenters or radicals, and one might imagine that Rogers, whose person-centred approach is also radical in its critique of the medical model, would have formed important connections with such individuals. The fact that he didn't may in part be because antipsychiatry was at its height after Rogers moved away from clinical practice. Rogers was certainly aware of the work of Laing and Szasz. A specially organised meeting with Laing at a conference in London in 1978 was not, however, a positive experience. Laing seems to have treated Rogers with contempt, referring to his 'California nice-guy bullshit' (described in Kirschenbaum, 2007: 277).

I imagine Rogers may have found Szasz far more congenial, although he was unsure (Rogers, 1975) about Szasz's view that mental illness is a 'myth' (Szasz, 1961). He certainly shared Szasz's concern about the control agenda of psychiatry. Szasz was an extreme libertarian who believed that psychiatrists had become agents of social control. Rogers, too, saw many of the damaging effects of psychiatry due to its potential to oppress, control and wield authoritarian power. I imagine Rogers and Szasz would have had an interesting and fruitful dialogue, although I am not aware they ever did. Anti-psychiatry is often derided within the psychiatric profession. It is unfortunate that the person-centred approach may suffer similar judgment by association, as a similarly radical approach to mental health problems.

Current challenges and hopes for the future

In highlighting some of the changes in the recent history of psychiatry, I touched on one of the dominant discourses within our culture – that of neurocentrism. However, this isn't the only powerful discourse shaping how we think about mental distress and disorder, and how we should respond to them. In this final section, I note briefly some of the other discourses and their underlying values. I believe it is important to understand how psychiatry and systems of mental healthcare are fundamentally built on human interests and values – as individuals, communities and whole societies. I have also found it important to hold in my awareness those values to which the person-centred approach runs counter. It is this clash of values that constitutes the challenge for person-centred practitioners working in healthcare organisations today, and outside them. While this represents a formidable challenge, there are beacons of hope, and I will close by highlighting a few of these.

A neurocentric and materialistic view of human beings is one that attempts to explain how human beings function in terms of cells, tissues and organs and the physiological and biochemical processes within them. As a culture, many of us routinely look for physical explanations when we think something is wrong in, or with, us, and we turn to medicine to provide this. Mental disturbance and distress are now commonly seen through a medical lens, with expectations (or at least the hope) that medicine will fix what is wrong. Within a traditional medical worldview is the notion that mental distress is abnormal, that it should be removed, and that we need experts to do this. It reflects a desire for our thoughts and feelings to be fully under our control, and our wish to avoid suffering. The desire for scientific knowledge also seems to reflect a craving for certainty and avoidance of the unknown and mysterious. Likewise, our culture champions what is (or claims to be) objective and known.

Many of these more dominant values fit nicely with those of free market economics. As is increasingly evident, healthcare organisations are run as businesses, their priorities determined by neoliberal economic principles. In order to run efficiently, they require the implementation of standardised pathways of care with pre-determined outcomes. It is no surprise that models of care, such as the person-centred approach, that prioritise relationship as a vehicle for healing, attend to subjective dimensions and to the *process* of care, and try to avoid forms of control, will find little or no place in organisations that control and regulate according to a target-driven culture aimed at maximising productivity and value for money. As for psychological therapies in mental healthcare organisations, it stands to reason that therapies most aligned to the medical model – for example, cognitive behavioural therapy, where the processes and goals of therapy are more easily defined and measured – will be afforded superior status.

It may be hard not to feel gloomy about the dwindling place of person-centred therapy in mental health care organisations today, with the exception of the recent development of Counselling for Depression in NHS IAPT services.[7] As a broader approach to helping, however, there may be more opportunities to influence the culture of care with person-centred attitudes and values. Indeed, this is already happening.

Challenges to the dominant discourses within psychiatry and the field of mental health have been growing in recent years. There is a deep hunger for real change in the provision of mental healthcare, as is evidenced by the work of organisations such as the Hearing Voices Network and the Soteria Network.[8] The inadequacies and limitations of the biomedical model in mental healthcare are increasingly voiced. The control agenda of psychiatry continues to be resisted. The desire for a more human, caring response that prioritises relationships, narratives, meanings and contexts was articulated clearly in a paper co-authored by some 30 UK psychiatrists, with the visionary title 'Psychiatry beyond the current paradigm' (Bracken et al, 2012). Within the psychiatric profession, there is a network of those critical about the dominance of the biomedical model in mental healthcare.[9] I

---

7. IAPT is an acronym for Improving Access to Psychological Therapies. Launched in 2008, this is a government-backed initiative to make psychological therapies more widely available within the NHS in England for people with mild-to-moderate depression and anxiety. The therapies have so far predominantly been CBT based, although counselling of a more humanistic nature, such as Counselling for Depression, couples therapy, and interpersonal psychotherapy (IPT), is becoming available in some areas.

8. See www.hearing-voices.org and www.soterianetwork.org.uk (accessed 30 November, 2016).

9. See www.criticalpsychiatry.co.uk (accessed 30 November, 2016).

doubt whether most of these psychiatrists would describe themselves as person-centred (in the Rogerian sense), but to my mind many of their concerns arise from values that seem aligned with those of the person-centred approach, particularly those that challenge psychiatric power and authority.

While a number of psychiatrists are calling for a new paradigm of mental healthcare, so are significant numbers of other mental health professionals, activists, patients and carers, many of whom are involved in the so-called Recovery Movement.[10] Although not a coordinated movement as such, recovery has become an increasingly used term in mental health settings, often as shorthand for values and beliefs that directly challenge the traditional biomedical approach. One of the most quoted descriptions of recovery is as follows:

> ... a deeply personal, unique process of changing one's attitudes, values, feelings and goals, skills, and/or roles. It is a way of living a satisfying, hopeful, and contributing life even within the limitations caused by illness. Recovery involves the development of new meaning and purpose in one's life as one grows beyond the catastrophic effects of mental illness. (Anthony, 1993)

In this description of recovery, what are prioritised are meanings and the importance for people to define their own goals and purpose (self-determination). It emphasises notions of growth rather than pathology. A recovery-orientated approach to helping also highlights the importance of healing relationships that convey person-centred attitudes, such as warmth, genuineness and empathy.

While there is a great deal here that will resonate with person-centred practitioners, the term 'recovery' is one to which other meanings are also attached. For example, mental health service-based definitions (sometimes termed 'clinical recovery') see the goal of recovery as remission of symptoms or achieving a certain level of functioning. Here, recovery is externally and objectively defined, as opposed to being a subjective experience defined by the patient him or herself. Recovery has, therefore, become a contested and ambiguous concept, reflecting sharply contrasting values. When it means self-determination, self-management and a process owned by the patient, a recovery approach clearly presents a radical challenge to the medical model. However, when the concept and goals of recovery reflect the interests of professionals, policy-makers and organisations, the survivor-led recovery movement appears to have been hijacked, or 'colonised' (O'Hagan, 2009), and its original values diluted, misunderstood and seriously compromised. It would seem, therefore, that the person-centred nature of recovery often needs to be rescued, certainly in order to challenge situations of 'coerced recovery' (Morgan & Felton, 2013), or when the term is applied as a corporate branding exercise.

It is also possible to be encouraged by a number of pioneering and alternative approaches to the provision of care that incorporate many aspects of the person-

---

10. There is now a wealth of literature on recovery in the field of mental health (for example, Slade, 2009).

centred approach. One example is Open Dialogue,[11] a community-based support system and approach to helping people experiencing psychosis or other severe mental health crises. It originally developed in Finland, but is receiving increasing interest in the UK, where training courses and pilot projects are now being developed. Open Dialogue is an approach that focuses on the social worlds of individuals and aims to support them, their families and support networks in a way that empowers and facilitates self-agency. It is fundamentally built on relationships, collaboration, dialogue and non-judgmental awareness of mental experiencing.

Another example, described by Venner and Noad (2013), is the Leeds Survivor-Led Crisis Service,[12] which was set up to provide sanctuary as an alternative to hospital admission and the medical model response to crisis. This service explicitly draws on the person-centred approach, including a belief in the human being's tendency to actualise, given facilitative conditions, and the importance of self-determination.

Conclusion

What I have learnt over the years is the importance of understanding the values and interests on which organisations operate (many of which will not be stated in the organisation's mission statement). The interests of the psychiatric profession are powerful, and such power needs to be challenged with care to minimise the risk of a backlash. Forming alliances is one way forward in this, as is learning the language of psychiatry and the dominant language of mental health settings in order to achieve more effective dialogue. This does not mean buying into the values and ideas such language symbolises. Of course, it is a considerable challenge to become bilingual, which any person-centred practitioner working in mental health settings needs to be. It is also demanding to work with several discourses, especially when they cannot be integrated.

Implicit throughout this chapter has been the question of whether it is possible for psychiatry and the person-centred approach to develop an alliance (which doesn't necessarily mean agreement). Clearly for me the answer is 'yes', but it is difficult. I have highlighted in this chapter some of the ways in which my person-centred values are compromised, not only by the tasks expected of me in my role as a psychiatrist but also by the general culture and ethos of the organisational setting, which is, in my experience, profoundly unhealthy. In my 20 years of psychiatric practice, patient expectations have also increased and our culture has, it seems, bought into the process of medicalisation.[13] The blame culture, too, adds increasing stress. For me, it doesn't get any easier. Would I set off on a similar voyage again? Despite the costs, it feels (so far) worth the effort. I continue to believe that the person-centred approach is one that is much-needed and can humanise psychiatry.

---

11. See www.opendialogueapproach.co.uk (accessed 30 November, 2016).

12. See www.lslcs.org.uk (accessed 30 November, 2016).

13. Medicalisation has been described as the process of pathologising normal psychological distress, or turning behaviours into medical conditions.

References

American Psychiatric Association (2013). *Diagnostic and Statistical Manual of Mental Disorders* (5th ed). Washington, DC: American Psychiatric Association.

Anthony WA (1993). Recovery from mental illness: the guiding vision of the mental health service system in the 1990s. *Psychosocial Rehabilitation Journal 16*: 11–23.

Bracken P et al (2012). Psychiatry beyond the current paradigm. *British Journal of Psychiatry 201*: 430–434.

Coulson WR, Rogers CR (1968). *Man and the Science of Man*. Columbus, OH: Charles E Merrill.

Davies J (2013). *Cracked. Why psychiatry is doing more harm than good*. London: Icon.

Evans R (ed) (1975). *Carl Rogers. The man and his ideas*. New York: EP Dutton.

Freeth R (2004). A psychiatrist's experience of person-centred supervision. In: Tudor K, Worrall M (eds). *Freedom to Practise: person-centred approaches to supervision*. Ross-on-Wye: PCCS Books (pp247–266).

Freeth R (2007). *Humanising Psychiatry and Mental Health Care: the challenge of the person-centred approach*. Oxford, UK: Radcliffe Publishing.

Joseph S (2011). *What Doesn't Kill Us: the new psychology of posttraumatic growth*. New York: Basic Books.

Kirschenbaum H (2007). *The Life and Work of Carl Rogers*. Ross-on-Wye, UK: PCCS Books.

Morgan A, Felton A (2013). From constructive engagement to coerced recovery. In: Coles S, Keenan S, Diamond B (eds). *Madness Contested: power and practice*. Ross-on-Wye: PCCS Books (pp56–73).

Murphy D, Joseph S (2014). Understanding posttraumatic stress and facilitating posttraumatic growth. In: Pearce P, Sommerbeck L (eds). *Person-Centred Practice at the Difficult Edge*. Ross-on-Wye, UK: PCCS Books (pp3–13).

O'Hagan M (2009). The colonisation of recovery. *Openmind 156*: 20.

Rogers CR, Gendlin ET, Keisler DJ, Truax CB (1967). *The Therapeutic Relationship and its Impact: a study of psychotherapy with schizophrenics*. Madison: The University of Wisconsin Press.

Rogers CR (1975). Cited in: Evans R. *Carl Rogers: the man and his ideas*. New York: EP Dutton.

Rogers CR (1980). *A Way of Being*. Boston: Houghton Mifflin.

Rogers CR, Russell D (2002). *Carl Rogers: the quiet revolutionary. An oral history*. Roseville, CA: Penmarin Books.

Satal S, Lilienfeld SO (2013). *Brainwashed: the seductive appeal of mindless neuroscience*. New York: Basic Books.

Sims A (2003). *Symptoms in the Mind: an introduction to descriptive psychopathology*. London: Saunders.

Slade M (2009). *Personal Recovery and Mental Illness: a guide for mental health professionals*. Cambridge: Cambridge University Press.

Sommerbeck L (2015). *Therapist Limits in Person-Centred Therapy*. Monmouth: PCCS Books.

Szasz T (1961). *The Myth of Mental Illness*. New York: Hueber-Harper.

van Blarikom J (2006). A person-centered approach to schizophrenia. *Person-Centered and Experiential Psychotherapies 5*: 155–173.

Venner F, Noad M (2013). A beacon of hope: alternative approaches to crisis – learning from Leeds Survivor Led Crisis Service. In: Coles S, Keenan S, Diamond B (eds). *Madness Contested: power and practice*. Ross-on-Wye: PCCS Books (pp332–348).

Warner M (2014). Client processes at the difficult edge. In: Pearce P, Sommerbeck L (eds). *Person-Centred Practice at the Difficult Edge*. Ross-on-Wye: PCCS Books (pp121–137).

World Health Organization (1992). *The ICD-10 Classification of Mental and Behavioural Disorders: clinical descriptions and diagnostic guidelines*. Geneva: World Health Organization.

21 Person-centred therapy and the regulation of counsellors and psychotherapists in the UK

Andy Rogers and David Murphy

Once the state begins to define in law the purposes of therapy, what therapeutic methods are valid, who is fit to practise, and which therapies and therapists prospective clients may choose, then freedom is curtailed. Indeed, the practice of person-centred therapy in the UK has benefited from the relative freedom afforded by the counselling and psychotherapy professions remaining outside of state regulation. Control, of course, can be exerted in more ways than through the law, and the state's increasing involvement with the psychological therapies via the overlapping fields of medicine, healthcare and welfare is having its own restricting and distorting effect on the kinds of theories, evidence and practices deemed legitimate. Yet, statutory regulation continues to pose a uniquely toxic threat to the authentic practice of person-centred therapy.

In this chapter, we discuss the implications for the person-centred approach of such state-controlled frameworks. Our aim is to engage practitioners, trainees and trainers of person-centred therapy in a thoughtful dialogue about the issues at stake. We consider the theoretical case against statutory regulation, highlighting the incongruence between systems of oppressive external control and the person-centred concepts of the actualising tendency, the locus of evaluation and the sovereign right to self-determination. For therapists to be useful companions to their clients in unblocking the inherent tendency towards self-direction and connectedness, they themselves must be sufficiently self-directing, free from external control and engaged in sufficiently authentic relationships with self and others, particularly around their therapeutic work. Highly directive, 'top-down' regulatory systems constrain such freedom, we argue, contaminating the therapeutic space with incongruent values, which inevitably limits what clients might gain from therapy. But what alternatives are there to these coercive systems of regulation, and are there any that can realistically be fit for purpose? We will also touch on this important issue and draw attention to some of the complexities involved.

State regulation

State regulation of counselling and psychotherapy has been a hot topic in the UK for several decades. Most recently, around 2008, the then Labour government proposed legally protecting the titles 'counsellor' and 'psychotherapist', making it illegal to use these titles without being on a register of practitioners intended to be held by the Health Professions Council (later renamed the Health and Care Professions Council (HCPC)). Practitioner psychologists were already regulated under the HCPC, and remain so, as are art psychotherapists and play therapists, but following a campaign involving thousands of counsellors, psychotherapists and psychoanalysts (Postle & House, 2009), the draft legislation for the psychological therapies was dropped in 2011 by the incoming coalition government, which implemented instead the Assured Voluntary Registration (AVR) scheme. Under this new, 'right touch' regulatory framework, a number of existing voluntary registers, such as those held by the United Kingdom Council for Psychotherapy (UKCP) and the British Association for Counselling & Psychotherapy (BACP), are endorsed, overseen and promoted by the Professional Standards Authority (PSA).

The debate over statutory regulation was fiercely argued and, in some quarters, highly divisive. An election for Chair of the UKCP was fought on the issue, and BACP backed the HCPC proposal until widespread concern among members provoked a last-minute U-turn. Across theoretical approaches, from humanistic therapies to psychoanalysis, colleagues found themselves at odds with each other. Yet, compared with the intense public conflicts in other groupings, the person-centred approach appeared relatively united against the HCPC proposal. At the height of the debate, two articles strongly criticising the plans from a person-centred perspective (Rogers, 2009; Thorne, 2009) were published in the same issue of the largest circulation professional counselling journal *Therapy Today*, but inspired no subsequent rebuttals. Meanwhile, following pressure from members (Florence et al, 2010), the British Association for the Person-Centred Approach (BAPCA) adopted a policy to reject the proposals and financially supported a campaign to take HCPC's conduct to judicial review – one of the clearest statements of opposition from any organisation in the field.

This relative unity is doubtless rooted in the history, traditions, theories, personalities and politics of the person-centred approach, and their incongruence with the HCPC proposals, which expressed a view of psychological distress and psychotherapeutic practice based on a rigid healthcare model. To therapists of many different persuasions, this highly medicalised interpretation of their work seemed inappropriate, but to person-centred practitioners it was an attack on the very core of their understanding of therapy and what it means to be a person in the world. As is well known, Carl Rogers himself became highly sceptical of the value of professional regulation and certification systems, and, indeed, of 'professionalism' itself. As he famously observed, 'there are as many certified charlatans and exploiters of people as there are uncertified' (Rogers, 1980: 235), deconstructing in that one statement the entire contemporary rationale for regulating the field. In terms of history, then, its founder left a clear marker for where the person-centred approach is positioned on matters of regulation. But, aside from these sentiments, a strong critique of state regulation is present in the theory and practice of the approach (Rogers, 2009), which emphasises not the expertise of the therapist but clients' capacities for change and their right to self-determination.

Within the person-centred approach, human beings are seen as having an inherent tendency towards growth and the fulfilment of potential, but this actualising tendency is facilitated or thwarted by environmental conditions. When our sense of worth in those environments is highly dependent on our satisfying often oppressive external conditions, then, in order to avoid losing the positive regard that we have come to learn we need (Standal, 1954), we can begin to behave – and ultimately think and feel – in ways that are incongruent with our own organismic valuing process (Mearns & Thorne, 1999). In doing so, our locus of evaluation becomes externalised – that is, how we evaluate both ourselves and our world becomes highly dependent on the judgment of others.

Person-centred therapy, it is argued, is in direct, creative relationship with this process. Where the person's environment is, or was, hostile and thwarts the fulfilment of potential, the therapeutic relationship creates the opportunity for our locus of evaluation to become internalised once more: this is 'an expected consequence of person-centred counselling' (Mearns & Thorne, 1999: 49). The relatively unconditional environment of good therapy (or other similarly engaged personal relationship) and the degree of freedom it provides – to think whatever we think, feel whatever we feel and be whoever we are – allows us to value our own experience and express it in more authentic ways, overcoming our previously internalised conditions of worth (Rogers, 1959).

This dynamic process is a matter of interpersonal and intrapersonal developmental psychology – one concerned principally with our relationships with significant others and how these affect our internal worlds, particularly through childhood and the processes of personality development. But we also exist in a social-cultural world; we are citizens of a society, and that society and its institutions and systems create powerful conditions of worth of their own. They too can be toxic, rather than growth promoting. To elaborate Carl Rogers' famous story of potatoes in a dark cellar still sending up fresh shoots towards the light from a small window (Rogers, 1980), if person-centred therapy is the soil, water and nutrients that might enable those potatoes not just to survive but to begin to achieve their potential, then what is the role of the wider environment? Surely it matters where our garden is and what the weather is like?

Say we replant our cellar-dwelling spuds in an attentively tended allotment. All would be well, surely? But what if the allotment is under threat because an aggressive housing developer wants to buy the land? What if the soil is affected by toxic leaks from a nearby factory? What if some fellow allotment holders want to sell their plots, and pressure us to do the same? What if they become highly critical of our gardening methods? Perhaps, against our better judgment, we feel pressured to change how we do things or to sell our plot too? Perhaps we become less attentive gardeners, or try to carry on as before but become overwhelmingly distressed or unwell ourselves? What then of the plants we intended to nourish?

The theoretical argument against a form of regulation in which the state defines practice and is legal gatekeeper and keyholder to the activity of therapy is that these are precisely the kind of disempowering conditions that will result. As the HCPC proposal demonstrated, such conditions are likely to actively corrode our ability to offer an opportunity for growth, and nowhere is this clearer than in the conflict of values between person-centred therapy and the state.

Person-centred values and the state

Psychological theories, as we know, are fallible. All have blind spots, areas of weakness and internal conflicts, and their construction can be motivated by a range of agendas, some more honourable than others. The person-centred approach is no exception, but person-centred therapy is not, like some other approaches, a matter of implementing theoretical insight via therapeutic technique in order to make good the hypothesised deficiencies in a client's psychology (Mearns & Thorne, 2000: 33–35). No doubt some therapists practice in such an instrumental way, but for many the approach is less a technique, less a set of theory-informed skills designed to have specific effects, less a treatment modality than a principled attitude to being a person in the world – what Carl Rogers called 'a way of being' (Rogers, 1980).

This approach to life, of which therapy practice is just one expression, is grounded in values: in beliefs about how to live, how to be with other people, how to respond to distress, how to organise and act collectively as groups and as a society. These are the politics of the person-centred approach, which have been described by Rogers and others as revolutionary (Rogers, 1977; Bozarth, 1998). The claimed radicalism here is that the person-centred approach subverts the tendency in other relationships – in families, education, work, organisations, politics and healthcare – towards the pursuit or uncritical acceptance of an oppressive level of power over others. In person-centred therapy, by contrast, we see the principled refusal of the role of expert technician: a disavowal of diagnosis and treatment in favour of *not-knowing*, *being-with* and *being-counter* (Schmid, 2002); a rejection of fear in favour of love (Thorne, 1985/2012). It is, in one view, the 'practice of freedom by free beings for free beings' (Grant, 2004: 163).

In state regulation of counselling and psychotherapy, by contrast, what is right for the people who access therapy – what the intentions, activities and outcomes should be – has to be approved by the government and its agencies. The problem is not only the inherently anti-person-centred principle of deferring to such a powerful and potentially coercive external authority on the intricately subjective matter of meeting another person in their distress – which inevitably means operating with a highly externalised professional locus of evaluation – but also that these institutions have very different agendas to those of many approaches to counselling and psychotherapy, and particularly the person-centred approach.

Never has this issue been more fraught than today. The UK government now views therapy as a treatment for discrete psychological disorders: a medicalised view of distress that garners ideological support in our culture from well-intentioned, celebrity-endorsed campaigns to destigmatise 'mental health' (Watts, 2015). Worse still, the state has come to see therapy as an intervention that can be mobilised to support the economy by reducing both sick leave and unemployment. This ideologically driven back-to-work agenda is explicit in the NHS Improving Access to the Psychological Therapies (IAPT) programme, and even more starkly apparent in the recent government move to co-locate IAPT-style therapists in or adjacent to jobcentres, with all the toxic power dynamics and devastating real-world impacts that such an overlap entails (Rogers & Atkinson, 2016).

The current predicament, though, is no simple policy matter. We live in a world in which everything can be bought and sold, everywhere is a potential marketplace, and therapy has not escaped – it too has become a commodity. We must be competitive to survive. We must show that we deliver the required outcome as efficiently as possible – that we are the fastest and cheapest. We need to market our product too, get our brand identity across, and when it comes to the marketplace of medicalised psychological treatment, this means being evidence-based. But not just any old evidence – it must be evidence that speaks the language of medicine and healthcare. And the closer the therapy field comes to identifying with medicine and healthcare, to seeing itself as a drug rather than a dialogue (Guy et al, 2011), the more it takes on board the risk-averse, reductionist, anxiety-driven, dehumanising and trust-eroding language and practices of those fields, as they have evolved over recent times (Rizq, 2013).

From the perspective of an approach that is actively opposed to the medicalising of distress (Sanders, 2005) and exists to counteract forces of disempowerment, it is hard to see any good in this increasingly cosy relationship between the state – via the enmeshed spheres of work, welfare and the NHS – and the field of counselling and psychotherapy. Historically, of course, the person-centred approach has always been something of a counter-cultural phenomenon, as have other humanistic approaches. But the language and culture of the therapy professions is becoming colonised by the values of healthcare and the neoliberal idea that everything is a commodity. When the market decides the value of everything, what else can we do but compete for acceptance? And what better way to demonstrate our worth than to seek the external validation of statutory regulation – to become a state-approved therapy or therapist?

It is a dilemma that person-centred theory is well placed to articulate. When therapy itself is subject to oppressive professional and socio-political conditions of worth – when what is demanded of us professionally is not congruent with our own experience – then, just to survive, we risk constructing a professional false self (Gladstone, personal communication) that is entirely at odds with that experience. In such a state, the therapist is acting as if the values internalised from these oppressive professional and socio-political environments are their own – an inherent incongruence that will inevitably stifle their capacity to fully experience the therapeutic attitudes, and thereby help others. How can a genuine and meaningful level of empathy and unconditional positive regard be achieved when, in relation to their work, the positive self-regard of the practitioner is deeply fractured, and a high degree of denial and distortion is required to maintain functioning as a therapist? Such a deep incongruence in both ourselves and our organisations can only be toxic for our encounters with those who come to us seeking greater congruence and meaning.

Far from protecting clients, then, by contaminating what the therapist brings to the co-created relationship, regulation potentially harms those who would wish to access person-centred and other relational therapies. At the very least, this must blunt the potential for clients to make use of the therapy space; at worst, the incongruence, or even complete dehumanisation, of the encounter might be actively harmful. Indeed, the enhanced status of the state-approved therapist means the role potentially 'attracts precisely the person who succumbs to the allurement of power, and who is therefore more likely to abuse it' (Thorne, 2002: 5). What is more, the 'public protection' rationale for regulation, which has been subject to extensive critique from a humanistic standpoint (Mowbray, 1995), might in itself be damaging:

> Creating the illusion that clients will be safe because of a state-registered system carries its own risks. As in wider society, the increasing dependence on other external sources to protect the vulnerable could serve to lessen the chances of clients following their own senses, thus limiting their ability to make their own judgements of perceived risk and threat. (Murphy, 2009: 44)

So we have a significant and daunting challenge. Given these huge obstacles, how do we create the right conditions for person-centred practice to thrive? Is any form of external regulation appropriate? While we might be aghast at some of the ways our field has become entangled with the agendas of the state, surely our clients – and society generally – are still entitled to require therapists to be accountable for their actions in some way?

Regulation, registration and accountability

While we do not have state regulation of counselling and psychotherapy via legal protection of title or function in the UK, the professional landscape is far from being an anarchic free-for-all. As mentioned above, we have a system of assured voluntary registers endorsed by a state body, the PSA, which sets standards, ensures compliance from these registers and promotes them to the public. The registers themselves are held by independent therapy organisations, and there is no legal compulsion for practitioners to sign up. But the reality is that it is practically impossible to get an employed position as a counsellor or psychotherapist without being on one of the bigger registers, such as that of BACP or UKCP. And the conventions around professional practice in the private sphere, where membership of these organisations is common, suggest that here too it is perceived as beneficial and responsible to join one such system of professional accountability.

As the scheme is quite new, many trainees, newly qualified therapists and some more experienced practitioners might be wondering whether or not to join a register. Access requires applicants to have completed a practitioner training. Depending on the professional body and the title used (counsellor or psychotherapist), this training will be at a level set by the professional body. Once registered, an annual fee is required to continue with membership of the organisation that grants admission to the register. Members are also required to maintain a level of continuing professional development, keep up a minimum level of practice, and be in regular supervision. By signing the approved register, a practitioner is agreeing to carry out their work in accordance with the ethical codes or frameworks developed by the professional body. When a client or colleague believes that the practitioner's standard of practice has fallen below the expected level, or that they have conducted themselves in a manner considered to bring the profession into disrepute, a complaint can be made. Depending on the seriousness of the issue, the practitioner might find they are either sanctioned to undertake further training or professional and personal development or they may be struck off the register altogether.

While each professional body has their own system for registering practitioners, membership benefits run across registers. Certainly, one important reason why practitioners join a register is because it demonstrates to potential employers and clients a certain level of qualification that is claimed to be commensurate with good professional practice. So there is an economic and career advantage, as well as the less tangible perks of professional status and esteem. There are benefits for a registered therapist's clients too, as they have a clear line for reporting a complaint, and can be assured that the complaint will be dealt with by the professional organisation. Few practitioners, we assume, join a register because they relish the prospect of being brought before an ethics committee, but it is a widely shared view across the professions that there is an ethical imperative for an individual's practice to be located within some sort of accountability framework.

So, the appeal of the system is clear. There is, however, an important question as to whether any professional body can effectively regulate the practice of a very wide range of therapeutic approaches and, crucially for the discussion here, whether any of the professional organisations, or indeed the AVR system itself, offers a system of accountability that is consistent with the person-centred approach. We have seen above the incongruence between person-centred principles and the most heavy-handed forms of state regulation, but how *values-congruent* with the person-centred approach are the organisational processes and procedures of the current 'assured voluntary' system?

One issue for person-centred practitioners is the nature of the complaints proceedings for the major organisations and registers, in which evidence is weighed by a committee or panel, which then passes down a verdict on guilt and decides on sanctions. The sanctions are often developmental (therapy, training, supervision, reflection), rather than simply punitive, but rarely, if ever, is some form of mediation offered in an effort to explore and work through the conflict. This hardly embodies the person-centred approach's commitment to and belief in the constructive potential of relationships. On the contrary, the complaints process can be a traumatic experience for both complainant and practitioner (Thomas, 2005). And these are not, of course, crimes that are being investigated. In the thankfully rare instances where a therapist does commit crimes against a client, there are existing legal processes to deal with that. More often, grievances in therapy involve complex relational matters. Sanctions and judgments might be necessary, but should we not expect therapist organisations to be able to deal with such conflicts more therapeutically than they do now?

Similarly problematic from a person-centred perspective is that wrongdoing in complaints procedures is defined by reference to an organisation's ethical code or framework, which may or may not accurately reflect the practitioner's own philosophy and practices, however embedded their practice is in an established approach to therapy. Historically, this has been complicated by therapists' own approaches not being sufficiently represented on the ethics/complaints panels judging their work, resulting in absurd sanctions based on entirely conflicting views about the purposes of therapy. Framing the cause of malpractice in theoretical terms does not in and of itself present a problem, so long as the practitioner intended in the first instance to be working in a way that is consistent with that theory. Khele, Symons and Wheeler (2008) point to this, reporting that, while the theoretical orientation of the therapist being complained against is not often recorded in complaint files, organisations such as Witness (now called the Centre for Boundary Studies), which exert significant pressure on both professional and public minds about therapeutic practitioners, claim that 'malpractice or abuse can occur through the therapist's *mismanagement of the transference*' (Khele, Symons & Wheeler, 2008: 130, emphasis added) – a point clearly meaningless to person-centred therapists (cf. Shlien, 1984).

But this question of conflicting worldviews has become about much more than just theoretical orientation. In the wake of the collapse of state regulation, the largest registering organisation, BACP, has revised its ethical framework in ways that draw therapy as a whole much closer to a state-endorsed healthcare model (Musgrave, 2014; Jenkins, 2015), uncritically adapting to cultural shifts that seem at odds with therapeutic values, especially person-centred ones. These are very much 'top-down' processes, with a small number of influential people in powerful positions making decisions about the trajectory of the professions. To use the analogy of therapy itself, it is as if the field has acquired a highly instrumental and directive team of therapists who interpret its disparate and at times counter-cultural complexity as a disorder that must be treated by alignment with the medical, healthcare and social welfare professions.

None of which is to say that it is impossible to work authentically as a person-centred practitioner within the existing system of approved registers. Many already do. But there are considerable tensions emerging, which will doubtless become harder to tolerate if the profession continues in its current direction. Even if, for now, we see AVR as sufficiently non-toxic to continue to practise, perhaps we can still find space to consider how else we might locate our work within a framework of civic accountability? Are there alternatives to the heavily 'top-down' approach: systems that can instead foster and support more organic, 'bottom-up' processes and achieve greater congruence with person-centred values?

Independent Practitioners Network

The most striking example – perhaps the only one – of a truly alternative model of professional accountability is the Independent Practitioners Network (IPN), which began in the early-to-mid 90s, partly in response to the proposed statutory regulation of psychotherapists and counsellors (see Totton, 1997/2011; IPN, 2016).

IPN is a 'self-generating practitioner community in which participatory ethics… are privileged over didactic, responsibility-eschewing institutional Codes of Ethics' (House, 2003: 253). It operates on a principle of peer-to-peer civic accountability, via a network of small groups. Each member group must meet regularly and include at least four individual practitioners who know about and are willing to 'stand by' one another's work, and are willing to respond to problems or conflicts in that work. The group meetings are not intended to replace supervision but instead offer a supplementary chance for practitioners to have their work reviewed and held accountable. Each group is linked to two other groups in a 'relationship of mutual validation and responsibility' (Totton, 1997/2011: 289). So the accountability of any single practitioner's work is through the other members of their own group, plus the two linked groups.

'The "standing-by" process means that each and every practitioner has a built-in and intrinsic interest in the quality of their colleagues' work' (House, 2003: 253). Should a problem arise in a member's practice, both their own group and the linked groups will be 'committed to seeking a resolution: not through a fixed and formal procedure, but in a way which is tailored to the specific situation, and to the specific outcomes sought by both client and practitioner' (Totton, 1997: 292). So the model is not one of trial and blame, but of conflict resolution.

Structurally, the network is 'non-hierarchical' and 'low bureaucracy', and operates on the basis that no single central organisation can or should have the right to decide who should practise therapy. All IPN participants are viewed as having equal status, and the network is open to practitioners of all levels of experience and all orientations and modes of practice. Instead of operating top-down, hierarchical processes and structures, it is both 'horizontal' and 'multi-centred'. There is no single standardised code of ethics: each member group creates and circulates its own guidelines, which are challenged, supported and validated by the linked groups. By stepping out of a centralised, top-down approach, it is argued, it is possible to recognise and respect the freedom to practise while maintaining a rigorous culture of challenge and openness. The network is grounded in the belief that best practice is achieved most effectively, not through rules, codes, registers and hierarchies, but through honesty, integrity and transparency in authentic relationships offering mutual support and challenge.

The IPN system seems to be highly consistent with the person-centred approach, and offers a very promising alternative to existing accountability systems. Indeed, some person-centred therapists are already participants. The model is certainly congruent with the person-centred approach's attitudes to relationships, groups and conflict resolution, and it is clearly more attuned to the kinds of power issues that concern person-centred practitioners, with accountability and validation coming through reflective engagement with authentically supportive and challenging personal relationships, rather than through conformity with a set of professional expectations defined by a powerful and distant external regulatory authority. Perhaps unintentionally, IPN seems to be a precise extrapolation of person-centred values into the domain of therapist accountability and ethical responsibility.

An authentic professional future?

Whether or not the IPN model is good enough for the demands of our culture and the contemporary anxieties of practitioners and clients alike is up for debate. Is it just too counter-cultural? Might some therapists and clients feel wary of the absence of an overarching authority that will define and police the activity of counselling and psychotherapy? Are we just too used to the illusory comforts of deferring to professional expertise and increasingly defensive and risk-averse bureaucracies? These are crucial questions around which much is at stake, not least ongoing access to authentic person-centred therapy for the clients of the future. So we invite readers of this chapter to consider their own affiliations, registrations and accreditations. What are your personal and professional motives for acquiring registration or pursuing regulation? Can these be disentangled from each other, and from the organisational, professional and socio-political pressures we face? When you sign up to, or argue for, any one system of accountability, what degree of congruence is there between the personal benefits for you of that system, your philosophy of practice, the effects on the therapeutic space, and the political implications of its widespread adoption?

These are certainly questions with which we, as authors and practitioners, continue to wrestle.

And there are issues for trainers, researchers and theoreticians of counselling and psychotherapy too. In these influential roles, we have to be mindful of the powerful messages conveyed to students and trainees of the approach – as well as to the profession and the culture at large – and the dangers of corrosive distortions and contradictions leaking into accepted person-centred and psychotherapeutic wisdom. It is simply not sufficient to be absent from such debates. It is our responsibility to engage critically in an authentic dialogue on these matters, even if that means being in tension with both the professional bodies and the political agendas that drive some of their policies. While the person-centred theory and practice of therapy often run counter to many of the toxic trends we have discussed, perhaps it is time to walk-the-talk in our professional organisations and frameworks. If we want a good enough environment for the flourishing of the person-centred approach and other relational approaches, perhaps we need to take the bold step of expressing our professional authentic selves out in the potentially hostile worlds of registration, regulation and civic accountability, embodying there the values we routinely bring to our therapeutic relationships?

References

Bozarth J (1998). *Person-Centred Therapy: a revolutionary paradigm*. Ross-on-Wye: PCCS Books.

Florence H, Freire E, Henn R, McGahey P, Murphy D, Rogers A, Shannon B (2010). *The future of the person-centred approach in the UK and the case against HPC and state regulation: an open letter to the British Association for the Person-Centred Approach (BAPCA)*. [Online]. www.bapca.org.uk/images/files/bapca_open_letter.pdf (accessed 12 June, 2016).

Grant B (2004). The imperative of ethical justification in psychotherapy: the special case of client-centred therapy. *Person-Centred and Experiential Psychotherapies* 3(3): 152–165.

Guy A, Thomas R, Stephenson S, Loewenthal D (2011). *NICE Under Scrutiny: the impact of the National Institute for Health and Clinical Excellence guidelines on the provision of psychotherapy in the UK*. London: University of Roehampton Research Centre for Therapeutic Education/ UKCP Research Unit.

House R (2003). Reflections and elaborations on 'post-professionalised' therapy practice. In: Bates Y, House R (eds). *Ethically Challenged Professions: enabling innovation and diversity in psychotherapy and counselling*. Ross-on-Wye: PCCS Books (pp237–256).

Independent Practitioners Network (IPN) (2016). Independent Practitioners Network. [Online]. http://ipnetwork.org.uk/sample-page/ (accessed 8 June, 2016).

Jenkins P (2015). What is wrong with the Ethical Framework? A consideration of the new BACP Ethical Framework and its implications. [Online]. *Contemporary Psychotherapy* 7(2). www.contemporarypsychotherapy.org/volume-7-no-2-winter-2015/what-is-wrong-with-the-ethical-framework/ (accessed 8 June, 2016).

Khele S, Symons C, Wheeler S (2008). An analysis of complaints to the British Association for Counselling and Psychotherapy, 1996–2006. *Counselling and Psychotherapy Research* 8: 124–132.

Mearns D, Thorne B (1999). *Person-Centred Counselling in Action* (2nd ed). London: Sage.

Mearns D, Thorne B (2000). *Person-Centred Therapy Today: new frontiers in theory and practice*. London: Sage.

Mowbray R (1995). *The Case Against Psychotherapy Registration: a conservation issue for the Human Potential Movement*. [Online.] London: Trans Marginal Press. www.transmarginalpress.co.uk (accessed 13 June, 2016).

Murphy D (2009). The politics of power. Letter to the editor. *Therapy Today* 20(9): 44

Musgrave A (2014). BACP's ethical framework revisions – the emergence of state-endorsed therapy? [Blog.] The Alliance for Counselling & Psychotherapy; 5 December. https://allianceblogs.wordpress.com/2014/12/05/bacp_state_endorsed_therapy/> (accessed 8 June, 2016).

Postle D, House R (eds) (2009). *Compliance? Ambivalence? Rejection? Nine papers challenging the Health Professions Council July 2009 proposals for the state regulation of the psychological therapies*. WLR London: [Online]. Wentworth Learning Resources. www.lulu.com/content/7709462 (accessed 8 June, 2016).

Rizq R (2013). The language of healthcare. *Therapy Today* 24(2): 20–24.

Rogers A (2009). Dare we do away with professionalism? *Therapy Today* 20(4): 26–29.

Rogers A, Atkinson P (2016). Ethical dialogue. *Self & Society* 43(4): 375–383.

Rogers CR (1959). A theory of therapy, personality, and interpersonal relationships, as developed in the client-centered framework. In: Koch S (ed). *Psychology: a study of science. Study 1, volume 3: formulations of the person and the social context*. New York: McGraw-Hill (pp184–256).

Rogers CR (1977). *On Personal Power*. London: Constable.

Rogers CR (1980). *A Way of Being*. Boston: Houghton Mifflin.

Sanders P (2005). Principled and strategic opposition to the medicalisation of distress and all of its apparatus. In: Joseph S, Worsley R. *Person-Centred Psychopathology: a positive psychology of mental health*. Ross-on-Wye: PCCS Books (pp21–42).

Schmid PF (2002). Knowledge or acknowledgement: psychotherapy as the art of 'not-knowing' – prospects on further developments of a radical paradigm. *Person-Centered and Experiential Psychotherapies* 1(1–2): 56–70.

Shlien J (1984). A counter-theory of transference. In: Levant RH, Shlien J (eds). *Client-Centered Therapy and the Person-Centered Approach*. New York: Praeger (pp153–181).

Standal SW (1954). *The need for positive regard: a contribution to client-centered theory*. Unpublished doctoral thesis. Chicago, IL: University of Chicago.

Thomas JT (2005). Licensing board complaints: minimizing the impact on the psychologist's defense and clinical practice. *Professional Psychology: Research and Practice* 36: 426–433.

Thorne B (1985/2012). The quality of tenderness. In: Thorne B. *Counselling and Spiritual Accompaniment: bridging faith and person-centred therapy*. Chichester: John Wiley (pp31–41).

Thorne B (2002). Guest editorial. Regulation – a treacherous path. *Counselling & Psychotherapy Journal* 13(2): 5.

Thorne B (2009). A collision of worlds. *Therapy Today* 20(4): 22–25.

Totton N (1997/2011). Independent Practitioners Network: a new model of accountability. In: House R, Totton N (eds). *Implausible Professions: arguments for pluralism and autonomy in psychotherapy and counselling* (2nd ed). Ross-on-Wye: PCCS Books (pp315–322).

Watts J (2015). Is mental suffering really 'just like any other illness'? [Blog]. Huffington Post Lifestyle; 5 November. www.huffingtonpost.co.uk/dr-jay-watts/mental-health-illness_b_8460340.html (accessed 23 March, 2016).

RESEARCH

22

Searching for the core: the interface of client-centred principles with other therapies[1]

Jerold D Bozarth and Noriko Motomasa

This chapter reviews first, Rogers' theory of client-centred psychotherapy; second, the conclusions of research on the 'necessary and sufficient conditions' postulated by Rogers (1957); third, the conclusions of psychotherapy outcome research over the last two decades, and fourth, the application of the results of psychotherapy outcome research. This exploration is considered in relation to the interface of client-centred principles in the mental health treatment system, which operate with a different view of psychotherapy. Vignettes of client-centred principles in therapeutic situations are presented.

Carl R Rogers (1951) formally introduced a revolutionary theory of psychotherapy identified as 'client-centered therapy'. The theory was identified as client-centred (to switch to the UK spelling) therapy after first being identified as 'non-directive' therapy (Rogers, 1942). The theory was revolutionary for several reasons. First, the locus of control was centred with the constructive organismic direction of the client. Second, the client was considered the source of the healing process. It was within a special relationship with the therapist that the client's development could become congruent with the constructive organismic process. The activities central to most theories of therapy were reversed, as Rogers' theory dismissed the importance of such activities as accurate diagnostic judgment and the use of techniques to alter the client's attitudes and behaviour. The power and control resting with the therapist was shifted to the client (Rogers, 1977: 3). The therapist's task was to create the opportunity for the client to connect with the constructive direction of the organism.

---

1. Sections of this chapter were published under the title 'The Art of "Being" in Psychotherapy' in *The Humanistic Psychologist Special Triple Issue: The Art of Psychotherapy 29*, 1–3, spring, summer, fall, 2001, 167–203. Reproduced with permission of the American Psychological Association, Division of Humanistic Psychology (Division 32).

The radical position of client-centred therapy is reviewed in relation to therapies that operate from other basic assumptions. Our examination suggests that the conditions of the therapeutic process postulated in client-centred therapy are the basic therapeutic ingredients for effectiveness in all approaches of psychotherapy. Rogers (1957) proposed this commonality in an 'integration' paper that generated over three decades of psychotherapy outcome research. Analyses of psychotherapy outcome research during the 1990s conclude that 70 per cent of successful therapy is predicated on the client-therapist relationship and client resources (Duncan & Miller, 2000; Hubble, Duncan & Miller, 1999; Lambert, 1992).

Client-centred therapy

Rogers (1959) was the first investigator to apply quantitative empirical research to the field of psychotherapy. He presented the only formal theory of therapy that delineates a format for scientific inquiry research. His self-proclaimed *magnum opus* identified only six conditions that are *necessary and sufficient* for the therapeutic process. Three of these conditions are attitudes to be held by the therapist. Specifically, he states:

1.   That two persons are in *contact*.

2.   That the first person, whom we shall term the client, is in a state of *incongruence*, being vulnerable, or anxious.

3.   That the second person, whom we shall term the therapist, is *congruent* in the *relationship*.

4.   That the therapist is *experiencing unconditional positive regard* toward the client.

5.   That the therapist is *experiencing* an *empathic* understanding of the client's *internal frame of reference*.

6.   That the client *perceives*, at least to a minimal degree, conditions 4 and 5, the *unconditional positive regard* of the therapist for him, and the *empathic* understanding of the therapist. (Rogers, 1959: 213)

The three postulates (3, 4 and 5) that are 'therapist conditions' can be construed as theoretical and pragmatic instructions for therapists. Brief definitions of these conditions are:

•   *Congruence* – The symbolization of the therapist's own experience in the relationship must be accurate. The therapist '… should accurately "be himself" in the relationship, whatever the self of that moment may be' (p214). Synonymous terms are: 'integrated, whole, genuine' (p206)

•   *Unconditional positive regard* – The self-experiences of the client are perceived as worthy of positive regard without discrimination by the therapist. In general, acceptance and prizing are synonymous terminology (p208)

- *Empathy* – 'The state of empathy, or being empathic, is to perceive the internal frame of reference of another with accuracy, and with the emotional components and meanings which pertain thereto, as if one were the other person, but without ever losing the "as if" condition' (p210).

The six conditions are the basic therapeutic assumptions that facilitate client change. The linear construction of the theory is that, if these conditions exist, there will be certain process and outcome changes in clients. The changes include increased freedom to express feelings through verbal and other modal channels; greater unconditional positive self-regard; one's self as the locus of evaluation, and the client experiencing themself less in terms of conditions of worth and more in terms of the organismic valuing process.

The outcome changes are predicated on the postulate that: 'The client is more *congruent*, more *open to his experience*, less *defensive*' (Rogers, 1959: 218). Hence, the client will be more psychologically adjusted, more objective, and more realistic. The client is more apt to observe the locus of evaluation and locus of choice as residing in self. Process and outcome variables are interchangeable, in that there are no intervening variables in the process conception of client-centred therapy (Rogers, 1959: 220).

The revolutionary difference between these assumptions and those of other theories has contributed to a chasm between client-centred and other therapeutic approaches. Ironically, Carl Rogers' (1957) abiding interest was to discover the common factors related to therapeutic effectiveness, regardless of the therapy or type of helping relationship.

The quagmire of different assumptions

The search for effectiveness is affected by basic assumptions about psychotherapy. An article in the *New York Times* (Carey, 2004) reported the intense strain between two directions of psychotherapy at the 2004 American Psychological Association convention. One direction is predicated on a particular view of scientific research requiring a focus on problems and defined treatment procedures. The other direction focuses on the therapist's more general therapeutic involvement with clients.

One view believes that there is empirical evidence that supports the thesis of specific treatments for particular diagnoses. These treatments can be administered with manualised guidelines. The proponents of this view believe that there are 'empirically-supported treatments' (EST) (Task Force on Promotion and Dissemination of Psychological Procedures, 1995). Others (Bozarth, 1998, 2002; Duncan & Miller, 2000; Hubble, Duncan & Miller, 1999; Messer & Wampold, 2002; Norcross, 2000; Wampold, 2001) challenge the premises and claims of these advocates. The latter view asserts that the research evidence supports the common factors of relationship and client resources as accounting for the major variance in psychotherapy outcomes. This view is discussed later.

Differences about effectiveness of treatment for mental problems have existed since the advent of psychotherapy. The 1985 Phoenix conference on 'The Evolution of Psychotherapy' dramatically illustrates this point (Zeig, 1987). In a report on the promotion of scientific psychotherapy, Joseph Wolpe (1987) described the conference '… as a babble of conflicting voices'. There is little evidence that there has been much change nearly 30 years later. The advent of empirically supported treatments and subsequent reactions have simply accelerated the babble.

The Phoenix conference exemplified two general assumptions about psychotherapy. One assumption is that humans are primarily reactive to external stimuli (eg. Skinner) that reinforce behaviour. The other is that humans react to internal stimuli identified as inner motivations (eg. Freud). The second assumption includes the conceptualisation that humans are in the process of becoming.

Rogers delineated a more radical position within the second assumption: namely, he referred to the 'self-actualization process' – a developmental process of the self that becomes congruent to the organismic 'actualizing tendency' when individuals experience unconditional positive regard and empathic understanding (Rogers, 1959).

Our conclusion is that the common factors embedded in the client–therapist relationship and the client's self-determination and own resources are the major contributors to therapeutic effectiveness. Client-centred principles have been integral elements of these, and at the forefront in the exploration of common therapeutic factors.

The necessary and sufficient conditions of therapeutic personality change

Early in his career, Rogers indicated that his abiding interest was to find the common variables related to successful outcome for all therapies. He crystallised this search in the early 1950s, as reported in discussion papers circulated at the Counseling Center of the University of Chicago. Rogers (1957, 1959) wrote two seminal articles emanating from these discussions. The first article (Rogers, 1957) was dubbed the 'Integration Statement' (Bozarth, 1998; Stubbs & Bozarth, 1996), and 'Conditions Therapy Theory' by Barrett-Lennard (1998).

As early as 1974, Patterson wrote: 'The days of schools in counseling and psychotherapy are drawing to a close' (pix). In several books, Patterson (1974; 1984; 1985; Patterson & Hidore, 1997) identified the common factors put forward by Rogers as the central assumptions for an eclectic psychotherapy. Patterson's (1984) review of the reviews of psychotherapy outcome research concluded that the conditions were the potent factors in successful therapy. Nevertheless, schools of psychotherapy multiplied throughout the decades of the 1980s and 1990s, and it was the behaviourally oriented schools, with their view of the reactive human being, that gained strong footholds in the mental health treatment system.

The research on the necessary and sufficient conditions dominated common factor psychotherapy outcome studies from the latter part of the 1950s into the 1980s (Bozarth, Zimring & Tausch, 2002). During this time, there was substantial research supporting Rogers' postulates of the attitudinal conditions. Confirmation of the research support from over three decades of findings was dismissed by many researchers with the rationale that the conditions had been found to be 'necessary but not sufficient', and that more specificity was needed. The assumption that the research on the conditions was not supported was predicated on fewer than half a dozen reviews. In addition, most of these reviews did not refute the research findings; rather, they called for more robust research designs (Bozarth et al, 2002). Studies concerned with congruence, unconditional positive regard and empathy diminished in the 1990s, alongside an increase in research on specificity. Later, overviews of the research and meta-analyses identified the greatest contributors to the effectiveness of psychotherapy as the common factors.

Conclusions of psychotherapy research over the last two decades

Rogers' 1957 paper was about the common factors in all therapies and helping relationships. Rogers' (1959) formal theory statement delineated his 'common factors' as the theoretical crux of the therapeutic process in client-centred therapy. In short, the common factors posited for all therapies became the foundation of the therapeutic process in client-centred therapy.

It was the 1957 integration paper that had the most profound influence on the entire field of psychotherapy. There was a shift from research that studied the difference of effectiveness among different therapeutic approaches to research that examined the attitudinal conditions in relation to the effectiveness of all therapies. Congruence, unconditional positive regard and empathy were central ingredients in much of this research (Bozarth, Zimring & Tausch, 2002).

The power of more broadly defined common factors in psychotherapy became increasingly recognised over the 1990s. Lambert (1992) classified the variability of psychotherapy success to conclude that the contributions of common factors accounted for most of the variance. His estimates were not derived directly from meta-analytic techniques but were, rather, '... the research findings of a wide range of treatments, disorders, and ways of measuring client and therapist characteristics' (Lambert & Barley, 2001: 357). The percentages of a subset of more than 100 statistical analyses that predicted outcome were averaged by the size of the contribution that each predictor made to the outcome. The relative contributions of variables that affececded outcome were identified. These variables and the estimated percentage of success variance accounted for were: 1) extra-therapeutic change (40%); 2) common factors (30%); 3) expectancy (or placebo) (15%), and

4) techniques (15%) (p97). Lambert's definitions are presented below (1992: 97):

- *extra-therapeutic change* – those factors that are a part of the client (such as ego strength and other homeostatic mechanisms) and part of the environment (such as fortuitous events, social support) that aid in recovery regardless of participation in therapy

- *expectancy (placebo effects)* – that portion of improvements that results from the client's knowledge that he/she is being treated and from the differential credibility of specific treatment techniques and rationale

- *techniques* – those factors unique to specific therapies (such as biofeedback, hypnosis, or systematic desensitization)

- *common factors* – the host of variables that are found in a variety of therapies regardless of the therapist's theoretical orientation: such as empathy, warmth, acceptance, encouragement of risk taking etc.

Others (Bozarth, 1998; Duncan & Miller, 2000; Hubble et al, 1999; Norcross, 1997) also cite these variables and extend the terminology. For example, common factors and relationship are used interchangeably, and extra-therapeutic change is periodically referred to as client resources (referring to the inner and external resources of the client). As noted, Lambert derived his conclusion from logical classification of the research results, rather than from statistical analyses. Later meta-analysis demonstrated through statistical analyses that 70 per cent of the success variance is accounted for by common rather than specific variance (Wampold, 2001).

Bozarth (1998) summarised major research reviews on psychotherapy outcome and came to the following conclusions:

1. Effective psychotherapy is primarily predicated upon (a) the relationship between the therapist and the client and (b) the inner and external resources of the client.

2. The type of therapy and technique is largely irrelevant in terms of successful outcome.

3. Training, credentials and experience of therapists are irrelevant to successful therapy.

4. Clients who receive psychotherapy improve more than clients who do not receive psychotherapy.

5. There is little evidence to support the position that there are specific treatments for particular disabilities.

6. The most consistent of the relationship variables related to effectiveness are the conditions of empathy, genuineness and unconditional positive regard. (p165)

Three decades later, the research reviews reflected the major notions observed by Berenson and Carkhuff (1967) and the Strupp, Fox and Lessler (1969) survey: namely, '... the importance of the client's involvement in their own treatment and the minuscule influence of "interventive" techniques' (Bozarth, 1998: 167).

There were two analyses of research that were especially revealing. First, Duncan and Moynihan (1994) summarised reviews of quantitative research studies and proposed a model of psychotherapy predicated upon the conclusions of the research. They suggested the intentional utilisation of the client's frame of reference. Their conclusion suggested that successful therapy called for '... a function of the client's unique perceptions and experience and requires that therapists respond flexibly to clients' needs, rather than from a particular theoretical frame of reference or behavioral set' (Duncan & Moynihan, 1994: 295).

The second was a qualitative review of psychotherapy efficacy research (Stubbs & Bozarth, 1994). A major finding from this study was that the general conclusion that the common conditions postulated by Rogers were necessary but 'not sufficient' was not consistent with the data. This conclusion was, at best, an extrapolation of flawed logic that lacked even one direct study to support the assertion. Evolving temporal categories of effective psychotherapy suggested that, first, the major thread running through more than four decades of efficacy research was the relationship of the therapist–client, and this thread included Rogers' attitudinal conditions of the therapist, and second, that the research basis for the 'specificity question' had 'abysmal research support', and the precursor of the 'specificity' assumption was the unsupported assertion that Rogers' conditions were necessary but not sufficient (Bozarth, 1998: 168).

It became clear that the increased investigation of specificity was not based on the results of previous research. In fact, research demonstrated that client perceptions of the relationship are the most consistent predictor of improvement (Gurman, 1977; Lafferty, Beutler & Crago, 1989).

Wampold's (2001) meta-analysis brought forth continued revelations of the efficacy of common factors over specificity. He compared the benefits of a 'contextual' versus a 'medical' meta-model of psychotherapy. The medical model is characterised by specific problem-solving ingredients; the contextual model is characterised by the essence of therapy being embodied in the client-therapist relationship. It became clear that the therapist who is delivering treatment is more crucial than the specific procedure used. Other meta-analyses (Ahn & Wampold, 2001; Elliott, 1997; Grissom, 1996; Smith & Glass, 1977; Wampold et al, 1997) yielded comparable results.

Several articles and books identified the client as her own best generator of self-change. One review of research asked, 'What makes psychotherapy work?', and answered, 'the active client' (Bohart & Tallman, 1996). They concluded that what makes therapy effective is not only the client's frame of reference and more reliance on the client, but also that '... we must truly understand that it is the whole person of the client who generates the processes and solutions that create change' (p26).

Duncan, Hubble & Miller's book (1997), summarising research findings and clinical discoveries, highlighted the '... clients' frame of reference, their worldview, as the determining "theory" for our work' (p206). Their later book on 'what works in therapy' (Hubble, Duncan & Miller, 1999) focused on the common factors culled from reviews of research studies.

Bohart (2004) brings attention to clients who act 'as active change agents who extract patterns of meaning from the therapy interaction, deduce implications, and use therapist empathy responses for purposes of self-support, validation, exploring experience, testing self-understanding, creating new meaning, and making connection with the therapist' (p104).

The major conclusion of psychotherapy outcome research is that the critical variables are the client–therapist relationship and extra-therapeutic variables (eg. client resources). However, this is a contentious conclusion between the different views about human beings.

There was a great push two decades ago by a task force of the Society of Clinical Psychology, Division 12 of the American Psychological Association, for the 'empirically supported treatments' proposal. Their efforts are founded on the assumption that there are specific treatments for particular dysfunctions (Task Force on Promotion and Dissemination of Psychological Procedures, 1995). The focus on empirically supported treatments has become a standard reference for the American Psychological Association.

Others identify intrinsic flaws of the empirically supported treatment paradigm that ignore, among other things, the examination of five decades of psychotherapy outcome research (Ahn & Wampold, 2001; Bozarth, 2002; Duncan & Miller, 2000; Quinn, 2015; Wampold, 2001). In particular, Quinn (2015) has revealed a sobering analysis and examination of the decades of previous research on the postulates of the therapeutic conditions. Among salient revelations in Quinn's book are: 1) that there was solid research from 1945 to 1975 that supported the effectiveness of client-centred therapy and the therapeutic conditions postulated by Rogers (ie. congruence, unconditional positive regard and empathy) as sufficient; 2) that the research shifted to dismissal and denigration of that research, starting in the late 1970s; 3) that this dismissal was based on inaccurate assumptions about the research designs and measurement procedures; 4) that the 'allegiance' factor of behavioural and psychoanalytic researchers drove the negative conclusions about the early research, and 5) that the research reviews after the late 1970s ignored the earlier studies and the reviews were founded on the basis of a few studies that were loaded with methodological problems of statistical design. The author goes further with his observation that contemporary 'person-centred therapies' using experiential, emotion-focused and pluralistic approaches cast Rogers' theoretical premises as obsolete and ineffective.

The bulk of the studies that compare different therapy modalities reveal that they are equally successful (Lambert, 1992; Hubble, Duncan & Miller, 1999). As noted previously, the reason for these findings is that it is the common elements, rather than differences, among these approaches that account for the success. The above variables are more general than Rogers' postulates, as indicated earlier by Lambert's (1992) definitions. Meta-analysis summaries (Ahn & Wampold, 2001; Wampold, 2001) have often identified the most familiar of the common factors to be the therapist–client alliance.

Horvath and Symonds (1991) found a correlation of .26 between alliance and outcome. Martin, Garske and Davis (2000) found a correlation of .22. These are medium effect sizes, accounting for seven per cent and five per cent of the outcome variance. Messer and Wampold indicate that: 'Clearly, the relationship accounts for dramatically more variability in outcome than specific ingredients' (p23). When these two meta-analyses were combined with 10 more recent published research studies, the overall effect size of .21 was compared with the overall effect size of .39 of psychotherapy (Smith & Glass, 1977). Horvath (2001), assuming quasi-independence of the active ingredients of therapy, concludes that: '… a little over half of the beneficial effects of psychotherapy accounted for in previous meta-analyses are linked to the quality of the alliance' (p366). The differentiation of alliance from relationship is somewhat questionable from both a conceptual and empirical review. Much of the empirical evidence uses therapeutic relationship and alliance synonymously. The conceptual base of alliance is from the authoritative stance of the therapist (eg. Freud's early papers) and theoretically, if not functionally, at odds with the view of the client as her/his own best expert about her/his life.

The researcher's allegiance reflecting the therapist's belief that her therapy is efficacious (referring to effectiveness determined through true research designs (Seligman, 1995)) turns out to have a whopping effect. Wampold (2001) and Luborsky et al (1999) suggest that 'almost 70% of the variability in effect sizes of treatment comparisons was due to allegiance' (Messer & Wampold, 2002: 23). In short, the researcher and therapist who believe strongly in the therapeutic approach are much more likely to have clients who improve, regardless of the particular approach. Factors such as acceptance, empathy and respect are generally embedded in the research findings that identify the relationship as the key factor. Lambert (1992: 97) refers directly to these conditions in his operational definition of 'common factors' (later referred to as the 'relationship'). The potency of the humanistic/experiential psychotherapies that focus on relationship in therapy has continued to be identified through meta-analysis designs (Elliott et al, 2013).

However, the specific variables of empathy and unconditional positive regard are often not explicitly included in the statistical analyses. Likewise, extra-therapeutic variables are embedded within the client's use of her resources in Rogers' conceptualisation. Rogers' assertion that it is the client's perception of the therapist's unconditional positive regard and empathic understanding that facilitates change is seldom a central focus of analysis in research studies.

Nevertheless, the overall conclusion of outcome research over the last two decades reaffirms that it is the client's active participation that accounts for successful therapy. Certain therapists facilitate more improvement in clients than do others, regardless of the therapist's therapy modality. The fundamental premises of client-centred therapy are embedded in the therapist–client relationship and in the focus on the client's frame of reference.

Use of the results of psychotherapy outcome research

Client-centred principles have been adopted in part by most therapies. These therapies, including behavioural, partially accept Rogers' (1957) 'necessary and sufficient' postulate. They accept the postulate as being necessary but do not consider it sufficient. Empathy and acceptance as necessary conditions have become common terminology for most therapies. However, these therapies believe that there must be something more that the therapist contributes. Generally, the idea of more therapist contribution refers to specific actions taken towards clients.

The Institute for the Study of Therapeutic Change (ISTC) group[2] insists that therapy that is change focused, client directed and outcome informed is based on psychotherapy outcome research. This approach to therapy can help the non-medical helping professions establish an identity separate from the field of medicine and provide clients with ethical and effective treatment. Hence, the ISTC group is involved in a systematic programme to focus on clients as the instruments of their own change. This group is spearheaded by the authors of *The Heroic Client* (Duncan & Miller, 2000). They transform the empirical 'facts' about successful therapy into practice dimensions. Their goals are to: 1) enhance the factors across theories that account for successful outcome; 2) use the client's theory of change to guide choice of techniques and integration of various therapy models, and 3) obtain valid and reliable feedback on the client's experience of the process and outcome of treatment (Duncan & Miller, 2000).

The emphasis of the ISTC group is different from that of the client-centred therapy model. The major difference is that the ISTC group provides – or more precisely, in their words, 'constructs with clients' – the intervention, whereas client-centred principles only instruct therapists to be congruent in their experiencing of unconditional positive regard toward the client and empathic understanding of the client's frame of reference. The ISTC group advocates selective listening, direct and pointed questions and responding to certain content of clients' stories for the purpose of providing 'more effective' therapy that reflects on clients' theories of change. Their approach assumes appropriate intervention is determined by the therapist. However, in client-centred therapy it is only the client's theory of change that is considered the substantial contribution. Nevertheless, the fundamental assumption about the client is the same: namely, the client is the real source of her own improvement. The ISTC group and client-centred practitioners are in

---

2. See www.talkingcure.com (accessed 21 January, 2017).

agreement about the major variables that are related to successful therapy: namely, the relationship and the client's unique resources.

Client-centred principles and the interface with other therapeutic approaches

There is striking correspondence with the core of client-centered principles and the crux of psychotherapy effectiveness. Correlation of success variance to the client-therapist relationship and the client's resources resonates with Rogers' basic postulates. However, nearly all therapies still focus on specific treatments and techniques, even though they account for only 15 per cent of the success variance. This percentage is comparable with the success variance of placebo effects. Messer and Wampold (2002: 24) advise:

> Because more variance is due to therapists than the nature of treatment, clients should seek the most competent therapist possible… whose theoretical orientation is compatible with their own outlook, rather than choosing a therapist strictly by expertise.

The fact that the crux of successful therapy for all therapies is related to common factors has little effect on the position status of client-centred therapy in most treatment programmes. The mental health treatment system continues to focus on the concept of specific treatment for particular diagnoses or dysfunction. The client-centred assumption that it is only the client's perception of the experiencing therapist that facilitates constructive client change does not resonate well with specific treatment models.

This fact often requires client-centred therapists to adjust when working in systems that are neither sympathetic nor understanding of the client-centred approach. Bozarth's (2001) description of his experience in mental health treatment and counselling centres suggests that such adjustment is possible.

Bozarth says that he learned client-centred therapy from long-term patients with severe mental health conditions in state mental institutions, before he was aware of client-centred therapy or the writings of Carl Rogers. Bozarth was employed as a psychiatric rehabilitation counsellor in two state mental hospitals. One was a conventional state hospital in the 1950s, and the other a training centre for psychiatrists that provided six-month treatment programmes for a wide variety of patients during the early 1960s. The rehabilitation programmes focused on vocational development that involved very specific objectives of facilitating patients toward independent living and employment. Financial resources were available to assist clients with obtaining these objectives. Thus, the operational philosophy of the client-centred approach was at odds with the hospital operational assumptions of medical diagnosis and with the operational assumptions of specific agency goals (eg. the goal of employment).

The following vignette offers one example of how the realities of institutional treatment goals and dedication to client-centred postulates were possible. The client, Howard, was in the conventional state hospital:

Howard had been in the hospital for over 20 years, diagnosed with schizophrenia, paranoid type. He spent several years in a special institution for the criminally insane because of brutal knife attacks on several people. When we first met, he said that he had heard about me from other residents and had asked his physician to refer him. We met for two or three formal appointments, during which he talked mostly about his jobs in the hospital. He had a paper round delivering the local paper to hospital staff who lived on the grounds. He also did yard work for some of the staff. We also discussed some of the resources available through the rehabilitation programme, including support for vocational training. He said that he was interested in some kind of training, and that staff had tried to help him get out of the hospital numerous times, but it just never worked out. He then concluded that he was really too afraid to get out of the hospital and decided to not see me for any more appointments. He felt that he would not be able to function outside of the hospital.

Over the next year, we casually chatted in the coffee shop or under a shady tree about his girlfriends, his work activities, and sometimes about world events. Nearly a year after our initial contact, Howard asked for an appointment and immediately picked up on our conversation of the first formal meetings, as though there had only been a few days' lapse. He thought that he might be interested in going to 'barbers' school'. We talked weekly for several months… Somewhere in that discussion, Howard decided to pursue training to become a barber. He was accepted for the programme but had to wait six months to begin the next class. He decided in the interim to try to find work outside the hospital. Hospital staff members were quite sceptical of his search for work, since the industrial community was in a severe recession. I agreed with Howard's wish to meet before and after his job interviews. However, Howard missed most of those meetings, and came by at the end of the week to report that he had three job offers. He decided to take the job where he would 'prep' hospital patients for surgery.

Howard finally went to barbers' school and was a barber until retirement 20 years later. I was able to follow Howard's life to some extent because my mother was the chief medical records administrator for the state hospital and was also acquainted with Howard's daughter. It still strikes me as ironic that this 'knife-wielding paranoid' and 'incarcerated psychotic' became a solid contributor to society through employment that involved the use of razors and scissors.

There were many variables that converged to help Howard return to society. If I was one of those helpful variables, what did I do that helped? One of my activities helped me examine this question. I kept copious notes of the sequential verbal responses of clients, recording them immediately after sessions. I would then try to determine their thematic 'I' statements. Interestingly, I seldom included my responses, except in a very general way. Howard's overall theme sequence was something like:

- I'm curious about this rehabilitation programme.
- I'm pretty successful in the hospital at making a little money.
- I have it made here. I have security and don't have to worry about a lot of things. I have girlfriends. I have spending money. I have a certain kind of respect.
- I don't think I could make it outside.
- I wonder if I could make it?
- I could give it a try. I could go to school while I am still in the hospital.
- I am pretty sure I can do it but I have to get out right away or I might change my mind. I can't wait for the starting date of the school.
- I am a successful man. I'm employed. I have contact with some of my family who disowned me years ago.

My sequential themes were along the following lines:

- I am willing to meet with Howard to just listen to him.
- I accept his fear of getting out of the hospital and will support him in his decision to not leave the hospital.
- I will go with Howard in his decision to seek employment even though others think that he 'is crazy' to search.

In short, my way of being with Howard was to be involved, responsive and willing to help him find ways to implement his decisions. I had no goals for him to get out of the hospital. I trusted his decisions at every level. I was willing to be with him on his terms. If I doubted his decisions, I would have shared this with him in depth, as I did with many clients.

> I learned from Howard as well as others that clear improvements did not depend upon exploration of their internal experiences; they did not delve into self-exploration; and that they did not focus on their feelings in the ways that are usually considered important in therapy. (Bozarth, 2001: 175–178)

Client-centred principles were central to the client's pursuit of goals that were also institutional criteria for success. We chose this vignette as an example of the client–therapist relationship and the use of the client's resources that enabled him to assimilate institutional/organisational resources into his personal vocational plan. The therapist's role was primarily that of listening to the client and facilitating the client with his development and implementation of concrete actions towards concrete goals.

Medically and behaviourally oriented organisations/agencies are often receptive to viable treatments that add to the overall benefit of their patients or clients. Primary health facilities in England that offer time-limited sessions for clients have accepted client-centred therapists on treatment teams (Bryant-Jefferies, 2003). Bryant-Jefferies offers detailed examples of client-centred sessions in a time-limited primary care setting. He presents fictional characterisations of some of his therapeutic relationships that describe specific struggles of client and therapist that are commonplace in the primary care setting in England. Experience with clients in the primary health facilities illustrates that a common ground between traditional problem-oriented approaches and client-centred principles can be reached.

Another scenario illustrates how a client-centred therapist worked with a client who came to a behaviourally oriented counselling centre seeking help with her four-year-old son.

Carolyn, a 33-year-old homemaker, came to the centre asking for help with controlling the behaviour of her four-year-old son. She described the boy as disrupting the entire household. He had temper tantrums and would not listen to either his mother or father. As she described specific behaviours, the therapist thought about a behavioural analysis that might identify specific acts and reinforce more acceptable behaviour from the boy. The centre orientation was behavioural, whereas the therapist was client-centred.

Carolyn continuously discussed the boy's disruption of the family as she covered myriad themes. These themes included: 1) that her husband worked late and was seldom there to help her; 2) that her husband did not care about the behaviour, but took the attitude that 'boys will be boys' – she frequently said that she did not receive emotional or practical support from her husband; 3) that she was dealing with everything alone. Her only friend was a neighbour who sometimes came over to try to talk to her son. He also cut their grass because her husband got home too late and worked weekends as well.

When asked if she wanted to return, she somewhat reluctantly said that she could return in two weeks.

When she returned, Carolyn did not mention her son at all, and nor did she raise issues about her son in future sessions. She briefly discussed her feeling of being alone and discontented with her life. Mainly, she talked about a sexual affair with her neighbour. But, again, she discontinued this discussion after this particular session. She focused more on her feelings of not being supported and being alone. She discontinued her therapy appointments after the eighth session. Three months later, she returned to say that things with her husband were going much better. They were going to church together and had bought a farm. She was instrumental in helping the farm to be a success. He was working 40 hours a week rather than 60 hours on his construction job. Carolyn's son had entered kindergarten and was 'pretty well' behaved.

Stubbs and Bozarth (1996) report an experiment with student counsellors using the scenario associated with Carolyn. The intention of the experiment was to explore the thesis that the personal embodiment of the conditions might transcend behaviour and method. A graduate student took the role of the client. The only information given to the 'client' was that of resisting discussion about the affair. Four graduate students followed models of therapy other than client-centred. The results were surprising in that the sessions went in a direction similar to the direction of the actual client:

> The actual client quit discussing the boy's behavior (never to be mentioned again) during the second session and discussed her affair. She then quit discussing the affair (never to be mentioned again) and talked about her feelings of being alone, discontented etc. This was the direction the role-play was going during the 10-minute integration model. (Stubbs & Bozarth, 1996: 30)

The student client thought that she might have been willing to discuss the client's affair with any of the therapists. Although the questions from the therapists were more focused on problems and resolution, the client believed that the questions kept her active and that she knew that the therapists were aware that, at some 'other level', there was more at issue than just the boy's disruptive behavior. One speculation was the following:

> This may be an example of the resiliency of individuals as clients but the point is that the client 'knew' at some level that the therapists 'knew', at least, vaguely that there was something else and that they were acceptant of her. (Stubbs & Bozarth, 1996: 30)

Most therapists, regardless of their theoretical orientation, are interested in the client's continued self-determination and self-authority. The data reveal little difference in the success among those with different theoretical orientations. It also suggests that common factors might be perceived in different ways. Rogers' sixth condition is crucial: namely, that the client perceives the therapist's experiencing of unconditional positive regard and empathic understanding.

Summary

The radical differences between the assumptions of client-centred therapy and those of other therapies have a common ground. The conclusions of psychotherapy outcome research identify this common ground. Seventy per cent of the success variance in psychotherapy is related to the client–therapist relationship (30%) and the client's own resources (extra-therapeutic variables – 40%). Client-centred therapy is more specific about the common variables in that the therapist's role in the relationship is defined as that of being congruent in experiencing unconditional positive regard towards the client and experiencing empathic understanding of the client's frame of reference.

It is the client's perception of the therapist's experiencing that facilitates the client's connection with her constructive organismic direction. It is the extent to which this connection exists that the individual is increasingly empowered to resolve her problems and dysfunctions. The therapist who has this therapeutic intent can work within the confines of organisational structures that operate from other theoretical foundations.

References

Ahn H, Wampold BE (2001). Where oh where are the specific ingredients? A meta-analysis of component studies in counseling and psychotherapy. *Journal of Counseling Psychology 48*: 251–257.

Barrett-Lennard GT (1998). *Carl Rogers' Helping System: journey and substance*. London: Sage.

Berenson BG, Carkhuff RR (eds) (1967). *Sources of Gain in Counseling and Psychotherapy*. New York: Holt, Rinehart & Winston.

Bohart AC (2004). How do clients make empathy work? *Person-Centered and Experiential Psychotherapies 3*: 102–116.

Bohart AC, Tallman K (1996). The active client: therapy as self-help. *Journal of Humanistic Psychology 36*: 7–30.

Bozarth JD (1998). *Person-Centered Therapy: a revolutionary paradigm*. Ross-on-Wye: PCCS Books.

Bozarth JD (2001). The art of 'Being' in psychotherapy. *The Humanistic Psychologist 29*(1–3): 167–203.

Bozarth JD (2002). Empirically supported treatment: epitome of the specificity myth. In: Watson JC, Goldman RN, Warner MS (eds). *Client-Centered and Experiential Psychotherapy in the 21st Century: advances in theory, research and practice*. Ross-on-Wye: PCCS Books (pp168–181).

Bozarth JD, Zimring F, Tausch, R (2002). Client-centered therapy: evolution of a revolution. In: Cain D, Seeman J (eds). *Handbook of Humanistic Psychotherapy: research and practice*. Washington, DC: American Psychological Association (pp147–188).

Bryant-Jeffries R (2003). *Time-Limited Therapy in Primary Care: a person-centered dialogue*. Abingdon: Radcliffe Medical Press.

Carey B (2004). For psychotherapies' claims, sceptics demand proof. *New York Times;* 10 August.

Duncan BL, Miller SD (2000). *The Heroic Client: doing client-directed, outcome-informed therapy*. San Francisco, CA: Jossey Bass.

Duncan BL, Moynihan D (1994). Applying outcome research: intentional utilization of the client's frame of reference. *Psychotherapy 31*: 294–301.

Duncan BL, Hubble MA, Miller SD (1997). *Psychotherapy with 'Impossible' Cases: the efficient treatment of therapy veterans*. New York: WW Norton & Company.

Elliott R (1997). Are client-centered/experiential therapies effective? A meta-analysis of outcome research. In: Esser U, Pabst H, Speierer GW (eds). *The Power of the Person-Centered Approach*. Köln, Germany: GwG Verlag (pp125–138).

Elliott RK, Greenberg LS, Watson J, Timulak L, Freire E (2013). Research on humanistic-experiential psychotherapies. In: Lambert MJ (ed). *Bergin and Garfield's Handbook of Psychotherapy and Behavior Change* (6th ed). New York: Wiley (pp495–538).

Grissom RJ (1996). The magic number: .7 +/– .2. Meta-meta-analysis of the probability of superior outcome in comparisons involving therapy, placebo, and control. *Journal of Consulting and Clinical Psychology* 64: 973–982.

Gurman AS (1977). The patient's perceptions of the therapeutic relationship. In: Gurman AS, Razin AM (eds). *Effective Psychotherapy*. New York: Pergamon (pp503–545).

Horvath AO (2001). The alliance. *Psychotherapy 38*: 365–372.

Horvath AO, Symonds BD (1991). Relation between working alliance and outcome in psychotherapy: a meta-analysis. *Journal of Counseling Psychology 38*: 139–149.

Hubble MA, Duncan BL, Miller SD (1999). *The Heart and Soul of Change: what works in therapy*. Washington, DC: American Psychological Association.

Lafferty P, Beutler LE, Crago M (1989). Differences between more and less effective psychotherapists: a study of select therapist variables. *Journal of Consulting and Clinical Psychology 57*: 76–80.

Lambert MJ (1992). Implications of outcome research for psychotherapy integration. In: Norcross JC, Goldfried MR (eds). *Handbook of Psychotherapy Integration*. New York: Basic Books (pp94–129).

Lambert MJ, Barley DE (2001). Research summary on the therapeutic relationship and psychotherapy outcome. *Psychotherapy 38*: 357–361.

Luborsky L, Diguer L, Seligman DA, Rosenthal R, Krause ED, Johnson S, Halperin G, Bishop M, Berman JS, Schweitzer E (1999). The researcher's own therapy allegiances: a 'wild card' in comparisons of treatment efficacy. *Clinical Psychology: science and practice 6*: 95–106.

Martin DJ, Garske JP, Davis MK (2000). Relation of the therapeutic alliance with outcome and other variables: a meta-analytic review. *Journal of Consulting and Clinical Psychology 68*: 438–450.

Messer SB, Wampold BE (2002). Let's face facts: common factors are more potent than specific therapy ingredients. *Clinical Psychology: science and practice 9*: 21–28.

Norcross JC (1997). Emerging breakthroughs in psychotherapy integration: three predictions and one fantasy. *Psychotherapy 34*: 86–90.

Norcross JC (2000). Empirically supported therapeutic relationships: a Division 29 task force. *Psychotherapy Bulletin 35*: 2–4.

Patterson CH (1974). *Relationship Counseling and Psychotherapy: theory and practice*. New York: Harper & Row.

Patterson CH (1984). Empathy, warmth, and genuineness in psychotherapy: a review of reviews. *Psychotherapy 21*: 431–438. Reprinted in: Patterson CH. *Understanding Psychotherapy: fifty years of person-centred theory and practice*. Ross-on-Wye: PCCS Books (pp161–174).

Patterson CH (1985). *The Therapeutic Relationship: foundations for an eclectic psychotherapy*. Monterey, CA: Brooks/Cole.

Patterson CH, Hidore S (1997). *Successful Psychotherapy: a caring loving relationship*. New Jersey: Jason Aronson Inc.

Quinn A (2015). *A Person-Centered Approach and the Rogerian Tradition: a handbook*. CreateSpace/Amazon.com.

Rogers CR (1942). *Counseling and Psychotherapy*. Boston: Houghton Mifflin.

Rogers CR (1951). *Client-Centered Therapy: its current practice, implications, and theory*. Boston: Houghton Mifflin.

Rogers CR (1957). The necessary and sufficient conditions of therapeutic personality change. *Journal of Consulting Psychology 21*: 95–103.

Rogers CR (1959). A theory of therapy, personality, and interpersonal relationships as developed in the client-centered framework. In: Koch S (ed). *Psychology: a study of science: vol. 3 formulation of the person and the social context*. New York: McGraw-Hill (pp184–256).

Rogers CR (1977). *Carl Rogers on Personal Power: inner strength and its revolutionary impact*. New York: Delacorte.

Seligman MEP (1995). The effectiveness of psychotherapy: the consumer report study. *American Psychologist 50*: 963–964.

Smith ML, Glass GV (1977). Meta-analysis of psychotherapy outcome studies. *American Psychologist 32*: 752–760.

Strupp HH, Fox RE, Lessler K (1969). *Patients View Their Psychotherapy*. Baltimore: The John Hopkins Press.

Stubbs JP, Bozarth, JD (1994). The dodo bird revisited: a qualitative study of psychotherapy efficacy research. *Journal of Applied and Preventive Psychology 3*: 109–120.

Stubbs JP, Bozarth JD (1996). The integrative statement of Carl Rogers. In: Hutterer R, Pawlowsky G, Schmid PF, Stipsits R (eds). *Client-Centered and Experiential Psychotherapy: a paradigm in motion*. New York: Peter Lang (pp25–33).

Task Force on Promotion and Dissemination of Psychological Procedures (1995). Training in and dissemination of empirically validated psychological treatments. Report and recommendations. *The Clinical Psychologist 48*: 3–23.

Wampold BE (2001). *The Great Psychotherapy Debate: models, methods, and findings*. Mahwah, NJ: Lawrence Erlbaum Associates.

Wampold BE, Mondin L, Moody M, Stich F, Benson K, Ahn H (1997). A meta-analysis of outcome studies comparing bonafide psychotherapies: empirically, 'all must have prizes'. *Psychological Bulletin 122*(3): 203–215.

Wolpe J (1987). The promotion of scientific psychotherapy. In: Zeig JK (ed). *The Evaluation of Psychotherapy*. New York: Brunner Mazel (pp133–142).

Zeig JK (1987). *The Evaluation of Psychotherapy*. New York: Brunner Mazel.

23 | Client-centred values limit the application of research findings: an issue for discussion[1]

Barbara Brodley

In this paper, I discuss the view that the values of client-centred theory and practice should significantly limit the role of research findings in a client-centred therapist's efforts to develop the practice and theory. Values should probably place limits on the use of research findings by therapists from any orientation, but the issue is especially obvious in client-centred therapy because it is based explicitly on values. Early in his writings on client-centred therapy, Rogers (1951) asserted that the 'philosophical orientation of the counselor' is crucial in therapist development. He wrote that the therapist 'can be only as "nondirective" as he has achieved respect for others in his own personality organization' (p21). He was explicit about the underlying role of values.

> How do we look upon others? Do we see each person as having worth and dignity in his own right? If we do hold this point of view at the verbal level, to what extent is it operationally evident at the behavior level? Do we tend to treat individuals as persons of worth, or do we subtly devalue them by our attitudes and behavior? Is our philosophy one in which respect for the individual is uppermost? Do we respect his capacity and his right to self-direction, or do we basically believe that his life would be best guided by us? To what extent do we have a need and a desire to dominate others? Are we willing for the individual to select and choose his own values, or are our actions guided by the conviction (usually unspoken) that he would be happiest if he permitted us to select for him his values and standards and goals? The answers to questions of this sort appear to be important as basic determiners of the therapist's approach. (p20)

1. This is a revision of a paper presented at the Annual Meeting of the Association for the Development of the Person-Centered Approach, Cleveland, Ohio, August 2002, and published as Brodley BT (2003). The relation of research to psychotherapy: a question for discussion. *Person-Centred Practice* 11(1): 52–55.

If one concurs with Rogers' view of the role of values, what should a client-centred therapist do with research findings that appear to suggest the efficacy of directive procedures or that omit or de-emphasise empathic understanding and acceptance of the client? A common response to such a question says 'since these techniques are effective... they should be used' (Bergin, 1970: 271). My contrary contention is that, 'Yes, one should mention these findings when discussing research, but ignore them in respect to theory and practice because research findings are not messages from a bank of truth.'

The dominating context of this discussion is psychologists' and counsellors' general belief that research findings are necessary to legitimise therapeutic practice and to improve theory. Rogers himself supported Thorndike's dictum that 'anything that exists, exists in some quantity that can be measured' (quoted in Gordon et al, 1954: 13), and he fostered many empirical studies of client-centred therapy, as well as pioneering the use of transcripts of sessions in psychotherapy research (Kirschenbaum & Henderson, 1989).

Some writers (Levant, 2004; McFall, 1996; Messer & Wampold, 2002; Peterson, 2004) qualify their general emphasis on empirical research by asserting that evidence-based practice should be integrated with clinical expertise. Some respond that it is true – so far, scientific procedures have not answered all the questions. But they argue that a wider range of questions and appropriate methods would keep therapy practice based on science and be best for clients (Beutler, 2004; Chambless, 2002; Rounsaville & Carroll, 2002).

Opinions vary about the role of not-strictly-scientific clinical expertise in modifying therapy. Still, all current writers on the subject appear to believe in and promote a scientific basis for therapy. None challenge the use of research for modifying practice, or assert the limiting role of values in incorporating research findings into therapy practice or theory.

Many of Rogers' descendants within the person-centred community use research findings to justify directive procedures and to change Rogers' theory. Outstanding examples are Gendlin (1969), Greenberg, Elliott and Lietaer (1998), Hendricks (2002), and Sachse and Elliott (2002). Rogers' own history as an innovative researcher and his encouragement of individualistic therapist development would seem, to some, to support letting the research chips fall where they may, even if it means abandoning non-directive client-centred therapy. Rogers' behaviour as a therapist, however, belies that impression.

Indeed, Rogers was a pioneer in psychotherapy research (Cain, 2002), but the research he fostered on outcome, on the concomitants of change, and on the specific processes involved in change (Rogers & Dymond, 1954; Halkides, 1958; Rogers, 1959, 1961a, 1967) does not appear to have had much influence on his own therapy practice other than to give it support. His therapy sessions in the 1980s are little changed from those in the mid-1940s (Bozarth, 1990, 2002; Brodley, 1994; Cain, 1993).

Rogers recorded, transcribed and studied his and his students' therapy behaviour, starting in 1940 (Rogers, 1942; Kirschenbaum, 1979). He critiqued his early therapy behaviour in relation to his theory, and on that basis made changes that are evident after 1942 (Brodley, 1994, 2004), but there is no evidence that any value-conflicting research findings available before his death influenced his therapy. He acknowledged that changes might be needed on the basis of research findings (Rogers, 1957, 1967), but he did not change his own behaviour with his individual clients on those grounds.

An example of Rogers' fidelity to his values can be found in his response to a study of his own therapy. In the late 1950s, Rogers listened to many of his therapy tapes and observed stages in clients' processes and manner of representing themselves as they improved (Rogers, 1961a). The pattern of therapeutic movement he observed in his clients was their response to his non-directive, congruent offering of unconditional positive regard and empathic understanding to his clients – behaviour consistent with his theory. For this good reason, Rogers did not interpret his own process research findings as instructions for directive procedures.

Some other therapists originally in the client-centred milieu did use this and other research to adopt directive procedures. For example, reports by Tomlinson and Hart (1962), Gendlin et al (1968), Gendlin (1969), Klein, Mathieu-Coughlan and Kiesler (1969), Friedman (1982), and Mathieu-Coughlan and Klein (1984) showed their shift to an experiential process-directive therapy, in part on the basis of Rogers' process findings.

A great deal of research shows the efficacy of client-centered therapy. For example, Truax and Carkhuff (1967) reported research results from 10 separate studies involving 850 clients. Those results 'overwhelmingly support' Rogers' hypothesis that therapist congruence, unconditional positive regard and empathic understanding result in constructive personality change (Friedman, 1982: 34). Rogers often reported such confirming studies, and it appears that Rogers embraced research findings when they tended to support his values about people and about therapy. However, he did not do this in a cavalier manner. In fact, Rogers (1961b) expressed a theoretical justification for the role of values in adopting scientific findings. He wrote:

> What I will do with the knowledge gained through scientific method… is a matter of subjective choice dependent upon the values which have personal meaning for me. (p223)

Rogers' client-centred therapy remained non-directive and empathic (Bozarth, 2002; Brodley, 1994; Merry, 1996; Van Belle, 1980) in respect to both content and process. After all the challenging research, his subsequent therapy remained consistent with his values.

Until the end of his life (early in 1987), Rogers continued to think that values determined what kind of therapy he would do, and that it is best to be aware of those values as one incorporates research findings. In a 1986 interview (Rogers & Russell, 2002: 188), Rogers asserted, 'Whatever philosophical views I hold I clearly implement in practice,' and said that client-centred therapy is 'an approach that simply lives a philosophy and puts its trust in the capacities of the client' (p259).

Rogers held to his description of client-centred therapy, written in 1946, for the rest of his career. He wrote:

> The therapist must… give up the temptation to subtly guide the individual, and must concentrate on one purpose only; that of providing deep understanding and acceptance of the attitudes consciously held at this moment by the client… (p421)

The obvious difference in Rogers' later-in-life therapy that I have observed from videos is that he manifests a less formal, less clinical presence with his clients. He changed in his non-verbal, expressive behaviour, but Rogers continued to exclusively communicate his non-directive, empathic intentions with clients, with only rare exceptions to this purity (Brodley, 1996).

Rogers expressed his values in an interview late in his life (Baldwin, 1987), stating that the 'suitable goals' in the therapy interaction are for the therapist's self. He said:

> I want to be as present to this person as possible. I want to really listen to what is going on [in the client]. I want to be real in this relationship… The goal has to be within myself, with the way I am… 'Am I really with this person in this moment? Not where they were a little while ago, or where they are going to be …' This is the most important thing. (pp47–48)

Also, in 1986, a few months before his death, Rogers expressed his non-directive client-centred attitudes, commenting to an interviewer:

> When the situation is most difficult, that's when a client-centered approach is most needed and… what is needed there is a deepening of the [therapeutic attitudes] and not trying something more technique-oriented. (Rogers & Russell, 2002: 258)

Research is useful. Outcome research can show some of the specific ways a therapy is helpful. It may also be useful for political or social purposes. For example, it may be used to justify a therapy to certification boards, or it may contribute to clients' decisions about who they would like to help them, by looking at the measures of benefits shown by research. Descriptive research using transcripts and tapes may help therapists evaluate the immediate effects of their behaviour on clients, or show how consistent or inconsistent their behaviour is in relation to their theory.

Research results, however, should not be viewed as providing an objective truth (Rogers, 1961b) as grounds for modifying a practice – especially if the research results have implications that contradict the underlying values of the therapy. Psychotherapy research itself – in its questions, in its methods, in the interpretation of results, and any move to apply results to a therapy – is influenced by the researcher's specific values and attitudes (Lietaer, 2002).

Consequently, one may legitimately argue that it is absurd to give credence to any research in respect to applying it to psychotherapy, given the proven role of the researcher's theoretical allegiance. Studies looking at theoretical allegiance are consistent in finding large effects (Messer & Wampold, 2002). There is as much as 69 per cent of the variability in effect sizes of treatment comparisons attributable to researcher theoretical allegiance (Luborsky et al, 1999, 2002). Given such powerful researcher contamination of findings, it is hard to understand why therapists and others trust psychotherapy research results at all.

Conclusion

Psychotherapy should be viewed as fundamentally a practical art and recognised as an ethical activity (Schmid, 2002; Grant, 1985). Consequently, a therapist should place severe limits on his or her use of research in the theory and practice of therapy. Therapy, and the research applied to a therapy – both – always express the therapist's values and attitudes about people, whether the therapist is conscious of this or not. Conversely, therapists should be aware of how their operational values may be impacted if they adopt changes in their therapy on the basis of research findings.

References

Baldwin M (1987). Interview with Carl Rogers on the use of the self in therapy. In: Baldwin M, Satir V (eds). *The Use of Self in Therapy*. New York: The Haworth Press (pp45–52).

Bergin AE (1970). Some implications of psychotherapy research for therapeutic practice. In: Hart JT, Tomlinson TM (eds). *New Directions in Client-Centered Therapy*. Boston, MA: Houghton Mifflin (pp257–276).

Beutler LE (2004). The empirically supported treatments movement: a scientist-practitioner's response. *Clinical Psychology: science and practice 11*: 225–229.

Bozarth JD (1990). The essence of client-centered therapy. In: Lietaer G, Rombauts J, Van Balen R (eds). *Client-Centered and Experiential Psychotherapy in the Nineties*. Leuven: Leuven University Press (pp59–64).

Bozarth JD (2002). The evolution of Carl Rogers as a therapist. In: Cain DJ (ed). *Classics in the Person-Centered Approach*. Ross-on-Wye: PCCS Books (pp43–47).

Brodley BT (1994). Some observations of Carl Rogers' behavior in therapy interviews. *Person-Centered Journal 1*: 37–48.

Brodley BT (1996). Uncharacteristic directiveness: the case of Rogers and the 'anger and hurt' client. In: Farber BA, Brink DC, Raskin PM (eds). *The Psychotherapy of Carl Rogers*. New York: Guilford Press (pp310–321).

Brodley BT (2004). Rogers' responses to clients' questions in client-centered therapy: some findings from a dissertation research by Claudia Kemp. Presented at the annual conference of the Association for the Development of the Person-Centered Approach. Anchorage, Alaska; July.

Cain DJ (1993). The uncertain future of client-centered counseling. *Journal of Humanistic Education and Development 31*: 133–139.

Cain DJ (2002). Preface. In: Cain DJ, Seeman J (eds). *Humanistic Psychotherapies Handbook of Research and Practice*. Washington, DC: American Psychological Association (pp*xix–xxvii*).

Chambless DL (2002). Beware the dodo bird: the dangers of overgeneralization. *Clinical Psychology: science and practice 9*: 13–16.

Friedman N (1982). *Experiential Therapy and Focusing*. New York: Half Court Press.

Gendlin ET (1969). Focusing. *Psychotherapy: theory, research and practice 6*: 4–15.

Gendlin ET, Beebe J, Cassens J, Klein M, Oberlander, M (1968). Focusing ability in psychotherapy, personality and creativity. In: Shlien JM (ed). *Research in Psychotherapy: Vol 3*. Washington, DC: American Psychological Association (pp217–241).

Gordon T, Grummon DL, Rogers CR, Seeman, J (1954). Developing a program of research in psychotherapy. In: Rogers CR, Dymond RF (eds). *Psychotherapy and Personality Change*. Chicago, IL: The University of Chicago Press (pp12–34).

Grant B (1985). The moral nature of psychotherapy. *Counseling and Values 29*: 141–150.

Greenberg LS, Elliott R, Lietaer G (1998). *Handbook of Experiential Psychotherapy*. New York: Guilford Press.

Halkides G (1958). An experimental study of four conditions necessary for therapeutic change. Unpublished doctoral dissertation. Chicago, IL: University of Chicago.

Hendricks M (2002). Focusing-oriented/experiential psychotherapy. In: Cain DJ, Seeman J (eds). *Humanistic Psychotherapies Handbook of Research and Practice*. Washington, DC: American Psychological Association (pp221–252).

Kirschenbaum H (1979). *On Becoming Carl Rogers*. A Delta Book. New York: Dell Publishing Company, Inc.

Kirschenbaum H, Henderson VL (eds) (1989). *The Carl Rogers Reader*. Boston, MA: Houghton Mifflin (pp*xi–xvi*).

Klein MH, Mathieu-Coughlan PL, Kiesler DJ (1969). *The Experiencing Scale: a research and training manual. Vol 1*. Madison, WI: University of Wisconsin.

Levant RF (2004). The empirically validated treatments movement: a practitioner/educator perspective. *Clinical Psychology: Science and Practice 11*: 219–224.

Lietaer G (2002). Paper presented on panel. Open discussion on person-centered research at the Carl R Rogers Symposium, La Jolla, CA; July.

Luborsky L, Diguer L, Seligman DA, Rosenthal R, Johnson S, Halperin G, Bishop M, Schweizer E (1999). The researcher's own therapeutic allegiances: a 'wild card' in comparisons of treatment efficacy. *Clinical Psychology: Science and Practice 6*: 95–132.

Luborsky L, Rosenthal R, Diguer L, Andrusyna TP, Berman JS, Levitt JT, Seligman DA, Krause ED (2002). The dodo bird verdict is alive and well – mostly. *Clinical Psychology: Science and Practice 9*: 2–12.

Mathieu-Coughlan PL, Klein MH (1984). Experiential psychotherapy: key events in client-therapist interaction. In: Rice LN, Greenburg LS (eds). *Patterns of Change*. New York: Guilford Press (pp213–248).

McFall RM (1996). Manifesto for a science of clinical psychology. *The Clinical Psychologist 44*: 75–88.

Merry T (1996). An analysis of ten demonstration interviews by Carl Rogers: implications for the training of client-centred counselors. In: Hutterer R, Pawlowsky G, Schmid PF, Stipsits R (eds). *Client-Centered and Experiential Psychotherapy: a paradigm in motion*. Frankfort am Main: Peter Lang (pp273–284).

Messer SB, Wampold BE (2002). Let's face facts: common factors are more potent than specific therapy ingredients. *Clinical Psychologist: Science and Practice 9*: 21–25.

Peterson DR (2004). Science, scientism, and professional responsibility. *Clinical Psychology: Science and Practice 11*: 196–210.

Rogers CR (1942). *Counseling and Psychotherapy*. Boston: Houghton Mifflin.

Rogers CR (1946). Significant aspects of client-centered therapy. *American Psychologist 1*: 415–422.

Rogers CR (1951). *Client-Centered Therapy*. Boston: Houghton Mifflin.

Rogers CR (1954). An overview of the research and some questions for the future. In: Rogers CR, Dymond RF(eds). *Psychotherapy and Personality Change*. Chicago, IL: University of Chicago Press (pp413–434).

Rogers CR (1957). The necessary and sufficient conditions of therapeutic personality change. *Journal of Consulting Psychology 21*: 95–103.

Rogers CR (1959). A theory of therapy, personality and interpersonal relationships as developed in the client-centered framework. In: Koch S (ed). *Psychology: a study of a science. Vol. III: formulations of the person and the social context*. New York: McGraw-Hill (pp184–256).

Rogers CR (1961a). A process conception of psychotherapy. In: Rogers CR. *On Becoming a Person*. Boston, MA: Houghton Mifflin (pp125–159).

Rogers CR (1961b). Persons or science? A philosophical question. In: Rogers CR. *On Becoming a Person*. Boston, MA: Houghton Mifflin (pp199–224).

Rogers CR (1967). *The Therapeutic Relationship and Its Impact: a study of psychotherapy with schizophrenics*. Westport, CT: Greenwood Press.

Rogers CR, Dymond RF (eds) (1954). *Psychotherapy and Personality Change*. Chicago: University of Chicago Press.

Rogers CR, Russell DE (2002). *Carl Rogers, the Quiet Revolutionary: an oral history*. Roseville, CA: Penmarin Books.

Rounsaville BJ, Carroll KM (2002). Commentary on dodo bird revisited: why aren't we dodos yet? *Clinical Psychology: Science and Practice 9*: 17–20.

Sachse R, Elliott R (2002). Process-outcome research on humanistic therapy variables. In: Cain DJ, Seeman J (eds). *Humanistic Psychotherapies Handbook of Research and Practice*. Washington, DC: American Psychological Association (pp83–115).

Schmid PF (2002). The characteristics of a person-centered approach to therapy and counseling: criteria for identity and coherence. Presentation given at the Carl R Rogers Centennial Celebration, La Jolla, CA; July.

Tomlinson TM, Hart JT (1962). A validation of the process scale. *Journal of Consulting Psychology 26*: 74–78.

Truax CB, Carkuff RR (1967). *Toward Effective Counseling and Psychotherapy: training and practice*. Chicago: Aldine Press.

Van Belle H (1980). *Basic Intent and Therapeutic Approach of Carl R Rogers*. Toronto: Wedge Publishing Foundation.

An evaluation of research, concepts and experiences pertaining to the universality of client-centred therapy and its application in psychiatric settings

24

Lisbeth Sommerbeck

There exists a myth that client-centred therapy is unsuitable for clients diagnosed with severe psychopathology. In this chapter, I identify five reasons for this myth and refute each of them, thereby demonstrating that the notion that client-centred therapy is only useful with less severe psychological disturbances is precisely what it is said to be: a myth.

Let me start by listing the five reasons for the existence of this myth, as I identify them:

1. the disappointing results of Rogers' own research with people diagnosed with schizophrenia (Rogers et al, 1967)

2. an erroneous notion that expression of empathic understanding of psychotic ideation is a collusion with or reinforcement of such ideation

3. a confusion of 'non-directive' with 'unstructured'

4. an erroneous notion that client-centred therapy is an in-depth, exploratory approach

5. a confusion of the theory of therapy with the theory of personality.

I will first deal with each of these reasons in turn. Then, in the final section, I will give my reasons, based on 36 years of experience with psychotherapeutic work in a psychiatric hospital, for regarding client-centred therapy not only as useful with clients diagnosed with serious psychiatric disturbances but also, with its pre-therapeutic extension (Prouty, 1994), as the only psychotherapeutic approach that is viable with people whom other approaches regard as being 'beyond psychotherapeutic reach'.

1. The disappointing results of the Wisconsin project

The material in this section is, mostly, edited excerpts of a previously published critique of the Wisconsin project (Sommerbeck, 2002). Unless otherwise stated, the quotations in this first major section are from Rogers et al's book about the Wisconsin project (1967).

In 1967, Rogers and his co-workers published the book about the scientifically impeccably and ingeniously designed large-scale research project that Rogers headed during his years as professor at the University of Wisconsin. The project investigated the effect of client-centred therapy on a group of 'normals', a group of 'acute schizophrenics', and a group of 'chronic schizophrenics', compared with matched and paired controls who did not receive client-centred therapy.

This book, as well as other commentaries on the Wisconsin project, bears witness to Rogers' disappointment with the results of the project. Most revealing is, I think, the following statement by Rogers (quoted by Shlien, 1992: 1083–1084):

> Our recent experience in psychotherapy with chronic and unmotivated schizophrenics raises the question whether we must modify our conception of this condition. Very tentatively it appears to me at the present time that, in dealing with the extremely immature or regressed individual, a conditional regard may be more effective in getting a relationship under way, than an unconditional positive regard.

In this quote Rogers is in effect saying that client-centred therapy doesn't work with these people. It is precisely the unconditionality of unconditional positive regard that is normally recognised as the primary therapeutic agent in client-centred therapy (see, for example, Bozarth, 1998), and advocating conditional regard as being more effective with these people is synonymous with advocating an approach that is, in its very essence, different from client-centred therapy.

Here are a few more quotes that illustrate the disappointing results of the Wisconsin project:

> In many respects the therapy group taken as a whole showed no better evidence of positive outcome than did the matched and paired control group. It had however a slightly better rate of release from the hospital, and this differential was maintained a year after the termination of therapy. The therapy group also showed a number of positive personality changes, which were not evidenced by the control group. The differences between the two groups, however, were not great. (Rogers, et al, 1967: 80)

The meaning of 'not great' is found on page 282:

> … it seemed probable that the discrepant ego strength scores for therapy and control groups accounted for their different hospitalization rates. While the therapy group continued to show a greater percentage of time out

of the hospital, the difference was no longer statistically significant. Thus,
when initial ego strength was controlled, the resultant findings became
consistent with those for other outcome measures, indicating no differential
improvement for the experimental and control groups.

Finally, Rogers accompanies the following quote with the explicit statement that
the finding reported 'was disappointing' (p82):

In general, there was no differential amount of process movement over
therapy in our schizophrenic group as a function of therapy.

Bearing these quotations in mind, I think it is no wonder that client-centred
therapy came to be regarded by everyone, including client-centred therapists, as
unsuitable for people diagnosed with schizophrenia. However, a careful reading of
the book about the project raises three important questions:

1.   Was it really the diagnosis of schizophrenia that was the relevant variable
     accounting for the disappointing results?
2.   Was the therapy offered really client-centred therapy?
3.   Were the therapists experienced with people diagnosed with schizophrenia?

My answer to all three questions is 'no'. Reading the book about the project, it seems
evident to me that the relevant variables accounting for the disappointing results
were 1) lack of client motivation for therapy; 2) that the therapy offered frequently
had nothing to do with client-centred therapy, and 3) that the therapists had no
experience with people diagnosed with schizophrenia. In the following sections,
each of these three points will be illustrated by quotations.

The research subjects lacked motivation for therapy

The following quotation should suffice to demonstrate the importance of the
variable of motivation for the disappointing results of the Wisconsin project:

The experience of most of the therapists on the project had been primarily
with outpatient clients who came voluntarily for help. They were faced with
many difficult problems in establishing a relationship with the hospitalized
schizophrenics and likewise with the normals, both of the groups being
composed of individuals who were not seeking help. The problems of the
therapist and the solutions to these problems were manifold: sometimes
pathetic, sometimes amusing. How is a male therapist to deal with a female
research client who dashes into the women's washroom when she sees
him coming? ... The therapists came to realize that they were dealing with
individuals who were unmotivated, often unreachable, largely without hope,

> lacking in any concept of therapy, and certainly lacking in any belief that a
> relationship could be helpful. (Rogers et al, 1967: 67–68)

It is important to note the reference to the 'normals' who, like the 'schizophrenics', were a group composed of 'individuals who were not seeking help'. Like the 'schizophrenics', these unmotivated 'normals' didn't benefit from therapy:

> With our normal individuals, who were not motivated for therapy, there
> was even a trend toward a more superficial level of experiencing in second
> halves of the therapeutic hours. This finding in the normal individuals seems
> explainable on the basis of their tendency to execute a defensive retreat from
> therapeutic engagements. (Rogers et al, 1967: 83)

It should be evident from the next to last quotation that the 'schizophrenics', surely, also executed 'a defensive retreat from therapeutic engagements' by, for example, hiding in the ladies' room. I see absolutely no reason to believe that this defensive retreat is of less importance for therapy outcome in people diagnosed with schizophrenia than in people regarded to be mentally healthy.

Although the pairs of control and research subjects were matched with respect to degree of disturbance, only one among more than 25 criteria for measuring degree of disturbance (Rogers et al, 1967: 551–552) was directly correlated with the clients' motivation for therapy. This criterion was 'awareness of need for help'. Among so many criteria for disturbance, the criterion of 'awareness of need for help' was not allowed to weigh as heavily as it should have been. The researchers did become aware of this. In a footnote on page 26, Rogers writes: 'With the wisdom of hindsight, we realize that motivation for help should probably have been another variable in our stratification, since this too has been judged to be related to therapeutic outcome. This factor was not, however, included in the design.'

To me, Rogers' laconic footnote has the flavour of a huge understatement. I think it is recognised by all psychotherapists, regardless of their orientation, that degree of motivation for therapy is a client variable that contributes much to the outcome of therapy, and that lack of motivation is certainly not confined to people diagnosed with schizophrenia. Lack of motivation is a client variable that is not correlated with any specific psychiatric diagnosis and, as a matter of fact, not even with psychopathology, as the unmotivated 'normals' of the Wisconsin project demonstrated. Thus far, therefore, the Wisconsin project has only demonstrated the rather self-evident fact that therapy with people who are not motivated for therapy has disappointing results.

Furthermore, imposing therapy on anybody seems to me to be contrary to the focus on respect for client autonomy that characterises client-centred therapy. It is inherent to client-centred therapy that it cannot be forced on people. If it is, it is no longer client-centred therapy. This will, I hope, become evident in the next section.

The therapeutic approach was not necessarily client-centred

As a consequence, it seems, of feeling rather helpless with their unmotivated clients, the therapists in Wisconsin did a lot of things that were not at all client-centred. The following quotations illustrate this point:

> … the therapists in our group found themselves trying out and developing many new and different modes of response behavior. The variety of specific behaviors among the therapists increased sharply. (Rogers et al, 1967: 12)

The following are examples of the kind of response behaviour that was tried out and developed (Hart & Tomlinson, 1970: 16–17):

> Patient did not wish to be seen after first two contacts. I told him 'that's okay with me' only to find that 'it isn't okay with me.' I called him back and asked him to come in ten times, then decide. Since we had already decided to play cards, since he refused to sit in silence, he then provided a cribbage board. After five hours he indicated that he would like to come in as long as he is here. Now I have a cribbage partner who cheats, or tries to.

> The patient refused right from the start to meet with me. To every mention of 'next time' and to every invitation to enter a room with me, he reacted with explicit anger and demands that I leave him alone. Over some weeks I accepted his feeling, anger, dislike of me: I *let* him leave; I had him brought by attendants; I argued with him; I was both honest and dishonest: I could not help but react negatively to his rejection and I felt he cut the ground from under my *right* to be with him. Because of these feelings in me I decided that he should not be further *coerced* to see me, since he would only discover a threatened and threatening person in me. (Italics my own.)

I find it evident that the approach of these therapists has nothing to do with client-centred therapy.

The therapists were inexperienced with people diagnosed with schizophrenia

There are many passages in the book about the Wisconsin project that illuminate the inexperience of the therapists with people diagnosed with schizophrenia:

> For the majority of the therapists this was the first extensive work with hospitalized psychotics… (Rogers et al, 1967: 8)

> Our therapists were sometimes baffled by the lack of self-exploration among our schizophrenic clients, since they had come to think of self-exploration as

characteristic of most psychotherapy. (p76)

... our therapists – competent and conscientious as they were – had over-optimistic and in some cases seriously invalid perceptions of the relationships in which they were involved. (p92)

Again, I think these quotations speak for themselves.

In the previous three sections, I think there is ample evidence that the disappointing results of the Wisconsin project had nothing to do with a failure of client-centred therapy to be of use to people diagnosed with schizophrenia. It had, rather, to do with the failure of a nondescript therapeutic approach, applied by inexperienced therapists, to be of use for people who were not motivated for therapy. There is, thus, no basis in the results of the Wisconsin project for the existence of the myth that client-centred therapy is unsuitable for clients diagnosed with severe psychopathology.

2. The erroneous notion that empathy colludes with or reinforces psychotic ideation

In the effort to follow the client's journey through his or her psychological landscape with consistent acceptant empathic understanding, the therapist must suspend his or her own conception of reality from start to finish of the session: the therapist puts his or her own conception of reality in parenthesis and out of the way of the client for the duration of the session. Raskin (quoted in Rogers, 1951: 25) expresses this beautifully:

At this level, counselor participation becomes an active experiencing with the client of the feelings to which he gives expression, the counselor makes a maximum effort to get under the skin of the person to whom he is communicating, he tries to get within and to live the attitudes expressed... to catch every nuance of their changing nature: in a word, to absorb himself completely in the attitude of the other. And in struggling to do this, *there is no room for any other type of counselor activity or attitude...* [italics my own]

There is, thus, no room for the therapist's own conception of reality, however unfamiliar or mistaken the client's conception of reality may seem to the therapist. This is also the case with clients who present with so-called psychotic ideation – ie. hallucinations and delusions – that do seem extremely unfamiliar to the therapist and quite at odds with the therapist's and others' more or less consensual conception of reality. With these clients, the therapist's capacity to suspend his or her own conception of reality is put to the test, and it is particularly important to remember that empathic understanding is neutral as far as confirmation or disconfirmation of the client's conception of reality is concerned. I've often seen empathic understanding confused with confirmation, even in psychotherapeutically well-informed circles. For example, the leader of the Danish Psychoanalytic Institute writes that 'empathic confirmation' is useful to strengthen the therapeutic alliance (Vitger, 1999: 200).

With a notion of empathic understanding as confirmative, it is little wonder that empathic understanding is dismissed as useless, and even harmful, with clients who present with psychotic experiences. In the psychiatric circles I'm acquainted with, there is a widespread fear that one is colluding with or reinforcing psychotic experiences if one responds with expressions of empathic understanding of it. Instead of expressions of empathic understanding, 'reality correction' is the favoured approach to patients' expression of psychotic ideation, particularly among psychiatric nurses. Sometimes psychiatric nurses seem to lean over backwards through fear of being misunderstood by the patient as agreeing with or confirming what they regard as the patient's psychotic conception of reality. They often feel that they are not doing their job properly if they do not try to correct the patient's conception of reality by telling them, directly or indirectly, what the correct conception of reality is. They often relate to patients as if not doing 'reality correction' is synonymous with collusion with the patients' conception of reality. For people who regard 'reality correction' as a necessary element in the treatment of people diagnosed with psychosis, client-centred therapy is seen as inconsequential at best, and harmful at worst.

There is, naturally, no guarantee that a client does not experience a therapist's expression of empathic understanding as confirmative (or disconfirmative, for that matter) of the client's conception of reality. It is, though, contrary to the essence of client-centred therapy to try to control client experiences in any way, including client experiences of the therapist. Client experiences of the therapist are received and followed with empathic understanding, just like all other client experiences.

Contrary to this myth of collusion, it has been my experience, from my work in a psychiatric hospital, that it is 'reality correction' that is potentially harmful to clients diagnosed with psychosis, not expressions of empathic understanding – and that it is expressions of empathic understanding that are beneficial, not 'reality correction'. 'Reality correction' is, by its very nature, confrontational, and patients with a diagnosis of psychosis feel, in general, threatened by confrontational approaches. Confronted with 'reality correction', they often tend to defend their conception of reality, thereby rigidifying and solidifying it and often expanding on it with more details and nuances, thereby developing their psychotic experiencing further. In short, they can become more psychotic when confronted with 'reality correction'.

In contrast, expression of accurate empathic understanding, non-confrontational as it is, gives the client no reason to defend his or her perception of reality. This is precisely what makes it possible for the client to consider alternative points of view. The client feels that his or her perception of reality is understood and accepted, which leaves the client feeling free to explore it further. In this climate of safety and acceptance, the client will then most often, very tentatively and in very minor ways at first, start to question some inconsistencies that the client discovers in his or her psychological landscape – inconsistencies that are normally very different from and much more concrete than the inconsistencies other people have tried to point out to the client. The client will also start to speak with less fear and fewer psychotic distortions about his or her experiences with the significant people in their life. This, of course, does not happen in dialogues that sometimes amount to a battle over whose conception of reality is the correct one. Every so often, clients diagnosed with psychosis have expressed to me that they feel our talks are little oases of safety and freedom to express themselves, contrasting our talks, implicitly or explicitly, with all the 'reality correction' they are exposed to in their talks with other people. This is not surprising from a client-centred point of view, since 'reality correction' is, basically, an expression of negative regard for the client's own perception of reality. These experiences of mine are thus in full accordance with the client-centred theory of therapy. Rogers writes (1951: 41):

> The therapist perceives the client's self as the client has known it, and accepts it; he perceives the contradictory aspects which have been denied to awareness and accepts those, too, as being part of the client; and both of these acceptances have in them the same warmth and respect. Thus it is that the client, experiencing in another an acceptance of both these aspects of himself, can take toward himself the same attitude.

Furthermore, it is in accordance with Rogers' concept of the fully functioning person (Rogers, 1959: 234–235) that it takes quite a high degree of openness to one's experiences to receive corrections of one's conception of reality non-defensively. Such openness to one's experiences is certainly not what normally characterises people diagnosed with psychosis; on the contrary.

The following excerpt of dialogue (factual content is changed so the client cannot be identified) is an example of a typical transition from the expression of relatively more to relatively less psychotic ideation in the course of a client-centred therapy session where, of course, no effort at 'reality correction' is made. It illustrates that expressions of empathic understanding (and the contact reflections of pre-therapy that characterise the first part of the session) are in no way reinforcing of psychotic ideation; on the contrary. The excerpt is from the sixth session, and the therapist is the one who has initiated, and continues to initiate, the contact between client and therapist (this is often the case in work with the most seriously disturbed patients in a psychiatric hospital). The therapist sees this patient in her room in the ward.

> Therapist: I thought that maybe… if there was anything you might like to tell me today, about how you feel, and about your situation, how you look on it?
>
> Client (in a very matter of fact, 'there's no discussing it' way): I feel well.
>
> T: You say you feel well, and you look very determinedly at me.

C: Yes, I feel well, and that's a fact.

(*Pause, C looks down at her lap.*)

T: You say it's a fact you feel well, and now you look down and are quiet.

C: Yes, I feel well when I drink coffee, juice, and things like that, but water is no good – and I've stopped eating.

T: As long as you can drink something that tastes good you feel well, but you've lost your appetite?

C: Yes, and I also feel well because I'm now totally out of the church.

T: It's a relief to be finally out of it.

C: Yes, well, I'm not totally out of it, I still receive their newsletter, and I can't read it, it was a mistake that I joined the church, I'm confused about it – I have to tell them to stop sending the newsletter.

T: The church was really too much, and now you need to get that newsletter off your back, that'll be a relief?

C: Yes, that's it, I need to stop the newsletter and to have my mail delivered here, then I can feel fine – but I do feel fine here.

T: You like to be here, and if you had these things settled you could enjoy it better, be more at ease?

C: Yes, precisely, that would be nice.

(*Pause, C moves her head around in abrupt jerks, staring at different spots.*)

T: You turn your head this way and that way and look around.

C: (grinding her teeth): My father is a Satan.

T: You grind your teeth and say 'My father is a Satan'.

C: He has slaughtered my mother, he is the real Satan, and the Danes are his devils and devils' brood.

T: He is the real Satan, because he has slaughtered your mother, and the Danes are his devils and devils' brood.

C: Not all Danes. People here are nice to me, but he has slaughtered my mother and if he does it again, I'll slaughter him.

T: You feel you'll slaughter him if…

(*C interrupts eagerly.*)

C: Yes, he has terrorised my mother all her life, psychological terror… her name is Maria, if Satan harmed Maria… Joseph would slaughter him, I'm Joseph.

T: You say 'I'm Joseph' and you feel like you think Joseph would feel if Satan harmed Maria, is that it?

C: (nodding her head and smiling): Yes, and I'm not afraid of Satan, I'm not afraid of anything.

T: You smile at the thought that you are not afraid of Satan or…

C: (interrupting): Yes, I'm not afraid, I'm glad of that, but why does he always have to be so rotten? Last time he visited, he brought some fruit from his back garden; it smelled real bad and then I took a bite and it tasted hellish… I threw it all away.

T: You think that everything he brings…

C: (interrupting): Yes, why does he have to be so provocative?

T: Like 'Why the hell can't you buy me some good fruit that I like, instead of bringing me the rotten leftovers from your back garden?'

C: Yes, I think he never spreads anything but shit around him – I can't bear being near him.

The client spends the rest of the session exploring her relationship with her father in a way that seems much more coherent and less infiltrated with psychotic ideation than in the first part of the session. Note how the generalisation about Danes becomes modified, and how her conception of her father is modified: at first he is, literally, Satan; later he takes on more humane proportions and is 'merely' unbearably provocative. Also, 'slaughter' becomes 'psychological terror'. I feel convinced that if someone else had pointed out to her these seeming inconsistencies in her conception of reality, in the name of 'reality correction', she would have persevered more rigidly in them than ever. It was acceptant, empathic following of her journey in her own psychological landscape that created the safety and space for her to consider alternatives in her conception of that landscape.

3. The confusion of 'non-directive' with 'unstructured'

It is common in psychiatric circles to believe that patients diagnosed with psychosis need 'structure'. What is meant by 'structure', though, is rarely defined. The practical implications of the conviction that psychotic patients need structure is normally that staff members in psychiatric hospitals try to make the patient follow a rather tightly scheduled daily routine, that 'limit-setting' is an important concept with these patients, and that an appropriate psychotherapeutic approach is assumed to be one that is goal directed and where the therapist structures the process by trying to keep the patient's focus on a certain issue, or on several issues in an ordered sequence. In my experience, some patients feel helped by this rather patronising approach, and others don't, and this has nothing to do with whether they are diagnosed with a psychotic condition or not.

As a consequence of the belief that psychotic patients need 'structure' of the above-mentioned kind, the non-directive attitude of the client-centred therapist is thought of as being potentially harmful, as a passive 'laissez-faire' attitude that leaves the psychotic client helpless in his/her world of hallucinations and delusions.

What is ignored is that the most important aspect of the notion of 'structure' is the reliability of the person's social environment. Patients diagnosed with psychosis are, in my experience, more vulnerable than people at large to 'surprises' in the way their significant others relate with them. In this sense, I think it is true that patients diagnosed with psychosis 'need structure'. They seem to thrive better (and exhibit fewer psychotic symptoms) when they know rather precisely what they can expect of others and when their expectations, once established, are not disappointed or nullified at a later time. One could also say that they, more than most other people, seem to need others to relate consistently (or congruently) with them.

In this sense, client-centred therapy is probably the most structured of all psychotherapeutic approaches. Any client, including clients diagnosed with psychosis, quickly learns what they can expect from their client-centred therapist: the therapist's very best effort at acceptant empathic understanding, neither more nor less. This is the consistent attitude of the therapist all through the course of therapy; the client-centred therapist doesn't change attitude in sudden and surprising – and thereby, to the psychotic client, potentially provocative or overstimulating – ways.

The client-centred therapist's non-directive attitude is, of course, precisely a consequence of the therapist's very active effort at following the client's process with acceptant empathic understanding. There is nothing 'passive' about it; no 'laissez-faire', no unstructured letting the client down, or leaving the client to his or her own devices, isolated and unaccompanied. It is truly unfortunate and sad that the therapist's non-directive attitude in client-centred therapy has been misunderstood in this way. It is particularly unfortunate and sad for patients diagnosed with psychosis, because the confusion between 'non-directive' and 'unstructured' is one of the reasons client-centred therapy has been dismissed as unsuitable for these people, when the truth is, in my experience, that it is eminently suitable for them (see Sommerbeck, 2003).

4. The erroneous notion that client-centred therapy is an in-depth exploratory approach

In the rather wide psychiatric circles that I'm acquainted with from 36 years' work in a psychiatric hospital, there is almost no knowledge of client-centred therapy, and to the extent that there is some slight knowledge, it contains many misunderstandings about client-centred therapy. Confusing the client-centred therapist's non-directive attitude with a passive 'laissez-faire' attitude is one of these misunderstandings. Another misunderstanding is that client-centred therapy is an in-depth exploratory approach on a par with psychodynamic therapy. Again, this is unfortunate and sad for patients diagnosed with psychosis. These patients are, in psychiatric circles, assumed not to benefit from an in-depth exploratory approach; on the contrary, they are assumed to be easily harmed by such an approach. The consequence of this misunderstanding is, therefore, that client-centred therapy is deemed unsuitable for these people.

In my experience, it is true that people diagnosed with psychosis are easily harmed by an in-depth exploratory approach that, more or less subtly, directs the client to still deeper levels of experiencing, and to still closer contact with emotionally stimulating material. The therapist who is biased towards 'deep is better than shallow' and 'close is better than distant', and therefore more or less systematically aims in the direction of 'deeper' and 'closer', does pose a risk to psychotic clients, who can easily be overwhelmed and overstimulated by what is normally regarded as 'deep' and 'close'. People with a diagnosis of psychosis tend to respond to feeling overwhelmed and overstimulated by displaying more rather than less so-called psychotic behaviours.

To the degree that this bias ('deep' is better than 'shallow' and 'close' is better than 'distant') is shared by client-centred therapists, to the same degree is it also true that they should not work with clients diagnosed with some kind of severe psychological disturbance. Unfortunately, this bias does exist in the group of client-centred therapists, probably because most client-centred therapists work with less disturbed clients in private practices, university clinics, outpatient clinics etc. They work, in short, mostly with clients who have never set foot in a psychiatric hospital, and never will. With these clients, the bias that 'deep and close is better than shallow and distant' is probably inconsequential, and it may even be helpful.

The existence of this bias among client-centred therapists is illustrated with the notion brought forth by some influential authors that 'additive empathy' (Mearns & Thorne, 1999: 45) or empathic understanding of 'edge of awareness experiences' (ibid: 52) is preferable to accurate empathy with what the client, in this moment, wants the therapist to understand about his or her psychological landscape. If I've understood Mearns and Thorne correctly, the client-centred therapist should, according to these authors, aim at additive empathy and empathy with 'edge of awareness experiences', as opposed to 'ordinary', accurate empathic understanding of the client's inner frame of reference or psychological landscape. This preference is, apparently, supported by research: Rainer Sachse (1990: 300–302) has shown that clients typically react with a deepening of their level of experience when the therapist systematically strives for 'deep' empathic understanding responses, and succeeds in this. However, the clients in this research were community clients, not inpatients in a psychiatric hospital. Inpatients in a psychiatric hospital are, of course, more seriously psychologically disturbed, probably psychotic, or in a so-called borderline condition, and they will typically react with withdrawal and/or intensification of psychotic symptoms to any effort to direct them to deeper levels of experiencing, whether it be by aiming systematically at 'additive empathy', or empathy with 'edge of awareness experiences', or by any other means. The tacit assumption that a deepening of the level of experiencing during the session is synonymous with therapeutic progress is not true for clients diagnosed with psychoses.

Therapist efforts at directing the client towards deeper levels of experiencing is, of course, an in-depth exploratory approach. But is it also client-centred therapy? I think not, because the therapist who more or less subtly directs the client towards deeper levels of experiencing is, surely, process directive and this has, in my mind, nothing to do with client-centred therapy, where the therapist is non-directive not only with respect to content but also to process. Raskin (1988: 33) puts it beautifully when he differentiates between systematic and unsystematic therapist responses and says that therapists making systematic responses have '... a preconceived notion of how they wish to change the client and work at it in systematic fashion, in contrast to the person-centered therapist who starts out being open and remains open to an emerging process orchestrated by the client'. Rogers has the following to say (1959: 229–30) about in-depth exploratory approaches:

> In the freedom of therapy, as the individual expresses more and more of himself, he finds himself on the verge of voicing a feeling which is obviously and undeniably true, but which is flatly contradictory to the conception of himself which he has held... Anxiety results, and if the situation is appropriate [*a later section discloses that this means if the core conditions are dominant (this author's comment)*], this anxiety is moderate, and the result is constructive. But if, through overzealous and effective interpretation by the therapist, or through some other means, the individual is brought face to face with more of his denied experiences than he can handle, disorganization ensues and a psychotic break occurs.

Aiming systematically at 'additive empathy' or empathy of 'edge of awareness experiences' is, in my experience, precisely such an over-zealous and effective means that can easily bring clients diagnosed with psychotic or near-psychotic conditions face to face with more of their denied experiences than they can handle.

The usefulness of client-centred therapy to clients diagnosed with psychosis or other forms of severe psychopathology hinges, precisely, on the non-directive attitude of the therapist with respect to content as well as to direction of the process. Psychotic clients, and clients with a 'borderline' diagnosis, will often flatten their level of experiencing as a sort of healthy recuperation, before they deepen it again. These clients can therefore talk about the latest fashion in shoes at one moment, only to talk about exceedingly painful experiences the next, and the therapist should follow the client in both directions, with equal interest and respect. Alternatively, and with expressions borrowed from Godfrey Barrett-Lennard (personal communication), with near-psychotic and psychotic clients the focus of the therapist will be on 'the thinking' rather than on 'the thinker' more often than is the case with the ordinary, less disturbed client population of client-centred therapy. This is no surprise, when one considers how easily these clients are overwhelmed and over-stimulated and disposed to process their experiences, particularly their emotionally disturbing experiences, in psychotic ways.

The following example (factual content has, again, been changed for reasons of confidentiality) illustrates how the therapist follows the client up and down the levels of experiencing, with no effort to direct the client to a deeper level of experiencing. The client was diagnosed with a borderline condition with paranoid features and was admitted to hospital after a suicide attempt in response to his first-ever girlfriend breaking up their relationship. Formally, he was a voluntary client, but a lot of pressure was put on him by his father and his GP to make him accept hospitalisation, and it was also after a lot of persuasion from staff members that he started to see the therapist.

In the session from which the excerpt is taken, he has been considering the possibility of writing a letter to his girlfriend when he stops talking and looks down to the floor, his face turned a little away from the therapist. The therapist has no idea of what is going on in his mind and remains silent. Finally, he looks up and evidently focuses his gaze on some photos on the wallboard in the therapist's office.

> Therapist: You look at the photos.
>
> Client: Yes, is it your dog?
>
> T: Yes.
>
> C: It looks sweet.
>
> T: It is very sweet.
>
> C (*seemingly pleased that he knows*): It's a beagle, isn't it?
>
> T: Yes… feel pleased to be able to recognise it?
>
> C: Yes… We used to have a basset. I did a lot of obedience training with him. Have you done that?
>
> T: Oh, yes, if you don't do that with a beagle, it is just all over the place.
>
> C (*laughing*): Just like with a basset.
>
> (*Falling silent again, and looking down on the floor. Then he looks at the therapist.*)
>
> C: Do you know what incest is?
>
> T: I know what the word means, but I'm not quite sure if that is what you are asking me?
>
> C (*quickly looking away from the therapist and down to the floor again*): Yes… No, incest is many things, isn't it?
>
> T: Yes (*the therapist feels that she has lost contact with the client again*).
>
> (*Client remains motionless and silent for a while; then he looks out of the window.*)
>
> T: You look out of the window.
>
> C: Yes, (*looking at the therapist again*) aren't you disturbed by all that noise from the birds (*a colony of crows in the big trees outside*)?
>
> T: No, not really. I'm so used to them, I seldom notice.
>
> C: You know, I… I don't know… that question about incest… I don't know.

> T: There is something about incest bothering you, and maybe it is too hard to talk about?
>
> C: Yes. (*Falls silent, seemingly thoughtful.*)
>
> C (*very quickly and abruptly, almost spitting it out*): It is about my father and maybe it was incest, I don't know, I don't want to talk about it.
>
> T: You just want me to know that you are troubled by something your father has done that maybe was incest, and you don't want to go into any details about it?
>
> C (*with evident relief*): Right, maybe later. I just wanted you to know that this is part of the picture, too.
>
> T: It's a relief that I know there are such things bothering you, too, and that you are not obliged to tell me any details about it?
>
> C: A huge relief, and maybe we can talk more about it next time?
>
> T: We sure can.

After a short silence, the client turned to other, much less emotionally provocative and more 'shallow' subjects. He didn't return to the issue of incest until three sessions later, when he associated to the topic after having described how he had had to give up his plan to watch television in the lounge, because the only seat left was next to a male nurse on a small sofa.

The approach of the therapist in this excerpt is non-directive, both with respect to content and with respect to process. The therapist does not aim to deepen the client's level of experience by systematically responding with 'additive empathy' or empathy for 'edge of awareness experiences'. The client is in full charge of the direction of the process towards flattening or deepening his level of experience, and the therapist follows the client with equal interest and acceptance when talking about client experiences of dogs and birds as when talking about client experiences of incest. This therapist's approach is, clearly, not an in-depth exploratory approach and it is, therefore, not a potentially harmful approach with people diagnosed with severe psychopathology – on the contrary, as I have already stated.

5. The confusion of the theory of therapy with the theory of personality

Rogers explains psychopathology as the result of more or less excessive exposure to conditions of worth (see, for example, Rogers, 1959). Present-day psychiatry, on the contrary, favours biological explanations for, particularly, the more serious psychological disturbances: ie. the disturbances of people diagnosed with a psychotic or near-psychotic (so-called borderline) condition. To the degree that it is assumed that a conviction of the truth of Rogers' theory of personality, including his explanatory theory of psychopathology, is a necessary prerequisite for practising client-centred therapy, to the same degree it is also true that client-centred therapy cannot be considered useful with the patients of 'heavy psychiatry' – at least not when viewed from the point of view of 'heavy psychiatry'. And when viewed from the point of view of those client-centred therapists who regard Rogers' explanation of psychopathology as the infallible truth, there will be a battle over 'who is right' with representatives of the psychiatric establishment.

It is my contention, however, that one does not need to be convinced of the truth of Rogers' explanatory theory of psychopathology in order to practise client-centred therapy. One only has to be convinced that offering the core conditions to the client is the best one can do, as a psychotherapist, to facilitate actualisation of the client's most constructive potentials. The actualisation of these constructive potentials may have been blocked for a variety of reasons, or the potentials, as such, may have been diminished permanently for a variety of reasons. The reasons may be biological, psychological, cultural, or whatever, but this is of no real consequence to the actual practice of client-centred therapy.

In this connection, it is important not to regard client-centred therapy as a curative treatment on a par with medical model treatments. People with severe somatic illnesses or handicaps benefit from client-centred therapy in the sense that they find better ways to live with their illness or handicap; they do not benefit in the sense that they are cured of their illness or handicap. This is, to a certain degree, also the case with many clients diagnosed with a psychotic condition. Client-centred therapy is useful to them, but not in the sense that they are cured of a presumed biological disposition to process stressful events in psychotic ways, but rather in the sense that they become better able to protect themselves against stress factors that used to release a psychotic breakdown. With these clients, client-centred therapy can be regarded as a preventive, rather than curative, treatment.

There exists, in my experience, no theory that, in a fully satisfying and unequivocal way, explains the existence of the so-called psychotic conditions, particularly those of schizophrenia and manic depression. It even seems increasingly probable that these conditions do not exist as discrete illnesses (Read & Sanders, 2010). I do not believe that Rogers' explanatory theory of psychopathology (excessive exposure to conditions of worth) goes all the way to telling the full story of how psychological disturbances come about, although I think it goes a long way in that direction. I think that other factors play a role, too: socio-economic factors, educational factors and, of course, cultural factors that are important for the definition of what a given culture regards as psychopathological behaviour. Finally, I can't disregard what to me seems to be convincing evidence that biological factors play a role, too, although they, in my opinion, play a more peripheral role than they are given by biologically oriented psychiatrists. Taken together, I think that the factors that determine what the psychiatry of western societies regard as psychopathological behaviour are many and are complexly intertwined.

In spite of the predominance of interest in biological etiological factors in modern psychiatry, psychiatry also takes environmental factors into account in the so-called stress/vulnerability model. This model hypothesises that there exists in the individual a more or less pronounced disposition (hereditary and biological) to react with psychosis, or depression, when under psychological/environmental stress – ie. when the conditions of the milieu of the person are too frustrating or burdening for the person to cope with. In this way, many psychiatrists today try to circumvent the 'nature/nurture' conflict by saying that it is a question of both: sometimes 'nature' is more pronounced than 'nurture', sometimes it is the other way around. This model corresponds quite well to my own experience that client-centred therapy with clients diagnosed with psychosis sometimes seems to result in a cure (more nurture than nature is probably involved); sometimes in better adaptation to an illness (more nature than nurture is probably involved). This, though, does not diminish my critical attitude to the predominance of the medical model in today's psychiatric establishment, as such. (See Chapter 7 for this author's discussion of the role of the critique of psychiatry in the client-centred therapist's daily work in the medical-model setting of a psychiatric hospital.)

The theory of psychopathology and personality to which one adheres is, as already stated, inconsequential as far as the practice of client-centred therapy is concerned. To the degree that client-centred therapy helps clients process experiences in more constructive ways, it will also help clients process experiences in less psychotic ways, even if a disposition to respond with psychotic ideation under stress is more or less biologically determined. Furthermore, and also in the face of a biological disposition, Rogers' explanation of psychotic breakdown may well go a long way to explain why the individual client responds with psychotic ideation to one particular stressor and not to others. In client-centred therapy, the client can find ways to handle individual 'risk factors' so they become less risky. None of this is fundamentally different from the process with other clients: the positive changes that take place during a course of client-centred therapy make all clients less vulnerable to the psychological 'risk factors' of their life, whether the risk is psychosis or something else.

Thus, confusing Rogers' theory of therapy with Rogers' theory of personality by regarding a conviction of the latter to be a prerequisite for practising the former propagates the myth, at least in psychiatric circles, that client-centred therapy is not useful for clients diagnosed with conditions that are, in these circles, regarded as predominantly biologically determined, and particularly the conditions diagnosed as schizophrenia and bipolar disorder. That it doesn't promote good communication between client-centred circles and psychiatric circles either is another matter worth mentioning, because it is probably an important reason that more client-centred therapists are not employed in psychiatry, although client-centred therapy is, in my experience, the only psychotherapeutic approach that can 'reach' the clients of 'heavy psychiatry'. I will give my reasons for this statement in the following and concluding section of this chapter.

6. Reaching the unreachable

It is common practice in other schools of psychotherapy to regard people with the most severe psychological disturbances as being 'beyond psychotherapeutic reach'. The basic reason for this is that these therapeutic approaches normally demand some degree of cooperation from the potential client, apart from this person allowing the therapist to make a 'perceived or subceived difference' (Rogers, 1959: 207) in his/her experiential field. At the very least, therapists of other approaches depend on experiencing a minimal degree of client ability to, and interest in: 1) keeping a sustained focus of attention; 2) making him or herself understood by the therapist; (3) changing something about him or herself, and 4) receiving and processing input/interventions from the therapist's frame. For various reasons, though, therapists will not have these experiences with many of the patients in the psychiatric back wards. Floridly psychotic patients rarely keep a sustained focus for any substantial length of time; withdrawn, so-called autistic patients seem without any wish that others shall understand anything about them; people diagnosed with delusions of persecution apparently don't feel in need of help to change anything about themselves – they feel in need of having the relevant authorities put a halt to the persecution; people diagnosed with delusions of grandeur seem to think that it is everybody else who is in need of their help, not the other way around; people diagnosed with a psychotic depression seem so depleted of energy and hope that they can't contribute with anything in a therapeutic relationship; and, finally, people diagnosed with a manic psychosis feel happily elated, without any worries they might want a therapist's help with. And the groups mentioned are all either incapable of, or uninterested in, receiving input/interventions from the therapist's frame. Since these are people whose behaviour is often within the area of applicability of laws of use of force in psychiatry, they are frequently involuntarily admitted to hospital and involuntarily treated with medication. Offers of help from psychiatry that they are free to refuse, like, for example, psychotherapy, they normally do refuse.

Of course, this list is a crude generalisation. It is stereotypical and leaves out all the nuances and individual degrees of variation with respect to the stereotype. Yet, in these stereotypes lie the reasons these patients are normally considered 'beyond psychotherapeutic reach'. They are, however, not beyond reach of client-centred therapy, often in combination with pre-therapy (see, Pörtner, 2000; Prouty, Van Werde & Pörtner, 2002; Van Werde, Chapter 12, this volume).

According to my experience, the reason for this is the non-directive attitude of the client-centred therapist and pre-therapist. This therapist makes no particular interventions in the hope that they will be helpful to the client. Of course, the therapist hopes that the relationship, in general, will benefit the client, but in a very basic sense he or she meets the client with an offer of interest rather than with an offer of help. The therapist tries to experience the client's momentary psychological landscape as the client experiences it; he or she has no wish to change the client in any way, only to get to know the client to the degree the client allows it. The patients described above are usually hypersensitive to other people's wishes to change them, and when they sense such wishes in another, they typically react with resistance and withdrawal. They do not normally resist or withdraw, though, when they are approached with a sincere interest in their experiences and points of view. In this case, they may put a limit to the contact because they have better things to do than be with the therapist, not because they are resistive or fearful of the contact, as such. And in many cases, they welcome the therapist's interest and some end up wishing the contact to continue because they feel helped by it and want further help. At this point, the relationship has developed into an ordinary client-centred therapy relationship that is motivated by the client's wish for help as much as, or more than, by the therapist's interest in the client.

A continuous effort at accurate empathic understanding is, by definition, post-dictive as opposed to pre-dictive, and the non-directive attitude is a consequence of this. Empathic understanding follows or accompanies the client's moves; it does not anticipate them. I feel convinced this is the reason that client-centred therapy can reach the patients in the psychiatric back wards, where other psychotherapeutic approaches cannot. To these people, the client-centred therapist's attitude seems often to be experienced as an oasis in a desert of what they experience as more or less dissimulated, manipulative, overprotective, patronising or coercive efforts to change them.

It is not the tendency of empathic understanding to stimulate self-exploration and clarification that is appreciated by these people. It is the unconditional interest and positive regard that is transmitted by the therapist's continuous effort at empathic understanding, devoid of any wish to change the client, that they appreciate. Only at a later point in the relationship will some of them, but far from all, come to appreciate the opportunity to clarify their psychological landscape that the empathic understanding of the therapist also offers them. As already mentioned, others will terminate the relationship with the therapist because they have found something more attractive to do. And of these, some will return with a request for renewed talks with the therapist at a later time. Client-centred therapists who want to relate with the patients in 'heavy psychiatry' must be flexible with regard to place, schedule, who takes the initiative in the contact and the length of the relationship. They must also know about pre-therapy.

The therapists in the Wisconsin project couldn't know of pre-therapy. Had they known, I feel convinced they would have been better able to remain more consistently in a non-directive empathic process with their clients and that the results of the research would have come closer to the positive results of Prouty's research (Rogers et al, 1967: 44–46). The contact reflections of pre-therapy respond to these clients' expressiveness on the extraordinarily concrete level that is often appropriate with clients diagnosed with severe psychopathology. It is the addition of pre-therapy to my ordinary client-centred approach that has enabled me to relate with the patients in psychiatry who seem most 'out of contact', in a non-imposing, non-intruding, non-demanding, unconditionally acceptant way. The contact reflections of pre-therapy help me meet these patients where they are, in a way that, to me, feels truly person-centred. With most clients today, I fluctuate rather effortlessly between the ordinary empathic understanding responses of client-centred therapy and the contact reflections of pre-therapy, depending on the variations I experience in the client's degree of being 'in contact' or 'out of contact' (see also Sommerbeck, 2003: 68–84).

Conclusion

It is, thus, not only a myth that client-centred therapy is not useful with clients diagnosed with severe psychopathology; it is the opposite of the truth: client-centred therapy is eminently suited for these clients and, with the extension of pre-therapy, client-centred therapy can reach patients in the most remote corners in the psychiatric back wards. The psychiatric nurses who participated in a training group in pre-therapy that I used to facilitate did not, as is normally the case, ask: 'Is this patient too disturbed to benefit from the approach?' On the contrary, they asked: 'Is this patient too *little* disturbed to benefit from the approach?' I feel touched by this, because it is evidence to me that, finally, there has been found an approach that makes it possible to reach the unreachable, an approach for those who are worst off, not another approach for those who are best off.

References

Bozarth JD (1998). *Person-Centered Therapy: a revolutionary paradigm.* Ross-on-Wye: PCCS Books.

Hart JT, Tomlinson TM (eds) (1970). *New Directions in Client-Centered Therapy.* Boston: Houghton Mifflin.

Mearns D, Thorne B (1999). *Person-Centred Counselling in Action.* London: Sage Publications.

Pörtner M (2000). *Trust and Understanding: the person-centred approach to everyday care for people with special needs.* Ross-on-Wye: PCCS Books.

Prouty G (1994). *Theoretical Evolutions in Person-Centered/Experiential Therapy: applications to schizophrenic and retarded psychoses.* Westport: Praeger.

Prouty G, Van Werde D, Pörtner M (2002). *Pre-Therapy: reaching contact-impaired clients.* Ross-on-Wye: PCCS Books.

Raskin N (1988). *What do we mean by person-centred therapy?* Paper presented at the second meeting of the Second Association for the Development of the Person-Centred Approach, New York, May.

Read J, Sanders P (2010). *The Causes of Mental Health Problems.* Ross-on-Wye: PCCS Books

Rogers CR (1951). *Client-Centered Therapy.* Boston: Houghton Mifflin.

Rogers CR (1959). A theory of therapy, personality, and interpersonal relationships as developed in the client-centered framework. In: Koch E (ed). *Psychology: a study of a science. Vol. 3*. New York: McGraw-Hill.

Rogers C, Gendlin E, Kiesler D, Truax CB (1967). *The Therapeutic Relationship with Schizophrenics*. Wisconsin: The University of Wisconsin Press.

Sachse R (1990). Concrete interventions are crucial: the influence of the therapist's processing proposals on the client's intrapersonal exploration in client-centered therapy. In: Lietaer G, Rombauts J, van Balen R (eds). *Client-Centered and Experiential Psychotherapy in the Nineties*. Leuven: Leuven University Press (pp295–308).

Shlien JM (1992). Theory as autobiography: the man and the movement. *Contemporary Psychology 37*(10). Reprinted in: Shlien JM (2003). *To Lead an Honorable Life: invitations to think about client-centered therapy and the person-centered approach*. Ross-on-Wye: PCCS Books (pp212–216).

Sommerbeck L (2002). The Wisconsin watershed – or the universality of CCT. *The Person-Centered Journal 9*: 140–157.

Sommerbeck L (2003). *The Client-Centred Therapist in Psychiatric Contexts: a therapist's guide to the psychiatric landscape and its inhabitants*. Ross-on-Wye: PCCS Books.

Vitger J (1999). Kurative Faktorer ved Psykoanalytiske Terapier. *Matrix 3*: 200.

25 | Small-scale research as personal development for mental health professionals[1]

Richard Worsley

Previously (Chapter 9, this volume), I argued that it is necessary for mental health workers to face within themselves the feelings and consequences, the undertow, of working with their clients' psychopathology. It is tempting to feign a sort of professional competence that seems to view objectively the client and their way of being. Clients have a real impact upon us. From time to time this impact will be major. Some psychopathological patterns are more difficult than others for any given individual to face. True professionalism involves developing the personal awareness to process these issues within us, lest they become stumbling blocks. In this chapter, I will demonstrate a model of small-scale, phenomenological research as a route to developing personal awareness. I will describe an encounter with a person who has known what it is to be anorexic; set out my initial responses to her; show how these develop and change within a two-hour encounter, and, in doing this, argue that even experienced therapists need to work on their awareness of the impact of clients' presenting material on them.

This chapter is a personal account of my encounter with Janet.[2] I had become aware that I felt discomfort at working with people with anorexia. This discomfort had a quality that suggested I needed to reflect in depth on it. Janet, who has known anorexia for a number of years, was willing to engage with me in this reflection. I sought her permission to do this, with the aim of facing the demon of my own apprehension. Psychopathology is personal just because we who are person-centred practitioners encounter others, as best we can, from the depths of our being.

---

1. This chapter was previously published in a slightly different version as 'Small is beautiful: small-scale phenomenological research for counsellor self-development' in *Person-Centered and Experiential Psychotherapies*, 2003; 2(2): 121–132. The chapter has thus been fully refereed in line with the policy of that journal.

2. Janet is not the co-researcher's real name. This article, in a previous version, has been seen by Janet and full and informed permission has been given for its use.

Mature, person-centred practitioners have had to develop a particular ability to be in tune with the phenomenal reality of their clients. We think phenomenologically, and strive to be aware of the impact of encounter upon us. Dave Mearns (1997: 151–152) has argued cogently that experientially-based research should be part of an extended period of counsellor development beyond the formal diploma training, in order to advance person-centred theory. Small-scale research can advance theory, but certainly can be a crucial element in the personal and professional development of the counsellor. It is part of the characteristic genius of the person-centred/experiential approach that its practitioners have, as an aspect of their daily experience of therapy, an immersion in phenomenological practice.

Personal development as research

The present project is an exploration of unconditional positive regard, of the quality of my relating. Martin Buber's (1958) work *I and Thou* is one of the foundation documents of the philosophical underpinning for being person-centred. Buber distinguishes between two primary categories of experiencing relationship. The I-It reduces the other to a mere object, a thing, that which can be used. By contrast, the I-Thou acknowledges that the other is a self, like the subject. Counsellors are committed in their daily work to the nurturing of the I-Thou relationship. I suggest that small-scale phenomenological research is truer to the I-Thou relationship. This is an ethical commitment, and one that is at the heart of person-centred thinking. To research through experiential learning is attractive to me, just because it resonates with the core activity of therapy, to which I commit my professional life. This paper sees experiencing-as-learning as firmly rooted in the I-Thou relationship. How this sits within the family of phenomenological research methods will be briefly addressed below.

I suggest that, in small-scale work, researching through the familiar I-Thou relationship can release the practitioner into confident action learning. The researcher is a stakeholder in her own effort because its outcomes feed back to the daily practice of her art. When research focuses on practitioner self-development, there is a deepening awareness of the very experience of learning, change and consequent improved practice. The remainder of this paper offers one such project by way of example.

A personal dilemma – a question in its context

Practice-based research begins with practice-based questions. I find that one practice issue comes round to haunt me: I struggle to accord unconditional positive regard to people with anorexia. I feel most uncertain that, in terms of others' bodies, small is beautiful. I need to learn and to grow.

In September 2002, I met Janet at a college reception. Grasping food and drink in our hands, I swiftly discovered something – but not much – of her life journey, and of her consequent research into the Christian pastoral care of those with eating disorders. I expressed my interest in what she was doing. I experienced myself as genuinely interested, but not at all willing to say what I felt about anorexia (which is to say, about Janet herself). I felt incongruent, and that was painful.

Janet offered to talk further with me about her work. I contacted her to request two hours of her time, so that I could explore in that context the issues that faced me. I felt aware that I might be using her – and indeed the language of co-researcher is about the possibility of exploitation. Her informed consent was crucial to me, but did not alleviate my anxiety that, in meeting Janet, I would meet difficult aspects of myself.

The ethics of personal encounter

To encounter another human being is to take a risk, not least when that person is vulnerable. In fact, in my encounter with Janet, both of us were vulnerable, but in different ways. I was acutely aware of her vulnerabilities that had led her to become anorexic, but equally aware of my limited positive regard for her in the first instance. Both point to ethical issues. It would seem most unwise for one person who believes another person to be a problem for them to blithely construct a meeting in which the co-researcher's vulnerability is open to the researcher's lack of positive regard.

It is simply not possible to work with a vulnerable co-researcher at random. In meeting Janet, I already knew that she had used her experience both for her own research and for subsequent teaching within faith communities. Her work with me was similar to other things she chose to do as part of her calling. Janet's strengths made it meaningful and safe to invite her to be a co-researcher. It was important to me throughout this to discuss the whole project with one of my supervisors, who herself has a psychotherapy research qualification.

I contracted verbally with Janet to meet with me for two hours, and then to review what I wrote from that. Her background in research and teaching was evidence that the consent she offered was both informed and genuine. At the end of the encounter, and after the writing of the first draft of this paper, Janet knew that she had the right to withdraw totally from the project. On each occasion, I had consent from her, on the first, verbally, but on the second in written form. I have subsequently updated her on the review and redrafting process.

Methodology

In essence, my method of exploration, as a person-centred practitioner, is to reflect on who I am in the light of my fear of working with people with anorexia, and then to meet both Janet and her research experience in order to investigate/instigate change. I am exploring the darker side of me in a research environment, so that I may work safely with clients with anorexia, as I need to. I want to engage in meeting with Janet, and to record systematically my awarenesses both before and after that encounter. This record, reflection and narrative, will constitute the second half of this paper. Stated thus, my methodology feels simplicity itself. It is congruent with a person-centred way of being. My aim is to meet with Janet with as little encumbrance as possible. I do not want to record and analyse our meeting. I seek to explore its meaning as it is manifested in the Me who exists before and after it.

I construe the issue as being about unconditional positive regard. It is not that I fail to offer this to people with anorexia. Rather, it is that I see before me an anorexic rather than a Thou (Buber, 1958). In the face of anorexia, I abstain to some unacceptable degree from encounter, from the Other. While I affirm, with Purton (1998), that all human beings are of absolute worth, I opt in the face of anorexia not to live this out. I am failing to acknowledge the very being of those who happen to have anorexia. The philosophical basis of acceptant responding has been spelled out by Peter Schmid (2002), who draws our attention in particular to the thought of Emmanuel Levinas:

> In his main work *Totalité et Infini* Levinas (1961) points out that to exist
> means to be entangled in oneself, caught in the totality of one's own world.
> According to Levinas the first alienation of the human being is not being able
> to get rid of oneself… [T]he awakening from the totality of the being-caught-
> in-oneself does not happen through 'being independent'. Rather, the Other is
> the power which liberates the I from oneself. (Schmid, 2002: 53)

My seeing some people as primarily anorexic, rather than as Thou, is a caughtness-in-myself. Active learning is a seeking the Other. I am not initially aware of why I carry these feelings, but I make a first guess, in the light of Rogers' (1961) description of what it is to move towards full functionality in process terms, that I am mis-symbolising. The Other who will liberate the I from myself will likely cause me to resymbolise anorexia to a sufficient degree. I note Orbach's argument (1993: 3–11) that anorexia is a powerful metaphor for our times. In what sense is it a powerfully misconstrued meaning for me?

My initial intuition, then, had been that I needed to resymbolise my engaging with people with anorexia, so as to reconstrue the multiple meanings of this for me. Phenomenological research methodologies offer a range of possibilities. (Moustakas, 1994: 1–22). However, my conceptualisation of the research process had been naïve, based upon two tools that were familiar to me. I set out below these two procedures, and then a *post factum* critical reflection on their use.

My first procedural tool was Moustakas' (1994: 84–101) procedure, based on Husserl's transcendental phenomenology. This procedure falls into four movements: bracketing (epoché), reduction, imaginative variation and synthesis. I had used it previously with a larger scale piece of work, but was aware of its limitations on the smaller scale. The aim is to reach a brief, phenomenological account of a particular experience, usually across a number of co-researchers. Thus, the method might look for the commonalities among a number of bereaved people. It seeks to set out the structure and the texture of their experience. The four stages are as follows.

1. *Bracketing.* The researcher seeks to become aware of her own prejudices, by stating them as clearly as possible. Husserl believed that they could be removed by making them fully open to the researcher. This is rather optimistic: limited awareness is as much as can be hoped for.

2. *Reduction.* The experience of a number of interviews, for example, can be reduced to a number of key themes. The researcher aims to describe each experience just as it is. In practice, this involves the identifying of 'horizons' – the limits of core experience – and the removal of duplication and irrelevancies.

3. *Imaginative variation.* The phenomenological truth is as much within the subject's grasp as within the 'out-there' world. Therefore, new understanding emerges as the researcher allows her imagination to experiment with the material derived from the reduction.

4. *Synthesis.* A complete account of the structure and texture of the experience is given. Husserl had seen this as a final truth. The more sceptical among us may well doubt that such a thing can be.

I abbreviated the Moustakas procedure by using time before my interview with Janet to reflect on my prejudices as a flow-of-consciousness exercise (bracketing) and then, after the interview itself, I reported to myself and recorded my immediate experience of recalling my encounter with Janet. In this, I combined the reduction with the imaginative variation – made possible by the smallness of scale of the project. I omitted the synthesis, partly because I doubt Husserl's claim that such a truth is available to us, but also because my attention was focused on my awareness of my own process and values. This shift of attention suggests that the Moustakas method is not a complete account of what I actually did (see below.)

David Kolb's (1984) cycle of experiential learning formed the other conceptual tool. Kolb's cycle consists of a four-phase process, which can be entered at any point, and which can be repeated at will. The phases are:

- Concrete experience. What is happening?
- Reflective observation. What did happen?
- Abstract conceptualisation. What does it mean?
- Active experimentation. What shall I do (be) as a result?

(Kolb, as summarised by Dainow & Bailey, 1988: 6)

The project can be conceptualised as three circuits of the Kolb cycle of experiential learning.

1. Experience my formulation of the question from practice. Reflect upon the texture and structure of this formulation. Lay open – acknowledge and own, or bracket and remove – its theoretical preconceptions. Integrate the methodology as action within the project.

2. (The overall bracketing.) Enter as deeply as possible into my experiencing of my fear of working with people with anorexia. Reflect on the texture and structure of that experience. Theoretise the experience in terms of what it would be for me to meet the Other without undue mis-symbolisation. Integrate this bracketing-off into an encounter with Janet and her research.

3. Meet with Janet. Reflect on the nature of that meeting for me. Theoretise this in terms of my resymbolisation of such encounters. Integrate this into practice by a summarising of my position as a starting point for any experience with an anorexic client.

Locating the methodology

The origin of this project was in life setting me a question about how I engaged as a therapist with people with anorexia. With some naïvety, I had allowed the question itself to dictate the methodology. I had used two tools with which I was familiar – Moustakas' procedure based on transcendental phenomenology, supplemented by Kolb's description of experiential learning. On reflection, I had done what I would do all over again, but it is only in the process of further reflection that I have located a more organised rationale for my way of working with Janet.

Formally, three approaches to phenomenological research are represented within what I did. Transcendental phenomenology is at the root of the process, in that I was already familiar with Moustakas' method. However, I altered this procedure in two ways. I put together the reduction with the imaginative variation. In part, this was simply a matter of economy of scale. In such a limited project, there is no good reason to rigidly separate these. However, this change, I now realise, shows a distrust within me for the rigidity of Husserl's conceptualisation of phenomenology. I was finally not interested in a methodologically pure statement of a phenomenological truth. I was interested in changing. I wanted to increase my positive regard for a particular client group.

I have come to recognise that my commitment was to a combination of heuristic and hermeneutical research. Moustakas (1990: 27) defines heuristic research in terms of six processes: initial engagement, immersion, incubation, illumination, explication and culmination. I find that what I did approximates to these. However, what I truly own is the underlying rationale:

> The deepest currents of meaning and knowledge take place within the
> individual through one's senses, perceptions, beliefs, and judgments. This
> requires a passionate, disciplined commitment to remain with the question

intensely and continuously until it is illuminated or answered.
(Moustakas, 1990: 15)

Although my conscious research procedure was derived from transcendental phenomenology, my dissatisfactions, which had caused me to modify the procedure, stemmed from a set of values largely in tune with heuristic principles.

I have also come to recognise that my belief, influenced by Rogers' process conception, that I was limiting my positive regard because I was mis-symbolising anorexia, also pushed me towards a hermeneutic turn. I was interested above all in the meaning of my experience and of Janet's for me. I wanted to change by finding new meaning within the metaphors of experience. I find myself resonating with the following passage of Paul Ricoeur:

> The subject who interprets himself while interpreting signs is no longer the *cogito*… he is a being who discovers exegesis of his own life, that he is placed in being before… he possesses himself. In this way hermeneutics would discover a manner of existing which would remain from start to finish a *being-interpreted*. (Ricoeur, 1989: 11 (original italics))

Ricoeur's perspective offers us the vision of a self that is continually in search of meaning through self-interpretation. When practitioner research has the courage to focus on the being of the researcher-as-subject, there emerges a researcher who is nearer to the deeply human way of being required of a therapist.

Bracketing

A week prior to meeting Janet, I reviewed my stance with my supervisor as an initial act of bracketing. Two days before our meeting, I spent half an hour making notes of my subjective flow of experience while focusing on the topic of this research. The following themes emerged. I have no sense that they connect or are ordered in any particular fashion, but rather that they represent a selection of significant symbolisations from a free-flowing reflection or meditation.

- A former tutor told me that people with anorexia cannot be counselled. I respect her opinions generally.
- Defiance is a key feeling. People with anorexia dare me to face their dying. They defy rescue.
- I become angry, helpless and vulnerable in the face of their defiance.
- They self-harm. (But other forms of self-harm do not worry me as much.)
- Is it OK to let you die? Will you die? I do not know.
- It is so *visible*. Everyone will see my failure as a therapist. I feel shame.

- The thinness reminds me of terminal cancer. My partner used to be a hospice chaplain. The staff always ate well to avoid thinness.

- As a therapist, I image myself as a provider. Am I rejected with the food? (Bulimia is OK?)

- All the while, frailty leaves *me* feeling attacked.

- My own (healthy and plump) body image becomes embarrassing – like drinking in front of an alcoholic.

- I cannot imagine the distress that leads to self-starvation.

- I work happily with addictions, but this seems like the very opposite. A not needing a thing. Why is that not OK?

- The anorexic body's image challenges my reality. I struggle for empathy. The schizophrenic's reality fascinates me, but not the anorexic's.

- As a person-centred practitioner, can I trust the actualising tendency of a self-starving human being? It felt as if the destructive urge might put an end to her fulfilment of her potential. This would be a view wholly at odds with my normal feelings about clients.

- It feels like trauma. I need to give up any notion of cure. There is an existential reality. How do people live healthily with anorexia? (Is this a shift, or a head-defence?)

- Can I form an alliance if I do not trust?

- Will my interest in Janet harm her? Can I protect her? Is that my job? Can I trust her to look after herself?

These notes are all I have before meeting Janet to resymbolise. They echo with associations and possible interpretations. The act of bracketing has left me feeling warmer. This feels like a vague awareness that no amount of reflection will substitute for meeting.

Meeting

Janet and I met for two hours. We agreed boundaries around confidentiality and Janet's right to see and change the final text of this project, or to withdraw from it completely. The day after the meeting I made notes in another act of free-flowing reflection. I deliberately left a short time for the experience of meeting to settle, and for a meaning-constructing process to happen within me. I note that, unlike more objective research, the resultant forgetting and recalling seems important. I hypothesise that the settling down involves a forgetting of surface detail in order to become more aware of felt-meaning (Gendlin, 1997).

My first awareness on sitting down was of my being challenged by Janet as to what in me had this particular need to understand anorexia as if it were an alien territory. Far from feeling threatened – as I might, for I wondered this about me too – I felt a great sense of comfort. I knew at the time, as well as on reflection, two truths. First, the firm, gentle congruence of the challenge told me that I was in the company of someone who could well look after herself. My anxiety that Janet might need protecting from my curiosity abated. From a practice perspective, I look now for those parts of the fragile client that need none of my protection. There is admittedly a major difference between Janet as a vigorous individual who happens to be in recovery from an eating disorder, and some clients who are, or seem to be, genuinely very fragile. Yet, being aware of and simultaneously letting go of fragility seems as though it might be crucial to respect. Second, I noted that my underlying anxiety was well outside of Janet's frame of reference. My apprehension in the face of anorexia is not at all an obvious or universal construct. Anorexia can be part of ordinary living. In response to her challenge, I talked of the tutor who had said that people with anorexia cannot be counselled, and dwelt on the impact this had on me. Yet, it felt defensive. Whatever the impact, there was more to it than that.

A second challenge came. How did I know that Janet had been anorexic? I resisted a fleck of defensiveness in me. I was completely perplexed. Had she not told me? Had I heard elsewhere? Was it not obvious? Why? On reflection, Janet shows no longer any signs how she might have been anorexic in the past. I have no answer to the literal question, but from it comes a sense of Janet's need to have control of her identity, a right to her personal boundaries. It would be easy to pathologise such a need. Is it any different from parallel needs in me? I suspect not.

All the while, I am aware now of my ambivalent feelings about what I was feeling. Was I listening to elements of control in Janet, or to my own fearful defendedness? I am reminded of the observation of Sheldon Cashdan (1988: 154–158) that the difference between therapeutic and personal countertransference is not knowable with certainty. There must be practised vigilance. I guess that my meeting with Janet will facilitate this in me in the years to come.

Before Janet and I had sat down together, she had expressed both an interest in counselling and a belief that person-centred work would be really valuable for people with anorexia. In conversation, this developed into an image about counselling being more difficult 'below the line'. The image is of a graph of the client's functionality. I needed to explore that in some depth. It spoke to a deep fear within me, about working beyond my competence and not knowing it – and perhaps of more than that. Janet clarified for me that when the body is weakest, special care must be taken to work in a way that avoids physical exhaustion. Within myself, I heard a distinct internal comment: So, it is not that 'below the line', psychological contact is absent (Rogers, 1957). It is sometimes the case that the question or fear only surfaces when the answer is in reach. At the level of practice, I will be loathe to doubt psychological contact without due evidence.

I am aware of the nature of Janet's personal story and her telling of it. She affirmed that she had needed to face deep issues within herself. Neither of us needed to talk about these. I profoundly do not know what they are or were for her, save that there is an element around control. At the surface level, this is simply a question of respect between co-researchers. Underneath, I began to feel my ability to live with the unsaid of clients. Janet spoke of her experience of a directive and abusive GP, and her sense of the need for openness and non-directivity. This she had found in the eating disorders unit she had attended. My underlying feeling was of warm acceptance. This was a strong and irrational sensation.

On reflection, my growing sense of acceptance, the fading of my fear of the unknown as I became more actively able to grant Janet her space, suggests to me that I have struggled with people with anorexia because their selves, their bodies, tend to be for me a metaphor of a largely irrational threat to my being with them. It is as if the therapy itself might starve. This too has been a strong and irrational sensation.

Talking about Janet's research could constitute for each of us a defence against the exploration we were committed to – a flight into the head. Yet, for me, even this aspect of our conversation was part of our I-Thou encounter.

The remainder of the conversation was a meandering between the personal – on both sides – and the research. From it, five themes emerged for me. As I write I am aware of the selectiveness of this. Again, the learning is what emerges for me, rather than an objective account. The first theme lives in the mental picture of Janet holding a chalice (cup) at the Eucharist. (Janet is training for the Christian ministry. At the heart of her being a priest will be her blessing and sharing with others bread and wine, symbolising the body and blood of Jesus Christ. Even to receive bread and wine has been a massive effort, a striving to confront fear at the very point where peace is hoped for.) It is tough for people with anorexia to share in a rite that requires even a minimal sign of eating. The road to recovery, if well negotiated and understood by the minister of that rite, can include a symbolising of gradual change. The chalice can be held without drinking. This is healing. To the extent that I have mis-symbolised within me elements of the experience of the person with anorexia, I also know that I can symbolise small and gradual elements of recovery, and thus of hope.

Second, Janet has made explicit for me a fact I thought I already knew. Anorexia is about protest, at least for her. I can empathise with protest. Third, Janet's awareness that people with anorexia often feel guilt that their condition is seen by others as a *voluntary* illness feels to me the correlate of my judgmentalism and fear of aggression, and hence of my own aggression. I can recognise a dynamic that is close to my own unwanted feelings.

Fourth, I had become fascinated by the fact that addiction, which I deal with more easily, is about a substance. This substance competes with the therapist, but at least it is a clear opponent (Worsley, 2002: 150–156). In anorexia, there is no substance. As therapist, I face nothing, as if a void. What is symbolised by me and within me are the feared existential voids. Last, I remember with great clarity my puzzlement that Janet said there was a time when she had forgotten how to eat. I explored this, and came gradually to see the texture and structure of her experience.

My clients will need to introduce me to those aspects of their experience that, in spite of words, are a long way from me. I come to sense the excitement again of learning from the client, even the client who happens in part of herself to have anorexia.

Conclusions

The project of my meeting with Janet leads me to a number of personal conclusions. When I allow myself to be curious about who she really is, I move away from a sort of phobic quality in my previous attitude towards those with anorexia. In this I face my aggressive and fearful self, and can begin to empathise with the protest element in anorexia. I notice that anorexic guilt seems to correspond to the punitive element in me. I become prepared to meet others with a different configuration in place. The symbol of protest and the symbol of the Eucharist as a place of experimenting with gradual change each allows me to move towards a re-symbolisation of anorexia for me as a therapist, particularly as I can own and then move away from the non-rational fear that the therapy itself might starve and perish. I appreciate in the case of at least one human being the strong perception that non-directiveness is essential to her recovery. All these, and other things yet to emerge, are personal outcomes of this research. It is in the act of meeting that I found a new flexibility and responsiveness for my internal models of anorexia, and so become open again to the reality of non-directiveness and acceptance. Meeting opened for me the possibility of a new congruence between my beliefs about my therapeutic practice and my internal experience of encounter.

More generally, this piece of small-scale research illustrates the need for workers to be aware of the detailed impact of clients' presentation on them; of their response to symptoms and diagnoses rather than persons; of the struggle at times to maintain unconditional positive regard for others in the face of one's own biases and projections. From a person-centred perspective, psychopathology is not an objective science but part of the journey of two individuals together. We meet not cases but others who, sometimes in spite of appearances, are distressingly like us.

References

Buber M (1958). *I and Thou*. Edinburgh: T & T Clark.

Cashdan S (1988). *Object Relations Therapy: using the relationship*. New York: WW Norton & Co.

Dainow S, Bailey C (1988). *Developing Skills with People*. London: Wiley.

Gendlin E (1997). *Experiencing and the Creation of Meaning: a philosophical and psychological approach to the subjective*. Evanston, IL: Northwestern University Press.

Kolb D (1984). *Experiential Learning*. Englewood Cliffs, NJ: Prentice Hall.

Levinas E (1961). *Totalité et Infini: essai sur l'extériorité*. Den Haag: Nijhoff.

Mearns D (1997). *Person-Centred Counselling Training*. London: Sage.

Moustakas C (1990). *Heuristic Research: design, methodology and applications*. London: Sage.

Moustakas C (1994). *Phenomenological Research Methods*. London: Sage.

Orbach S (1993). *Hunger Strike*. Harmondsworth: Penguin.

Purton C (1998). Unconditional positive regard and its spiritual implication. In: Thorne B, Lambers E (eds). *Person-Centered Therapy: a European perspective*. London: Sage (pp23–37).

Ricoeur P (1989). *The Conflict of Interpretations: essays on hermeneutics*. London: Continuum.

Rogers, CR (1957). The necessary and sufficient conditions of therapeutic personality change. *Journal of Consulting Psychology 21*: 95–103.

Rogers CR (1961). A process conception of psychotherapy. In: Rogers CR. *On Becoming a Person*. Boston: Houghton Mifflin (pp125–159).

Schmid PF (2002). Acknowledgement: the art of responding. Dialogical and ethical perspectives on the challenge of unconditional relationships in therapy and beyond. In: Bozarth JD, Wilkins P (eds). *Rogers' Therapeutic Conditions: evolution, theory and practice. Volume 3: Unconditional positive regard*. Ross-on-Wye: PCCS Books (pp49–64).

Worsley RJ (2001). *Process Work in Person-Centred Therapy: phenomenological and existential perspectives*. Basingstoke: Palgrave.

26 Assessing efficacy and effectiveness in person-centred therapy: challenges and opportunities.

Tom G Patterson

Person-centred theory (Rogers, 1959) presents us with a unique and comprehensive model for understanding psychological distress that is informed by a substantial body of research (Barrett-Lennard, 1998; Murphy & Joseph, 2016; Rogers & Dymond, 1954). However, in the current context of evidence-based healthcare commissioning and provision, person-centred practitioners face pressure to further demonstrate the efficacy and effectiveness of their approach. This task is perhaps made more challenging by the dominance of the medical model conceptualisation of psychopathology in the literature concerned with efficacy and effectiveness research.

This chapter considers ways in which person-centred practitioners and researchers might engage with the task of further developing the evidence base for person-centred psychotherapy and counselling within the current context. After consideration of the particular challenges that this proposition raises for person-centred practitioners, I argue that theoretically congruent measures offer a promising way forward and, in line with this, describe a range of formal measures that fulfil this criterion. Some of those measures are drawn from research into person-centred theory and therapy. However, given that only a small number of such measures exist, I will also consider the relevance of measures developed by academic psychologists and, in particular, those measures from positive psychology research that appear to be consistent with the principles of person-centred theory and the goals of person-centred therapy. Finally, I consider potential future directions, including reflections on whether some degree of compromise might be required if person-centred researchers and practitioners choose to engage with the challenges inherent in the current environment of mental healthcare commissioning and provision.

The current context of mental healthcare commissioning and provision

In a time of austerity politics, the quest for greater efficiency in financially squeezed public and voluntary sector organisations has left all those who practise psychotherapy and counselling facing pressures to provide evidence of therapeutic efficacy and effectiveness. This represents a particular challenge to person-centred practitioners, given that the discourse has largely developed around a medical model conceptualisation of mental health difficulties, most clearly exemplified in the *Diagnostic and Statistical Manual of Mental Disorders* produced by the American Psychiatric Association (2013; *DSM-5*). The medical model and the *DSM* classification system share the assumption that psychological distress and mental health difficulties can be reliably broken down into a taxonomy of specific medical conditions, and that the central goal of therapeutic interventions should be to achieve alleviation or cure of the medicalised symptoms assumed to underpin the particular condition. Commissioners of mental healthcare services, as well as provider organisations, have become accustomed to discourse framed in the language of conditions and symptoms – an obvious challenge for person-centred practitioners.

In the UK context, where the NHS is the leading provider of mental health services, those who practise psychotherapy or counselling in the NHS are expected to follow the National Institute for Health and Care Excellence (NICE) guidelines on therapies or treatments considered effective for particular mental health *conditions*. Those guidelines are predominantly based on evidence from randomised control trials (RCT), considered the 'gold standard' in terms of quality of healthcare research design. Although medical model-informed RCT studies represent a further challenge to therapies that do not view symptom reduction as the key indicator of therapeutic effectiveness, person-centred therapy and other humanistic therapies still perform relatively well in RCT studies (see Elliott, 1996; Friedli et al, 1997; King et al, 2000).

However, while RCTs can provide useful information about the *efficacy* (the probable effectiveness) of different therapies, their reliance on symptom-focused measures, such as measures of depression or anxiety, serves to reinforce a medical model conceptualisation of mental health difficulties. In addition, due to their need to adopt stringent criteria regarding who can and cannot be included in a study, they tend to exclude people with taxonomically unclear or 'complex' presentations. Consequently, the findings from RCTs will not always reflect the real-world *effectiveness* of the therapies they evaluate for the broad range of individuals seen by counsellors and psychotherapists.

A brief illustration of the limitations of making inferences about therapeutic effectiveness based solely on RCT findings comes from a study by Hansen, Lambert and Forman (2002). Reviewing data from more than 6,000 people who had received therapeutic support in routine clinical care contexts in the US, these authors found that only 20 per cent of clients who had attended therapy showed improvement, compared with rates of between 50 and 80 per cent improvement reported in RCT studies, indicating that RCT efficacy findings do not necessarily translate into real-world therapeutic effectiveness. Despite such limitations, RCT research designs do have methodological strengths. Given that the findings from these studies inform commissioning of psychotherapy and counselling provision, it would seem naïve to suggest that engagement with research into therapeutic efficacy and effectiveness, including RCT studies, should not be the concern of person-centred practitioners. Rather, I would argue that demonstrating efficacy and effectiveness merits a proactive response, and that serious consideration should be given to determining precisely how person-centred practitioners can best engage in such research.

The challenge of engaging in the assessment of therapeutic efficacy and effectiveness

While some may not agree with the use of any formal measurement in the evaluation of person-centred counselling and psychotherapy, I would argue that there is a strong rationale for engaging in formal measurement and evaluation in light of the increasing emphasis placed on empirical evidence of efficacy and effectiveness by those who commission and provide public and third-sector mental healthcare services. This, of course, requires a willingness on the part of person-centred practitioners and researchers to engage in the measurement of therapy outcomes. However, it is suggested here that a pragmatic approach, involving the use of measures that are consistent with the person-centred theoretical account of how psychopathology develops and how therapy works, may represent an acceptable way forward.

Person-centred personality theory proposes that people are intrinsically and naturally motivated towards their full potential and optimal functioning unless this motivational tendency is usurped and thwarted by social-environmental factors, resulting in psychological distress (Joseph & Linley, 2006). A thwarted potential perspective views vulnerability to psychopathology as arising from the internalisation of conditions of worth during childhood, with a consequent alienation of the individual from his or her organismic needs. Defensive processes of denial and/or distortion of self-experiences that do not fit with the individual's conditions of worth result in a state of incongruence between self and experience, whereby the individual's self-regard, or valuing of themselves, becomes increasingly conditional on maintaining the standards demanded by their internalised conditions of worth (Rogers, 1959).

As all psychopathology is viewed as stemming from inaccurate conscious representations of experiencing due to alienation from the organismic self, this then becomes the focus of counselling and psychotherapy. Rather than developing specific interventions for specific symptoms, it is understood that all mental health problems can be helped through accepting, empathic and genuine relationships that foster the client's agency. This understanding informed the early years of research into person-centred theory and client-centred therapy, resulting in innovative approaches to assessing therapeutic process and, to a lesser degree, therapeutic outcome, including the use of formal measures of some person-centred constructs, to which I will return later in this chapter.

A shared challenge

Person-centred practitioners are not alone in rejecting a medical model understanding of mental distress. Interestingly, there is much criticism of the medical model of mental health difficulties from within core healthcare professions, such as psychiatry and clinical psychology, which have also challenged the validity and reliability of medical model diagnostic systems (for example, Bentall, 2003; Marzillier, 2004; Johnstone, 2014). These critiques also emphasise the importance of socio-environmental factors and serve as a reminder that there is support from various quarters for alternatives to the medical model of psychopathology.

Nor are person-centred practitioners alone in having to face the dilemma of whether and how to engage with a therapeutic effectiveness agenda that does not fit with their fundamental understanding of mental distress. To give just one example, the medical model of psychopathology also presents a serious challenge for narrative therapy practitioners. Narrative therapy focuses on how people make or construe meaning from experience; it values individual subjective differences in interpretation and meaning-making, while also recognising that the narratives we develop about ourselves emerge within a social and relational context (White & Epston, 1990).

The approach is radically opposed to the labelling inherent in diagnostic categories, seeing this as restricting possibilities for people to make sense of their lives in alternative ways. Nonetheless, therapists and practitioners from within this approach have started to explore ways in which they can develop the evidence-base for narrative therapy in a theoretically consistent manner. One approach involves assessing how the quality of self-experience within narratives of self and illness changes over the course of therapy. For example, using a formal measure of personal narrative, the Scale To Assess Narrative Development (STAND), researchers found that higher STAND total scores for clients (ie. having a higher quality of personal narrative) were associated with greater social functioning in individuals with schizophrenia or schizoaffective disorder diagnoses (Lysaker et al, 2008, 2010, 2006). Social functioning is a key indicator of wellbeing and, through this innovative work, narrative therapy is being evaluated in a way that focuses on measuring outcomes that are congruent with the approach, while also providing empirical evidence of the effectiveness of the approach.

Existential counsellors and psychotherapists similarly reject the medical model and the dominant discourse about demonstrating conventional therapeutic outcomes, such as symptom-reduction. Nonetheless, they are also beginning to consider whether and how to engage with the challenges presented by the current context of healthcare provision in the UK, such as the calls for increased efficiency in NHS and third-sector services, with therapists expected to achieve specified outcomes in their work with clients within a specified number of sessions. Cooper (2003) explains that the idea of producing results within a limited time frame goes against the existential therapy view of therapy, its understanding of the therapeutic relationship and its understanding that the existential challenges of life, which are the focus of existential therapy, do not simply disappear after six or 12 sessions. Nonetheless, he encourages engagement with this challenge, pointing out that some existential therapists are exploring how therapy could be practised in a time-limited manner, which would allow existential practitioners to '... begin to move away from an attitude of resignation towards the current calls for efficiency and to constructively and creatively grapple with the givens of the current climate' (Cooper, 2003: 148). Thus, we can see that practitioners and researchers from various therapeutic orientations face similar challenges to engagement with the demands of the current mental healthcare context.

Opportunities presented by recent developments in positive psychology

It has already been noted that person-centred personality theory (Rogers, 1959) provides a distinct and alternative conceptualisation of how psychological problems develop, where the emphasis of therapy is on facilitating the development of a healthier, more positive mode of functioning, rather than a narrow focus on achieving symptom reduction. Positive functioning is not something that has traditionally been a concern of psychiatry; however, it has come to the fore over recent years as the focus of the positive psychology (Linley & Joseph 2004a; Seligman & Csikzentmihalyi, 2000) and positive clinical psychology (Joseph & Patterson, 2016; Wood & Johnson, 2016) disciplines.

Person-centred researchers and practitioners may be interested in developments stemming from positive psychology because there is much theoretical overlap. For example, it has been shown that one of the major theories of positive psychology, self-determination theory (SDT) (Ryan & Deci, 2000), shares the same meta-theoretical assumptions as person-centred personality theory, as well as providing a substantial body of empirical evidence that both supports person-centred personality theory and, in some areas, advances person-centred theory (Joseph & Patterson, 2008; Patterson & Joseph, 2007a; Joseph, 2015). The SDT model of extrinsic regulation explains (using different language) how conditions of worth become internalised, and offers a parallel, and more nuanced, evidence-based understanding of how conditions of worth develop (see Joseph, 2015). Furthermore, in contrast to the dysfunction focus of the medical-model approach to psychopathology, positive psychology conceptualises mental health difficulties in a way that encourages a focus on growth, personal strengths and potential for becoming more fully functioning. For example, some positive psychologists have argued that psychosocial wellbeing and ill-being have many common drivers (Huppert, 2009), while others have argued that positive and negative functioning are separate continuums but are both facets of a higher-order subjective wellbeing continuum (Diener et al, 1999). Elsewhere, Joseph and Maltby (2014), drawing on the circumplex model of emotions (Russell, 1980; Russell & Barrett, 1998), propose that states of psychological distress such as depression or anxiety may share a single continuum with states of positive functioning. Positive psychologists tend to adopt a dimensional or continuum approach to conceptualising mental health, which allows a focus on strengths as well as difficulties.

Psychosocial wellbeing is one of the most widely researched constructs in positive psychology, and has been defined as broadly having two aspects. The first aspect refers to how happy and content a person feels in their life. It has a cognitive component (the sum of life satisfaction), and an affective component (positive affect minus negative affect), and is referred to as hedonic or subjective wellbeing (SWB). In contrast, the second facet is concerned with feeling that one's life and actions are meaningful, and is referred to as eudaimonic or psychological wellbeing (PWB).

PWB reflects engagement with the existential challenges of life (Ryan & Deci, 2001), and is often operationalised as involving autonomy, self-acceptance, environmental mastery, purpose in life, positive relationships with others, and personal growth (Ryff & Keyes, 1995). Although SWB and PWB are related philosophically (Ryff, 1996; Ryff & Keyes, 1995) and empirically, they can be considered separable (Compton et al, 1996; Keyes, Shmotkin & Ryff, 2002), and this is reflected in the different measures that have been developed to measure psychosocial wellbeing, which are discussed in more detail later in this chapter. Given their focus on evaluating positive functioning and applying a dimensional approach to conceptualising mental health, they are likely to be of interest to person-centred researchers and practitioners.

Revisiting formal assessment

The formal assessment of therapeutic process and change is not new to person-centred practice. The early years of person-centred theory and client-centred therapy were characterised by important developments in theory, research and practice. Research using a wide range of methodologies, including formal measurement scales, was an integral part of person-centred therapy during this period, with a significant focus on variables associated with therapeutic process, including the necessary and sufficient conditions (see Barrett-Lennard, 1998 for an historical overview). For example, the use of client self-rating methods to investigate the change process was a feature of person-centred research in the early 1950s, with both the introduction of the Q-sort method for ranking a series of self-descriptive statements (eg. Butler & Haigh, 1954), and the use of self-report attitudinal scales such as the Self-Other Scale (eg. Gordon & Cartwright, 1954).

Although researchers throughout the 1950s and 1960s developed a considerable evidence base for person-centred therapy, Carl Rogers' own move away from the academic world of the university was followed by a decline in the level of research into person-centred therapy. Nonetheless, a number of self-report scales were developed to measure the self-actualisation process, based on broader humanistic conceptualisations of self-actualisation that reflect the theoretical work of both Abraham Maslow and Carl Rogers (see, for example, Shostrom, 1966; Sorochan, 1976; Lefrancois et al, 1997).

The most widely used of these is the Personal Orientation Inventory (POI) (Shostrom, 1966), a 150-item scale composed of two subscales measuring *time competence* and *inner directedness*. High scores on the POI indicate the presence of positive functioning, while low scores are indicative of psychopathology, consistent with a person-centred and humanistic understanding. A number of research studies have confirmed the validity and reliability of the POI (eg. Shostrom & Knapp, 1967; Fox, Knapp & Michael, 1968). Although the POI is well validated and could potentially be applied to the current context of outcome evaluation, one limitation of the measure is that, due to the large number of scale items, it takes approximately 35–45 minutes to complete, and would therefore be relatively burdensome for both therapists and clients in terms of time demands.

To address this issue, Jones and Crandall (1986) developed the Short Index of Self-Actualization, or Self-Actualization Scale (SAS). This 15-item scale was developed, based on modified terms from the POI and a closely related measure, the Personal Orientation Dimensions (Knapp & Knapp, 1978), with example items including: 'I do not feel ashamed of any of my emotions,' and 'It is better to be yourself than to be popular.' The initial validation study of the measure found a slightly low level of internal consistency reliability of .65, but a good test-retest reliability of .69. There was also evidence of construct validity, with a strong positive correlation of the scale with the POI (r = .67). Factor analysis of the measure suggests it is comprised of five underlying factors: autonomy or self-direction; self-acceptance and self-esteem; acceptance of emotions and freedom of expression of emotions; trust and responsibility in interpersonal relations, and ability to deal with undesirable aspects of life (Jones & Crandall, 1986). The measure has been widely used in studies of self-actualisation, although the precise factor structure has been an issue of debate (eg. Flett, Blankstein & Hewitt, 1991). More recently, a study that used confirmatory as well as exploratory factor analysis has raised further questions about the theoretical structure of the measure (Faraci & Cannistraci, 2015), indicating a need for further research into this. Nonetheless, it illustrates that brief, theoretically consistent measures have been used over many decades to study humanistic and person-centred constructs such as self-actualisation.

Assessing efficacy and effectiveness in the current context

The person-centred theory of therapy is an *if-then* theory wherein, given the presence of necessary and sufficient social-environmental conditions within the context of the therapeutic relationship, certain measurable process changes and outcomes will occur (Rogers, 1959). This suggests that there are few obstacles preventing the development of theoretically grounded outcome measures that evaluate therapeutic change and effectiveness in terms of the process outcomes predicted by the person-centred theory of therapy (Patterson & Joseph, 2007b). Rogers and colleagues (Rogers, 1951, 1959; Rogers & Dymond, 1954) identified a number of anticipated process outcomes that result from successful therapy, including less rigid adherence to conditions of worth, increased congruence, more openness to experience, reduced defensiveness, greater unconditional positive self-regard and more autonomous functioning. These are all constructs with clear theoretical definitions that can be operationally defined and formally measured.

In this section, I will describe a number of self-report measures that are either based on person-centred constructs or theoretically consistent with person-centred theory and a person-centred conceptualisation of psychopathology. This brief overview of existing measures will include both instruments that were developed specifically to assess person-centred constructs (of which there are relatively few) and measures that are theoretically consistent with person-centred theory but that have been developed by researchers in positive psychology and social psychology. While the latter have not been developed as person-centred measures, they do focus on aspects of positive functioning, such as growth and wellbeing, that will resonate with person-centred practitioners. These measures appear to be entirely consistent with a person-centred theoretical understanding of psychopathology, as well as with the broad goals of therapy, and I believe that they illustrate a rich potential that resides in drawing on the work of positive psychology and social psychology researchers to inform person-centred assessment of therapeutic efficacy and effectiveness.

Measuring unconditional positive self-regard

An important therapeutic goal of person-centred counselling and psychotherapy is a loosening of the client's rigid internalised rules and values in order to allow them freedom to grow and develop. This is facilitated by the creation of necessary and sufficient relationship conditions within the therapeutic encounter (Rogers, 1957a). Person-centred theory argues that it is through establishing and maintaining these relationship conditions that the client is enabled to achieve positive therapeutic change, evidenced by an increase in the individual's unconditional positive self-regard (UPSR) and a decrease in conditions of worth (Rogers, 1959). As such, UPSR would seem to be an important indicator of therapeutic change and outcome.

The Unconditional Positive Self-Regard Scale (UPSRS) (Patterson & Joseph, 2006) was developed in line with an operational definition of the construct based on Rogers' (1959) formal definition:

> When the individual perceives himself in such a way that no self-experience can be discriminated as more or less worthy of positive regard than any other, then he is experiencing unconditional positive self-regard. (Rogers, 1959: 209)

According to this definition, there are two distinguishable facets of UPSR. The first element refers to the expression or withholding of positive regard towards oneself, or positive self-regard. Whether or not positive self-regard is expressed is conditional on the individual's perception of his/her self-experiences as differentially worthy of positive regard. This conditionality, or conditional–unconditional continuum, is the second component of the construct of UPSR. It follows then, that UPSR attempts to capture an attitude that is characterised by the individual's self-regard being positive while at the same time being non-contingently self-accepting.

The measure consists of 12 items: six that measure the person's level of positive self-regard (self-regard subscale) and six that measure levels of unconditional self-regard (conditionality subscale), with responses to the items scored on a five-point Likert-type scale from 'strongly agree' to 'strongly disagree'. After taking reverse-scored items into account, a total score for each subscale is calculated by adding up the subscale item scores. Psychometric evaluation carried out in the development of the UPSRS showed that the scale has a two-factor structure, high levels of internal consistency reliability (Cronbach's alpha = .88 for the self-regard subscale and .79 for the conditionality subscale), good construct validity and good convergent and discriminant validity in relation to other measures (Patterson & Joseph, 2006).

In a separate study, internal consistency reliability was found to be .81 for full-scale UPSR, .89 for the self-regard subscale and .66 for the conditionality subscale (Griffiths & Griffiths, 2013). In addition, initial research using the UPSRS has demonstrated associations between presence of unconditional positive self-regard and a range of other indicators of psychological wellbeing. For example, higher levels of unconditional positive self-regard have been associated with greater self-esteem, less contingent self-worth, less depressive symptomatology and less overall psychopathology (Patterson & Joseph, 2006; Patterson & Joseph, 2013). Further studies have shown UPSR to be positively correlated with both self-compassion (Griffiths & Griffiths, 2013) and post-traumatic growth (Flanagan et al, 2015), and negatively correlated with depression and anxiety (Griffiths & Griffiths, 2013). The measure therefore offers person-centred practitioners and researchers a useful and theoretically congruent way of assessing therapeutic change.

Measuring authenticity

Authenticity is an important concept in person-centred therapy, where it is seen as an essential component of becoming a more fully functioning individual. Becoming more authentic implies a more accurate symbolisation of experience (ie. less alienation between organismic self and experience). Tudor (2008) points out that authenticity is sometimes used interchangeably with the word 'congruence' in the person-centred literature, and points to the importance of authenticity/ congruence for psychological health, as understood from a person-centred perspective, writing that:

> For Rogers, congruence is synonymous with authenticity and in this context I think authenticity is a more precise word. Rogers (1975) sees a deep concern for authenticity as a quality of the multifaceted, emerging person. He goes on to describe this person in polemical and political terms, citing examples of people who are prepared to reject a culture they see as hypocritical, to confront those in authority, to refuse orders, to work for civil rights, and to take full personal responsibility in situations. (Tudor, 2008: 167)

One measure that seems particularly appropriate to measuring authenticity is the Authenticity Scale (Wood et al, 2008), which was designed from a combined humanistic and social psychological perspective to be consistent with person-centred theory. The measure views absence of authenticity as arising through a lack of congruence between conscious awareness, inner emotional and cognitive states and the social environment (Joseph & Worsley, 2005; Wood et al, 2008).

The Authenticity Scale consists of 12 items that are grouped into three subscales measuring resistance to external influence, self-alienation and authentic behaviour. Each item is rated on a seven-point Likert-type scale, such that scores on each subscale have a possible range of four to 28, with higher scores indicating greater external influence (measuring tendency to accept external influence rather than being self-directing), greater self-alienation (providing an indication of incongruence between self and experience) and greater authentic behaviour (a measure of living and acting in ways consistent with one's own beliefs and values). Together, the subscales constitute a tripartite model of authenticity that can be used to help clients track their progress in relation to each of the three underlying factors.

Measuring autonomy

Rogers (1957b) coined the term *fully functioning person* to describe a state of more optimal psychological functioning that occurs when self-actualisation and the actualising tendency are concordant. The term captures the contrast between process and stasis, describing the individual as a continually changing person-in-process (Rogers, 1959). The development of increasing autonomy is a further characteristic of the more fully functioning person. Person-centred theory's conceptualisation of organismically congruent self-actualisation is described as involving '... the development toward autonomy and away from heteronomy, or control by external forces' (Rogers, 1959: 196). Autonomy in person-centred theory is synonymous with internal freedom, the psychological freedom to move in any direction, and it develops in line with the individual's increasing organismic valuing.

The Self-Determination Scale (SDS) (Sheldon & Deci, 1996) was designed to assess individual differences in the extent to which people tend to function in a more autonomous or self-determined way, such that self-determination equates to autonomous functioning, posited by Rogers (1959) as one of the key goals of client-centred therapy. As has been described elsewhere, self-determination theory holds similar meta-theoretical assumptions to person-centred theory (Patterson & Joseph, 2007a; Joseph & Patterson, 2008; Joseph, 2015).

The SDS measure has been shown to consist of two underlying factors: *self-contact*, or awareness of oneself (being more aware of one's feelings and sense of self), and *choicefulness*, or perceived choice (feeling a sense of choice with respect to one's behaviour) (Sheldon, Ryan & Reis, 1996). The 10-item scale is composed of two five-item subscales. For each item, participants indicate which of two statements feels most true for them: for example, a) 'My emotions sometimes seem alien to me,' versus b) 'My emotions always seem to belong to me' (a self-contact item); or a) 'I sometimes feel that it's not really me choosing the things I do,' versus b) 'I always feel like I choose the things I do' (a choicefulness item). Participants respond to each item by scoring from one to nine on a Likert-type scale and, after recoding reversed items, responses are added together. The subscales can either be used separately or combined into an overall SDS score.

The SDS has been psychometrically evaluated and shown to have good internal consistency, adequate test-retest reliability, and to be a strong predictor of a wide variety of psychological health outcomes, including self-actualisation, empathy and life satisfaction (Sheldon & Deci, 1996). It has also been used in several published research studies (Sheldon, 1995; Sheldon, Ryan & Reis, 1996; Elliot & McGregor, 2001).

Measuring conditions of worth

Conditions of worth refer to the internalised rules and values upon which the individual's self-regard has become contingent (Rogers, 1959). Until recently, there was no way of measuring Rogerian conditions of worth. However, a self-report scale developed by researchers concerned with understanding self-esteem appears to hold particular relevance for person-centred practitioners interested in studying changes in conditions of worth. *Contingencies of self-worth* represent a construct that is conceptually similar to person-centred conditions of worth, where the individual is seen to be guided more by external influences and introjected rules and values, in contrast to a more autonomous mode of functioning where the individual displays greater internal freedom regarding how they will act or respond.

The Contingencies of Self-Worth Scale (CSWS) (Crocker et al, 2003) was designed to measure the degree to which a person's level of self-esteem is tied to certain domains of self-worth within which achievements, or successful outcomes, are perceived by the individual as essential to his/her worth as a person. As such, the individual's feelings of self-worth, or self-esteem, are contingent upon perceived success or failure in those domains in which self-esteem is invested, which may differ from person to person (Crocker & Wolfe, 2001; Crocker et al, 2003). In other words, the introjected rules and values, or conditions of worth in person-centred terminology, are viewed as being linked to certain domains of life that are particularly valued or prized by the individual.

The CSWS is a 35-item scale designed to assess seven sources of self-worth (others' approval, appearance, competition, academic competence, family support, virtue, God's love). Example items include, 'When my family members are proud of me, my sense of self-worth increases,' or, 'My self-worth is influenced by how well I do on competitive tasks.' Responses are given on a seven-point Likert-type scale, and are then summed for each subscale. The seven subscales all have high internal consistency (Cronbach's alpha values range from .82 to .96), and a three-month test-retest reliability ranging from .68 to .92 (Crocker et al, 2003).

Measuring growth following adversity

Post-traumatic growth, also referred to as growth following adversity, describes how the survivors of trauma may develop new perspectives on the self and the world that move them beyond their pre-trauma levels of functioning (Joseph, 2005, 2011; see also Chapter 14, this volume). For example, survivors may become aware of newly discovered strengths within themselves, go on to build more intimate and meaningful relationships, and reorder their priorities in life (Tedeschi & Calhoun, 2004; Calhoun & Tedeschi, 2006), leading to greater psychological wellbeing (Joseph & Linley, 2008). Post-traumatic growth has been reported following a wide range of traumatic life events, and it has been estimated that between 30 and 70 per cent of people who experience trauma commonly report some form of positive change (Linley & Joseph, 2004b).

The topic of traumatic stress has been conceptualised from a person-centred perspective, leading to a new understanding that the natural endpoint of cognitive-emotional processing following trauma is growth (Joseph, 2003, 2004, 2005; Joseph & Linley, 2005). The traditional medical model conceptualisation of post-traumatic stress has viewed it in terms of dysfunction, as a psychiatric disorder. However, when post-traumatic stress is considered alongside post-traumatic growth, a different conceptualisation emerges, wherein post-traumatic stress can be seen as a process, rather than an outcome variable, and post-traumatic growth can be seen as the desirable endpoint or outcome of successful processing of cognitions and affect arising from the adverse event(s) (Joseph, 2005; Joseph & Linley, 2005).

The theory that informs this account of the complex interplay between post-traumatic stress processes and post-traumatic growth is the Organismic Valuing Process theory of growth following adversity (OVP theory). OVP theory is a person-centred theory that is underpinned by the assumption that people are intrinsically motivated towards growth and that, even in the face of adverse events, given the right social-environmental conditions (ie. a facilitating therapeutic/social environment that provides the conditions for growth), the person will process the traumatic experience in a way that leads to growth (Joseph & Linley, 2005).

While recognising and validating the distress experienced by people who have been diagnosed with post-traumatic stress disorder, OVP theory points to the potential for those who are currently in a state of experiencing post-traumatic stress, or who have been diagnosed with post-traumatic stress disorder, to eventually move from that state of stress and distress to a state of growth. This involves a process of resolving discrepancies between the new trauma-related information and the pre-existing assumptive world, leading to the rebuilding of the assumptive world in new ways that allow the person to be more fully functioning (Joseph, 2004).

Interestingly, findings from a recent study demonstrate that higher unconditional positive self-regard (ie. relating in a less rigid/conditional manner to internal/organismic experiencing) is associated with subsequent post-traumatic growth (at three-month follow-up) in individuals who have experienced traumatic events, so lending further support to the person-centred conceptualisation of post-traumatic growth (Flanagan et al, 2015).

A number of measures that assess post-traumatic growth and positive change through adversity have been developed. Here, I will focus on just two of those measures. The Changes in Outlook Questionnaire (CiOQ) (Joseph, Williams & Yule, 1993) was the first measure of post-traumatic growth to be developed. The CiOQ provides a self-report assessment of the extent to which a person has experienced both positive and negative changes following adversity and trauma. The CiOQ consists of 26 items: 11 assess positive changes and 15 assess negative changes. The 11 positive items are added together to give a total score ranging from 11 to 66. Similarly, the 15 negative items are added together to give a total score ranging from 15 to 90. The CiOQ has been psychometrically validated and provides practitioners with a useful tool when working with clients who have experienced trauma and adversity (Joseph et al, 1993, 2005). For practitioners who may need to use brief and quick-to-administer measures, a short version of the CiOQ is also available (Joseph et al, 2006). As indicated above, the measure has been used in several studies, where findings have provided further evidence that it is a psychometrically robust measure (Joseph et al, 2005, 2006; Flanagan et al, 2015).

A more recently developed measure of post-traumatic growth is the Psychological Wellbeing Post-Traumatic Changes Questionnaire (PWB-PTCQ) (Joseph et al, 2012). The scale consists of 18 items focusing on both positive and negative changes (as perceived by the respondent), in a similar vein to the CiOQ. In addition to capturing positive and negative changes in the aftermath of a traumatic event, the measure also provides an indication of level of subjective wellbeing.

Initial research has demonstrated good internal reliability, as well as convergent validity with measures of gratitude and authenticity and a strong correlation with actual changes in psychological wellbeing (Joseph et al, 2012).

Measuring psychosocial wellbeing

As described previously, measures of psychosocial wellbeing are widely used in positive psychology research, and may be of interest to person-centred researchers and practitioners, given their focus on evaluating positive or growth-oriented aspects of a person's functioning. They include measures designed to capture both hedonic and eudaimonic aspects of wellbeing, others that focus solely on subjective wellbeing, and yet others that are concerned with measuring only psychological wellbeing. I will, therefore, briefly describe some of the more commonly used measures.

A measure that assesses both positive functioning (wellbeing) and negative functioning (psychological distress) is the Positive Functioning Inventory (PFI-12) (Joseph & Maltby, 2014). This 12-item self-report questionnaire consists of six items asking about positive thoughts, feelings and bodily sensations ('I felt happy'; 'I felt pleased with the way I am'), and a further six items asking about negative thoughts, feelings and bodily experiences ('I felt worried'; 'I felt dissatisfied with my life'). In terms of measuring wellbeing, the PFI-12 includes items that capture aspects of both SWB (eg. positive affect) and PWB (eg. items focusing on self-acceptance and meaning). Each item is rated on a four-point scale from 'never' to 'often', and items are summed to give a total in the range 0–36. Higher scores indicate greater positive functioning; lower scores indicate greater psychological distress (depression and anxiety). However, instead of viewing depression and anxiety as categories, they are viewed as problems in living that are continuous with more positive functioning. This measure is unique in providing a single assessment that can detect depressive and anxious states but can also assess the extent to which the person is moving towards positive functioning.

The Warwick-Edinburgh Mental Well-Being Scale (WEMWBS) (Tennant et al, 2007) was designed to measure psychosocial wellbeing, including affective-emotional aspects, cognitive-evaluative dimensions and psychological functioning, and it has been validated on a representative general population sample of British, Chinese and Pakistani adults (Tennant et al, 2007). It is a relatively short measure, comprised 14 items relating to different aspects of positive mental health, including both hedonic and eudaimonic aspects. Examples include 'I've been feeling optimistic about the future', 'I've been feeling interested in other people', 'I've been dealing with problems well', and 'I've been feeling good about myself'. For each statement, responses are scored on a five-point Likert scale ranging from 'none of the time' to 'all of the time', where the individual rates their experience over the previous two weeks. Confirmatory factor analysis suggests measurement of a single underlying construct. The WEMWBS has been reported to have good content validity, strong internal consistency reliability of .91 in a population sample, and a one-week test re-test reliability of 0.83. It also showed high correlations with other mental health and wellbeing scales (Tennant et al, 2007).

Focusing more specifically on SWB, the Subjective Happiness Scale (SHS) (Lyubomirsky & Lepper, 1999) is a four-item measure of global subjective happiness scale, with high internal consistency reliability and strong test-retest reliability, which has also been shown to have good convergent and discriminant validity. Similarly concerned with positive evaluations, although adopting a cognitive-evaluative focus, the Satisfaction with Life Scale (Diener et al, 1985) is a seven-item scale that was designed to measure the individual's subjective rating of overall satisfaction with his or her life. The measure has been shown to have robust psychometric properties across a number of studies and with a range of different populations (Diener et al, 1985; Pavot & Diener, 1993, 2008).

The Questionnaire for Eudaimonic Wellbeing (Waterman et al, 2010) is a 21-item scale that was developed to measure PWB and, based on initial psychometric evaluation, has strong internal reliability (alpha = 0.86), as well as good convergent, discriminant and construct validity (Waterman et al, 2010). With a similar, but more multi-dimensionally rich conceptualisation of PWB, the Scales of Psychological Well-being (Ryff, 1989; Ryff & Singer, 1996) provide a detailed assessment of six aspects of psychological wellbeing, including autonomy, environmental mastery, personal growth, positive relations with others, purpose in life and self-acceptance. There are long (84-item), medium (54-item) and short (42-item) versions available, and the long and medium versions in particular have been shown to have robust psychometric qualities (Ryff, 1989; Ryff & Singer, 1996).

Dilemmas and future directions

This chapter serves as an invitation to person-centred practitioners and researchers to consider the use of theoretically congruent measures of therapy outcomes as one potential way of responding to current pressures to demonstrate the efficacy and effectiveness of person-centred therapy and counselling. This proposal carries with it a number of challenges, not least of which is the fact that person-centred practitioners commit to work within the client's frame of reference, which may not include any motivation for monitoring or measuring therapeutic outcome. This clearly presents a dilemma for person-centred practitioners. However, for those who practise in the NHS, or other, similar public or third-sector healthcare provider organisations, the administration of formal outcome measures is almost certainly already a routine requirement of their job. It seems likely, moving forward, that therapeutic modalities that do not engage in assessing efficacy and effectiveness may not be commissioned, restricting them to the realm of private practice. By proactively engaging with this challenge, person-centred practitioners and researchers can influence the evidence-based practice agenda by promoting the use of measurement instruments that are theoretically consistent with their approach and therefore more ethically appropriate to their work with the clients they see.

Up until now I have avoided the difficult issue of whether, when engaging in outcome evaluation, only theoretically congruent measures should be used, or whether theoretically congruent measures should be used alongside symptom measures. While the former option is preferable, the latter may well need to be considered, particularly by researchers aiming to carry out or collaborate on large-scale therapy outcome studies. Drawing on developments in positive psychology by using measures such as the Positive Functioning Inventory (Joseph & Maltby, 2014), a measure of both positive and negative aspects of functioning, appears to offer one potential solution to this dilemma. However, while person-centred practitioners may find that they are more comfortable with the dimensional approach to psychopathology and wellbeing adopted by positive psychologists, other mental health practitioners who favour a categorical understanding of psychopathology are unlikely to want to participate in large-scale therapy comparison studies that do not include symptom-focused measures.

In addition, as mentioned previously, such measures are being routinely used in many services where person-centred psychotherapists and counsellors already practise and, hence, research using symptom measures may be difficult to avoid altogether. Furthermore, commissioners of mental health services as well as provider organisations have become accustomed to discourse around treatment outcomes, therapeutic efficacy and effectiveness that is largely framed in psychiatric language, where symptom reduction is viewed as a key indicator of a successful intervention. While no solution is offered here, it is important to acknowledge the pressures on person-centred practitioners and others who practise within a non-medical model framework to consider whether any compromise may be needed. This is a challenging issue for person-centred practitioners and researchers, and one that will need to be given serious consideration when looking to the future.

Finally, it is clear that the challenges of demonstrating therapeutic efficacy and effectiveness are also shared by practitioners of other therapeutic modalities that do not accept the medical-model approach to psychopathology. Establishing ongoing dialogue with practitioners and researchers from other approaches and sharing ideas and learning may be helpful in determining how best to address some of the challenges posed by the current dominant discourse on therapeutic effectiveness.

Conclusion

In the current context of mental healthcare provision, it is becoming increasingly important for person-centred practitioners to engage with demands from both funders and providers of mental healthcare, psychotherapy and counselling services to empirically demonstrate therapeutic effectiveness and efficiency. The use of theoretically congruent self-report measurement scales, which this chapter advocates, offers one potential way in which this challenge might be addressed. A number of appropriate measures already exist and there would seem to be a strong rationale for their use by person-centred practitioners and researchers, not simply as a pragmatic way forward but primarily because these measures can be seen to be congruent with person-centred theory and consistent with the goals of person-centred therapy.

References

American Psychiatric Association (2013). *Diagnostic and Statistical Manual of Mental Disorders* (5th edition). American Psychiatric Press, Washington, DC: American Psychiatric Press.

Barrett-Lennard GT (1998). *Carl Rogers' Helping System: journey and substance.* London: Sage.

Bentall R (2003). *Madness Explained: psychosis and human nature.* London: Allen Lane.

Butler JM, Haigh GV (1954). Changes in the relation between self-concepts and ideal concepts consequent upon client-centred counselling. In: Rogers CR, Dymond RF (eds). *Psychotherapy and Personality Change.* Chicago: University of Chicago Press (pp55–75).

Calhoun LG, Tedeschi RG (2006). *Handbook of Post-Traumatic Growth: research and practice.* Mahwah, NJ: Lawrence Erlbaum Associates Publishers.

Compton WC, Smith ML, Cornish KA, Qualls DL (1996). Factor structure of mental health measures. *Journal of Personality and Social Psychology 71*: 406–413.

Cooper M (2003). *Existential Therapies.* London: Sage.

Crocker J, Wolfe CT (2001). Contingencies of self-worth. *Psychological Review 108*: 593–623.

Crocker J, Luhtanen RK, Cooper ML, Bouvrette A (2003). Contingencies of self-worth in college students: theory and measurement. *Journal of Personality and Social Psychology 85*: 894–908.

Diener E, Emmons RA, Larsen RJ, Griffin S (1985). The Satisfaction with Life Scale. *Journal of Personality Assessment 49*: 71–75.

Diener E, Suh EM, Lucas RE, Smith H (1999). Subjective well-being: three decades of progress. *Psychological Bulletin 125*: 276–302.

Elliot AJ, McGregor HA (2001). A 2x2 achievement goal framework. *Journal of Personality and Social Psychology 80*: 501–519.

Elliott R (1996). Are client-centred/experiential therapies effective? A meta-analysis of outcome research. In: Esser U, Pbast H, Speierer GW (eds). *The Power of the Person-Centred Approach: new challenges-perspectives-answers.* Koln: GwG Verlag (pp125–138).

Faraci P, Cannistraci S (2015). The Short Index of Self-Actualization: a factor analysis study in an Italian sample. *International Journal of Psychological Research 8*(2): 23–33.

Flanagan S, Patterson TG, Hume I, Joseph S (2015). A longitudinal investigation of the relationship between unconditional positive self-regard and post-traumatic growth. *Person-Centered and Experiential Psychotherapies 14*(3): 191–200.

Flett GL, Blankstein KR, Hewitt PL (1991). Factor structure of the Short Index of Self-Actualization. *Journal of Social Behavior and Personality 6*: 321

Friedli K, King M, Lloyd M, Horder J (1997). Randomised controlled assessment of non-directive psychotherapy versus routine general practitioner care. *The Lancet 350*: 1662–1665.

Fox J, Knapp RR, Michael WB (1968). Assessment of self-actualisation of psychiatric patients: validity of the Personal Orientation Inventory. *Educational and Psychological Measurement 28*: 565–569.

Gordon T, Cartwright D (1954). The effect of psychotherapy upon certain attitudes towards others. In: Rogers CR, Dymond RF (eds). *Psychotherapy and Personality Change*. Chicago: University of Chicago Press (pp167–195).

Griffiths L, Griffiths C (2013). Unconditional positive self-regard (UPSR) and self-compassion: the internal consistency and convergent/divergent validity of Patterson & Joseph's UPSR Scale. *Open Journal of Medical Psychology 2*(4): 168–174.

Hansen N, Lambert M, Forman E (2002). The psychotherapy dose-effect and its implications for treatment delivery services. *Clinical Psychology: Science and Practice 9*: 329–343.

Huppert A (2009). Psychological wellbeing: evidence regarding its causes and consequences. *Applied Psychology: Health and Wellbeing 1*: 137–161.

Johnstone L (2014). *A Straight Talking Introduction to Psychiatric Diagnosis*. Ross-on-Wye: PCCS Books.

Jones A, Crandall R (1986). Validation of a short index of self-actualization. *Personality and Social Psychology Bulletin 12*: 63–73.

Joseph S (2003). Person-centred approach to understanding post-traumatic stress. *Person-Centred Practice 11*: 70–75.

Joseph S (2004). Client-centred therapy, post-traumatic stress, and post-traumatic growth: theoretical perspectives and practical implications. *Psychology and Psychotherapy: Theory, Research and Practice 77*: 101–120.

Joseph S (2005). Understanding post-traumatic stress from the person-centred perspective. In: Joseph S, Worsley R (eds). *Person-centred psychopathology: a positive psychology of mental health*. PCCS Books: Ross-on-Wye (pp190–201).

Joseph S (2011). *What Doesn't Kill Us: the new psychology of post-traumatic growth*. New York: Basic Books.

Joseph S (2015). *Positive Therapy: building bridges between positive psychology and person-centred psychotherapy* (2nd ed). Hove: Routledge.

Joseph S, Linley PA (2005). Positive adjustment to threatening events: an organismic valuing theory of growth through adversity. *Review of General Psychology 9*: 262–280.

Joseph S, Linley PA (2006). *Positive Therapy: a meta-theory for positive psychological practice*. Hove: Routledge.

Joseph S, Linley PA (2008). Psychological assessment of growth following adversity: a review. In: Joseph S, Linley PA (eds). *Trauma, Recovery, and Growth: positive psychological perspectives on post-traumatic stress*. Hoboken, NJ: John Wiley & Sons (pp21–38).

Joseph S, Linley PA, Andrews L, Harris G, Howle B, Woodward C, Shevlin M (2005). Assessing positive and negative changes in the aftermath of adversity: psychometric evaluation of the Changes in Outlook Questionnaire. *Psychological Assessment 17*: 70–80.

Joseph S, Linley PA, Shevlin M, Goodfellow B, Butler L (2006). Assessing positive and negative changes in the aftermath of adversity: a short form of the changes in Outlook Questionnaire. *Journal of Loss and Trauma 11*: 85–99.

Joseph S, Maltby J (2014). Positive functioning inventory: initial validation of a 12-item self-report measure of well-being. *Psychology of Well-being: Theory, Research and Practice 4*: 15.

Joseph S, Maltby J, Wood AM, Stockton H, Hunt N, Regel S (2012). The Psychological Well-Being—Post-Traumatic Changes Questionnaire (PWB-PTCQ): reliability and validity. *Psychological Trauma: Theory, Research, Practice, and Policy 4*: 420-428.

Joseph S, Patterson TG (2008). The actualising tendency: a meta-theoretical perspective for positive psychology. In: Levitt BE (ed). *Reflections on Human Potential: bridging the person-centred approach and positive psychology*. Ross-on-Wye: PCCS Books (pp1–16).

Joseph S, Patterson TG (2016). A practical guide to positive functioning assessment in clinical psychology. In: Wood AM, Johnson J (eds). *The Wiley Handbook of Positive Clinical Psychology*. Chichester: Wiley (pp47–56).

Joseph S, Williams R, Yule W (1993). Changes in outlook following disaster: the preliminary development of a measure to assess positive and negative responses. *Journal of Traumatic Stress 6*: 271–279.

Joseph S, Worsley R (2005). A positive psychology of mental health: the person-centred perspective. In: Joseph S, Worsley R (eds). *Person-Centred Psychopathology: a positive psychology of mental health*. PCCS Books: Ross-on-Wye (pp348–357).

Keyes CLM, Shmotkin D, Ryff CD (2002). Optimizing well-being: the empirical encounter of two traditions. *Journal of Personality and Social Psychology 82*: 1007–1022.

King M, Sibbald B, Ward E, Bower P, Lloyd M, Gabbay M, Byford S (2000). Randomised controlled trial of non-directive counselling cognitive behaviour therapy and usual general practitioner care in the management of depression as well as mixed anxiety and depression in primary care. *British Medical Journal 321*: 1383–1388.

Knapp RR, Knapp L (1978). Conceptual and statistical refinement and extension of the measurement of actualizing concurrent validity of the Personal Orientation Dimensions (POD). *Educational and Psychological Measurement 38*: 523–526.

Lefrancois R, Leclerc G, Dube M, Herbert R, Gaulin P (1997). The development and validation of a self-report measure of self-actualisation. *Social Behaviour & Personality 25*: 353–366.

Linley PA, Joseph S (2004a). *Positive Psychology in Practice*. Hoboken, NJ: Wiley.

Linley PA, Joseph S (2004b). Positive change following trauma and adversity: a review. *Journal of Traumatic Stress 17*(1): 11–21.

Lysaker PH, Buck KD, Taylor AC, Roe D (2008). Associations of metacognition and internalized stigma with quantitative assessments of self-experience in narratives of schizophrenia. *Psychiatry Research 157*: 31–38.

Lysaker PH, Ringer J, Maxwell C, McGuire A, Lecomte T (2010). Personal narratives and recovery from schizophrenia. *Schizophrenia Research 121*: 271–276.

Lysaker PH, Taylor A, Miller A, Beattie N, Strasburger A, Davis LW (2006). The Scale to Assess Narrative Development: associations with other measures of self and readiness for recovery in schizophrenia spectrum disorders. *The Journal of Nervous and Mental Disease 194*: 223–225.

Lyubomirsky S, Lepper HS (1999). A measure of subjective happiness: preliminary reliability and construct validation. *Social Indicators Research 46*: 137–155.

Marzillier J (2004). The myth of evidence-based psychotherapy. *The Psychologist 17*: 392–395.

Murphy D, Joseph S (2016). Person-centered therapy: past, present and future orientations. In: Cain DJ, Keenan K, Rubin S (eds). *Humanistic Psychotherapies: Handbook of Research and Practice*. Washington, DC: American Psychological Association (pp185–218).

Patterson TG, Joseph S (2006). Development of a measure of unconditional positive self-regard. *Psychology and Psychotherapy: Theory, Research, and Practice 79*: 557–570.

Patterson TG, Joseph S (2007a). Person-centred personality theory: support from self-determination theory and positive psychology. *Journal of Humanistic Psychology 47*: 117–139.

Patterson TG, Joseph S (2007b). Outcome measurement in person-centred practice. In: Worsley R, Joseph S (eds). *Person-Centred Practice: case studies in positive psychology*. Ross-on-Wye: PCCS Books (pp200–217).

Patterson TG, Joseph S (2013). Unconditional positive self-regard. In: Bernard ME (ed). *The Strength of Self-Acceptance*. New York: Springer (pp93–106).

Pavot W, Diener E (1993). Review of the Satisfaction with Life Scale. *Psychological Assessment 5*: 164–172.

Pavot W, Diener E (2008). The Satisfaction with Life Scale and the emerging construct of life satisfaction. *Journal of Positive Psychology 3*: 137–152.

Rogers CR (1951). Client-Centered Therapy. Boston: Houghton Mifflin.

Rogers CR (1957a). The necessary and sufficient conditions of therapeutic personality change. *Journal of Consulting Psychology 21*: 95–103.

Rogers CR (1957b). A therapist's view of the good life. *The Humanist 17*: 291–300.

Rogers CR (1959). A theory of therapy, personality, and interpersonal relationships as developed in the client-centered framework. In: Koch S (ed). *Psychology: a Study of a Science. Vol. 3: Formulations of the person and the social context*. New York: McGraw-Hill (pp184–256).

Rogers CR (1975). The emerging person: a new revolution. In: Evans RI (ed). *Carl Rogers: the man and his ideas*. New York: EP Dutton & Co (pp147–175).

Rogers CR, Dymond RF (eds) (1954). Psychotherapy and Personality Change. Chicago: University of Chicago Press.

Russell JA (1980). A circumplex model of affect. *Journal of Personality and Social Psychology 39*: 1161–1178.

Russell JA, Barrett L (1998). Independence and bipolarity in the structure of current affect. *Journal of Personality and Social Psychology 74*: 967–984.

Ryan RM, Deci EL (2000). Self-determination and the facilitation of intrinsic motivation, social development and well-being. *American Psychologist 55*: 68–78.

Ryan RM, Deci EL (2001). On happiness and human potentials: a review of research on hedonic and eudaimonic well-being. *Annual Review of Psychology 52*: 141–166.

Ryff CD (1989). Happiness is everything, or is it? Explorations on the meaning of psychological well-being. *Journal of Personality and Social Psychology 57*: 1069-1081.

Ryff CD, Keyes CLM (1995). The structure of psychological well-being revisited. *Journal of Personality and Social Psychology 69*: 719–727.

Ryff CD, Singer BH (1996). Psychological well-being: meaning, measurement, and implications for psychotherapy research. *Psychotherapy and Psychosomatics 65*: 14–23.

Seligman MEP, Csikszentmihalyi M (2000). Positive psychology: an introduction. *American Psychologist 55*: 5–14.

Sheldon KM (1995). Creativity and self-determination in personality. *Creativity Research Journal 8*: 61–72.

Sheldon KM, Deci EL (1996). *The Self-Determination Scale*. Unpublished manuscript. Rochester, NY: University of Rochester.

Sheldon KM, Ryan RM, Reis H (1996). What makes for a good day? Competence and autonomy in the day and in the person. *Personality and Social Psychology Bulletin 22*: 1270–1279.

Shostrom EL (1966). A test for the measurement of self-actualisation. *Educational and Psychological Measurement 24*: 207–218.

Shostrom EL, Knapp RR (1967). The relationship of a measure of self-actualisation to a measure of pathology and therapeutic growth. *American Journal of Psychotherapy 20*: 192–203.

Sorochan D (1976). *Personal Health Appraisal.* New York: Wiley & Sons.

Tedeschi RG, Calhoun LG (2004). Post-traumatic growth: conceptual foundations and empirical evidence. *Psychological Inquiry 15*(1): 1–18.

Tennant R, Hiller L, Fishwick R, Platt S, Joseph S, Weich S, Brown S (2007). The Warwick-Edinburgh Mental Well-Being Scale (WEMWBS): development and UK validation. *Health and Quality of Life Outcomes 5*: 63.

Tudor K (2008). Psychological health: autonomy and homonomy. In: Levitt BE (ed). *Reflections on Human Potential: bridging the person-centered approach and positive psychology.* Ross-on-Wye: PCCS Books (pp161–174).

Waterman AS, Schwartz SJ, Zamboanga BL, Ravert RD, Williams MK, Agocha VB, Donnellan MB (2010). The Questionnaire for Eudaimonic Well-Being: psychometric properties, demographic comparisons, and evidence of validity. *The Journal of Positive Psychology 5*: 41–61.

White M, Epston D (1990). *Narrative means to therapeutic ends.* New York: WW Norton & Co.

Wood AM, Linley PA, Maltby J, Baliousis M, Joseph S (2008). The authentic personality: a theoretical and empirical conceptualization and the development of the authenticity scale. *Journal of Counselling Psychology 55*: 385–399

Wood AM, Johnson J (eds) (2016). *The Wiley Handbook of Positive Clinical Psychology.* Chichester: Wiley.

CONCLUSION

27 | Taking stock of the person-centred approach and moving forward

Stephen Joseph

Ten years ago, in the first edition of this book, Richard Worlsey and I wrote that the dominance of the medical model was being seriously challenged from all quarters. We said it was likely that, in the coming decade, the discipline of psychology would come to contain a strong voice for the humanisation of professional practice. A lot has happened in the past decade that has indeed seen practice begin to change.

The fifth edition of the American Psychiatric Association's *Diagnostic and Statistical Manual of Mental Disorders* (*DSM-5*) has appeared since the first edition of this book (American Psychiatric Association, 2013). This generated much discussion and debate among the mental health professions. Increasingly, other professionals are also coming out as critical of the use of psychiatric terminology and looking for alternatives to the medical model. For example, the Division of Clinical Psychology of the British Psychological Society (BPS) released guidelines on the use of psychiatric terminology in 2015 in which it was stated that: '... there is a large and growing body of evidence suggesting that the experiences described in functional diagnostic terms may be better understood as a response to psychosocial factors such as loss, trauma, poverty, inequality, unemployment, discrimination, and other social, relational and societal factors. As a profession, we have publicly affirming [sic] the need to move towards a system which is no longer based on a "disease" model.' The guidelines go on to describe three principles. The first is to avoid the use of diagnostic language in relation to the functional psychiatric presentations, whenever possible. The second is to replace terms that assume a diagnostic or narrow biomedical perspective with psychological or ordinary language equivalents. Finally, the third is to indicate awareness of its contested nature in situations where the use of diagnostic terminology is difficult to avoid.

Person-centred practitioners may long have seen clinical psychology as one of the mental health professions that has actually condoned medicalisation. As such, it may seem ironic that clinical psychology now positions itself at the forefront of developments. Nonetheless, these principles are welcome, and these newer critics follow in the wake of those who have long voiced their objections, such as Newnes et al (1999), Bentall (2004), Read, Mosher and Bentall, (2004), Maddux (2002) and Maddux and Lopez (2015), who themselves continued and augmented a tradition of anti-psychiatry in which the names of Laing and Szasz are perhaps the best-known representatives. But yet, in all these discussions challenging medicalisation, the person-centred approach remains largely overlooked as an alternative.

There are three defining features of the medical model:

1. the focus on the individual. In the medical model the origins of distress and dysfunction are seen as within the person

2. the role of the practitioner as expert on what the patient needs. In the medical model, it is the practitioner who knows what is best for the patient

3. the emphasis on distress and dysfunction. In the medical model the clinician is interested in what is weak and defective about people.

Ultimately, the challenge posed by the person-centred approach is to rethink the nature of human suffering. As we have seen in this book, Rogers' person-centred theory offers a meta-theoretical perspective on human nature founded on the assumption that human beings have an inherent tendency toward growth, development and optimal functioning (see Rogers, 1959, 1961, 1969). Unpacking the implications of this for practice, the person-centred approach is in direct opposition to each of these three features of the medical model:

1. person-centred therapists are concerned with the social systems of family and community and how external forces act on the person, leading to the development of conditions of worth, which in turn affect their processing style

2. person-centred therapists focus on the client as expert on what is best for them and seek to form collaborative relationships in which it is the client who directs the therapeutic process. The therapist is non-directive because the direction comes from the client, hence the term 'client-centred'

3. person-centred therapists are interested in the constructive and healthy potential of people and their movement towards becoming fully functioning, consistent with the aims of positive psychology.

Various individuals and professional groups may seize on one of these three points of opposition to define themselves, but still hold fast to the other features of the medical model. In this way, practitioners may perceive themselves as standing against the medical model when, in fact, they continue to promote others of its features. Only the person-centred approach offers an alternative to the medical model in all three ways – by looking to health and wellness, seeking to understand the social processes, and taking the stance that people are the best experts on themselves. At least, that is the theoretical stance of the person-centred approach; in reality, these ideas may not always have been put into practice so well. The approach has been most successful at promoting the idea that people are their own best experts, but less so in the promotion of health and wellness. In my view, many person-centred therapists have themselves forgotten their theoretical roots, so immersed and besotted have they become with the medical model and its ideas of deficit and dysfunction. It has become so commonplace for many therapists to use the language and terminology of psychiatry themselves that they have forgotten that theirs is a potentiality model. And as Proctor (Chapter 19, in this book) argues, we have not stood against the societal causes of distress as successfully as would seem needed. In looking to the future, we need to ensure that all three aspects of person-centred theory are now given equal attention.

The chapters in this book illustrate the richness of theory and the applicability of the approach in a number of clinical contexts, such as working in residential psychiatric settings (Van Werde, Chapter 12 in this book), and caring for people with 'special needs' (Pörtner, Chapter 17 in this book), as well as the difficulties and challenges faced by its practitioners working in psychiatric settings (eg. Sommerbeck, Chapter 7 in this book). It will seem self-evident to many that the person-centred approach offers a more ethical and effective way of helping, but that is not enough. It must be shown to be so. There is already substantial evidence for the therapeutic role of relationships (Bozarth & Motomasa, Chapter 22 in this book), but there is a long way to go yet if the person-centred approach is to gain credibility in the current mental health system. If that is ever to happen, we need to take research more seriously and get new evidence behind the person-centred approach that shows that it really is an alternative that makes a difference in our understanding of how problems arise and how people can be helped. Furthermore, we need to do more than convince ourselves. The person-centred approach is not widely represented in our universities, where such research often takes place. Awareness of the person-centred approach among other professionals is minimal; if we want the approach to be taken more seriously, we also need to communicate the research beyond the person-centred community. As I see it, future research developments are needed in a number of areas.

First, we need to see new research that accommodates the ideas of evidence-based practice as they are framed through the lens of the medical model. Such research would develop person-centred conceptualisations of the various diagnostic categories and test the effectiveness of person-centred therapy for specific conditions, not to provide a justification for the medical model, but to show that there are other more humane ways of thinking about and working with people who have a diagnosis. We need research that meets the standards of professional journals in psychology and psychiatry and speaks directly to these audiences in ways that they understand and that mean that the person-centred approach gets taken more seriously. However, in doing this research, we must be open to learning about the strengths and the limitations of person-centred therapy. Such research may not always show us what we expect or want to find. There may be conditions that really are not well-suited to person-centred therapy, but it seems a safe assumption that it will be possible to understand the majority of conditions for which people currently seek help from the person-centred approach. We have begun to see some conceptual work in this direction, most notably with the topics of post-traumatic stress (Joseph, Chapter 14 in this book), and attachment styles (Tickle & Joseph, Chapter 11 in this book). In terms of therapy for specific conditions, the most significant development of recent years has been the Counselling for Depression (CfD) programme, as described by Sanders and Hill (2014). Some may see such research as an example of what Sanders (Chapter 2 in this book) describes as a compromise of the principles of the person-centred approach, insofar as it adopts the language of the medical model. For example, CfD by definition involves the diagnosis of depression. On the other hand, those involved in CfD may see this as a necessary compromise that has led the person-centred approach to be taken seriously in the NHS and by funding bodies.

Second, for those whose stance is to reject any involvement with the medical model, there is other research and scholarship needed. Our own understandings of the person-centred approach from its own frame of reference cannot stand still. We do need to continue to define our assessment procedures (eg. Wilkins, Chapter 8 in this book). We do need to describe our own use of models of dysfunction (eg. Warner, Chapter 6 in this book). We need an understanding of social and cultural forces (eg. Lago, Chapter 10 in this book). Research that develops person-centred theory in its own right, and not as a compromise to other positions, is vital if the approach is to maintain and develop its own distinct stance to mental health. Such research can continue to build in the specialist humanistic and person-centred journals.

Third, rather than remain isolated, person-centred practitioners can also begin to see themselves in alignment with other professionals who hold similar views on some of the same theoretical aspects. Such research need not compromise the principles of the person-centred approach, but simply take it to new and influential audiences that will be receptive to its ideas and values. In promoting social justice, we would do well to look to the profession of social work, which shares our concern about the societal causes of distress and dysfunction and their prevention. In terms of health and wellness, recent years have seen much interest in positive psychology. It seems self-evident to me that the person-centred approach is a positive psychology (Joseph, 2015), and we would benefit from thinking in terms of the absence of full functioning rather than the language of deficit and disorder. But, in saying that the person-centred approach is a form of positive psychology, let me be clear that not all positive psychology is person-centred. What makes the person-centred approach a unique form of positive psychology is its underlying metatheoretical stance that human beings are organismically motivated toward developing to their full potential. Research will benefit from a broader positive psychological conceptualisation of measurement that embraces a theoretically consistent approach, as discussed by Patterson in Chapter 26. We need new research that can show that mental health problems are better understood as expressions of thwarted potential, and that person-centred therapy leads to increases in people becoming more fully functioning, not only to reductions in distress and dysfunction. Imagine, instead of diagnostic assessment, a new system that was based on these ideas and that therapists no longer think about symptom reduction but about the promotion of a person's potential.

In these three ways – 1) researching person-centred therapy in medical model contexts and using person-centred theory to understand psychiatric concepts; 2) building strong theory and scholarship within the person-centred approach, and 3) aligning the person-centred approach with contemporary developments such as positive psychology – we can begin to advance new evidence for the person-centred approach to mental health.

References

American Psychiatric Association (2013). *Diagnostic and statistical manual of mental disorders* (5th ed.). Washington, DC: American Psychiatric Press.

Bentall RP (2004). *Madness Explained: psychosis and human nature.* Harmondsworth: Penguin.

BPS Division of Clinical Psychology (2015). *Guidelines on language in relation to functional psychiatric diagnosis.* British Psychological Society. Leicester. www.bps.org.uk/system/files/Public%20files/guidelines_on_language_web.pdf (accessed 28 November, 2016).

Joseph S (2015). *Positive therapy: building bridges between positive psychology and person-centred psychotherapy.* London. Routledge.

Maddux JE (2002). Stopping the 'madness': positive psychology and the deconstruction of the illness ideology and the DSM. In: Snyder CR, Lopez SJ (eds). *Handbook of Positive Psychology.* New York: Oxford University Press (pp13–25).

Maddux JE, Lopez SJ (2015). Toward a positive clinical psychology: deconstructing the illness ideology and constructing an ideology of human strengths and potential in clinical psychology. In: Joseph S (ed). *Positive Psychology in Practice: promoting human flourishing in work, health, education, and everyday life* (2nd ed). New York: John Wiley (pp411–427).

Newnes C, Holmes G, Dunn C (1999). *This is Madness: a critical look at psychiatry and the future of mental health services.* Ross-on-Wye: PCCS Books.

Read, J, Mosher, LR, Bentall RP (2004). *Models of Madness: psychological, social and biological approaches to schizophrenia.* Hove/New York: Brunner Routledge.

Sanders P, Hill A (2014). *Counselling for Depression.* Sage. London.

Rogers CR (1959). A theory of therapy, personality, and interpersonal relationships as developed in the client-centered framework. In: Koch S (ed). *Psychology: a study of a science. Vol. 3: Formulations of the person and the social context.* New York: McGraw-Hill (pp184–256).

Rogers, CR (1961). *On Becoming a Person.* Boston, MA: Houghton Mifflin.

Rogers CR (1969). *Freedom to Learn.* Columbus, OH: Merrill.

Contributors

Jerold D Bozarth PhD learned client-centered therapy from working with chronic psychotic, hospitalised clients. He has published over 400 articles and book chapters and three books, and has consulted with person-centred training programmes in Austria, Brazil, Czech Republic, England, Portugal and Slovakia. He is Professor Emeritus at the University of Georgia.

Barbara Temaner Brodley has, sadly, died (in December 2007) since the first edition of this book was published. She was an adjunct professor at the Illinois School of Professional Psychology (Argosy University). She received her doctorate in clinical psychology at the University of Chicago, where she was on the staff of the Counseling Center founded by Carl Rogers. She published many articles that expressed her interest in preserving recognition of non-directive client-centred therapy as a continuing form of effective psychotherapy.

Elaine Catterall is a BACP-accredited counsellor and qualified supervisor. Her personal and professional interest in perinatal mental health came out of her own experience of postnatal depression, and listening to and working with the needs of other women. Much of her counselling work is now focused on children, young people and their families in school settings, where she continues to witness the therapeutic benefits of providing a person-centred, creative approach to distressed parents and their children.

Mick Cooper is a professor of counselling psychology at the University of Roehampton and a chartered psychologist. Mick is author and editor of a range of texts on person-centred, existential and relational approaches to therapy, including *Existential Therapies* (Sage, 2003), *Working at Relational Depth in Counselling and Psychotherapy* (Sage, 2005, with Dave Mearns), and *Pluralistic Counselling and Psychotherapy* (Sage, 2011, with John McLeod). Mick has also led a range of research studies exploring the process and outcomes of humanistic counselling with young people. Mick's latest book is *Existential Psychotherapy and Counselling: contributions to a pluralistic practice* (Sage, 2015).

Rachel Freeth is a psychiatrist working in an NHS community team in Herefordshire. She also works as a counsellor for a counselling charity in Gloucestershire, having trained in the person-centred approach. In both these roles, she bridges the worlds of psychiatry and counselling and the contrasting worlds of psychiatry and the person-centred approach. She is author of *Humanising Psychiatry and Mental Healthcare: the challenge of the person-centred approach* (CRC Press, 2007), and has also written a number of other chapters and articles, details of which can be found at www.rachelfreeth.com

Jan Hawkins is a person-centred therapist, supervisor and freelance trainer, passionate about providing opportunities for experiential continual personal and professional development to allow practitioners to nourish the way of being that is the person-centred approach. Jan welcomes all, and has particular experience with people who have learning disabilities, autistic spectrum disorder, and also survivors of childhood abuse. Thirty years a therapist next year, Jan continues to love her work and to hold in her heart all those clients who have become more of who they are, and healed from extraordinary trauma throughout those years. Jan can be contacted on www.janhawkins.co.uk or jan@janhawkins.co.uk

Stephen Joseph PhD is at the University of Nottingham, where he is Professor of Psychology, Health and Social Care and the Convenor of the Counselling and Psychotherapy Cluster in the School of Education. He is an HCPC-registered health and counselling psychologist, and Senior Practitioner member of the British Psychological Society's Register of Psychologists Specialising in Psychotherapy.

Jacky Knibbs is a consultant clinical psychologist with experience of working in the NHS. She has been responsible for initiating and developing local services for children, young people and their families where there may be a diagnosis of the autism spectrum.

Colin Lago DLitt was Director of the Counselling Service at the University of Sheffield, UK from 1987–2003. He now works as an independent counsellor/psychotherapist, trainer, supervisor and consultant. Trained initially as an engineer, Colin went on to become a full-time youth worker in London and a teacher in Jamaica before becoming a counselling practitioner. He is a Fellow of BACP. Deeply committed to transcultural concerns in psychotherapy, he has published articles, videos and books on the subject.

Noriko Motomasa PsyD gained her PCA/CCT training from the experienced clinicians associated with the Chicago Counseling Psychotherapy Center and earned her doctorate from Illinois School of Professional Psychology, Chicago, Argosy University. Noriko appreciates Hawaii's variety of cross-cultural experiences, including the use of her bilingual skills (English-Japanese), in her clinical practice at Psychology Hawaii. She lives in Honolulu with her husband Graeme, and enjoys the tropical lifestyle. nm.phawaii@gmail.com

David Murphy PhD, CPsychol, AFBPsS is on the British Psychological Society Register of Psychologists Specialising in Psychotherapy. He works as a person-centred experiential psychotherapist with particular interest in the field of trauma. David is the course director for the MA in Person-Centred Experiential Counselling and Psychotherapy at the University of Nottingham, UK. He is author of *Relational Depth: new perspective and developments* (Palgrave Macmillan, 2012), *Trauma and the Therapeutic Relationship* (Palgrave Macmillan, 2013), and is currently editing the BPS-Wiley *Textbook on Counselling Psychology*. He is editor of the international journal *Person-Centered & Experiential Psychotherapies*.

Tom Patterson is a clinical psychologist who has worked across both adult and older adult clinical psychology services. He is currently Senior Lecturer and Academic Director of the Clinical Psychology Doctorate Programme at Coventry University, UK. His research and clinical interests include the non-medicalised evaluation of therapeutic outcome, self-conscious emotions in dementia, caregiving in dementia, positive factors in mental health, and applications of the person-centred paradigm in clinical psychology.

Marlis Pörtner, psychologist, trained as a person-centred psychotherapist in Switzerland and the US. Since 1983, she has worked for many years in private practice, with people with special needs among her clients. In addition, she has been, and occasionally still is, a consultant and trainer of staff members of social organisations in Switzerland, Germany and Austria. In her books, published in German and several other languages, she has developed specific person-centred concepts for different professional fields.

Gillian Proctor is an independent clinical psychologist and person-centred therapist. She is a lecturer in counselling at Leeds University. Her latest book is *Values and Ethics in Counselling and Psychotherapy* (Sage, 2014).

Andy Rogers trained at the University of East Anglia in the late 1990s, and has worked in and written about the therapy field ever since. He now coordinates a counselling service in a large college of further and higher education, and is an active participant in the Alliance for Counselling & Psychotherapy. Andy is also a father, contemporary music obsessive, occasional blogger and keen home cook.

Kirshen Rundle is a BACP-accredited person-centred therapist and has just completed her doctoral thesis that investigated subjective accounts of hearing voices and of having person-centred therapy. She has worked with clients in psychiatric, prison, university and other agency settings. She has also contributed several chapters to books and presented at conferences in the UK and internationally. Her particular interest is in promoting a person-centred, non-medical approach towards helping people in distress who have unusual experiences. She lives and works in Norwich, UK.

Anja Rutten is Senior Lecturer and Programme Director for Counselling at Keele University. As well as lecturing, Anja has worked extensively with people on the autism spectrum and their families in a variety of settings, including the voluntary sector, an NHS-commissioned service and private practice. Anja's research interests are the lived experiences of people on the autism spectrum, especially their therapeutic experiences, general wellbeing and self-perspectives.

Lisbeth Sommerbeck is a clinical psychologist, accredited as a specialist in psychotherapy and supervision by the Danish Psychological Association. Since 1974 and until she retired in 2011, she was employed in Danish psychiatry, where the bulk of her work consisted in psychotherapy, supervision, consultation and teaching. She has written books, book chapters and articles about various aspects of client-centred therapy, and in 2002 she initiated the Danish Carl Rogers Forum.

Pete Sanders retired from practice after more than 25 years as a counsellor, trainer and supervisor. He is now a director of PCCS Books. He continues to have an interest in mental health issues and following the developing theory and practice of client-centred therapy.

Peter F Schmid is founder of person-centred training in Austria and co-founder of both the World Association (WAPCEPC) and the European Network (PCE-Europe). Cooperation with Carl Rogers in the 1980s. Teacher at the Sigmund Freud University, Vienna; psychotherapist and trainer at the Institute for Person-Centred Studies (APG-IPS) in Austria; author and co-editor of 27 books and more than 350 academic publications about the foundations of the person-centred approach and anthropological, epistemological and ethical issues of person-centred psychotherapy and counselling; co-founder of the two major international academic person-centred journals: the German language journal PERSON and the English language journal *Person-Centered & Experiential Psychotherapies*. Websites: www.pfs-online.at and www.pca-online.net

Emma Tickle is an assistant professor in counselling at Nottingham University. She teaches part time on the MA PCEP course and delivers Counselling for Depression for qualified therapists practising in the NHS. Emma has taught counselling at certificate, diploma, degree and master's level. Emma has clinical experience in multi-disciplinary teams in education, health and corporate contexts, offering one-to-one, group, short- and long-term counselling. Emma is interested in the capacity of the person-centred approach to empower the individual in all of these contexts, in the role of both teacher and therapist.

Margaret Warner PhD is a client-centered teacher and theorist who has written extensively about client-centred therapy with clients with more serious psychological disorders, and on client-centred theory as it relates to other disciplines in clinical psychology and the behavioural sciences. She trained in client-centred therapy at the Chicago Counseling Center, and has a doctorate in Behavioral Sciences from the University of Chicago, and is currently a professor at the Illinois School of Professional Psychology. With help of other faculties at the Illinois School, she has developed a Client-Centered and Experiential Minor and Client-Centered Clinical Practice Organization.

Paul Wilkins is a semi-retired person-centred academic, therapist and supervisor, now in private practice, with an interest in collaborative approaches to research and how the person-centred paradigm applies not only to psychotherapy but to ways of being in relationship to the world. He once headed a local authority 'mental health' team and, besides 'work', his interests include good food, walking, music and the wild places of the planet.

Richard Worsley has worked for a number of years as a person-centred counsellor, supervisor and trainer. He is also an Anglican priest. He has particular interests in process in therapy, in spirituality, in philosophy and therapy, and in therapeutic groups. He worked at the University of Warwick as a staff and student counsellor. In experiencing high-volume work with people with a wide range of presenting distress, he is even more convinced that people are unique, and process their experience in unique and creative ways.

Dion Van Werde is a Belgian psychologist with a postgraduate specialisation in client-centred/experiential psychotherapy (Katholieke Universiteit Leuven). He is co-founder, national and international trainer and coordinator of the Pre-Therapy International Network, based at Psychiatrisch Ziekenhuis Sint-Camillus, Gent. There, 'Contact' was created, a ward where Prouty's pre-therapy continues to be translated into a model in residential care for people diagnosed as psychotic. He is a former board member of the Netherlands/Flanders chapter of ISPS (International Society for Psychological and Social Approaches to Psychosis); member of the editorial board of *Person-Centered & Experiential Psychotherapies*, and guest editor (with Sommerbeck and Sanders) of its December 2015 issue on pre-therapy. His publications can be found under References at www.pre-therapy.com, among which is *Pre-Therapy*, by Prouty, Van Werde & Pörtner (PCCS Books, 2002), now available in four languages.

Name index

Subject index